.NET Application Development

with C#, ASP.NET, ADO.NET and Web Services

Hanspeter Mössenböck,
Dietrich Birngruber and Alb
University of Linz

Translators
David Lightfoot and Albrecht Wöß

PEARSON
Addison
Wesley

Harlow, England • London • New York • Boston • San Francisco • Toronto • Sydney • Singapore • Hong Kong
Tokyo • Seoul • Taipei • New Delhi • Cape Town • Madrid • Mexico City • Amsterdam • Munich • Paris • Milan

Pearson Education Limited
Edinburgh Gate
Harlow
Essex CM20 2JE
England

and Associated Companies throughout the world

Visit us on the World Wide Web at:
www.pearsoned.co.uk

ISBN 0 321 17349 X

British Library Cataloguing-in-Publication Data
A catalogue record for this book is available from the British Library

Library of Congress Cataloging-in-Publication Data
A catalog record for this book is available from the Library of Congress

10 9 8 7 6 5 4 3 2 1
08 07 06 05 04

Printed in Great Britain by Henry Ling Ltd, at the Dorset Press, Dorchester, Dorset

The publisher's policy is to use paper manufactured from sustainable forests.

Preface

.NET is Microsoft's new software platform which largely unifies the development of client applications (written in several languages) and web applications. It is touted as a revolution that will completely change the way in which software is written in the future. This sounds like marketing speak and makes one suspicious. Were we not told yesterday that COM, CORBA, STL, ATL or XML was the decisive breakthrough in software development? Is .NET just the next fad?

The mistrust of many software developers is understandable, though this time not well founded. In fact, .NET is revolutionary, at least in the Windows world, where it represents the biggest change in architecture for ten years, comparable with the change from DOS to Windows. .NET is a platform on which programs written in different languages can cooperate seamlessly. The Internet plays a central role in .NET. Programming dynamic web pages or accessing remote programs (so-called *web services*) becomes as simple as developing local applications.

On the other hand .NET is not really revolutionary, in the sense that it is based on ideas that have already been put into practice elsewhere for several years and are well tried. In some respects .NET is a further development of Java (cynics even call it a remake). Many concepts have been carried over from the Java world, such as the idea of a run-time environment with garbage collection, code verification and other security mechanisms. In addition, the new language C# is essentially a dialect of Java. However, in the areas of web pages and web services .NET goes further than Java and offers sophisticated concepts and tools.

In contrast to Java, whose aim is to offer a single programming language (namely Java) under as many operating systems as possible, .NET aims to support many different languages on a single system (namely Windows). Microsoft won't want to hear that last part: .NET can of course be implemented on systems other than Windows and there are already .NET implementations for Linux, FreeBSD-Unix and MacOS X. However, the best support for .NET will probably always come from Windows.

.NET is definitely the way that Microsoft will go in the future. It will be part of the next generation of the Windows operating system (codename *Longhorn*). More and more Windows applications are already using it. So if you are a Windows developer there is probably no way to get around .NET.

Content and Aims

This book gives an overview of the entire .NET technology. It introduces its architecture, describes the language C#, gives an overview of the class library, and then deals in detail with the use of .NET in the areas of ASP.NET, ADO.NET and web services.

The .NET technology is quite extensive. Each of the above aspects could warrant its own book. For this reason we prefer not to go into every detail, but instead we concentrate on the fundamental concepts of .NET. This book will make readers understand those concepts and will put them in a position to develop .NET applications of average complexity. By making use of the excellent online documentation ([SDKDoc]) that comes with the .NET Framework readers should be able to explore any further details of .NET themselves.

Who Should Read this Book?

Our book is aimed at a wide readership, including:

- ❏ Students, who can use the book as a textbook for a course on C#, object-oriented programming, component technology or web engineering;
- ❏ Practitioners, who wish to obtain an overview of .NET, in order to assess whether they can use this technology in their own work;
- ❏ Java programmers, who wish to learn about the differences between Java and .NET;
- ❏ C++ developers, who are seeking greater safety and convenience;
- ❏ COM developers, who feel that using IDL, GUIDs and the Registry is not the ultimate end of technology;
- ❏ CORBA developers, who are looking for a simpler alternative for distributed object-oriented systems;
- ❏ Web programmers, who regard technologies such as ASP or Java servlets and JSP as too cumbersome;
- ❏ Developers, who have written their software in languages such as C++, Visual Basic, Fortran, Cobol or Eiffel and now wish to combine it with programs written in other languages.

How Should You Read this Book?

The individual chapters of this book have been designed to be read in sequence, though selective reading is possible as well. In any case, Chapter 1 should be read first; it gives an overview of .NET. Chapter 2, which is about C#, is effectively a prerequisite, because C# is used in all the examples in the remaining chapters. Chapter 3 offers a view behind the scenes of .NET and can be skimmed on a first reading. Details about the architecture of .NET can be gleaned from a targeted reading later. The remaining chapters of this book are largely independent of each other and can be read in any desired order.

We assume that the reader can already program, preferably in Java or C++. A certain familiarity with HTML and the development of dynamic web pages is useful for Chapter 6, but not essential.

The Future of .NET

While this book was being translated from German to English, Microsoft announced version 2.0 of the .NET Framework (codename *Whidbey*). This will be an integral part of the next version of the Windows operating system (codename *Longhorn*). Version 2.0 of .NET will offer a wealth of new features, such as generics, partial types and anonymous methods in C#, master pages, themes and customization in ASP.NET, as well as transactions and better security in web services. Since most of these features are still under development and are likely to change, we decided not to integrate them into the regular text of this book, but to give an extensive overview of them in Chapter 9.

Exercises

In order to help the reader to practise and digest the concepts in this book, every chapter comes with a collection of exercises. Sample solutions are available from http://dotnet.jku.at.

System Requirements

All the examples in this book have been tested with the English version 1.1 of .NET under Windows 2000 and Windows XP (Professional), Microsoft Internet Information Server 5.0 and Microsoft Internet Explorer 6.0.

Contents of the CD

This book comes with a CD that contains the following material:

- ❑ *Microsoft .NET Framework SDK 1.1*. This is the development environment that is used throughout the book. It consists of the .NET Framework with the common language runtime, the .NET class library, the C# compiler and various tools, as well as the entire API documentation. Visual Studio .NET is not included, because it is not free of charge.
- ❑ *SharpDevelop IDE*. This is an open source IDE for C#.

❑ *Microsoft ASP.NET Web Matrix*. This tool offers approximately the same functionality as Visual Studio .NET with respect to ASP.NET applications (a web page designer as well as mechanisms for database connectivity).

❑ *.NET Webservice Studio*. This is a tool for invoking and testing web service methods interactively.

❑ *Coco/R*. This is an open source compiler generator written in C#. It can be used to translate the grammer of a language into a scanner and a parser for this language.

The .NET Framework comes with excellent online documentation that not only describes all the APIs, but also contains tutorials and examples of the whole .NET technology, as well as the language specification of C#. Links to other technical documentation are listed in the reference section at the end of this book.

This Book's Web Site

Because .NET will be developed further in the next few years, this book has been supplemented by a web site:

  http://dotnet.jku.at

It contains not only the source code for all the examples in the book but also the solutions to the exercises at the end of each chapter in the book, as well as teaching material and useful links to .NET topics.

Acknowledgements

A book such as this can only originate with the help of many persons. We wish to take this opportunity to thank the staff of Microsoft at Redmond, Cambridge and Vienna who were always available to help with questions, above all Jim Miller, Eric Gunnerson, David Stutz, Van Eden, Ralph Zeller and Andreas Schabus. Christoph Ertl, Christian Nagel, Christoph Steindl, Rainer Stütz, Josef Templ, Thomas Thalhammer and Sandra Wöß deserve our thanks for their careful reading of the manuscript and valuable suggestions for improvements. David Lightfoot and Albrecht Wöß did an excellent job in translating the book and Pat Terry carefully proofread the translation. Karin Haudum prepared some of the diagrams and Kurt Prünner as well as Herman Lacheiner helped with the layout of the book's web site.

  Hanspeter Mössenböck
  Wolfgang Beer
  Dietrich Birngruber
  Albrecht Wöß
  Linz, January 2004

Table of Contents

3 The .NET Architecture

4   The .NET Class Library   185

7 Web Services   403

8 Working with the .NET Framework SDK   445

9 A Preview of .NET 2.0

References

Index

1 What is .NET?

At the beginning of 2002, after several years of research and development, Microsoft brought .NET (pronounced: *dot net*) to market. .NET is not an operating system in the narrow sense of the word and so it is not a successor to Windows. It is more a layer on top of Windows (and perhaps on other operating systems in the future). It mainly adds the following two things:

❏ A **run-time environment** that offers automatic garbage collection, security, versioning and, above all, interoperability between programs written in different languages.

❏ An **object-oriented class library**, providing a rich set of functionality for graphical user interfaces (*Windows forms*), web interfaces (*web forms*), database connectivity (*ADO.NET*), collections, threads, reflection and much more. In many cases it replaces the current Windows API and goes beyond it.

However, .NET is more than that. It is an open platform that Microsoft developed to merge diverging streams of software development and thus to offer their clients a uniform technology again.

❏ Web applications (for example online stores) are currently developed with a technology that differs from that with which desktop applications are written. Desktop applications are programmed with compiled languages such as C++ or Pascal and make use of object-oriented class libraries and frameworks. Web applications, on the other hand, are written in HTML, ASP, CGI and interpreted languages such as JavaScript or PHP. With .NET both styles of applications can now be developed with the same techniques, for example with compiled languages such as C# or Visual Basic .NET, as well as with a comprehensive object-oriented class library.

❏ In recent years, organizations have invested a great deal of money in software developed in various languages such as C++, Visual Basic or Fortran. They don't feel like throwing these investments away. They are much more interested in seeing programs that have been written in different languages working together smoothly. .NET makes this possible with an unprecedented degree of interoperability.

❑ Recently there has been a huge growth in the use of small computers such as hand-helds, palmtops and systems with embedded micro-controllers. Special languages and operating systems have been developed for them too. With .NET they can be programmed with the same languages and libraries as PCs and web servers. This allows the development of software for mobile and embedded systems to move closer to conventional programming.

A field that has had an underrated role so far is that of distributed systems that co-operate via the Internet to perform tasks that cannot be done locally. In the future such systems will have a much greater significance. For this sort of work .NET offers *web services*. Web services are implemented by means of remote procedure calls and work together by using XML and protocols such as HTTP.

.NET also makes a range of tools available, the most prominent of which is Visual Studio .NET. This is a multi-language development environment with a debugger and a GUI designer that is specially developed for use with web forms or web services.

Under the title .NET Microsoft also subsumes various servers such as the *SQL Server*™ [MSSQL] and the *BizTalk*™ *Server* [MSBiz] as well as a range of ready-made services such as the *.NET Passport service* [Pass] that provide frequently needed information and operations via web services.

So what then is .NET? It is a concerted set of system components, libraries, tools, web services and servers that is hard to define in a single sentence. In combination it aims to make the programming of Windows and web applications more straightforward and more uniform. Software development under .NET is radically different from the current style of programming for Windows and the web. It is simpler, safer and more elegant. However, one must be prepared to learn new APIs and new concepts.

1.1   The .NET Framework

The .NET Framework forms the core of the .NET technology (see Figure 1.1). It consists of a run-time environment and an object-oriented class library that covers all areas of Windows and web programming. With this comes the new programming language C# that has been specially designed for .NET. This chapter will briefly describe the various parts of the framework. The remaining chapters of the book look at each topic in more detail.

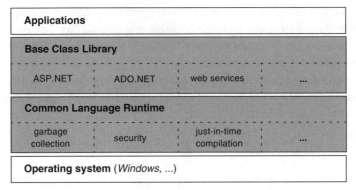

Figure 1.1 *Outline of the .NET Framework architecture*

Common Language Runtime

The Common Language Runtime (CLR) is the run-time environment under which .NET programs are executed. It provides, among other things, garbage collection, security and interoperability.

Similarly to the Java environment, the CLR is based on a *virtual machine*, with its own instruction set (CIL–*Common Intermediate Language*) into which programs written in any .NET language are translated. Just before they are run, CIL programs are compiled (*just in time*) into the code of the target machine. The CIL code guarantees interoperability between different languages as well as code portability. JIT compilation (*just-in-time compilation*), on the other hand, ensures that programs are nonetheless efficient.

However, for different languages to be able to cooperate it is not enough for them just to be translated into CIL. They must also use the same sort of data types. Therefore the CLR defines a *Common Type System* (CTS) that describes how classes, interfaces and primitive types are represented. The CTS not only allows a class, implemented in C#, to be used in a Visual Basic .NET program, but it even allows the C# class to be extended by a subclass written in Visual Basic .NET. Similarly, an exception raised by a C# program can be handled by a program written in any other .NET language.

The *Common Language Specification* (CLS) is the minimal subset of the CTS that all languages must support if they wish to make use of .NET's language interoperability. At the moment there are more than 20 such languages, both from industry and from academia. Alongside the Microsoft languages such as C#, Visual Basic .NET and Managed C++ are Fortran, Eiffel, Java, ML, Oberon, Pascal, Perl, Python and Smalltalk. Managed C++ is a variant of C++ that is translated into *managed code* that runs under the control of the CLR.

The CLR offers mechanisms for making .NET programs safer and more robust. Among these are the *garbage collector*, which is responsible for reclaiming the storage of objects once they are no longer needed. In older languages such as C and C++ programmers themselves were responsible for freeing this space. So it could happen that an object's space was freed when it was still in use by other objects. This left the other objects staring into a void and could lead to unrelated storage areas being destroyed. Similarly a programmer could forget to release the space of an object. This then remained in the memory as a *memory leak*, wasting space. Such errors are hard to find but, thanks to the garbage collector, can never occur under .NET.

When a program is loaded and translated into machine code the CLR uses a *verifier* to check that the type rules of the CTS have not been violated. For example, it is illegal to treat a number as an address and use it to access storage areas that belong to other programs.

The CLR defines a common platform for all .NET programs irrespective of what language they are written in and what machine they run on. A system of well-thought-out rules ensures that all programs have the same view of types and methods, and that method calls, exceptions and threads are all handled in the same way. The CLR as a part of the .NET architecture is described in Chapter 3.

Assemblies

.NET supports component-based software development. The components are called *assemblies* and are the smallest units that can be individually deployed. An assembly is a collection of classes and other resources (for example, images). It is stored either as an executable EXE file or as a DLL file (*Dynamic Link Library*). In some cases an assembly is even made up of multiple files.

Each assembly also contains *metadata* in addition to code. The metadata holds the full type information of the classes, fields, methods and other program elements in the assembly. An assembly also contains a *manifest*, which can be thought of as a table of contents. Thus assemblies are self-describing and can be inspected and used by loaders, compilers and other tools, by means of *reflection*.

Assemblies are also used for version control. Each has a multi-level version number that also applies to all the classes within the assembly. When a class is compiled, the version numbers of referenced classes are recorded in its object code. The loader then asks for those classes (i.e. assemblies) that correspond to the expected version numbers.

Under .NET several DLLs with the same name but different version numbers can coexist without getting in the way of each other. This spells the end of "*DLL hell*" under Windows, where the installation of new software could cause old DLLs to be overwritten by new ones with the same names so that existing software would suddenly cease to work.

Assemblies do not have to be recorded in the Windows registry. They are simply copied into the application directory or into the so-called *global assembly cache* and they are equally easy to remove when they are no longer needed.

Assemblies are effectively the successors of COM components. Unlike under COM (*Component Object Model*), one doesn't have to describe them via an IDL (*Interface Definition Language*), because they contain comprehensive metadata that has been gathered by the compiler from the source code. The common type system guarantees that software written in different languages uses the same sort of metadata and is thus binary compatible. However, investment in COM components is not lost. It is still possible to use COM components from .NET classes and vice versa.

The Language C#

Although .NET programs can be written in many different languages, Microsoft has developed a new "in-house" language that fully exploits the power of the CTS. C# is an object-oriented language that looks like Java at first sight but goes beyond Java in its capabilities.

C# supports single code inheritance and multiple interface inheritance. It facilitates the development of components in the sense of component-oriented programming by providing *properties*, *events* and *delegates*. All types in C# (and in other .NET languages) form a uniform type system that allows primitive types such as numbers and characters to be treated as objects. In addition to *reference types*, such as classes and arrays, there are also *value types* that get stored not on the heap but on the method stack. This relieves the garbage collector from keeping track of those objects and so makes the programs more efficient.

Number-crunching applications often work with multi-dimensional arrays. Unlike in Java, such arrays can be stored in contiguous memory locations in C#. This increases the efficiency of such applications.

User-defined indexing operators (so-called *indexers*) allow accessing the elements of lists and other collections with the familiar array-index notation. A new loop construct—the *foreach loop*—makes working with such object collections particularly simple and readable.

C# is one of the first languages that can be extended by using so-called *attributes*. Attributes are metadata that can be attached to almost all program elements (classes, fields, methods, parameters etc.) and that can be queried at run time by means of *reflection*. This is how conditional compilation, serialization of objects, COM interoperability and other useful mechanisms are implemented in .NET.

Reflection not only allows access to attributes but also to other metadata. One can, for example, discover at run time what methods a class has. It is even possible to call methods or to access fields whose names were still unknown at compile time. This makes it straightforward to implement debuggers, analysis tools and test environments.

Other notable features of C# are *exception handling, operator overloading* and user-defined *conversion operators* between different types.

Many of the characteristics of C# are also found in other languages. So C# is not revolutionary but, rather, a mixture of the best features of other programming languages. It is a practically oriented selection of modern software engineering concepts that every .NET programmer needs. Therefore C# has a chapter of this book dedicated to it.

The Base Class Library

The Base Class Library (BCL) contains the most important classes of .NET and can be used by all .NET languages. It provides functionality for a wide range of purposes. In most cases it supersedes the current Windows APIs which were infamous for their complexity and inconvenience. However, it is still possible to call classical Windows functions from .NET. The BCL is divided into namespaces, each of which deals with a particular functionality. Among the most important namespaces are the following:

❑ System.Collections contains classes that manage collections of objects. These include lists, sets, trees, dynamic and associative arrays and hash tables.

❑ System.IO contains classes for input and output, including general data streams, files, directories as well as formatted input and output of data.

❑ System.Threading provides classes for parallel programming. Among these are threads and thread pools as well as synchronization mechanisms such as semaphores and monitors.

❑ System.Net deals with network programming. It includes sockets and net-work streams, protocols, such as HTTP, and the corresponding request and response classes as well as cookies.

❑ System.Reflection allows access to metadata and thus to run-time type infor-mation. It contains classes such as Assembly, Type, MemberInfo and MethodInfo that can be used not only to get information about programs but also to manipulate them dynamically. It is even possible to create and exe-cute programs at run time.

❑ System.Windows.Forms is concerned with graphical user interfaces. There are classes for windows, dialogs and other user-interface elements. This namespace is one of the richest and most complex parts of the BCL and largely replaces the *Microsoft Foundation Classes*. Visual Studio .NET makes it possible to build graphical user interfaces by drag-and-drop and to install methods that will react to user input.

❑ System.XML contains classes for the creation and reading of data in XML (*Extensible Markup Language* [XML]) format. XML plays an important role in web services and other parts of .NET.

This core of the BCL is discussed in Chapter 4. Further important namespaces are System.Web which is used for programming dynamic web pages under ASP.NET, and System.Data which contains classes for accessing databases under ADO.NET. Both of these are described in their own chapters of this book.

ADO.NET

ADO.NET comprises all the classes of the .NET library that are concerned with accessing databases and other data sources (such as XML files). In contrast to its predecessor technology ADO (*ActiveX Data Objects*), ADO.NET is object-oriented and therefore more structured and straightforward to use.

ADO.NET supports the relational data model, with transactions and locking mechanisms. Therefore it is independent of different data providers and database architectures. The differences between concrete data sources like MS SQL Server, OLE DB (*Object Linking and Embedding Database*) and ODBC (*Open Database Connectivity*) are abstracted away with common interfaces.

Database access can be *connection-oriented* or *connectionless*. In the first case, a permanent connection to a data source is established. In the second, a snapshot of a part of the database is fetched into a DataSet object and then processed locally. In both cases the data can be accessed by SQL statements (*Structured Query Language*). ADO.NET is described in Chapter 5 of this book.

ASP.NET

ASP.NET is the part of the .NET technology that deals with programming dynamic web pages. Its name is reminiscent of the predecessor technology ASP (*Active Server Pages*). However, the programming model is fundamentally different.

With ASP.NET, web pages are constructed dynamically on the server from current data and are sent to the client in the form of pure HTML, so that any web browser can display them. In contrast to ASP, ASP.NET uses an object-oriented model. Web pages, as well as the GUI elements that appear in them, are objects whose fields and methods can be accessed in programs. All this is done in a compiled language such as C# or Visual Basic .NET and not, as in ASP, in an interpreted language such as JavaScript or VBScript. Thus web pages can take advantage of the entire class library of .NET.

User input is handled in an event-driven way. When a user fills out a text field, clicks a button or selects an item from a list, this raises an event that can be handled by code on the server side. Although the server is stateless—as is usual for the

Internet—state information is retained automatically between individual user inter-
actions, in fact in the HTML code itself. This represents a considerable simplification over the former programming model, where the programmer was responsible
for maintaining state information.

ASP.NET offers a rich library of GUI elements that go far beyond what is supported by HTML, although all GUI elements are eventually translated to HTML.
Programmers can even build their own GUI elements and thus adapt the user
interface of their web pages to their particular needs. It is particularly straightforward to display the results of database queries as lists and tables, since ASP.NET
has largely automated this. Validators are a further new feature. They allow user
input to be checked for validity.

Authentication of user access to protected web pages is supported by various
methods, ranging from standard Windows authentication through cookie-based
authentication to Microsoft's external passport authentication service.

Visual Studio .NET allows the user interface of a web page to be built interactively, in a way familiar from the development of desktop applications. GUI elements can be dragged into windows with the mouse. Values of properties can be
assigned using menus and property windows, and methods can be specified that
will be called in response to user input. All this sweeps away the difference between programming desktop applications and web applications and simplifies the
development of online stores and pages that show frequently updated information
(for example, stock data). ASP.NET is treated in depth in Chapter 6 of this book.

Web Services

Web services are regarded as a core of the .NET technology, although they also
exist outside .NET. They work via *remote method calls* using textual protocols
such as HTTP and SOAP (an application of XML).

The Internet has proved itself to be tremendously powerful for accessing information and services distributed around the world. Currently, access is mainly
through web browsers such as Internet Explorer or Netscape Navigator. Web services, on the other hand, allow a new style of cooperation between *applications* by
making them communicate without web browsers. Ordinary desktop applications
can fetch information such as current exchange rates or booking data from one
or more web services running as methods of applications on other computers and
responding over the Internet.

The calls and their parameters are generally coded to conform to SOAP, an
XML-based standard that is supported by most large firms. Programmers need to
know nothing of this. They call a web service in just the same way as a normal
method and .NET takes care of translating the call into SOAP, sending it over the
Internet and decoding it on the target machine. On the target machine the chosen
method is invoked and its result is transmitted back to the caller transparently,

again using SOAP. The caller and the callee can therefore be written in quite different languages and can run under different operating systems.

In order for .NET to be able to carry out the coding and decoding correctly, the web services, together with their parameters, are described in WSDL (*Web Services Description Language*). This is also done automatically by .NET.

Microsoft expects that there will be countless web services worldwide that will offer useful information. To find the right web service, UDDI (*Universal Description, Discovery and Integration*) has been developed. This can be regarded as an address book that helps find the appropriate service for a particular requirement. Thus UDDI takes over the role of a search engine for web services. Web services are described further in Chapter 7.

1.2   What Does .NET Offer?

Compared to current Windows and web programming .NET contains many new features. But what tangible benefits does it offer? How is .NET useful to programmers and users?

Robustness and Safety

Type checking and verification of CIL code make sure that programs cannot perform illegal instructions and so cannot, for example, access the memory of other programs or manipulate pointers. The garbage collector guarantees that there will not be any storage reclamation errors. All this eliminates the majority of the problems that used to bring programmers to the brink of despair.

The versioning of assemblies permits DLLs of the same name to coexist and avoids the complications that can arise when an old DLL is overwritten by a new one. Some call it the end of "*DLL Hell*".

System administrators can not only define access rights for individual persons (*role-based rights*) but also for particular parts of code (*code-based rights*), which are checked regardless of who is running the code. Assemblies can be signed using *public key cryptography* so as to be sure that they are in their original form and have not been altered or extended later. This significantly reduces the problem of viruses.

Simple Installation and De-installation of Software

Software is installed under .NET simply by copying all the program files into a directory. DLLs no longer have to be kept in a global system directory nor recorded in the Windows registry. Assemblies that are used by many programs can be stored in the so-called *Global Assembly Cache* in which there can also be several

DLLs with the same name but different version numbers. De-installation is equally easy. The files are simply deleted from the disk. No registry entry or other remnant is left behind.

Interoperability

Under .NET the various parts of a program do not all have to be written in the same language. For each part the appropriate language can be chosen—for example, Managed C++ might be used for the system-level parts, C# or Visual Basic .NET for the user interface, and ML for those parts that are best expressed in a functional language.

Program parts written in different languages can work together seamlessly, thanks to the common language runtime and its common type system. Not only is it permissible to call methods from another language, but it is also possible, for example, to create in Visual Basic .NET an object of a class that has been declared in Eiffel, or to handle in a C# program an exception that has been thrown in a Managed C++ program.

The object-oriented programming model defined by the common type system assists the development of software that is object-oriented and thus modular, extensible and easy to maintain.

Uniform Software for Desktop and Web

With .NET, object-oriented programming is now available for web programming in the same way as it has been in desktop programming for many years. Web pages and their contents are objects with fields and methods that can be used in server page code. Cryptic mixtures of HTML and script code, as were usual with ASP, are a thing of the past. Furthermore, web services make accesses to programs that run on remote computers appear as conventional method calls.

Thus, software development techniques for desktop and web applications, which have diverged in recent years, come closer together again under .NET.

Standards

Although the .NET technology originated at Microsoft, its core consists of several open standards. The ECMA standard 335 [CLI], for example, defines the *Common Language Infrastructure* (CLI), including the CLR and part of the BCL. The ECMA standard 334 [C#Std] defines the language C#. SOAP is based on the W3C standards for HTML and XML. It is itself presented as an IETF standard (*Internet Engineering Task Force*) [SOAP]. WSDL will also become a W3C standard [WSDL]. Finally, UDDI is a de facto standard that is supported by more than

200 firms, including Boeing, Cisco, Fujitsu, Hitachi, HP, IBM, Intel, Microsoft, Oracle, SAP and Sun [UDDI].

1.3 Differences from Java

.NET bears considerable resemblance to Java and so is often compared with it. As with Java, .NET is based on a virtual machine that presents a run-time environment into whose code all programs are translated.

Whereas CIL programs are *always* translated into machine code, programs in Java bytecode are initially interpreted. Only when a Java method has been called a certain number of times does it get translated into machine code by a background task. This has the advantage that Java programs can start up immediately in the interpreted mode. Under .NET the JIT compiler must always run first and so a program experiences some tenths of a second delay when it is called for the first time. On the positive side, however, there is no need for an interpreter under .NET. The designers of the CIL code also had more degrees of freedom because the CIL code was never intended for interpretation.

At first sight, the languages Java and C# are very similar. Indeed there are dialects of Pascal that differ from one another more than C# does from Java. Closer inspection, however, shows C# to be more powerful than Java, even given that many C# features are mere syntactic sugar and can also be accomplished in Java in some way or another. For example, C# has a uniform type system. It offers value types as well as reference types, has reference parameters and many other useful features such as properties, indexers, enumerations, delegates and attributes. On the other hand, Java is simpler and stricter: there is, for example, no notion of code parts being marked as "unsafe", meaning that type rules can be quietly broken there. Java is also stricter regarding exceptions. It insists that the programmer must always handle them, which is not the case in C#.

The class libraries of Java and .NET are very similar, indeed so much so that the names of many classes and methods are the same in both systems.

In place of ASP.NET, Java has a technology called JSP (*Java Server Pages*) which is in turn derived from the old ASP technology. As in .NET, JSP pages are translated into classes (*servlets*) that generate a specific HTML stream for the client. The main difference between JSP and ASP.NET is the fact that under .NET there is a clean separation between the HTML description of a web page and its program code. Under .NET, they can be in different files whereas in Java the HTML code is mixed up with the Java code fragments. In addition, the state management of a page, the object-oriented access to GUI elements and the event-driven style of reacting to user input are better engineered under ASP.NET.

For web services there is also a corresponding Java technology from Sun Microsystems called ONE (*Open Network Environment* [ONE]). As with web services under .NET, it is based on SOAP, WSDL and UDDI. Web services under

.NET, however, are more closely integrated into the system than in Java. Here Microsoft is slightly ahead.

The main difference between Java and .NET lies in the different objectives of these systems. Whereas Java aims to support a single language on many different operating systems, .NET has the exactly opposite aim, namely, to support many different languages on a single platform. Just because the platform is currently called Windows does not mean that it must always be that way. There are already implementations of .NET for other operating systems (for example, Linux and FreeBSD) and other processors (for example, SPARC and PowerPC) [Mono]. However, the best support of .NET is likely always to be under Windows.

1.4 Further Reading

This book gives an overview and introduction to the whole of the .NET technology. For the individual aspects of .NET (for example, CLR, C#, ASP.NET, or web services) there are specialized books that treat them in considerably more detail than is possible here. Some of these books are listed in the bibliography.

There are also numerous online sources, from introductions, through tutorials, to detailed specifications. New developments are picked up and described more rapidly through the Internet than is possible in the printed form. Some of the more important .NET portals are listed here:

- ❏ www.microsoft.com/net/
  This is Microsoft's official .NET site, with general information about .NET, specifications and example programs. The latest version of the .NET Framework SDK can be downloaded from here. It contains the CLR, the base class library, compilers for C# and other languages, but not, however, Visual Studio .NET.
- ❏ msdn.microsoft.com/net/
  This is the site of the Microsoft Developer Network, with all kinds of technical information on various aspects of .NET.
- ❏ www.gotdotnet.com
  Another rich source of examples, articles and other useful information about .NET.
- ❏ www.devhood.com
  A site with many examples, tutorials and training modules on .NET.
- ❏ www.iBuySpy.com
  A well-documented example of a web-shop implementation with ASP.NET.
- ❏ dotnet.jku.at
  This is the web site for this book, with sample solutions for the exercises and the source code of all the examples in this book, as well as links, tools and various information on .NET.

One of the most useful sources for .NET is the online documentation [SDKDoc] that comes with the .NET Framework SDK (see the CD in this book). It contains introductory texts, tutorials, examples and detailed specifications. In particular, the reference documentation is an indispensable companion for all .NET developers. The documentation is thorough and readable. With this book as a guide and the online reference documentation it should not be difficult to become an expert in all details of the .NET Framework.

1.4   Exercises

1. **Getting started.** Install the .NET software development kit (SDK) from the CD that comes with this book. Look at the documentation which can be opened by Start I Programs I Microsoft .NET Framework SDK I Documentation and browse through the pages named *Getting Started*.

2. **Common language runtime.** What services does the .NET common language runtime provide on top of the services that are offered by Windows? What are the benefits of these services?

3. **.NET versus Java.** Which features of the .NET Framework resemble those of the Java environment? Which features are not supported by Java?

4. **C#.** Which software engineering principles are supported by C#? How does this language help in the development of large software systems?

5. **Assemblies.** Why are .NET assemblies easier to install and to de-install than COM objects?

6. **ASP.NET.** What are the major differences between ASP.NET and the older ASP technology?

7. **Web services.** Describe several scenarios in which web services could be useful.

8. **Web search.** Visit the web sites www.microsoft.com/net, msdn.microsoft.com/net, www.gotdotnet.com and www.devhood.com and look at the information they offer about .NET. The web site www.go-mono.com describes the port of .NET to the Linux operating system.

2 The Language C#

C# (pronounced: *see sharp*) is Microsoft's new programming language for the .NET platform. Although .NET can also be programmed in many other languages (for example, Visual Basic .NET, or C++), C# is Microsoft's preferred language; it supports .NET best and is best supported by .NET.

C# is not a revolutionary new language. It is more a combination of Java, C++ and Visual Basic. The aim has been to adopt the best features of each of these languages while avoiding their more complex features. C# has been carefully developed by a small team led by *Anders Hejlsberg*. Hejlsberg is an experienced language expert. At Borland he was the chief designer of Delphi. He is known to design his languages with the needs of practitioners in mind.

In this chapter we assume that the reader already has some programming experience, preferably in Java or C++. While we are explaining the concepts of C# we will also compare them with Java and C++.

2.1 Overview

Similarities to Java

At first sight C# programs look much like Java programs. Any Java programmer should be able to read them. As well as having almost identical syntax the following concepts have been carried across from Java:

- ❏ *Object-orientation*. Like Java, C# is an object-oriented language with single inheritance. Classes can inherit from just one base class but can implement several interfaces.
- ❏ *Type safety*. C# is a type-safe language. Programming errors that arise from incompatible types in statements and expressions are detected by the compiler. There is no arbitrary pointer arithmetic and no unchecked type casts as in C++. At run time there are checks to ensure that array indices lie in the appropriate range, that objects are not referenced via uninitialized pointers and that a type cast leads to a well-defined result.

- *Garbage collection.* Dynamically allocated objects are not released by the programmer, but are automatically disposed of by a garbage collector as soon as they are no longer referenced. This eliminates many awkward errors that can occur, for example, in C++ programs.
- *Namespaces.* What Java calls packages C# calls namespaces. A namespace is a collection of type declarations. It allows the same names for classes, structures or interfaces to be used in different contexts.
- *Threads.* C# supports lightweight parallel processes in the form of threads. As in Java, there are mechanisms for synchronization and communication between threads.
- *Reflection.* As in Java, type information about a program can be accessed at run time, classes can be loaded dynamically, and it is even possible to compose executable programs at run time.
- *Libraries.* Many types in the C# library resemble those in the Java library. There are familiar classes such as Object, String, Hashtable or Stream, often even with the same methods as in Java.

Various features are also taken from C++, for example operator overloading, pointer arithmetic in system-level classes (which must be marked as unsafe) as well as some syntactical details, for example in connection with inheritance. From Visual Basic comes the foreach loop, for example.

Differences from Java

Beside these similarities, however, C# has several characteristics that go beyond Java. Most of them also apply to the other .NET languages:

- *Reference parameters.* Parameters can be passed not only *by value* but also *by reference.* Because of this, not only input parameters but also output and transient parameters can be used.
- *Objects on the stack.* Whereas in Java all objects are kept on the heap, in C# an object can also be stored in the method-call stack. Such objects are lightweight, that is, they make no demands of the garbage collector.
- *Block matrices.* For numerical applications the Java storage model for multi-dimensional arrays is too inefficient. C# allows the programmer to choose whether to have a matrix laid out as in Java (that is, as an array of arrays) or as a compact block matrix, as in C, Fortran or Pascal.
- *Enumerations.* As in Pascal or C, there are enumeration types whose values are denoted by names.
- *Goto statement.* The much-maligned goto statement has been reintroduced in C#, but with restrictions that make it scarcely possible to misuse it.

❑ *Uniform type system*. In C# all types are derived from the type object. In contrast to Java, numbers or character values can also be stored in object variables. The C# mechanism for this is called *boxing*.

❑ *Versioning*. Classes are given a version number during compilation. Thus a class can be available in several versions at the same time. Each application uses the version of a class with which it was compiled and tested.

Finally there are many features of C# that are convenient to use, although they don't really increase the power of the language. They can be viewed as "*syntactic sugar*", because they allow one to do things that are also possible in other languages, but the way of doing them in C# is simpler and more elegant. Among them are the following:

❑ *Properties and events*. These features facilitate component technology. Properties are special fields of an object. When they are accessed the system automatically calls getter or setter methods. Events can be declared and triggered by components and handled by other components.

❑ *Indexers*. An index operation like that for arrays can be declared for custom collections via getter and setter methods.

❑ *Delegates*. Delegates are essentially the same as *procedure variables* in Pascal or *function pointers* in C. However, they are more powerful. For example, several methods can be stored in a delegate variable at the same time.

❑ *foreach loop*. This loop statement can be used for iterating through arrays, lists or sets in a convenient manner.

❑ *Boxing/unboxing*. Values such as numbers or characters can be assigned to variables of type object. To do this they are automatically wrapped into an auxiliary object (*boxing*). On assignment to a number or a character variable they are automatically unwrapped again (*unboxing*). This feature allows the construction of generic container types.

❑ *Attributes*. The programmer can attach metadata to classes, methods or fields. This information can be accessed at run time by means of reflection. .NET uses this mechanism, for example, for serializing data structures.

Hello World

Now it is time for a first example. The well-known Hello World program looks like this in C#:

```
using System;
class Hello {
    public static void Main() {
        Console.WriteLine("Hello World");
    }
}
```

It consists of a class Hello and a method Main (note that upper and lower case letters are considered to be different in C#). Each program has exactly one Main method, which is called when the program is started. Console.WriteLine("...") is an output statement, where WriteLine is a method of the class Console that comes from the namespace System. In order to make Console known, System must be imported in the first line by writing using System;.

The simplest development environment for .NET is Microsoft's *Software Development Kit* (SDK). It is command-line oriented. In addition to a compiler (csc) it provides several other software tools (such as al or ildasm). These are described in Chapter 8. C# programs are stored in files with the suffix .cs. If we store our Hello World program in a file Hello.cs it can be compiled by typing

    csc Hello.cs

and executed by typing

    Hello

The output appears in the console window.

Under .NET the file name does not have to match the class name, although this is recommended for readability. A file can consist of several classes. In this case it should be named after the principal class it defines.

Structuring Programs

The source text of a C# program can be spread across several files. Each file can consist of one or more namespaces. Each namespace can contain one or more classes or other types. Figure 2.1 shows this structure.

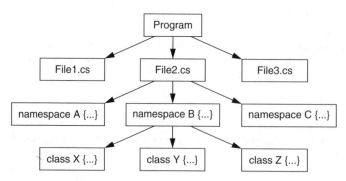

Figure 2.1 *Structure of programs*

Our Hello World program consists of a single file and a single class. No namespace is specified. Thus the class Hello belongs to an anonymous default namespace created for us by .NET. Namespaces are dealt with in Section 2.5 and 2.13; classes in Section 2.8.

Multi-file Programs

If a program consists of several files, they can be compiled either together or separately. In the first case a single executable is generated. In the second case an executable and one or more DLL (*Dynamic Link Library*) files are created.

Let's consider a class Counter in a file Counter.cs used by a class Prog in a file Prog.cs:

```
public class Counter {          // in file Counter.cs
    int val = 0;
    public void Add(int x) { val = val + x; }
    public int Val() { return val; }
}

using System;                   // in file Prog.cs
public class Prog {
    static void Main() {
        Counter c = new Counter();
        c.Add(3); c.Add(5);
        Console.WriteLine("val = " + c.Val());
    }
}
```

We can compile these two files with a single command

```
csc prog.cs Counter.cs
```

which creates the executable file Prog.exe which contains both classes. Alternatively we can make a library (DLL) from Counter by writing:

```
csc /target:library Counter.cs
```

In this case the compiler creates a file Counter.dll, and we have to specify it as follows when compiling Prog.cs

```
csc /reference:Counter.dll Prog.cs
```

This compilation also creates a file Prog.exe, but this time it contains only the class Prog. The class Counter remains in the file Counter.dll and is dynamically loaded when Prog is invoked. The compilation command and its options are detailed in Section 8.2.

2.2 Symbols

C# programs are made up of names, keywords, numbers, characters, strings, operators and comments.

Names. A name consists of letters, digits and the character "_". The first character must be a letter or a "_". Upper and lower case letters are considered as distinct (for example, red is not the same as Red). Because C# uses Unicode characters [UniC], names can also contain Greek, Arabic or Chinese symbols. However, with Western keyboards these symbols must be input using numeric codes. For example, the code \u03C0 denotes π and the name b\u0061ck means back.

Keywords. C# has 76 keywords; Java has only 47. This already suggests that C# is more complex than Java. Keywords are reserved; that means they cannot be used as names.

abstract	as	base	bool	break	byte
case	catch	char	checked	class	const
continue	decimal	default	delegate	do	double
else	enum	event	explicit	extern	false
finally	fixed	float	for	foreach	goto
if	implicit	in	int	interface	internal
is	lock	long	namespace	new	null
object	operator	out	override	params	private
protected	public	readonly	ref	return	sbyte
sealed	short	sizeof	stackalloc	static	string
struct	switch	this	throw	true	try
typeof	uint	ulong	unchecked	unsafe	ushort
using	virtual	void	while		

Naming conventions. The following rules should be followed when choosing names and deciding whether to use upper or lower case (they are also followed in the C# class library):

- ❏ Names begin with capital letters (e.g., Length, WriteLine) except for local variables and parameters (e.g., i, len) or fields that are not visible outside their class.
- ❏ In composite words each word begins with a capital letter (for example, WriteLine). Joining words with "_" is seldom used in C#.
- ❏ Methods that do not return a value should begin with a verb (for example, DrawLine). All other names should generally begin with a noun (for example, Size, IndexOf, Collection). Fields or methods of type bool can also begin with an adjective if they express some boolean value (for example, Empty).

Characters and strings. Character constants are written between single quotes (for example, 'x'). String constants are written between double quotes (for example, "John"). In each, any characters can appear except the terminating quote, a line break or the character \, which is used as an *escape character*. The following escape sequences allow the expression of special characters in character or string constants:

```
\     "
\     ""
\\    \
\0    0x0000 (the character with the value 0)
\a    0x0007 (alert)
\b    0x0008 (backspace)
\f    0x000c (form feed)
\n    0x000a (new line)
\r    0x000d (carriage return)
\t    0x0009 (horizontal tab)
\v    0x000b (vertical tab)
```

In order to write, for example

```
file "C:\sample.txt"
```

as a string constant we have to write:

```
"file \"C:\\sample.txt\""
```

As in names, Unicode values (for example, \u0061) can also be used in character or string constants.

If a string constant is preceded by the character @, it may contain line breaks, escape sequences remain unprocessed, and quotes must be doubled. So the above example can also be written:

```
@"file ""C:sample.txt"""
```

Integer constants. They can be expressed in decimal (e.g. 123) or hexadecimal (e.g. 0x007b). Their type is the smallest type from int, uint, long or ulong that their value will fit into. The suffix u or U (e.g. 123u) defines the constant to be of the smallest suitable unsigned type (uint or ulong). The suffix l or L (e.g. 0x007bl) indicates that the value has the smallest type of the set long and ulong.

Floating-point constants. They consist of an integer part, a decimal part and an exponent (e.g. 3.14E0 means $3.14 * 10^0$). Any of these parts can be omitted, but at least one must appear. The numbers 3.14, 314E-2 and .314E1 are valid notations for the same value. The type of a floating-point constant is double. Appending f or F (e.g. 1f) determines the type to be float. Appending m or M (e.g. 12.3m) determines the type to be decimal.

Comments. There are two forms of comments. *Single-line comments* begin with // and extend until the end of the line, for example:

```
// a comment
```

Delimited comments begin with /* and end with */. They can extend over several lines but cannot be nested. Example:

```
/*  a comment
    that takes two lines */
```

Single-line comments are used for short annotations and delimited comments mainly for commenting-out code.

2.3   Types

The data types of C# form a hierarchy, shown in Figure 2.2. There are value types and reference types. *Value types* are primitive types such as char, int or float, as well as enumerations and structs. Variables of these types directly contain a value (such as 'x', 123 or 3.14). *Reference types* are classes, interfaces, arrays and delegates. Variables of these types hold a reference to an object that is stored in the dynamic storage area (the *heap*).

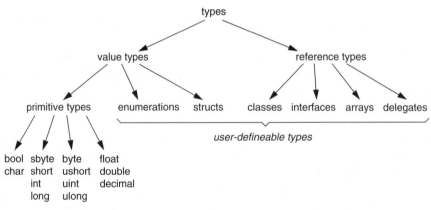

Figure 2.2 *Type hierarchy*

Uniform Type System

C# has a uniform type system, which means that all types, whether value types or reference types, are compatible with the type object (see Section 2.3.7): values of any type can be assigned to object variables and understand object operations. This makes it easy to design algorithms that can work with any kind of data. Table 2.1 summarizes the differences between value types and reference types.

Table 2.1 *Value types and reference types*

	value types	reference types
Variable contains	a value	a reference to an object
Variable is stored	on the method stack or in the containing object	on the heap
Assignment	copies the value	copies the reference
Example	int i = 17; int j = i;	string s = "Hello"; string s1 = s;

The type string, used in Table 2.1, is a predefined class and thus a reference type. Actually string is a keyword that the compiler expands into the class System.String (that is, the class String in the namespace System). Similarly, object is expanded into the class System.Object.

2.3.1 Primitive Types

As with all languages, C# has predefined types for numbers, characters and boolean values. Numeric types are divided into integer types and floating-point types. Within these groups the types differ in range and accuracy. Table 2.2 shows an overview of all primitive types.

Table 2.2 *Primitive types*

	range of values	expanded to
sbyte	−128 .. 127	System.SByte
short	−32768 .. 32767	System.Int16
int	−2147483648 .. 2147483647	System.Int32
long	-2^{63} .. $2^{63}-1$	System.Int64
byte	0 .. 255	System.Byte
ushort	0 .. 65535	System.UInt16
uint	0 .. 4294967295	System.UInt32
ulong	0 .. $2^{64}-1$	System.UInt64
float	±1.4E-45 .. ±3.4E38 (32 Bit, IEEE 754)	System.Single
double	±5E-324 .. ±1.7E308 (64 Bit, IEEE 754)	System.Double
decimal	±1E-28 .. ±7.9E28 (128 Bit)	System.Decimal
bool	true, false	System.Boolean
char	Unicode characters	System.Char

The unsigned types byte, ushort, uint and ulong are mainly used for systems programming and for compatibility with other languages. The type decimal allows the representation of large decimal numbers with high accuracy and is mainly used for financial mathematics.

The compiler maps all primitive types to struct types defined in the namespace System. For example, the type int is mapped to System.Int32. All the operations defined there (including those inherited from System.Object) are thus applicable to int.

There is a compatibility relationship between most of the primitive types. This is shown in Figure 2.3. An arrow between char and ushort means, for example, that char values can be assigned to a ushort variable (ushort includes all char values). The relationship is transitive. That means that char values can also be assigned to int or float variables. An assignment to decimal is, however, only permitted with an explicit type cast (e.g., decimal d = (decimal) 3;). In assigning values of type long or ulong to float there can be a loss of accuracy if there are insufficient bits in the mantissa to represent the result.

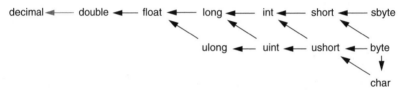

Figure 2.3 *Compatibility relationship between primitive types*

2.3.2   Enumerations

Enumerations are types whose values are explicitly given by a list of named constants, for example:

```
enum Color { red, blue, green }
```

Variables of type Color can take the values red, blue or green, and the compiler maps these values to the numbers 0, 1 and 2. However, enumerations are not numeric types; they cannot be assigned to numeric variables, and numbers cannot be assigned to Color variables. If desired, the value of an enumeration constant can be specified in the declaration, as in

```
enum Color { red=1, blue=2, green=4 }
enum Direction { left=0, right, up=4, down }   // left=0, right=1, up=4, down=5
```

Enumerations usually occupy four bytes. However, a different type size can be chosen by writing a (numeric) base type after the enumeration type name. For example:

```
enum Access: byte { personal=1, group=2, all=4 }
```

Variables of type Access are thus one byte long. Enumerations can be used as follows:

```
Color c = Color.blue;
Access a = Access.personal | Access.group;
if ((a & Access.personal) != 0) Console.WriteLine("access granted");
```

When using enumeration constants they must be qualified with their type names. If values are chosen to be powers of two (as in the type Access) one can form bit sets using the logical operators &, | and ~. In this way an enumeration variable can hold a set of values. If an operation yields a value for which there is no enumeration constant, that does not bother the compiler (for example, Access.personal | Access.group yields the value 3). The following operations are allowed with enumerations:

```
==, !=, <, <=, >, >=     if (c == Color.red) ...
                         if (c > Color.red && c <= Color.green) ...
+, -                     c = c + 2;
++, --                   c++;
&                        if ((a & Access.personal) != 0) ...
|                        a = a | Access.group;
~                        a = ~ Access.all;   // one's complement
```

As with the logical operations, an arithmetic operation can yield a value that does not map to any enumeration constant. The compiler accepts this.

Enumerations inherit all the operations of object, such as Equals or ToString (see Section 2.3.7). There is also a class System.Enum that provides special operations on enumerations.

2.3.3 Arrays

Arrays are one- or multi-dimensional vectors of elements. The elements are selected by an index, where the indexing begins at 0.

One-dimensional arrays. One-dimensional arrays are declared by stating their element type followed by empty square brackets:

```
int[] a;                            // declares an array variable a
int[] b = new int[3];               // initializes b with an array of 3 elements, all 0
int[] c = new int[] {3, 4, 5};      // initializes c with the values 3, 4, 5
int[] d = {3, 4, 5};                // initializes d with the values 3, 4, 5
SomeClass[] e = new SomeClass[10];  // creates an array of references
SomeStruct[] f = new SomeStruct[10]; // creates an array of values (directly in the array)
```

An array declaration does not allocate storage. Therefore it does not specify an array length. In order to create an array object we have to use the new operator with the desired element type and length. For example, new int[3] creates an array of three int elements. The values of a newly created array are initialized to 0 (or '\0', false, null as appropriate), except when explicit initial values are specified in curly braces. In the declaration of an array the initialization can also be given directly (without using the new operator), in which case the compiler creates an array of the necessary length.

Note that an array of classes contains *references*, whereas an array of structs holds the *values* directly.

Multi-dimensional arrays. Multi-dimensional arrays can be either jagged or rectangular. Jagged arrays hold references to other arrays, whereas the elements of rectangular arrays form a contiguous block of memory (see Figure 2.4). Rectangular arrays are not only more compact, but also allow a more efficient indexing. Here are some examples of multi-dimensional arrays:

```
// jagged arrays (declared with [][])
int[][] a = new int[2][];       // two rows, the columns of which are still undefined
a[0] = {1, 2, 3};               // row 0 has three columns
a[1] = {4, 5, 6, 7, 8};         // row 1 has five columns

// rectangular arrays (declared with [,])
int[,] a = new int[2, 3];       // two rows with three columns each
int[,] b = {{1, 2, 3}, {4, 5, 6}};   // initialization of the two rows and three columns
int[,,] c = new int[2, 4, 2];   // two blocks with four rows with two columns each
```

In jagged arrays the rows can have different lengths. For this reason only the length of the first dimension is specified in the new operation and not the length of all dimensions, as with rectangular arrays. Figure 2.4 shows the difference between the two styles of array.

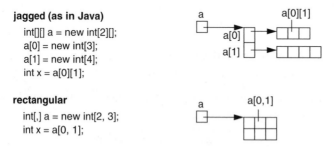

jagged (as in Java)
```
int[][] a = new int[2][];
a[0] = new int[3];
a[1] = new int[4];
int x = a[0][1];
```

rectangular
```
int[,] a = new int[2, 3];
int x = a[0, 1];
```

Figure 2.4 *Jagged and rectangular multi-dimensional arrays*

Array operations. As can be seen from Figure 2.4, array variables hold references. Therefore an array assignment is a *reference assignment*, i.e., the array itself is not copied. Indexing always begins at 0. The length of an array can be determined with the Length operator.

```
int[] a = new int[3];
int[][] b = new int[2][];
b[0] = new int[4];
b[1] = new int[4];
Console.WriteLine(a.Length);          // 3
Console.WriteLine(b.Length);          // 2
Console.WriteLine(b[0].Length);       // 4
```

In rectangular arrays Length gives the total number of elements. In order to get the number of elements in a certain dimension we must use the GetLength method.

```
int[,] a = new int[3, 4];
Console.WriteLine(a.Length);          // 12
Console.WriteLine(a.GetLength(0));    // 3
Console.WriteLine(a.GetLength(1));    // 4
```

The class System.Array contains some useful operations for copying, sorting and searching in arrays.

```
int[] a = new int[2];
int[] b = {7, 2, 4};
Array.Copy(b, a, 2);                  // copies b[0..1] to a
Array.Sort(b);                        // sorts b into ascending order
```

Variable-length arrays. Once an array has been allocated, its length is fixed. However, there is a class System.Collections.ArrayList which implements arrays of *variable* length (see Section 4.1.5). The method Add can be used to add elements of any type to the array. The elements can then be selected by indexing:

```
using System;
using System.Collections;

class Test {
    static void Main() {
        ArrayList a = new ArrayList();      // creates an empty array of variable length
        a.Add("Alice");                     // appends "Alice" to the end of the array
        a.Add("Bob");
        a.Add("Cecil");
        for (int i = 0; i < a.Count; i++)   // a.Count returns the number of elements
            Console.WriteLine(a[i]);        // output: "Alice", "Bob", "Cecil"
    }
}
```

Associative arrays. The class System.Collections.Hashtable allows arrays not only to be indexed by numbers but also, for example, by strings:

```
using System;
using System.Collections;

class Test {
    static void Main() {
        Hashtable phone = new Hashtable();      // creates an empty associative array
        phone["Jones"] = 4362671;
        phone["Miller"] = 2564439;
        phone["Smith"] = 6451162;
        foreach (DictionaryEntry x in phone) {  // foreach: see Section 2.6.9
            Console.Write(x.Key + " = ");        // key, e.g. "Miller"
            Console.WriteLine(x.Value);          // value, e.g. 2564439
        }
    }
}
```

2.3.4   Strings

Character arrays (strings) occur so often that C# provides a special type string for them. The compiler expands this into the class System.String. A string constant or a string variable can be assigned to another string variable:

```
string s = "Hello";
string s2 = s;
```

Strings can be indexed like arrays (e.g. s[i]), but they are not actually arrays. In particular, they cannot be modified. If we need strings that can be modified we should use the class System.Text.StringBuilder instead:

```
using System;
using System.Text;

class Test {
    static void Main(string[] arg) {
        StringBuilder buffer = new StringBuilder();
        buffer.Append(arg[0]);
        buffer.Insert(0, "myfiles\\");
        buffer.Replace(".cs", ".exe");
        Console.WriteLine(buffer.ToString());
    }
}
```

This example also shows that the Main method can be declared as having a string array parameter to which command-line arguments are passed. If the above program were to be called as

```
Test sample.cs
```

the output would be myfiles\sample.exe.

Strings are reference types, that is, a string variable holds a reference to a string object. String assignments are therefore *reference assignments*; the value of the string is not copied. However, the operations == and != are, in contrast to Java, value comparisons. The comparison

> (s+ " World") == "Hello World"

returns the value true. The compare operations <, <=, >, >= are not allowed for strings; instead, the method CompareTo must be used (see Table 2.3). Strings can be concatenated with + (e.g. s + " World" gives "Hello World"). This creates a new string object (so s is not changed). The length of a string can be obtained by using s.Length, as for arrays. The class System.String offers many useful operations (see Table 2.3).

Table 2.3 *String operations (extract)*

operation	returns
s.CompareTo(s1)	−1, 0 or 1 according to whether s < s1, s == s1 or s > s1
s.IndexOf(s1)	the index of the first occurrence of s1 in s
s.LastIndexOf(s1)	the index of the last occurrence of s1 in s
s.Substring(from, length)	the substring s[from..from+length−1]
s.StartsWith(s1)	true if s starts with s1
s.EndsWith(s1)	true if s ends with s1
s.ToUpper()	a copy of s in upper case letters
s.ToLower()	a copy of s in lower case letters
String.Copy(s)	a copy of s

2.3.5 Structs

Structs are user-defined types that hold data and possibly methods. They are declared as follows:

```
struct Point {
    public int x, y;                                        // fields
    public Point(int a, int b) { x = a; y = b; }            // constructor
    public void MoveTo(int x, int y) { this.x = x; this.y = y; }   // method
}
```

Structs are *value types*. Therefore variables of type Point hold the values of the fields x and y directly. An assignment between structs is a value assignment and not a reference assignment.

```
Point p;                  // p is so far uninitialized
p.x = 1; p.y = 2;         // field access
Point q = p;              // value assignment (q.x == 1, q.y == 2)
```

Structs can be initialized with a *constructor*. The declaration

```
Point p = new Point(3, 4);
```

declares a new struct object p on the stack and calls the constructor of Point, which initializes the fields to the values 3 and 4. A constructor must always have the same name as the struct type. The method MoveTo is called as follows:

```
p.MoveTo(10, 20);
```

In the code of the called method the object p, on which the method was called, can be referred to by this (the so-called *receiver* of the message MoveTo). Thus this.x denotes the field x of the object p, whereas x denotes the formal parameter of the method MoveTo. When there is no ambiguity this can be omitted from the field access, as above in the constructor of Point.

Structs may not declare parameterless constructors. However, a parameterless constructor may be used on structs, because the compiler creates one for every struct type. The constructor in the declaration

```
Point p = new Point();
```

initializes the fields of p with the value 0. Section 2.8 goes into further detail on structs and constructors.

2.3.6   Classes

Like structs, classes are types consisting of data and methods. In contrast to structs, however, they are *reference types*. That is, a variable of a class type holds a reference to an object that is stored in the heap. Classes are declared as follows:

```
class Rectangle {
    Point origin;   // bottom-left corner
    public int width, height;
    public Rectangle() { origin = new Point(0, 0); width = height = 1; }
    public Rectangle(Point p, int w, int h) { origin = p; width = w; height = h; }
    public void MoveTo(Point p) { origin = p; }
}
```

A Rectangle variable can only be used if a Rectangle object has been installed in it:

```
Rectangle r = new Rectangle(new Point(10, 20), 5, 5);
int area = r.width * r.height;
```

Whenever an object is created with the new operator the appropriate constructor is automatically called. This initializes the fields of the object. The class Rectangle has two constructors that differ in their parameter lists. The parameters of the second constructor match the actual parameters of the new operator in the example above and so this constructor is chosen. The declaration of constructors or methods with the same name in a class is called *overloading*. This will be discussed further in Section 2.8.

Created objects are never explicitly released in C#. Instead this task is left to the *garbage collector*, which automatically releases objects once they are no longer referenced. This removes the source of many awkward errors that C++ programmers have to struggle with: if objects are released too soon, some references may point into a void. On the other hand, if a C++ programmer forgets to release objects they remain as "memory leaks". Under .NET such errors cannot occur, because the garbage collector takes care of releasing objects.

Because a variable of a class type holds a reference, the assignment

```
Rectangle r1 = r;
```

is a *reference assignment*: afterwards r and r1 point to the same object. Methods are called as for structs:

```
r.MoveTo(new Point(3, 3));
```

In the implementation of the method MoveTo the predefined name this again denotes the object r on which the method was called. Because the field name origin is unambiguous there it does not need to be qualified as this.origin.

Table 2.4 compares classes and structs again. Some of these differences are covered in detail in later sections.

Table 2.4 *Classes versus structs*

classes	structs
reference types (variables reference objects on the heap)	value types (variables contain objects)
support inheritance (all classes are derived from object)	do not support inheritance (but are compatible with object)
can implement interfaces	can implement interfaces
parameterless constructor can be declared	parameterless constructor cannot be declared

Structs are lightweight types which are often used for temporary data. Because they are not stored on the heap they do not burden the garbage collector. Classes are mainly used for more complex objects which are often linked into dynamic data structures. Objects of a class can outlive the methods that created them.

2.3.7   object

The type object, which is expanded into System.Object, has a special meaning in C#. It is the root of the entire type hierarchy. That means that all types are compatible with it. So a value of any type can be assigned to an object variable:

```
object obj = new Rectangle();       // assignment of Rectangle to object
Rectangle r = (Rectangle) obj;      // type cast
obj = new int[3];                   // assignment of int[] to object
int[] a = (int[]) obj;              // type cast
```

In particular, object allows the implementation of generic container classes. For example, a stack that stores objects of any type can have a method

```
void Push(object x) {...}
```

which can then be called with parameters of any type:

```
Push(new Rectangle());
Push(new int[3]);
```

The class System.Object (covered in detail in Section 2.9.8) contains several methods that are inherited by all classes and structs (and are mostly overridden). The most important methods are:

```
class Object {
    public virtual bool Equals(object o) {...}   // compares the values of the receiver and o
    public virtual string ToString() {...}       // converts the object into a string
    public virtual int GetHashCode() {...}       // calculates a hash code for the object
    ...
}
```

These methods can be applied to objects of any type and even to constants:

```
string s = 123.ToString();   // s == "123"
```

2.3.8   Boxing and Unboxing

Not only reference types are compatible with object but also value types such as int, structs or enumerations. In the assignment

```
object obj = 3;
```

the value 3 is wrapped up by an object of a temporary class that is then assigned to the variable obj (see Figure 2.5). This is called *boxing*.

Figure 2.5 Boxing of an int value

Assignment in the opposite direction needs a type cast:

```
int x = (int) obj;
```

In this, the value is unwrapped from the temporary object and treated as an int value. This is called *unboxing*.

Boxing and unboxing are particularly useful with container types because these can then be used not only with elements of reference types, but also with elements of value types. For example, if a class Queue has been declared as follows:

```
class Queue {
    object[] values = new object[10];
    public void Enqueue(object x) {...}
    public object Dequeue() {...}
}
```

it can be used like this:

```
Queue q = new Queue();
q.Enqueue(new Rectangle());          // used with a reference type
q.Enqueue(3);                         // used with a value type (boxing)
...
Rectangle r = (Rectangle) q.Dequeue();  // type cast: object -> Rectangle
int x = (int) q.Dequeue();              // type cast: object -> int (unboxing)
```

Calls to object methods are forwarded to the boxed object. For example, the code fragment:

```
object obj = 123;
string s = obj.ToString();
```

assigns the value "123" to s.

2.4 Expressions

Expressions consist of operands and operators and calculate values. Table 2.5 shows the operators of C# ordered by priority. Operators higher up in the list have priority over operators lower down in the list. Binary operators at the same level are evaluated from left to right in an expression, for example:

```
... a + b - c ...      // ... (a + b) - c ...
```

The unary operators +, -, !, ~, as well as type casts are right-associative, that is, they are evaluated from right to left, for example:

```
... - (int) x ...      // ... - ((int) x) ...
```

Table 2.5 *Operators ordered by priority*

operator class	operators
primary operators	(x) x.y f(x) a[x] x++ x-- new typeof sizeof checked unchecked
unary operators	+ - ~ ! ++x --x (T)x
multiplication operators	* / %
addition operators	+ -
shift operators	<< >>
relational operators	< > <= >= is as
equality operators	== !=
bitwise and	&
bitwise exclusive or	^
bitwise or	|
conditional and	&&
conditional or	||
conditional expression	condition?value1:value2
assignment operators	= += -= *= /= %= <<= >>= &= ^= |=

2.4.1   Arithmetic Expressions

Arithmetic expressions are formed with the operators +, -, *, /, % (*remainder*), ++
(*increment*) and -- (*decrement*). Their operands must have a numeric type or the
type char. The operators ++ and -- also apply to enumerations. However, they can
only be applied to variables, not to constants or expressions.

The result type of an arithmetic expression is the smallest numeric type that
includes both operand types (according to Section 2.3), but at least int. With operands of enumeration types the result type is the same enumeration type again.
Here are some examples:

```
short s; int i; float f; char ch; Color c;
... s + f ...      // float
... s + s ...      // int
... i + ch ...     // int
... c++ ...        // Color
```

There are some special rules for unsigned operands: the negation of a uint value,
as well as the combination of a uint value with an sbyte, short or int value, gives a
long value because the range of the result can fall outside that of uint. The negation
of a ulong value, as well as the combination of a ulong value with an sbyte, short, int
or long value is forbidden, as is the combination of a decimal value with a float or
double value.

2.4.2   Relational Expressions

The operators <, >, <=, >=, == (*equality*) and != (*inequality*) compare numeric operands, characters or enumeration values with one another. The operators == and

!= are also applicable to boolean values, references and delegates. If values of different numeric types (e.g. int and long) are compared then the smaller type is converted to the larger type before the comparison.

The operator is performs a type test; the operator as combines a type test with a cast; these operators are described further in Section 2.9.2. In the expression x is T or x as T, x can be an expression of any type and T must be a reference type. For example:

```
r is Rectangle      // does r reference a Rectangle object?
3 is object         // is 3 of type object?
a is int[]          // does a reference an int array?
```

The result of a relational expression is always of type bool.

2.4.3   Boolean Expressions

The operators && (*and*), || (*or*) and ! (*negation*) apply to boolean operands and yield a result of type bool. The operators && and || are evaluated using *conditional* (or *short-circuit*) *evaluation*. This means that the evaluation will stop as soon as the result is known. Formally stated:

```
a && b      is evaluated as: if (!a) false else b
a || b      is evaluated as: if (a) true else b
```

This evaluation order is useful for computing compound expressions where the second term should only be evaluated if the first term is true (or false):

```
if (p != null && p.val > 0) ...     // p.val is only evaluated if p != null
if (y == 0 || x / y > 2) ...        // x / y is only evaluated if y != 0
```

The conditional expression *condition* ? *value1* : *value2* yields *value1* if *condition* is true and *value2* otherwise. For example:

```
int max = x > y ? x : y;            // if (x > y) max = x; else max = y;
```

2.4.4   Bit Expressions

The operators & (*bitwise and*), | (*bitwise or*), ^ (*bitwise exclusive or*) and ~ (*bitwise negation*) can be applied to numeric operands, char values and enumerations. The operators &, |, ^ are also allowed with boolean operands, but they do not result in short-circuit evaluation. With operands of different types the smaller type is converted to the larger type before the evaluation. The result type is the larger of the two operand types. However, with numeric or char operands the result type is at least int. The following examples show how bit expressions work. x is assumed to have the value 5 and y the value 6 (in two's complement representation):

```
x & y      // 00000101 & 00000110 => 00000100 (4)
x | y      // 00000101 | 00000110 => 00000111 (7)
x ^ y      // 00000101 ^ 00000110 => 00000011 (3)
~ x        // ~ 00000101 => 11111010 (-6)
```

2.4.5   Shift Expressions

Shift expressions are mainly used in systems programming. They allow for efficient multiplication or division by powers of two. The expression x << y (respectively x >> y) denotes a left shift (respectively a right shift) of the bit pattern of x by y bits. With x << y zero-bits are shifted in from the right. With x >> y bits with the value b are shifted in from the left, where b is zero for unsigned types and the value of the sign bit for signed types. The type of x must be an integer type or char and the type of y must be int. The result type is the type of x, but at least int. The following examples assume that the int variables a and b hold the values 7 and -7, respectively:

```
a >> 1     // 00000111 >> 1 = 00000011 (3)  = a / 2
a << 3     // 00000111 << 3 = 00111000 (56) = a * 8
b >> 2     // 11111001 >> 2 = 11111110 (-2)
b << 1     // 11111001 << 1 = 11110010 (-14)
```

2.4.6   Overflow Checking

If the result of an arithmetic expression is out of range no error is reported but the result will simply be truncated. For example:

```
int x = 1000000;
x = x * x;   // -727379968, no error is reported
```

In some situations—such as when implementing a random-number generator—this behaviour is desired. In many others we might wish to check for overflow, which can be done using the checked operator or the checked statement like this:

```
x = checked(x * x); // checked operator: throws OverflowException in case of an overflow
...
checked {            // checked statement
   ...
   x = x * x;        // throws OverflowException in case of an overflow
   ...
}
```

Overflow checking can also be turned on for an entire compilation unit by using the checked compiler option:

```
csc /checked Test.cs
```

2.4.7 typeof

The typeof operator can be applied to a type name and it yields the corresponding type object (of type System.Type). This object contains type information and can be used for reflection (see Section 4.5).

```
Type t = typeof(int);
Console.WriteLine(t.Name);   // prints Int32
```

The type of an *object* or a value can be found by using the method GetType inherited from System.Object:

```
Type t = 123.GetType();
Console.WriteLine(t.Name);   // prints Int32
```

2.4.8 sizeof

The sizeof operator can be applied to value types and gives their size in bytes. Because the storage required by a struct can be platform dependent, programs that use sizeof are not easily portable. This operator should normally be avoided, but if it is needed it must be used in an unsafe block:

```
unsafe {
    Console.WriteLine(sizeof(int));   // prints 4
}
```

Furthermore, this code must be compiled with the unsafe option and can only be executed in an environment that has been configured to be fully trusted:

```
csc /unsafe Test.cs
```

2.5 Declarations

Declarations introduce names by defining their types and sometimes also their initial values. For example:

```
int x = 3;             // declares an int variable x with the value 3
void Foo ( ) { ... }   // declares a method Foo without a result type
```

Each name belongs to a particular *declaration space*. C# has four of these:

- ❏ **Namespace:** can contain classes, interfaces, structs, enumerations, delegates and further namespaces.
- ❏ **Class, interface, struct:** can contain fields, methods, constructors, destructors, properties, indexers, events and nested types.
- ❏ **Enum:** contains enumeration constants.
- ❏ **Block:** can contain local variables.

The following rules apply to declarations:

1. No name can be declared more than once in the same declaration space at the same level. It may, however, be redeclared in an inner declaration space, except in a nested statement block.
2. The use of a name may precede its declaration, except for local variables, which must be declared before they are used.

The declaration space that a name belongs to determines its *visibility*:

1. A name is visible in its whole declaration space (local variables only from the point of their declaration onwards). If a name is redeclared in an inner declaration space, it hides the same name from the outer declaration space.
2. In general, no name is visible outside its declaration space.
3. The visibility of names declared in namespaces, classes, structs and interfaces can be controlled by the modifiers public, private, protected or internal. Names of enumeration constants can be accessed if they are qualified with their enumeration type name.

2.5.1 Declarations in Namespaces

Namespaces allow the grouping of type declarations that belong together. They also permit the use of the same name in different parts of a program. By declaring classes and other types in a separate namespace we can avoid collisions with identically named types from other namespaces. Namespaces can be nested. This can be used to create a hierarchy of namespaces:

```
namespace A {
    ... classes ...
    ... interfaces ...
    ... structs ...
    ... enumerations ...
    ... delegates ...
    namespace B {   // full name: A.B
        ...
    }
}
```

A namespace is declared by the keyword namespace and its name. After that, the types and possible nested namespaces follow in braces. The full name of a namespace B nested in a namespace A is A.B.

If a type is declared outside a namespace it belongs to an anonymous default namespace. The class Hello from Section 2.1 is an example of this.

As an example, assume that we have a namespace Persons with two classes Student and Teacher.

```
namespace Persons {
    public class Student {...}
    public class Teacher {...}
}
```

The types declared in Persons are of course visible in Persons. But because they are declared public, they can also be used in other namespaces that *import* Persons by incorporating a using clause:

```
namespace School {
    using Persons;        // imports all public types from Persons

    class Course {
        Student s;        // Student is known here
        Teacher t;        // Teacher is known here
    }
}
```

Instead of making Student and Teacher visible by importing Persons, they can be qualified with their namespace.

```
namespace School {
    class Course {
        Persons.Student s;     // qualification of a type with its namespace
        Persons.Teacher t;
    }
}
```

The explicit qualification of a type name is mainly used if types with the same names are to be imported from different namespaces.

Almost every program needs the namespace System (for example to be able to use the type Console for input and output). For this reason almost every program begins with using System;. We describe namespaces in more detail in Section 2.13.

2.5.2 Declarations in Classes, Structs and Interfaces

Classes, structs and interfaces can contain the following members:

```
class C {
    ... fields, constants ...
    ... methods ...
    ... constructors, destructors ...
    ... properties ...
    ... indexers ...
    ... events ...
    ... overloaded operators ...
    ... nested types (classes, structs, interfaces, enumerations, delegates) ...
}
```

```
struct S {
    ... as for classes ...
}

interface I {    // see Section 2.10
    ... methods ...
    ... properties ...
    ... indexers ...
    ... events ...
}
```

If classes are extended by inheritance (see Section 2.9) the superclass and the sub-class belong to different declaration spaces. Therefore the same names can be used for members in both classes.

Interfaces must not contain any data fields. Also, in contrast to Java, no constants are allowed. As a replacement, properties can be used.

2.5.3   Declarations in Enumeration Types

An enumeration type may only contain enumeration constants. When used, these must be qualified by the name of the enumeration type.

```
enum E {
    ... enumeration constants ...
}
```

2.5.4   Declarations in Blocks

A block is a sequence of statements enclosed in braces. It forms the body of a method or a sequence of related statements. Only local variables may be declared in a block.

```
void Foo(int x) {                   // method block
    ... local variables ...
    if (...) {                      // nested block of an if statement
        ... local variables ...
    }
    for (int i = 0; ...) {          // nested block of a for statement
        ... local variables ...
    }
}
```

Blocks can be nested. The declaration space of a block includes the declaration spaces of its nested blocks. Thus, in contrast to many other languages, a name must not be declared in a nested block if it has already been declared in its enclosing block.

Formal parameters (e.g. x in the method Foo) belong to the declaration space of the method block even though they are declared outside the block. Their names must not collide with other names declared in the method.

Similarly, the loop variable of a for statement (e.g. the variable i in the for loop above) belongs to the declaration space of the for block. Therefore different for statements may declare loop variables with the same name.

As already indicated, the declaration of a local variable must precede its use. The following example shows several errors that arise from violating the above rules. These errors are reported by the compiler:

```
void Foo(int a) {
   int b;
   if (...) {
      int b;              // error: b is already declared in the outer block
      int c;
      int d;
   } else {
      int a;              // error: a is already declared in the outer block (parameter)
      int d;              // OK, no conflict with d from the previous block
   }
   for (int i = 0; ...) {...}
   for (int i = 0; ...) {...}   // OK, no conflict with i from the previous loop
   int c;              // error: c is already declared in a nested block
}
```

It is permissible to declare a local variable with the same name as a field of the enclosing class. However, this field must not be used before the variable declaration in the method. The following program is therefore wrong:

```
class C {
   int x = 1, y = 2;
   void Foo() {
      int x = 2;          // OK, hides field x
      Console.WriteLine(y);
      int y = 3;          // error: y has already been used before in Foo
      ...
   }
}
```

This situation is forbidden, because y would otherwise denote two different objects in Foo.

2.6   Statements

The statements of C# do not differ very much from those of other programming languages. In addition to assignments and method calls there are various sorts of selections and loops, as well as branch statements and statements for exception handling.

2.6.1   Empty Statement

Every non-structured statement in C# must be terminated by a semicolon. A semicolon by itself is an empty statement that indicates no action and is used, for example, to express an empty loop body.

2.6.2   Assignment

An assignment evaluates an expression and assigns its value to a variable. The assignment itself is also an expression, so multiple assignments are possible:

```
x = 3 * y + 1;        // x becomes 3 * y + 1
a = b = 0;            // multiple assignment: a and b both get the value 0
```

The type of the expression must be assignment compatible with the type of the variable. This is the case if the two types are the same or if the type of the variable includes the type of the expression according to Figure 2.3 (e.g. short values can be assigned to int variables). Assignment compatibility also holds if the type of the expression is a subclass of the variable's type (see Section 2.9).

Assignments can be combined with various binary operators. For example:

```
x += y;
```

is a short form of

```
x = x + y
```

These short forms are useful in the case where x is a composite name (e.g. a[i].f). They reduce the typing effort and make it easier for the compiler to optimize an assignment. Combined assignments are possible with the operators +=, -=, *=, /=, %=, <<=, >>=, &=, !=, ^=.

2.6.3   Method Call

A method is called through its name and a parameter list. The details of method calls and parameter passing are covered in Section 2.8.3. Here are some examples of calls with methods of class String:

```
string s = "a,b,c";
string[] parts = s.Split(',');        // calls the method s.Split (non-static)
s = String.Join(" + ", parts);        // calls the method String.Join (static)
char[] arr = new char[10];
s.CopyTo(0, arr, 0, s.Length);
```

As Section 2.8.3 will show, methods can be *static* or *non-static*. A *non-static* method (for example, Split) is applied to a specific object (e.g. s). For example, s.Split(',') returns the substrings of s, which are delimited by occurrences of ',' (here "a", "b" and "c").

A *static* method (e.g. Join) is not applied to an object but to a class (e.g. String). It is comparable with an ordinary function in C. For example, String.Join(" + ", parts) concatenates the strings in the array parts together with " + ". The result here is "a + b + c".

Both Split and Join are *function methods*. They are called as operands in expressions and return a value. However, there are also methods that do *not* deliver a function result. They have the method type void and are called as stand-alone statements. For example, s.CopyTo(from, arr, to, len) copies len characters of the string s starting at the position from into the array arr beginning at the position to.

2.6.4 if Statement

An if statement has the form

if (*BooleanExpression***)** *Statement* **else** *Statement*

If the Boolean expression is true, the then branch (the first statement) is executed, otherwise the else branch (the second statement). The else branch may also be omitted. If the then branch or the else branch consists of several statements then they must be written as a *statement block* in braces. Here are some examples of if statements:

```
if (x > max) max = x;                 // without else branch
if (x > y) max = x; else max = y;     // with else branch
if ('0' <= ch && ch <= '9')
    val = ch - '0';
else if ('A' <= ch && ch <= 'F')      // nested if
    val = 10 + ch - 'A';
else {                                // else branch consists of a statement sequence
    val = 0;
    Console.WriteLine("invalid character: " + ch);
}
```

In contrast to C and C++ the if expression must be of type bool. In particular, it is not permissible to interpret the value 0 or null as false.

2.6.5   switch Statement

The switch statement is a *multi-way selection*. It consists of an expression and several statement sequences each prefixed by case labels. The switch statement branches to the case label that corresponds to the value of the expression. If there is no matching case label it jumps to the default label and if there is none then to the end of the switch statement. Here is an example:

```
switch (country) {
   case "England": case "USA":
      language = "English";
      break;
   case "Germany": case "Austria": case "Switzerland":
      language = "German";
      break;
   case null:
      Console.WriteLine("no country specified");
      break;
   default:
      Console.WriteLine("don't know the language of " + country);
      break;
}
```

The expression in the head of the switch statement must be numeric, an enumeration or of the type char or string. The case labels must be disjoint constant values whose type must be assignment compatible with the type of the expression.

In contrast to most other languages, C# allows the expression to be of type string (including case labels with the value null). In this case the switch statement is treated by the compiler as a series of nested if statements, whereas in the other cases it is implemented as a direct jump to the matching case label.

Each statement sequence between the case labels *must* end with a statement to break out. The most common of these is the *break statement* which jumps to the end of the switch statement. Other statements allowed are return, goto and throw. We discuss these later. In contrast to most other languages, C# does not allow a program to *fall through* a (non-empty) case branch to the next. If this is what we want we must implement it with a goto statement.

2.6.6   while Statement

The while statement is the most common form of loop. It consists of a Boolean expression and a *loop body* which is repeatedly executed as long as the expression remains true. The expression is tested before each execution of the loop body. If the loop body consists of more than one statement then it must be written as a statement block in braces.

```
while (x > y) x = x / 2;        // loop body consists of a single statement
while (i < n) {                 // loop body consists of a statement sequence
   sum += i;
   i++;
}
```

2.6.7 do-while Statement

The do-while statement differs from the while statement only in that the Boolean expression is tested *after* the loop body. So the body will be executed at least once.

```
do i = 10 * i while (i < n);    // loop body consists of a single statement
do {                            // loop body consists of a statement sequence
   sum += a[i]; i--;
} while (i >= 0);
```

2.6.8 for Statement

The for statement is the most flexible but also the most complicated form of loop. It has the form:

```
for (Initialization; Condition; Increment) Statement
```

Before the first run through the loop the initialization is executed. This usually assigns a value to a loop variable. Before each execution of the loop the condition is tested and at the end of each iteration the increment is carried out. The loop body is executed as long as the condition is true. The statement

```
for (int i = 0; i < n; i++)
   sum += i;
```

can be regarded as a short form of the while loop

```
int i = 0;
while (i < n) {
   sum += i;
   i++;
}
```

It is treated by the compiler in exactly the same way as the while loop (except that i is local to the for loop). Both the initialization and the increment can comprise of more than one statement. These are then separated by a comma instead of being terminated by a semicolon. For example:

```
for (int i = 0, j = n-1; i < n; i++, j--)
   sum += a[i] + b[j];
```

2.6.9   foreach Statement

The foreach statement offers a convenient way of iterating over an array, a string or some other collection of elements that implements the interface IEnumerable (see Section 4.1.1). It has the form:

foreach (*ElementVarDecl* **in** *Collection***)** *Statement*

Here are two examples of foreach statements:

```
int[] a = {3, 17, 4, 8, 2, 29};
sum = 0;
foreach (int x in a) sum += x;

string s = "Hello";
foreach (char ch in s) Console.WriteLine(ch);
```

The first loop sums the elements of the array a. The second prints all the characters of the string s. The following example is also interesting:

```
Queue q = new Queue();
q.Enqueue("John"); q.Enqueue("Alice"); ...
foreach (string s in q) Console.WriteLine(s);
```

The elements of a queue are stored as data of type object. The compiler knows, however, that the loop variable s of the foreach statement is of type string. Therefore it generates a checked type cast from object to string when it retrieves the elements from q.

2.6.10 break and continue Statements

We have already seen the break statement in connection with the switch statement. However, it can also be used to terminate the execution of a loop:

```
for (;;) {
    int x = stream.ReadByte();
    if (x < 0) break;
    sum += x;
}
```

This example shows the use of a for statement as an *endless loop*. If the initialization part, the condition and the increment are omitted then the loop cycles forever—or until, as in this case, it is terminated by executing a break statement. The break statement can also be used in while, do-while and foreach loops. With nested loops, however, it only leaves the innermost loop. In order to break right out of a nested loop structure a goto statement must be used.

The continue statement (written as continue;) may likewise be used in any kind of loop. It indicates that the rest of the loop body should be skipped, any increment should be carried out (only in for loops) and the continuation condition should be tested again before the next run through the loop begins.

2.6.11 goto Statement

The goto statement jumps to a label that is written in front of another statement. The label consists of a name followed by a colon. For example, the do-while statement could also be coded by means of a goto and a label:

```
top:                    // do {
   sum += i;            //    sum += i;
   i++;                 //    i++;
   if (i <= n) goto top;   // } while (i <= n);
```

This is not recommended because it obscures the structure of the program. A sensible use of a goto statement is, for example, to break out of an inner loop, because this cannot be done with a break statement.

Because the unrestricted use of the goto statement can have a negative impact on the quality of a program there are certain restrictions pertaining to jumps. So, for example, it is illegal to jump into a block or to jump out of a finally block during exception handling (see Section 2.12).

Goto statements can also be used within a switch statement to jump to a case label. This is a sensible use of a goto because it allows so-called *finite-state machines* to be implemented efficiently. A finite-state machine consists of a set of states between which transitions are defined that are triggered by a sequence of input symbols. Figure 2.6 shows such a state machine where the states are denoted by circles and the transitions by arrows.

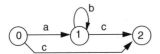

Figure 2.6 *Finite-state machine*

This state machine can be implemented in the following way by using goto statements:

```
int state = 0;                     // starts in state 0
int ch = Console.Read();           // reads first input symbol
switch (state) {
   case 0:  if (ch == 'a') { ch = Console.Read(); goto case 1; }
            else if (ch == 'c') goto case 2;
            else goto default;
```

```
case 1:  if (ch == 'b') { ch = Console.Read(); goto case 1; }
         else if (ch == 'c') goto case 2;
         else goto default;
case 2:  Console.WriteLine("input valid!");
         break;
default: Console.WriteLine("illegal character: " + (char) ch);
         break;
}
```

It would be even shorter in this case to discard the switch statement and jump directly to labels named state0, state1, state2 and illegal.

2.6.12 return Statement

The return statement allows the (early) termination of methods. There are two forms of it: one for void methods and one for functions. Void methods can be terminated by a return statement without an argument. For example:

```
void P(int x) {
   if (x < 0) return;
   ...
}
```

Of course, the method also ends after its last statement. Function methods must be dynamically terminated by a return statement that has the return value as its argument. For example:

```
int Max(int a, int b) {
   if (a > b) return a; else return b;
}
```

The type of the return value must be assignment compatible with the return type declared in the method heading. A function method must not reach its end without executing a return statement, because it always has to return a value.

The Main method of a program may also be declared as a function. Its return value of type int will be interpreted as an error code that is stored in a system variable (under Windows the variable errorlevel).

```
class Test {
   static int Main() {
      ...
      if (...) return -1;
      ...
   }
}
```

2.7 Input and Output

Like most modern languages, C# has no dedicated statements for input and output of data. Instead there are library classes for this. In this chapter we will see how one can write to the screen and read from the keyboard, as well as use files for input and output. Section 4.2 goes even further into input and output.

2.7.1 Output to the Screen

The console window on the screen is represented by the class System.Console. This class contains two output methods:

```
Console.Write(x);      // writes the value of x to the console
Console.WriteLine(x);  // writes the value of x to the console and then skips to the next line
```

The parameter x can be an expression of any primitive type (int, char, float, ...) as well as of type string. If x is of some other type (e.g. a reference type) it is automatically converted to a string by calling x.ToString() prior to output.

Formatted Output

Write and WriteLine also allow formatted output of values. For this purpose one has to supply a format string and a variable number of argument values. The format string has numbered placeholders for the other arguments. The call

```
Console.WriteLine("{0} = {1}", x, y);
```

replaces {0} by x and {1} by y and then prints the resulting string. Here is another example that prints the values of an array in a neatly formatted way:

```
using System;

class Test {
    static void Main() {
        string[] a = {"Alice", "Bob", "Cecil"};
        for (int i = 0; i < a.Length; i++)
            Console.WriteLine("a[{0}] = {1}", i, a[i]);
    }
}
```

The output looks as follows:

```
a[0] = Alice
a[1] = Bob
a[2] = Cecil
```

Placeholder Syntax

A placeholder in a format string allows the specification of a field width, an output format and the desired number of decimal places. Its syntax

```
"{" n ["," width] [":" format [precision]] "}"
```

has the following meaning (square brackets indicate that the bracketed part can be omitted):

n	argument number (begins at 0)
width	field width (if too small it will be extended)
	positive = right aligned, negative = left aligned
format	formatting code, for example d, f, e, x (see below)
precision	number of decimal places (sometimes number of digits)

For example, the placeholder

```
{0, 10:f2)
```

indicates the right-aligned output of argument 0 in a field that is 10 characters wide. The output will be in fixed-point format f with 2 decimal places. Table 2.6 shows the most important formatting codes and their meanings.

Table 2.6 *The most important formatting codes*

Code	Meaning	Output image
d, D	**decimal format** (integer number with leading zeros) precision = number of digits	-xxxxx
f, F	**fixed-point format** precision = number of decimal places (default = 2)	-xxxxx.xx
n, N	**number format** (with thousands separator) precision = number of decimal places (default = 2)	-xx,xxx.xx
e, E	**floating-point format** (upper and lower case is significant) precision = number of decimal places	-x.xxxE+xxx
c, C	**currency format** precision = number of decimal places negative values shown in brackets	$xx,xxx.xx ($xx,xxx.xx)
x, X	**hexadecimal format** (upper and lower case is significant) precision = number of hex digits (possibly leading zeros)	xxxx
g, G	**general** (selects the most compact format for the arguments; this is the default if no other formatting code has been specified)	

The following examples show the output of a value with different formatting codes:

```
int x = 26;

Console.WriteLine("{0}", x);        //  26
Console.WriteLine("{0, 5}", x);     //     26

Console.WriteLine("{0:d}", x);      //  26
Console.WriteLine("{0:d5}", x);     //  00026

Console.WriteLine("{0:f}", x);      //  26.00
Console.WriteLine("{0:f1}", x);     //  26.0

Console.WriteLine("{0:E}", x);      //  2.600000E+001
Console.WriteLine("{0:e1}", x);     //  2.6e+001

Console.WriteLine("{0:X}", x);      //  1A
Console.WriteLine("{0:x4}", x);     //  001a
```

String Formatting

Numbers can be converted to strings by the method ToString. Just as with Write and WriteLine, formatting codes can be given for ToString to specify the format, field width and decimal places. Here are some examples:

```
string s;
int i = 12;
s = i.ToString();       // "12"
s = i.ToString("x4");   // "000c"
s = i.ToString("f");    // "12.00"
```

ToString even allows country-specific formatting, affecting for example the currency format:

```
s = i.ToString("c");                           // "$12.00" -- US format
s = i.ToString("c", new CultureInfo("en-GB")); // "£12.00" -- British format
```

Finally the class String has a method Format for general formatting of strings, as in:

```
s = String.Format("{0} = {1,6:x4}", name, i);   // "myName =   000c"
```

2.7.2 Output to a File

Write and WriteLine can also be used to write formatted output to a file. For this we have to create an output stream of type FileStream and attach a StreamWriter to it. Like Console, StreamWriter provides the methods Write and WriteLine. The following example creates a file "myfile.txt" in the current directory and writes a table with the squares of the numbers 1 to 10.

```
using System.IO;                        // imports FileStream and StreamWriter
class Test {
    static void Main() {
        FileStream s = new FileStream("myfile.txt", FileMode.Create);
        StreamWriter w = new StreamWriter(s);
        w.WriteLine("Table of squares:");
        for (int i = 1; i < 10; i++)
            w.WriteLine("{0,3}: {1,5}", i, i*i);
        w.Close();                      // necessary to flush the output buffer
    }
}
```

2.7.3 Input from the Keyboard

The class System.Console can be used not only for output to the screen, but also for input from the keyboard. Each call of the method:

```
int ch = Console.Read();
```

returns the next character from the keyboard as an int number. At the end of the input (under Windows if control-Z is typed at the start of a line) it gives the value -1. Read blocks until the user has entered a whole line terminated by the return key and then reads all characters of this line. If the input is abc followed by the return key then successive calls of Read yield the sequence 'a', 'b', 'c', '\r', and '\n'. To read the entire line at once the method

```
string line = Console.ReadLine();
```

can be used. This too blocks until the user presses the return key and then it returns the input line without the '\r' and '\n'. At the end of the input ReadLine returns the value null.

Unfortunately, the current version of the class library does not provide methods for formatted input of numbers or boolean values. Programmers have to implement these themselves. For example:

```
static int ReadInt() {
    int ch = Console.Read();
    while (0 <= ch && ch <= ' ') ch = Console.Read();   // skip insignificant characters
    int val = 0;
    while ('0' <= ch && ch <= '9') {
        val = 10 * val + (ch - '0');
        ch = Console.Read();
    }
    return val;
}
```

The user can download a class In from [JKU] with various methods for formatted input.

2.7.4 Input from a File

Read and ReadLine can also be used to read from a file. For this we have to open a FileStream and attach a StreamReader to it, which provides the methods Read and ReadLine:

```
using System.IO;   // imports FileStream and StreamReader
class Test {
    static void Main() {
        FileStream s = new FileStream("myfile.txt", FileMode.Open);
        StreamReader r = new StreamReader(s);
        string line = r.ReadLine();
        while (line != null) {
            ...
            line = r.ReadLine();
        }
        r.Close();
    }
}
```

Unfortunately, it is not possible to attach more than one StreamReader at a time to a single file in order to read from different places in the file.

2.7.5 Reading Command-line Arguments

To run a program we type its name in the command line, followed by a sequence of words separated by spaces. These command-line arguments are passed to the Main method as a string array:

```
using System;
class Test {
    static void Main(string[] arg) {
        for (int i = 0; i < arg.Length; i++)
            Console.WriteLine("{0}: {1}", i, arg[i]);
    }
}
```

If this program is called like this:

```
Test value = 3
```

it prints

```
0: value
1: =
2: 3
```

2.8   Classes and Structs

Both classes and structs are types that allow related data and operations to be grouped. Classes and structs can contain a selection of the following members, explanations of which will follow:

- ❏ fields and constants
- ❏ methods
- ❏ constructors and destructors
- ❏ properties
- ❏ indexers
- ❏ events
- ❏ overloaded operators
- ❏ nested types (classes, structs, interfaces, enumerations, delegates).

Here is an example of the class Counter, which provides methods to accumulate some values and to compute their average:

```
class Counter {
    public int value = 0;                          // fields
    private int n = 0;
    public void Add(int x) { value += x; n++; }    // methods
    public float Mean() { return (float) value / n; }
}
```

Before a Counter object can be used it must be created in the following way:

```
Counter c = new Counter();
```

After creation the public fields and methods can be accessed. For example:

```
c.Add(3); c.Add(17); ...
Console.WriteLine("sum: {0}, average: {1}", c.value, c.Mean());
```

Classes are *reference types*. Their objects are stored on the heap and are referenced through pointers. Structs, on the other hand, are *value types* that are kept on the method stack (or are embedded in other objects) and are stored directly in variables. The following example shows a struct for representing fractional numbers:

```
struct Fraction {
    public int n, d;                               // fields
                                                   // (numerator, denominator)
    public Fraction(int n, int d) { this.n = n; this.d = d; }     // constructor
    public Add(Fraction f) { n = n * f.d + d * f.n; d = d * f.d; } // methods
    public Multiply(Fraction f) { n = n * f.n; d = d * f.d; }
}
```

When a struct variable is declared, its fields are as yet uninitialized but values can already be assigned to them. For example,

```
Fraction f;
f.n = 1; f.d = 1;
```

However, it is better to initialize a struct via a constructor (see Section 2.8.4):

```
Fraction f = new Fraction();        // does not create a new object, but initializes
Fraction g = new Fraction(1, 2);    // the objects f and g on the stack
g.Add(new Fraction(1, 3));          // creates a new Fraction object on the stack
```

Every struct type automatically has a parameterless default constructor that initializes its fields to 0. The constructor called in the creation of g sets g.n to 1 and g.d to 2. The call g.Add(new Fraction(1, 3)) creates a new Fraction object on the method stack with the value 1/3 and adds it to g so that g.n is assigned the value 5 and g.d the value 6.

Because of a limitation in the common language runtime it is illegal to initialize struct fields in their declarations. Thus the compiler will report errors for the following example:

```
struct Fraction {
    public int n = 1;// error!
    public int d = 1;// error!
    ...
}
```

Struct objects (which are stored on the method stack) are automatically released when the execution of the declaring method is completed. Class objects (which are stored on the heap) are never explicitly released but are removed by the garbage collector as soon as they are no longer referenced.

2.8.1   Access Modifiers

An important role of classes and structs is to abstract from the implementation of their data by concealing it from other classes (*information hiding, data abstraction*). This can be achieved by restricting the visibility of their members by access modifiers such as public, private, protected and internal.

public. Declarations that have the access modifier public are visible wherever their enclosing namespace is known. Members of interfaces and enumerations are public by default. Members of structs and classes must, however, be explicitly declared as public if they are to be publicly visible, otherwise they are private.

Types at the outermost level of a namespace (classes, structs, interfaces, enumerations and delegates) can also be declared as public. Otherwise they have the visibility internal, which means that they are only known within the assembly in which they are declared. Roughly speaking, an *assembly* consists of all types that are compiled in the same compilation run. In Section 2.13 we will deal with assemblies in greater detail.

Public members of types are of course only visible if the type to which they belong is also visible.

private. Declarations that have the access modifier private are only visible in the class or struct in which they are declared. Members of classes and structs are private by default. To make them publicly visible we have to declare them as public. Here is an example that shows the use of access modifiers:

```
struct Fraction {                               // internal
    public int n, d;                            // public
    private int auxiliary1;                     // private
    int auxiliary2;                             // private
    void Reduce() {...}                         // private
    public void Add(Fraction f) {...}           // public
}
```

The following example shows where private members can be accessed:

```
class A {
    private int x;
}

class B {
    private int y;

    public void F(B b) {
        y = ...;            // B methods can access private B members
        b.y = ...;          // B methods can access private members of other B objects
        A a = new A();
        a.x = ...;          // wrong! B methods must not access private members of A objects
    }
}
```

Beside public, private and internal there are also the access modifiers protected and protected internal. These are described in Section 2.9.1.

2.8.2 Fields

The data within classes and structs are called *fields* and can be variables or constants. The following example shows some valid declarations:

```
class C {
    int value = 0;                              // field variable
    const long size = ((long)int.MaxValue + 1) / 4);    // field constant
    readonly DateTime date;                     // read-only field
    ...
}
```

Variables. Field variables such as value are declared by stating their type and their name. In classes they can also be initialized, as in the above example. In structs, however, they cannot. This has to do with a limitation of the common language runtime. The initialization of a struct must always be done in a constructor. If a field is initialized in its declaration the initialization code must not access other fields and methods of the same object.

Constants. A field constant such as size is a name for a value, which is computed at compile time and is used in all places where the name appears. Constants are declared with the keyword const and must be initialized (also in structs).

Read-only fields. If a field is declared with the keyword readonly it must be given its value either in the declaration or in a constructor. Later it may be read but not written. In contrast to constants, read-only fields occupy memory, which is accessed in later use. Read-only fields are initialized at run time, constant fields at compile time. The advantage lies in the fact that the value of a read-only field can, for example, be obtained from a file. This is not possible for constants.

Within their class, fields can be referenced simply by their names (e.g., value or this.value). The fields of another object must be qualified with the object's name. (e.g., c.value).

Static Fields

The fields of a class exist either in each of its objects or only once per class. If they are to exist only once per class then they are called *static fields* and must be declared with the modifier static.

```
class Rectangle {
    static Color defaultColor;       // only once per class
    static readonly int scale = 1;   // only once per class
    int x, y, width, height;         // stored in every object
    ...
}
```

The fields defaultColor and scale belong to the Rectangle class itself and are allocated just once. The fields x, y, width and height, on the other hand, are stored in every Rectangle object (see Figure 2.7).

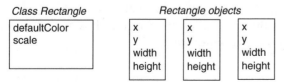

Figure 2.7 *Static and non-static fields*

All methods of a class can access the static fields of this class (e.g. through defaultColor or Rectangle.defaultColor). To access the static fields of a different class the field name must be qualified with the class name (e.g. String.Empty).

For constant fields no memory is allocated. Therefore the static modifier makes no sense and is forbidden.

2.8.3   Methods

The operations of a class are called *methods*. They are declared by their name, a (possibly empty) parameter list and their code body.

```
class Counter {
    int sum = 0, n = 0;

    public void Add(int x) {          // procedure
        sum = sum + x; n++;
    }
    public float Mean() {             // function (must return a value)
        return (float)sum / n;
    }
}
```

Methods can be procedures or functions. A *procedure* is called as a statement on its own. For example:

```
counter.Add(3);
```

It returns no value and is therefore declared as void. A *function* on the other hand is called as an operand of an expression. For example:

```
float result = 10 + counter.Mean();
```

It returns a *function value* and is therefore declared with the type of this value (for example, Mean() returns a float result). The result must be returned by a return statement, otherwise the compiler reports an error.

Static Methods

Just as with fields, methods can be associated either with a class itself or with the objects of the class. Methods that are associated with the class are called *static methods* and are declared with the keyword static.

```
class Rectangle {
    static Color defaultColor;

    public static void ResetColor() { defaultColor = Color.white; }
    ...
}
```

Static methods are applied to their classes, whereas non-static methods are applied to the objects of their classes. Static methods are mainly used to initialize static fields. Within the declaring class they can be accessed by their names (e.g. ResetColor or Rectangle.ResetColor). Static methods of other classes must be qualified with the class name (e.g. String.Format).

Parameters

Parameters are values that are passed from the caller to the method or back from the method to the caller. A method declaration contains a (possibly empty) list of *formal parameters*, which correspond to the *actual parameters* specified in the method call. Parameters are declared just like variables except that they are separated by commas, rather than terminated by semicolons. For example:

```
void PrintMessage (string msg, int x, int y) {...}
```

C# supports three kinds of parameter, which are passed in different ways.

Value parameters. A value parameter is an *input parameter* that is passed from the caller to the method (*call by value*). The actual parameter must be an expression, whose value is calculated before the call and is then copied into the corresponding formal parameter. In the following example:

```
void Inc(int x) { x = x + 1; }

void F() {
    int val = 3;
    Inc(val);        // after this call, val still has the value 3
}
```

the value of val is copied into the formal parameter x before Inc is called. When x is increased in Inc the value of val remains unchanged because x is only a copy of val. With value parameters, the types of the actual and formal parameters must be assignment compatible. That is the case here, because both val and x have the type int.

ref parameters. A reference parameter is an *input/output parameter*. It can be used to pass a value to a method, to change it there, and then to pass it back to the caller for further use. The actual parameter must be a variable, for which the corresponding formal parameter is an alias name. Technically this is achieved by passing the address of the actual parameter (*call by reference*). The corresponding formal parameter then simply gets the same address as the actual one. Both the formal and the actual parameter must be marked with the keyword ref. In the example:

```
void Inc(ref int x) { x = x + 1; }

void F() {
    int val = 3;
    Inc(ref val);      // val has the value 4 after the call
}
```

val and x refer to the same variable. If Inc increases x, then val is increased as well. The compiler makes sure that val already has a value before it is passed to Inc. The method may alter this value and then passes it back to the caller. With reference parameters the actual and formal parameters must have the same type because they designate the same variable.

Out parameters. An out parameter is an *output parameter*, which is passed back from the method to its caller. As for reference parameters, the parameter-passing mode is *call by reference*. The actual parameter need not have a value before the call, but the compiler checks that the formal parameter gets a value before it is passed back. The actual parameter must be a variable that has the same type as the corresponding formal parameter. Both formal and actual parameters must be marked with the keyword out.

```
void Read(out int first, out int next) {
    first = Console.Read();
    next = Console.Read();
}

void F() {
    int a, b;
    Read(out a, out b);
}
```

In this example, a and first are two names for the same variable, as are b and next. Out parameters are mainly used when a method needs to return more than one value. Otherwise the result can be returned as a function value.

Variable Number of Parameters

C# methods can have a variable number of parameters. To be precise, the last parameter can be declared as an array, to which a sequence of values can be passed in the call. Such a parameter must be declared with the keyword params, as in the following example:

```
void Add(out int sum, params int[] val) {
    sum = 0;
    foreach (int i in val) sum += i;
}
```

If the method is called as follows:

```
Add(out sum, 3, 4, 2, 9);
```

the values 3, 4, 2 and 9 are collected into an int array which is passed to val, and the value 18 is returned in sum.

Other familiar examples of methods with a variable number of parameters are Write and WriteLine from the class Console. They are declared as follows:

```
public void WriteLine(string format, params object[] arg) {...}
```

and can have any number of arguments after the format string.

One restriction must be mentioned: the keyword params must not be combined with ref or out. So there can be a variable number of input parameters, but not a variable number of output or input/output parameters.

Method Overloading

Within a class, methods can have the same name as long as they differ in their formal parameters, i.e. if they have

❑ a different *number* of parameters, or
❑ different parameter *types*, or
❑ different parameter kinds (value, ref/out).

In the following example, five methods with the name P are declared. They differ according to the above criteria.

```
void P(int x) {...}
void P(char x) {...}
void P(int x, long y) {...}
void P(long x, int y) {...}
void P(ref int x) {...}
```

In a call of the method P the compiler selects the best-fitting variant according to the types of the actual parameters, so:

```
int i; long n; short s;
P(i);        // P(int x)
P(ref i);    // P(ref int x)
P('a');      // P(char x)
P(i, n);     // P(int x, long y)
P(n, s);     // P(long x, int y)
P(i, s);     // ambiguous between P(int x, long y) and P(long x, int y) => error
P(i, i);     // ambiguous between P(int x, long y) and P(long x, int y) => error
```

If the choice is ambiguous, as in the last two lines of the example, the compiler reports an error.

Overloaded methods may not differ only in their function types, as in the following example:

```
int F() {...}
string F() {...}
```

Since any function can also be called as a procedure

```
F();   // return value is ignored
```

the compiler cannot determine which of the two functions is meant. Therefore this case is forbidden.

Furthermore, the keyword params, as well as ref versus out, may not be used as distinguishing criteria with overloaded methods. The following declarations are therefore wrong:

```
void P(int[] a) {...}
void P(params int[] a) {...}    // error: ambiguous
void Q(ref int x) {...}
void Q(out int x) {...}         // error: ambiguous
```

The reason for the latter restriction is not obvious, since Q must be called as either Q(ref x); or Q(out x); so the compiler should be able to distinguish between the two methods. For some reason, however, the compiler generates the same CIL code in both cases and so the JIT compiler cannot distinguish the two calls.

2.8.4 Constructors

Constructors are special methods for initializing objects. We will first discuss constructors in classes, then constructors in structs and finally static constructors.

Constructors in Classes

A constructor is a method that is called automatically right after the creation of an object in order to initialize it. Constructors have the same name as the class in which they are declared and have no function type. The class Rectangle in the following example has three overloaded constructors:

```
class Rectangle {
    int x, y, width, height;
    public Rectangle(int x, int y, int w, int h) { this.x = x; this.y = y; width = w; height = h; }
    public Rectangle(int w, int h) : this(0, 0, w, h) {}
    public Rectangle() : this(0, 0, 0, 0) {}
    ...
}
```

The statement

```
Rectangle r1 = new Rectangle(2, 2, 10, 5);
```

creates a new Rectangle object and calls the appropriate constructor (in this case the one with four parameters), which initializes the fields x, y, width and height with the values 2, 2, 10, 5. Creation and initialization of an object are thus combined in an atomic action. Creating an object with

```
Rectangle r2 = new Rectangle(10, 5);
```

calls the constructor with two parameters. In the heading of its declaration the call

```
... : this(0, 0, w, h)
```

denotes that another constructor of this class should be called (the one with four parameters) before the former constructor is executed. The implementation of a constructor can thus reuse the implementation of another constructor. The same applies to the third constructor.

After the creation of an object and before the call of the constructor, initializations in the field declarations are executed, if there are any. Any fields of an object that are not initialized explicitly are given a null value (i.e. 0, '\0', null, false).

Default constructor. If no constructor was declared for a class, a parameterless default constructor is automatically created. So if a class looks like this

```
class C {
    int x;
    bool y;
}
```

an object of this class can be created as usual:

```
C obj = new C();
```

This causes the default constructor to be called, which initializes the fields of the object as follows (depending on their types):

numeric type:	0
enumeration:	constant that corresponds to the value 0
bool:	false
char:	'\0'
reference type:	null

If a class has at least one explicit constructor then no default constructor is created. So if a class looks like this

```
class C {
    int x;
    public C(int y) { x = y; }
}
```

a parameter must be given when creating an object:

```
C c1 = new C(3);      // OK
C c2 = new C();       // compiler reports an error
```

Constructors in Structs

In principle, constructors for structs have the same form and meaning as those for classes. However, for structs, no parameterless constructors may be declared (the reason lies in the implementation of the common language runtime). Instead, the compiler itself creates a parameterless default constructor that initializes the fields to null values as described above. Here is an example:

```
struct Complex {
    double re, im;
    public Complex(double re, double im) { this.re = re; this.im = im; }
    public Complex(double re) : this(re, 0) {}
    ...
}
...
Complex c0;                          // c0.re and c0.im are not yet initialized
Complex c1 = new Complex();          // c1.re == 0, c1.im == 0
Complex c2 = new Complex(5);         // c2.re == 5, c2.im == 0
Complex c3 = new Complex(10, 3);     // c3.re == 10, c3.im == 3
```

Static Constructors

Like methods, constructors can be marked with the keyword static. A static constructor serves mainly to initialize a class or struct (i.e. its static fields) and is automatically called before the type is used for the first time. Here are two examples:

```
class Rectangle {
    static Color defaultColor;
    static Rectangle() { defaultColor = Color.black; }
    ...
}
struct Point {
    ...
    static Point() { Console.WriteLine("Point initialized"); }
}
```

Static constructors must be parameterless (even for structs) and must not have an access modifier (such as public or private). There can only be a single static constructor for each type.

Before a static constructor is called the initializations specified in the declarations of the static fields are executed, if there are any. If a class has no static constructor then all its static fields that do not have explicit initializations are initialized to null values (0, false, '\0' etc.).

The order in which the static constructors of the individual types are called is undefined. It is only guaranteed that they will be called before the types are used.

2.8.5 Destructors

Destructors are the counterpart of constructors. They clean up objects (e.g. they close files that an object has opened) and are automatically called—if they exist—before the garbage collector releases an object of the corresponding class. If the superclass also has a destructor, this is automatically called after the destructor of the subclass. A destructor has the same name as its class, is parameterless, neither public nor private and is declared with a tilde (~). For example:

```
class Buffer {
    FileStream s = new FileStream("scratch.txt", FileMode.Create);
    ...
    ~Buffer() {          // destructor
        s.Close();       // cleanup work
    }
}
```

Most classes do not need a destructor, because normally the cleanup consists only of releasing the objects that are no longer needed, and this is carried out automatically by the garbage collector. .NET does not specify the order in which destructors will be called, nor even that they will be called at all before the program ends. Besides, objects with destructors take longer to create and to release. Therefore: hands off destructors! In contrast to C++, they are hardly ever needed.

2.8.6 Properties

Properties are smart fields that are used through get and set accessors. The declaration of such a field and its accessors forms a syntactic unit, for example:

```
class Data {
    FileStream s;

    public string FileName {  // property with the name FileName and the type string
        set { s = new FileStream(value, FileMode.Create); }   // set accessor
        get { return s.Name; }                                // get accessor
    }
    ...
}
```

The property FileName can be used as if it were a field of type string. If a value is assigned to it, e.g.:

```
Data d = new Data();
d.FileName = "myFile.txt";
```

the set accessor of FileName is automatically called, and the string "myFile.txt" is passed as a hidden parameter. The hidden parameter always has the name value and the type of the property (here string). The assignment thus leads to the execution of

```
s = new FileStream("myFile.txt", FileMode.Create);
```

If the property is accessed in read mode

```
string str = d.FileName;
```

the get accessor of FileName is called and returns a string value in this case. Strictly speaking, get and set are not called as methods but their code is *in-lined* by the JIT compiler. Thus properties are almost as efficient as fields.

Properties can also be static, in which case they belong to a class rather than to an object. In addition to the plain assignment, all combined assignment operators are allowed (+=, -=, etc):

```
class C {
    private static int size;

    public static int Size {
        get { return size; }
        set { size = value; }
    }
}
...
C.Size = 3;        // plain assignment
C.Size += 2;       // combined assignment: C.Size = C.Size + 2;
```

Not all properties must have a set as well as a get accessor. If the set accessor is omitted then the property is read-only. If the get accessor is omitted then it is write-only. The restriction to reading is useful, for example, in the following class Account where it is possible to enquire about the balance of an account, but not to change it.

```
class Account {
    long balance;

    public long Balance {
        get { return balance; }
    }
}
...
long x = account.Balance;      // OK
account.Balance = 0;           // forbidden: compiler reports an error
```

Since properties are compiled into methods we cannot use them as ref or out parameters, because there the actual parameter must be a variable in which the parameter can be returned.

Benefits of properties. Properties are a concept that is absent from both C++ and Java. In fact, in Java there is a naming convention that a private field xxx should be accessed via a pair of methods getXxx and setXxx, but this is just a convention. Properties have the following advantages:

❑ The interface and the implementation of data can differ, as in the example for FileName. Clients use FileName as a string field. In reality, however, it is stored as a FileStream that is automatically opened when the property is set.

❑ When assigning to a property, validity checks, trace output or other operations can be done in the background. If the size field in our example should have a value in the range 0 to 100 this can be checked in the set accessor of the property Size.

❑ As already mentioned, properties can be used to implement read-only or write-only fields.

❑ Interfaces (see Section 2.10) cannot have fields, but can have properties. Properties are thus a replacement for fields in interfaces.

❑ Properties can easily be recognized through reflection (see Section 4.5). This is important in component-based programs where we often plug components together in a builder environment and must know what properties a component has in order to configure it correctly.

2.8.7 Indexers

A class often represents a collection of elements (e.g. a list, a set or a file) that one would like to access with the array indexing notation. In C# we can use an *indexer* for this.

An indexer is a user-defined operation for indexing a sequence of elements. Like a property, it has a pair of get and set accessors. In addition, it has one or more index parameters that serve as keys. The access is written in array indexing notation, for example list[i].

This is best explained through an example. Assume that we have a file and we want to access its bytes in the form file[i]. The class File and its indexer could be implemented as follows:

```
class File {
    private FileStream s;

    public int this [int offset] {
        get {
            s.Seek(offset, SeekOrigin.Begin);
            return s.ReadByte();
        }
```

```
set {
    s.Seek(offset, SeekOrigin.Begin);
    s.WriteByte((byte)value);
}
}
...
}
```

An indexer always has the name this. Its type (in the above example, int) gives the type of the returned element. Instead of a parameter an index is declared in square brackets (here [int offset]). It serves as the key for the access. As with properties, the value that is passed to the set method always has the name value. The indexer can be used as follows:

```
File f = new File();
int x = f[10];          // calls f.get(10) => offset == 10
f[10] = 'A';            // calls f.set(10, 'A') => offset == 10, value == 'A'
```

For read access the get accessor is called, in which offset has the value 10 here. For write access the set accessor is called, in which offset has the value 10 and value the value 'A'.

As for methods, indexers can be overloaded by declaring index values with different types. This is illustrated in the following example, which also shows that the index parameter need not be of type int and that the get or set accessors can be omitted:

```
class MonthlySales {
    int[] sales = new int[12];   // sales figures for the last 12 months

    public int this [int i] {
        get { return sales[i-1]; }
    }

    public int this [string month] {
        get {
            switch (month) {
                case "Jan": return sales[0];
                case "Feb": return sales[1];
                ...
            }
        }
    }
}
```

If s is a variable of type MonthlySales then the sales figures for February can be accessed by s[2] or s["Feb"]. This is more readable than calling a method such as s.getSales(2) or s.getSales("Feb"). Indexers are heavily used in the .NET class library, for example in accessing the elements of a string, an ArrayList or a Hashtable (see Section 4.1).

2.8.8   Operators

In general, built-in operators such as + and * have a fixed meaning, defined by the language. C#, however, allows such operators to be implemented as methods and thus to be given a user-defined meaning. This is called *operator overloading*.

Overloaded operators are useful, for example, for fractional or complex numbers where they are natural in a mathematical sense. Two fractions a and b can then be added by writing a + b instead of a clumsy method call a.Add(b). The following example shows the declaration of a type Fraction with an overloaded operator +.

```
struct Fraction {       // fractional numbers
    int n, d;           // numerator, denominator

    public Fraction(int n, int d) { this.n = n; this.d = d; }

    public static Fraction operator + (Fraction a, Fraction b) {
        return new Fraction(a.n * b.d + b.n * a.d, a.d * b.d);
    }
    ...
}
```

An overloaded operator must always be declared as a static method that returns a function result (most often an object of the same type for which the operator is declared). The name of the method is the operator itself (for example, +) preceded by keyword operator.

There are unary and binary operators. Methods for unary operators have a single parameter. Methods for binary operators have two parameters. In both cases the parameters must be of the type to which the method belongs (in the above example, Fraction).

Now we can use Fraction variables as follows:

```
Fraction a = new Fraction(1, 2);
Fraction b = new Fraction(3, 4);
Fraction c = a + b;                     // c.n == 10, c.d == 8
```

In the expression a + b the static method + of the class Fraction is called with a and b as parameters. The method returns a new Fraction object that represents the result of the expression.

Table 2.7 shows the operators that can be overloaded in C#. If the operator == (respectively <, <=, true) is overloaded, then so must be the operator != (respectively >, >=, false).

Table 2.7 *Operators that can be overloaded*

unary arithmetic operators	+, -, ++, --
binary arithmetic operators	+, -, *, /, %
unary bit operators	!, ~, true, false
binary bit operators	&, |, ^, <<, >>
relational operators	==, !=, <, >, <=, >=

The operators ++ and -- do not have to be distinguished into prefix and postfix form. With x++ the overloaded operator applies to the retrieved value of x and with ++x to the variable x.

The operators && and \|\| cannot be overloaded directly, but only by overloading &, \|, true and false. This will in turn affect the operators && and \|\|. To exemplify this, assume that we need values with three possible states: true, false and undecided. We can implement such values through a class TriState which contains, among others, the operators &, \|, true and false:

```
class TriState {
    private int state;   // -1 == false, 0 == undecided, 1 == true
    public TriState (int s) { state = s; }

    public static bool operator true (TriState x) { return x.state > 0; }
    public static bool operator false (TriState x) { return x.state <= 0; }

    public static TriState operator & (TriState x, TriState y) {
        if (x.state == -1 || y.state == -1) return new TriState(-1);   // false
        if (x.state == 1 && y.state == 1) return new TriState(1);      // true
        return new TriState(0);                                        // undecided
    }
    public static TriState operator | (TriState x, TriState y) {
        if (x.state == 1 || y.state == 1) return new TriState(1);      // true
        if (x.state == -1 && y.state == -1) return new TriState(-1);   // false
        return new TriState(0);                                        // undecided
    }
}
```

The operators && and \|\| can now be used on any objects that support the operators &, \|, true and false. The compiler translates these operators as follows:

```
x && y      ⇒    false(x) ? x : (x & y)
x || y      ⇒    true(x) ? x : (x | y)
```

We can then write the following program and obtain the output true, false, true and false:

```
TriState x = new TriState(1);
TriState y = new TriState(0);
if (x) Console.WriteLine("true"); else Console.WriteLine("false");
if (y) Console.WriteLine("true"); else Console.WriteLine("false");
if (x || y) Console.WriteLine("true"); else Console.WriteLine("false");
if (x && y) Console.WriteLine("true"); else Console.WriteLine("false");
```

Conversion Operators

We have already seen several examples of type conversion. Strictly speaking, we distinguish two styles of conversion:

❏ **Implicit conversions** occur in expressions and assignments without being visible in source code. For example, if an int value is assigned to a long variable it is first converted into a long value. Implicit conversions are always possible and lead to no loss of precision.

❏ **Explicit conversion**s are expressed by a type cast (for example, intVar = (int) longVar;). With reference types they lead to a run-time type check. With primitive types the result may be truncated.

In addition to the implicit and explicit conversions defined by C#, we can define conversion operators for our own classes and structs. Using these operators, we can then, for example, convert between Fraction and int values like this:

```
Fraction f = 3;       // implicit conversion
int i = (int) f;      // explicit conversion
```

The first line represents an implicit conversion because an int value can be converted into a fractional number without loss of precision. The second line represents an explicit conversion, because when assigning a fractional value to an int number the fractional part must be cut off.

In order to accomplish both these conversions, implicit and explicit conversion operators must be declared as follows in the class Fraction:

```
class Fraction {
    ...
    public static implicit operator Fraction (int x) { return new Fraction(x, 1); }
    public static explicit operator int (Fraction f) { return f.n / f.d; }
}
```

The *name* of the operator method is the *target type* into which the value is to be converted. The *parameter* of the method represents the *value* to be converted. The keyword implicit or explicit specifies whether the conversion is to be applied automatically during an assignment, or whether it must be requested explicitly by a type cast operator. Having these two conversion methods we can now assign between Fraction and int values as shown above.

2.8.9 Nested Types

Classes and structs can themselves contain types (i.e., further classes, structs, interfaces, enumerations or delegates). Mostly these are auxiliary types that are only used locally in a class or a struct. By embedding these types we can make their dependence explicit and restrict their visibility. The following code fragment shows an example of a class A and two classes B and C nested within it.

```
class A {
    int x;
    B b = new B(this);              // object of the local class B
    public void MA() { b.MB(); }    // uses a method of the local class B

    class B {                       // local class B; only visible inside A
        A a;
        public B(A a) { this.a = a; }
        public void MB() { a.x = 3; a.MA(); }  // can access all members of A
    }

    public class C {                // local class C; also visible outside A
        public int y = 0;
        ...
    }
}

class D {
    A.C c = new A.C();              // A.C is visible here, A.B is not
    void MD() { c.y = 1; }
}
```

Nested types see all the members of their enclosing type, even the private ones. So B can access the private field x of A. However, outer types see only the public members of their inner types. A can call the method MB from B, but cannot access the private field a. External types only see a nested type if it is declared as public. So D can access A.C, but not A.B.

The fields of inner and outer types belong to different objects. In order to access them, we must specify the object to which they belong (for example, a.x or c.y). This is different from Java, where inner classes can access the fields of outer classes as if they were their own.

2.8.10 Differences from Java and C++

In contrast to Java, C# has no *anonymous classes* that can be declared without a name directly in the creation of an object. In Java, anonymous classes are mainly used to implement so-called *listeners* that react to events. In C#, the reaction to events is implemented by means of *delegates* (see Section 2.11).

Unlike C++, but as in Java, C# has no *generic types* (*templates*) that can be parameterized with other types. However, generic types are planned for inclusion in version 2.0 of C# (see Section 9.1).

C# and Java also differ in the default visibility of members in classes and structs. If a member has no access modifier, then in C# it has the visibility private, whereas in Java it has the visibility package. Classes without access modifiers have visibility internal (see Section 2.9.1) in C#, but package in Java.

2.9 Inheritance

As an object-oriented language, C# allows a class to be derived from another class. It is then called a *subclass* and inherits all members of its *superclass* as if they had been declared in the subclass. The subclass can declare additional members and can override inherited methods, properties and indexers.

2.9.1 Declaration of Subclasses

In declaring a class we can state what other class it should be derived from. Here is an example of a superclass (or base class) A and a subclass B derived from it:

```
class A {                     // superclass (or base class)
   int a;
   public A() {...}
   public void F() {...}
}

class B : A {                 // subclass: inherits from A and extends A
   int b;
   public B() {...}
   public void G() {...}
}
```

Writing B : A indicates that B is a subclass of A. It inherits the field a and the method F from A and introduces a new field b and a method G. Constructors are not inherited but must be declared afresh for each class. If no superclass is specified (as for example in A) then it is implicitly assumed to be System.Object. Therefore all classes inherit directly or indirectly from System.Object.

In C# a class may only be derived from a single superclass. That means that C# supports only *single inheritance* and not *multiple inheritance* as is allowed in C++. However, a class can implement multiple interfaces (see Section 2.10) and can thus achieve most of the effects that come with multiple inheritance.

Inheritance is only supported for classes and not for structs. A struct cannot be extended by other structs. Like classes, however, a struct can implement any number of interfaces. Furthermore, structs are compatible with object by means of *boxing* (see Section 2.3.8). Of course, a class can only inherit from a class, not from a struct.

Access modifier protected. The private members of a superclass are not visible in its subclasses, only those declared as public. Public elements, however, are also visible in other classes, and in certain circumstances this is undesirable. For this reason there is the access modifier protected. If a member is declared as protected it is visible only in the declaring class and its subclasses (which can use it for accessing the implementation of the superclass). Other classes simply cannot not see it. This is shown in the following example, in which the fields of a class Stack are used in the implementation of the method Contains in a subclass BetterStack.

```
class Stack {
    protected int[] val = new int[32];
    protected int top = -1;
    public void Push(int x) {...}
    public int Pop() {...}
}

class BetterStack : Stack {
    public bool Contains(int x) {
        for (int i = 0; i <= top; i++) if (x == val[i]) return true;
        return false;
    }
}
...
Stack s = new Stack();
s.val = ...;                    // forbidden
```

Access modifier internal. Finally, there is also the access modifier internal. If a name is declared as internal it is known in the entire assembly to which the declaration belongs. An assembly is, roughly speaking, the set of all types that are compiled in the same compilation. Assemblies are treated in more detail in Section 2.13. Types at the outermost level of a namespace are internal if no other access modifier is given.

The modifiers protected and internal can also be combined. This means that if a name is declared as protected internal in class C it is known in the declaring assembly and also in subclasses of C that are declared in other assemblies. However, this style of visibility is rarely used.

2.9.2 Compatibility Between Classes

A subclass inherits all the characteristics of its superclass. It is therefore a special case of its superclass and can be used at all places where the superclass is expected. In particular, an object of a subclass can be assigned to a variable of its superclass. The following examples show three classes A, B and C that are derived from each other as follows:

```
class A {...}
class B : A {...}
class C : B {...}
```

A variable of type A can reference objects of class B and C, because B and C are special cases of A:

```
A a = new A();
a = new B();
a = new C();
```

The inverse assignment, however, is forbidden:

```
B b = new A();   // forbidden
```

An A object cannot be assigned to a B variable because A does not contain all the fields and methods of B and thus cannot be used as a B object.

What does it mean then, when an A variable references a B object? We say that this variable is then of the *dynamic type* B, whereas its *static type* is always the type with which it was declared. Thus, the dynamic type of a variable can be an extension of the variable's static type. Table 2.8 shows the static and dynamic types of a variable after various assignments.

Table 2.8 *Static and dynamic types of a variable*

	static type of a	dynamic type of a
A a = new A();	A	A
a = new B();	A	B
a = new C();	A	C

Run-time type test. The dynamic type of a variable can be tested at run time. The *type test*

```
v is T
```

checks whether the variable v is of dynamic type T or a subtype of T, i.e. whether it can be used as a T object. This is illustrated by the following example:

```
A a = new C();      // dynamic type of a is C
if (a is C) ...     // true
if (a is B) ...     // true (dynamic type of a is C, which is an extension of B)
if (a is A) ...     // warning, because this is always true
a = null;
if (a is C) ...     // false: type tests always return false for null values
```

Type cast. If we know that a is of dynamic type B it should be possible to use this variable as a B variable. For this a type cast is needed. The type cast

```
(T) v
```

tests whether v is of dynamic type T. If so, it changes the static type of v to T in this expression so that we may access v here as if it were a T object. If not, an Invalid-CastException is thrown. Type casts in C# are thus safe operations: the type of an object cannot be converted to a type that the object does not have. The following example shows how assignments become possible after type casts:

```
A a = new C();        // dynamic type of a is C
B b = (B) a;          // because "a is B" holds, a is cast into a B object and assigned to b
C c = (C) a;          // because "a is C" holds, a is cast into a C object and assigned to c
a = null;
c = (C) a;            // OK: null can be converted into any reference type; c == null
```

In C# there is also a second form of type cast. The expression

```
v as T
```

is equivalent to (T) v, but with the difference that no exception will be thrown if the dynamic type is not T. Instead, the result of the expression will be null. Here are some further examples:

```
A a = new B();        // dynamic type of a is B
B b = a as B;         // because "a is B" holds, a is cast into a B object and assigned to b
C c = a as C;         // because "a is C" does not hold, c gets the value null
a = null;
c = a as C;           // c == null
```

2.9.3   Overriding and Hiding of Elements

A subclass can redeclare a method inherited from a superclass. In doing so, we can choose whether the inherited method should be *hidden* or *overridden*. In both cases, the inherited method is replaced by the new one. Methods that override others can be called with *dynamic binding* (see Section 2.9.4), methods that hide others cannot.

If a method is to be overridden, we must declare it as virtual in the superclass and as override in the subclass, whereas any method of a superclass can be hidden in a subclass by declaring it there as new. The following example shows some valid and invalid cases of overriding and hiding of methods.

```
class A {
    public          void P() {...}
    public          void Q() {...}
    public virtual  void R() {...}
    public virtual  void S() {...}
    public virtual  void T() {...}
    public virtual  void U() {...}
}
```

```
class B : A {
    public           void P() {...}      // error: "new" required
    public new       void Q() {...}      // OK: hides the inherited Q
    public           void R() {...}      // error: "override" or "new" required
    public virtual   void S() {...}      // error: "override" or "new" required
    public override  void T() {...}      // OK: overrides the inherited T
    public new       void U() {...}      // OK: overrides the inherited U
}
```

Methods that override or hide others must have the same signature as the corresponding method in the superclass. If the signature changes then this is *overloading*, rather than overriding or hiding (that is, this method is an alternative implementation of the operation with different parameters, see Section 2.8.3). Methods are said to have the same signature if:

- ❑ they have the same number of parameters, and corresponding parameters have the same types (including the function type) as well as the same parameter-passing modes (value, ref/out).
- ❑ they have the same access modifiers (e.g. public).

An overriding or hiding method M can still use the corresponding method of the superclass by referring to it as base.M. In this way, we can use the inherited functionality in addition to adding new functionality.

```
class B : A {
    public override void T() {
        base.T();      // calls the overridden method T of the superclass
        ...            // new functionality
    }
    ...
}
```

Like methods, properties and indexers can also be overridden or hidden. The keywords virtual, override and new have to be used here as well.

Static methods cannot be overridden but they can be hidden. The reason for not being able to override them is that dynamic binding does not work with static methods.

Hiding (but not overriding) also works with fields. An inherited field can be hidden in a subclass and can even have a different type there. The following example shows how hidden fields can still be accessed:

```
class A {
    public int x = 0;
    public void P() {...}
}
```

```
class B : A {
    public new bool x = true;    // hides x from A
    public new void P() {...}     // hides P from A
}
...
B b = new B();
b.x = false;                      // refers to x from B
b.P();                            // calls P from B
...
((A)b).x = 3;                     // refers to the hidden x from A
((A)b).P();                       // calls the hidden P from A
```

Hiding and overriding of members only works if the corresponding members of the superclass are visible in the subclass, i.e. if they are declared as public or protected. In the following example:

```
class A {
    private int x;
    private void P() {...}
    ...
}

class B : A {
    public int x;
    public void P() {...}
}
```

B actually inherits the private members x and P from A, but because they are not visible in B they need not be hidden with new there.

2.9.4 Dynamic Binding

As we have already seen, a variable x of a class C may reference objects of any subclass of C. If C has a virtual method M and a subclass overrides this, which method is then called by x.M()? The M method of C or that of the subclass?

The following rule holds: a call x.M() invokes the M method that belongs to the *dynamic type* of x, i.e. the method of the object that x currently references. This is called *dynamic binding*: the same call can have a different effect depending on the content of x.

Assume that a class Animal has a method WhoAreYou that is overridden in the subclass Dog:

```
class Animal {
    public virtual void WhoAreYou() { Console.WriteLine("I am an animal"); }
}
class Dog : Animal {
    public override void WhoAreYou() { Console.WriteLine("I am a dog"); }
}
```

If a Dog object is now assigned to an Animal variable:

```
Anmal animal = new Dog();
```

then the call

```
animal.WhoAreYou();
```

produces the output "I am a dog". The dynamic type of animal is Dog, therefore the WhoAreYou method of Dog is called.

Dynamic binding allows programs to work with arbitrary subclasses without having to distinguish them. The method:

```
void TakeCareOf(Animal animal) {
    animal.WhoAreYou();
    ...
}
```

for example, can work with objects of any subclass of Animal:

```
TakeCareOf(new Animal());        // output: "I am an animal"
TakeCareOf(new Dog());           // output: "I am a dog"
TakeCareOf(new Cat());           // output: "I am a cat"
```

However, dynamic binding only works for overridden methods, not for hidden methods. Thus in order to use this mechanism, the corresponding methods must be declared with virtual in the superclass and with override in the subclass.

Dynamic Binding and Method Hiding

The possibility of hiding methods gives dynamic binding a complicated semantics in C#. Namely, the call x.M() invokes the M method of the dynamic type of x only if M is not hidden in any superclass. The following example shows the problem. The class Beagle hides the method WhoAreYou that is inherited from Dog, but at the same time declares it as virtual so that it can again be overridden in the subclass AmericanBeagle.

```
class Animal {
    public virtual WhoAreYou() { Console.WriteLine("I am an animal"); }
}
class Dog : Animal {
    public override WhoAreYou() { Console.WriteLine("I am a dog"); }
}
class Beagle : Dog {
    public new virtual WhoAreYou() { Console.WriteLine("I am a beagle"); }
}
class AmericanBeagle : Beagle {
    public override WhoAreYou() { Console.WriteLine("I am an American beagle"); }
}
```

Now if we have an AmericanBeagle object it behaves differently depending on which variable refers to it:

```
Beagle beagle = new AmericanBeagle();
beagle.WhoAreYou();          // "I am an American beagle"

Animal animal = beagle;
animal.WhoAreYou();          // "I am a dog"
```

Although animal is of dynamic type AmericanBeagle, the WhoAreYou method of Dog is called here, because the WhoAreYou method has been hidden in Beagle. In C# we have to inspect the entire inheritance chain from the static type (Animal) to the dynamic type (AmericanBeagle) of animal and check whether the called method has been hidden anywhere. This is awkward and more complicated than in other object-oriented languages such as Java and C++.

The Fragile Base Class Problem

One of the reasons why dynamic binding is so complicated in C# is that its designers wanted to be able to deal with the *fragile base class problem* [Szy97]. This problem can crop up in languages such as Java, for example, if a method that already exists in a subclass is introduced in a superclass.

As an example, assume that someone uses a class LibraryClass from an external provider and derives a class MyClass from it (note: the following code is Java, not C#!):

```
class LibraryClass {
    public void Setup() {...}
    ...
}

class MyClass extends LibraryClass {
    public void Clear() {... /* erases the hard disk */ ...}
}
```

In the next version of LibraryClass the provider also introduces a method Clear, which is called from Setup:

```
class LibraryClass {   // new version
    String name;
    public void Clear() { name = ""; }
    public void Setup() { this.Clear(); ... }
    ...
}
```

If the programmer had used MyClass as follows

```
MyClass c = new MyClass();
c.Setup();
```

the Setup method will now call this.Clear(). Due to dynamic binding in Java, this will invoke the Clear method of MyClass, which erases the hard disk. The apparently harmless introduction of a method in the superclass led to a dangerous situation in the subclass.

In C# this problem cannot occur. If the provider suddenly delivers LibraryClass with a new method Clear, this does not change anything, as long as we do not recompile MyClass. MyClass continues to use the old version of LibraryClass that does not contain a Clear. If MyClass is recompiled at some time, the C# compiler will report an error, because Clear in MyClass is not declared with new and thus the inherited Clear is not correctly hidden. In any case, dynamic binding would not be applied in C# if we did not declare Clear as virtual in LibraryClass.

Here we see an example of *versioning* in .NET. The compiler assigns each DLL a unique version number, which the client classes remember during their own compilation. When a client class is loaded, it requests the DLLs in the expected version. If a DLL exists in several versions, the correct one is chosen, namely the one that was seen during the compilation of the client class.

The modifier new should be used sparingly, however; that is, only if we cannot, or do not wish to, resolve a name conflict by renaming the subclass method. In most cases it is better to choose unique names for the methods in the subclass.

2.9.5   Constructors in Superclasses and Subclasses

The constructors of a class are not inherited by its subclasses; instead the subclass must define its own constructors. However, these can call the constructors of the superclass and thus delegate the initialization of the superclass fields to the superclass. The call of the superclass constructor appears in the heading of the subclass constructor, as in the following example:

```
class Animal {
    string name;
    public Animal(string name) { this.name = name; }
    ...
}

class Dog : Animal {
    string breed;
    public Dog(string name, string breed) : base(name) { this.breed = breed; }
    ...
}
```

If a new Dog object is allocated

```
Dog dog = new Dog("Snoopy", "Beagle");
```

the constructor of Animal is executed first. It sets the name of the animal to "Snoopy". Then the constructor of Dog is executed, which sets the breed of the dog to "Beagle".

If the subclass constructor makes *no* reference to base() then the parameterless default constructor of the superclass is automatically called. Table 2.9 shows the cases that can occur and which of them are legal.

Table 2.9 Implicit calls of the parameterless default constructors of the superclass

class A {
    ...
}
class B : A {
    public B(int x) {...}
}
 	
B b = new B(3);
 	
OK. The automatically created default constructor of A is called, and then B(int x).
	class A {
	    public A() {...}
	}
	class B : A {
	    public B(int x) {...}
	}
	
	B b = new B(3);
	
	OK. The constructor A() is called and then B(int x).
		class A {
		    public A(int y) {...}
		}
		class B : A {
		    public B(int x) {...}
		}
		
		B b = new B(3);
		
		Wrong. No default constructor A() was created, because there is already a constructor A(int y) and so A() cannot be called. We must write:
		public B(int x) : base(x) {...}

2.9.6 Abstract Classes

A superclass sometimes declares methods that can only be given meaningful implementations in its subclasses. Nevertheless, those methods are already declared in the superclass (with their signatures but without code) in order to be able to use them through variables of the superclass by means of dynamic binding. Such methods are called *abstract*. If a class contains at least *one* abstract method it is itself abstract. Both abstract classes and abstract methods must be declared with the keyword abstract. Here is an example:

```
abstract class Stream {
    public abstract void Write(char ch);  // no code yet
    public void WriteString(string s) { foreach (char ch in s) this.Write(ch); }
}

class File : Stream {
    public override void Write(char ch) {... /*write ch to disk*/ ...}
}
```

Stream is an abstract class. It contains the abstract method Write, which has no body and is overridden in the subclass File, where it is implemented. Abstract methods are implicitly virtual because they are intended to be overridden in subclasses.

No objects of an abstract class can be created because they have unimplemented methods. However, we can declare variables of an abstract class and store objects of their subclasses in them:

```
Stream s = new File();
s.Write('x');              // calls Write from File (dynamic binding)
s.WriteString("Hello");    // calls WriteString from Stream, which calls
                           // Write from File using dynamic binding.
```

Abstract classes serve as templates for future subclasses. They indicate which methods a subclass must override. In addition to File we can also derive classes such as MemoryStream or NetworkStream from Stream, each of which must override Write. Abstract classes therefore combine several subclasses into a *family*, whose members share similar behaviour.

Abstract Properties and Indexers

As with methods, we can also declare properties and indexers as abstract. Again they have no statement parts and must be overridden in subclasses, as shown in the following example.

```
abstract class Sequence {
    public abstract void Add(object x);          // abstract method
    public abstract string Name { get; }         // abstract property
    public abstract object this [int i] { get; set; }   // abstract indexer
}

class List : Sequence {
    public override void Add(object x) {...}
    public override string Name { get {...} }
    public override object this [int i] { get {...} set {...} }
}
```

With abstract properties and indexers the empty get and set accessors are expressed simply by get and set and a semicolon. When overriding such properties and indexers they must have the same get and set accessors as in the superclass, since otherwise their signatures would be changed.

2.9.7 Sealed Classes

Sometimes we want to prevent programmers from extending a class and overriding or hiding some of its methods. This can be achieved by declaring the class with the keyword sealed:

```
abstract class Account {
    public abstract void Deposit(long x);
    public abstract void Withdraw(long x);
    public abstract long Balance { get; }
}
sealed class SafeAccount : Account {
    long balance;
    public override void Deposit(long x) { balance += x; }
    public override void Withdraw(long x) { balance -= x; }
    public override long Balance { get { return balance; } }
}
```

The class SafeAccount is sealed. If we try to make a subclass from it then the compiler will report an error. Instead of sealing a whole class, methods, properties or indexers that *override* others can be sealed selectively. So we can write:

```
class SafeAccount : Account {
    long balance;
    public sealed override void Deposit(long x) { balance += x; }
    public sealed override void Withdraw(long x) { balance -= x; }
    public override long Balance { get { return balance; } }
}
```

In this case, subclasses can be derived from SafeAccount but the methods Deposit and Withdraw cannot be overridden in them. The property Balance is not sealed and can therefore be overridden in subclasses.

Sealed classes or methods promote safety. Programmers cannot accidentally or deliberately change the semantics of methods by overriding them. Furthermore, sealed methods are more efficient to call, because the compiler can use static binding rather than dynamic binding in certain situations.

2.9.8   The Class Object

The class System.Object, into which the standard type object is translated, assumes a special role in C#. It is the root of the entire class hierarchy; all classes are directly or indirectly derived from it and inherit its characteristics. Through boxing, value types (structs, int, char, bool, etc.) are also compatible with Object, that is, int values can be stored in an object variable. The following code fragment shows the most important methods of Object:

```
class Object {
    public Type GetType() {...}
    public virtual bool Equals(object o) {...}
    public virtual string ToString() {...}
    public virtual int GetHashCode() {...}
    protected object MemberwiseClone() {...}
}
```

GetType returns the type of a variable, a constant or even an expression. For example:

```
Animal a = new Dog();
Type t = a.GetType(); Console.WriteLine(t.Name);   // prints "Dog"
t = 17.GetType(); Console.WriteLine(t.Name);       // prints "Int32"
long x = 5;
t = (x+1).GetType(); Console.WriteLine(t.Name);    // prints "Int64"
```

GetType returns an object of class System.Type, which is used for reflection (see Section 4.5), and which we do not describe further here.

The methods Equals, ToString and GetHashCode are only implemented in a rudimentary form in Object and should be overridden in subclasses. x.Equals(y) should test there whether x and y hold the same values, x.ToString() should convert x into a string and x.GetHashCode() should calculate a numeric hash code from x, i.e. a number that is as far as possible unique for x.

The standard implementation of Equals in Object does a pointer comparison, x.ToString() returns the class name of x and x.GetHashCode() calculates a unique value from x; but be careful: this value might be reused for other objects once x has been freed by the garbage collector.

The method x.MemberwiseClone() returns a shallow copy of x. However, it is protected and can therefore only be used in the class of x or in its subclasses.

For a clean implementation of our own classes, we should override all the inherited methods of Object. The following example demonstrates this for the class Fraction:

```
class Fraction {
    int n, d;  // numerator, denominator
    public Fraction(int n, int d) { this.n = n; this.d = d; }
    ...
    public override string ToString() {
        return String.Format("{0}/{1}", n, d);
    }

    public override bool Equals(object o) {
        Fraction f = o as Fraction; return f != null && f.n == n && f.d == d;
    }

    public override int GetHashCode() {
        return n ^ d;   // exclusive or operation
    }

    public Fraction ShallowCopy() {
        return (Fraction) MemberwiseClone();
    }
}
```

This class can then be used as follows:

```
Fraction a = new Fraction(1, 2);
Fraction b = new Fraction(1, 2);
Fraction c = new Fraction(3, 4);

Console.WriteLine(a.ToString());        // 1/2
Console.WriteLine(a);                   // 1/2  (ToString is automatically applied)

Console.WriteLine(a.Equals(b));         // true (value comparison)
Console.WriteLine(a == b);              // false (pointer comparison)

Console.WriteLine(a.GetHashCode());     // 3 (formed from 1^2)

a = c.ShallowCopy();
Console.WriteLine(a);                   // 3/4
```

In this example the following should be noted:

- ❑ WriteLine(a) automatically transforms the object a into a string by calling a.ToString().
- ❑ a.Equals(b) compares the *values* of the objects referenced by a and b and therefore returns true, whereas a == b compares the *references* a and b and thus returns false.
- ❑ MemberwiseClone cannot be called from classes other than Fraction because it is protected. However, we can call it from a method ShallowCopy within Fraction. ShallowCopy can then be called from any class.

Many classes also overload the operators == and != so that they perform a value comparison. We therefore extend our class Fraction in this way as well:

```
class Fraction {
    ...
    public static bool operator == (Fraction a, Fraction b) {
        return ((object) a == null && (object) b == null) || ((object) a != null && a.Equals(b));
    }
    public static bool operator != (Fraction a, Fraction b) {
        return ! (a == b);
    }
}
```

The compiler will report an error if only one of these operators is overloaded. It also prints a warning if one overloads == and != but does not override Equals. Fraction objects can now be used as follows:

```
// assume that a and b reference different objects with the same value
Console.WriteLine(a == b);                   // true
Console.WriteLine((object) a == (object) b); // false
Console.WriteLine(a.Equals(b));              // true
```

2.10 Interfaces

Interfaces can be regarded as fully abstract classes. They contain the signatures of methods, properties, indexers and events; the implementations of these members are omitted. Interfaces cannot contain fields, constants, constructors, destructors, overloaded operators or nested types. They are a mere collection of operations. Here is an example of a simple interface IWriter (by convention the name of an interface always begins with an I):

```
interface IWriter {
    void Write(char ch);
}
```

The interface IWriter defines only a single method Write and its parameters. In general, however, interfaces have several methods. All members of an interface are implicitly public and abstract (and thus also virtual). They are intended to be overridden in classes that implement this interface. Therefore the members of an interface must not be static, because static members cannot be overridden.

Classes and structs can *implement* one or more interfaces. This means that they inherit all members of the interface and must override them. Here are two examples of classes that implement IWriter:

```
class TextField : GUIComponent, IWriter {
    public void Write(char ch) {...}   // implements IWriter.Write, but is not itself virtual
}

struct Buffer : IWriter {
    char[] buf = new char[128];
    public virtual void Write(char ch) {...}   // implements IWriter.Write as a virtual method
}
```

A class can only inherit from *one* other class, but may implement any number of interfaces. For example, TextField inherits from GUIComponent and implements IWriter (the base class must be given *before* the interfaces). If a class inherits from another class this is called *subclassing*; if a class implements an interface this is called *subtyping*.

A method that implements an interface method must be public, because it is also public in the interface. However, we do not have to declare it as override. The compiler knows that it is overriding the corresponding method of the interface. However, if the method should also be overridable in subclasses we must declare it as virtual, even though the corresponding method is already virtual in the interface.

Instead of implementing Write, TextField could also inherit it from GUIComponent. The only important thing is that TextField has an implementation of Write.

Each object whose type implements the interface IWriter can be used as an IWriter. We can store it in an IWriter variable and apply the method Write to it, in which case dynamic binding is used:

```
IWriter w = new TextField();
w.Write('x');                     // invokes the Write method of TextField
w = new Buffer();
w.Write('x');                     // invokes the Write method of Buffer
```

From this example it should already be clear what interfaces are used for: they permit otherwise unrelated types to be treated in the same way by performing the same operations on them.

An interface variable is like a *slot* into which we can plug objects of any class that implements this interface. For example, if a client works with a variable of a class type (e.g. list) and calls its methods (e.g. list.Add or list.Remove) then it is tightly bound to this class. However, if it works with an interface variable (e.g. iList) calling its methods (e.g. iList.Add, iList.Remove) then we can later assign objects of any suitable class to this interface variable, and the coupling between the client and the classes used is not so fixed (see Figure 2.8).

Interfaces are the foundation of *object-oriented frameworks*. A framework is a semi-finished piece of software with slots (so-called *hot spots*) into which we can plug custom objects in order to build a finished product.

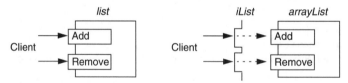

Figure 2.8 *Working with an object directly versus working with an interface variable*

The following example shows again which operations are permitted on interfaces. It uses a class MyClass that inherits from a class MyBaseClass and implements two interfaces IList and ISerializable from the .NET class library:

```
class MyClass : MyBaseClass, IList, ISerializable {
    //----- methods, properties and indexers from IList
    public int Add(object o) {...}
    public bool Contains(object o) {...}
    public bool IsReadOnly { get {...} }
    public object this[int i] { get {...} set {...} }
    //----- method from ISerializable
    public void GetObjectData(SerializationInfo i, StreamingContext c) {...}
    //----- own members
    ...
}
```

As we already know, a MyClass object can be assigned to a variable of type IList or ISerializable:

```
MyClass obj = new MyClass();
IList list = obj;
```

Subsequently we can use all IList operations on list:

```
list.Add("Tom");    // dynamic binding => Add from MyClass
```

Also, type tests are allowed on interface variables:

```
if (list is MyClass) ...    // yields true here
```

Finally, we can also use type casts:

```
obj = (MyClass) list;
obj = list as MyClass;
```

Because MyClass implements both IList and ISerializable, a MyClass object that is referenced by an IList variable can even be cast to ISerializable:

```
ISerializable ser = (ISerializable) list;
```

If an interface declares properties or indexers with only a get accessor then these can be implemented by properties or indexers that have both a get and a set accessor. This is in contrast to overriding properties or indexers inherited from a class, where the number of get and set accessors must be the same as in the superclass.

Extending Interfaces

Just as classes can extend other classes, so too interfaces can be derived from other interfaces. The following example shows an interface ISimpleReader with a method Read as well as an interface IReader that is derived from it. IReader inherits Read and adds two new methods Open and Close:

```
interface ISimpleReader {
    int Read();
}

interface IReader : ISimpleReader {// inherits Read
    void Open(string name);
    void Close();
}
```

Classes and structs can now implement either ISimpleReader or IReader. In the first case they need only to override the method Read, in the second case also Open and Close.

```
class Terminal : ISimpleReader {
    public int Read() {...}
}

class File : IReader {
    public int Read() {...}
    public void Open(string name) {...}
    public void Close() {...}
}
```

The inheritance relationships between the interfaces and classes in the above example are shown in Figure 2.9 as a UML class diagram [RJB99], [Fow03].

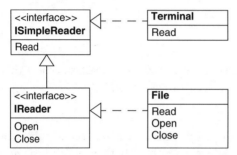

Figure 2.9 *Dependencies between ISimpleReader, IReader, Terminal and File*

File and Terminal inherit no code from each other. However, they both implement the interface ISimpleReader (Terminal implements it directly; File implements it indirectly through IReader). Thus objects of these two classes can be assigned to an ISimpleReader variable.

```
ISimpleReader sr = null;   // null can be assigned to any interface variable
sr = new Terminal();
sr = new File();
```

File implements the interface IReader and can thus be assigned to both an IReader variable and an ISimpleReader variable.

```
IReader r = new File();
sr = r;
```

Name Conflicts

If a class implements two interfaces that have members with the same names and signatures then a conflict arises. The question is whether the class must implement those members separately, once per interface, or whether a single implementation suffices for both interfaces.

In C# we have both possibilities. In the following example the two F methods of the interfaces I1 and I2 are implemented by a single method in the class C:

```
interface I1 {
    void F();
}

interface I2 {
    void F();
}

class C : I1, I2 {
    public void F() { Console.WriteLine("C.F"); }   // implements both I1.F and I2.F
}
```

The implementation of F matches both interfaces:

```
C c = new C();
c.F();                         // output: C.F
I1 i1 = c; i1.F();             // output: C.F
I2 i2 = c; i2.F();             // output: C.F
```

However, we can also implement each of the methods separately. To do so, we must qualify their names with the name of the interface from which they originate, as shown in the following example:

```
class D : I1, I2 {
    void I1.F() { Console.WriteLine("I1.F"); }       // must not be declared public!
    void I2.F() { Console.WriteLine("I2.F"); }       // -- " --
}
```

In this case we can use F only with a variable of type I1 or I2, but not with a variable of type D.

```
D d = new D();
d.F();                         // compiler reports an error: F can only be called via interfaces
I1 i1 = d; i1.F();             // output: I1.F
I2 i2 = d; i2.F();             // output: I2.F
((I1)d).F();                   // output: I1.F
```

2.11 Delegates and Events

A delegate type is a *method type* and allows the declaration of variables in which methods can be stored. It is declared with the keyword delegate and a method signature:

```
delegate void Notifier(string sender);
```

The name of this type is Notifier. Like any other type, it can be used in the declaration of variables:

```
Notifier notify;
```

A variable of a delegate type can hold any method that has the same signature as the delegate type, that is, the same number of parameters, the same parameter types (including the return type) and the same parameter-passing modes (ref, out, value):

```
void SayHello(string sender) {
    Console.WriteLine("Hello from " + sender);
}

notify = new Notifier(SayHello);   // stores the method SayHello in notify
```

The variable notify can now be assigned to other variables, passed as a parameter to methods, and called like a method:

```
notify("Alice");
```

Calling a delegate variable invokes the method that is stored in it (in this case SayHello). In this case the output would be:

```
Hello from Alice
```

Of course, we could have assigned any other method whose signature matches Notifier to the variable notify:

```
void SayGoodBye(string sender) {
    Console.WriteLine("Good bye from " + sender);
}

notify = new Notifier(SayGoodBye);
...
notify("Bob");           // "Good bye from Bob"
notify = null;           // null can also be assigned to delegate variables
```

Delegates are reference types. Therefore the value null can be assigned to delegate variables. However, if we attempt to call a delegate variable that has the value null a run-time error occurs (NullReferenceException).

Maybe delegates sound familiar to you. This is because they resemble procedure variables in Delphi or function pointers in C++.

Multicasts

The attraction of delegate variables lies in the fact that they can hold multiple methods at the same time. If we call such a delegate variable, all methods that are stored in it are invoked. We can add methods to a delegate variable with += and remove them with -=.

```
notify = new Notifier(SayHello);
notify += new Notifier(SayGoodBye);
notify("Alice");                        // "Hello from Alice"
                                        // "Good bye from Alice"

notify -= new Notifier(SayHello);
notify("Bob");                          // "Good bye from Bob"
```

The invocation of several methods through a single delegate variable is called a *multicast*. Multicast delegates are often used for event handling in the .NET Framework. Several methods can be registered for an event (e.g. a mouse click) by installing them in a delegate variable. If the event occurs then the delegate variable is called and the methods registered in it are invoked.

If we install several *function methods* in a delegate variable then the return value of the delegate call is the value that comes from the function that is the last to be called. The same applies for multicasts with out parameters.

Creation of Delegate Values

In creating a delegate value with new we have simplified things so far. To be precise, a delegate value consists not only of a method but also of the object to which the method will be applied (the receiver of the message). Both are stored in the delegate variable. The creation of a delegate value looks as follows:

delegateVar = new *DelegateType*(**obj.Method**)

In the examples so far, the object to which the method was to be applied was this and therefore was omitted. We can also store method calls for quite different objects in a delegate variable:

```
delegate void Adder(int x);

class Counter {
    int value = 0;
    public void Add(int x) { value += x; }
}

class Test {
    static void Main() {
        Counter a = new Counter();
        Counter b = new Counter();
        Adder add = new Adder(a.Add);
        add += new Adder(b.Add);
        add(3);  // calls a.Add(3) and b.Add(3)
    }
}
```

The methods to be called can also be static. In this case the class name must be given instead of the object. It can be omitted, however, if it is the class in which the delegate value is created:

```
class StaticCounter {
    static int value = 0;
    public static void Add(int x) { value += x; }
}

class Test {
    static void Main() {
        Adder add = new Adder(StaticCounter.Add);
        add(3);   // calls StaticCounter.Add
    }
}
```

A method that is to be stored in a delegate variable must not be abstract, but it can be declared with virtual, override or new.

Events

Events are special delegate variables that are declared as fields of a class. They are denoted by the keyword event:

```
class Model {
    public event Notifier notifyViews;
    public void Change() { notifyViews("Model"); }
}
```

As with normal delegate variables, multiple methods can be stored in them:

```
class View1 {
    public View1(Model m) { m.notifyViews += new Notifier(this.Update); }
    void Update(string sender) { Console.WriteLine("View1 changed by " + sender); }
}

class View2 {
    public View2(Model m) { m.notifyViews += new Notifier(this.Update); }
    void Update(string sender) { Console.WriteLine("View2 changed by " + sender); }
}
```

In their constructors the classes View1 and View2 register their Update methods in the variable notifyViews of the model. If the method Change is called due to a change of the model this leads to a call of notifyViews and thus to the invocation of the two Update methods of View1 and View2.

```
class Test {
    static void Main() {
        Model m = new Model();
        View1 v1 = new View1(m);
        View2 v2 = new View2(m);
        m.Change();    // "View1 changed by Model", "View2 changed by Model"
    }
}
```

What is the difference between events and normal delegate variables? The difference is that events can only be activated from within the class in which they are declared. The class Model may call m.notifyViews but not the class Test. This rule prevents the deliberate or inadvertent activation of events that are declared in other classes. Furthermore, classes other than Model may only assign to m by using the += and -= operators, not a normal assignment.

Events are useful in the implementation of graphical user interfaces. In such applications there are many events, such as key strokes, mouse clicks or window events that must be reacted to. We will develop this theme further in Section 4.6.

2.12 Exceptions

Exceptions provide a systematic way of error handling in which the error-handling code can be cleanly separated from the normal program logic. Instead of reporting errors by error codes that are returned by methods, they are reported by exception objects, which are "thrown" at the error point and "caught" and dealt with at some other point in the program.

Central to exception handling is the try statement which consists of a *protected statement sequence* and one or more *exception handlers*. It may be best to explain these concepts with an example:

```
FileStream s = null;

try {                                    // protected statement sequence
    s = new FileStream(name, FileMode.Open);
    ...
} catch (FileNotFoundException e) {      // exception handler for FileNotFoundException
    Console.WriteLine("file {0} not found", e.FileName);
} catch (IOException) {                   // exception handler for IOException
    Console.WriteLine("some IO exception occurred");
} catch {                                 // exception handler for other exceptions
    Console.WriteLine("some unknown exception occurred");
} finally {                               // cleanup code
    if (s != null) s.Close();
}
```

The meaning of this statement is as follows: if an exception occurs in the protected block, or in a method called from it, execution of the block is terminated and control is diverted to a suitable catch clause (exception handler). The catch clauses are checked in sequential order. Each clause handles an exception of a particular exception class (and its subclasses). If for example a FileNotFoundException occurs, the first catch clause is executed and the exception object is passed to it as a parameter. Exception objects contain information about the cause of the exception and can be retrieved in the catch clause.

As the example shows, a catch clause may also contain just an exception type without a parameter variable (e.g. IOException). In this case no exception object is available in the exception handler.

It is even possible to specify a catch clause without an exception type. Such a clause catches *all* exceptions. Of course, it is important to write this clause last, because otherwise the clauses that appear later could never be reached. The compiler reports an error if more general clauses appear before more specific ones.

A try statement can also contain a finally clause, which is *always* executed at the end of the try statement, no matter whether an exception occurred or not. The compiler ensures that the finally clause is not terminated prematurely by means of a return, goto or break.

If there is no matching catch clause then—after the execution of the finally clause—the exception is passed to the (dynamically) enclosing try statement (or rather, one of its catch clauses). Note that this try statement can also be in one of the callers (see Figure 2.11). If no matching catch clause is found in any of the enclosing try statements the program is aborted with an error. In the above example this cannot happen, however, because the third catch clause catches all exceptions.

A catch clause can again throw an exception, which is then caught by one of the outer catch clauses. If we wish to rethrow the exception that has just been handled we can simply write a throw statement without argument, thus:

```
... catch (FileNotFoundException e) {
    ...
    throw;   // passes FileNotFoundException further upwards
}
```

As we can see, the try statement separates the error-free program logic in the protected block from the various error cases that are handled in the catch clauses. This makes the program more readable.

Exception Classes

An exception is an object of an exception class. All exception classes are derived from the class System.Exception. Here is an overview of this class:

```
class Exception {
    public Exception() {...}
    public Exception(string message) {...}
    public virtual string Message { get {...} }
    public virtual string Source { get {...} set {...} }
    public MethodBase TargetSite { get {...} }
    public virtual string StackTrace { get {...} }
    public override string ToString() {...}

    ...

}
```

When creating an Exception object e we can specify an error message that can later be accessed by the property e.Message.

```
new Exception("error in message Foo");
```

The property e.Source returns the name of the program (i.e. the assembly) in which the exception occurred. e.Source can also be assigned a user-defined name which specifies more precisely where the exception was thrown.

The property e.TargetSite provides information about the method in which the exception occurred. For example, e.TargetSite.Name yields the name of this method.

The property e.StackTrace returns the method-call chain, starting with the method in which the exception occurred and ending with the Main method where the program began. For example:

```
at Test.Foo() in C:\Samples\Test.cs: line 8
at Test.Bar() in C:\Samples\Test.cs: line 14
at Test.Main() in C:\Samples\Test.cs: line 19
```

In this way we can find out how the program reached the point where the error occurred. In order to get detailed trace information with file names and line numbers, however, the program must be compiled with the debug option:

```
csc /debug Test.cs
```

Finally, the method e.ToString() returns full information about the exception e, i.e. the name of the exception class as well as the value of e.Message and e.StackTrace.

The .NET library already contains many predefined exception classes such as FileNotFoundException and IOException which are derived from Exception. However, programmers may also declare their own exception classes and place error-specific information and methods in them. User-defined exception classes should be declared as subclasses of ApplicationException.

Figure 2.10 shows an extract from the Exception hierarchy.

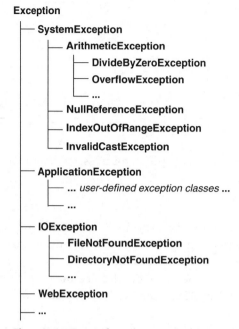

Exception
— **SystemException**
    — **ArithmeticException**
        — **DivideByZeroException**
        — **OverflowException**
        — **...**
    — **NullReferenceException**
    — **IndexOutOfRangeException**
    — **InvalidCastException**
— **ApplicationException**
    — **...** *user-defined exception classes* **...**
    — **...**
— **IOException**
    — **FileNotFoundException**
    — **DirectoryNotFoundException**
    — **...**
— **WebException**
— **...**

Figure 2.10 *Extract from the exception class hierarchy*

Throwing Exceptions

Exceptions can be thrown in the following two ways:

❏ *Implicit exceptions* are thrown by the common language runtime as a result of invalid operations such as divisions by zero, array accesses with an index outside the legal bounds, or member accesses with a null reference.

❏ *Explicit exceptions* are thrown by the programmer using a throw statement.

A throw statement has the form

```
throw exceptionObject;
```

and is often combined with the creation of this exception object. For example:

```
throw new Exception("invalid parameter in Foo");
```

Here is an example of a custom exception class and its handling in a try statement:

```
class InvalidParameterException : ApplicationException {
    object parameter;
    public InvalidParameterException(string msg, object par) : base(msg) {
        parameter = par;
    }
    public object Parameter { get { return parameter; } }
}
```

```
class Test {

    static void Foo(int par) {
        if (par < 0)
            throw new InvalidParameterException("invalid parameter", par);
        ...
    }

    static void Main() {
        try {
            ...
            Foo(-10);
            ...
        } catch (InvalidParameterException e) {
            Console.WriteLine(e.Message + ": " + e.Parameter);
        }
    }
}
```

The method Foo throws an InvalidParameterException which is handled in the caller Main. An error message, as well as the conflicting parameter, is stored in the exception object and printed in the catch clause. The output is:

```
invalid parameter: -10
```

Figure 2.11 demonstrates that the search for a matching case clause can become more complex.

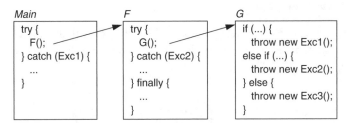

Figure 2.11 *Search for a matching catch clause*

If an exception of type Exc1 is thrown in G, the system first searches there for an enclosing try statement with a suitable catch clause. Since there is no try statement in G, the search is continued in F. This method indeed has a try statement but it has no catch clause for Exc1 and thus the search continues in Main. There a catch clause for Exc1 is finally found. The program terminates the execution of G, executes the finally clause in F, jumps to the catch clause in Main and then continues after the try statement in Main.

If an exception of type Exc2 is thrown in G, the matching catch clause in F is executed, followed by the finally clause in F; and thereafter the program continues after the try statement in F.

If an exception of type Exc3 is thrown in G, no suitable catch clause can be found in any of the currently running methods. The program is therefore aborted with a run-time error.

Exceptions Thrown by Methods

In Java, a method must either handle all exceptions that can occur in it or specify them in the throws clause of its signature. If they appear in the method signature either the caller of the method must handle them or in turn specify them in its own method signature. In this way the Java compiler can check that every exception is eventually handled. The case that no suitable catch clause is found cannot arise in Java (at least for checked exceptions).

In C#, exceptions do *not* need to be specified in method signatures and also need not be handled in catch clauses. That might seem questionable from a software engineering view but was done for reasons of compatibility with other .NET languages. Moreover, many programmers find it annoying that they are forced to write a catch clause even if they know that a particular exception cannot arise.

Exception handling in C# is safe, however, in the sense that no exception can go undetected. If it is not handled in any catch clause then the program is at least aborted with an error message.

Exceptions in Multicast Delegates

If several methods are called via a delegate variable and one of them throws an exception it is possible that the other methods stored in the variable will never be executed. Figure 2.12 explains this with an example.

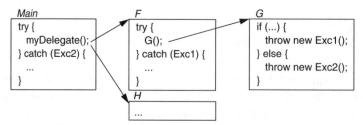

Figure 2.12 *Search for a catch clause in multicast delegates*

Assume that the variable myDelegate contains two methods F and H which are called in that order. F in turn calls G. If an exception Exc1 occurs in G then it is handled in F, F continues to run to completion and then the second method H stored in myDelegate is called. However, if the exception Exc2 occurs, it is only handled in Main. The calls in myDelegate are aborted and H is not executed.

2.13 Namespaces and Assemblies

Namespaces have already been introduced in Section 2.5 and used in several examples. We want to look at them in more detail now and compare them with the concept of *packages* in Java.

Namespaces combine several classes, structs, interfaces, enumerations and delegates into a logical unit. However, they are merely a compile-time concept that controls the visibility of names for the compiler. At run time they no longer have great importance and are replaced by *assemblies* which combine several types into a separately loadable and versioned component. Assemblies and namespaces are orthogonal, i.e. they are independent of each other. Before exploring this further, let us summarize what we know about namespaces.

A source file can contain several namespaces although in general it contains just one. Here is an example of a file with several namespaces:

```
namespace Util {
    public enum Color {red, blue, green};

    namespace Figures {
        public class Rectangle {...}
        public class Circle {...}
    }
}

namespace Drawing {
    public enum Color {black, white}
    public class Rectangle {...}
}

class Test {...}
```

There is no name conflict between the types Util.Color and Drawing.Color because they are declared in different namespaces. The same holds for the types Util.Figures.Rectangle and Drawing.Rectangle. The class Test is not declared in any namespace and therefore belongs to an anonymous default namespace.

A namespace can extend over several source files. For example, the namespaces Util and Util.Figures can be opened again in another source file and extended with further types:

```
namespace Util {
    public class Random {...}
}

namespace Util.Figures {
    public class Triangle {...}
}
```

The types of a namespace are visible in its nested namespaces. The type Color of the namespace Util can therefore be used in Util.Figures. In other namespaces, however, they are only visible if their names are qualified by their namespace or are imported into the namespace with a using clause. The following example shows this:

```
namespace MyProgram {
    using Util.Figures;        // imports all public types from Util.Figures

    class Test {
        Rectangle r;           // used without qualification (because imported with using)
        Triangle t;
        Util.Color c;          // used with qualification
        ...
    }
}
```

Note that the import of Util.Figures does not imply the import of its enclosing namespace Util. Therefore we must qualify Util.Color or import it with a using clause. Types that are to be imported in other namespaces should have the visibility public or internal.

C# Namespaces Versus Java Packages

A *package* in Java is similar to a namespace in C#. A package is also a collection of classes and interfaces that belong together. However, there are certain differences. A C# file can, for example, contain several namespaces,

```
namespace A {...}
namespace B {...}
namespace C {...}
```

whereas a Java file always belongs to just one package. The first line of a Java file gives the name of the package to which all the declarations in that file belong:

```
package A;   // this is Java code!
class C {...}
class D {...}
```

A further difference is that Java packages are mapped to directories, C# namespaces are not. For each Java package there is a directory with the same name. Nested packages lead to nested subdirectories. A class C that belongs to a package A is compiled into a file C.class that is stored in the directory A. In C# a class is not translated into a separate file, but several classes (e.g. C and D) can be compiled into a single file MyLib.dll. Namespaces are also not mapped to directories: MyLib.dll can be stored in any directory (see Figure 2.13).

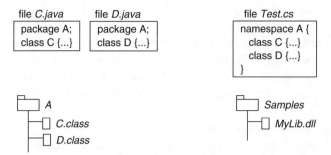

Figure 2.13 *Packages are mapped to directories in Java, but not in C#*

Whereas in C# the using clause

```
using A;
```

imports *all* public types of the namespace A, in Java one can import either *specific* types or *all* types of a package:

```
import java.util.LinkedList;   // Java code: imports only the class LinkedList
import java.awt.*;             // Java code: imports all public types of the package java.awt
```

In C#, the using clause can also be used to define an alias for a namespace, as in the example:

```
using F = System.Windows.Forms;   // F is another name for System.Windows.Forms
F.Button b;
```

This possibility does not exist in Java.

In C#, all declarations of a namespace are known in inner namespaces. In Java, there are also sub-packages, but these cannot access the names of the enclosing packages without explicitly importing them.

Finally, in Java there is package visibility. All names that are declared without an access modifier in Java are only known in their declaring package and cannot be imported into other packages:

```
package A;
class C {                      // C is only known in A
    void f() {...}             // f is only known in A
}
public class D {...}           // D is also known outside of A
```

In C#, we cannot restrict the visibility of a name to a single namespace. If a type has the visibility public or internal it can also be imported into other namespaces. The visibility internal restricts a name to an assembly, but that is not the same as a namespace.

Assemblies

Assemblies are a concept that is initially hard to understand for C# programmers. There is no syntactic construct in the language that is equivalent to an assembly. An assembly is rather a run-time construct, a collection of compiled classes and other resources (for example icons) that are loaded together and have the same version number.

For Java programmers, assemblies can best be compared with *jar files*: an assembly is a library of several classes with a table of contents (a so-called *manifest*) and a description of the types and other members that it contains (the *metadata*). Under .NET assemblies are stored either as executable files with the extension **exe** or as library files with the extension **dll**.

Assemblies are usually created during compilation. All files (i.e. their classes) that are compiled together form an assembly. The compilation command:

```
csc A.cs B.cs C.cs
```

creates an assembly **A.exe**. By using compiler options the name of the assembly or its kind (**exe** or **dll**) can be defined (see Section 8.2). There is also an assembly linker **al.exe**, which can be used to create assemblies that consist of individual modules (e.g. modules that are not written in C#) and other resources.

It is important to understand the difference between assemblies and namespaces. A namespace is a compile-time construct: it establishes the visibility of names for the compiler. An assembly on the other hand is a run-time construct: it can contain classes from quite different namespaces. A namespace can also be split across several assemblies. Figure 2.14 shows an assembly that consists of the classes A.C2 and B.C5 as well as an icon.

Further details about assemblies can be found in Section 3.6.

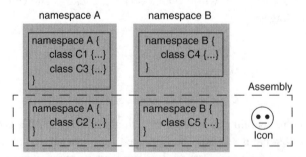

Figure 2.14 *An assembly consisting of the classes A.C2 and B.C5 as well as an iconp*

2.14 Attributes

In any programming language the number of language features is limited. In part this limitation is offset by the fact that additional features such as input/output or threading are provided by library classes, where new functionality can be added at any time. If, however, we wish to extend *existing* features (for example classes or methods) with new characteristics such as serializability or COM interoperability, that must be done in a different way. C# offers the concept of *attributes* for this.

Attributes are user-defined annotations that can be attached to program elements such as classes, methods, parameters or assemblies at compile time and can be queried and evaluated at run time. They extend the set of predefined attributes such as public, sealed or abstract.

Attributes are written in square brackets in front of the relevant language construct. For example, to make a class serializable, so that its objects can be written to a file and read back in automatically (for details see later), we simply write the attribute [Serializable] in front of the class declaration.

```
[Serializable]
class C {
    ...
}
```

We can also attach multiple attributes to a language construct. For example:

```
[Serializable] [Obsolete]
class C {...}
```

or for short

```
[Serializable, Obsolete]
class C {...}
```

Many of these attributes are already predefined in the .NET library. However, we can also declare custom attributes and attach them to program elements. Attributes are just simple classes that are derived from the class System.Attribute. So we only have to derive our own class from System.Attribute to be able to use it as an attribute in its own right.

Attributes with Parameters

Attributes can also have parameters. As an example, consider the predefined attribute Obsolete. If we put this in front of a class or method, the compiler issues a warning if this class or method is used, saying that the corresponding element is outdated and that it would be better to use something else. Obsolete has the following parameters:

```
[Obsolete("Use class C1 instead", IsError=true)]
public class C {...}
```

The first parameter is a *positional parameter*, the second a *named parameter*. We
know positional parameters from method calls: they are mapped to the corresponding formal parameters at the same position. Named parameters consist of a
name and a constant value. They can be written in any order, but must come *after*
the positional parameters.

Positional parameters correspond to the formal parameters of the constructors
of the attribute class. Named parameters on the other hand specify assignments to
properties of the attribute class and are optional.

The Obsolete attribute is implemented by the class ObsoleteAttribute. Attribute
classes normally end in Attribute, although this part of the name can be omitted
when the attribute is used.

```
public sealed class ObsoleteAttribute : Attribute {
    string message;
    bool isError;
    public string Message { get { return message; } }
    public bool IsError { get { return isError; } }
    public ObsoleteAttribute() { message = ""; isError = false; }
    public ObsoleteAttribute(string msg) { message = msg; isError = false; }
    public ObsoleteAttribute(string msg, bool error) { message = msg; isError = error; }
}
```

In this declaration we can see that Obsolete can be used in various ways:

```
[Obsolete]
```

calls the parameterless constructor ObsoleteAtribute(), in which message is set to ""
and isError is set to false.

```
[Obsolete("some message")}
```

calls the second constructor, where message is set to "some message" and isError
is set to false.

```
[Obsolete("some Message", true)]
```

calls the third constructor which initializes both fields with the parameter
values. If the property isError had a set accessor we could also set it with a named
parameter:

```
[Obsolete("some Message", IsError=true)]
```

However, this is not allowed here, because isError only has a get accessor. The example with the Obsolete attribute at the start of this section was, in fact, incorrect
and was used only to introduce the concept of named parameters.

For example, if we annotate the class MyClass with the Obsolete attribute, an ObsoleteAttribute object is created and attached to the class MyClass. We can query its data at run time as follows:

```
class AttributeTest {
    static void Main() {
        Type t = typeof(MyClass);
        object[] a = t.GetCustomAttributes(typeof(ObsoleteAttribute), true);
        ObsoleteAttribute attr = (ObsoleteAttribute)a[0];
        Console.WriteLine("{0}, IsError = {1}", attr.Message, attr.IsError);
    }
}
```

The function t.GetCustomAttributes(attrType, subclasses) returns all attributes of type attrType that are attached to t. The second parameter determines whether attributes of t's subclasses should also be returned.

We will now look at three further examples of predefined attributes: namely Serializable, which makes a class serializable, Conditional, which causes the conditional compilation of a method, and DllImport, which allows the calling of a function that was not implemented under .NET.

Serializable

In many applications it is necessary to make a data structure *persistent*, that is to store it to a file so that it can be read in again on a later run of the program.

Because a data structure can be nonlinear (e.g. a graph of objects) it must be *serialized* (i.e. flattened) before it can be written to a file. When the sequence of objects is read in again, the pointers between them must be set up again so that they point to the same objects as before. Fortunately, .NET takes care of this nontrivial task automatically. One just has to write the attribute Serializable in front of the classes whose objects are to be serialized.

Suppose that we have a class List which implements a linked list of Node objects. In order to serialize this data structure we write the attribute Serializable in front of both classes. As a consequence we can automatically write all their fields to a file. If we do not wish a field to be written we mark it with the attribute NonSerialized.

```
[Serializable]
class Node {
    public int value;
    [NonSerialized] public string temp;
    public Node next;
}
```

```
[Serializable]
class List {
    Node head = null;
    public void Add(int value, string temp) {...}
    public bool Contains(int value) {...}
    ...
}
```

Now we only need to start the serialization by using a BinaryFormatter object and its method Serialize. The following example shows the construction of the list as well as its serialization and deserialization.

```
using System;
using System.IO;                                    // FileStream
using System.Runtime.Serialization;                 // IFormatter
using System.Runtime.Serialization.Formatters.Binary;  // BinaryFormatter

class SerializationTest {

    static void Main() {
        //----- construct the list
        List list = new List();
        list.Add(1, "xxx"); list.Add(2, "yyy"); list.Add(3, "zzz");

        //----- serialize the list
        FileStream s = new FileStream("myfile", FileMode.Create);
        IFormatter f = new BinaryFormatter();
        f.Serialize(s, list);
        s.Close();

        //----- deserialize the list
        s = new FileStream("myfile", FileMode.Open);
        List newList = f.Deserialize(s) as List;
        s.Close();
        if (newList != null) newList.Print();
    }
}
```

After deserialization newList holds a copy of the original list. Because the field temp was not serialized, it gets the value null in the reloaded list (see Figure 2.15).

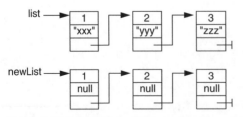

Figure 2.15 *Original list and the new list after serialization and deserialization*

Occasionally, we wish to serialize objects in a way that is different from that in which they are stored in main memory. If a field, for example, references a file stream we do not wish to store the FileStream object itself, but rather the file name from which the FileStream object can be reconstructed. To achieve this, the .NET library offers the interface ISerializable, which can be used to control serialization on a finer level (see [SDKDoc]).

Conditional

The Conditional attribute from the namespace System.Diagnostics can be attached to void methods and means that these methods will be called only if a certain symbol (specified as a parameter of the Conditional attribute) has been defined with a preprocessor command. This is best shown by an example:

```
#define debug                 // preprocessor command defining the symbol debug
using System;
using System.Diagnostics;     // imports ConditionalAttribute

class Test {

  [Conditional("debug")]
  static void Assert(bool ok, string errorMsg) {
    if (!ok) {
      Console.WriteLine(errorMsg);
      System.Environment.Exit(0);   // deliberate termination of the program
    }
  }

  static void Main(string[] arg) {
    Assert(arg.Length > 0, "no arguments specified");
    Assert(arg[0] == "dir", "invalid argument");
    ...
  }
}
```

The method Assert terminates the program with an error message if a certain condition is not satisfied. It is marked with the attribute [Conditional("debug")] meaning that the method will only be called if the symbol debug has been defined with the preprocessor command #define debug. If the preprocessor command is missing the compiler does not generate any calls to Assert.

Conditional calls like these are quite useful for testing. For example, Assert can be used to provide a program with extensive validity checks. After the test phase the preprocessor command can simply be removed but the validity checks remain in place. A recompilation at this stage will have the effect of suppressing the calls to Assert and so the efficiency of the program will not be impaired. Should the program be changed later, validity checking is easily reactivated by inserting the preprocessor command again.

The Conditional attribute is also useful for marking trace output routines, which can then be activated and deactivated with a preprocessor command.

DllImport

Although the .NET library provides classes and methods for almost any situation (see Chapter 4), it is sometimes necessary to call functions that were not developed under .NET, but are, for example, part of a Win32 DLL. The interoperability with such *native DLLs* is controlled by the attribute DllImport.

Suppose that we wish to call the Win32 function MessageBox, whose signature looks like this in C:

```
int MessageBox(HWND hParent, BSTR lpText, BSTR lpCaption, uint uType);
```

To do this we have to declare the method as external in C#:

```
[DllImport("user32.dll")]
static extern int MessageBox(int hParent, string text, string caption, int type);
```

The attribute DllImport states in which DLL the function can be found. Further parameters of this attribute allow us to specify the function's real name in the DLL (in case a different name is used in C#), the calling conventions and so on (details are to be found in the online documentation of the .NET Framework [SDKDoc]). However, in most cases it suffices to specify the DLL. In our example we can use the function as follows:

```
using System;
using System.Runtime.InteropServices;   // imports DllImportAttribute

class DLLTest {

    [DllImport("user32.dll")]
    static extern int MessageBox(int hParent, string text, string caption, int type);

    public static void Main() {
        int res = MessageBox(0, "Isn't that cool?", "", 1);
        Console.WriteLine("res=" + res);
    }
}
```

The function pops up the window that is shown in Figure 2.16.

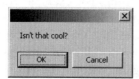

Figure 2.16 *A window opened by the native function MessageBox*

Declaring Your Own Attributes

As already mentioned, we can declare our own attributes as subclasses of System.Attribute. For every custom attribute we have to specify to which program elements (classes, methods, etc.) it should be applicable. This is done with the predefined attribute AttributeUsage:

```
public sealed class AttributeUsageAttribute : Attribute {
    public AttributeUsageAttribute(AttributeTargets validOn) {...}
    public bool AllowMultiple { get {...} set {...} }
    public bool Inherited { get {...} set {...} }
}
```

The constructor has a parameter validOn that specifies the set of program elements to which the attribute should be applicable. If an attribute should be applicable to methods and constructors, we would supply the value:

```
AttributeTargets.Method | AttributeTargets.Constructor
```

The property AllowMultiple determines whether the attribute may be attached to a program element several times or just once. The property Inherited specifies whether the attribute should also be inherited by subclasses.

As an example, let us now declare an attribute Comment that can be applied to classes and interfaces, and in which we can store comments and the author of the program element. The declaration of this attribute looks as follows:

```
[AttributeUsage(AttributeTargets.Class | AttributeTargets.Interface, Inherited=true)]
public class CommentAttribute : Attribute {
    string comment, author;
    public string Comment { get { return comment; } }
    public string Author { get { return author; } set { author = value; } }
    public CommentAttribute(string comment) {
        this.comment = comment; author = "unknown";
    }
}
```

This attribute might then be used in the following way to annotate classes and interfaces with comments that can be queried at run time.

```
[Comment("A demo class", Author="HM")]
class Demo {...}
```

At run time the attribute can be accessed like this:

```
Type t = obj.GetType();
object[] a = t.GetCustomAttributes(typeof(CommentAttribute), true);
CommentAttribute attr = a[0] as CommentAttribute;
if (attr != null)
    Console.WriteLine("comment = {0}, author = {1}", attr.Comment, attr.Author);
```

2.15 Automatically Generated Comments

Like Java, C# supports special comments from which the compiler can automatically generate documentation files. Comments of this sort begin with three slashes and must be placed in front of a program element's declaration. For example:

```
/// ... comments for MyClass ...
class MyClass {
    /// ... comments for Foo ...
    public void Foo() {...}
    ...
}
```

If this file is compiled with the /doc option

```
csc /doc:MyClass.xml MyClass.cs
```

the compiler translates the special comments into a documentation file (in this case MyClass.xml), which is in XML format. By using mechanisms such as XSL (*extensible stylesheet language*) and CSS (*cascading stylesheets*) we can transform the XML file into a neatly formatted HTML document.

Documentation comments contain XML tags with information about the individual program elements. The following XML tags can be placed in front of any program element:

```
<summary>short description of a program element</summary>
<remarks>detailed description of a program element</remarks>
<example>code sample</example>
```

For methods we can also describe the parameters and the return value, as well as any exceptions that are thrown in the method:

```
<param name="ParamName">description of the parameter</param>
<returns>description of the return value</returns>
<exception cref="ExceptionType">description of the exception</exception>
```

Furthermore, the text within XML elements can contain the following tags:

```
<code>multi-line code fragment</code>
<c>single-line code fragment</c>
<see cref="ProgramElement">text for a link to another program element</see>
<paramref name="ParamName">text for a link to a parameter</paramref>
```

The <include> tag allows the inclusion of text pieces (such as copyright notes or authors' names) that are stored at one place and then included at several other places. To do this we must describe the text piece in an XML file (e.g. MyTexts.xml):

```
<?xml version="1.0"?>
<doc>
   <member name="copyright">
      <remarks>Copyright 2003-2006 University of Linz</remarks>
   </member>
   <member name="HM">
      <remarks>Hanspeter Moessenboeck</remarks>
   </member>
</doc>
```

Such text pieces can then be used in a documentation comment like this:

```
/// <summary> ... </summary>
/// <include file='MyTexts.xml' path='doc/member[@name="copyright"]/*'/>
class C {...}
```

Because documentation comments are ordinary XML texts we can also add any user-specific elements (e.g. <author> or <version>), but must handle these later with user-defined XSL specifications.

Some parts of the documentation are checked for consistency by the compiler. It checks, for example, whether names in <param>, <exception> and <see> tags are correctly written. For methods it also ensures that either none or all of the parameters are documented.

Unfortunately, the compiler does not write the type of fields, properties and methods into the XML file. A tool that transforms the XML file into a formatted HTML documentation must therefore retrieve the types of these members by using reflection.

Example

The following example shows the source code of a class Counter that is annotated with documentation comments.

```
/// <summary>
///   A counter for accumulating values and computing the mean value.
/// </summary>
class Counter {
   /// <summary>The accumulated values</summary>
   private int value;

   /// <summary>The number of added values</summary>
   public int n;

   /// <summary>Adds a value to the counter</summary>
   /// <param name="x">The value to be added</param>
   public void Add(int x) {
      value += x; n++;
   }
```

```
/// <summary>Returns the mean value of all accumulated values</summary>
/// <returns>The mean value, i.e. <see cref="value"/> / <see cref="n"/></returns>
public float Mean() {
    return (float)value / n;
}
}
```

From this the compiler creates the following XML file:

```
<?xml version="1.0"?>
<doc>
    <assembly>
        <name>MyFile</name>
    </assembly>
    <members>
        <member name="T:Counter">
            <summary>
                A counter for accumulating values and computing the mean value.
            </summary>
        </member>
        <member name="F:Counter.value">
            <summary>The accumulated values</summary>
        </member>
        <member name="F:Counter.n">
            <summary>The number of added values</summary>
        </member>
        <member name="M:Counter.Add(System.Int32)">
            <summary>Adds a value to the counter</summary>
            <param name="x">The value to be added</param>
        </member>
        <member name="M:Counter.Mean">
            <summary>Returns the mean value of all accumulated values</summary>
            <returns>
                The mean value, i.e. <see cref="F:Counter.value"/> /
                <see cref="F:Counter.n"/>
            </returns>
        </member>
    </members>
</doc>
```

In this XML text we can observe several things: firstly, there are <member> sections for the class as well as for all its fields and methods. All these sections have the same nesting level and must be put into a suitable hierarchy by means of an XSL style sheet. Secondly, we see that the names of the program elements are qualified as follows:

types	T:*typename*
fields	F:*typename.fieldname*
methods	M:*typename.methodname*
properties	P:*typename.propertyname*
events	E:*typename.eventname*

In order to format such an XML file with XSL we can, for example, write the following stylesheet directive as the second line of the XML file:

```
<?xml:stylesheet href="doc.xsl" type="text/xsl"?>
```

The stylesheet doc.xsl analyses the XML file, brings its elements into the desired order and adds HTML formatting (one can download doc.xsl and the style sheet doc.css that is used by it from [JKU]). With these transformations, a web browser can display the documentation in a neat form.

2.16 Exercises

1. **Safety.** Explain why C# is a safe language. Which kinds of programming errors or other dangerous effects are prevented by C# and the CLR?

2. **Enumerations.** What are the advantages of an enumeration type

    ```
    enum Color {red, blue, green}
    ```

    versus named int constants

    ```
    const int red = 0, blue = 1, green = 2;
    ```

3. **Enumerations.** Look up the class Enum in the online documentation of the .NET SDK and implement two methods for reading and writing values of a specific enumeration type in textual form. Can you make the methods general enough that they can be used for *any* enumeration type?

4. **Arrays.** Write a method double[,] MatrixMult(double[,] a, double[,] b), which multiplies the matrices a and b and returns the result as a function value. If a and b cannot be multiplied due to incompatible dimensions the method should throw an exception.

5. **Strings.** Write a method which takes a file path (e.g. c:\dotnet\myfile.cs) and extracts the file name from it (e.g. myfile.cs).

6. **Expressions.** What are the result types of the following expressions?

    ```
    short s = 1; int i = 2; long x = 3; float f = 4f; char c = 'a'; Color col = Color.red;
    ... s + 1 ...
    ... s + 100000000000 ...
    ... i + f ...
    ... c + 1 ...
    ```

```
... col + 1 ...
... 10 * x + (x - '0') ...
... s + 1.0 ...
```

7. **Short-circuit evaluation.** Why is short-circuit evaluation important in the following loop header?

    ```
    while (p != null && p.name != "John") {...}
    ```

8. **Switch statement.** Write a switch statement that computes the number of days in a given month (ignoring leap years). Implement one version in which the month is given as an integer and another one in which it is given as a string. Compare the resulting code by using *ildasm* (see Chapter 8).

9. **Input and output.** Write a program which removes all comments from a C# source text. The program should read the text character by character and write the result to a new file.

10. **Formatted output.** Write a program which prints a nicely formatted table with the square roots of the numbers 1 to n. Use the function Math.Sqrt(x) to compute the square root of the integer x. The value n should be passed as a command-line argument.

11. **Classes and structs.** In which situations would you use classes and in which structs?

12. **Structs.** Implement a struct Complex representing a complex number. Write a constructor as well as properties for accessing the real part and the imaginary part of the complex number. The operations +, -, *, /, == and != should be implemented with operator overloading. Add an implicit and an explicit conversion operator that can be used to convert between complex numbers and double. Finally, override the methods Equals, ToString and GetHashCode, which are inherited from Object.

13. **Classes.** Implement a class GrowableArray representing a dynamically growing array of arbitrary objects. Write an indexer for accessing the elements. If the index value is greater than the array length the array should grow, that is, it should be replaced by a longer array with the elements of the old array at its start.

14. **foreach, interfaces.** Modify the class GrowableArray such that the array elements can be enumerated with a foreach loop. For this purpose the class GrowableArray must implement the interface System.Collections.IEnumerable. Study this interface in the online documentation of the .NET SDK or in Section 4.1.1 of this book.

15. **Classes.** Write a class In that has methods for reading numbers, words, strings, characters and boolean values (i.e. the words true and false) from the keyboard. Use the class Console for reading from the keyboard.

16. **Classes.** Modify the class In such that you can use it to read either from the keyboard, from a file or from a string.

17. **Static variables and methods.** Assume that we want to know how many objects of a class C are allocated by a program. Implement such a class C with a static counter variable for holding the number of allocated C objects. Also implement a static method for resetting the counter. Where must the counter be increased?

18. **Structs and properties.** Implement a struct Time representing a time of day. Internally, a time should be stored in seconds. There should, however, be properties, which return the hours, minutes and seconds of a time (for example, 5000 seconds are 1 hour, 23 minutes and 20 seconds). Also write a constructor as well as overloaded operators + and - for adding and subtracting times.

19. **Parameters.** Discuss the advantages and disadvantages of ref parameters, out parameters and function return values.

20. **Variable number of parameters.** Write a method Clear that can be used to set an arbitrary number of elements in an int array to 0 (for example, Clear(arr, 3, 4, 9, 12); should set arr[3] = arr[4] = arr[9] = arr[12] = 0;).

21. **Cross-reference list.** Write a program that generates a cross-reference list (or index) of a C# source text. The cross-reference list should contain the input text with line numbers as well as a list of all names in the text with the line numbers where they occur in the text. Keywords should not be counted as names. Hint: Use a SortedList for the names and one ArrayList per name for the line numbers. Study these classes either in Chapter 4 of this book or in the on-line documentation of the .NET SDK.

22. **Object-orientation.** Model the acticles of a web shop as classes and subclasses. Articles can be books, CDs or videos. Each article has an ID and a price. The various kinds of articles have further data that you can define (e.g. an author, a list of songs, etc.). Implement constructors as well as a property Price for retrieving and modifying the price of an article. The base class should have a virtual method Description() that is overridden in every subclass. It should return a string consisting of the article's description. Implement also a shopping cart that can hold several articles. On demand, the cart should return a string with the descriptions of all articles in it together with their prices and the total price.

23. **Object-orientation and dynamic binding.** Modify the example with the classes Animal and Dog from Section 2.9.4 by adding Cat and Cow as subclasses of Animal. Each subclass should implement a method Likes(string food), which

returns true if the animal likes the food that was passed as a parameter. Each animal should also have a method Speak(), which returns a string with the sound that is produced by this animal (e.g. "woof" for Dog). An animal farm should then be usable as follows:

```
foreach (Animal animal in animalArray)
    if (animal.likes("fish")) animal.Speak();
```

24. **Abstract classes.** What is the difference between an abstract class and an interface?

25. **Delegates.** Assume that we have an array arr with elements of the same kind (for example, strings, fractional numbers, or other objects). Write a method Sort(arr, compare), which sorts the array arr using a method compare(x, y) that is passed as a delegate and determines whether x is less than, equal, or greater than y.

26. **Delegates.** Write a class Counter with a method Add(x), which adds x to the counter value, as well as a method Clear(), which clears the counter. If the counter value satisfies a certain condition (e.g. value > n), one or several actions should be performed. Both the condition and the actions to be performed should be passed to a Counter object as delegates.

27. **Exceptions.** The method Convert.ToInt32(s) converts a digit string s into an int value. If s does not contain digits or if it has the wrong format several exceptions can be thrown by this method. Study those exceptions in the online documentation of the .NET SDK and write a program that calls Convert.ToInt32(s) and catches all possible exceptions.

28. **Namespaces.** The namespace System.Drawing contains a type Color. Implement your own type Color in a namespace Util and use both types in a third namespace. Look up the possible usage of System.Drawing.Color in the online documentation of the .NET SDK.

29. **Namespaces, assemblies, and DLLs.** Use the online documentation of the .NET SDK to find out the namespaces and assemblies to which the types Pen, Directory, FieldInfo, StringBuilder, Stack and Page belong. In which DLLs are they stored?

30. **Attributes.** Use the attribute System.Diagnostics.ConditionalAttribute to define trace ouput methods that can be switched on and off on demand. Use these methods in the implementation of a class Stack.

31. **XML comments.** Annotate one of your classes with XML comments and look at the result that is produced by the compiler when it is called as

```
csc /doc:myfile.xml myfile.cs
```

3 The .NET Architecture

With the new architecture of the .NET Framework Microsoft has given both programming for Windows and programming for the Web a completely new direction. In order to understand it better and therefore be able to use it to advantage, we should get to know the most important pillars, innovations, underlying principles and new features that are covered by the term .NET.

This chapter covers the internals of the CLR with the aim of contributing to an understanding, but this are not actually essential for working with .NET. Readers who are not currently interested in this background can skim this chapter on a first reading.

As we have already seen in the introductory chapter, the .NET platform consists essentially of two layers (see Section 1.1). The *Common Language Runtime* (CLR) lies at the base of this framework. It is directly connected to the operating system and is the run-time environment in which all .NET programs are executed. The CLR understands an intermediate language (*Common Intermediate Language*, CIL) into which all .NET programs are compiled (see Section 3.4). However, intermediate-language statements alone are not enough for the CLR. It needs further information about the programs. This is held in *metadata* that contains descriptions of the types of the executed program (see Section 3.5).

In addition to this, the CLR requires all programs to conform to certain rules (*Common Type System*, CTS). In return, it provides a convenient infrastructure (see Section 3.2). If two programs written in different programming languages are to work together they must use only a restricted set (the *Common Language Specification*, CLS) of the otherwise very large-scale infrastructure features. These rules are also more restrictive (see Section 3.3).

For delivery, all parts of a .NET program are packed into an *assembly* that contains information about the publisher as well as CIL statements and metadata (see Section 3.6) that are necessary for the execution of the program (see Section 3.7).

Some of the points to be covered here have a considerable similarity to concepts already explained in Chapter 2. This is understandable, because C# was developed to be suitable for the CLR and therefore shares many of its characteristics.

However, C# does not exploit the full potential of the CLR and so we find certain aspects that are not used by C# and that are intended for other—possibly future—languages. Because one of the main goals of .NET is a widespread language independence, some readers might not be interested in the capabilities of C# but only in certain features of the Common Language Runtime, the Common Type System, the Common Language Specification or the Common Intermediate Language. Here we collect together some of this information.

In order to emphasize the language independence of the .NET architecture, most of the code examples of this chapter are expressed in the real language of the CLR: the Common Intermediate Language (CIL), coupled with metadata. The .NET Framework SDK is supplied with a useful software tool for accessing this information—the IL Disassembler (ildasm.exe, see Section 8.5.1). It allows the user to view the CIL and metadata of any program, irrespective of the programming language in which it was originally developed. To make understanding of this information easier for the reader, we attempt to make some of it familiar in this chapter.

The code fragments we present are therefore mainly expressed in the syntax of the output of the IL disassembler. For reasons of readability, we have allowed ourselves to show only the relevant parts and to reformat some aspects. This means that the examples cannot actually be used directly as input to the IL assembler (ilasm.exe) to create .NET PE files (see Section 3.6). However, as said before, our goal is not to make you an IL programmer but only to enable you to understand the output of the IL disassembler. The precise specification of the CIL, which mixes code and metadata in readable code, is found in [CLI].

We begin with some general discussion of the motivation behind the new architecture.

3.1   Why a Virtual Machine?

The Common Language Runtime is at the heart of the .NET architecture. It is the motor that runs all applications that are written for this new technology.

The CLR is a virtual machine (similar to those already known from Java or Smalltalk). So it is a processor that is built in software, not in hardware. As with the virtual machine of Java, the virtual machine of the CLR is basically a stack machine. An alternative computation model that originates from hardware is the register machine used, for example, in the Intel Pentium processor. The difference between the two models is the following: in a stack machine, the operands of operations have to be loaded in the correct order on to a "stack" and then taken off again (with a stack, a value can either be placed on the top of the stack or taken off the top of the stack). This storage model is also called LIFO (*last in, first out*). A register machine, on the other hand, allows direct access to specified storage cells (registers) that hold the values for operands.

A virtual machine itself of course runs on a real machine, as does every program. Thus it leads to an additional level in between the code generated from the high-level language and that of the machine on which the program will run.

Formerly under Windows, programs in C++, for example, were compiled directly into the machine code of a possible target platform (for example Intel x86) and therefore led to an immediately executable program. Under .NET the program is first of all compiled into the intermediate language—in this case the Common Intermediate Language (CIL). The CLR then loads this intermediate-language program and the run-time environment produces a machine-code program. So what benefits result from this additional layer?

Platform and language independence. Firstly, the platform independence of the program is increased, because porting the CLR to a new platform is all that is needed for all existing .NET programs to be able to run without being compiled afresh. It is also possible to implement .NET programs in languages other than C# and all that is needed is one compiler that translates the desired programming language into the intermediate language.

Developers working in a classical scenario with m different programming languages on n machines need a compiler for every language and every platform, thus $m * n$, since each compiler depends on the language as well as on the platform (see Figure 3.1).

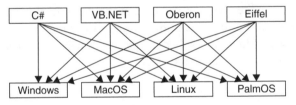

Figure 3.1 *One compiler for each language on each platform (here 4*4 = 16)*

With an intermediate language as a connecting layer, we need only one compiler for each language, because it compiles into the intermediate language (front-end). The only thing now required is a further compiler that translates the intermediate language, usually just in time, into the machine language of the platform (back-end). Back-ends are language independent, because they always work from the intermediate language.

In this way, the work needed to implement m programming languages on n platforms is reduced to merely implementing m front-ends and n back-ends, that is, $m + n$ compilers (see Figure 3.2).

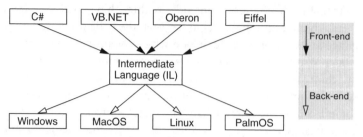

Figure 3.2 *Only one compiler per language and one CLR per platform (here 4 + 4 = 8)*

Compactness. Program code is more compact in intermediate language than in source language. There can indeed often be many intermediate-language statements for one source language statement, but these are usually only one byte long. Also, in comparison with native code, there are advantages regarding storage requirements, because compiler optimizations such as function in-lining and loop unrolling can indeed make a program faster but also make it bigger. This compactness shows the usefulness of the intermediate language and is particularly advantageous if programs are loaded over a network.

Optimized code. The route via an intermediate language does not necessarily incur a speed cost. Because the translation of the intermediate language into the machine's own language is delayed until the execution of the program on a concrete computer, the just-in-time compiler has the opportunity to analyze the current configuration of the machine and to use this information in the compilation process. Code created this way can therefore be better optimized, which has positive effects on execution time and resource demands.

Comparison of Two Virtual Machines: CLR versus JVM

The advantages described above hold for virtual machines in general. To show some particular features of .NET CLR we compare it briefly with the Java Virtual Machine (JVM).

An advantage of the CLR with respect to the JVM is its versatility, which allows the use of different programming languages. In theory it is possible to compile many languages just as easily into JVM bytecode as into CLR intermediate language. However, in practice certain restrictions of the JVM hinder the equivalent translation of certain language-specific features. The examples cited cannot be implemented in their real form and can at best be simulated by JVM constructs. This naturally has a negative effect on performance.

Objects on the stack (records, unions). In the JVM, structured data types can only be declared as classes (= reference types) whose objects lie on the heap. Variables of these types consist of a pointer to the object. It is not possible to store the actual data directly in a local variable on the stack. On the other hand, the CLR supports such constructs (see Section 3.2.2). It even contains instructions to store an object of a value type on the heap (boxing/unboxing, see Section 3.2.4).

Reference parameters. In the JVM, all parameters of methods are passed by the call-by-value technique. The CLR on the other hand, offers call-by-reference parameters as well as call-by-value parameters.

Varargs. The JVM only allows a method to have a fixed number of arguments. We have already seen in Section 2.8.3 that C# allows a variable number of arguments in a method declaration. Thus the number of arguments is unknown and variable. Their type, however, must be provided in the declaration and all the (optional) parameters must have this same type. In the intermediate language this variability vanishes: there an array with the specified type is used.

However, the CLR even allows methods where not only the number, but even the type of the arguments need not be known in the declaration of the method. In this case the CLR uses a type-safe iterator (System.ArgIterator) to read all the arguments of a variable-length method parameter list (see Section 3.7.5).

Function pointers. The CLR makes a special sort of pointer available for referencing methods (see Figure 3.4 and Section 3.2.1). In Java, we have to declare an interface with the method that we wish to access. A variable of interface type is then a sort of function pointer.

Block matrices. If we wish to use multi-dimensional arrays with the JVM, only the jagged variant is available, that is, chained single dimensions of arrays (see Figure 3.3). That means that each dimension stores only a pointer to the elements of the next dimension and only the last dimension reaches the actual values. So each dimension constitutes a further indirection, which has a negative effect on performance.

Block matrices ("rectangular" multi-dimensional arrays) are much more compact and efficient. Here, the elements are stored contiguously in the memory. Admittedly all the elements of a dimension must have the same number of elements (see Figure 3.3). The CLR supports both variants (see Section 3.2.3).

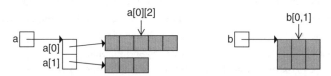

Figure 3.3 Two-dimensional arrays: "jagged" a and "rectangular" b

Overflow checking. For all the arithmetic operators (add, sub, mul) and type conversion (conv) the CLR offers a version with overflow checking (*.ovf). If an overflow takes place at run time, the CLR throws the appropriate exception (of type System.OverflowException, see Section 3.4).

Tail calls. The CLR can erase the stack frame of a method call before branching to the called method. Programming languages that work intensively with recursion (such as Haskell or Mercury) need this feature.

Reference types. The JVM only supports one form of pointer, namely a reference to an object on the heap. The CLR permits much greater flexibility, because it makes fine distinctions between different styles of pointers (see Figure 3.4).

Natural type size. Whereas with the JVM all memory cells are always exactly 32 bits wide, the CLR allows the size of a type to be determined by the JIT, that is at run time. Because all pointers (see Section 3.2.1) are represented by this natural size type the JIT can make addressing suit local conditions, without changing the intermediate-language code. Thus without recompilation of the source code we get 32-bit addresses on a 32-bit architecture and 64-bit addresses on a 64-bit architecture.

Multi-language capability. The CLR is basically intended to support many languages and thus many language constructs, whereas the JVM was basically only developed for the Java language. That does not mean, however, that the CLR is some sort of "wonder machine" that offers a perfect run-time environment for every language. At present it is well suited for imperative languages (COBOL, Pascal, C, etc.) and statically typed, object-oriented languages (C#, Oberon, Eiffel, etc.). However, Microsoft intends to support further language paradigms. Currently there are also .NET compilers for functional languages, such as Haskell and ML.

Boxing of value types. In Java, all classes are derived directly or indirectly from java.lang.Object. For reasons of efficiency there is also a handful of value types (int, float, ...) that are not derived from the class java.lang.Object. This means, for example, that generic containers such as arrays of type java.lang.Object cannot contain int values unless so-called wrapper classes (Integer, ...) are used to pack int values.

The CLR likewise treats value and reference types very differently, but when a value type needs to be treated as a reference type this can be done without having to create wrapper classes (see Section 3.2.4). Classes for the objects created on the heap are generated automatically. They are derived directly from System.ValueType and so indirectly from System.Object. In this way we can, for example, assign an int value to a reference of type System.Object.

Furthermore, it is possible to add user-defined value types to the predefined ones (see Section 3.2.2). Such values can also just as easily be copied into equivalent heap objects. In Java, only classes—that is, reference types—can be defined.

Compilation versus interpretation. An essential difference between the JVM and the CLR lies in the mode of program execution. The Java bytecode was developed for interpretation by a virtual machine. It is run by being interpreted by the JVM. (Some JVMs, such as, for example, the HotSpot JVM, provide a JIT compiler that translates individual methods into machine code after a certain number of calls.) On the other hand, the CIL code is never interpreted by the CLR but instead, on the first call of a method, it is translated into machine code, just in time, and is then run directly on the CPU (see Section 3.7).

Besides the advantages mentioned above, a run-time environment such as the CLR has even more effects. Because it lies at the centre of the architecture, it determines what programs may do, what they may not do and how they must do certain things. It can offer a range of services and functions and so, for example, increase the safety and stability of programs, bring simplifications and support to developers, and much more.

3.2 Common Type System (CTS)

The *Common Type System* is the centre point of the proposed standard *Common Language Infrastructure* (CLI). It sets rules by which types are declared, used and managed. It describes everything that .NET can do, and what languages targeting the .NET platform can expect. The CTS is, so to speak, what .NET offers to developers. .NET can only do what is defined here.

Because .NET is an object-oriented platform, we start with a brief summary of object-oriented programming. The programmer working in the object-oriented style mainly implements classes (in the .NET documentation and specification "class" is synonymous with "type"). A class is a construct consisting of data and its access methods. Objects of these types can be created at run time. These objects can be given concrete values for their data fields and thus put into different states. They interact with other objects by sending messages (= calling methods).

In general, we can say that a type is a set of values and operators defined on them. Values are held in particular locations in the memory (see memory management in Section 3.7.5). In a type-safe environment such as the CLR, all these locations are marked with a type that determines which values can be stored at the location and what operations can be performed on them.

An aim of .NET is to be capable of being installed on various platforms. That means not only that .NET applications, in principle, can run under various operating systems, but also that they can be developed in various programming languages. It is even possible to implement different parts of a project in different programming languages, as, for example, in the following situation: a type is developed in C# (as many classes in the .NET class library are). Another type, described in Visual Basic .NET, can now use methods and properties of the C# type and not only that—it can even be derived from it!

In the introduction to this chapter we have already mentioned that all .NET programs are packed in assemblies that hold CIL code and metadata. This is the first step for the interoperability of programs in different programming languages: after compilation, all programs are represented as CIL code and metadata. They look the same to the CLR irrespective of what language they were originally written in.

Despite this, sometimes different languages use different data types, so that, for example, a method implemented in Visual Basic might return a floating-point number in a format not supported by C++. Avoiding such situations is the purpose of the CTS, which provides a large set of data types and determines their format. Each programming language can then choose types from this superset that best fit its needs (see Figure 3.8). Types other than those so defined cannot be offered, supported or used by .NET languages. (To be precise, the compiler can use only these types in the generated intermediate code. It must thus attempt to represent all types of the original language as types of the CTS.)

Data Types

In contrast to Java, where simple data types such as int or float are not compatible with object references, there are *no* exceptions under .NET. All types are either directly derived from System.Object (see Sections 2.3.7 and 2.9.8) (= reference types) or can be converted into a compatible form by the CLR (boxing, see Section 3.2.4). The range of types supported by the CLR is shown in Figure 3.4 (the shaded types are predefined and the others can be further extended by users).

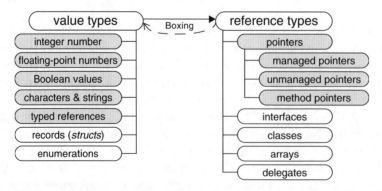

Figure 3.4 *The data types of the CLR*

All .NET types are derived from exactly one other type (*single implementation inheritance (subclassing)*) and can implement any number of interfaces (*multiple interface inheritance (subtyping)*). The only exception is the class System.Object, which has no base type.

The CLR distinguishes between two basic sorts of types: *value types*, which represent a value and whose objects are stored directly at the memory location assigned to their variable, and *reference types*, which are realized by a pointer to an object on the heap.

3.2.1 Predefined Types

The CLR supports a range of predefined data types. The value types include numbers, characters and a Boolean type. The CTS, in contrast to Java, supports more than one elementary reference type. For all these types CIL uses special notations. Table 3.1 shows these notations, as well as the types from the .NET class library (namespace System) from which they are formed.

Table 3.1 *Predefined data types of the CLR*

CIL notation	mapped to	description
bool	System.Boolean	1 byte: 0 (= false), 1–255 (= true)
char	System.Char	16-bit Unicode character
string	System.String	Unicode character string
object	System.Object	managed pointer to object on heap
typedref	System. TypedReference	value type from type and type description (used for varargs)
		IEEE 754 floating-point numbers
float32	System.Single (Epsilon)	32 bit: [−3,402823 E 38 .. 3,402823 E 38] (smallest positive number: 1.4 E−45)
float64	System.Double	64 bit: [[−1,79769313486232 E 308 .. 1,79769313486232 E 308]
	(Epsilon)	(smallest positive number: 4,94065645841247 E−324)
		signed integer numbers
int8	System.SByte	8 bit: [−128 .. 127]
int16	System.Int16	16 bit: [−32768 .. 32767]
int32	System.Int32	32 bit: [−2147483648 .. 2147483647]
int64	System.Int64	64 bit: [−9223372036854775808 .. 9223372036854775807]
		unsigned integer numbers
unsigned int8	System.Byte	8 bit: [0 .. 255]
unsigned int16	System.UInt16	16 bit: [0 .. 65535]
unsigned int32	System.UInt32	32 bit: [0 .. 4294967296]
unsigned int64	System.UInt64	64 bit: [0 .. 18446744073709551616]

Table 3.1 *Predefined data types of the CLR (cont.)*

CIL notation	mapped to	description
		numbers of machine-dependent size
native int	System.IntPtr	2's-complement integer number
native unsigned int	System.UIntPtr	unsigned integer number

Object pointers. An object pointer (object) points to an object of a class or array on the heap. Object pointers can be created by using the statement newobj or newarr and can be used as method arguments or results, as object and class fields, as local variables and as array elements.

Arithmetic operations with object pointers are forbidden! In CIL user-defined value types or reference types are marked with the keyword valuetype or class. The example

```
.field valuetype Point p
.field class Node[] nodeArr

.method valuetype Point m (class Node n) {
    .locals (valuetype Point V_0, class Node V_1)
}
```

shows possible characteristics of object pointers:

❑ a field p of value type Point,
❑ a further field nodeArr that is an array of Node objects, and
❑ a method m that returns an object of value type Point and takes as argument an object pointer to a Node object and has the local variables V_0 of value type Point and V_1 of reference type Node.

Managed pointers. Object pointers can only point to whole objects or arrays in the heap, that is, to their start position in the memory. There are, however, cases when a pointer to a field within an object or an element of an array is needed (for example with a reference parameter). This is forbidden with object pointers. Therefore, a further sort of pointer that is allowed to point into the middle of objects is needed. This is expressed in CIL by appending an & symbol to the description of the type. In the example

```
.method instance void RefParMethod (int32& i, valuetype Point& p, class Node& n)
```

a method is declared with reference parameters of type int32, of value type Point and of reference type Node. These pointers are, however, not simple pointers as known from C or C++, but are typed and type-safe, that is, the CLR checks at run time that they actually point to objects of the stated types. Furthermore, they are subject to the control of the memory management, so that their values (exactly as for the object pointers) can be adjusted if the position of the object in the memory changes (this can happen, for example, during a garbage collection (see Section

3.7.5)). For this reason, these pointers are called *managed pointers*. They can be used as method arguments or local variables, but not as object or class fields or array elements.

Unmanaged pointers. The kinds of pointers seen so far were all type safe, that is, information about the referenced type was provided which could be checked at run time. Pointers as known from C and C++ do not have that characteristic. They are merely unsigned integer values that do not have any meaning as numbers, but only as addresses in memory. They are not controlled by the memory management and are therefore called *unmanaged pointers*. In order not to disrupt the working of the garbage collector, under .NET they cannot point to classes or arrays, i.e. not to objects on the heap. Unmanaged pointers are defined as native unsigned int (and are handled as such by the CLR) or by appending the symbol * to the type description. All arithmetic operations are allowed with unmanaged pointers.

The use of unmanaged pointers conceals safety risks and makes the code type un-safe and not verifiable (see Section 3.7.3). Therefore, unmanaged pointers can only be used in blocks that have been marked with the keyword unsafe. In addition, the C# compiler must be informed by the use of the option /unsafe. In the C# example

```
unsafe {
    int x = 10;
    int* pX = &x;
}
```

an int variable x is assigned the value 10 and an unmanaged pointer pX then points to this value.

Transient pointers. Internally, the CLR also uses a further kind of pointer: so-called *transient pointers*. This form is invisible to the user and forms a sort of intermediate step between managed and unmanaged pointers. It can be used wherever one of the two styles is expected. For example, such pointers can be created by instructions that return addresses outside the managed heap (ldloca, ldarga, ldsfla, ...).

Method pointers. A further extra feature of the CLR compared to Java is the method pointer. They are identified by the keyword method, the result type, the symbol * to replace the method name, and the argument types. The example

```
.field method int32 * (int32&) intMeth

.method static method void * () getMeth ()
```

declares a field intMeth as a pointer to a method that returns an int32 value and which contains a reference parameter of type int32. It also declares a static method getMeth() that returns a pointer to a parameterless procedure.

Fixed objects. The CLR allows supplementary control over memory management by adding the attribute

> *type* **pinned**

to a type description. This prevents the object to which the variable points from being moved by the garbage collector (see Section 3.7.5).

Machine-dependent word length. Some of the data types described above defer determining the size of stored values from compile time to run time (JIT compilation). These *generic* types include all native types, as well as object, managed (&) and unmanaged (*) pointers. The CLR can use these to choose the optimal size for the current processor, that is, the word length depends on the target platform. For example, a variable of type native int on an Intel Pentium processor is 32 bits long (and thus converted into int32), whereas the same variable on an IA64 processor is allocated 64 bits (int64).

3.2.2   Value Types

A value type is essentially the same as the familiar struct in C or record in Pascal. The difference between this and a reference type is that the values are not stored in the heap, but in situ, that is, in the method stack in the case of a local variable or directly inside the object in the case of a field of an object. Because there is no extra indirection into the heap, accessing a value type is faster than for a reference type. However, there must be enough contiguous memory space available at the location of the variable to hold *all* the data of the object, whereas with a reference type only the 4 (or 8) bytes for a pointer to the object are needed. For this reason, value types are suitable for storing small structures, often for representing temporary results, which are deleted immediately after leaving the current method, in the case of a local variable, and so do not require the work of the garbage collector.

Figure 3.5 shows a simple example (the individual memory areas, such as heap, method state and stack are explained in more detail in Section 3.7.5). Here we consider two local variables of a method that is currently being executed. We assume that in the active method objects of the two types

```
.class RPoint extends System.Object {        .class VPoint extends System.ValueType {
    .field int32 x                                .field int32 x
    .field int32 y                                .field int32 y
}                                             }
```

have been created and assigned to two local variables

> .locals (**class** RPoint **rp**, **valuetype** VPoint **vp**)

The structures of RPoint and VPoint are entirely identical. The difference lies only in that RPoint is a reference type and VPoint is a value type.

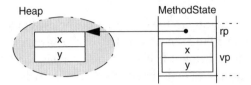

Figure 3.5 *Objects of value and reference types in memory*

The local variables are stored as part of the method's state in the method stack. One of them (rp) points to an object of the reference type RPoint on the heap. The other (vp) contains the value for an object of value type VPoint. RPoint objects and VPoint objects can store the same information, but the extra indirection in the use of the reference type and the greater storage space requirement in the method stack for the data of the value type are clearly visible.

Figure 3.6 *Remainder of value-type and reference-type objects after leaving the method*

After leaving the method, the entire method state, including all local variables, is deleted (see Figure 3.6). Thus the object of the value type disappears from the memory, whereas the object of the reference type still exists on the heap. Nevertheless, it can no longer be used, since the only reference to it, in the local variable rp, has been deleted. The object remains unused in memory until the garbage collector is activated and removes it.

User-defined Value Types

In contrast to Java, .NET allows users to define their own value types in addition to using the predefined types of Table 3.1. Such user-defined value types are always derived from System.ValueType and no further derivation from them is permitted (attribute sealed). There are three different styles:

❑ **Structure** (struct). With this, the CLR determines the order of fields in the memory (attribute auto) and the layout of the object can be made optimal for the target platform. The struct in the example describes a person by their name and age.

```
.class auto sealed Person extends System.ValueType {
  .field string name
  .field int32 age
}
```

It is also possible, however, to indicate to the CLR that the fields should be laid out in a particular order (attribute sequential). This can be given explicitly (as in the example for union below). If it is left unspecified, the CLR lays out the fields in the order they were declared. This form is used by the C# compiler when a struct is defined.

```
.class sequential sealed TwoNums extends System.ValueType {
  .field float32 f
  .field int32 i
}
```

❑ **Union.** If we do not wish to leave the memory layout to the CLR, we can give the memory position of the fields explicitly (attribute explicit). In particular, we may thus also allocate the same memory location to several fields. In this way it is possible to define a value type that has either an integer number or a floating-point number in the same position. An IntFloat object is thus only four bytes long, because both values are stored in the same location, whereas a TwoNums object requires eight bytes, because the four-byte-wide fields are allocated one after another.

```
.class explicit sealed IntFloat extends System.ValueType {
  .field [0] float32 f
  .field [0] int32 i
}
```

The layout attributes sequential and explicit are distinguished mainly by the fact that explicit allows overlapping of memory areas, which the CLR prohibits for sequential. Moreover, omitting the position specification with explicit leads to a run-time error.

❑ **Enumeration.** An enumeration assigns numeric constants to names. It extends System.Enum, which is in turn directly derived from System.ValueType. In the following example, a set of three colours (red, green, blue) is defined. As can be seen, the names are mapped on to int32 constants 0, 1 and 2.

```
.class sealed Color extends System.Enum {
  .field static literal valuetype Color red = int32(0x00000000)
  .field static literal valuetype Color green = int32(0x00000001)
  .field static literal valuetype Color blue = int32(0x00000002)
}
```

It is also possible to specify the type of the constants and thereby the size of the object of the enumeration type. Variables of type Color are four bytes wide, whereas ColorB variables only require one byte.

```
.class sealed ColorB extends System.Enum {
    .field static literal valuetype Color red = int8(0x00)
    .field static literal valuetype Color green = int8(0x01)
    .field static literal valuetype Color blue = int8(0x02)
}
```

Like classes, structs can declare constructors, methods, properties and indexers.

3.2.3   Reference Types

The reference types include all constructs that do not store a value in their variables, but are instead a pointer to the position where the value is stored. These are classes, interfaces, arrays, and delegates.

Classes

Classes encapsulate fields (data) and methods (operations). The CTS additionally supports properties and events. These can be defined as special object components. The very simplest C# class looks like this:

```
class Bar {   }
```

The C# compiler translates this into the following CIL class definition:

```
.class Bar extends System.Object {
    .method instance void .ctor () {          // constructors are always called .ctor
        ldarg.0                               // load this pointer (argument 0) onto stack
        call instance void System.Object::.ctor()// call constructor of System.Object
        ret                                   // end of method, return to caller
    }
}
```

So we see that in the intermediate language every class is explicitly derived from a base class (here System.Object). A class may extend more than one base class, because the CTS only allows single implementation inheritance. Furthermore, each class must have at least one constructor (.ctor) that at least calls the constructor of the base class to initialize the inherited fields. If an explicit constructor is missing from the source code, then the compiler must produce one, as above.

Creation of an object. In Java, the necessary memory space is reserved by means of a bytecode instruction and then a further instruction calls the appropriate constructor, as shown in the following Java bytecode example:

```
new Bar                              // allocate storage space
dup                                  // duplicate reference to new object
invokespecial Bar.<init>()           // constructor call
```

Because the allocation of memory space and the initialization of the object fields are separated, the Java bytecode verifier must perform a complex dataflow analysis to be sure that an object is not used before its initialization and that it is not initialized more than once.

The CLR avoids this by combining memory-space reservation with initialization into a single atomic statement:

```
newobj instance void Bar::.ctor()
```

After this, an object pointer (object) lies on the stack and it points to the new object on the heap.

Methods. The CLR offers not only the statically bound class methods and dynamically bound (thus overridable) object methods as known from Java, but also permits the definition of statically bound (not overridable) object methods. The class

```
.class Bar extends System.Object {
    .method static           void foo  () { ... }
    .method instance virtual void goo () { ... }
    .method instance         void hoo  () { ... }
}
```

contains one method of each sort.

The method foo is a *static* method or class method (attribute static). It differs from the other two methods in that it is not connected to any particular object and thus cannot access any object component. It can only use the static components of its class.

The two object methods (attribute instance) goo and hoo are passed a pointer to an object on the heap (this pointer in C#) as the *first* argument. They use this to access the data of this object.

The method goo is a so-called *virtual* object method (attribute virtual), as known from Java. It can be overridden in derived classes.

These two kinds of method do not support all possible constructs of many programming languages, because, for example, C++ and C# also support non-overridable object methods. The method hoo is one of these.

Method call. The CLR distinguishes between two styles of calls. It takes the binding as the criterion for the call instruction. If a method call is bound to the appropriate method *early* or statically, that is, at compile time, then the invocation is expressed by the call instruction. This works for class methods and both sorts of object methods. In the following example, we call the methods of a variable bar of type Bar:

```
.locals ( class Bar bar )            // see above for declaration of Bar
call void Bar::foo()                 // statically bound call of a static method
ldloc.0                              // load local variable 0 (= bar) onto the stack
call instance void Bar::goo()        // statically bound call of a virtual object method
ldloc.0
call instance void Bar::hoo()        // statically bound call of a non-overridable object method
```

The two sorts of object method-call (attribute instance) require the this pointer as first method argument. It is loaded on to the operand stack by ldloc. It is noticeable that the call of bar.goo() is not dynamically bound to the *run-time type* of bar, but *statically* to the method goo() of the class Bar, although it is a virtual method. Thus, through the use of the call instruction, it is possible to disable dynamic binding, if necessary.

In order to bind method calls *late* or dynamically, that is at run time, the callvirt instruction must be used.

```
ldloc.0
callvirt instance void Bar::goo()  // dynamically bound call of a virtual object method
ldloc.0
callvirt instance void Bar::hoo()  // statically bound call of a non-overridable object method
```

Here the call of bar.goo() is *dynamically* bound to the run-time type of the variable bar, whereas bar.hoo() is still bound statically to the hoo() method of the class Bar. Thus dynamic binding cannot be enforced for methods that are not declared as virtual.

Interfaces

The purpose of interfaces lies essentially in listing the operations (virtual object methods) that can be used on data of the interface type. Interfaces are declared in CIL as classes with the keyword .class and are identified as interfaces by use of the additional keyword interface. This attribute has some effects on the further declarations of the interface class.

Interface classes must always be marked as abstract, because no objects may be created from them. Because the CTS allows multiple interface inheritance, i.e. each type may implement any number of interfaces, there are some special rules for the declarable components.

So interfaces may define:
- ❑ no object fields
- ❑ no non-overridable object methods
- ❑ no inner classes
- ❑ no value types

... but may have:
- ❑ class fields (not in C#)
- ❑ properties
- ❑ static methods (not in C#)
- ❑ virtual object methods

The virtual object methods must always be declared as public and abstract in order to force all concrete classes to implement all supported methods of an interface type.

The interfaces that are implemented by a data type must be listed in the type declaration after the name of the base type and after the keyword implements. A type is not compatible with any interface not listed here even if it does in fact implement the appropriate methods. Thus the existence of implementations of methods does *not* imply the support of an interface.

```
.class interface abstract ILockable {
    .method public abstract instance virtual void Lock () { }
}
```

The example shows an interface that describes lockable objects; these must contain a Lock method. Now here is an example of a door that is known to be lockable:

```
.class Door extends System.Object implements ILockable {
    .method public instance virtual void Lock () { . . . }
}
```

Also, windows of the sort

```
.class Window extends System.Object {
    .method public instance virtual void Lock () { . . . }
}
```

can be similarly locked. However, they are not considered lockable, because they lack the special mark. The statement

```
newobj instance void Window::.ctor()    // puts pointer to new window object onto the stack
callvirt instance void ILockable::Lock() // calls Lock method of the ILockable interface
```

results in a run-time error, because of the attempt to access the Lock method of the ILockable interface type, whereas the this pointer on the stack only points to an object of type Window. Although this does indeed contain a Lock method, because of the lack of a corresponding declaration, it is still not compatible with ILockable. Therefore even a type cast does not help:

```
newobj instance void Window::.ctor()
castclass ILockable
callvirt instance void ILockable::Lock()
```

In this case a System.InvalidCastException is thrown.

Arrays

In contrast to classes, whose data elements are addressed via names and can be of different types, the elements of an array are accessed by means of an index value and must all be of the same type. Array types are indicated by following their element type by square brackets (for example, char[], object[][], int32[,,,]). The CLR distinguishes between several sorts of arrays, which are all derived from System.Array and thus can use the methods defined there (see Sections 2.3.3 and 4.1.4).

Vectors. The simplest variant is so-called vectors: one-dimensional arrays whose indexing begins with 0. They are supported by the CLR through individual CIL instructions (newarr, ldelem, stelem, ...). So-called "jagged" multidimensional arrays also count as vectors as long as their indexing begins at 0. They are a form of one-dimensional array whose elements are themselves one-dimensional arrays, and so on. Only vectors can be created with the newarr instruction. The following code examples show array creation in C# on the left and the result of the compilation into CIL on the right:

```
int[]   a;                     .locals (int32[]  a,
int[][]  aj;                              int32[][]  aj )
// one-dimensional array
a = new int[6];                Idc.i4.6
                               newarr System.Int32
                               stloc a
// two-dimensional jagged array
aj = new int[1][];             Idc.i4.1
                               newarr int32[]
                               stloc aj
aj[0] = new int[3];            ldloc aj
                               Idc.i4.0
                               Idc.i4.3
                               newarr System.Int32
                               stelem.ref
```

Arrays as objects. All the other sorts of arrays come into this category, that is, rectangular multi-dimensional arrays and arrays whose indexing does not begin at 0. They are not created by the newarr instruction, but as objects of classes with the instruction newobj. For example:

```
int[,] ab;                     .locals ( int32[0...,0...] ab )
// two-dimensional block array
ab = new int[2,3];             Idc.i4.2
                               Idc.i4.3
                               newobj instance void int32[0...,0...]::.ctor(int32,int32)
                               stloc ab
```

Arrays whose indexing does not begin at 0 can only be created with the CreateInstance method of the class System.Array followed by a cast to the desired type, because there is no CIL instruction for this.

Just as a method of System.Array must be called in order to create such an array, so must elements of such arrays be accessed by means of set and get methods. The CIL statements Idelem and stelem only work for vectors.

Delegates

The fourth form of reference type in CTS is the so-called delegate. It represents a type-safe variant of a method pointer. The type safety is achieved by encapsulating it in a compiler-generated class that is managed by the run-time environment.

We have already shown in Section 2.11 how to define and use a delegate type in C#. The C# declaration

```
delegate int Adder(int a, int b);
```

is translated by the C# compiler into the following CIL declaration:

```
.class sealed Adder extends System.MulticastDelegate {
    .method instance void .ctor (object receiver, native int method) runtime { }
    .method virtual instance int32 Invoke(int32 a, int32 b) runtime { }
    .method virtual instance class System.IAsyncResult BeginInvoke
        (int32 a, int32 b, class System.AsyncCallback acb, object asyncState) runtime { }
    .method virtual instance int32 EndInvoke(class System.IAsyncResult result) runtime { }
}
```

Each delegate type always directly extends System.MulticastDelegate and may not be used to derive any further type (attribute sealed)—exactly as for value types. A peculiarity of the delegate types is also that their methods are marked with the attribute runtime. This indicates that no CIL code is provided for the methods of a delegate type, but instead the CLR alone determines the behaviour of the method. Usually we find the attribute cil here and the behaviour of the method is specified through CIL code in the method body (between curly braces).

Each delegate type contains at least one constructor and one method named Invoke to call the method encapsulated in the delegate. The constructor is passed the receiver of the method (receiver) call as well as a pointer to the method to be invoked (method). In the case where the delegate invokes a static method, the receiver is set to null. The signature (= return type and parameter types) of the method Invoke is equivalent to the delegate definition (here: two parameters of type int32 (a, b), return type int32). It determines which methods may be assigned to an object of a delegate type.

In the above example, we also see two further methods BeginInvoke and EndInvoke which are used for asynchronous calls of the delegate method. It is thus possible to begin the execution of the delegate method with BeginInvoke and then *not* to wait for the result, but to carry on the processing in the calling method. We can access the state of the call by using the IAsyncResult object returned from BeginInvoke, for example to determine if the calculation has already terminated.

The caller must take care of collecting the results of the invocation. This is done with the method EndInvoke, which takes a reference to the corresponding IAsyncResult object, in order to determine which invocation to end.

There is also the possibility of registering an AsyncCallback delegate with BeginInvoke. This is called by the CLR as soon as the delegate method terminates. In the last parameter of the BeginInvoke method the caller can install an arbitrary object that manages information about the call.

Because the asynchronous use of the delegate is not described in Section 2.11, we show the following C# example which contrasts a synchronous and an asynchronous call of a delegate:

```
static int Add(int a, int b) { return a + b; }

static void Main() {
    Adder a = new Adder(Add);

    // synchronous call of the delegate method
    Console.WriteLine("3 + 5 = " + a(3,5));

    // asynchronous call of the delegate method
    IAsyncResult asyncCall = a.BeginInvoke(5, 8, null, null);
    . . .
    while (! asyncCall.IsCompleted)              // wait until computation is done
        System.Threading.Thread.Sleep(0);
    int result = a.EndInvoke(asyncCall);
    Console.WriteLine("5 + 8 = " + result);
}
```

3.2.4   From Value Type to Reference Type and Back

In Java, simple data types such as int and float are not derived from java.lang.Object and so are not assignment compatible with objects of that class. However, there are situations in which we need an Object-compatible representation for these value types. For example, if we wish to make a list of numbers, we can use a library class for lists of objects (for example, java.util.Vector) and then pack the numbers in a *wrapper* object. The following Java code uses such a wrapper class Integer to store int values in a Vector.

```
java.util.Vector v = new java.util.Vector();
Integer intObj = new Integer(5);
v.addElement(intObj);
```

We must thus create an object of the appropriate wrapper class (here: Integer) in order to pack a value in an object of a reference type. In Java this solution may indeed be practical. Because it is not possible to define our own value types, pre-defined wrapper classes for the primitive data types suffice.

However, we have seen in Section 3.2.2 that the CTS allows the definition of arbitrary value types. In order not to bother the user with having to implement a wrapper class for every user-defined value class, a mechanism for converting value types into reference types and back again is provided.

The CIL statement box makes an equivalent reference type from any value type. Space is reserved on the heap and the contents of the fields of the value-type object are copied into the fields of the object on the heap. So we can say that every value type has two representations:

❑ *raw*: a raw version, which can be used if the value-type object either lies on the stack or is directly embedded in an object on the heap.

❑ *boxed*: a 'packed' version, in which the value-type object is replaced by a new reference object on the heap.

The CIL instruction unbox, however, does not, as suggested by its name, trigger the exact reversal of the box operation. This reversal would mean that the values of the fields of an object on the heap were copied, for example, into a local variable. Actually only the reference of type object that lies on the operand stack before the unbox call is converted into a managed pointer to the data of the value type (which is packed inside the object on the heap). If we wish to put this data into a variable of the value type, we must load the values from the address indicated by the managed pointer on to the stack and then store them in the variable.

An example should clarify this. We have already shown in Section 2.3.8 how boxing and unboxing work in C#:

```
object obj = 3;      // Boxing
int x = (int) obj;   // Unboxing
```

Apart from the type cast, all storage-management operations are concealed from the high-level-language programmer. Study of the disassembled code, however, reveals explicit statements for the packing and unpacking of value objects:

```
.locals ( object obj, int32 x )

        // object obj = 3;
1    ldc.i4.3              // load constant 3 on to the stack
2    box System.Int32      // create value from stack as int32 object on heap
                           // and put pointer to it on the stack
3    stloc obj             // store object pointer from stack in local variable

        // int x = (int) obj;
4    ldloc obj             // load object pointer from local variable on to stack
5    unbox System.Int32    // convert to managed pointer to value in object
6    ldind.i4              // load value from target of managed pointer on to stack
7    stloc x               // store value from stack in local variable
```

Figure 3.7 shows how to picture the flow of this procedure inside the CLR. The numbers after the arrows correspond to the numbers next to the statements in the code fragment above. The comments explain exactly what happens in each step. The individual memory areas, such as heap, method state and stack, are described in more detail in Section 3.7.5.

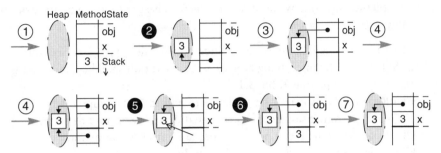

Figure 3.7 *Boxing and unboxing in the CLR*

The programmer should be aware that boxing and unboxing always signify some background processing work for the machine, and so have an effect on performance.

3.3 Common Language Specification (CLS)

The CTS describes the entire set of possible characteristics that can be used by a programming language. The *Common Language Specification*, however, reflects the minimal requirements for any programming language. It is the subset of the CTS features and types that must be supported by a compiler if the language is to be able to work with other .NET types. Of the predefined CLR types from Table 3.1, the following are not CLS-compliant: typedref, int8, unsigned int16, unsigned int32, unsigned int64, native unsigned int. Figure 3.8 shows the relationship between CTS, CLS and various programming languages.

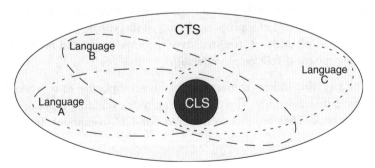

Figure 3.8 *Relationship between CTS, CLS and programming languages*

Additionally, a developer who wishes to exploit the merits of .NET with respect to language interoperability has to take care that all exported types and interfaces observe the CLS guidelines. If a language fulfils all these requirements, then it is guaranteed that types from this language can interoperate with types from other CLS-compliant languages without any problem. These rules include, for example, the following:

CLS Rule 3: The CLS does not include boxed value types (see Section 3.2.4).

CLS Rule 7: The underlying type of an enumeration shall be a built-in integer type (see Table 3.1).

CLS Rule 16: Arrays shall have elements with a CLS-compliant type and all dimensions of the array shall have lower bounds of zero. ...

CLS Rule 17: Unmanaged pointer types are not CLS-compliant.

CLS Rule 23: System.Object is CLS-compliant. ...

An exhaustive list of all 41 CLS rules can be found in [CLI] (Partition I, Section 10 'Collected Rules'), for example. We indicate once more that only "externally visible" parts must adhere to these rules to guarantee compatibility between types of different source languages. "Externally visible" includes all types which are visible outside their assemblies, as well as all components of such types that allow public, family or family-or-assembly access (see Table 3.7, page 154).

3.3.1   Attribute CLSCompliant

In order to simplify conformance to the CLS rules, the attribute System.CLSCompliantAttribute is provided in the .NET library. It is used to make the compiler check the CLS compliance of assemblies, types or components of a type ([CLSCompliant(true)]). The following rules apply:

1. An assembly is only CLS-compliant if that is explicitly required ([assembly: CLSCompliant(**true**)]).

2. A type is CLS-compliant if its assembly is; a nested type, if its outer type is; a component (method, field, property, event), if its type is.

3. The elements listed under 2. ((nested) types, components) can be declared non-CLS-compliant ([CLSCompliant(**false**)]).

The compiler (or assembly linker (al.exe)) checks CLS-compliance only when this is required for the entire assembly. The third rule permits excluding types or components from the check. They are then considered non-CLS-compliant. In C# the attribute CLSCompliant is used as follows:

```
using System;
```

[assembly: CLSCompliant(true)]

```
public class VisibleType {
    public sbyte Accessible() { ... }
}
```

In the example, the entire assembly should be CLS-compliant. Therefore the compiler must check the compliance of all exported types and their externally accessible components. Because here the return value of the Accessible method does not belong to the CLS-compliant types, the C# compiler reports the following error:

```
error CS3002: Return type of 'VisibleType.Accessible()' is not CLS-compliant
```

This error can be avoided by changing the type of the return value or stating that this method does not need to be CLS-compliant:

```
[CLSCompliant(false)]
public sbyte Accessible() { ... }
```

3.4 Common Intermediate Language (CIL)

The *Common Intermediate Language* (CIL) (also often referred to as *Microsoft Intermediate Language* (MSIL)) is the intermediate language into which programs written for the CLR are translated. Because this chapter has already introduced some CIL statements and will show others later, we will not list them all here (there are over 220 of them). In addition, [CLI] documents the entire CLI instruction set extensively. We recommend [Gou02] as an excellent description of the CIL instructions (with special attention to implementing your own compiler for the CLR). Here we will only briefly touch on a few aspects of the CIL.

It is notable that in contrast to the bytecode instructions of the JVM, CLI instructions often have no indication of the type of their arguments. Table 3.2 shows an illustrative example: it loads the values of two local variables on to the stack, adds them, and stores the result in a third local variable. In one case it uses integers and in the other floating-point numbers.

Table 3.2 *Comparison: type information about operands in Java bytecode and CIL*

Java bytecode for integers	Java bytecode for floats	CIL (for integers or floats)
iload_0	fload_0	ldloc.0
iload_1	fload_1	ldloc.1
iadd	fadd	add
istore_2	fstore_2	stloc.2

The CIL instructions are completely independent of the type of their arguments. However, the Java bytecode uses a specific instruction for every argument type.

Because it is known from the instruction what types will follow as arguments, the Java bytecode is easier to interpret. Through discarding this type information, Microsoft has made creating a compiler to CIL easier, but at the same time the work of the JIT compiler has become more difficult, because it must now determine for itself what types it is dealing with. Because multi-language support is a declared goal of the .NET platform, it is understandable that development of source-to-IL compilers has been made as easy as possible. Not without reason is an entire namespace of the .NET class library (System.Reflection.Emit, see Section 4.5.5) filled with types that further facilitate the generation of CIL. Apart from that, the .NET SDK includes no fewer than three example compilers (*SMC*, *MyC*, *CList*) to illustrate the implementation of one's own compiler.

As a rule, the CIL instructions work with values that lie on the stack, that is, they take their arguments from the stack and return their results there. Therefore [CLI] presents for every instruction a so-called *Stack Transition Diagram* which shows what should lie on the stack before the execution of the instruction and what will lie there afterwards. For example:

> **add**:   ..., value1, value2   ➡   ..., result (=*value1+value2*)

An interesting detail here is that the CLR stores values on the stack differently from all other memory locations. Only a limited set of types are available on the stack, namely:

> ❏ for integer numbers: native int (i), int32 (i4), int64 (i8)
> ❏ for floating-point numbers: F (here there is only one format)
> ❏ for pointers: object, native unsigned int, &, * (here all is left unchanged).

The CLI statements thus work only with a subset of the types shown in Table 3.1. All other types that are used by the CLR must be converted by means of the appropriate load and store instructions during transfer from and to the stack. For some of these instructions (ldloc, stloc, ldarg, starg) there is only a generic form and the CLR has to determine the type of source and target, whereas other instructions provide the type of the storage cell explicitly. For example, the statements for indirect loading that find a storage address on the stack and load a value from the thus-specified location belong to the last group:

> **ldind.<*type*>**:   e.g. ldind.i2, ldind.r8, ...

Here the data type of the value to which the address on the stack points is indicated. There are also statements in the CIL for explicit conversion between the restricted stack types and the types of the CLR:

> **conv.<*target type*>**:   e.g. conv.i, conv.i1, conv.i2, conv.u8, conv.r4, ...

For example, conv.i1 takes the top value off the stack and changes it so as to guarantee that the converted value (which still lies as an int32 value on the stack) can be stored as int8, by selecting only the last byte and ignoring the higher three bytes.

Besides these, there exist special formats for some instructions that interpret integer values on the stack as unsigned without this value being known to be such (there is no unsigned whole-number type on the stack). This is expressed in CIL by appending the suffix .un to the CIL statement:

> div.**un**, rem.**un**, ..., shr.**un**, ..., bgt.**un**, ble.**un**, ..., add.ovf.**un**, conv.ovf.**un**, ...

For all arithmetic operations and type conversions there are equivalent instructions that carry out an overflow test and throw an exception (System.OverflowException) if it fails:

> add.**ovf**, sub.**ovf**, mul.**ovf**, conv.**ovf**.*<target type>*

3.5 Metadata

A .NET program not only consists of machine instructions for the CLR (CIL), but also always contains metadata in the form of tables. The lines of these tables contain extensive descriptions of the types defined in the module (see Section 3.6) and their components. They are referred to via so-called tokens. These are four-byte values where the highest byte gives the type of the token—i.e. the table to which it refers—and the remaining three bytes the index (line number) of the entry in the appropriate table (see Figure 3.9).

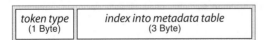

Figure 3.9 *Structure of a metadata token*

There are three sorts of metadata tables:

- ❏ *Definition tables* describe elements that are defined in the module itself (see Table 3.3).
- ❏ *Reference tables* describe elements that are not defined in the module, but are used there (see Table 3.4).
- ❏ *Manifest tables* form that part of the metadata that is referred to as manifest (see Table 3.6, page 152). We go into this in Section 3.6.

We can say that metadata is a sort of superset of older technologies for type description (for example, type libraries or IDL files). It is more powerful than its predecessors, because firstly it contains more and more-detailed information, and secondly it is always bound to the code to which it refers. It must be stored in the

Table 3.3 *Metadata tables with information about definitions in a module*

Table name	*CIL tag*	*1st token byte*
Description:	*Number of entries per module* *– extract of contained information*	
Module	.module	0x00
Always only one entry. – complete file name of the original module file		
TypeDef	.class	0x02
One entry for each type defined in the module. – fully-qualified name – reference to base type (=TypeDef token if base type is defined in module, or TypeRef token if defined in another module) – attributes: visibility (public, internal), Layout (auto, sequential,…), String format, ... – reference to list of fields in field table – reference to list of methods in method table		
Field	.field	0x04
One entry for each field defined in module. – name – signature (metadata uses an extended signature concept) – attributes: access rights (public, protected, private, ...), Static, InitOnly, ...		
Method	.method	0x06
One entry for each method defined in module. – name – signature – list of parameters (= Param tokens) – attributes: access rights, Static, Final, Virtual,…, Code style (CIL, Native,...) Synchronized,... – position of the CIL code of the method		
Param	.param	0x08
One entry for each parameter defined in module. – name – attributes: In, Out, Optional, HasDefault, ... – sequence: 0 (= return value), 1..n (= arguments)		
PropertyMap	.property	0x15
One entry for each type with properties defined in the module. – reference to type which defined the properties (= TypeDef token) – reference to list of properties in Property table		
Property	.property	0x17
One entry for each property defined in module. – name – signature – attributes: HasDefault, …		
MethodSemantics	.get, .set, .addon, .removeon, .fire, .other	0x18
One entry for each property-to-method or event-to-method relation. – reference to method in method table – reference to property or event in Property or Event table – semantics: Setter/Getter, AddOn/RemoveOn, Fire, Other		

Table 3.4 *Metadata tables with information about references from the module*

Table name	CIL tag	1st token byte

Description:	Number of entries per method – extract of contained information	

AssemblyRef	.assembly extern	0x23

One entry for each external assembly referenced from within the module.
– name of the assembly (without file extension or path)
– version: (2 bytes each for) major, minor, build, revision
– language
– hash value
– public key (128 bytes) or public key token (8-byte hash value of the entire key)

ModuleRef	.module extern	0x1A

One entry for each module file whose types are referenced from within the module.
– file name of the module file (with extension, without path)

TypeRef	[*assemblyName* or .module *moduleName*]*typeName*	0x01

One entry for each external type referenced from within the module.
– namespace and name of the type
– reference to implementation

MemberRef		0x0A

One entry for each type component referenced from within the module.
– name of the component
– signature of the component
– reference to implementation (= mainly TypeRef token)

same file as the CIL by any compiler that creates code for the .NET platform. It is thus not possible to separate type description and code, so that it is guaranteed that the type description always matches the current code.

The metadata tables listed in this section are only a small extract of the information that can be stored in metadata. Despite that, we can get an idea of how powerful metadata is. In [CLI] there is a detailed list of all metadata tables. In the following tables the column marked CIL tag shows the keywords that are used by the IL disassembler to describe the corresponding metadata information. The designation of the table number (= 1st token byte) should be a unique identification and makes it easier to find detailed information in the documentation.

In order to show how the metadata tables interact, we will briefly explain how properties are managed under .NET. Properties (and also events, which are realized by the same scheme) are basically nothing other than an aggregation of several methods under one name. A property can have one get method, which is called for read access to the property and which returns its current value, and one set method, which is called for write access and which changes the value of the property.

Like any other method, the get and set methods are entered in the Method table of the metadata. The MethodSemantics table associates the methods with the property. The PropertyMap table relates the property to its type. Figure 3.10 shows an example of a class Person that contains a property Age with a get method get_Age and a set method set_Age (these access methods for properties are automatically created by the C# compiler).

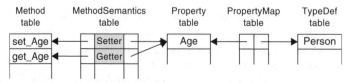

Figure 3.10 *Metadata tables for properties*

Attributes

As already explained in Section 2.14, attributes are for determining characteristics of program elements that can be interrogated at run time. There are a number of predefined attributes that are specified by bit masks in the metadata tables (Public, Static, Final, ...). It is, however, also possible to define one's own attributes (*custom attributes*). These must then be derived from System.Attribute. Some of these user-defined attributes are already made available by the .NET library. Table 3.5 shows examples that should give an impression of the many possibilities of application. A list of the attributes directly derived from System.Attribute can be found in the documentation of .NET SDK, for example.

Table 3.5 *Attributes of the class library*

Attribute name (System. *)	Description
AttributeUsageAttribute	determines how an attribute may be used
CLSCompliantAttribute	indicates whether a program element is CLS-compliant or not (see Section 3.3.1)
CodeAccessSecurityAttribute	base attribute for realizing declarative security

Table 3.5 *Attributes of the class library (cont.)*

Attribute name (System.*)	Description
ObsoleteAttribute	marks program elements that should no longer be used (Usage see Section 2.14)
WebMethodAttribute	declares a method as an XML web service (see Section 7.2)

User-defined attributes can be attached to any element of the metadata except other user-defined attributes. In CIL an attribute is referenced through the constructor of the attribute class and is preceded by the keyword .custom. In the following example we want to indicate that the class OurBook should be serializable. For this we use the System.SerializableAttribute from the class library. In addition, we have defined our own attribute TooLowAttribute and assigned it to the field ourPrice.

```
.class serializable OurBook extends System.Object {
    .field int32 ourPrice
        .custom instance void TooLowAttribute::.ctor()
}
```

Because attributes are embedded in the metadata, we can query and evaluate them at run time, like all other metadata. That means that programs can store any additional information about themselves with the help of attributes. It is thus possible to extend metadata in any way and to adjust it to individual needs.

3.6 Assemblies and Modules

In most cases programs are not delivered as source code but in a binary format, which usually matches the targeted operating system. This is also true for .NET, if one regards the CLR as being the ".NET operating system". Because .NET was primarily developed for the Windows platform, a binary format that is compatible with Windows binary format PE (*Portable Executable*) has been chosen. Such PE files can be loaded directly by the Windows loader. That means, for example, that a file HelloWorld.exe can be run by entering HelloWorld at the command line, or double clicking it in Windows Explorer. Figure 3.11 shows the layout of a typical .NET PE file.

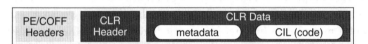

Figure 3.11 *Layout of a .NET PE file*

The first part is left over from DOS days. It contains a short program that tells the user who tries to run this program under DOS that this is just not possible. This is followed by information about the further segments of the file and their positions within the file.

The distinguishing feature of a .NET PE file, compared to previous Window PE files, is the contents of both the other segments shown in Figure 3.11. Here the CLR finds .NET-specific information that it needs in order to be able to run the program.

The CLR header stores the version number of the CLR for which the program was written. This means that it is possible to have many versions of the CLR installed on the same machine at the same time and the .NET program will nonetheless always be run by the correct CLR. If it is an executable file (.exe), the CLR header indicates the method where execution should begin. Finally the size and position of metadata tables appear in the CLR header.

Perhaps seeing this Windows-specific file format makes you wonder how this affects the much-vaunted platform independence. Few users of other operating systems are going to be willing to change their loader to a Windows loader just to be able to run .NET programs. Thus what will happen on other operating systems is that the CLR must be explicitly started and the .NET application to be carried out passed as a parameter—exactly in the way that is already familiar from Java applications. For example, we would perhaps write clr HelloWorld instead of java HelloWorld to start a HelloWorld program. In Microsoft's Shared Source Version of the CLI (Project "Rotor") [SSCLI] it is already like that. There clix.exe starts the CLR, and clix HelloWorld runs the HelloWorld program under Rotor.

However, talking of program files under .NET, the expression ".NET PE file" is not frequently used. Mainly it is assemblies that are spoken of, rather than modules. Because these concepts have no correspondence in programming languages they often give rise to confusion. Figure 3.12 and the description following it aim to clarify the two concepts and their difference.

Module (*managed module*). Each .NET PE file is a *module*. A module contains the definitions of types with metadata and the CIL code of the defined methods. The reason why programmers so seldom deal with modules is that the CLR cannot directly use a module alone. For this, special meta-information called a *manifest* is needed (see Table 3.6).

When this information is added, the module becomes an assembly. Besides other tools, the C# compiler can also do this. It produces a single file as a result of the compilation process and because—at least in the beginning—we usually compiles all types of a program in one step, we immediately get a complete assembly (.exe or .dll) from the compiler and are thus inclined to think that an assembly is the same as a module.

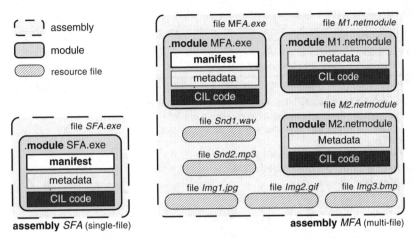

Figure 3.12 *Difference: Assembly (= logical unit) — Module (= physical unit)*

Assembly. Actually, however, an *assembly* is the .NET unit for delivery, encapsulation (see Section 3.6.1), versioning (see Section 3.6.2) and security (see Section 3.8). We can also say that assemblies are .NET components [MeSz01].

Whereas a module is always a single physical file, an assembly represents a purely logical unit. It can consist of a single .NET PE file (*single-file assembly*) or several separate files (modules and resource data, such as picture, HTML, XML files, ...) combined together (*multi-file assembly*, see Figure 3.13). In an assembly exactly one module holds the manifest, which refers to possible other modules and resources and holds the assembly together. If the assembly is a directly executable program (.exe), in contrast to a dynamically linkable library (.dll), then the module with the entry point (Main method) should also contain the manifest.

Manifest. The manifest holds information that is necessary to find all definitions of an assembly. This information is again stored in metadata tables of which Table 3.6 shows an extract.

Only a single module of an assembly may have an entry in the assembly table that identifies the assembly itself. This is the manifest module. With multi-file assemblies all other files are listed in the File table. Only the PE file of the manifest module itself is not found there; this must already be loaded in any case, because otherwise the File table itself would not be available.

The ExportedType table describes types that are defined in other modules of the assembly and should be visible outside the assembly (CIL keyword public). If a program needs such a type, first of all the manifest module is loaded. There the ExportedType table indicates the module in which the type requested is implemented. Only then can this module be loaded.

Table 3.6 *Metadata tables of an assembly manifest*

Table name	CIL tag	1st token byte
Description:	Number of entries per module – extract of contained information	
Assembly	.assembly	0x20
One entry in the case that this module is the manifest module of an assembly. – name of the assembly (without file extension or path) – version: (2 bytes each for) major, minor, build, revision – culture – hash algorithm: None, MD5, SHA1 – attributes: PublicKey, NonSideBySide, ... – public key		
File	.file	0x26
One entry for each further file of the assembly. – file name (with file extension, without path) – attributes: ContainsMetaData, ContainsNoMetaData, ... – hash value		
ExportedType	.class extern	0x27
One entry for each externally visible (public) type defined in another module of this assembly. – namespace and name of the type – attributes: visibility, layout, string format, ... – reference to TypeDef entry of the module that defines the type – reference to the implementation (mostly a File token of the file with the implementation)		

Multi-file assemblies can be used if the individual modules are written in different languages or if we wish to avoid loading all parts of the application at once for each run of the program. Particularly in distributed applications it is advisable only to pack essential types in the manifest module. In this way we avoid loading modules or resource files if their types or data are not needed during a particular program run. (For details about loading see Section 3.7.2.)

The multi-file assembly sketched in Figure 3.13 was created with the following compilations (a more detailed explanation of the compiler options can be found in Section 8.2).

```
csc /target:module /out:priv.mod PrivateType.cs
csc /target:module /out:pub.mod /addmodule:priv.mod PublicType.cs
csc /addmodule:priv.mod,pub.mod MFAApp.cs
```

The assembly from Figure 3.13 consists of the three files MFAApp.exe, pub.mod, and priv.mod. All three are independent .NET PE files, and so are modules in the sense of .NET, but only one of the three, the module MFAApp.exe, is responsible for indicating that this a multi-file assembly. It contains the manifest mentioned

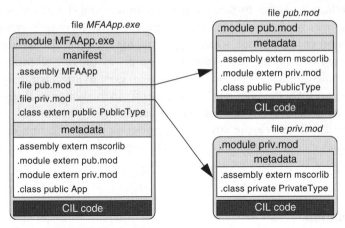

Figure 3.13 *Multi-file assembly*

above. This indicates that the name of the assembly is MFAApp, that two further files (pub.mod and priv.mod) belong to the assembly and that a type PublicType is exported from the assembly.

Another assembly, OtherApp, which uses the type PublicType, merely finds in its metadata the information that PublicType is part of assembly MFAApp (see (1) in Figure 3.14). Therefore the file pub.mod cannot be loaded immediately. The manifest of the file MFAApp.exe must first be consulted (2) in order to find out that PublicType is implemented in the file pub.mod (3). Figure 3.14 illustrates this process.

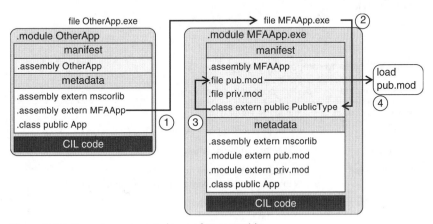

Figure 3.14 *Access to an exported type of an assembly*

Zero-impact installation. The information in the manifest and the heuristic on locating assemblies that we describe in Section 3.7.2 make a .NET program entirely independent from other information sources, such as, for example, the Windows Registry. So it is possible to install .NET programs simply by copying all program files into an application directory. As long as there is no need to interoperate with old COM components there does not need to be any entry in the Windows Registry. If a program has been installed in this way, it can just as easily be removed from the computer again, without leaving any trace, by deleting the application directory (and all the files it contains). This is called *zero-impact installation*, that is, a form of program installation without any side effects.

3.6.1   Encapsulation

An assembly makes a module into a unit and thus controls:

❏ *visibility*: which of the types defined in the assembly are visible outside the assembly;
❏ *accessibility*: from where and to which components access is allowed.

Thus it forms a capsule of all the component elements. It is possible to prevent types from being visible from outside (keyword private) or to allow their export (keyword public). If a type is not visible externally then other assemblies cannot access its components and inner types. Otherwise the determining of the access permissions depends on the relative position of the reference to the referenced component. Table 3.7 shows the access attributes for components (starting with the most restrictive).

Table 3.7 *Access to components of a type*

Access attribute	permits access to references ...
private	... within the same type
family	... within the same or a derived type
assembly	... within the same assembly
famandassem	... within the same type ... within one of the derived types of the same assembly
famorassem	... within the same or a derived type ... within the same assembly
public	... from any place

3.6.2 Versioning

In .NET, two approaches have been considered for managing different versions of the same program simultaneously in a system. These approaches are based on the difference between the two sorts of assemblies:

1. *Private assemblies* are known only within an application directory. Different versions lie in different directories and cannot come into conflict.
2. *Shared assemblies* are held in a system-wide repository, the so-called *Global Assembly Cache* (GAC), and must be identified by a so-called *strong name* (see below). The system can now distinguish versions of assemblies from each other, even when they are held in files of the same name, and so they can coexist alongside each other.

Strong name. Each assembly contains in its manifest a metadata entry that identifies it uniquely (see *Assembly* in Table 3.6). Other assemblies that reference it have a corresponding entry in their AssemblyRef tables (see Table 3.4). Now two assembly references are only considered to be the same if the following four characteristics match. Together they form the strong name of the assembly:

❑ **Name:** The name of an assembly should match the name of the PE file to enable finding the assembly.
❑ **Version:** The version number consists of four numbers separated by periods: major.minor.build.revision. It can be determined either in the source code with the attribute System.Reflection.AssemblyVersionAttribute or during the creation of the assembly with the assembly linker (al.exe). Any parts of the version number not provided are set to 0. Additionally, the build and revision values can be generated automatically by putting a *. Build then consists of the number of the days since 1 January 2000, and revision of the number of seconds since midnight (local time), divided by two. Table 3.8 shows different possibilities for assigning the version number.

Table 3.8 Assembly version number (created on 15 January 2002 at 10:00:00 local time)

declared value	created version number	
	0.0.0.0	
1	1.0.0.0	
1.2	1.2.0.0	
1.2.3	1.2.3.0	
1.2.3.4	1.2.3.4	
1.2.*	1.2.745.18000	(745 = 366 + 365 + 14)
1.2.3.*	1.2.3.18000	(18000 = 10 * 3600 / 2)

❑ **Culture:** This assigns language or country-specific information to the assembly. If no value is given here the language is set to "neutral". This mark can also be set through an attribute (System.Reflection.AssemblyCultureAttribute) or with the assembly linker (al.exe), where a string that corresponds to a language specification according to IETF RFC 1766 ([RFC]) must be given: for example, "en-US" for U.S. English, "de-AT" for Austrian German, and so on.

❑ **Public key:** This key identifies the producer of the assembly. Because the key is 128 bytes (1024 bits) long, often only a reduced version of 8-byte (64-bit) length (*public key token*) is used for referencing assemblies with strong names. Details about the generation of pairs of public and private keys and the signing of assemblies are available in Section 8.5.2 where we deal with the *strong name tool* (sn.exe).

In order to be able to reference assemblies by their strong names both in source code and in configuration files a special format has been specified. We explain this briefly with two examples:

```
MyAssembly, Version=1.2.745.18000, Culture=en-US, PublicKeyToken=13a3f300fff94cef
AnotherAssembly, Version=0.0.0.0, Culture=neutral, PublicKeyToken=null
```

Side-by-Side Execution and the End of the DLL Hell

The slogans "side-by-side execution" and the "end of the DLL hell" are often heard in connection with the .NET Framework. The first concerns different versions of a component working alongside each other in the same process. "DLL hell" refers to the following situation, which is unfortunately familiar to Window users:

During the installation of a program, existing versions of dynamic link libraries (DLLs) are overwritten by newly delivered versions. Now, other programs that worked with old versions of the DLLs suddenly cease to do so.

In order to make side-by-side execution possible and to come to grips with the DLL hell, two measures are considered for .NET:

Different versions of a DLL have different strong names, because they differ at least in their version number. This prevents assemblies overwriting each other simply because they have the same file name. (How that functions internally is described in Section 8.5.3.)

In addition, because each program declares exactly which version of a component it needs, a new version of the component can be installed on a computer without the risk that, because of this, other programs will suddenly cease to work.

3.7 Virtual Execution System (VES)

The CLR is the run-time environment of the .NET Framework. It controls the execution of all programs that are developed for this platform. In order to get an idea of what the CLR does, we will now go through the entire process of program execution and thereby bring particular aspects of the CLR under the microscope. Figure 3.15 gives an overview of the most important players that work together to

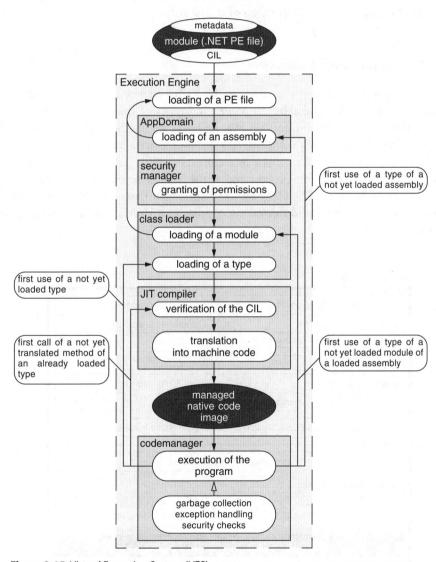

Figure 3.15 *Virtual Execution System (VES)*

run .NET programs. These are known collectively by the name *Virtual Execution System* (VES).

Every execution of a .NET application under Windows begins with the starting of a .exe file. In this, the .NET program code (*managed code*) is packed so that it conforms to the Windows PE file format (see Section 3.6). This packing lets the Windows loader call the function _CorExeMain from mscoree.dll (in the Windows System32 directory). mscoree.dll is just a small, central switchboard that decides which version of the CLR should execute the .NET application and then starts it. Everything after that is the concern of the CLR.

3.7.1   Application Domains

Every application that is executed by the CLR receives its own area within the CLR processes. All assemblies, modules and types of the application are loaded into this. The application domain also manages the method tables of the loaded types and the static fields and objects associated with the application domain. With these application domains a mechanism has been created that allows several applications to run in one process and at the same time ensures that these do not influence each other. The class System.AppDomain from the .NET class library represents such application domains. Figure 3.16 shows a process with several AppDomains.

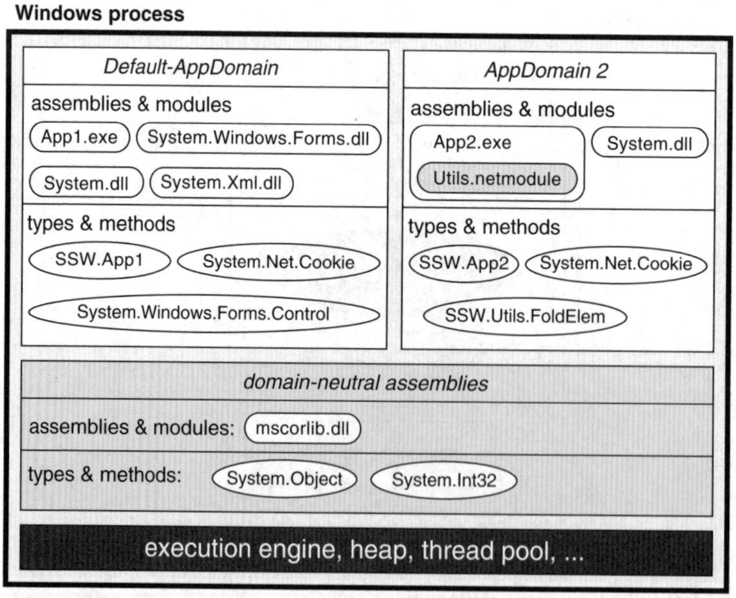

Windows process

Default-AppDomain	AppDomain 2
assemblies & modules	assemblies & modules
(App1.exe) (System.Windows.Forms.dll)	(App2.exe) (System.dll)
(System.dll) (System.Xml.dll)	(Utils.netmodule)
types & methods	types & methods
(SSW.App1) (System.Net.Cookie)	(SSW.App2) (System.Net.Cookie)
(System.Windows.Forms.Control)	(SSW.Utils.FoldElem)

domain-neutral assemblies

assemblies & modules: (mscorlib.dll)

types & methods: (System.Object) (System.Int32)

execution engine, heap, thread pool, ...

Figure 3.16 *Several application domains in one process*

The CLR always creates at least one so-called Default-AppDomain. This remains in existence until the entire process is terminated. Other application domains can be created either directly in the program code (System.AppDomain.CreateDomain) or by the current host of the CLR. These additional AppDomains can be unloaded again without exiting the CLR. Besides the AppDomain there is another area that manages assemblies and types that will be used together by different applications. They are reachable from all application domains (domain neutral) and are only loaded once per process.

Note that assemblies that are used by several applications are loaded independently of one another into each application domain (here: System.dll). Also, all types, static fields and so on are loaded once per AppDomain (here: System.Net.Cookie).

3.7.2 Loading and Execution of Managed Code

In order to be able to start the execution of a .NET program, the CLR must first find an entry point in the program; that is, the methods that are marked by the keyword .entrypoint in the executable assembly (.exe instead of .dll). As with every method, this belongs to a type, which in turn belongs to an assembly, which is implemented in a module (see Section 3.6). This module consists of a .NET PE file on the hard disk.

So the first task of the execution engine consists of loading a PE file. This is also the only loading process that actually accesses a peripheral storage medium. All other activities designated as "loading" in Figure 3.15 only create different representations of data already existing in storage.

Thus the responsible application domain uses the PE file object already in storage, in order to retrieve from it all necessary information for the creation of an assembly (*loading of an assembly*).

Subsequently, the security manager checks what rights the assembly may be granted (see Section 3.8.1). This then holds for all modules and types of the assembly.

From the assembly representation, the class loader obtains the information necessary to create a module object. This might require the loading of a further PE file.

Finally the module information exists in the memory in an adequate form and so the class loader creates a class object for the type to be loaded.

The CLR has only a single class loader and, unlike Java, does not permit users to use their own class loaders. However, the CLR loading also functions dynamically, that is, all assemblies, modules and types are not loaded at the start of the program, but only when they are first needed, that is, only as soon as components (fields, methods, properties, events) are accessed for the first time.

Locating an Assembly

As soon as an assembly has been loaded, the CLR has all the information available for locating the further parts of the assembly (modules, types, resources). However, if the CLR needs to load an unknown assembly, it must try to find it with the following information:

❑ name of the sought assembly
❑ version information, which was determined during compilation
❑ information about the application domain that wants to load the assembly
❑ information from various configuration files.

The so-called assembly resolver is responsible for this locating process. It uses the following strategy:

First it considers whether the assembly to be found is private or shared (see Section 3.6.2). Only shared assemblies must be identified by a strong name that contains precise information about the identity, version and culture of the assembly. Only they can be installed in the *Global Assembly Cache* (GAC), a data structure for managing assembly files, and thus made available system-wide. Private assemblies must lie in the directory of the current application (or a subdirectory of it) and are always sought through *probing* (see below). Shared assemblies are only searched by probing if the following four steps do not lead to a result:

1. Determine the version of the assembly to be loaded, by considering the application and machine configuration files.
2. If the sought version is already loaded, then this is used.
3. If it is not loaded, it will first be searched for in the GAC.
4. If the assembly is not found there, the search is continued in one of the two following ways:
   – if a so-called *codebase* (URI) is specified in a configuration file, the assembly is only searched for in this place. If it is not there, then the search will be terminated unsuccessfully.
   – otherwise so-called probing is employed.

Probing. While probing, the assembly resolver of the CLR uses the following information to determine the location of the sought assembly:

- the base directory of the application which wants to load the assembly (see System.AppDomain.BaseDirectory);
- (if available) the culture of the assembly to be loaded;
- the name of the assembly to be loaded;
- (if available) the private search path of the application (see System.AppDomain.RelativeSearchPath). This list of subdirectories of the application directory can be provided either in the application configuration file or directly in the code.

In order to demonstrate this with a small example, we search for the public assembly with the name MyAssembly (in full: MyAssembly, Version=1.1.0.0, Culture=neutral, PublicKeyToken= a9ba664985e79673). The base directory of the application is http://dotnet.jku.at/. As private search path only the subdirectory bin has been provided in the application configuration file (see Section 8.3). In the search for MyAssembly the following URIs are now scanned in the order given here:

```
http://dotnet.jku.at / MyAssembly.dll
http://dotnet.jku.at / MyAssembly / MyAssembly.dll
http://dotnet.jku.at / bin / MyAssembly.dll
http://dotnet.jku.at / bin / MyAssembly / MyAssembly.dll

http://dotnet.jku.at / MyAssembly.exe
http://dotnet.jku.at / MyAssembly / MyAssembly.exe
http://dotnet.jku.at / bin / MyAssembly.exe
http://dotnet.jku.at / bin / MyAssembly / MyAssembly.exe
```

Because only the name of the assembly reference is stored in the metadata, and not the complete file name, the file extension must be "guessed". Therefore .dll files are searched and then .exe files. Further extensions will not be tried.

MyAssembly has no special culture attribute defined (Culture=neutral). The search strategy for assemblies with the special language mark looks somewhat different: here the search is always conducted in a subdirectory that corresponds to the culture attribute, for example probing for

```
AustrianText, Version=2.3.0.0, Culture=de-AT, PublicKeyToken=a9ba664985e79673

http://dotnet.jku.at / de-AT / AustrianText.dll
http://dotnet.jku.at / de-AT / AustrianText / AustrianText.dll
http://dotnet.jku.at / bin / de-AT / AustrianText.dll
http://dotnet.jku.at / bin / de-AT / AustrianText / AustrianText.dll

http://dotnet.jku.at / de-AT / AustrianText.exe
http://dotnet.jku.at / de-AT / AustrianText / AustrianText.exe
http://dotnet.jku.at / bin / de-AT / AustrianText.exe
http://dotnet.jku.at / bin / de-AT / AustrianText / AustrianText.exe
```

However, the locating and loading of the assembly is only the first step. When loading a type T the class loader also deals with the following things:

- ❏ Determining the necessary memory space for an object of type T.
- ❏ Determining the memory layout for T objects.
- ❏ Resolving all references from T to types already loaded. Here the consistent use of references is checked and the named references are converted into direct references.
- ❏ Testing the consistency of all references to T from already loaded types.
- ❏ References from T to types not yet loaded are either
  - – resolved through immediate loading of the referenced type, or
  - – only registered so that their consistency can be checked when loading the referred types later on.
- ❏ Creation of stubs for all implemented methods of T that will trigger the JIT translation of the CIL code on the first call of the method.

With the above-mentioned consistency tests, the class loader already supports the security web which the CLR ties around the executed programs. These minimal tests must always be carried out and represent the first level of the security checks. Another part of the VES—the verifier (see below)—is responsible for a more complex but optional formal testing of the type safety of a program, the so-called verification.

As soon as a type has been loaded completely, objects of this type can be instantiated, their fields and properties can be used and methods can be carried out. In order to do the latter, it is necessary for the code of methods that is in CIL to be translated (see Section 3.7.4). In many situations that require a high measure of security, the CIL must have previously been verified.

3.7.3 Verification of CIL Code

The VES is responsible for the safe execution of program. In order to guarantee that, the type safety of a program must be proven before its translation into machine code! This is referred to as *verification*. Verification is in parts the task of the class loader and in others the task of the verifier.

Type safety. Type-safe programs only access memory areas that have actually been allocated for them. Additionally, they only use objects according to their interfaces. These restrictions permit objects to exist in the same address space without getting in each other's way. They also prevent possible circumvention of security tests (see Section 3.8).

The VES examines the CIL code of a compiled method and performs a control-flow analysis with the help of the type information, in order to show that

1. the code is type safe, if all type information is correct, and that
2. the implementation guarantees the correctness of the type information.

Unfortunately, a perfect verification algorithm that shows that every type-safe program is indeed type safe is not possible. Therefore the CLR uses a conservative algorithm that at least guarantees that each successfully verified program is type safe. It can thus happen that a program fails verification, even though it is type safe. This leads to the following categorization of CIL code:

- ❑ **Invalid:** For invalid CIL code the JIT compiler cannot create machine code. The code either does not conform to CIL format or contains undefined instruction codes. Also, a jump instruction that does not lead to the start of a statement makes the code invalid.
- ❑ **Valid:** All CIL programs that do not fall into the first group belong to this category. Machine code can be generated for them. Their syntax corresponds to the CIL format. However, they can contain statements that are not type safe (e.g. pointer arithmetic).
- ❑ **Type safe:** These CIL programs represent a proper subset of the valid ones. In type-safe CIL code all statements conform strictly to the contracts implemented by the referenced types.
- ❑ **Verifiable:** Such CIL code can be proven to be type safe. As mentioned above, one cannot verify all type-safe programs; therefore this last category is a proper subset of the previous one.

The verifier is a part of the JIT compiler. Therefore it is only called for single methods, without knowing the contexts of their invocations. For this reason the verifier cannot test a further necessary condition for the type safety of a program:

3. all input values must conform to the prescribed signature.

Here the class loader helps out. It uses its consistency conditions and checks to ensure that the type signatures of all uses of methods and fields match their implementation. For this it mainly considers the metadata of an assembly. For example, it checks whether the used metadata tokens also correctly point into the corresponding tables, or whether string constants have enough buffer space (avoidance of buffer overflow).

Many tests that the class loader carries out may well already have been performed by the compiler; most compilers actually do this. However, because one does not know which compiler was used to create the assembly that is to be loaded, the loader must check many things again at run time.

3.7.4 Translation of CIL into Machine Code

The CLR cannot simply interpret intermediate-language programs, as the JVM sometimes does. On the .NET platform only machine code is executed. That means CIL code is always converted to machine code before the first execution. However, it does not mean that the CLR translates every program in full when loading it. Instead, the translation of the program code is done dynamically, while the program is running—exactly as with the loading of data types. Each method is then translated when it is invoked for the first time, thus as late as possible, but nevertheless just in time. For this reason this translation strategy is called *just in time* (JIT) compilation. The programs responsible for it are referred to as *JIT compilers*, and what they do is sometimes described as *jitting*.

This jitting proceeds as follows: a method call first reaches the stub created for every method by the class loader. The stub contains information about the JIT status of the method, that is, whether it has already been translated into machine code or not. If not, the JIT compiler is called to translate the method into a so-called *native code image*. The information in the stub is changed correspondingly, so that further calls to the just-translated method no longer activate the JIT compiler, but instead immediately run the just-generated machine code.

The JIT translation is carried out at most once per method, and only if the method is actually called. However, as soon as the program ends, the JIT-translated native code images are deleted and must be translated once again in another run of the program.

To avoid this, .NET offers the possibility of translating a program just once, by using the *Native Image Generator* (ngen.exe). This creates a complete machine code at installation time and puts the result in the *Native Image Cache*, which is part of the GAC. In this way the start-up times of such pre-compiled programs can be reduced.

In the documentation, this activity is often called *preJIT*, but in our opinion this is misleading, because in this case the compilation is undertaken in advance, and not just in time. When installing the CLR, the following assemblies are pre-compiled by default: CustomMarshallers, mscorlib, System, System.Design, System.Drawing, System.Drawing.Design, System.Windows.Forms, System.Xml.

The JIT Compilers of the CLR

In order to be capable of being installed on different platforms and conforming to different requirements, the CLR offers three different forms of JIT compilers: JIT, EconoJIT, OptJIT.

JIT is the standard JIT compiler that the CLR normally uses (and the only one that is already contained in version 1.1 of the .NET Framework). It takes into consideration the current computer architecture and configuration in order to carry out code optimizations, thus fully exploiting the advantages of JIT compilation.

EconoJIT is a variant that was developed with the aim of using as few time and space resources as possible during compilation. The availability of the EconoJit is also a reason why the interpretation of JIT codes can be forgone. The frugality and simplicity of the EconoJITter also offer many of the advantages of interpretation with respect to uncomplicated porting to any platform. The code generation strategy of EconoJIT allows it to throw away generated machine code, so that even large CIL programs can get by with very small memory space. For this reason, the EconoJIT is well suited for mobile devices such as PDAs, and is intended to be used for the Windows CE version of the .NET Framework. The JIT compiler *FJIT* in the Shared Source Implementation of the CLI [SSCLI] uses a JIT compiler equivalent to the EconoJIT.

OptJIT differs from the other two variants above all in one respect: it does not understand the full extent of CIL, but merely a subset of it, called OptIL. OptIL contains additional information that facilitates compiler optimization. Through the already optimized input, the OptJIT achieves similar results as the Standard JIT, although its resource needs are almost as frugal as EconoJIT's. Thus with OptJIT, a part of the JIT effort at run time is transferred to the compiler. Standard source-to-CIL compilers undertake only very rudimentary optimizations (if any at all). They translate the source code more or less statement by statement into the intermediate language. The result of this is that the JIT compiler must then work harder in order to create efficient machine code. The OptJIT, on the other hand, expects an already optimizing source-to-CIL compiler that creates additional information about control flow or register allocation. Unfortunately, it seems that Microsoft have put the OptJIT project on ice, so that for the time being the CLR will not be equipped with an OptJIT compiler.

In order to improve the flexibility of the JIT compilation, there are standardized interfaces between the CLR and the JIT compiler that enable the use of user-implemented JIT compilers.

3.7.5   Code Management

Within the VES of the .NET Framework the code manager has the following responsibilities:

- ❑ memory management
- ❑ garbage collection
- ❑ exception handling (see Section 2.1)
- ❑ security checking (see Section 3.8)
- ❑ support for developer services such as debugging (see Section 8.4) or profiling.

As with JIT compilation, .NET also allows the implementation of one's own code manager. For this purpose, a standardized interface will be provided in a later version. The code manager is closely bound to the JIT compiler, because the code created by the JIT compiler must be compatible with the memory layout assumed by the code manager.

Memory Management

In order to keep track of the state of the virtual machine at every point in time, a lot of information about the running program must be stored. The CLR distinguishes between its global state (see Figure 3.17) and the state of the method currently running (see Figure 3.18).

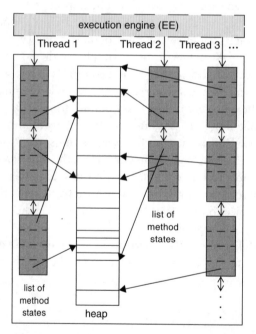

Figure 3.17 *Memory partitioning of the CLR at run time*

The CLR can carry out several independent threads of control in parallel (strictly, interleaved), in the same process. It manages these by maintaining dedicated lists of method states. Besides this, the shared address space also contains the heap, where space is reserved for storing dynamically created objects.

All the information needed immediately for running a method is kept in a method state (often called a *stack frame*). The list of method states shown in Figure 3.17 is often referred to as the method or procedure stack. On each call of a method, a new method state is created, appended to the end of the corresponding list, and linked to its predecessor. The current method is thus always the last in the list (on top of the procedure stack). On leaving a method, any results are copied to their destinations, the method state is removed from the list and all its data is deleted. Its predecessor then becomes the current method state.

In order to find its predecessor, each method must know the method from which it was called. This chaining is ensured by means of the so-called *return-state handle*. This corresponds to the concept of the *dynamic link* in compiler construction ([ASU86], [Wir96]).

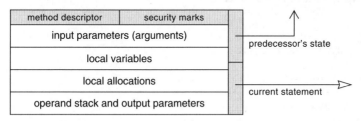

Figure 3.18 *Method state*

The method descriptor holds the type signature of the method, that is, the method name and the types of its input and output parameters. In addition, there is information about the types of the local variables and information for handling exceptions. The descriptor can be read at run time but cannot be changed.

The description of the security marks of the method cannot be read directly by managed program code. It merely helps the security mechanism of the CLR to determine the corresponding rights of a method.

Because the CLR must know what a method is doing at any point in time, each method state contains a pointer to the CIL statement that is currently being executed (*instruction pointer*).

Alongside these informative parts, the method state also contains four areas for the dynamic storage of data.

Input parameters. Unlike the JVM, input parameters do not count as local variables. They are stored in a list that is addressed via an index. Special instructions (ldarg, starg) are used to access each argument of the current method for reading or writing. It is also possible to load the address of a parameter on to the stack (ldarga). The order of the arguments in the list corresponds to the declaration order in the method signature. The first argument in the list has the index zero. With an object method, the first argument is always a pointer to the object on which the method is called (this).

When using variable-length argument lists, System.ArgIterator permits a type-safe access to the arguments, despite the fact that their type is not known in the method declaration. For those especially interested, we illustrate this in the following with a CIL code example.

In the example we take a method VarArgMethod that requires one parameter of type System.Int32 and subsequently allows any number of parameters of any type (keyword vararg).

```
.method static vararg void VarArgMethod (int32 x) { ... }
```

Calls to this method always have an int number as their first parameter and then possible further parameters. Figure 3.19 shows two calls of this method: one without, and one with, additional parameters.

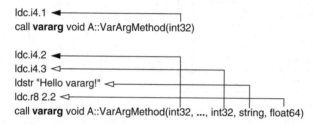

Figure 3.19 *Call of a method with variable number of parameters*

The first call contains no further parameters and thus after the keyword vararg it looks like a familiar method call. The second call is interesting, because it makes use of the possibility of having further parameters. All parameters are loaded on to the stack before the call, as usual. The call itself contains the type of the parameters in the corresponding order. An ellipsis separates the fixed from the optional parameters.

A System.ArgIterator is used to access the additional parameters in the body of the method. This is done in the following way:

```
.locals init (valuetype System.ArgIterator iter)
```

The iterator is loaded into a local variable.

```
ldloca iter
arglist
call instance void System.ArgIterator::.ctor(valuetype System.RuntimeArgumentHandle)
```

The instruction arglist obtains a pointer to the list of optional parameters and this is passed to the constructor of the iterator.

```
ldloca iter
call instance typedref System.ArgIterator::GetNextArg()
call object System.TypedReference::ToObject(typedref)
```

On each call, the method GetNextArg returns another optional parameter. The returned value is of the predefined value type typedref (System.TypedReference), a pointer–type pair (see Table 3.1) and can be cast into an object reference.

This form of variable parameters is entirely different from what is permitted by C# with the keyword params (see Section 2.8.3). There, simply an array of a particular element type can be passed. That means that although the number of parameters is indeed determined only at run time, the type of each parameter is already fixed at compilation. The only simplification, compared to Java, is that in calling such a method we are not obliged to pack the arguments into an array ourselves, but can simply write them in a comma-separated list. In the CIL nothing remains from this simplification. The C# compiler inserts the necessary statements for creating and filling the array to be passed.

Local variables. The local variables, like the method arguments, are stored in a list indexed from zero. For accessing local variables we have the instructions ldloc and stloc. The ldloca instruction loads the address of a local variable on to the stack. The keyword init can be used to signify that all local variables should be assigned their associated null value on entry to the method.

Local allocations (*local memory pool*). The instruction localloc allows dynamic allocation of storage space that will not be freed by the garbage collector, but automatically at the end of the method. This means that we cannot tidy up this memory area as long as the method is still running. The instruction localloc can be used, for example, to achieve the functionality supported by the C statement alloca.

Operand stack and output parameters. This is the "stack" that we have already mentioned so often and on which the functioning of the entire virtual machine is essentially based. On entry to a method it is always initially empty. On leaving a method it contains only the return value and any possible output parameters. This area of the method state is the only one that is not individually addressable, that is, we cannot access individual elements, just the top (last-loaded) element. Only when this has been removed does the next below it become visible.

The operand stack must not be confused with the method stack. On each call, a stack frame with the local variables of the method is loaded on to the method stack. The operand stack, on the other hand, serves merely for intermediate storage of values during the execution of instructions and is somewhat comparable to registers.

Garbage Collection

An essential innovation for Windows programming (especially for C programmers) is automatic garbage collection, which the CLR provides. Programmers moving from C/C++ to C# are changing to an environment in which they no longer have to concern themselves with freeing of memory, but can leave this to the *garbage collector*. In fact, there is no possibility of explicitly freeing memory space.

During the execution of an object-oriented program, all dynamically created objects are loaded on to a so-called *heap*. The life cycle of such objects can in general be split into five phases:

1. *Allocation*: reserve storage space for the object.
2. *Initialization*: assign suitable initial values.
3. *Use of the object*, while it is still reachable by at least one object reference.
4. *Finalization*: release possibly used resources (files, database connections, etc.).
5. *Freeing* of the storage space of the object.

If we are obliged to free the storage space of objects manually, this—in itself simple—scheme holds two sources of severe (and common) programming errors:

❑ Memory space is never freed.
❑ Memory space is freed, although a reference still exists which then points into the void.

These errors are very problematic because they are hard to locate, in that they can come to light at quite a different point from where they originate. As long as we work within an environment where a garbage collector takes full control of such matters neither of the two errors can ever occur!

Managed heap. The heap is a contiguous storage area where all objects of classes and arrays must be created. Only the garbage collector may free storage on the heap. An internal pointer (NextObjPtr) refers to the position where the next object can be allocated (see Figure 3.20).

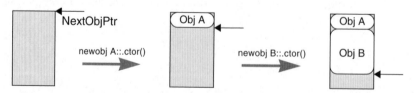

Figure 3.20 *Managed Heap: empty, after allocating one object, and then a further object*

Allocation. An object is created on the heap by the instruction newobj. First there is a check to see whether enough memory space is available. If so, the object is placed at the location indicated by NextObjPtr, its constructor is called and its address is loaded on to the operand stack. Subsequently, NextObjPtr is set to the end of the object just created and thus once again points to the start of the available memory area (see Figure 3.20).

The creation of the object is thus very quick. It simply consists of adjusting a pointer. Also, to test whether enough space is available, it is simply necessary to compare the difference between NewObjPtr and the end of the heap with the size of the object to be created.

In a typical C++ run-time environment, on the other hand, it is necessary to work through a chain of free storage blocks to find a sufficiently large block. This must then be partitioned and the unused part must be connected back into the list of free blocks. The faster allocation strategy of .NET is made possible because the garbage collector takes care of keeping the heap compacted. The allocated objects always come first, tightly packed against each other, followed by the entire free storage in one single piece.

Garbage collection algorithm. If there is not enough memory space available for the object to be created, the garbage collector is activated to obtain some space. However, before it can start, all active threads must be suspended in order to ensure that no new objects are created, or references changed, during the work of the garbage collector. This suspension of the program execution is the major disadvantage of automatic memory management, because it means that the running time of the program often becomes decidedly longer. Especially for real-time applications the unpredictable starting time and duration of a garbage collection is often unacceptable.

Once all threads are suspended, the first phase is the marking of "live" objects. An object is live, if it is reachable, either directly or indirectly, from a "root". Roots are all references in global variables or in local variables and parameters of the currently executing method (in Figure 3.17 for example, all pointers that point from the method states to the heap are roots).

Then the second phase can begin. In this, the live objects are shifted so that they are contiguous and all references to these objects are updated. NextObjPtr then again points to the end of the used part of the heap area.

Only now can the threads be restarted and the program execution continued. Figure 3.21 sketches the situation of the heap before and after a garbage collection.

A more precise description of garbage collection under .NET can be found in [Rich00a], [Rich00b] as well as [Rich02]. These also explain the problems of finalization and the different generations that are used by the CLR to optimize the garbage collection algorithm.

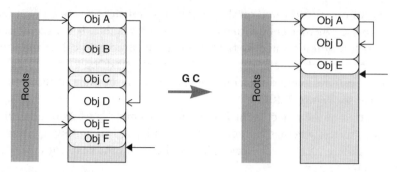

Figure 3.21 *Heap and pointers before and after a garbage collection*

3.8   Security

Performing security checks is actually the work of the VES, but since security is such a central theme of .NET, we have devoted an entire section to it. Because this topic was not covered in the chapter on C#, we will give the code examples here in C#, instead of the CIL used so far.

.NET was developed to support, among others, distributed applications that are called over a network (intranet or internet). As always when running binary code, we do not know exactly what this will do. Therefore a certain security risk has always existed. The situation is made drastically more acute now, because code from anywhere in the world can be downloaded and run on the user's own machine. There must therefore be mechanisms to prevent programs from doing damage to the user's computer.

A common way is the so-called *role-based security* that is supported by most operating systems (Windows 2000, MacOS, Linux, ...). The administrator authorizes each user (or user group) to have certain rights, which allow or forbid access to system resources. This means, however, that every program receives the same rights as the user who runs it. For example, a system administrator has full access to all resources. At the same time, all the programs that he or she executes have all rights. This is a situation that must be avoided at all costs. Therefore the model of *code-based security* was developed for .NET.

3.8.1   Code-based Security

.NET does not grant rights for users, but for individual assemblies, and for this it uses information about the assemblies themselves, completely independently from the rights of the current user. This is called *Code Access Security* (CAS) because, as the name suggests, it works essentially by determining whether an assembly (=

code) should have access to a particular resource or not. It is the assembly that here again is the smallest unit for which access rights are granted.

It can happen that assemblies receive rights from the CLR that the current user executing them under Windows does not have. However, in this case the operating system prevents unauthorized access. Security features of the operating system are thus not undermined by .NET.

The CAS is based essentially on the following three assumptions:

1. At load time, the CLR must be able to determine the rights of an assembly and assign them to it.
2. At run time it must be possible to check whether an assembly has the necessary rights of access to a resource (*security stack walk*).
3. In implementing types that need access to critical resources, the programmer must take care to check the rights of the caller before each access (Demand).

Determining the Rights of an Assembly

The process of determining the rights of an assembly can be shown diagrammatically, as in Figure 3.22. The ideas embodied there are explained in what follows.

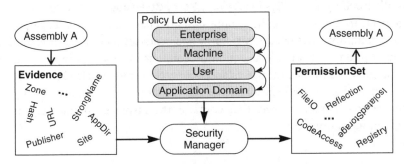

Figure 3.22 *Determining the rights of an assembly*

Each assembly carries information about its identity, origin, producer and so on. This is called *evidence*. The security manager (System.Security.SecurityManager) determines the set of permissions (System.Security.PermissionSet) that may be assigned to the assembly by matching the evidence to the security policies available in the system. It thus composes a permission set by using evidence (information about the assembly) and policy (the rules about granting of rights set on the target machine).

Evidence. The class System.Security.Policy.Evidence represents a collection of objects that contain specific information about an assembly. These include, for example, the URL (System.Security.Policy.Url) from which the assembly was loaded, the zone (System.Security.Policy.Zone) from which it originates (possible zones are listed in the enumeration System.Security.SecurityZone), and the producer of the assembly (System.Security.Policy.Publisher). Additionally, objects of user-defined evidence classes can complete the assembly description. These will be ignored by the standard configuration of the security system, but an administrator can set the configuration so that additional evidence is taken into account.

Security policy. The security policy guides the mapping of the assembly description (evidence) to permissions that is carried out by the security manager. As Figure 3.22 shows, the security manager sees four levels of the security policy (System.Security.Policy.PolicyLevel). The top three can be adapted by administrators via the configuration files mentioned in Section 8.3. The lowest depends on the host of the application (more detailed information about this can be obtained from the online documentation). The levels of the security policy are queried one after another when trying to ascertain the permissions for an assembly. The result is the *intersection* of all four resulting PermissionSets. An assembly thus receives only those permissions that are actually assigned to assemblies with the given characteristics by *all* levels of the security policy.

We can think of these levels as a tree structure (see Figure 3.24) whose nodes are so-called code groups (System.Security.Policy.CodeGroup). A code group can have an arbitrary number of child groups and attaches a name of a set of permissions to a condition (System.Security.Policy.IMembershipCondition). All assemblies whose descriptions conform to the condition count as members of this code group and the permissions of the group (System.Security.NamedPermissionSet) are associated with them. Figure 3.23 shows such a relationship between a code group and the NamedPermissionSet *Internet* that contains the displayed permissions in the standard configuration.

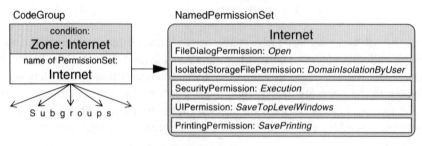

Figure 3.23 *Code group with NamedPermissionSet*

If an assembly description corresponds to the condition of the code group, the conditions of the corresponding child groups must also be tested. An assembly can thus belong to several code groups. The set of permissions that are assigned to an assembly is the *union* of the NamedPermissionSets of all the code groups of which the assembly is a member. Figure 3.24 shows how a code group tree could be configured for a level of the security policy.

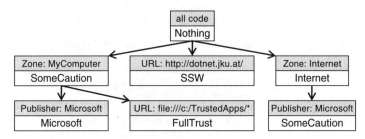

Figure 3.24 *Security Policy Level*

In order to ascertain the rights of the assembly c:\TrustedApps\MSApp.exe for the level of the security policy shown in Figure 3.24, the security manager proceeds as follows. It always starts from the root node of the code group tree. Every assembly fulfils the condition "*all code*" hence MSApp gets the rights from the NamedPermissionSet *Nothing* (which contains no permissions) and now the first child group is tested. Because MSApp.exe is in a local directory, it fulfils the condition "*Zone: MyComputer*". It is assigned the rights from the NamedPermissionSet *SomeCaution* and the security manager tests the condition of the first child group of this group. Because MSApp.exe was produced by Microsoft, it additionally receives the right from the NamedPermissionSet *Microsoft*. This node has no offspring, and so now the condition in its sibling is tested. MSApp.exe lies in the directory c:\TrustedApps and so it also receives the rights from the NamedPermissionSet *Full-Trust*. This node also has no offspring and there are no further nodes on this level. Thus the security manager takes a step back and checks whether the assembly has been loaded from http://dotnet.jku.at and then whether it originates from the Internet or not. Neither condition is fulfilled and so the security manager has finished determining the permissions at this level. As a result, the PermissionSet of MSApp now contains the permissions from the union *Nothing, SomeCaution, Microsoft* and *FullTrust*. While *Nothing* and *FullTrust* are predefined NamedPermissionSets, *SomeCaution* and *Microsoft* have been defined specifically for the security policy at this level.

Permission. A Permission object describes the set of operations that should be secured for a given resource. In the .NET class library a range of such permissions is already available. Table 3.9 gives a short overview.

Table 3.9 *Permissions of the .NET library (Namespace System.Security.Permisssion)*

Name	Description
EnvironmentPermission	for controlling access to system and user environment variables.
FileDialogPermission	for controlling access to files and directories through the use of file dialogs. Can be used, for example, to obtain at least read access to some files or directories via file dialogs without having a FileIOPermission.
FileIOPermission	for controlling access to files and directories.
IsolatedStorageFilePermission	for controlling access to files in the *isolated storage* area. This is a separate area in the file system only available to one component (see Section 4.2.3).
ReflectionPermission	for controlling the access to metadata information with the help of the reflection API (see Section 4.5).
RegistryPermission	for controlling the access to values and keys of the Windows registry.
SecurityPermission	manages elementary permissions, for example, – *Execution*: may code be executed? – *UnmanagedCode*: may unmanaged code be called? – *SkipVerification*: may verification be skipped? – and so on.
UIPermission	manages permissions that concern user interfaces, for example, firing events in a window, or use of the clipboard.

The abstract type System.Security.CodeAccessPermission defines the base class for all permissions that wish to carry out a *security stack walk* (see below) for checking the rights of an assembly. All types in Table 3.9 are derived from this type. We describe what the interface of a permission looks like and how it is used further below, where we go into some implementation details.

Security Stack Walk

In the section on memory management (in Section 3.7.5) we explained how the method states are chained together into so-called *threads of control*. Such a thread of control can be imagined as a stack of method states. At the beginning, there is always the state of the start method. If this calls a further method, then a method state for the new method is created and put on to the method stack. The method state on top always represents the currently executing method and all the method states lying beneath it are referred to as callers of this method.

If the current method now accesses resources, it can be that the rights of the callers must also be checked. The callers are those methods whose states currently lie on the method stack. Because the checking involves a traversal of the method stack, this is called a *stack walk*. Figure 3.25 depicts this process.

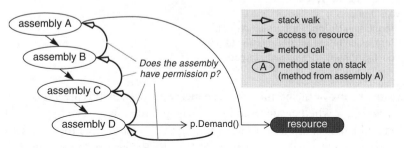

Figure 3.25 *Security stack walk*

In Figure 3.25 a method from assembly D attempts to access a resource that is protected by a permission p. Before this access, the method uses p.Demand() to check its callers. In this, each method state on the stack is checked to see whether the assembly to which it belongs has the permission p. Only if all the callers fulfil this condition may the access take place. If even one method is from an assembly that does not have p, the security manager throws a System.Security.SecurityException and blocks access to the resource.

So a security stack walk either throws an exception and interrupts the "normal" execution of the program, or everything is all right and the program can continue. Therefore, action taken after the call of the Demand method can assume that the assembly has the demanded permissions.

Implementation

For the security system to function at all, developers must carry out or request the appropriate security tests whenever they implement programs or libraries that access security critical resources. Therefore .NET offers the following possibilities:

- ❑ User-defined permissions can be created to protect new kinds of accesses or resources.
- ❑ Before the access to a resource, all callers of a method can be checked for specified permissions (Demand).
- ❑ The check for the permissions can be modified.
- ❑ The execution of an assembly can be adapted according to the rights granted.

User-defined permissions. The interface System.Security.IPermission defines the following contract which every permission must implement so that the security manager can also work with it:

```
public interface IPermission : ISecurityEncodable {
    IPermission Copy();
    void Demand();
    IPermission Union(IPermission target);
    IPermission Intersect(IPermission target);
    bool IsSubsetOf(IPermission target);
}
```

Copy creates a copy of the permission. The method p.Demand() is always called if it is necessary to test whether an assembly has the permission p (see Figure 3.25).

Union and Intersect are used in determining the PermissionSet for an assembly. Within a particular level of the security policy the PermissionSets resulting from the code groups are united (Union) (see Figure 3.24). In a final step these union sets of the different policy levels are intersected (Intersect) to yield the result of the rights assignment. In this, the PermissionSets delegate the Union and Intersect operations to their permissions.

p1.IsSubsetOf(p2) tests whether p1 is a subset of p2, or in other words, if p2 implies permission p1. This is the case, if p1 does not allow more accesses than p2. If, for example, p1 allows only read access to a particular directory, but p2 has full access, then p1 is a subset of p2. Also, if p1 allows a particular kind of access to a directory D and p3 allows the same kind of access to a directory that contains D, then p1 is a subset of p3. The three example permissions from the situations described here are declared and created in C# in the following way:

```
CodeAccessPermission
    p1 = new FileIOPermission(FileIOPermissionAccess.Read, "c:\\Temp"),
    p2 = new FileIOPermission(FileIOPermissionAccess.AllAccess, "c:\\Temp"),
    p3 = new FileIOPermission(FileIOPermissionAccess.Read, "c:\\");
```

The following holds:

```
p1.IsSubsetOf(p2);   // true
p1.IsSubsetOf(p3);   // true
```

It is important always to be aware that particular permissions can imply others. In this way it can happen that assemblies hold permissions that are not explicitly visible in their code, which can lead to security holes being opened by mistake.

Demand. Library types usually make available functions for accessing resources. For example, System.IO.File and System.IO.FileStream support access to the file system of a computer. Because no one can know in advance how, or from what programs, the library types will be used, the methods that ultimately access a resource must always take care of checking the necessary security permissions. This is done by creating an appropriate Permission object (or PermissionSet) and calling its

Demand method. In the following example, a file c:\F.txt is to be read. Before that, a check of the permissions of all callers is requested:

```
CodeAccessPermission p;
p = new FileIOPermission(FileIOPermissionAccess.Read, "c:\\F.txt");
p.Demand();
// now the file can be read (without security risks)
...
```

In Figure 3.25, D is an assembly that offers types for accessing resources and re-quests a security stack walk before each access. This implementation requirement is thus particularly relevant to developers of library types.

Customizing the security stack walk. Developers also have the possibility to mod-ify the course of a security stack walk as shown in Figure 3.25. It is not always the case that all callers, without exception, have to be tested before an access is al-lowed or rejected. At run time three special sets of permissions can be defined for every method state. For this, the class System.SecurityCodeAccessPermission makes the following methods available:

- ❏ Assert: for early positive termination of the stack walk. With this a method can vouch for its callers. These are then no longer checked for rights, and access can still take place, as long as the vouching party itself holds the per-missions vouched for. Because of the obviously increased security risk this should only be used with great caution!
- ❏ Deny: for early negative termination of the stack walk. This allows it to be made explicit that a method may not access a resource. If it is already known at the time of development that a certain access will be denied in any case, then this can be done with the Deny method.
- ❏ PermitOnly: for early negative termination of the stack walk. In contrast to Deny, here those permissions are given for which further callers must still be tested. In this way all accesses except the set of chosen ones can be blocked.

Assert, Deny and PermitOnly permissions are always only valid for the method in which they have been set. On leaving a method those permission sets that have been set by the caller become valid again. In using these methods, we must keep in mind that each method has at any time only one Permission or one PermissionSet stored for Assert, Deny or PermitOnly and any call of these methods overrides all previous ones. If one of the three methods is called several times in the body of a method, then it is only the Permission or PermissionSet of the last one that applies. In the example, we call Deny twice in succession, with two different permissions p1 and p2, and then cause a stack walk for each by calling Demand (the comments describe the results of the statements).

```
void SomeMethod() {
    p1.Deny();          // permission p1 may now no longer be granted
    p1.Demand();        // must fail, because p1 is in the Deny set
    p2.Demand();        // normal stack walk; only p1 is in the Deny set

    p2.Deny();          // permission p2 may now no longer be granted
    p1.Demand();        // normal stack walk; only p2 is in the Deny set
    p2.Demand();        // must fail, because p2 is in the Deny set
}
```

The second stack walk for p1 is carried out entirely normally and does not fail immediately as it does the first time, because after p2.Deny, only p2 is in the Deny set and the p1.Deny() carried out previously now no longer applies to the stack walk.

In order to remove these additional constraints for the security stack walk, that is, empty the special permission sets, there are corresponding revert methods: RevertAll, RevertAssert, RevertDeny, RevertPermitOnly.

Granting rights. The permissions that an assembly may have according to the security policy need not be same ones that it actually gets. After determining the allowed permissions, the permissions are only granted in a second pass. By means of attributes and the enumeration System.Security.Permissions.SecurityAction each assembly is allowed to give three special sets of permissions, which are evaluated at load time and influence the rights assignment. Only if none of the three sets is given are all the allowed permissions actually granted to the assembly. These three sets are:

❏ *Minimum necessary permissions* (SecurityAction.RequestMinimum): If the security manager realizes that not all the permissions requested herein may be granted, it forbids further progress of the program by throwing the exception System.SecurityPolicy.PolicyException.

❏ *Refused permissions* (SecurityAction.RequestRefuse): In order to avoid possible security risks, the developer has the possibility of forbidding the assembly in advance from receiving certain permissions.

❏ *Optional permissions* (SecurityAction.RequestOptional): In the case that these permissions may not be granted, the program should proceed nonetheless. It can possibly not offer certain functionality.

Under .NET, security mechanisms can be implemented in two ways: namely declarative and imperative.

Declarative security. Expressing security requirements declaratively means that they are associated with a program element in the form of user-defined attributes (more details on the use of attributes can be found in Section 2.14).

All attributes for declarative security are derived from the abstract base attribute System.Security.Permissions.SecurityAttribute. It has the following public interface:

```
public abstract class SecurityAttribute : Attribute {
    //----- constructors
    public SecurityAttribute (SecurityAction action);
    //----- properties
    public SecurityAction Action { get; set; }
    public bool Unrestricted { get; set; }
    //----- methods
    public abstract IPermission CreatePermission();
}
```

We can thus indicate a desired action for each permission as the first positional parameter, and then add further characteristics as named parameters. The declaration

```
[ FileIOPermission(SecurityAction.Demand, Read="c:\\Temp") ]
public void ReadFile (string filename) { /* read file filename */ }
```

demands, for example, that before executing the ReadFile method a stack walk should be carried out (SecurityAction.Demand) to check whether all the callers have read access rights to the directory c:\Temp.

The advantage of the declarative implementation variant is that the security requirements are stored in the metadata and can thus be queried by other programs and tools via reflection. In addition, there are certain security requirements that can only be formulated in this style, such as, for example, the Request sets described above.

A disadvantage of the declarative implementation is its coarse granularity: security attributes can only apply to entire assemblies, types or methods, and also they can only be granted at compile time.

Imperative security. Imperatively security is expressed through the creation of a permission object, and a subsequent call of a method such as Demand or Assert. The requirement

```
p = new FileIOPermission(FileIOPermissionAccess.Read, "c:\\Temp");
p.Demand();
```

is the imperative equivalent of the declarative requirement from the example above. Here, the advantage of the imperative over the declarative style is already visible: it is possible to provide different permissions at run time for different execution paths through the program. This allows the permissions to be specified more precisely, and that reduces the chance of overlooking security holes.

The ReadFile method from the example of declarative security tests the access rights for the entire directory, although only an individual file is to be read. However, its name may only be determined at run time and thus there is no way to provide a more exact indication of the necessary permissions declaratively. The imperative method can look like this:

```
public void ReadFile (string filename) {
    CodeAccessPermission p;
    p = new FileIOPermission(FileIOPermissionAccess.Read, filename);
    p.Demand();
    ... // read file filename
}
```

Here only a subset of the declaratively required rights is necessary to realize the same functionality. For two reasons it is advisable always to try to require only the minimal set of permissions: firstly, with fewer rights, an assembly can also do less damage, and secondly, it reduces the possibility of opening security holes though implicit permissions (see IsSubsetOf method further above).

3.8.2   Role-based Security

Role-based security is supported by most operating systems, as already mentioned at the beginning of this section. Thus if .NET runs on such an operating system, it can be sure that no program can carry out accesses that are not allowed for the user who is running it.

In many cases the identity or role of the user will differ from those assigned by the operating system. For example, if the user connects to a web service. Therefore .NET provides the means to assign a user identity or a user role to a thread. .NET programs can thus define and grant their own identities and roles.

The most important types supporting role-based security are in the namespace System.Security.Principal where two interfaces are particularly relevant:

❑ IIdentity represents the identity of the user in whose name the program is executed.

```
public interface IIdentity {
    string Name { get; }
    bool IsAuthenticated { get; }
    string AuthenticationType { get; }
}
```

All these properties of an identity are set either by the operating system or by another authenticating instance (for example, ASP.NET).

❑ IPrincipal represents the roles that a user can be assigned. Under Windows that is determined by the user groups to which the user belongs.

```
public interface IPrincipal {
    //----- properties
    IIdentity Identity { get; }
    //----- methods
    bool IsInRole (string role);
}
```

Each principal must be assigned exactly one identity. The method IsInRole determines whether the principal belongs to a given role or not. A thread can belong to exactly one principal. This assignment is made by the static method CurrentPrinicpal of the type System.Threading.Thread.

For both interfaces there is a standard implementation in the form of the classes GenericIdentity and GenericPrincipal, as well as a binding to the security system of the Windows operating system in WindowsIdentity and WindowsPrincipal.

3.9 Exercises

1. **Virtual machines.** What are the advantages of using a programming language that is based on a virtual machine?

2. **CLR versus JVM.** Which platform is better suited as a target for different programming languages: the .NET common language runtime or the Java virtual machine? Justify your answer.

3. **Value types and reference types.** What is the fundamental difference between a value type and a reference type? What effect does this difference have at run time?

4. **Type compatibility.** In spite of the differences between value types and reference types all .NET types are compatible with System.Object. How is this compatibility achieved for value types?

5. **Attribute CLSCompliant.** Consider the following code fragments and decide which classes, methods and fields are checked for CLS compliance by the C# compiler (the compiler will not report an error in any of these cases). Give a short justification of your answers.

```
public class A {
    public int F1;
    public void M1 (int p1) { }
}

[assembly: System.CLSCompliant(true)]
public class B {
    public int F1;
    public void M1 (int p1) { }
}

[assembly: System.CLSCompliant(true)]
public class C {
    public int F1;
    void M1 (sbyte p1) { }
}
```

6. **Metadata.** What kinds of metadata exist under .NET? What are they used for?

7. **Assemblies and modules.** What is the difference between an assembly and a module?

8. **Strong names.** Describe the parts of a strong name. When and why does an assembly need to have a strong name?

9. **Versioning.** Assume that an assembly with the version number 1.2.1088.3792 was created from a source file containing the attribute:

   ```
   [assembly: AssemblyVersion("1.2.*")]
   ```

   When was this assembly created?

10. **Application domains.** Write a C# program AppLauncher that can launch and run other applications. Each of these applications should run in its own application domain (not in a separate process!).

11. **Probing.** Assume that the private assembly Utils is needed for the execution of the application MyApp that was loaded from c:\Programs\MyAppDir\. Where does the CLR look for this assembly?

12. **Code-based security.** The security policy under .NET is defined on four levels: the enterprise level, the machine level, the user level and the application-domain level. Assume that all assemblies have full rights (that is, their permission set is FullTrust) on the enterprise, the user, and the application-domain level. The security policy on the machine level is defined as follows:

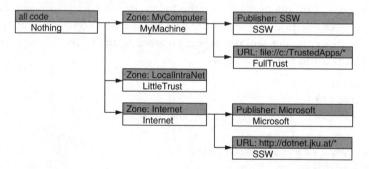

What rights does an assembly MSApp get, which comes from Microsoft, is signed, and was loaded from http://dotnet.jku.at/pub/apps? To which code groups does it belong on the machine level?

4 The .NET Class Library

The class library of .NET (Base Class Library or BCL) consists of about 100 namespaces and over 2000 types. It is the programming interface to the .NET Framework and contains APIs for all conceivable areas, beginning with simple data structures, through input and output streams, database access, XML, threads, network access, reflection to GUI- and Web programming. Figure 4.1 gives a basic overview.

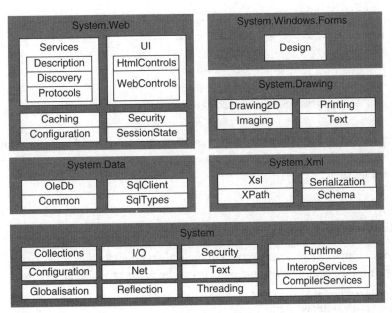

Figure 4.1 The .NET Class Library (BCL, Base Class Library)

In the following sections of this chapter we will now look at the most important namespaces of this library. Although the extracts and examples are given here in C#, the BCL is *language independent* and can be used by all .NET languages.

Obviously, we cannot describe all namespaces and classes here and we have even condensed the classes we do cover by making a choice from their functionality. The complete reference information for the BCL can be found in the online documentation of the .NET Framework SDK [SDKDoc]. When executing the examples it is important to start them from a local drive. If you start them from a networked drive (mapped drive) you can get a SecurityException, because of restrictions in the default security configuration.

4.1   Collections

The C# language syntax directly supports only arrays. Other sorts of object collections are provided in the namespace System.Collections and its sub-namespaces. Figure 4.2 shows some of the collection types and their inheritance hierarchy.

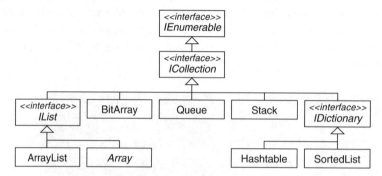

Figure 4.2 *Extract of the Collections hierarchy with its classes and interfaces*

All collection classes implement the interface ICollection and usually add new functionality to it. In the following sections we go further into the classes and interfaces from Figure 4.2.

4.1.1   IEnumerable

The interface IEnumerable describes all enumerable types. All collection classes implement this interface. IEnumberable objects can be traversed with an *iterator*:

```
interface IEnumerable {
    IEnumerator GetEnumerator();
}
```

A call of c.GetEnumerator returns an iterator that can be used to work though the elements of a collection c. An *iterator* is a design pattern that allows a set of elements to be traversed without needing to give details of the internal structure of the object set. Each kind of collection offers its own iterator, but all iterators support the following interface IEnumerator:

```
interface IEnumerator {
    object Current { get; }
    bool MoveNext();
    void Reset();
}
```

The property Current returns the currently visited element of the collection currently visited. The method MoveNext advances Current so that it points to the next element (the value false is returned if there is no further element). The method Reset sets Current back to the first element of the collection. The following example shows how to iterate across an array (which counts as a collection and which implements IEnumerable):

```
using System; using System.Collections;
...
string[] a = { "Mike", "Tom", "Pam" };
IEnumerator e = a.GetEnumerator();
while (e.MoveNext())
    Console.WriteLine(e.Current);
```

4.1.2 ICollection

The interface ICollection is the base interface for all classes that implement collections of data:

```
public interface ICollection : IEnumerable {
    //----- properties
    int Count { get; }
    bool IsSynchronized { get; }
    object SyncRoot { get; }
    //----- methods
    void CopyTo(Array a, int index);
}
```

Count returns the number of elements in the collection. In order to allow synchronized access to a collection, SyncRoot returns an object to which a lock can be applied (see Section 4.3.5). The enquiry IsSynchronized determines whether access will be synchronized. Details about synchronization and resource management are in Section 4.3. The method c.CopyTo(a, i) copies the collection c into the array a starting at position i. The following example shows how SyncRoot can be used to provide synchronized access to an array a:

```
static int[] a = { 1, 2, 3 };

void SetSynchronized(int i, int value) {
    lock (a.SyncRoot) {   // exclusive access to array a for this thread
        a[i] = value;
    }
}
```

4.1.3 IList

The interface IList is the base interface of all object collections that are implemented as lists (for example, Array and ArrayList):

```
public interface IList : ICollection, IEnumerable {
    //----- properties
    bool IsFixedSize { get; }
    bool IsReadOnly { get; }
    object this[int index] { get; set; }     // indexer for access to individual elements
    //----- methods
    void Clear();
    int Add(object o);                        // appends o at end of list
    void Insert(object o, int i);             // inserts o at position i
    void Remove(object o);                    // removes first occurrence of o from list
    void RemoveAt(int i);                     // removes element at position i
    bool Contains(object o);
    int IndexOf(object o);
}
```

IList defines typical list operations such as Insert and Remove. IsFixedSize determines whether the list has a fixed size that cannot be changed. IsReadOnly indicates whether the elements of the list are write protected. IList also defines an *indexer* that can be used to access the elements of the list via an index operator as known from accessing array elements.

4.1.4 Array

All arrays declared in programs are in fact instantiations of run-time generated subclasses of the abstract class Array that is in namespace System rather than System.Collections.

```
public abstract class Array : ICloneable, IList, ICollection, IEnumerable {
    //----- implements properties and methods of the following interfaces
    // IEnumerable: GetEnumerator
    // ICollection: Count, CopyTo, ...
    // IList: Clear, Add, Insert, Remove, RemoveAt, Contains, IndexOf, Indexer, ...
    // ICloneable: Clone
    //----- properties
    public int Length { get; }    // number of elements in an array
    public int Rank { get; }      // number of dimensions of an array
    //----- methods
    public static void Clear(Array a, int index, int length);   // initializes with 0, false, null, ...
    public void Initialize();     // initializes value types in the array by calling their constructors
    public static void Copy(Array srcArray, Array destArray, int len);
    public static void Copy(Array srcArray, int srcIdx, Array destArray, int destIdx, int len);
    public static int IndexOf(Array a, object val);
    public static int IndexOf(Array a, object val, int startIndex);
```

```
public static int LastIndexOf(Array a, object value);
public static int LastIndexOf(Array a, object value, int startIndex);
public static Array CreateInstance(Type elementType, int len);
public static Array CreateInstance(Type elementType, int[] len);
public int GetLength(int dimension);      // number of elements in the given dimension
public int GetLowerBound(int dimension);
public int GetUpperBound(int dimension);
public object GetValue(int idx);      // returns the element at position idx (1-dim array)
public object GetValue(int[] idx);      // returns the element at position idx (n-dim array)
public void SetValue(object obj, int idx);      // sets obj at position idx (1-dim array)
public void SetValue(object obj, int[] idx);      // sets obj at position idx (n-dim array)
public static void Reverse(Array a);      // reverses order of elements in array a
public static int BinarySearch(Array a, object val);
public static int BinarySearch(Array a, object val, IComparer c);
public static int BinarySearch(Array a, int index, int len, object val);
public static int BinarySearch(Array a, int index, int len, object val, IComparer c);
public static void Sort(Array a);      // sorts the elements in array a
public static void Sort(Array keys, Array values);      // sorts pairs based on the keys
public static void Sort(Array a, IComparer comparer);      // special sorting
// ... + overloaded methods
}
```

The class Array defines a vector of elements that has a fixed size which cannot be changed after the storage space has been allocated. So for this, the returned value of IsFixedSize inherited from IList is always true. The following example shows how a C# array can use the functionality of the class Array:

```
int[] a = { 3, 1, 5, 2, 9, 4 };
Array.Sort(a);                     // sorts the elements in array a
foreach (int elem in a)
    Console.Write("{0} ", elem);   // prints the (sorted!) elements to the console: 1 2 3 4 5 9
```

In C# an Array object can be created as follows:

```
int[] a = new int[6];
```

The same result is achieved by calling the method CreateInstance of the class Array:

```
int[] a = (int[]) Array.CreateInstance(typeof(int), 6);
```

a.Clone() creates a shallow copy of the array a. If the array contains references to objects, only the references are copied, *not* the objects themselves.

Multi-dimensional Arrays

The class array allows single and multi-dimensional arrays to be created with the help of the CreateInstance method:

```
Array a = Array.CreateInstance(typeof(int), 10, 20, 30);
```

This statement creates an array object a with three dimensions, where the first has 10 elements, the second 20 and the third 30.

The Rank property of an array returns the number of dimensions with which it was defined. The following example creates a two-dimensional matrix and displays its number of dimensions on the console:

```
Array matrix = Array.CreateInstance(typeof(int), 10, 20);
Console.Write("Dimensions:{0}", matrix.Rank);   // prints "Dimensions: 2" to the console
```

The property Length gets the total number of elements in *all* dimensions of the array. So matrix.Length yields 10×20 elements:

The Length property of an array returns the number of elements in *all* dimensions. If one displays matrix.Length the value is 10×20 elements, so 200.

```
Console.Write("{0} elements", matrix.Length);   // prints "200 elements"
```

In order to determine the number of elements in dimension n, one has to use the method GetLength(n):

```
int count = matrix.GetLength(0);     // count = 10
count = matrix.GetLength(1);         // count = 20
```

In C#, array indexing always begins at 0 but other languages often define different start indexes. The method Array.CreateInstance(Type t, int[], dim, int[] bounds) can be used to define an array with any start indexes. Here dim gives the number of elements per dimension and bounds the start index of each dimension. Arrays with start index of 0 and arrays with different start indexes count as different types.

The methods a.GetLowerBound(n) and a.GetUpperBound(n) can be used to get the index bounds in dimension n of array a. The first method returns the lower bound, thus usually 0, and the second the highest permissible index. The following code sequence shows a use of both methods:

```
for (int i = matrix.GetLowerBound(0); i <= matrix.GetUpperBound(0); i++) {
    for(int j = matrix.GetLowerBound(1); j <= matrix.GetUpperBound(1); j++)
        Console.Write("{0} ", matrix.GetValue(i, j));
    Console.WriteLine();
}
```

The call matrix.GetUpperBound(0) returns the higher index bound of dimension 0 of matrix, so in this case, 9.

The static method Array.Clear() clears the values of all elements in the array. They are set to the value 0, '\0', null or according to the element type.

Sorting, Reversing and Searching

The class Array extends the functionality of IList with some useful operations. The static method Array.Sort(a) sorts the elements of an array a. To specify the sorting order one can supply an object of type IComparer. The interface IComparer defines a method Compare(x, y) that returns an integer to indicate whether x is less than, equal to, or greater than y.

```
public interface IComparer {
    int Compare(object x, object y);   // returns <0 if x < y  |  0 if x == y  |  >0 if x > y
}
```

Thus IComparer allows customization of comparison operations. If the standard comparison strategy suffices, no IComparer object has to be provided when invoking Sort. The class library offers some implementations of IComparer:

IComparer allows the use of user-defined comparison operations. If the comparison of the two objects should follow the standard mechanism, then there is no need for an IComparer object. Examples of pre-implemented IComparer types in the library are:

❑ Comparer: character string comparison, case sensitive
❑ CaseInsensitiveComparer: character string comparison, case insensitive

The following example shows the implementation of an IComparer object that performs a string comparison on the basis of length. Note here that, in conformance with Microsoft documentation, a null reference is considered the smallest element:

```
using System; using System.Collections;

public class StringLengthComparer : IComparer {
    public int Compare(object x, object y) {
        if (x == null && y == null) return 0;                         // x == y
        if (x == null) return -1;                                     // x < y
        if (y == null) return 1;                                      // x > y

        if (x.ToString().Length == y.ToString().Length) return 0;// x == y
        if (x.ToString().Length < y.ToString().Length) return -1;    // x < y
        return 1;                                                     // x > y
    }
}
public class TestComparer {
    public static void Main() {
        string[] a = { "Birngruber", "Woess", "Moessenboeck", "Beer" };
        Array.Sort(a, new StringLengthComparer());
        foreach (string s in a) Console.WriteLine("{0}", s);
    }
}
```

The class TestComparer tests the sorting of a character-string array with the newly implemented StringLengthComparer. The following output appears on the console:

```
Beer
Woess
Birngruber
Moessenboeck
```

The static method Array.Reverse(a) reverses the order of the elements in array a. The following example shows how an array can be sorted and then reversed:

```
int[] a = { 1, 0, 4, 3, 2 };
Array.Sort(a);
foreach (int elem in a) Console.Write("{0} ", elem);   // output: 0 1 2 3 4
Array.Reverse(a);
foreach (int elem in a) Console.Write("{0} ", elem);   // output: 4 3 2 1 0
```

A further typical array operation is searching for a given element. Here the class Array offers the useful methods Array.IndexOf(a, o) and Array.BinarySearch(a, o). Both methods return the value of the index of the object o in a or the value -1 if it was not found. The method BinarySearch, in contrast to IndexOf, performs a binary search and requires that the array is sorted. The binary search in a sorted array is significantly faster than a sequential search. The next code sequence shows how a set of string objects can be searched for the position of a certain object:

```
string[] a = { "This", "is", "a", "test"};
int pos = Array.IndexOf(a, "is");
Console.WriteLine("Position of 'is': {0}", pos);   // prints "Position of 'is': 1"
```

4.1.5 ArrayList

Just as Array implements the interface IList, so does the class ArrayList. Thus ArrayList belongs to the family of lists. ArrayList represents lists that have dynamic size, so in contrast to the arrays we have seen so far, can grow and contract. The interface of ArrayList is defined as follows

```
public class ArrayList : IList, ICollection, IEnumerable, ICloneable {
    //----- implements properties and methods of the following interfaces
    // IEnumerable: GetEnumerator
    // ICollection: Count, CopyTo, ...
    // IList: Clear, Add, Insert, Remove, RemoveAt, Contains, IndexOf, indexer, ...
    // ICloneable: Clone
    //----- constructors
    public ArrayList();
    public ArrayList(ICollection c);
    public ArrayList(int capacity);
    //----- properties
    virtual int Capacity { get; set; }   // reserved size of the ArrayList
    //----- methods
    public virtual ArrayList GetRange(int index, int count);   // returns a subset of the
            // elements as a new ArrayList where the elements are not copied
    public virtual void SetRange(int i, ICollection c);   // replaces the elements of the
            // ArrayList starting at index i by the elements of c
    public virtual void AddRange(ICollection c);   // appends c
    public virtual void InsertRange(int i, ICollection c);   // inserts c at index position i
    public virtual void RemoveRange(int index, int count);   // removes subset of elements
```

```
    public virtual void CopyTo(Array a);    // copies the ArrayList into the array a
    public virtual int LastIndexOf(object o); // returns the last index of the element o
                                             // or -1 if the element was not found
    public virtual int BinarySearch(object o); // returns the first index of the element o
                                             // or -1 if the element was not found
    public virtual void Sort();    // sorts the elements of the ArrayList
    public virtual void Reverse();    // reverses the order of the elements in the ArrayList
    public virtual object[] ToArray();    // copies the elements into an object array
    public virtual void TrimToSize();    // sets capacity to current number of elements
    public static ArrayList Repeat(object o, int n);// creates n copies of the element o
                                             // and returns these in a new ArrayList
    public static ArrayList Adapter(IList list);    // creates an ArrayList wrapper for list
}
```

The following example creates an ArrayList, inserts some elements and carries out some operations, such as sorting and reversing:

```
using System; using System.Collections;

...

ArrayList a = new ArrayList();
a.Add(3); a.Add(1); a.Add(2); a.Add(4); a.Add(9);
a.Sort();
foreach (int i in a) Console.Write("{0} ", i);          // output: 1 2 3 4 9
a.Reverse();
for (int i = 0; i < a.Length; i++) Console.Write("{0} ", a[i]);    // output: 9 4 3 2 1
```

The method a.BinarySearch(obj) searches for the element obj in the sorted list a. It can have an object of type IComparer passed as its second parameter. This compares obj with the elements of the array. BinarySearch only works with sorted lists. The following example shows the binary search in an array as well as the conversion of the ArrayList into an array of fixed size:

```
using System; using System.Collections;

...

ArrayList a = new ArrayList();
a.Add("Axel"); a.Add("Diana"); a.Add("Bill"); a.Add("Edward"); a.Add("Carl");
a.Sort();
int i = a.BinarySearch("Edward");
Console.WriteLine("Pos. {0}: {1}", i, a[i]);        // prints "Pos. 4: Edward"
i = a.BinarySearch("bill", new CaseInsensitiveComparer());
Console.WriteLine("Pos. {0}: {1}", i, a[i]);        // prints "Pos. 1: Bill"
object[] arr = a.ToArray();                         // conversion into static array
foreach (string s in arr) Console.Write("{0} ", s); // prints "Axel Diana Bill Edward Carl"
```

4.1.6   BitArray

The class BitArray represents a dynamic list of binary values each of which can be either true or false. Among others, the permitted operations are And, Or, Xor, and Not, as well as an indexer for access to individual binary values. The interface of the class BitArray is defined as follows:

```
public sealed class BitArray : ICollection, IEnumerable, ICloneable {
    //----- implements properties and methods of the following interfaces
    // IEnumerable: GetEnumerator
    // ICollection: Count, CopyTo, ...
    // ICloneable: Clone
    //----- extract of the constructors
    public BitArray(int length);
    public BitArray(bool[] values);
    public BitArray(byte[] bytes);
    //----- properties
    public bool this[int index] { get; set; }   // indexer for access to individual elements
    public int Length { get; set; }   // returns the number of bit positions
    //----- methods
    public bool Get(int index);   // returns the bit value of the given position index
    public void Set(int index, bool val);   // sets the bit value at position index to val
    public void SetAll(bool val);   // sets each position to the given bit value val
    public BitArray And(BitArray val);   // binary and operation
    public BitArray Or(BitArray a);   // binary or operation
    public BitArray Xor(BitArray a);   // binary exclusive-or operation
    public BitArray Not();   // binary not operation
    public void CopyTo(Array a, int i);   // copies the bit array into the array a from position i
}
```

Here is an example of the use of bit arrays:

```
BitArray a = new BitArray(8);   // creates a bit array with 8 elements, all false
BitArray b = new BitArray(new bool[] { true, true, true, true, false, false, false, false });
// or: BitArray b = new BitArray(new byte[] { 0x0F });   // bit string = 00001111
a[1] = a[2] = a[5] = true;      // a == 00100110, b == 00001111
a = a.Not();                    // a == 11011001
a = a.Or(b);                    // a == 11011111
if (b[0]) b = b.Xor(a);         // b == 11010000
foreach (bool x in a) Console.WriteLine(x);
for (int i = 0; i < b.Length; i++) Console.WriteLine(b[i]);
```

4.1.7   Queue

A *queue* is a data structure (also known as a buffer) where objects join at one end and are removed from the other end. Because the first element to enter is the first to leave this is called a FIFO (*first-in, first-out*) strategy. A typical use for a queue is a sequence of reports (for example, print requests) that must be processed in the order in which they joined. The interface of the class Queue is defined as follows:

```
public class Queue : ICollection, IEnumerable, ICloneable {
    //----- implements properties and methods of the following interfaces
    // IEnumerable: GetEnumerator
    // ICollection: Count, CopyTo, ...
    // ICloneable: Clone
    //---- constructors
    public Queue();   // creates an empty queue
    public Queue(ICollection c);   // creates a queue and carries over the elements of c
    //----- methods
    public virtual void Enqueue(object o);   // appends an element to the end of the queue
    public virtual object Dequeue();   // returns the first element from the start of the queue
    public virtual object Peek();   // returns the first element without removing it
    public virtual bool Contains(object o);   // tests whether the queue contains the object
    public virtual void Clear();   // removes all elements from the queue
    public virtual object[] ToArray();   // returns a copy of the queue as an object array
    public virtual void TrimToSize();   // sets capacity to the current number of elements
    public static Queue Synchronized(Queue q);   // returns a synchronized wrapper
}
```

The call q.Enqueue(obj) adds the object obj to the queue q; q.Dequeue() removes and returns the oldest object in q. Here is an example:

```
using System; using System.Collections;
...
Queue q = new Queue();
q.Enqueue("Axel"); q.Enqueue("Bill"); q.Enqueue("Carl"); q.Enqueue("Diana");
while (q.Count > 0) Console.Write(q.Dequeue() + " ");
```

This program produces the following output:

```
Axel Bill Carl Diana
```

The working of a queue is shown graphically in Figure 4.3.

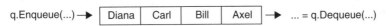

q.Enqueue(...) ➔ | Diana | Carl | Bill | Axel | ➔ ... = q.Dequeue(...)

Figure 4.3 *Working of a queue*

When using a queue as a waiting list it is important that threads accessing the queue do not conflict. For this reason Queue provides a static method Queue.Synchronized(q) that returns a wrapper object that guarantees synchronized access to individual elements.

4.1.8   Stack

A *stack* is a data structure where the objects are added at one end and removed again from the same end. The object added last is the first to be removed again and so this is called a LIFO (*last-in first-out*) strategy. The interface of the class Stack is shown here:

```
public class Stack : ICollection, IEnumerable, ICloneable {
    //----- implements properties and methods of the following interfaces
    // IEnumerable: GetEnumerator
    // ICollection: Count, CopyTo, ...
    // ICloneable: Clone
    //----- constructors
    public Stack();
    public Stack(ICollection c);
    public Stack(int capacity);
    //----- methods
    public virtual void Push(object o);   // puts object o as the first element of the stack
    public virtual object Pop();   // returns the first element of the stack and removes it
    public virtual object Peek();   // returns the first element of the stack without removing it
    public virtual bool Contains(object o);   // tests if object o is contained in the stack
    public virtual void Clear();   // removes all elements from the stack
    public virtual object[] ToArray();   // copies all elements of the stack into an object array
    public static Stack Synchronized(Stack s);   // returns a synchronized wrapper
}
```

s.Push(obj) inserts obj in the stack s; s.Pop() removes and returns the last inserted element. s.Peek() returns the last inserted element, like Pop, but does not remove it from the stack. In the following example a stack is used instead of a queue:

```
using System;
using System.Collections;
...
Stack s = new Stack();
s.Push("Axel"); s.Push("Bill"); s.Push("Carl"); s.Push("Diana");
while (s.Count > 0) Console.Write(s.Pop() + " ");
```

This program produces the following output:

```
Diana Carl Bill Axel
```

The working of a stack is shown graphically in Figure 4.4.

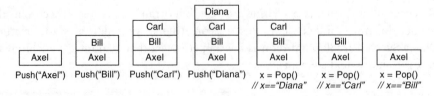

Figure 4.4 *Working of a stack*

4.1.9 IDictionary

Classes that implement the interface IDictionary form a family of lists that work with key–value pairs. Each value is associated with a unique key of type object and which cannot be null. The value is likewise of type object and may even be null. IDictionary does not imply any sorting order. Here is an extract from IDictionary:

```
interface IDictionary : ICollection, IEnumerable {
    // inherits from ICollection: Count, CopyTo, ...
    //----- properties
    ICollection Keys { get; }
    ICollection Values { get; }
    object this[object key] { get; set; }   // indexer for access to individual elements
    bool IsFixedSize { get; }
    bool IsReadOnly { get; }
    //----- methods
    void Add(object key, object value);
    void Remove(object key);
    bool Contains(object key);
    void Clear();   // removes all elements of the IDictionary
    IDictionaryEnumerator GetEnumerator();
}
```

Because IDictionary is derived from IEnumerable one can use an iterator to traverse all the key–value pairs. The returned iterator is of the special type IDictionaryEnumerator which also provides the key and value via properties:

```
public interface IDictionaryEnumerator : IEnumerator {
    // inherits from IEnumerator: Current, MoveNext, Reset
    //----- properties
    public object Key { get; }
    public object Value { get; }
    public DictionaryEntry Entry { get; }
}
```

The interface to this key–value pair is defined by a struct type DictionaryEntry:

```
public struct DictionaryEntry {
    // ----- constructor
    public DictionaryEntry(object key, object value);   // creates a key–value pair
    // ----- properties
    public object Key { get; set; }     // returns the key of a key–value pair
    public object Value { get; set; }   // returns the value of a key–value pair
}
```

IDictionary also defines an indexer which uses the key as an index and returns the corresponding value. The properties Keys and Values return a list of the keys and values of an IDictionary object. The method d.Add(key, value) can be used to insert a key–value pair in the dictionary d and d.Remove(key) removes the key and its corresponding value.

4.1.10 Hashtable

The class Hashtable is a concrete implementation of IDictionary and represents a *hash table*. Hash tables permit a very efficient searching and insertion of objects. The interface of Hashtable looks like this:

```
public class Hashtable : IDictionary, ICollection, IEnumerable, ISerializable, ICloneable,
                         IDeserializableCallback {
    //----- implements properties and methods of the following interfaces
    // ICollection: Count, CopyTo, ...
    // IDictionary: Clear, Add, Remove, Contains, GetEnumerator, Indexer, ...
    // ICloneable: Clone
    //----- constructors
    public Hashtable();   // creates a hash table of standard size
    public Hashtable(int capacity);   // creates a hash table of the given size
    public Hashtable(int capacity, float loadfactor);
    public Hashtable(IDictionary d);   // creates new hash table, fills it with elements from d
    ...
    //----- methods
    public virtual bool ContainsKey(object key);
    public virtual bool ContainsValue(object val);
    public static Hashtable Synchronized(Hashtable h);   // returns a synchronized wrapper
    ...
}
```

The key inserted into a hash table must override the methods GetHashCode and Equals from Object. k.GetHashCode() should convert k to an int value with the best possible spread. This is then used by the hash table to determine the storage location for the key–value pair.

In the constructor of Hashtable a *load factor* between 0.1 and 1.0 can be given to specify the maximum percentage of usage of the table. The smaller the load factor the more efficient the searching and insertion of elements, but the greater the storage requirement. If the maximum load factor is exceeded by inserting elements then the table is automatically increased in size.

In the following example persons are inserted into a hash table and the social security number is used as key:

```
public class Person {
    string lastName;
    string firstName;
    public Person(string firstName, string lastName) {
        this.firstName = firstName; this.lastName = lastName;
    }
    public override string ToString() {
        return firstName + " " + lastName;
    }
    ...
}
```

```
public class HashtableExample {
    public static void Main() {
        Hashtable tab = new Hashtable();
        tab.Add(3181030750, new Person("Mike", "Miller"));
        tab.Add(1245010770, new Person("Susanne", "Parker"));
        tab.Add(2345020588, new Person("Roland", "Howard"));
        tab.Add(1245300881, new Person("Douglas", "Adams"));
        foreach (DictionaryEntry e in tab)
            Console.WriteLine(e.Value + ": " + e.Key);
        if (tab.Contains(1245010770))
            Console.WriteLine("Person with SSN 1245010770: " + tab[1245010770]);
    }
}
```

The output of this program is as follows:

```
Mike Miller: 3181030750
Susanne Parker: 1245010770
Roland Howard: 2345020588
Douglas Adams: 1245300881
Person with SSN 1245010770: Susanne Parker
```

4.1.11 SortedList

The class SortedList, like Hashtable, implements the interface IDictionary. It too represents a list of key–value pairs. However, in contrast to Hashtable, these are sorted on their key. SortedList is a mixture of an array and a hash table, because elements can be identified by their key as well as by their index. The interface of the class SortedList is as follows:

```
public class SortedList : IDictionary, ICollection, IEnumerable, ICloneable {
    //----- implements properties and methods of the following  interfaces
    // ICollection: Count, CopyTo, ...
    // IDictionary: Clear, Add, Remove, Contains, GetEnumerator, Indexer, ...
    // ICloneable: Clone
    //----- constructors
    public SortedList();
    public SortedList(IComparer c);
    public SortedList(IDictionary d);
    public SortedList(IDictionary d, IComparer c);
    ...
    //----- properties
    public virtual int Capacity { get; set; }   // reserved size of the SortedList
    //----- methods
    public virtual void RemoveAt(int i);   // removed the key–value pair with index i
    public virtual bool ContainsKey(object key);
    public virtual bool ContainsValue(object val);
    public virtual int IndexOfKey(object key);   // returns the index for a key
    public virtual int IndexOfValue(object value);   // returns the index for an element
```

```
public virtual object GetByIndex(int i);    // returns the element with the index i
public virtual void SetByIndex(int i, object val);    // replaces value with index i by val
public virtual object GetKey(int i);    // returns the key with the index i
public virtual IList GetKeyList();    // returns a list of all keys of the hash table
public virtual IList GetValueList();    // returns a list of the values of the hash table
public virtual void TrimToSize();    // sets Capacity to the current number of elements
public static SortedList Synchronized(SortedList list);    // returns synchronized wrapper
}
```

As already mentioned in connection with the sort methods of Array and ArrayList, the sorting can be influenced by an IComparer object that is passed to the constructor of a SortedList.

If a key–value pair is inserted into a sorted list, it must be different from any element already there.

Operations on sorted lists are slower than operations on hash tables. Therefore sorted lists are mainly used when it is necessary to work with the elements in a sorted order and to access them by an index.

4.2   Input / Output

The namespaces System.IO and System.IO.IsolatedStorage contain types for the input and output of data with various media. The entire input and output works with data streams that permit the byte-oriented reading and writing of data. The base class of all data streams is the abstract class Stream. It hides system-dependent details. There are subclasses of Stream: for example for files (System.IO.FileStream), network streams (System.Net.Sockets.NetworkStream) and ciphered streams (System.Security.Cryptography.CryptoStream).

4.2.1   Streams

All classes that represent a data stream are derived from System.IO.Stream. The class Stream is abstract and specifies only one input or output stream. Instead it defines the underlying operations that are applicable to all data streams, namely:

❑ reading of data from a data stream;
❑ writing of data to a data stream;
❑ searching for or changing a position within a data stream.

Programs that work with Stream can also work with any subclass of it. Substituting the concrete Stream implementation automatically allows the same algorithm to function for different input and output media. The interface of the abstract class Stream is defined as follows:

```
public abstract class Stream : MarshalByRefObject, IDisposable {
    //----- properties
    public abstract long Length { get; }   // returns the length of the data stream
    public abstract long Position { get; set; }   // gets or sets current position in the stream
    public abstract bool CanRead { get; }   // can the stream be read?
    public abstract bool CanSeek { get; }   // does the stream support searching?
    public abstract bool CanWrite { get; }   // can the data stream be written to?
    //----- methods
    public abstract int Read(out byte[] buff, int offset, int count);   // reads a byte array
    public abstract void Write(byte[] buff, int offset, int count);   // writes a byte array
    public virtual int ReadByte();   // reads one byte from the data stream, or -1 at the end
    public virtual void WriteByte(byte value);   // writes one byte
    public abstract long Seek(long offset, SeekOrigin origin);   // sets the read/write position
    public abstract void SetLength(long value);   // sets the desired length of the stream
    public abstract void Flush();   // clears the stream's buffer
    public virtual void Close();   // closes the stream and releases all resources
    ...
}
```

The properties CanRead, CanWrite and CanSeek determine whether the respective operation is permitted for the stream. A NetworkStream, for example, does not support searching for a position within a data stream because the data is constantly delivered by the communication partner and returning to a previous position is not possible. Figure 4.5 shows different data streams that are specialized for different media and different application purposes.

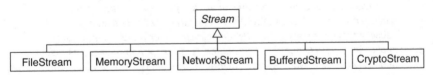

Figure 4.5 *Inheritance hierarchy of the abstract class Stream*

FileStream works with files. MemoryStreams works with data streams that are used for temporary storage of files in main memory. NetworkStreams are used in network communication to exchange data between communication partners. CryptoStream works with ciphered data streams. BufferedStream uses a data buffer to increase the efficiency of the read and write operations. Here it is necessary to note that at the end of the output the buffer must be emptied by using Flush(). Close() first calls Flush() before it closes the data stream and releases all resources.

The classes TextReader and TextWriter play a role in input and output, alongside Stream (see Figure 4.6). They are responsible for the formatting of data (e.g. *Unicode, XML, ASCII*), whereas a stream is used to perform the reading and writing on the appropriate medium. This model is very flexible, because both the medium and the formatting can vary. While subclasses such as StreamReader and StreamWriter work with streams, other classes, such as StringReader and

StringWriter, use character strings. The classes BinaryReader and BinaryWriter are not derived from TextReader and TextWriter, but similarly use a Stream object as their data source. BinaryReader and BinaryWriter can be used to read and write primitive data types such as int, char, bool or string in binary format.

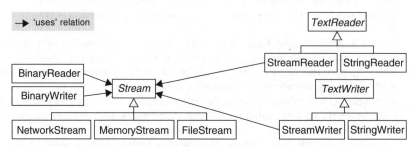

Figure 4.6 *Streams with different reader and writer classes*

Here are the interfaces of the abstract base classes TextReader and TextWriter:

```
public abstract class TextReader : MarshalByRefObject, IDisposable {
    public virtual int Read();   // reads the next character and removes it from the stream
    public virtual int Read(out char[] buf, int idx, int count);   // reads up to count characters
        // into the buffer buf from position idx and returns the number of characters read
    public virtual int ReadBlock(out char[] buf, int index, int count);   // blocking variant
    public virtual string ReadLine();   // reads a line from the data stream as a string.
        // The line ends with '\r' (carriage return), or '\n' (line feed) or '\r' followed by '\n'.
        // The returned string does not contain any of these characters.
    public virtual string ReadToEnd();   // reads to end of data stream
    public virtual int Peek();   // reads the next character without removing it
    public virtual void Close();   // closes the TextReader and releases its resources
    public static TextReader Synchronized(TextReader r);   // returns synchron. wrapper
}

public abstract class TextWriter : MarshalByRefObject, IDisposable {
    public virtual void Write(bool val);   // writes a boolean value
    public virtual void Write(string s);   // writes a string
    public virtual void Write(int val);   // writes an integer value
    ...   // + overloaded methods for writing all primitive data types
    public virtual void WriteLine();   // causes line break
    public virtual void WriteLine(bool val);   // write val followed by line break
    ...   // + overloaded methods for writing all primitive data types with line break
    public virtual void Flush();   // empties the TextWriter's buffer
    public virtual void Close();   // closes the TextWriter and releases all its resources
    public virtual string NewLine { get; set; }   // returns the characters that
                                    // mark the end of line (standard "\r\n")
    public abstract Encoding Encoding { get; }   // returns the encoding object (see later)
    public static TextWriter Synchronized(TextWriter w);   // returns synchronized wrapper
}
```

FileStream

FileStreams allow reading and writing of a file. The interface of the class FileStream is defined as follows:

```
public class FileStream : Stream {
    //----- constructors
    public FileStream(string path, FileMode m);    // creates a FileStream on the file path
    public FileStream(string path, FileMode mode, FileAccess access);
    public FileStream(string path, FileMode mode, FileAccess access, FileShare share);
    ...
    //----- properties
    public string Name { get; }    // returns the name of the file stream
    //----- methods
    public virtual void Lock(long pos, long len);      // locks access to a part of a file
    public virtual void Unlock(long pos, long len);   // removes a lock
    ...
}
```

The Read and Write methods are inherited from Stream and are appropriately overridden. As already mentioned, special reader and writer classes (StreamReader and StreamWriter) are used to work with formatted data. StreamWriter is a subclass of TextWriter and StreamReader is a subclass of TextReader.

```
public class StreamWriter : TextWriter {
    public StreamWriter(Stream s);
    public StreamWriter(Stream s, Encoding e);
    ...  // remainder same as TextWriter
}
public class StreamReader : TextReader {
    public StreamReader(Stream s);
    public StreamReader(Stream s, Encoding e);
    ...  // remainder same as TextReader
}
```

The StreamWriter can have the coding style passed as a parameter. In the following example the coding Encoding.Unicode is chosen. ASCIIEncoding, UTF7Encoding and UTF8Encoding are also available.

To set the read or write position to the end of the file the method FileStream.Seek(0, SeekOrigin.End) must be called. The method takes an offset as its first parameter. This refers to a second parameter (here the end position of the file). When the write process is finished, the method Close should be called to implicitly write any buffered data to the file by using Flush and to release the resources of the data stream.

```
using System;
using System.IO;
using System.Text;   // for encoding definitions
public class StreamWriterExample {
    public static void Main() {
        FileStream fs;
        fs = new FileStream("log.txt", FileMode.OpenOrCreate, FileAccess.Write);
        // Connects a StreamWriter object to the FileStream fs.
        // For the matter of simplicity, this example does not catch any exceptions.
        StreamWriter sw = new StreamWriter(fs, Encoding.Unicode);
        sw.BaseStream.Seek(0, SeekOrigin.End);
        sw.WriteLine("log entry 1");
        sw.WriteLine("log entry 2");
        sw.Close();
        fs.Close();
    }
}
```

Three access attributes can be specified in FileStream's constructor. They are defined by the enumerations FileMode, FileAccess and FileShare:

```
public enum FileAccess {
    Read,            // file can be read
    ReadWrite,       // file can be read and written
    Write            // file can be written
}
```

```
public enum FileMode {
    Append,          // opens existing file or creates a new one and appends data to its end
    Create,          // creates new file or overwrites an existing one
    CreateNew,       // creates new file; if it already exists, throws IOException
    Open,            // opens existing file; if it does not exist, throws FileNotFoundException
    OpenOrCreate,    // opens an existing file or creates a new one
    Truncate         // opens an existing file and deletes its content
}
```

```
public enum FileShare {
    Inheritable,     // makes the file handle inheritable by child processes
    None,            // declines subsequent opening of the file
    Read,            // allows subsequent opening of the file for reading
    ReadWrite,       // allows subsequent opening of the file for reading and writing
    Write            // allows subsequent opening of the file for writing
}
```

4.2.2 Files and Directories

In addition to data streams, System.IO offers extensive support for working with files and directories.

Directories

System.IO.Directory has a range of static methods for working with directories.

```
public sealed class Directory {
    public static DirectoryInfo CreateDirectory(string path);    // creates all directories
        // and subdirectories as specified by path
    public static void Move(string src, string dest);    // moves directory src to dest
    public static void Delete(string path);    // deletes an empty directory
    public static void Delete(string path, bool recursive);    // deletes directory with contents
    public static bool Exists(string path);    // checks if directory exists
    public static string[] GetFiles(string path);    // returns all file names in path
    public static string[] GetFiles(string path, string searchPattern);
    public static string[] GetDirectories(string path);    // returns all directory names in path
    public static string[] GetDirectories(string path, string searchPattern);
    public static DirectoryInfo GetParent(string path);    // returns the parent directory
    public static string GetCurrentDirectory();    // returns current working directory
    public static void SetCurrentDirectory(string path);    // sets current working directory
    public static string[] GetLogicalDrives();    // returns names of logical drives (e.g. "c:\")
    public static DateTime GetCreationTime(string path);    // returns creation date & time
    public static DateTime GetLastAccessTime(string path);
    public static DateTime GetLastWriteTime(string path);
    public static void SetCreationTime(string path, DateTime t);    // sets creation date & time
    public static void SetLastAccessTime(string path, DateTime t);
    public static void SetLastWriteTime(string path, DateTime t);
}
```

In order to create a new directory or to open an existing directory, the method Directory.CreateDirectory should be called. It returns an object of type DirectoryInfo. This object can be used to make enquiries about the directory. Paths for directories or files can either be specified as relative, or by using the *UNC* path (*Universal Naming Convention*) [UNC]. Note that the path name is restricted to 248 characters. The following calls of CreateDirectory are valid:

```
Directory.CreateDirectory("\\tmp\\log.txt");
Directory.CreateDirectory("c:\\tmp");
Directory.CreateDirectory("\\\\140.78.195.112\\tmp");
```

In the case where the directory does not already exist and must be newly created, every user gets full access rights to it. Access rights can be set by using the namespace System.Security.Permissions. In an access to a directory with the static methods of the class Directory each call leads to a security test being carried out. This has an adverse effect on performance. If the accesses to the same directory are frequent, one should therefore use the equivalent methods from the class DirectoryInfo. These do not make the security checks on each call and are thus more efficient. The interface of DirectoryInfo is defined as follows:

```
public sealed class DirectoryInfo : FileSystemInfo {
    //----- constructor
    public DirectoryInfo(string path);   // path specifies the directory
    //----- properties
    public override string Name { get; }   // returns the directory name without the path
    public override bool Exists { get; }    // indicates if this directory exists
    public DirectoryInfo Parent { get; }   // returns the parent directory
    public DirectoryInfo Root { get; }   // returns the root directory
    //----- methods
    public void Create();   // create a new directory, if it does not exist
    public DirectoryInfo CreateSubdirectory(string path);   // creates a subdirectory
    public void MoveTo(string destDir);   // moves this directory to destDir
    public void Delete();   // deletes this directory, if it is empty
    public void Delete(bool recursive);   // deletes this directory and its contents
    public FileInfo[] GetFiles();   // returns all files in this directory
    public FileInfo[] GetFiles(string pattern);   // returns matching files in this directory
    public DirectoryInfo[] GetDirectories();   // returns all directories in this directory
    public DirectoryInfo[] GetDirectories(string pattern);   // returns all matching directories
            // (e.g.: '*s' returns all subdirectories ending with 's')
    public FileSystemInfo[] GetFileSystemInfos();   // returns all files and directories
    public FileSystemInfo[] GetFileSystemInfos(string pattern);
    public override ToString();   // returns the path given in the constructor
}
```

Files

The class System.IO.File, as with the class Directory, offers a range of static methods for carrying out the typical file operations (creation, deletion, renaming).

```
public sealed class File {
    public static FileStream Open(string path, FileMode mode);
    public static FileStream Open(string path, FileMode m, FileAccess a);
    public static FileStream Open(string p, FileMode m, FileAccess a, FileShare s);
    public static FileStream OpenRead(string path);
    public static FileStream OpenWrite(string path);
    public static StreamReader OpenText(string path);   // returns Reader for reading text
    public static StreamWriter AppendText(string path);   // returns Writer for appending text
    public static FileStream Create(string path);   // create a new file
    public static FileStream Create(string path, int bufferSize);
    public static StreamWriter CreateText(string path);
    public static void Move(string src, string dest);
    public static void Copy(string src, string dest);   // copies file src to dest
    public static void Copy(string src, string dest, bool overwrite);
    public static void Delete(string path);
    public static bool Exists(string path);
    public static FileAttributes GetAttributes(string path);
    public static DateTime GetCreationTime(string path);
    public static DateTime GetLastAccessTime(string path);
    public static DateTime GetLastWriteTime(string path);
```

```
        public static void SetAttributes(string path, FileAttributes fileAttributes);
        public static void SetCreationTime(string path, DateTime creationTime);
        public static void SetLastAccessTime(string path, DateTime lastAccessTime);
        public static void SetLastWriteTime(string path, DateTime lastWriteTime);
    }
```

As with the class Directory, the class File carries out security checks before each operation. Here too the corresponding methods of the class FileInfo are more efficient in that they only carry out the checks when the file is created.

```
    public sealed class FileInfo : FileSystemInfo {
        //----- constructors
        public FileInfo(string fileName);    // creates a new FileInfo object for a file fileName
        //----- properties
        public override string Name { get; }    // name of this file
        public long Length { get; }    // size of this file
        public override bool Exists { get; }    // indicates if this file exists
        public DirectoryInfo Directory { get; }    // directory containing this file
        public string DirectoryName { get; }    // name of the directory containing this file
        //----- methods
        public FileStream Open(FileMode m);    // open a FileStream to this file
        public FileStream Open(FileMode m, FileAccess a);
        public FileStream Open(FileMode m, FileAccess a, FileShare s);
        public FileStream OpenRead();    // opens a read-only FileStream to this file
        public FileStream OpenWrite();    // open a write-only FileStream to this file
        public StreamReader OpenText();    // returns a UTF8 reader for reading text
        public StreamWriter AppendText();    // returns a StreamWriter for appending text
        public FileStream Create();    // returns FileStream to this newly created file
        public StreamWriter CreateText();    // returns Writer to this newly created text file
        public void MoveTo(string dest);    // move this file to dest
        public FileInfo CopyTo(string dest);    // copies this file to dest
        public FileInfo CopyTo(string dest, bool overwrite);    // copies to and overwrites dest
        public override Delete();    // deletes this file
        public override string ToString();    // returns entire path of this file
    }
```

In the following example, all the subdirectories of the logical drive "c:\\" and then all its files are output to the console.

```
    using System; using System.IO;

    public class DirectoryExample {
        public static void Main() {
            DirectoryInfo dir = Directory.CreateDirectory("c:\\");
            Console.WriteLine("---------- Directories ----------");
            DirectoryInfo[] dirs = dir.GetDirectories();
            foreach (DirectoryInfo d in dirs) Console.WriteLine(d.Name);
            Console.WriteLine ("---------- Files ----------");
            FileInfo[] files = info.GetFiles();
            foreach (FileInfo f in files) Console.WriteLine(f.Name);
        }
    }
```

This example of course gives differing output according to the content of the directory "c:\\". The output might look like this:

```
---------- Directories ----------
Documents and Settings
I386
Program Files
System Volume Information
WINNT
---------- Files ----------
AUTOEXEC.BAT
boot.ini
CONFIG.SYS
IO.SYS
MSDOS.SYS
NTDETECT.COM
ntldr
pagefile.sys
```

Monitoring the File System

The .NET class System.IO.FileSystemWatcher offers a useful facility for monitoring of the file system that can be used to check whether any changes are made to a specified directory. This monitoring can be applied to a local disk and also to a networked drive, as long as the operating system is at least Windows NT 4.0. Monitoring of DVD or CD drives is not possible, because their file attributes cannot be changed. An excerpt from the class FileSystemWatcher is given here:

```csharp
public class FileSystemWatcher : Component, ISupportInitialize {
    //----- constructors
    public FileSystemWatcher(string path);   // creates a monitoring object
    public FileSystemWatcher(string path, string filter);   // uses a filter (e.g. "*.log")
    //----- properties
    public string Path { get; set; }   // returns or sets the monitored path
    public string Filter { get; set; }   // returns or sets the monitor filter
    public bool EnableRaisingEvents { get; set; }   // activates monitoring
    public bool IncludeSubdirectories { get; set; }   // includes subdirectories
    //----- methods
    public WaitForChangedResult WaitForChanged(WatcherChangeTypes types);
            // blocks until a monitored event occurs and then returns information about it
    ...
    //----- events
    public event FileSystemEventHandler Changed;   // reports all changes
    public event FileSystemEventHandler Created;   // reports creation of file or directory
    public event FileSystemEventHandler Deleted;   // reports deletion of file or directory
    public event RenamedEventHandler Renamed;   // reports renaming of file or directory
}
```

A path and possible file filter are passed to the constructor of the class FileSystemWatcher. The path specifies the directory or logical drive where the monitoring is to take place and the filter specifies the sort of files to monitor:

```
FileSystemWatcher fsw = new FileSystemWatcher("c:\\", "*.log");
```

Here all the files with the extensions ".log" of the logical drive "c:\\" are to be monitored. The following example shows a simple program that monitors all changes to files on the logical drive "c:\\" and creates an output on the console. The class FileSystemWatcher supports a variety of results that report information about changes in file system to registered observers:

```
using System; using System.IO;

public class WatcherEventExample {
    public static void Changed(object sender, FileSystemEventArgs args) {
        Console.WriteLine("Changed -> {0}", args.Name);
    }
    public static void Created(object sender, FileSystemEventArgs args) {
        Console.WriteLine("Created -> {0}", args.Name);
    }
    public static void Deleted(object sender, FileSystemEventArgs args) {
        Console.WriteLine("Deleted -> {0}", args.Name);
    }
    public static void Renamed(object sender, RenamedEventArgs args) {
        Console.WriteLine("Renamed -> {0}", args.Name);
    }
    public static void Main() {
        FileSystemWatcher fsw = new FileSystemWatcher("c:\\");
        //----- register all event handlers:
        fsw.Changed += new FileSystemEventHandler(Changed);
        fsw.Created += new FileSystemEventHandler(Created);
        fsw.Deleted += new FileSystemEventHandler(Deleted);
        fsw.Renamed += new RenamedEventHandler(Renamed);
        fsw.IncludeSubdirectories = true;
        fsw.EnableRaisingEvents = true;
        fsw.Filter = "*.*";
        while ( ... ) fsw.WaitForChanged(WatcherChangeTypes.All);
    }
}
```

4.2.3 Isolated Storage

The namespace System.IO.IsolatedStorage provides facilities for putting data into an isolated storage area that can only be accessed by certain persons or modules. Isolated storage areas are protected against unauthorized changes or destruction. The various access groups are defined in the enumeration IsolatedStorageScope:

```
public enum IsolatedStorageScope {
    Assembly,   // access for all modules of this assembly
    Domain,     // access for all programs in this application domain
    None,       // unrestricted access for all (no isolation)
    Roaming,    // the isolated storage area roams with the user account
    User        // access for this user
}
```

The two classes IsolatedStorageFile and IsolatedStorageFileStream (derived from IsolatedStorage and FileStream) can be used to set up an isolated storage area, as the following example demonstrates:

```
using System; using System.IO; using System.IO.IsolatedStorage;

public class IsolatedStorageExample {
    public static void Main() {
        // create an isolated file
        IsolatedStorageFile iso = IsolatedStorageFile.GetStore
            (IsolatedStorageScope.User | IsolatedStorageScope.Assembly, null, null);
        // create a data stream that writes to the isolated file
        IsolatedStorageFileStream ifs = new IsolatedStorageFileStream
            ("test", FileMode.OpenOrCreate, iso);
        // redirect output to StreamWrite to be able to write strings more conveniently
        StreamWriter sw = new StreamWriter(ifs);
        // store a test string in the isolated storage area
        sw.Write("This is a test.");
        // close all output streams (with implicit Flush of data buffer)
        sw.Close(); ifs.Close(); iso.Close();
    }
}
```

The *Isolated Storage Tool* can be used to print a list of all isolated storage areas. The command for this tool looks like this

```
StoreAdm /List
```

and leads to the following output

```
Microsoft (R) .NET Framework Store Admin 1.1.4322.573
Copyright (C) Microsoft Corporation 1998-2002. All rights reserved.

Record #1
[Assembly]
<System.Security.Policy.Url version="1">
    <Url>file://C:/tmp/Examples/IsolatedStorageExample.exe</Url>
</System.Security.Policy.Url>
    Size : 1024
```

The isolated file "test" is stored in the user's local profile in the directory "...\LocalSettings\AppplicationData\IsolatedStorage\". The XML element <Url> determines what program asked for the isolated storage area to be set up. In this case it is the program *IsolatedStorageExample*.

4.3 Threading

The namespace System.Threading contains classes and interfaces that are useful for working with lightweight processes (*threads*). It supports the sequencing of threads as well as their synchronization. The following section describes how to work with threads by showing an example in C#. Further details are contained in the online documentation.

4.3.1 Creating Threads

The class System.Threading.Thread makes lightweight processes available and has this interface (somewhat simplified):

```
public sealed class Thread {
    //----- constructor
    public Thread(ThreadStart start);
    //----- properties
    public string Name { get; set; }   // determines a name for this thread
    public ThreadPriority Priority { get; set; }   // determines the priority of this thread
    public ThreadState ThreadState { get; }   // returns the current state of this thread
    public bool IsAlive { get; }   // checks if this thread is currently active
    public bool IsBackground { get; set; }   // determines if this is a background thread
    public static Thread CurrentThread { get; }   // returns the currently running thread
    ...
    //----- methods
    public void Start();   // sets this thread to ThreadState.Running
    public static void Sleep(int time);   // blocks the current thread for time milliseconds
    public void Suspend();   // suspends this thread
    public void Resume();   // resumes processing of the suspended thread
    public void Join();   // blocks this thread until another thread terminates
    public void Interrupt();   // interrupts this thread while it is in WaitSleepJoin state
    public void Abort();   // raises ThreadAbortException to begin termination of this thread
    public static void ResetAbort();   // cancel Abort request for the current thread
}
```

At the outset every program consists of just one thread which executes the Main method. However, it can create additional threads and launch them. The currently running thread can be discovered by a call of Thread.CurrentThread. To set up a thread we create an object of the class Thread and give it a ThreadStart delegate that represents a parameterless method that will be processed by the new thread:

```
public delegate void ThreadStart();
```

The execution of this method begins as soon as the thread's Start method is called. Multiple calls of Start give rise to a ThreadStateException. We can call the static method Thread.Sleep(d) to halt the thread for a specified time d (in milliseconds). When the time interval has elapsed the thread continues its work. The following example creates two threads t0 and t1 that print a series of characters to the console:

```
using System; using System.Threading;
public class ThreadExample {
    public static void RunT0() {
        for (int i = 0; i < 10; i++) {
            Console.Write("x");
            Thread.Sleep(100);
        }
    }
    public static void RunT1() {
        for (int i = 0; i < 10; i++) {
            Console.Write("o");
            Thread.Sleep(100);
        }
    }
    public static void Main() {
        Thread t0 = new Thread(new ThreadStart(RunT0));
        t0.Start();
        Thread t1 = new Thread(new ThreadStart(RunT1));
        t1.Start();
    }
}
```

This example uses two methods RunT0 and RunT1 to output the corresponding characters to the console. The methods are passed as ThreadStart delegates in the creation of the threads. Then the two threads are started by t0.Start() and t1.Start() at which point the delegate methods continue to work in a quasi-parallel manner. This example could produce outputs such as the following (depending on which thread gets processor time first):

```
xoxoxoxoxoxoxoxoxoxo    xoxoxoxoxoxooxoxoxox    xoxoxoxooxoxoxoxxoxo   ...
```

4.3.2   Thread State

From the time of creation any thread is in a certain state, which can be determined by the property Thread.ThreadState. These various states are declared in the enumeration ThreadState. Figure 4.7 shows a graphical illustration of these states.

```
public enum ThreadState {
    Aborted, AbortRequested, Background, Running, Stopped,
    StopRequested, Suspended, SuspendRequested, Unstarted, WaitSleepJoin
}
```

After creation, a thread t is initially in the state Unstarted. The call of t.Start() starts it and changes its state to Running. The method Start is called asynchronously. Thus it is possible that it has already returned to the caller before the thread has started running. From Running, the thread can be moved into a waiting state (WaitSleepJoin), an interrupted state (Suspended) or a termination state (Stopped).

Thread.Sleep(0) has the effect that the thread passes control to another thread, but remains ready to be run. Thread.Sleep(Timeout.Infinite) leaves the thread in the wait state until it is interrupted by t.Interrupt(). The method Interrupt can cancel the blocked state of a thread. A blocked state can come about because of waiting for a resource or because of an infinite wait time (Timeout.Infinite) in the method Sleep.

In contrast to the call Thread.Sleep(d) which puts the current thread into the state WaitSleepJoin immediately, the call Suspend() puts it into a state SuspendRequested and continues running until it arrives at a safe point at which it can be interrupted safely. Only then does it go into the state Suspended. Figure 4.7 shows typical state changes of a thread.

The ThreadState property can often consist of several states at the same time. For example, several states can come about if a thread is in the WaitSleepJoin state and it contains a suspend statement. Then it is in the state WaitSleepJoin + SuspendRequested. If the thread then leaves the WaitSleepJoin state the suspend statement is carried out and it goes into the Suspended state.

A thread arrives in the end state if its method reaches its end or in response to an Abort request (AbortRequested). Once in the Stopped state a thread can no longer be restarted. If one tries to do that it results in a ThreadStateException.

The call t.Abort() causes the CLR (*Common Language Runtime*) to throw a ThreadAbortException in order to stop the thread. Before that, however, all open finally blocks must be carried out. The interruption process of a thread can be reversed by means of Thread.ResetAbort(). The following example shows how a thread can be interrupted with the method Abort:

```
using System; using System.Threading;

public class ThreadAbort {

    public static void Go() {
        try { while (...) Console.Write("X"); }
        catch (ThreadAbortException e) { Console.WriteLine(e.Message); }
    }
    public static void Main() {
        Thread t = new Thread(new ThreadStart(Go));
        t.Start();
        Thread.Sleep(5000);    // Main thread is blocked for 5000ms, while thread t continues
        t.Abort();
        t.Join();
        Console.WriteLine("ready");
    }
}
```

The asynchronous call of t.Abort() can result in problems, because it does not guarantee that the thread will be interrupted immediately. It is possible that the interruption is delayed by a computation-intensive task in a finally block. To wait for a thread t to be interrupted one should call t.Join(), as shown in the above example.

It is more elegant to terminate a thread by letting it reach the end of its work. In the following example this is achieved by setting running to false.

```
public class ThreadAbortAlternative {
    static bool running = true;

    public static void Go() {
        while (running) Console.Write ("X");
    }

    public static void StopThread() {
        running = false;
    }

    public static void Main() {
        Thread t = new Thread(new ThreadStart(Go));
        t.Start();
        StopThread();
    }
}
```

Figure 4.7 shows the various states and state transitions of a thread.

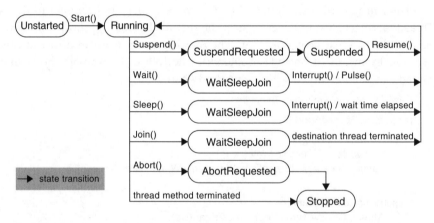

Figure 4.7 *Thread state diagram*

4.3.3 Background Threads

There are two sorts of threads, known as foreground threads and background threads. So far we have only considered foreground threads. As long as at least one foreground thread is running, the entire program will not be interrupted. Background threads, on the other hand, are interrupted if no foreground thread is still running. To mark a thread t as being a background thread we must set the property t.IsBackground to true.

4.3.4 Grouping of Threads into a Thread Pool

In many applications a thread can spend most of its time in a waiting state. That is the case, for example, if a network socket is waiting for a client connection (see Section 4.4). Such a process should run in the background and possibly not require threads of its own because the thread spends most of its time in the state WaitSleepJoin.

The class ThreadPool can bring together tasks that can then be processed by a set of threads (called *worker threads*). The programmer can leave their optimization and management to the system. Once a task is registered with a thread pool the worker threads take care that this task is carried out in a timely manner. When the task comes to an end, the worker thread becomes available for other tasks. In this way it is possible for a worker thread to handle many different tasks.

After the registration of a task with a thread pool, this task can no longer be directly accessed, because its management has been delegated to the system. The interface of the class ThreadPool is defined as follows:

```
public sealed class ThreadPool {
    public static void GetAvailableThreads(out int workers, out int asyncIOs);
        // returns number of currently available worker and asynchronous I/O threads
    public static void GetMaxThreads(out int workers, out int asyncIOs);
        // returns number of worker and async. I/O threads that can be active concurrently
    public static bool QueueUserWorkItem(WaitCallback task);   // registers a task
    public static bool QueueUserWorkItem(WaitCallback task, object state);   // with state
    ...
}
```

In order to register a task called task in the form of a WaitCallback delegate with a thread pool, the method ThreadPool.QueueUserWorkItem must be called. The thread pool is created as soon as the first WaitCallback delegate is registered.

```
public delegate void WaitCallback(object state);
```

There is always only *a single* thread pool per application domain. The following example shows how different sorts of tasks can be registered with a thread pool. Two sorts of task are registered: WorkerProcess is suitable for long-running tasks and TinyWorkerProcess for short tasks that are finished within 5000 ms. In addition, the Main method continuously monitors the number of worker threads currently available and displays this on the console:

```
using System; using System.Threading;

public class ThreadPooling {
    public static void WorkerProcess(object state) {
        for (;;) {   // infinite task
            Thread.Sleep(2000);
            Console.WriteLine("WorkerProcess: {0}", state);
        }
    }
}
```

```
public static void TinyWorkerProcess(object state) {
    Thread.Sleep(5000);   // short task
    Console.WriteLine("TinyWorkerProcess: {0}", state);
}

public static void Main(string[] argv) {
    int workers;        // worker threads
    int asyncIOs;       // asynchronous I/O threads

    // How many worker and async. I/O threads are at most available for the various tasks?
    ThreadPool.GetMaxThreads(out workers,out asyncIOs);
    Console.WriteLine("max. worker threads: {0}", workers);
    Console.WriteLine("max. asynchronous I/O threads: {0}", asyncIOs);

    // register three tasks that run forever
    for(int i = 0; i < 3; i++)
        ThreadPool.QueueUserWorkItem(new WaitCallback(WorkerProcess), i);

    // add three further tasks that take at most 5000 ms before they terminate
    for(int i = 0; i < 3; i++)
        ThreadPool.QueueUserWorkItem(new WaitCallback(TinyWorkerProcess), i);

    // permanently monitor the number of available worker threads
    for (;;) {
        Thread.Sleep(5000);
        ThreadPool.GetAvailableThreads(out workers, out asyncIOs);
        Console.WriteLine("currently available worker threads: {0}", workers);
    }
}
}
```

The example produces the following output on the console:

```
max. worker threads: 25
max. asynchronous I/O threads: 1000
WorkerProcess: 0
WorkerProcess: 1
WorkerProcess: 2
WorkerProcess: 0
WorkerProcess: 1
currently available worker threads: 19
WorkerProcess: 2
WorkerProcess: 0
TinyWorkerProcess: 0
WorkerProcess: 1
TinyWorkerProcess: 1
WorkerProcess: 2
TinyWorkerProcess: 2
WorkerProcess: 0
WorkerProcess: 1
WorkerProcess: 2
currently available worker threads: 22
. . .
```

Note that in this example, the thread pool has 25 free worker threads available at the start. After the input of the six tasks six worker threads are therefore reserved. Thus the thread pool has 19 remaining free worker threads available. After the processing time of about 5000 ms all the TinyWorkerProcesses are finished and their worker processes are released again. Then the thread pool again has 22 worker threads available.

The following guidelines should simplify the decision about the application of a thread pool:

- ❑ No priorities can be given to the individual tasks in the thread pool!
- ❑ If a task requires a great deal of processor time, then a thread pool is not suitable.
- ❑ If we wish to have current access to a task, for example so as to be able to stop it, then a thread pool is again not suitable.

4.3.5 Synchronization

Threads that share resources (for example, shared data fields) must access these in a synchronized manner, that is one after another, and not at the same time. If threads are not correctly synchronized, unforeseeable results can arise. The following sections will show the various possibilities for synchronization of threads in C#.

The lock Statement

In the example ThreadExample at the beginning of this chapter, two threads produced a sequence of different characters in the output console. The resource System.Console was used as a common output medium simultaneously by the two threads. The accesses were not synchronized and so the outputs varied according to the distribution of processor time between the two processes. C# offers a *lock statement* that can be used to prevent this.

A lock statement sets a lock on a specified object (usually the shared resource itself). While a thread executes a lock statement no other thread can carry out a lock statement on the same object. This guarantees *mutual exclusion* for a critical region that must not be simultaneously executed by several threads.

```
using System; using System.Threading;

public class LockExample {
    public static void RunT0() {
        lock (Console.Out) {
            for (int i = 0; i < 10; i++) { Console.Write('x'); Thread.Sleep(100); }
        }
    }
}
```

```
public static void RunT1() {
    lock (Console.Out) {
        for (int i = 0; i < 10; i++) { Console.Write('o'); Thread.Sleep(100); }
    }
}
public static void Main() {
    new Thread(new ThreadStart(RunT0)).Start();
    new Thread(new ThreadStart(RunT1)).Start();
}
}
```

Immediately after the start the first thread (RunT0) locks the object of the share resource (Console.Out, the console output) and only releases it once the letter 'x' has been written ten times. The second thread (RunT1) must wait at the beginning until the first thread releases the lock. Only then may it reserve the shared resource object for itself and output its ten 'o's. This example always produces the following output:

xxxxxxxxxxooooooooooo

Class Monitor

As well as by using the lock statement, synchronization of threads can also be achieved by using the class Monitor, which can also attach a lock to a code region and then release it again.

```
public sealed class Monitor {
    public static void Enter(object obj);     // acquires an exclusive lock on the object obj
    public static bool TryEnter(object obj);   // attempts to lock object obj
    public static bool TryEnter(object obj, int millies);  // attempts to lock obj for millies ms
    public static void Exit(object obj);    // releases an exclusive lock on the object obj
    public static bool Wait(object obj);   // releases the lock on obj and blocks the
                                      // current thread until it reacquires the lock
    public static bool Wait(object obj, int millies);
    public static bool Wait(object obj, int millies, bool exitContext);
    public static void Pulse(object obj);    // notifies the next thread in the waiting queue
                                      // about a change in obj's locked state
    public static void PulseAll(object obj);   // notifies all waiting threads
    ...
}
```

The lock statement

```
lock (obj) { ... }
```

is actually nothing other than a short form of

```
Monitor.Enter(obj);
try { ... }
finally { Monitor.Exit(obj); }
```

The difference from the lock statement appears only when using Monitor.TryEnter(obj). This method returns the value false if there is already a lock on the specified object. This does not block the method and it permits immediate reaction when a lock was refused. The following example demonstrates the use of the class Monitor:

```
using System; using System.Collections; using System.Threading;

public class MonitorExample {
    Queue lpt;   // line printer queue

    public void AddBlocking(object elem) {
        lock (lpt.SyncRoot) {
            lpt.Enqueue(elem);
        }
    }

    public bool AddNonBlocking(object elem) {
        if (! Monitor.TryEnter(lpt.SyncRoot)) return false;
        try { lpt.Enqueue(elem); }
        finally { Monitor.Exit(lpt.SyncRoot); }
        return true;
    }
}
```

Wait and Pulse

It often happens that a thread finds itself in a monitor and must wait for a condition that can only be set by another thread, which must itself refer to the monitor. Because that is not possible as long as the first thread still holds the lock, things can come to a *deadlock*. The first thread must temporarily release the monitor until the condition on which it is waiting is satisfied. For this purpose the class Monitor provides two methods: Wait and Pulse.

Monitor.Wait(obj) sets the current thread into a waiting state (that means, appends it to a waiting queue on object obj) and releases the lock on object obj. Monitor.Pulse(obj) awakes the next thread waiting in the queue for obj. If another thread holds the lock it must wait until the lock is free. The following example shows how synchronization with Wait and Pulse works:

```
// thread A                         // thread B
lock (obj) /*1*/ {                  lock (obj) /*3*/ {

    ...                                 ...
    /*2*/ Monitor.Wait(obj); /*5*/      /*4*/ Monitor.Pulse(obj);

    ...                                 ...
}                                  } /*6*/
```

1. Thread A comes to a lock statement and enters the monitor because the lock is free.
2. A comes to Wait, blocks and releases the lock.

3. Thread B comes to the lock statement and enters the monitor because the lock is free.

4. B comes to Pulse and this awakes A but it also continues running.

5. A attempts to obtain the lock on obj once again, but that is not allowed, because B still holds it. So A must wait.

6. B comes to the end of the lock statement and releases the lock on obj. Thus A can obtain the lock, continue running and end its lock statement.

The following example shows a classic buffer synchronization using Wait and Pulse. A buffer is used by several threads that can use buf.Put(ch) to introduce a character ch into the buffer and ch = buf.Get() to take a character out of the buffer. If the buffer is full or empty the executing thread must wait until another thread takes out or respectively puts in a character.

```
public class Buffer {
    const int size = 16;
    char[] buf = new char[size];
    int head = 0, tail = 0, n = 0;                      // n ... fill level

    public void Put(char ch) {
        lock(this) {
            while (n >= size) Monitor.Wait(this);       // buffer full
            buf[tail] = ch; tail = (tail + 1) % size; n++;
            Monitor.Pulse(this);                        // notify possibly waiting Get thread
        }
    }
    public char Get() {
        lock(this) {
            while (n <= 0) Monitor.Wait(this);          // buffer empty
            char ch = buf[head]; head = (head + 1) % size; n--;
            Monitor.Pulse(this);                        // notify possibly waiting Put thread
            return ch;
        }
    }
}
```

Note that the Wait call must be in a loop. A waiting Put thread is certainly only awakened if a Get thread has made space in the buffer but it can be that yet another Put thread has already filled up the buffer space again. For this reason the awakened Put thread can only continue running if n is less than size.

4.4 Network Communication

The .NET Framework arrives in an era when communication across a network is already commonplace, so such communication became an inseparable part of .NET from the outset.

This chapter gives an overview of network communication under .NET. *Web services* are kept separate because they will be developed in Chapter 7. Furthermore, only the most important classes and methods are explained, because an extensive discussion of this material could fill entire books. The classes described here belong to the namespaces System.Net and System.Net.Sockets.

4.4.1 Addressing

Before two computers can communicate with each other across a network, they must establish a connection. Connections are made with endpoints that are identified by the *IP address* (Internet Protocol address) of the computers and the unique *port number*. While the port numbers 0 to 1024 are reserved for the standard protocols such as HTTP (*Hypertext Transfer Protocol*, Port 80) [HTTP] or SMTP (*Simple Mail Transfer Protocol*, Port 25) [SMTP], other numbers can generally be used for individual connections.

In the following example an endpoint for the IP address 254.10.120.3 and port number 50000 is created:

```
IPAddress ip = IPAddress.Parse("254.10.120.3");
IPEndPoint ep = new IPEndPoint(ip, 50000);
```

IP addresses are hard to remember. Therefore one works instead with *DNS names* (Domain Name System names) such as dotnet.jku.at. These are translated into IP addresses by a DNS server. The class Dns helps in this. The call

```
IPHostEntry host = Dns.Resolve("dotnet.jku.at");
```

returns a description of all alias names and IP addresses that are authorized for the DNS name dotnet.jku.at. The following code fragment outputs the assigned lists of IP addresses and alias names:

```
foreach (IPAddress ip in host.AddressList) Console.WriteLine(ip.ToString());
foreach (string alias in host.Aliases) Console.WriteLine(alias);
```

If we do not only want to address an endpoint on a computer but rather a resource located there (e.g. a file) we use URIs (*Universal Resource Identifier*) [URI] which are a superset of the URLs (*Universal Resource Locator*). Here are three examples of URIs:

```
http://www.jku.at/Courses/index.html?id=12345
file:///Samples/DotNet/first.aspx
/Joe/index.html
```

The first URI refers to a web resource, the second a file on a local computer and the third is a relative URI which corresponds to another URI. The addressing schema (for example, "http://" or "file://") determines which access protocol applies.

The classes Uri and UriBuilder support analysis and compilation of URIs but are not further described here.

4.4.2   Sockets

Sockets are bi-directional communication points through which data can be sent and received. Before data can be passed both the client and the server must create a socket and connect it.

The following example shows what code is necessary at the server and at the client, to allow a client to establish a connection to port 50000 on a computer with the IP address 254.10.120.3:

```
// Server                                    // Client
IPAddress ip =                               IPAddess ip =
    IPAddress.Parse("254.10.120.3");             IPAddress.Parse("254.10.120.3");
IPEndPoint ep =                              IPEndPoint ep =
    new IPEndPoint(ip, 50000);                   new IPEndPoint(ip, 50000);
Socket s0 = new Socket(...);                 Socket s2 = new Socket(...);
server.Bind(ep);
server.Listen(10);
```

The server creates a socket s0 and binds to an endpoint with the desired address. Then it carries out s0.Listen(10) which signals its availability and that it can serve up to ten clients that simultaneously try to make a connection.

The client similarly declares a socket s2 without connecting to an endpoint at that stage. Figure 4.8 shows the situation after these code fragments have been carried out.

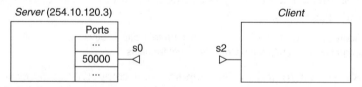

Figure 4.8 Sockets on server and client (still not connected)

The server now uses s0.Accept() to wait for a connection and the client establishes this by means of s2.Connect(ep):

```
// Server                                    // Client
Socket s1 = s0.Accept();                     s2.Connect(ep);
```

The Accept call blocks until the connection is established. As a result it returns a new socket s1 that is connected to the client socket s2. The socket s0 is now ready again to establish new connections. Figure 4.9 illustrates this situation.

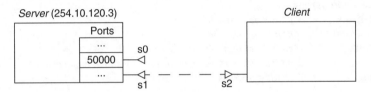

Figure 4.9 *Sockets s1 and s2 are connected and ready for communication*

After the connection has been established the client and the server can communicate with one another by using Send and Receive:

```
// Server
s1.Receive(msg1);

...

s1.Send(msg2);
s1.Shutdown(SocketShutdown.Both);
s1.Close();
```

```
// Client
s2.Send(msg1);

...

s2.Receive(msg2);
s2.Shutdown(SocketShutdown.Both);
s2.Close();
```

The details of the Socket interface can be seen from the following extract:

```
public class Socket : IDisposable {
    //----- constructor
    public Socket(AddressFamily af, SocketType st, ProtocolType pt);
    //----- properties
    public AddressFamily AddressFamily { get; }
    public SocketType SocketType { get; }
    public ProtocolType ProtocolType { get; }
    public bool Connected  { get; }
    public EndPoint LocalEndPoint { get; }
    public EndPoint RemoteEndPoint { get; }
    public int Available { get; }
    //----- methods
    public void Bind(EndPoint localEndPoint);
    public void Listen(int backlog);
    public Socket Accept();
    public void Connect(EndPoint remoteEP);
    public int Send(byte[] buffer);
    public int Receive(byte[] buffer);
    public void Shutdown(SocketShutdown how);
    public void Close();

    ...

}
```

If we create a socket we must specify the desired addressing schema, the socket type and the transfer protocol. The type AddressFamily determines the addressing schema:

```
public enum AddressFamily {
    InterNetwork,       // IP address version 4
    InterNetworkV6,     // IP address version 6
    AppleTalk,          // address of AppleTalk protocol
    IrDa,               // address for infrared communication via IrDA protocol
    NetBios,            // NetBios address
    ...
}
```

The enumeration SocketType gives the type of the desired socket. A socket can, for example, permit connection-oriented or connectionless packet data transfer.

```
public enum SocketType {
    Dgram,        // packet-oriented transfer via UDP; packets may get lost
    Rdm,          // packet-oriented transfer; guarantees that no packets get lost and
                  // that they arrive in the proper order
    Seqpacket,    // connection-oriented transfer in both directions
    Stream        // connection-oriented transfer in both directions with TCP protocol
    Raw,          // access lower levels of OSI model, e.g. for sending ICMP packets (Ping)
    Unknown,      // specifies an unknown kind of socket
    ...
}
```

Finally, we must indicate, by means of ProtocolType, which transfer protocol should be used:

```
public enum ProtocolType {
    Icmp,     // Internet Control Message Protocol (e.g. for implementing Ping)
    IP,       // IP protocol
    TCP,      // Transmission Control Protocol
    UDP,      // User Datagram Protocol
    ...
}
```

Once a socket has been created its addressing schema, socket type and protocol type can be queried. Connected returns whether a socket is connected to another one. LocalEndPoint and RemoteEndPoint provide the endpoints of the connection. The property Available states how many bytes are available to be received.

Example Echo Server

We now wish to implement an *echo server* as an example. It will receive data and return it unchanged to the sender. To simplify matters, the echo server and its clients can all run on the local computer. Therefore the local address of the computer is given. It is known as *loopback address* (IPAddress.Loopback). To run the example on different computers only the loopback address needs to be changed to the other IP address.

The echo server is kept very simple and so can only serve one client at a time because the connection is closed after each data transfer.

```
using System; using System.Net; using System.Net.Sockets;

class EchoServer {
    Socket s;

    public bool StartUp(IPAddress ip, int port) {
        try {
            s = new Socket(AddressFamily.InterNetwork, SocketType.Stream,
                           ProtocolType.Tcp);
            s.Bind(new IPEndPoint(ip, port));
            s.Listen(10);
        } catch (Exception e) {
            Console.WriteLine(e.Message);
            return false;
        }
        for(;;) {
            Socket newSocket = s.Accept();   // Accept blocks until a client connects
            Communicate(newSocket);
        }
    }

    void Communicate(Socket clSock) {
        try {
            byte[] buffer = new byte[1024];
            while (clSock.Receive(buffer) > 0)   // Receive blocks until data arrives
                clSock.Send(buffer);
            clSock.Shutdown(SocketShutdown.Both);
            clSock.Close ();
        } catch (Exception e) {
            Console.WriteLine(e.Message);
        }
    }

    public static void Main() {
        EchoServer server = new EchoServer( );
        if (! server.StartUp(IPAddress.Loopback, 50000))
            Console.WriteLine("Starting echo server failed");
    }
}
```

The client is implemented by means of the following class EchoClient. It creates a socket and gives IPAddress.Loopback as target. Then a sequence of bytes is sent to the echo server and the answer is received by the server and output on the console:

```
using System; using System.Text; using System.Net; using System.Net.Sockets;

class EchoClient {
    public static void Main() {
        try {
            //----- establish connection
            Socket s = new Socket(AddressFamily.InterNetwork, SocketType.Stream,
                                  ProtocolType.Tcp);
            s.Connect(new IPEndPoint(IPAddress.Loopback, 50000));
```

```
//----- send
byte[] msg = Encoding.ASCII.GetBytes("This is a test.");
s.Send(msg);
//----- receive
byte[] retMsg = new byte[1024];
s.Receive(retMsg);
string str = Encoding.ASCII.GetString(retMsg);
Console.WriteLine(str);
  } catch (Exception e) {
    Console.WriteLine(e.Message);
  }
}
}
```

4.4.3   NetworkStream

In the examples up to now the data was sent and received directly via sockets. However, we can read and write via a data stream connected to a socket object. This has the advantage that we do not have to deal with byte arrays.

The constructor of the class NetworkStream receives a socket object as a data source on which reading and writing processes should operate:

```
Socket s = new Socket(...);
s.Connect(new IPEndPoint(ip, port));
NetworkStream ns = new NetworkStream(s);
```

The NetworkStream ns can then be used as by a *reader* or a *writer* to work with formatted data such as, for example, ASCII character strings or XML code (see Section 4.7). The following example shows how ns can be used as a data source of an XMLTextReader in order to read XML text from a server:

```
XMLTextReader r = new XMLTextReader(ns);
for (int i = 0; i < r.AttributeCount; i++) {
    r.MoveToAttribute(i);
    Console.Write("{0} = {1}", r.Name, r.Value);
}
```

4.4.4   WebRequest and WebReponse

The communication via sockets described above requires countless low-level operations. The .NET Framework also offers communication classes at a higher level that can be conveniently used with the commonly used protocols such as http:// and file://.

The basis for this style of communication is the abstract classes WebRequest and WebResponse which permit access to web resources (in general files) by means of a *request/response* protocol. The client sends a request to the server and the server returns the requested web resource in its response. For example, a request object is created by the call

```
WebRequest reqest = WebRequest.Create("http://dotnet.jku.at/index.html");
```

The kind of URI passed determines which class the object created will belong to. If it begins with http:// then an HttpWebRequest object comes back. If it begins with file:// then a FileWebRequest object is returned. HttpWebRequest and FileWebRequest are subclasses of WebRequest. Other subclasses and their prefixes can be registered with the method RegisterPrefix. The request object can be configured by means of properties such as Method (for example, "GET" or "POST"), ContentType (for example, "text/html") or Headers. With POST request parameters can be written to the data stream that can be obtained with GetRequestStream. However, for the majority of requests we do not need these configurations. Here is an extract from the interface of WebRequest:

```
public abstract class WebRequest : MarshalByRefObject, ISerializable {
    //----- properties
    public virtual string Method { get; set; }
    public virtual string ContentType { get; set; }
    public virtual WebHeaderCollection Headers { get; set; }
    ...
    //----- methods
    public static WebRequest Create(string uri);
    public virtual Stream GetRequestStream();
    public virtual WebResponse GetResponse();
    public static bool RegisterPrefix(string prefix, IWebRequestCreate creator);
    ...
}
```

As soon as we have called the method request.GetResponse() the request is sent and the reply received in the WebResponse object which can be of type HttpWebResponse or FileWebRespose depending on the protocol. Here again is an extract from the abstract class WebResponse:

```
public abstract class WebResponse : MarshalByRefObject, ISerializable, IDisposable {
    //----- properties
    public virtual long ContentLength { get; set; }
    public virtual string ContentType { get; set; }
    public virtual WebHeaderCollection Headers { get; }
    public virtual Uri ResponseUri { get; }
    ...
    //----- methods
    public virtual Stream GetResponseStream();
    public virtual void Close();
    ...
}
```

The response object received can now be inspected via its properties. We can access the reply stream (for example the content of the HTML file) by means of

GetResponseStream(). In the following example, an HTML file is requested and output on the console:

```
using System;
using System.IO;                    // for StreamReader
using System.Net;                   // for WebRequest, WebResponse

class WebTest {
    static void Main() {
        WebRequest request = WebRequest.Create("http://dotnet.jku.at");
        WebResponse response = request.GetResponse();
        StreamReader r = new StreamReader(response.GetResponseStream());
        for (string line = r.ReadLine(); line != null; line = r.ReadLine())
            Console.WriteLine(line);
    }
}
```

4.5   Reflection

The term *reflection* means the access of type information at run time. The name-spaces System.Reflection and System.Reflection.Emit offer classes that make meta-information about assemblies, modules (see Section 3.6) and types available. An assembly can contain one or more modules in which various types are defined and these individual types consist of members such as fields, methods, events, proper-ties or inner classes. In this context reflection is used for the following tasks:

❑ reading of meta-information about assemblies, modules and types;
❑ reading of meta-information about elements of a type;
❑ creation of objects of a specified type;
❑ *dynamic invocation* of method objects and access to values of fields and properties via meta-information;
❑ creation of a new type at run time, with the help of the types in namespace System.Reflection.Emit.

In addition, the namespace System.Reflection.Emit offers support for the program-ming of compilers and interpreters. It contains classes that one can use to create intermediate code in CIL (*Common Intermediate Language*) and which can be stored in PE files (*Portable Executable*). Thus types can be created at run time.

4.5.1   System.Reflection.Assembly

We can use reflection to load an assembly and information about its modules and types. For this purpose the namespace System.Reflection provides the class Assembly. It offers meta-information at the assembly level. Here is an extract from its interface:

```
public class Assembly : IEvidenceFactory, ICustomAttributeProvider, ISerializable {
    //----- properties
    public virtual string FullName { get; }   // = name, version, culture, public key token
    public virtual string Location { get; }   // returns filename with path of this assembly
    public virtual MethodInfo EntryPoint { get; }   // returns Main method or null
    public bool GlobalAssemblyCache { get; }   // loaded from GAC?
    ...
    //----- methods
    public static Assembly Load(string name);   // loads assembly called name
    public static Assembly LoadFrom(string file);   // load assembly from file
    public static Assembly LoadFrom(string file, Evidence securityEvidence);
    public static Assembly GetAssembly(Type t);   // returns assembly containing type t
    public static Assembly GetEntryAssembly();   // returns assembly of main program
    public static Assembly GetExecutingAssembly();   // returns currently running assembly
    public virtual AssemblyName GetName();   // returns name object of this assembly
    public Module[] GetModules();   // returns all modules of this assembly
    public Module[] GetLoadedModules();   // returns loaded modules of this assembly
    public Module GetModule(string name);   // returns the specified module
    public virtual Type[] GetTypes();   // returns all types of this assembly
    public virtual Type[] GetExportedTypes();   // returns all public types of this assembly
    public virtual Type GetType(string typeName);   // returns the specified type
    public object CreateInstance(string typeName);   // creates instance of type typeName
    public virtual object[] GetCustomAttributes(bool inherit);
        // returns all custom attributes of this assembly (parameter inherit is ignored)
    public virtual object[] GetCustomAttributes(Type attributeType, bool inherit);
        // returns custom attributes of this assembly that are of type attributeType
    ...
}
```

In order to obtain information about an assembly we must first obtain a reference to it, for example by loading the assembly:

```
Assembly a = Assembly.Load("mscorlib");
```

In this example, the assembly mscorlib.dll is loaded. It contains many of the base classes of the .NET library. After a successful loading the metadata about these classes can be queried. The following code lists all the types of the assembly a on the console.

```
Type[] types = a.GetTypes();
foreach (Type t in types) Console.WriteLine(t.FullName);
```

Here is an extract from the output:

```
...
System.Reflection.Emit.AssemblyBuilder
System.Reflection.Emit.AssemblyBuilderData
System.Reflection.Emit.ResWriterData
System.Reflection.Emit.NativeVersionInfo
...
```

4.5.2   System.Type

The abstract class Type declared in the namespace System forms the basis of all reflection operations. Type is the abstract description of all types that can exist in the run-time environment. These include classes, interfaces, structs, arrays, enums and delegates. The class Type allows information about a type to be acquired at run time (by the way, this information is also be obtained via the disassembler tool ildasm.exe). Here is an extract from the interface of Type:

```
public abstract class Type : MemberInfo, IReflect {
    //----- properties
    public abstract string FullName { get; }   // fully qualified name (= with namespace)
    public abstract Type BaseType { get; }    // direct base type or null (for System.Object)
    public abstract Assembly Assembly { get; }  // returns assembly that declares this type
    public TypeAttributes Attributes { get; }   // returns attributes of this type
    public bool IsAbstract { get; }   // is this type abstract?
    public bool IsClass { get; }   // is this type a class?
    public bool IsPublic { get; }    // is this type declared public?
    ...
    //----- methods
    public ConstructorInfo[] GetConstructors();   // returns public constructors of this type
    public Type[] GetInterfaces();   // returns all interfaces that this type implements or inherits
    public FieldInfo[] GetFields();   // returns public fields of this type
    public MethodInfo[] GetMethods();   // returns public methods of this type
    public MethodInfo GetMethod(string name);   // returns specified public method
    public MethodInfo GetMethod(string name, Type[] argTypes);
    public PropertyInfo[] GetProperties();   // returns public properties of this type
    public virtual EventInfo[] GetEvents();   // returns public events of this type
    public MemberInfo[] GetMembers();   // returns all public members of this type
    public abstract MemberInfo[] GetMembers(BindingFlags bindAttr);
        // returns all members that match the specified constraints
        // (e.g. BindingFlags.NonPublic, BindingFlags.Static | BindingFlags.DeclaredOnly)
    ...
}
```

In order to enquire about a particular type we must obtain a Type object for the type. This is done in the following manner:

```
Type t1 = Type.GetType("System.String");
Type t2 = typeof(System.String);
string s = "Hello";
Type t3 = s.GetType();   // GetType is inherited from Object
```

As soon as we have a Type object we can obtain meta-information about its elements, as shown in the following examples:

```
using System; using System.Reflection;
...
string s = "Hello";
Type t = s.GetType();
```

```
Console.WriteLine("type: {0}", t.FullName);
Console.WriteLine("direct base type: {0}", t.BaseType);

Console.WriteLine("implemented interfaces:");
foreach (Type i in t.GetInterfaces()) Console.WriteLine("\t{0}", i.FullName);

Console.WriteLine("public constructors:");
foreach (ConstructorInfo i in t.GetConstructors()) Console.WriteLine("\t{0}", i);

Console.WriteLine("public properties:");
foreach (PropertyInfo i in t.GetProperties()) Console.WriteLine("\t{0}", i);
```

The example produces the following output:

```
type: System.String
direct base type: System.Object
implemented interfaces:
        System.IComparable
        System.ICloneable
        System.IConvertible
        System.Collections.IEnumerable
public constructors:
        Void .ctor(Char*)
        Void .ctor(Char*, Int32, Int32)
        Void .ctor(SByte*)
        Void .ctor(SByte*, Int32, Int32)
        Void .ctor(SByte*, Int32, Int32, System.Text.Encoding)
        Void .ctor(Char[], Int32, Int32)
        Void .ctor(Char[])
        Void .ctor(Char, Int32)
public properties:
        Char Chars [Int32]                      // indexer counts as property
        Int32 Length
```

Meta-information about types, fields, methods, properties and events is described by the abstract class MemberInfo and its subclasses (see Figure 4.10).

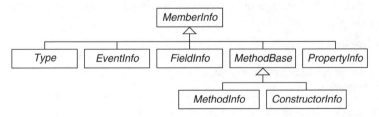

Figure 4.10 *Inheritance hierarchy for the MemberInfo classes*

For example, if we wish to obtain meta-information about all constructors of a type t we call t.GetConstructors() and receive a list of ConstructorInfo objects. MethodInfo and ConstructorInfo have the same base class, MethodBase, whose interface looks like this:

```
public abstract class MethodBase : MemberInfo {
    //----- properties
    public abstract MethodAttributes Attributes { get; }    // returns attributes of this method
    public virtual CallingConventions CallingConvention { get; };
    public bool IsAbstract { get; }
    public bool IsPublic { get; }
    public bool IsStatic { get; }
    public bool IsVirtual { get; }
    ...
    //----- methods
    public static MethodBase GetCurrentMethod();    // returns currently running method
    public abstract ParameterInfo[] GetParameters();    // returns parameters of this method
    public object Invoke(object obj, object[] params);
    ...
}
```

The call meth.Invoke(obj, args) carries out the method described by meth for the object obj and passes the parameters collected in args. In this way we can dynamically invoke a method that has been retrieved by reflection (see Section 4.5.4).

4.5.3   Dynamic Object Creation

In order to create an object of a particular type, we use the class Activator from the namespace System:

```
public sealed class Activator {
    public static object CreateInstance(Type type);
    public static object CreateInstance(Type type, object[] args);
    ...
}
```

An object of the specified type is created by the call Activator.CreateInstance(type). In the call Activator.CreateInstance(type, args) arguments in the form of an object array can be passed. These arguments are used to choose the correct constructor. Here is an example:

```
Type t = Type.GetType("System.String");
object[] args = new object[] { new char[]{'T','e','s','t'} };
string s = (string) Activator.CreateInstance(t, args);
Console.WriteLine(s);
```

The type of args[0] selects the constructor

```
String(char[] c)
```

which creates a String object and initializes it with "Test". WriteLine displays "Test".

The class Activator also contains methods for creating COM objects and proxy objects for network communication. However, we cannot go into details here (see [Ram02]).

4.5.4   Dynamic Execution of Methods

Through the meta-information made available by the class Type we can search for
a method of a type at run time and execute it with the desired parameters. This is
also called *late binding*, or *custom binding*, of the method.

Searching for a Method

Information about the methods of a type can be read with the help of the class
MethodInfo:

```
Type t = typeof(System.String);
MethodInfo[] methods = t.GetMethods();
foreach (MethodInfo m in methods) Console.WriteLine(m);
```

This code fragment returns all the public methods of the class System.String:

```
...
Int32 LastIndexOf(System.String, Int32)
System.String PadLeft(Int32)
System.String PadLeft(Int32, Char)
System.String PadRight(Int32)
System.String PadRight(Int32, Char)
Boolean StartsWith(System.String)
System.String ToLower()
...
```

We can also limit the search by using flags. For example, if we only want to search
for static methods that are declared public, one can write

```
Type t = typeof(string);
MethodInfo[] methods = t.GetMethods(BindingFlags.Static | BindingFlags.Public);
foreach (MethodInfo m in methods) Console.WriteLine(m);
```

and obtain

```
...
System.String Format(System.String, System.Object[])
System.String Format(System.IFormatProvider, System.String, System.Object[])
System.String Copy(System.String)
...
```

If we already know the name of the method, we can enquire about its meta-
information directly by using t.GetMethod(name, argTypes). In this, the case of the
method name (upper or lower) is significant. If the method does not exist, null is
returned. The following example shows the search for a method with and without
parameters:

```
Type t = typeof(string);
MethodInfo m1 = t.GetMethod("Clone");        // search for 'Clone()'
if (m1 != null) Console.WriteLine(m1);
```

```
Type[] args = {typeof(char), typeof(int)};
MethodInfo m2 = t.GetMethod("IndexOf", args);    // search for 'IndexOf(char, int)'
if (m2 != null) Console.WriteLine(m2);
```

The output produced in this case is:

```
System.Object Clone()
Int32 IndexOf(Char, Int32)
```

Executing a Method

Once we have the MethodInfo object of a method, we can use the method by calling
it with methodInfo.Invoke(obj, args).

The following example shows this process, from the search for the methods,
through the dynamic object creation to the dynamic call of the method found:

```
//----- create a String object
Type t = typeof(string);
object[] args = new object[] { new char[] {'F','o','O','B','A','r'} };
string s = (string) Activator.CreateInstance(t, args);
Console.WriteLine("s before invoking method s.ToLower(): {0}", s);
//----- search for and invoke s.ToLower()
MethodInfo method = t.GetMethod("ToLower", new Type[0]);    // no parameters
object result = method.Invoke(s, new object[0]);    // no parameters
Console.WriteLine("result of method s.ToLower(): {0}", result);
```

As a result we receive the following output:

```
s before invoking method s.ToLower(): FoOBAr
result of method s.ToLower(): foobar
```

In contrast to the direct call of a method, here the method name and parameters
only need to be known at run time: for example, they can be read in from a file.
The search and call of the method are carried out dynamically.

As a second example, we now see the call of s.IndexOf('B', 1) where a method
with parameters is called.

```
// String object s taken from previous example ("FoOBAr").
Type[] parTypes = { typeof(char), typeof(int) };
MethodInfo method = t.GetMethod("IndexOf", parTypes);
object[] parameters = { 'B', 1 };
object result = method.Invoke(s, parameters);
Console.WriteLine("result of method s.IndexOf('B', 1): {0}", result);
```

The output shows the index of the first occurrence of a 'B' after position 1: So 3 is
shown on the console.

4.5.5 System.Reflection.Emit

The namespace System.Reflection.Emit is mainly used by compilers and interpreters in order to translate source code into CIL (*Common Intermediate Language*). It allows the possibility of creating new types in CIL code according to metadata and using these immediately or storing them in PE (*Portable Executable*) files. In particular it supports the following tasks:

- ❏ creation of *assemblies* with the possibility of executing them, or storing them in PE files;
- ❏ creation of modules with the possibility of placing them in assemblies;
- ❏ creation of types with the possibility of creating objects of these types at run time and executing methods of these objects;
- ❏ creation of meta-information for particular modules to support profiling and debugging.

As a small example we show here how a class HelloWorld can be created dynamically and its method SayHelloTo executed:

```
//----- create an assembly
AssemblyName assemblyName = new AssemblyName();
assemblyName.Name = "HelloWorldAssembly";
AssemblyBuilder newAssembly = AppDomain.CurrentDomain.DefineDynamicAssembly
                            (assemblyName, AssemblyBuilderAccess.Run);
//----- create a module within the new assembly
ModuleBuilder newModule = newAssembly.DefineDynamicModule("HelloWorldModule");
//----- create a type within the new module
TypeBuilder newType = newModule.DefineType("HelloWorld", TypeAttributes.Public);
//----- create a method with its signature within the new type
Type[] paramTypes = { typeof(string) };
Type retType = typeof(string);
MethodBuilder newMethod = newType.DefineMethod("SayHelloTo",
        MethodAttributes.Public | MethodAttributes.Virtual, retType, paramTypes);
//----- insert CIL instructions into the new method
ILGenerator ilGen = newMethod.GetILGenerator();
ilGen.Emit(OpCodes.Ldstr, "Hello ");
ilGen.Emit(OpCodes.Ldarg_1);
Type t = typeof(string);
MethodInfo mi = t.GetMethod("Concat", new Type[] { typeof(string),typeof(string) });
ilGen.Emit(OpCodes.Call, mi);
ilGen.Emit(OpCodes.Ret);
//----- finish new type
newType.CreateType();
//----- execute the newly created method SayHelloTo("Wolfgang")
MethodInfo method = newType.GetMethod("SayHelloTo", new Type[] { typeof(string) });
object obj = Activator.CreateInstance(newType);
object result = method.Invoke(obj, new string[] {"Wolfgang"});
Console.WriteLine(result);
```

This example produces the output "Hello Wolfgang".

4.6   Graphical User Interfaces with Windows.Forms

Up until now all the examples in this book have been console programs, that is, the input and output were restricted to the console. The namespace System.Windows.Forms allows the *Windows* graphical user interface to be used. The classes in System.Windows.Forms make an object-oriented graphical interface model available. This replaces previous models such as MFC (*Microsoft Foundation Classes*) or ATL (*Active Template Library*) and thus substantially simplifies Windows GUI programming.

In using graphical user interfaces it is necessary at present to distinguish between two different principles:

- ❏ *Windows applications* (System.Windows.Forms): This style of application runs locally on a single computer and is used if an application needs considerable processing power. A further advantage of a Windows application is the simple access to local resources such as disks and other devices. Examples of such applications are graphics programs, visualizations, games or numerical calculations;

- ❏ *Web applications* (System.Web): Web applications consist of graphical user interfaces that are presented by a browser. Because they built from standard HTML these interfaces are indeed platform and browser independent but are at present somewhat restricted in their capabilities. Details of web-based graphical user interfaces are discussed in Chapter 6 on ASP.NET.

It is possible that these two principles will be brought together in a unified model so that there is no longer any difference between local and web interfaces.

Because the programming of graphical user interfaces is an extensive topic we restrict ourselves in this chapter to an explanation of the basic structure and the presentation of some small examples which can be realized without *Visual Studio*.

4.6.1   Controls

Every graphical user interface consists of controls that represent information and display results. These tasks are fulfilled by objects of the type Control and UserControl. The class Control is the base class of all graphical controls defined in the namespace System.Windows.Forms. Controls are displayed in windows that are called *forms* under .NET and that are represented by the class Form (see Section 4.6.2). Here is an extract from the interface of Control:

```
public class Control : Component, ISynchronizeInvoke, IWin32Window {
    //----- constructors
    public Control();
    public Control(string text);   // creates a control with the specified text to display
    public Control(Control parent, string text);   // creates a child control for parent
    ...
```

```
//----- properties
public string Name { get; set; }
public virtual string Text { get; set; }   // text to display
public virtual Color ForeColor { get; set; }
public virtual Color BackColor { get; set; }
public Size Size { get; set; }
public Rectangle Bounds { get; set; }   // current size and position of this control
public Point Location { get; set; }   // position of upper-left corner relative to container
public bool Visible { get; set; }   // is the control visible?
public Control.ControlCollection Controls { get; }   // embedded controls
public virtual Cursor Cursor { get; set; }   // how to display mouse pointer above control
public virtual bool AllowDrop { get; set; }   // can accept dragged data?
...

//----- methods
public void Show();   // makes the control visible
public void Hide();   // makes the control invisible
public void Invalidate();   // invalidates the entire bounding box of this control
public void Invalidate(Rectangle region);   // invalidates only the specified region
public void Update();   // causes immediate repainting of all invalid regions
public virtual void Refresh();   // forces this control to repaint itself immediately
public void Select();   // selects this control
public bool Focus();   // sets the focus to this control
public void Scale(float ratioX, float ratioY);   // scales this control by the given factors
public void SetBounds(int x, int y, int width, int height);   // set size and position
public void BringToFront();
public void SendToBack();
public bool Contains(Control ctl);
public Control GetChildAtPoint(Point p);
public Control GetNextControl(Control ctl, bool forward); // returns the control that
        // will receive the focus after this one when the Tab key is pressed
public IContainerControl GetContainerControl();
public Form FindForm();   // returns the form that contains this control
public DragDropEffects DoDragDrop(object data, DragDropEffects allowedEffects);
...

//----- events
public event EventHandler Click;
public event EventHandler DoubleClick;
public event KeyEventHandler KeyDown;
public event EventHandler GotFocus;
public event EventHandler LostFocus;
public event EventHandler MouseEnter;   // mouse pointer enters this controls
public event EventHandler MouseHover;   // mouse pointer is above this control
public event EventHandler MouseLeave;   // mouse pointer leaves this control
public event MouseEventHandler MouseDown;   // mouse button pressed above control
public event MouseEventHandler MouseMove;
public event MouseEventHandler MouseUp;   // mouse button release above control
public event EventHandler TextChanged;   // Text property has changed
public event EventHandler BackColorChanged;
public event ControlEventHandler ControlAdded;
public event ControlEventHandler ControlRemoved;
```

```
public event DragEventHandler DragEnter;
public event PaintEventHandler Paint;   // control has been repainted
...
}
```

.NET already offers a set of useful controls that are all derived from Control (see Table 4.1). Each of them adds functionality to Control. So there is, for example, a control MonthCalendar that displays a calendar where an individual day can be chosen (see Figure 4.11).

Figure 4.11 *Example of a control: MonthCalendar*

Table 4.1 *Various controls*

Button	
CheckBox	
CheckedListBox	
ComboBox	
DataGrid	
GroupBox	
Label	
ListBox	
ListView	
Menu	
Panel	
ProgressBar	

Table 4.1 *Various controls (cont.)*

RadioButton	RadioButton
ScrollBar	
StatusBar	Ready
TabControl	Tab1 Tab2
TextBox	Text contents
ToolBar	
TreeView	⊟ root ⋯ child

4.6.2   Windows Form

The class Form is likewise derived from Control and presents a window of a Windows application. A Form object can contain and display controls such as *buttons*, *scrollbars*, *menus*, *toolbars* and so on. Here is an extract from the interface of Form:

```
public class Form : ContainerControl {
    //----- constructor
    public Form();
    //----- properties
    public new Size Size { get; set; }
    public new Size ClientSize { get; set; }   // size of this window with menu and border
    public Point DesktopLocation { get; set; }
    public Rectangle DesktopBounds { get; set; }   // bounds including menu and border
    public FormBorderStyle FormBorderStyle { get; set; }
    public double Opacity { get; set; }   // between 0.00 and 1.00
    public bool Modal { get; }
    public MainMenu Menu { get; set; }
    public bool MinimizeBox { get; set; }   // has minimize button in title bar?
    public bool MaximizeBox { get; set; }   // has maximize button in title bar?
    public bool ShowInTaskbar { get; set; }   // has task bar representation?
    public IButtonControl AcceptButton { get; set; }   // button activated by pressing ENTER
    public IButtonControl CancelButton { get; set; }   // button activated by pressing ESC
    public DialogResult DialogResult { get; set; }   // result of a modal dialog
    public bool IsMdiChild { get; }
    public bool IsMdiContainer { get; set; }
    public Form[] MdiChildren { get; }   // returns all MDI child windows
    public Form MdiParent { get; set; }   // returns this window's MDI parent window
    public Form ActiveMdiChild { get; }   // returns currently active MDI child window
    public static Form ActiveForm { get; }   // returns application's currently active window
    ...
```

```
//----- methods
public DialogResult ShowDialog();   // displays the form as a modal dialog
public DialogResult ShowDialog(IWin32Window owner);   // dialog with specified owner
public void Activate();   // activates this window and sets the focus to it
public void Close();
public void AddOwnedForm(Form ownedForm);   // makes this form owner of another
public void RemoveOwnedForm(Form ownedForm);
protected void CenterToParent();
protected void CenterToScreen();
public void LayoutMdi(MdiLayout value);   // arranges the MDI child windows
public void SetDesktopBounds(int x, int y, int width, int height);
public void SetDesktopLocation(int x, int y);
...
//----- events
public event EventHandler Load;   // occurs before this window is first displayed
public event EventHandler Closed;   // occurs after this window is closed
public event CancelEventHandler Closing;   // occurs before this window is closed
public event EventHandler Activated;
public event EventHandler Deactivate;
public event EventHandler MaximizedBoundsChanged;
public event EventHandler MaximumSizeChanged;
public event EventHandler MinimumSizeChanged;
public event EventHandler MdiChildActivate;
public event EventHandler MenuStart;
public event EventHandler MenuComplete;
...
}
```

By setting the properties of a Form window it can also be converted into a modal dialog window or into a MDI window (*Multiple Document Interface*). An MDI window can contain multiple child windows and is recognizable by its IsMdiContainer property being set to true. To open a window as a dialog window the method form.ShowDialog() must be called. Objects of predefined dialog window classes can also be displayed in this way. The following example opens a dialog for the selecting a file:

```
OpenFileDialog openDialog = new OpenFileDialog();
openDialog.InitialDirectory = "c:\\";
openDialog.Filter = "All files|*.*";   // "filter name | filter pattern"
if (openDialog.ShowDialog() == DialogResult.OK){
    Stream file = openDialog.OpenFile();
    if (file != null) {
        ... // the selected file has been opened for editing
        file.Close ();
    }
}
```

In the next example, we wish to convert the console program HelloWorld into an application for a graphical user interface (see Figure 4.12). We therefore declare a new window class as a subclass of Form:

```
using System; using System.Windows.Forms; using System.Drawing;

class HelloWorldForm : Form {
    Label lab;                          // Label realizes a static text field

    HelloWorldForm() {
        this.Text = "Hello World Form";  // window title
        this.Size = new Size (240, 60);  // window size
        lab = new Label();
        lab.Text = "Hello World";
        lab.Location = new Point(10, 10); // position of the label in the window
        this.Controls.Add(lab);          // insert label into window
    }
    public static void Main() {
        Application.Run(new HelloWorldForm());   // start form as Windows application
    }
}
```

Calling Application.Run starts a Windows application. It opens a new window and couples it to the event-driven programming model of .NET (see Section 4.6.3).

Figure 4.12 *HelloWorldForm window*

As well as the namespace System.Windows.Forms there are other namespaces for programming Windows applications. For example, the namespace System.Drawing and its sub-namespaces offer functions for graphical output. In the example above, this namespace was used with the class Point to determine the coordinates of the text field.

4.6.3   Event-driven Programming Model

Windows applications are based on an event-oriented model. The task of an application is to watch for events and react to them accordingly. Events can be initiated by the user, by controls or even by the operating system. To take part in the system's event model an application must announce its window form to the system by using Application.Run(form). By using the class Application an application can be started, monitored and stopped:

```
public sealed class Application {
    //----- properties
```

```
public static string StartupPath { get; }
public static bool AllowQuit { get; }
public static CultureInfo CurrentCulture { get; set; }
...
//----- methods
public static void Run(Form mainForm);
public static void Exit();
public static void AddMessageFilter(IMessageFilter value);
public static void RemoveMessageFilter(IMessageFilter value);
...
//----- events
public static event EventHandler ApplicationExit;
public static event EventHandler ThreadExit;
public static event EventHandler Idle;
public static event ThreadExceptionEventHandler ThreadException;
}
```

As soon as an application has been started it reacts to events such as Click or TextChanged initiated by the controls (and in turn by the user). Because all controls (including Form) are derived from Control they already inherit a large set of pre-defined events. Each control can, however, define additional events.

If an object wants register for an event it must install an event-handling method (*delegate*) in the control that triggers the event. Details about *events* and *delegates* are given in Section 2.11. The most commonly used event-handling type is the delegate EventHandler:

```
public delegate void EventHandler(object sender, EventArgs e);
```

The parameter sender denotes the object that has initiated the event and e is a list of additional arguments. The following example shows how one installs a method OnMouseEnter as event handler for the event MouseEnter of the control elem:

```
elem.MouseEnter += new EventHandler(OnMouseEnter);
```

If the mouse pointer enters the graphical region of elem, a MouseEnter event is initiated and the method OnMouseEnter is called (as well as possible other installed methods). If the mouse pointer leaves the region of elem again, a MouseLeave event occurs. The following example uses these two events to colour a panel red when the mouse pointer is outside it and green when the mouse is within it.

```
class MouseEventTest : Form {
    Panel p;

    MouseEventTest() {
        p = new Panel();
        p.BackColor = Color.Red;
        p.MouseEnter += new EventHandler(OnMouseEnter);
        p.MouseLeave += new EventHandler(OnMouseLeave);
        Controls.Add(p);
    }
```

```
public void OnMouseEnter (object sender, EventArgs args) {
    p.BackColor = Color.Green;
}

public void OnMouseLeave (object sender, EventArgs args) {
    p.BackColor = Color.Red;
}

public static void Main() { Application.Run(new MouseEventTest()); }
}
```

Some events need additional parameters and thus delegate types that vary from the type EventHandler. By convention such delegates are called *Name*EventHandler and the arguments bound to them *Name*EventArgs. As an example we show the event MouseDown which returns the mouse position and the mouse button that was pressed as arguments. The delegate type for the event handler method is here called MouseEventHandler and the arguments passed are called MouseEventArgs:

```
class MouseEventExample : Form {
    Label lab;

    MouseEventExample (){
        lab = new Label();
        lab.BackColor = Color.White;
        lab.Size = new Size(300, 80);
        lab.Font = new Font(lab.Font.FontFamily, 20.0f);
        lab.MouseDown += new MouseEventHandler(OnMouseDown);
        Controls.Add(lab);
        ClientSize = lab.Size;
    }

    public void OnMouseDown(object sender, MouseEventArgs args) {
        lab.Text = String.Format("Button: {0}\nx:{1} y:{2}", args.Button, args.X, args.Y);;
    }

    public static void Main() { Application.Run(new MouseEventExample()); }
}
```

Information about the event can be queried, as in the above example, from the MouseEventArgs. So we can determine which mouse button was pressed and where the mouse pointer was located. A mouse click in a window leads to the output that is seen in Figure 4.13.

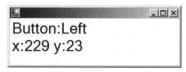

Figure 4.13 *Using MouseEventArgs*

4.6.4 User-defined Controls

As well as the controls already defined in the .NET library, we can develop our own controls and then use them in various applications. To develop a control the class System.Windows.Forms.UserControl must be extended.

As an example, we now want to develop a control BarChartControl that shows a sequence of values as a bar chart. BarChartControl extends the functionality of UserControl and overrides the method OnPaint which is responsible for drawing the graphical representation onto the screen. To have drawing functionality available (for example, Color, Graphics, Point) we must import the namespace System.Drawing.

In order to demonstrate the use of standard controls in conjunction with our user-defined controls we introduce a text (Label) in the BarChartControl. If one clicks there with the mouse, the bars in the chart are displayed in sorted order. On a new click they are returned to their original order. The values displayed in the bar charts are set by the property Values:

```
using System; using System.Collections;
using System.Windows.Forms; using System.Drawing;

class BarChartControl : UserControl {
    int[] show, original, sorted;   // displayed, original, sorted list of values for the bar chart
    Label state = new Label();

    public BarChartControl() {
        state.Location = new Point(1, Height - 15);
        state.Click += new EventHandler(OnSortLabelClick);
        this.Controls.Add(state);
    }
    public int[] Values {
        set {
            show = original = (int[]) value.Clone();
            sorted = (int[]) original.Clone(); Array.Sort(sorted);
            state.Text = "unsorted";
            Refresh();
        }
    }
    protected void OnSortLabelClick(object sender, EventArgs args) {
        if (show == sorted) { show = original;  state.Text = "unsorted"; }
        else                { show = sorted;    state.Text = "sorted"; }
        Refresh();
    }
```

```
protected override void OnPaint(PaintEventArgs e) {
    Brush b = new SolidBrush(ForeColor);        // fill colour for bars
    int w = Width / (show.Length * 2 - 1);      // width of and spacing between bars
    int x = w;                                  // position of first bar
    foreach (int i in show) {
        e.Graphics.FillRectangle(b, x, Height - i - 20, w, i);
        x += w * 2;
    }
}

public static void Main() {
    Form f = new Form();
    BarChartControl chart = new BarChartControl();
    chart.Values = new int[] { 30, 20, 50, 10, 15, 40, 100, 70, 80, 99 };
    f.Controls.Add(chart);
    f.ClientSize = chart.Size;
    Application.Run(f);
}
```

The Main method creates a BarChartControl, fills it with values and introduces it to a new window. On a click on the text "sorted" or "unsorted" the bar chart switches between the sorted and unsorted display (see Figure 4.14).

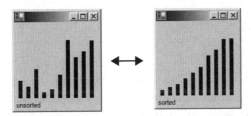

Figure 4.14 *BarChartControl in unsorted and sorted order*

4.7 XML

XML (*eXtensible Markup Language*) is a platform-independent format for hierarchically structured data. It was defined by the W3C (*World Wide Web Consortium*) [W3C] and has been accepted as a standard for data exchange. XML is a text-based format. XML-coded information is also human readable. Many new standards, such as *SOAP* or *UDDI*, are built on XML. Microsoft gives the following reasons for the tight integration of XML into the .NET Framework.

❑ *Use of existing standards*: Using existing and openly available standards such as XML enables data exchange between applications and platforms.

❑ *Consistent use*: XML is used consistently in all areas of the .NET Framework (ADO.NET, web services, configuration and so on). Therefore it represents a familiar notation for developers.

❑ *Extensibility*: XML can be extended by the user. XML classes in the .NET library (for example, XmlReader, XmlWriter) are abstract and can be extended to individual needs.

❑ *Performance*: The XML classes in the library are efficient and form the best basis for application-specific use of XML.

.NET uses XML-based formats for database access, web services, configuration files, for documentation of source code and much more. The .NET library contains a namespace System.Xml with very many classes and interfaces for working with XML data. In this section we describe some of the most important aspects.

4.7.1 XML Architecture

Tools for processing with XML files have the following tasks:

❑ reading of XML data;
❑ handling and transforming XML data;
❑ verification of XML data;
❑ writing of XML data.

The namespace System.Xml and its sub-namespaces offer classes for these tasks. The basis for all XML reading operations is the abstract class XmlReader. If XML data is read by an XmlReader, it can be stored in an intermediate form for further processing with the help of the classes XmlDocument and XPathDocument. The class XmlWriter is intended for writing XML data.

XSL (*eXtensible Stylesheet Language*) is a notation for transforming XML data into another XML representation (for example, HTML). The class XslTransform changes an XmlDocument or an XmlPathDocument into another representation with the help of XSL stylesheets. The inter-relationship of these classes is shown in Figure 4.15 and is described further in Section 4.7.5.

There are two different styles for reading XML data:

❑ **SAX** (*Simple API for XML*): The XML data is read sequentially and no data structure is formed in the main memory. The analysis of the XML is carried out with an event mechanism: if the parser reaches a part that is of

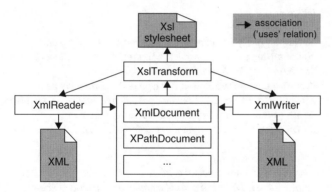

Figure 4.15 *Relationship of XML classes under .NET*

interest to the application it sends it an event. Irrelevant XML parts are skipped. So parsing of XML documents of arbitrary length can be efficient.

❑ **DOM** (*Document Object Model*): A DOM parser builds an XML data structure in the main memory and this can later be processed. Thus documents of any particular length can be read and put into intermediate storage. It is also possible for a SAX parser to create a DOM structure in the memory.

4.7.2   Sequential Reading with an XmlReader

The class XmlReader allows sequential reading of XML data without using intermediate storage. An XmlReader displays some of the characteristics of a SAX parser. The difference from a SAX parser is that an XmlReader follows the *Pull model*, where applications request XML data. In contrast, a SAX parser follows the *Push model*, where the parser informs the application of the content of the XML data by means of events.

The classes XmlTextReader, XmlNodeReader and XmlValidatingReader are extensions of the abstract class XmlReader. The most efficient variant is XmlTextReader because it does not perform any validation on the XML data when reading. Validation with respect to a DTD document (*Document Type Definition*) or an XML schema is done by the XmlValidatingReader. An XmlNodeReader is used for read operations on an object of type XmlNode. The class XmlNode as a representative of an XML element is described in Section 4.7.3. The interface of the abstract class XmlReader is defined as follows:

```
public abstract class XmlReader {
    //----- properties
    public abstract string Name { get; }   // name of current element (including prefix)
    public abstract string LocalName { get; }   // name of current element (without prefix)
    public abstract string Value { get; }   // value of the current element
    public abstract XmlNodeType NodeType { get; }  // type of the current element
    public abstract int AttributeCount { get; }   // number of attributes of the current element
    public abstract int Depth { get; }   // nesting level of the current element
    public abstract bool EOF { get; }   // is the reader at the end of the file?
    ...
    //----- methods
    public abstract bool Read();   // reads the next element
    public virtual void Skip();   // skips over the current element and its child elements
    public abstract string GetAttribute(int i);   // returns the i-th attribute of the element
    public virtual XmlNodeType MoveToContent();   // moves to the next content node
    public virtual bool IsStartElement(string name);   // is the current element a start tag?
    public abstract void Close();   // releases resources, sets ReadState to Closed
    ...
}
```

The following XML document contains an extract of an address book. It will be
used as a basis for various examples:

```
<?xml version='1.0' encoding="utf-8"?>
<addressbook owner="1">
    <person id="1">
        <firstname>Wolfgang</firstname>
        <lastname>Beer</lastname>
        <email>beer@uni-linz.at</email>
    </person>
    <person id="2">
        <firstname>Dietrich</firstname>
        <lastname>Birngruber</lastname>
        <email>birngruber@uni-linz.at</email>
    </person>
    <person id="3">
        <firstname>Hanspeter</firstname>
        <lastname>Moessenboeck</lastname>
        <email>moessenboeck@uni-linz.at</email>
    </person>
    <person id="4">
        <firstname>Albrecht</firstname>
        <lastname>Woess</lastname>
        <email>woess@uni-linz.at</email>
    </person>
</addressbook>
```

The method r.Read() of the class XmlReader reads the next XML element on each
successive call (for example, <person>, <firstname>, Wolfgang, ...). If the end of the
document is reached the method returns false. If an element has been read, so that

it is now in the read buffer, we can check whether it is an XML start element with the name name by using r.IsStartElement(name).

An element can only be read once, because the reading process is sequential. Elements and sub-elements can be skipped over by calling r.Skip(). The properties of the class **XmlReader** can be used to enquire about the element in the read buffer. The following example shows how all the last names from an XML address book can be read:

```
XmlTextReader r = new XmlTextReader("addressbook.xml");
while (r.Read()) {
    if (r.IsStartElement("lastname")) {      // is <lastname> element?
        r.Read();                            //  read the name
        Console.Write("{0}, ", r.Value);     // print name to console
    }
}
r.Close();
```

The following names are output to the console:

```
Beer, Birngruber, Moessenboeck, Woess,
```

4.7.3   Reading with a DOM Parser

A DOM parser (*Document Object Model* parser) allows an XML document to be read and transformed into a data structure in main memory. There the XML data can be manipulated conveniently. This is not possible with the sequential reading of an **XmlReader**. A disadvantage of the DOM data structure is its storage requirement which can lead to problems with large XML documents. Figure 4.16 shows an extract of the data structure that is constructed when loading the XML address book with a DOM parser. In this diagram the XML elements are shown as ellipses and their attributes as rectangles.

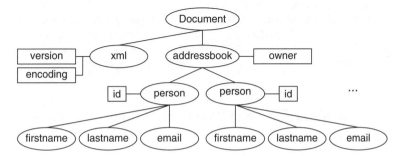

Figure 4.16 *Extract from the DOM data structure of the XML address book*

XmlNode

XML elements are represented by the abstract class XmlNode of the namespace System.Xml. It supports the traversing of DOM data structures as well as the insertion and deletion of elements. Here is an extract of its interface:

```
public abstract class XmlNode : ICloneable, IEnumerable, IXPathNavigable {
    //----- properties
    public abstract string Name { get; }
    public abstract string LocalName { get; }
    public abstract XmlNodeType NodeType { get; }
    public virtual string Value { get; set; }
    public virtual XmlAttributeCollection Attributes { get; }
    public virtual XmlDocument OwnerDocument { get; }
    public virtual bool IsReadOnly { get; }
    public virtual bool HasChildNodes { get; }
    public virtual XmlNodeList ChildNodes { get; }
    public virtual XmlNode FirstChild { get; }
    public virtual XmlNode LastChild { get; }
    public virtual XmlNode NextSibling { get; }    // returns the node following this one
    public virtual XmlNode PreviousSibling { get; }    // returns the note preceding this one
    public virtual XmlElement this[string name] { get; }    // indexer to access child elements
    public virtual XmlElement this[string localname, string ns] { get; }
    public virtual XmlNode ParentNode { get; }
    public virtual string Prefix { get; set; }
    public virtual string BaseURI { get; }    // where has this node been loaded from?
    public virtual string NamespaceURI { get; }
    ...
    //----- methods
    public virtual XmlNode AppendChild(XmlNode newChild);
    public virtual XmlNode PrependChild(XmlNode newChild);
    public virtual XmlNode InsertAfter(XmlNode newChild, XmlNode refChild);
    public virtual XmlNode InsertBefore(XmlNode newChild, XmlNode refChild);
    public virtual XmlNode RemoveChild(XmlNode oldChild);
    public virtual void RemoveAll();
    public XPathNavigator CreateNavigator();
    public XmlNodeList SelectNodes(string xpath);    // returns all nodes matching xpath
    public XmlNode SelectSingleNode(string xpath);    // returns first match for xpath
    public abstract void WriteContentTo(XmlWriter w);    // writes child nodes to w
    public abstract void WriteTo(XmlWriter w);    // writes this node to w
    ...
}
```

The different types of elements of a DOM data structure are given in the enumeration XmlNodeType:

```
public enum XmlNodeType {
    Attribute,              // XML attribute: id="1"
    CDATA,                  // text not recognized as markup: <![CDATA[escaped text]]>
    Comment,                // XML comment: <!-- my comment -->
    Document,               // contains the root element of the entire XML document
    DocumentFragment,       // element or subtree that is not actually a part of the document
    DocumentType,           // specifies the type of the XML document: <!DOCTYPE: ... >
    Element,                // XML element: <person>
    EndElement,             // end of an XML element: </person>
    EndEntity,              // end of an entity during processing of call to ResolveEntity
    Entity,                 // declaration of an XML entity: <!ENTITY ...>
    EntityReference,        // a reference to an XML entity: &num;
    None,                   // returned by XmlReader before first call to Read
    Notation,               // notation in a DTD: <!NOTATION ...>
    ProcessingInstruction,  // processing instruction: <?pi test ?>
    SignificantWhitespace,  // for example, whitespace in a xml:space="preserve" section
    Text,                   // text contents of an XML element
    Whitespace,             // whitespace between markup
    XmlDeclaration          // the xml declaration: <?xml version='1.0'?>
}
```

XmlDocument

The class XmlDocument is derived from XmlNode and it facilitates the loading and storing of XML documents. It also contains methods with which XML documents can be collected together. Here is an extract from its interface:

```
public class XmlDocument : XmlNode {
    //----- constructors
    public XmlDocument();
    ...
    //----- properties
    public XmlElement DocumentElement { get; }   // returns this document's root element
    public virtual XmlDocumentType DocumentType { get; }
    XmlResolver XmlResolver { set; }
    ...
    //----- methods
    public virtual void Load(Stream in);    // loads an XML document from a data stream
    public virtual void Load(string url);   // loads an XML document from a file
    public virtual void LoadXml(string data);   // creates an XML document for a string
    public virtual void Save(Stream out);   // save the XML document to the data stream
    public virtual void Save(string url);   // saves the XML document to a file
    public virtual XmlDeclaration CreateXmlDeclaration( string version, string encoding,
                                                        string standalone);
    public XmlElement CreateElement(string name);
    public XmlElement CreateElement(string qualifiedName, string namespaceURI);
    public virtual XmlElement CreateElement(string prefix, string lName, string nsURI);
    public virtual XmlText CreateTextNode(string text);
    public virtual XmlComment CreateComment(string data);
    ...
```

```
//----- events
public event XmlNodeChangedEventHandler NodeChanged;
public event XmlNodeChangedEventHandler NodeChanging;
public event XmlNodeChangedEventHandler NodeInserted;
public event XmlNodeChangedEventHandler NodeInserting;
public event XmlNodeChangedEventHandler NodeRemoved;
public event XmlNodeChangedEventHandler NodeRemoving;
}
```

The following example creates an XML document from a character string:

```
XmlDocument doc = new XmlDocument();
doc.LoadXml("<?xml version='1.0' encoding=\"utf-8\"?>" +
            "<addressbook owner=\"1\">" +
            "</addressbook>");
```

After the execution of this code sequence the framework of the XML document is in the object doc. The XML data can also be loaded from a file or from a URL:

```
doc.Load("addressbook.xml");
doc.Load("http://www.test.com/addressbook.xml");
```

If the parser encounters an error in the XML data it throws an XmlException. The method doc.Save(stream) can be used to store the XML data structure again. The call

```
doc.Save(Console.Out);
```

produces the following output on the console;

```
<?xml version="1.0" encoding="IBM437"?>
<addressbook owner="1">
</addressbook>
```

Creation of XML Documents

The class XmlDocument also facilitates constructing XML documents by hand. As an example of this we now wish to build an XML document for our address book. Firstly we declare a new XML document object:

```
XmlDocument doc = new XmlDocument();
```

In the next step we use doc.CreateDeclaration(version, encoding, standalone) to create the declaration part of the XML document. There we pass the XML version *1.0*. The encoding styles are defined in the class Encoding; we pass the value null to get the default encoding (IBM437) as above. For standalone we pass the value null. The XML declaration is inserted into the XML document:

```
XmlDeclaration decl = doc.CreateXmlDeclaration("1.0", null, null);
doc.AppendChild(decl);
```

Now we create the hierarchy for the XML elements. We begin with the root element addressbook according to its attribute owner, as well as sub-elements for persons, names and e-mail addresses. This is achieved by the following code:

```
//----- create the root element 'addressbook'
XmlElement rootElem = doc.CreateElement("addressbook");
rootElem.SetAttribute("owner", "1");
doc.AppendChild(rootElem);
//----- create a 'person' element
XmlElement person = doc.CreateElement("person");
person.SetAttribute("id", "1");
XmlElement e = doc.CreateElement("firstname");      // first name
e.AppendChild(doc.CreateTextNode("Wolfgang"));
person.AppendChild(e);
e = doc.CreateElement("lastname");                  // last name
e.AppendChild(doc.CreateTextNode("Beer"));
person.AppendChild(e);
e = doc.CreateElement("email");                     // e-mail address
e.AppendChild(doc.CreateTextNode("beer@uni-linz.at"));
person.AppendChild(e);
doc.DocumentElement.AppendChild(person);
//----- create further 'person' elements ...
...
//----- test output on the console
doc.Save(Console.Out);
```

This code fragment produces the following text on the console:

```
<?xml version="1.0" encoding="IBM437"?>
<addressbook owner="1">
   <person id="1">
      <firstname>Wolfgang</firstname>
      <lastname>Beer</lastname>
      <email>beer@uni-linz.at</email>
   </person>
</addressbook>
```

4.7.4 XPath

XPath (*XML Path Language*) is a notation for navigation in XML documents. It is possible with the help of a query syntax to select individual XML elements or a whole group of them. The exact definition of the XPath syntax is found in [XPath]. Example of XPath queries are:

- ❏ "*": returns all XML elements beneath the root elements.
- ❏ "/addressbook/*": returns all elements beneath the addressbook element.
- ❏ "/addressbook/person[1]": returns the person element with the index 1.
- ❏ "/addressbook/*/firstname": returns the firstname element of all persons.

The interface System.Xml.XPath.IXpathNavigable, implemented by XmlNode, contains methods that return an XPathNavigator:

```
public interface IXPathNavigable {
    XPathNavigator CreateNavigator();
}
```

The class System.Xml.XPath.XPathNavigator can carry out XPath queries. Here is an extract from its interface:

```
public abstract class XPathNavigator : ICloneable {
    //----- properties
    public abstract string Name { get; }
    public abstract string LocalName { get; }
    public abstract XPathNodeType NodeType { get; }
    public abstract string Value { get; }
    public abstract bool HasAttributes { get; }
    public abstract bool HasChildren { get; }

    ...

    //----- methods
    public virtual XPathNodeIterator Select(string xpath);
    public virtual XPathNodeIterator Select(XPathExpression expr);
    public virtual XPathExpression Compile(string xpath);
    public abstract bool MoveToNext();
    public abstract bool MoveToFirstChild();
    public abstract bool MoveToParent();

    ...

}
```

Next we print the first names of all persons in the address book to the console:

```
XmlDocument doc = new XmlDocument();
doc.Load("addressbook.xml");
XPathNavigator nav = doc.CreateNavigator();
XPathNodeIterator iterator = nav.Select("/addressbook/*/firstname");
while (iterator.MoveNext()) Console.WriteLine(iterator.Current.Value);
```

If the same query is to be carried out many times it is more efficient to translate this into an object of the class XPathExpression that can also be used by the method Select. To read out the e-mail addresses of all persons in the address book that have the first name *Wolfgang*, the following code can be used:

```
XPathExpression expr = nav.Compile("/addressbook/person[firstname='Wolfgang']/email");
iterator = nav.Select(expr);
while (iterator.MoveNext()) Console.WriteLine(iterator.Current.Value);
```

Instead of traversing the elements with an XPathNodeIterator we can also use the methods MoveToNext, MoveToFirstChild and MoveToParent of the class XPathNavigator. iterator.Current returns an XPathNavigator object that can be used for navigation. The properties of XPathNavigator can be used to find out about the characteristics of the sought node.

4.7.5 XSL Transformation

XSL (*eXtensible Stylesheet Language*) is a notation for compilation of so-called *stylesheets* that describe the formatting of the contents of XML documents. The namespace System.Xml.Xsl offers classes and interfaces for working with stylesheets.

Stylesheets are closely tied to the XPath standard described already. To navigate through XML documents an XPathNavigator must exist.

The class XslTransform can transform an XML document into another XML representation, with the help of stylesheets. However, XslTransform only works with data sources that implement the interface XPathNavigable. Only these data sources return an XPathNavigator, which is needed by the class XslTransform to carry out a transformation. The interface of the class XslTransform is defined as follows:

```
public class XslTransform {
    //----- constructor
    public XslTransform();
    //----- methods
    public void Load(string url);    // loads an XSLT stylesheet from a URL
    public void Transform(string infile, string outfile, XmlResolver resolver);
            // transforms XML file infile to outfile using an XmlResolver
    ... // + numerous overloads for the methods Load and Transform
}
```

The method Load can be used to load a stylesheet. Transform can be used to perform the transformation of the given XML data source into another XML representation. Since version 1.1 of the .NET Framework, an additional parameter of type System.Xml.XmlResolver is required for all Transform methods. All versions of the Transform method without this parameter have now been declared obsolete. The XmlResolver is used to resolve external XSLT resources referenced from within the stylesheet and process include or import elements found in the stylesheet.

The following example shows how the address book described above can be converted into an HTML representation. First, the following stylesheet (in the file addressbook.xsl) must be created:

```
<xsl:stylesheet version="1.0" xmlns:xsl="http://www.w3.org/1999/XSL/Transform">

<xsl:template match="/">
    <html>
        <head> <title>XML Address Book</title> </head>
        <body>
            <table border="3" cellspacing="10" cellpadding="5">
                <xsl:apply-templates/>
            </table>
        </body>
    </html>
</xsl:template>
```

```
<xsl:template match="addressbook">
   <xsl:apply-templates select="person"/>
</xsl:template>

<xsl:template match="person">
   <tr>
      <td> <xsl:value-of select="firstname"/> </td>
      <td> <b><xsl:value-of select="lastname"/></b> </td>
      <td> <xsl:value-of select="email"/> </td>
   </tr>
</xsl:template>

</xsl:stylesheet>
```

The following code fragment performs the transformation into an HTML representation according to the stylesheet.

```
XslTransform xt = new XslTransform();
xt.Load("addressbook.xsl");
xt.Transform("addressbook.xml", "addressbook.html", );
```

As result of this transformation a file addressbook.html is created. It contains the following HTML code:

```
<html>
   <head>
      <META http-equiv="Content-Type" content="text/html; charset=utf-8">
      <title>XML-AddressBook</title>
   </head>
   <body>
      <table border="3" cellspacing="10" cellpadding="5">
         <tr>
            <td>Wolfgang</td>
            <td><b>Beer</b></td>
            <td>beer@uni-linz.at</td>
         </tr>
         <tr>
            <td>Dietrich</td>
            <td><b>Birngruber</b></td>
            <td>birngruber@uni-linz.at</td>
         </tr>
         <tr>
            <td>Hanspeter</td> <td><b>Moessenboeck</b></td>
            <td>moessenboeck@uni-linz.at</td>
         </tr>
         <tr>
            <td>Albrecht</td> <td><b>Woess</b></td>
            <td>woess@uni-linz.at</td>
         </tr>
      </table>
   </body>
</html>
```

The web browser displays this document as shown in Figure 4.17.

Figure 4.17 *Representation of the generated HTML code by a browser*

4.8 Exercises

1. **IEnumerable.** Write a class that maintains a linked list of nodes each of which holds a char value. The class should implement IEnumerable so that users can traverse the list. Implement the list from scratch, that is, do not use ArrayList or any of the other list classes of the library.

2. **Sorting vectors.** Write a class Vector that represents a pair of double numbers (for example, (0.0, 0.0) or (10.5, 3.14)). Vector should also implement the interface IComparable so that an array of Vector objects can be sorted by length using the method Array.Sort(). The length of a vector (x, y) can be computed as Math.Sqrt(x*x + y*y).

3. **Calculator.** Implement a calculator that works according to the stack principle (using class Stack). It should have the following commands, which are entered in the console window together with any integer arguments that they require:

    Create creates a new calculator
    Put x   pushes the value x on to the stack
    Get   removes the topmost stack element and displays it on the console
    Add   adds the two topmost stack elements and pushes the result
    Sub   subtracts the two topmost stack elements and pushes the result
    Mul   multiplies the two topmost stack elements and pushes the result
    Div   divides the two topmost stack elements and pushes the result
    Flush   clears the stack

4. **Statistics.** Write a program that counts and displays the frequencies of all words in a text. The words should be kept in a hash table.

5. **Directories and files.** Write a method TreeDump(string path, int tabs), which lists the names of all files and directories recursively starting with the directory given in path. The parameter tabs denotes the number of tabulator characters by which every line for this directory should be indented.

6. **Reading a file.** Write a program that displays the contents of a text file on the console. The file name should be specified as a command-line argument.

7. **Copying a file.** Write a program that reads a file and copies it to some other file. Both file names should be specified as command-line arguments.

8. **Isolated storage.** Create an isolated storage area that can only be accessed by the user that is currently logged in. Write some data to this area and check the result using the *StoreAdm* tool.

9. **Isolated storage.** Discuss possible usages for isolated storage areas.

10. **Print server.** Write a program that simulates a print server as a separate thread. The print server should accept print jobs (i.e. the name of a job and the number of pages to print). Print jobs should arrive at random intervals (use the class System.Random for that) and should be stored in a Queue object. A second thread should process the queue and list the name and the number of pages for every job on the console. Note: you don't really have to print anything; you just have to simulate the processing of the jobs.

11. **Print server (extension).** Extend the previous example such that there are three printers (implemented as separate threads). The duration of a print job can be calculated by the number of pages to be printed and a printer-specific constant (e.g. 20 ms per page). Simulate the processing of a print job by putting the printer to sleep for the calculated amount of time (Thread.Sleep()). When a printer has finished a print job it should write the job name and the number of pages to the console and look for further print jobs in the queue.

12. **Dining philosophers.** Five philosophers are sitting at a round table and eat spaghetti. To the left and to the right of every philosopher there is a fork on the table, which they share with their neighbours.

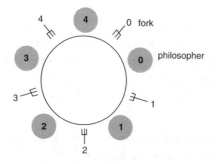

The philosophers do nothing else but think, eat, and then think again. If a philosopher wants to eat he has to pick up both forks. If one of his neighbours is holding the forks he has to wait until the neighbour has finished eating and has put the forks back on the table. Although the philosophers think and eat at different speeds it can happen that all of them get hungry at the same time. If every philosopher picks up the left fork first he will notice that his right fork is already in use. This would lead to a deadlock and the philosophers would starve.

Write a program that simulates this situation and guarantees each philosopher a fair chance of survival. Implement every philosopher as a thread and model their thinking and eating times with Thread.Sleep() and the class System.Random. Implement the forks as an array of bool with 5 elements. If fork i is in use fork[i] should be true otherwise false. Hint: the philosophers would appreciate it if you guarded access to the forks with a monitor.

13. **Domain names.** Read all IP addresses of the domain www.microsoft.com using the class Dns.

14. **Network resources.** Open the network resource http://dotnet.jku.at/index.html and display its HTML contents on the console.

15. **Time server.** Implement a network server that returns the time of day on request. Use sockets for the communication.

16. **Time server (parallel requests).** Extend your time server from the previous example so that it can accept requests from multiple clients concurrently. The server should be implemented as a thread that waits for requests and creates a new thread for every request. This new thread should handle the request.

17. **Dynamic loading.** Write a class TestReflection with the following two methods:

```
public void WithoutParameters() {...}
public bool WithParameters(string p1) {...}
```

Compile this class into an assembly TestReflection.dll and load it using Assembly.LoadFrom(). Display all relevant information about your assembly on the console.

18. **Reflection.** Use reflection to retrieve information about the two methods in TestReflection.dll. Display all relevant information on the console.

19. **Dynamic object creation.** Dynamically load TestReflection.dll and use reflection to create an object of the class TestReflection.

20. **Dynamic method call.** Dynamically load TestReflection.dll and call both of its methods using reflection.

21. **System.Reflection.Emit.** Study the documentation of System.Reflection.Emit in this book and in the online documentation of the .NET SDK and describe several scenarios in which one could use this namespace.

22. **Dynamic code generation.** Use the tool *ildasm* to inspect the CIL code of the methods WithoutParameters() and WithParameters() from the example above. Try to generate a similar assembly using System.Reflection.Emit.

23. **Color dialogs.** Study the class ColorDialog in the online documentation of the .NET SDK and use it to select a colour from the dialog and to display its value.

24. **Events.** Write a Windows form with three buttons labelled "red", "blue" and "green". A click on one of these buttons should set the background colour of the form according to the button's label.

25. **Pie charts.** Write a user control that takes a set of integer values and generates a pie chart in a Windows form. Use the BarChartControl from Section 4.6.4 as an example.

26. **Multiple document interface.** Write an MDI window which can contain other MDI windows as children. Every window should have a toolbar with a button to create a new child window and another button to close this window.

27. **SAX versus DOM.** Discuss the advantages and disadvantages of the SAX approach versus the DOM approach for reading XML data.

28. **SAX parser versus XmlReader.** What is the difference between the *push model* of a SAX parser (as used in the Java XML API) and the *pull model* of an XmlReader?

29. **XML files.** Write a class that maintains a list of tasks. Every task should consist of a date, a start time, an end time and a task description. The class should have a method Store(string fileName), which stores the list to an XML file. It should also have a method Load(string fileName), which reads the XML file and creates a new task list.

30. **SAX parsing.** Read the XML file that was generated in the previous example using a SAX parser. Accumulate the working times of all tasks in this file and display the result on the console.

31. **XSL transformations.** Write an XSL style sheet which maps the XML file that was generated in the example above to HTML. Use the class XslTransform to transform the XML file into an HTML file.

5 ADO.NET

Very many programs work with external data. ADO.NET is the part of the .NET Framework that handles structured data from databases, XML files and other sources.

The predecessor of ADO.NET is called ADO (*ActiveX Data Objects*). Readers familiar with ADO might expect ADO.NET to be nothing more than an adaptation of ADO for the .NET platform. That is correct to some extent, but here lies the potential of ADO.NET: it has not simply been adapted to fit into the .NET platform, but it is now strongly integrated within large parts of the .NET library. This integration spans different GUI frameworks, such as *web forms* (see Chapter 6), *Mobile Forms* and *Win Forms* (see Section 4.6), as well as distributed *web services* (see Chapter 7).

This chapter deals with accessing databases and XML files with ADO.NET.

5.1 Overview

ADO.NET constitutes one of a number of layers for accessing data sources in Microsoft's architecture (see Figure 5.1). It is built on top of OLE DB (*Object Linking and Embedding DataBase*), which abstracts from the concrete data source. OLE DB comprises a number of interfaces and components for accessing structured data. ODBC (*Open DataBase Connectivity*) was one of the predecessors of OLE DB, allowing only access to database systems, while OLE DB extended this functionality to different kinds of data sources, such as mainframes or XML files.

ADO.NET simplifies the access to OLE DB as well as other database-specific access protocols such as ODBC. ADO.NET works as a link between .NET applications and OLE DB, ODBC and other data providers.

ODBC, OLE DB and ADO are part of the MDAC library (*Microsoft Data Access Components*). In order to use ADO.NET, the MDAC library version 2.7 (or higher) has to be installed. This is done automatically during the installation of the .NET SDK.

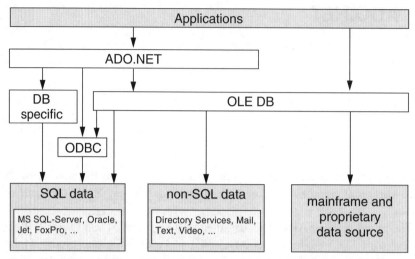

Figure 5.1 *Microsoft's data access architecture and parts of the MDAC Library*

All libraries for data access (such as ADO.NET) exhibit a similar architecture. Their common task is to connect the realm of (object-oriented) software development with the realm of (set-oriented) data storage. This is shown schematically in Figure 5.2.

At one level we find the applications, also known as *data consumers*. They retrieve data stored in data sources. Depending on the programming language employed, different programming models are applied by the consumers. An example is the object-oriented model, where data is manipulated in form of classes (see Section 2.8) or collections (see Section 4.1).

On another level we find database systems and other data sources, where data is stored in a structured or set-oriented way (for example, in tables). Those are known as *managed providers*. Such database systems usually guarantee the so-called *ACID properties* (*Atomicity, Consistency, Isolation, Durability*) [ElNa00]. Tabular data is defined and manipulated with the language SQL (*Structured Query Language*). There are efforts to standardize SQL, for example, ANSI-SQL92 [MeSi92]. However, in practice database providers often choose to use proprietary SQL dialects for their products.

There are two principal tasks for ADO.NET: firstly, it facilitates the definition and manipulation of data independent of the kind and location of its source. Secondly, it supports the transformation of .NET data types into data-source-specific types. ADO.NET allows us to query data with SQL instructions, such as SELECT, UPDATE and DELETE, and also supports SQL's data definition facilities (CREATE TABLE, DROP TABLE, etc.) to define database schemas.

This chapter primarily looks at ADO.NET from a data consumer's perspective. The data provider level is more relevant for database producers, who need to be able to address different data sources with ADO.NET. However, application developers should have a basic understanding of the data provider level—at least enough to be able to choose the appropriate data source and access mode for their applications.

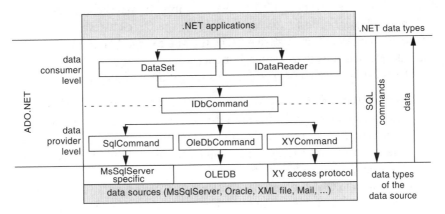

Figure 5.2 *Schematic architecture of ADO.NET*

ADO.NET supports two basic access modes: *connection-oriented* access with the interface IDataReader and *connectionless* access with the class DataSet (see Figure 5.2). IDataReader is a database cursor. DataSet was introduced with ADO.NET and is an in-memory representation of selected data from possibly different data sources.

An access itself is represented by a command object of type IDbCommand. The implementations of the IDbCommand interface take care of the appropriate physical access to OLE DB or some proprietary access protocol, in order to query, for example, the data from a customer table of an SQL database.

Besides the access mode, we must also choose the appropriate data provider implementation. ADO.NET offers several implementations: two rather general implementations for accessing OLE DB-compatible data sources and ODBC-compatible databases, and a number of implementations that are optimized for certain database servers. The .NET SDK contains data provider implementations for database servers from Oracle and for the Microsoft SQL Server Version 7.0 or higher (we will refer to it as MsSqlServer from now on). Using the general OLE DB-capable implementation makes the .NET application independent of the selected data source, whereas using one of the implementations for MsSqlServer or Oracle binds the application to these products. We expect still further implementations of other data providers to become available for ADO.NET in the future. These implementations can be downloaded from Microsoft's web site [MSData] and [MSDL]. It is also possible to access ODBC-compatible data sources or Oracle databases via OLD DB. Accessing ODBC via OLE DB requires an "OLE DB for ODBC" data provider, which is already part of the MDAC library.

The classes and interfaces in the assembly System.Data.dll implement the ADO.NET architecture and provide some data provider implementations, whereas the types in the assembly System.Xml.dll are responsible for exchanging data via XML (see Section 4.7). In the assembly System.Data.OracleClient.dll we find the implementation for data providers for the Oracle database server and in the assembly System.Data.SqlServerCE.dll the one for the MsSqlServer version for smart devices (such as PDAs and cellphones).

The assembly System.Data.dll contains the following namespaces:

❑ System.Data is the core of the ADO.NET framework. This namespace contains classes and interfaces for accessing various data sources in a connectionless or connection-oriented manner. Consumers who want to be independent of the data source implementation should use these interfaces for accessing data defined here.

❑ System.Data.OleDb offers the most general implementation of a data provider. This namespace contains types for accessing OLE DB-compatible data sources, transmitting SQL commands and reading their results. Some of these types extend types from System.Data or System.Data.Common.

❑ System.Data.SqlClient offers a special data provider implementation. This namespace contains types for accessing MsSqlServer databases, transmitting SQL commands and reading their results. The types from System.Data.SqlClient are similar to those from System.Data.OleDb, except that they are optimized for use with MS SQL Server 7.0 and its successors.

❑ System.Data.Common contains types that are used or extended by data providers and their implementations.

❑ System.Data.SqlTypes contains special types for the MsSqlServer implementation. With these types, MsSqlServer data types can be converted to .NET data types and vice versa. The namespace System.Data has implementations for more general mappings of SQL data types (e.g. varchar) to .NET data types (e.g. string).

❑ System.Data.Odbc offers a special implementation for ODBC-compatible data sources.

In the following sections we will discuss in more detail some of the classes and interfaces from the assembly System.Data.dll, which are used for creating connections and executing SQL statements.

5.2 Connection-oriented and Connectionless Access

System.Data.IDataReader and System.Data.DataSet allow the programmer to access data from various data sources. Implementations of the interface IDataReader are used for connection-oriented access, whereas the class DataSet is used for connectionless access.

A *connection-oriented* access keeps the connection to the database alive. An IDataReader represents a kind of database cursor for reading data in one direction. Like an iterator, it steps through a table row by row. It keeps the connection to the database open during the entire reading process. Therefore any modifications of the data in the data source done by other applications become immediately visible at the next reading step. If we move the cursor (IDataReader) in our .NET application to the next packet of data, it will be read from the database.

This mode of access is intended for applications which require up-to-date data for each access and which take only very little time for processing the data between consecutive accesses. ADO.NET offers various implementations for IDataReader.

With a *connectionless* access, all data is read from the data source in one step and is stored in a DataSet object. Before further processing of the data in the .NET application, the connection to the database is closed. Thus the data in the DataSet is a "snapshot", reflecting the momentary state of the database. It may already differ from the actual database immediately after the DataSet has been filled, because another application may have modified the original data in the meantime. Changes to the data in the DataSet will not be reflected in the database and vice versa. If we want to carry over our modification of the data in the DataSet into the database, we must open a connection to the database again and explicitly update the data in the underlying database.

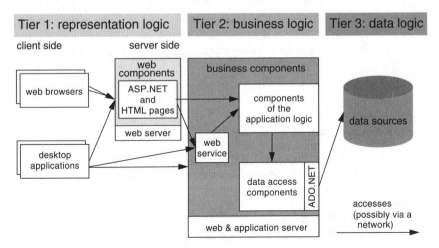

Figure 5.3 *Three-tier architecture of distributed applications*

The connectionless mode of access is mainly intended for distributed scenarios that operate without direct attachment to the data source and where scalability plays an important role. Applications of this kind typically possess a three-tier architecture as shown in Figure 5.3. Tier 1 is responsible for the user interface and can run at the server (e.g. with web forms) or at the client (e.g. with Windows forms). The second tier contains components implementing the application logic and the access to the database. Examples for the application logic and its business processes are parallel queries for goods in stock, ordering in a web shop or the log-in to a computer system. Data consistency is achieved by having all applications, no matter whether web or desktop applications, manipulate the data only via the second tier and by preventing them from directly accessing the data source in the third tier. Examples of such distributed applications are ASP.NET applications (see Chapter 6) or web services (see Chapter 7).

The following example should illustrate the differences between connection-less and connection-oriented access. Assume that 500 users simultaneously access data storage for an extended period of time. In the case of connection-oriented access this results in 500 connections to the data source being open at the same time and active for a long time—not a very efficient solution. Connectionless accesses, on the other hand, only require *at most* 500 connections being open for only a *short* period of time, while the data is transferred to the second tier and buffered in a DataSet there. In this way concurrent data accesses do not lead to permanent connections to the database.

5.3   Connection-oriented Access

An ADO.NET application uses at least the namespace System.Data and one namespace of a data provider implementation. The pseudo-code fragment shown below illustrates the structure of a typical connection-oriented ADO.NET application. After opening a connection to the data source, we can read and manipulate the data. At the end, we must release the resources used, such as IDataReader.

```
using System.Data;
...
DECLARE CONNECTION;
try {   // optional
    REQUEST CONNECTION TO DATABASE;
    EXECUTE SQL STATEMENTS;
    RELEASE CREATED RESOURCES;
} catch ( Exception ) { HANDLE ERROR OR FORWARD EXCEPTION TO CALLER;
} finally {
    try {   // optional
        CLOSE CONNECTION;
    } catch ( Exception ) { HANDLE ERROR; }
}
```

In .NET we are not forced to handle exceptions, but we should be aware that any unhandled exception will lead to a program crash. That is why we marked the try-statements in the pseudo code with // *optional*. However, in ADO.NET applications various exceptions can occur. For example, the connection to the data source could break down, the data source could not be found, etc. Therefore it makes sense to react to these exceptions.

ADO.NET has two base classes for exceptions that mainly occur when using DataSets (see Section 5.4): System.Data.DataException and System.Data.DBConcurrencyException. The latter has no subclasses and can occur when synchronizing a DataSet with a database. The subclasses of DataException in the namespace System.Data are listed here:

ConstraintException   NoNullAllowedException
DeletedRowInaccessibleException   ReadOnlyException
DuplicateNameException   RowNotInTableException
InRowChangingEventException   StrongTypingException
InvalidConstraintException   TypedDataSetGeneratorException
InvalidExpressionException   VersionNotFoundException
MissingPrimaryKeyException

Data provider implementations often provide their own exceptions, such as System.Data.SqlClient.SqlException or System.Data.OleDbException. These do not necessarily extend System.Data.DataException.

Before we go further into the types for the connection-oriented access, we will look at an example that opens a connection to a database, reads the rows of a table and outputs them to the console.

The .NET-SDK contains a developer version of MsSqlServer (MSDE) with some sample databases, such as the *Northwind database* which holds data for a food store. In the following example the information about the employees of the Northwind company is retrieved from the database and printed to the console.

```
using System; using System.Data; using System.Data.OleDb;

public class EmployeeReader {
    public static void Main () {
        //----- open connection to Northwind database on the local machine
        Console.WriteLine("Opening connection");
        string conStr =   "provider=SQLOLEDB; data source=127.0.0.1\\NetSDK; " +
                          "initial catalog=Northwind; user id=sa; password=;";
        IDbConnection con = null;   // declare connection
        try {
            con = new OleDbConnection(conStr);
            con.Open();   // request connection to database
            //----- build SQL command to query ID and names of all employees
            IDbCommand cmd = con.CreateCommand(); // create an OleDbCommand object
            cmd.CommandText = "SELECT EmployeeID, LastName, FirstName " +
                            "FROM Employees";
```

```
        //----- execute SQL command; it yields an OleDbDataReader object
        IDataReader reader = cmd.ExecuteReader();
        object[] dataRow = new object[reader.FieldCount];
        //----- read data row by row and process them
        while (reader.Read()) {   // as long as more data are available
            int cols = reader.GetValues(dataRow);   // actual reading
            for (int i = 0; i < cols; i++) Console.Write("| {0} " , dataRow[i]);
            Console.WriteLine();
        }
        //----- close reader
        reader.Close();
    } catch (Exception e) {  // handle error
        Console.WriteLine(e.Message);
    } finally {
        try {
            if (con != null) con.Close();   // close connection
        } catch (Exception e) { Console.WriteLine(e.Message); }
    }
  }
}
```

This example demonstrates three basic elements of connection-oriented accesses:

- ❏ a connection to the database (IDbConnection),
- ❏ one or more command objects (IDbCommand) that wrap the SQL statements to be executed,
- ❏ an IDataReader object for reading the results of a SELECT statement.

In the following sections we will discusses these three elements in more detail.

5.3.1   Connections

Before we can access data via a command object, we must open a connection to the data source. The kind of connection can range from a simple file access, to a connection to a database system on a remote machine. The different types of connections are abstracted by the interface System.Data.IDbConnection, which is partly shown below. Two implementations of this interface come with ADO.NET: System.Data.SqlClient.SqlConnection for connecting to an MsSqlServer and System.Data.OleDb.OleDbConnection for an OLE DB-compatible data source.

```
public interface IDbConnection : IDisposable {
    //----- properties
    string ConnectionString { get; set; }
    int ConnectionTimeout { get; }
    ...
```

```
//----- methods
IDbTransaction BeginTransaction();
IDbTransaction BeginTransaction(IsolationLevel lvl);
void Close();
void Open();
IDbCommand CreateCommand();

...

}
```

Calling Open establishes a connection. Because this can become a time-intensive matter, it makes sense to share one connection to the same data source among several command objects in order to speed up database accesses. A so-called *connection pool* manages connections. When establishing a connection, ADO.NET checks whether a connection with the same name (property ConnectionString) already exists in the connection pool. If this is the case, the connection will be used, otherwise a new connection will be created.

The method Close closes the current connection and returns it to the connection pool, if this is being used. A connection should always be closed as soon as it is no longer needed. Trying to close a connection that has not been opened will not cause an exception. That means that we can call Close more than once.

IDbConnection extends the interface System.IDisposable, which contains the method void Dispose(). IDisposable marks types that manage resources that are not under the control of the CLR (*unmanaged resources*). With the Dispose method we can free those resources. For some types it appears more intuitive to close them than to dispose of them. Such types can offer an additional Close method that should then invoke Dispose. The interested reader can find a thorough discussion of the *dispose pattern* and IDisposable in [Rich00b] or [Rich02].

A connection is identified by its name. The name consists of several parts that depend on the data provider implementation. These parts configure the connection. In the example above we use the OLE DB implementation to connect to an MsSqlServer database on the local machine. If the Northwind database was in an ORACLE database system, all we would need to change is the name of the connection. Thanks to OLE DB we need *not* change the SQL statements. The connection name in the above example looks like this:

```
"provider=SQLOLEDB; data source=127.0.0.1\\NetSDK; "
"initial catalog=Northwind; user id=sa; password=; "
```

It contains the following parts which are each terminated by a semicolon:

❑ provider specifies the name of the OLE DB implementation for the access from OLE DB to the actual database. SQLOLEDB is the name of the OLEDB driver for the MsSqlServer. The field provider is only required for OleDbConnection and not for SqlConnection.

❑ data source describes the IP address or the DNS name of the database server. Here NetSDK is the name of the database server on the local machine. The local host is specified by the IP number 127.0.0.1 or with (local).

❑ inital catalog holds the name of the database.

❑ user id specifies the user. In this example we use the standard administrator "sa" which, for obvious reasons, should not be used in practice.

❑ password contains the password used.

In the ConnectionString property of an OleDbConnection or an SqlConnection to an MsSqlServer we can specify further configuration attributes (such as Connection Time or Packet Size). These are described in more detail in the .NET online documentation. Here we show some more examples for connection names:

```
"provider=Microsoft.Jet.OLEDB.4.0; data source=c:\bin\LocalAccess40.mdb;"
```

```
"provider=MSDAORA; data source=ORACLE8i7; user id=OLEDB; password=OLEDB;"
```

```
"data source=(local)\\NetSDK; initial catalog=MyDB; user id=sa;
  pooling=false; Integrated Security=SSPI;"
```

The first two examples are names for OLE DB connections: the first to an MS Access database and the second to an Oracle8i database. For any OLE DB connection we must at least specify the fields provider and data source. The last example specifies a connection name for an MsSqlServer connection (System.Data.SqlClient.SqlConnection) to the local database MyDB. We use pooling=false to advise ADO.NET not to add this SqlConnection to the connection pool and not to look for it there, but always to create a new connection. Integrated Security is an MsSqlServer-specific attribute which describes the method of authorization to use.

The property ConnectionTimeout of IDbConnection determines the maximum period of time in seconds that establishing a new connection may take. If the connection cannot be established within this time period after Open() has been invoked, a corresponding exception will be thrown. By setting this property to 0 we indicate that we want to wait for an arbitrary amount of time. However, we do not recommend using this value, to avoid the situation arising in exceptional circumstances that your program never finishes waiting (for example, when the server cannot be found). We can set the value of ConnectionTimeout in the ConnectionString, for example:

```
"data source=(local)\\NetSDK; initial catalog=MyDB; user id=sa; connection timeout=20;"
```

The IDbConnection method CreateCommand creates a command object that can then be executed via the connection. Section 5.3.3 deals with command objects.

The overloaded method BeginTransaction initiates a user-defined transaction and creates an ADO.NET transaction object. But more on transactions in the next section.

5.3.2 Transactions, Isolation Levels, and Deadlocks

Many database accesses consist of several elementary operations. For example, when transferring money from one bank account to another we must withdraw the desired amount from the first account and then deposit it to the second. In order to keep the data consistent, we must either carry out both steps completely or not at all. We call such a sequence of steps that leads a database from one consistent state into a new consistent state, a *transaction* (see also [LBK01]).

In ADO.NET, there are two kinds of transactions: automatic and custom. *Automatic transactions* make sure that the database carries out each SQL statement within a separate transaction. For *custom transactions* the user can determine the isolation level as well as the beginning and end of the transaction. In this way a sequence of SQL statements (for example, for withdrawing and depositing money from and to the corresponding accounts) can be combined into a single transaction. Correspondingly, IDbConnection offers the method BeginTransaction to start a transaction. The connection must already be open. Depending on the data provider implementation BeginTransaction can start one or more transactions in parallel.

The transaction itself is represented by an object of the interface type System.Data.IDbTransaction. IDbTransaction offers methods to complete a transaction successfully (Commit) or abort a transaction (Rollback). An unfinished transaction will also be aborted if its database connection is shut down with Close.

```
public interface IDbTransaction : IDisposable {
    //----- properties
    IDbConnection Connection  { get; }
    IsolationLevel IsolationLevel  { get; }
    //----- methods
    void Commit();
    void Rollback();
}
```

Command objects encapsulate SQL statements and can be combined into a transaction by setting the property Transaction. If the property Transaction is not set, the SQL statement of the command object is carried out within an automatic transaction.

In the following example we delete a certain order from the Northwind database. The header of the order is in the table Orders and the ordered articles in the table [Order Details]. For the MsSqlServer, names of database objects containing spaces must be enclosed in square brackets ([...]). Deleting an entire order requires two DELETE statements combined to form a custom transaction. If one of the DELETE statements fails, neither the header nor the details of the order will be deleted (see trans.Rollback).

```
SqlConnection con = new SqlConnection(connStr);
IDbTransaction trans = null;
try {
   con.Open ();
   //----- create command object
   IDbCommand cmd = con.CreateCommand();
   //----- start a custom transaction with two SQL statements
   trans = con.BeginTransaction(IsolationLevel.ReadCommitted);
   cmd.Transaction = trans;
   // delete the order
   cmd.CommandText = "DELETE [Order Details] WHERE OrderID = 10258";
   cmd.ExecuteNonQuery();
   // delete the header of the order
   cmd.CommandText = "DELETE Orders WHERE OrderID = 10258";
   cmd.ExecuteNonQuery();
   trans.Commit();   // complete transaction successfully
} catch (Exception e) {
   if (trans != null) trans.Rollback();   // abort transaction and rollback all modifications
   Console.WriteLine(e.ToString());
} finally {
   try { con.Close(); } catch (Exception e) { Console.WriteLine(e.ToString()); }
}
```

On starting the transaction with BeginTransaction(IsolationLevel.ReadCommitted)
we provided an isolation level, which is described in the next section.

Isolation levels

The ACID property *isolation* determines that transactions running in parallel
are isolated and cannot interfere with each other. Thus the result of concurrent
transactions should be same as the result of the same transactions carried out
sequentially.

A custom transaction can use different isolation levels given by the enumeration System.Data.IsolationLevel (see Table 5.1).

Using locks is one way of implementing isolation levels. In order to keep data
consistent when different transactions access the same data at the same time, we
can use locks to synchronize the read and write accesses. Locks are usually maintained until a transaction is terminated by a Commit or a Rollback. Locks prevent
concurrent accesses, but at the same time decrease performance. We can distinguish between read and write locks. For SELECT statements we can use a read
lock, because we only want to read the data. Write locks are for INSERT, UPDATE
and DELETE statements. At the start of a transaction, locks are requested for all
the objects that are accessed by the SQL statements of the transaction. The following questions arise:

❑ What should be locked (entire table, single row)?

❑ When should the locks be released (at the end of the transaction or immediately after executing the SQL statement)?

So-called locking protocols determine the possible options. These are described by the ANSI Standard *isolation levels* (see [LBK01]). The developer cannot directly request locks, but only determines a certain isolation level when starting the transaction.

We can distinguish the isolation levels by the phenomena or anomalies that can occur. These phenomena are *dirty reads, phantom rows* and *repeatable reads*. Isolation levels are sorted strictly monotonically: phenomena that are prevented in one level can no longer occur in a higher level. The levels are (lowest to highest): *read uncommitted, read committed, repeatable read* and *serializable* (see Table 5.1). A higher level decreases the chance that a transaction aborts because of write/write or write/read conflicts. But at the same time this decreases the possibility of executing transactions in parallel and thus decreases performance. By selecting an isolation level the programmer determines the degree of parallelism for transactions and which phenomena may or may not occur.

Isolation levels can be implemented in various ways, mostly with locks. Each level uses read locks in a different way (for example, regarding the duration of the lock or what actually gets locked). Write locks are released at the end of the transactions in all isolation levels.

Let us look at an example: transaction T1 contains the following SELECT statement to read all Peter's accounts.

```
SELECT * FROM Accounts WHERE Name = 'Peter';
```

Here the question arises as to whether to lock the entire table Accounts which has more than 10,000 tuples (rows) when only a few will be read, or whether only the affected tuples should be locked. Should we lock anything at all?

If we only lock the affected tuples, *phantom rows* can occur. They can be caused by another transaction T2. Let us assume that T1 locks only the tuples that are affected by the WHERE condition and not the entire table. In this case T2 can insert a new account for Peter, even before T1 terminates. *Repeatable read* describes another phenomenon and means only that throughout the whole transaction repeated reads always yield the same data. So, in order to see possible modifications executed concurrently with T1 (for example, deleting Peter's accounts), T1 has to terminate and then run again. If the same query can yield different results during the same transactions, we call this *non-repeatable reads*.

In ADO.NET, creating the transaction with BeginTransaction also determines the isolation level. Different transactions can thus have different isolation levels. If setting an isolation level requests a lock and this is granted, the statements can begin to modify or read the data. If the lock is not granted, the statements must wait until it is granted (unless isolation level ReadCommitted is chosen) or until a waiting period has elapsed (see command property CommandTimeout in Section 5.3.3).

Table 5.1 lists the most important isolation levels with a short description.

Table 5.1 *The most important isolation levels for transactions*

IsolationLevel	Description
ReadUncommitted	A transaction can read any data, even data that has been written, locked and not yet committed by another transaction.
	Thus the data read can be in an inconsistent state (*dirty read*).
ReadCommitted	This is the default setting of the SQL Server. It guarantees that data that has been written by a transaction T1 can only be read by another transaction T2 after T1 has terminated. However, it is permissible for T1 and T2 to modify different rows of the same table at the same time.
	Dirty Reads can no longer occur. But phantom rows cannot be avoided and the same SELECT statement can produce different results (*non-repeatable read*).
RepeatableRead	This isolation level is a little more restrictive than ReadCommitted. It guarantees that within a transaction the same query will always yield the same result, independent of modifications by other transactions. All rows affected by a query are reserved (locked) for the transaction T1. Other transactions cannot modify these rows, but they can insert new rows. When repeating the query these new rows will still not be selected (*phantom rows*).
	Non-repeatable reads are no longer possible. Phantom rows are not avoided, but they do not affect the result of reads.
Serializable	This is the most restrictive isolation level. It serializes the accesses of multiple transactions to the same data. The transactions may not access the data simultaneously, but only sequentially. This isolation level is also used when filling DataSets (see Section 5.4).
	Phantom rows can no longer occur.

Deadlocks

Let us assume that two transactions access certain data at the same time and both want to modify it. If the SQL statements of these transactions request locks, they can possibly block each other and so a *deadlock* will occur. Figure 5.4 illustrates such a situation.

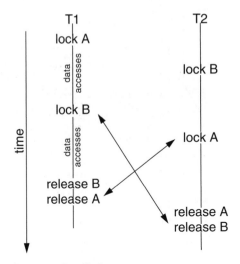

Figure 5.4 *Deadlock*

Transactions T1 and T2 start at the same time. Early on, an SQL statement in T1 locks table A and one in T2 locks table B. If T1 now requests a lock for B or T2 a lock for A, a deadlock occurs.

If T2 did not request a lock on A, there would be no deadlock, because the SQL statement (that is, the ADO.NET command object) in T1 would wait until B is released at the end of T2. In this case only T1 would be blocked temporarily.

Most database systems detect deadlocks and react to them differently. By setting timeouts for SQL commands we can at least avoid waiting infinitely long for the release of locked data. However, ADO.NET does not define how to react to a transaction or a command that is not executed. This is the responsibility of the application developer.

5.3.3   SQL Command Objects

In ADO.NET, SQL statements are represented by command objects that implement the interface System.Data.IDbCommand. A command object contains either an SQL statement or a database procedure (*stored procedure*) that it executes on the database. As mentioned in the previous section, multiple command objects can share a connection and can be combined to form a transaction.

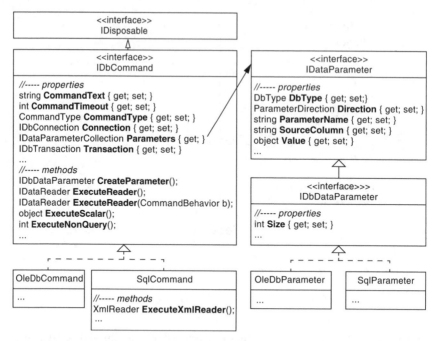

Figure 5.5 *Overview of IDbCommand and IDataParameter*

IDbCommand contains various Execute methods for read (SELECT) and write accesses (INSERT, UPDATE, DELETE, DROP TABLE). Figure 5.5 shows the most important properties for configuring command objects, as well as the various Execute methods for executing a command and the method CreateParameter for creating parameters. We will now explain these properties and Execute methods with some examples. Later on we will devote a separate subsection to parameters. The Execute methods require an open connection and correct syntax of the SQL statements.

```
cmd.CommandText = "UPDATE Employees SET City = 'Seattle' WHERE EmployeeID=8";
```

The property CommandText represents the SQL statement that the Execute method will execute at the data source. CommandText can consist of any SQL statement (including those for manipulating the database schema, for example CREATE TABLE), the name of a stored procedure, or even just the name of a table of the database. The property CommandType distinguishes between different kinds of CommandText.

```
CommandType t = cmd.CommandType;
cmd.CommandType = CommandType.Text;
cmd.CommandType = CommandType.StoredProcedure;
```

This property encodes the type of the command with the enumeration CommandType. The default setting Text means that the property CommandText holds an SQL statement, whereas CommandType.StoredProcedure indicates that it contains the name of a stored procedure. If we want to retrieve the entire contents of one or more tables, we can set CommandType to TableDirect and CommandText to the names of those tables. So far TableDirect is only supported by data provider implementations for the MsSqlServer.

```
IDataParameterCollection params = cmd.Parameters;
```

returns the input and output parameters of the command. The parameters themselves are described by objects of the interface IDataParameter. At the end of this section we show an example of the use of parameters.

```
IDbTransaction trans = cmd.Transaction;
cmd.Transaction = trans;
```

The property Transaction represents the custom transaction (see Section 5.3.1) to which the command belongs.

```
int sec = cmd.CommandTimeout;
cmd.CommandTimeout = 30;
```

CommandTimeout gives the maximum period of time in seconds that the execution of the command may take. The setting here is 30 seconds.

```
IDataReader reader = cmd.ExecuteReader();
IDataReader reader = cmd.ExecuteReader(CommandBehavior.CloseConnection);
IDataReader reader = cmd.ExecuteReader(CommandBehavior.SchemaOnly);
```

The ExecuteReader methods execute a SELECT command and return an IDataReader to iterate over the result. The enumeration CommandBehavior determines additional properties of the command, for example whether the connection should be closed together with the IDataReader (CloseConnection) or whether schema information (i.e. information about the columns of the table) should be returned instead of data (SchemaOnly). Besides CloseConnection and SchemaOnly the enumeration type CommandBehavior also offers Default, KeyInfo, SequentialAccess, SingleResult, and SingleRow.

```
int affectedRows = cmd.ExecuteNonQuery();
```

executes a write access (such as INSERT, UPDATE, DELETE, CREATE TABLE) and returns the number of affected rows. For SQL statements that do not affect any rows (e.g. CREATE TABLE), -1 is returned. In case of an error a System.InvalidOperationException is thrown.

```
object o = cmd.ExecuteScalar();
```

executes a aggregation function (e.g. count(*)) in the context of a SELECT command. In the following example we determine the number of rows in the employees table.

```
IDbCommand cmd = new SqlCommand("SELECT count(*) FROM Employees",
                                new SqlConnection(connStr));
cmd.Connection.Open();
int count = (int) cmd.ExecuteScalar();
cmd.Connection.Close();
```

MsSqlServer databases offer the proprietary SQL extensions FOR XML AUTO, FOR XML RAW and FOR XML EXPLICIT to receive the results of SELECT queries as XML data streams. The class SqlCommand supports this functionality with the method ExecuteXmlReader. The following example writes the information about employees of Northwind to the console in an XML format.

```
SqlConnection con = new SqlConnection(connStr);
con.Open ();
SqlCommand cmd = new SqlCommand( "SELECT EmployeeID, LastName, FirstName "
                                + "FROM Employees FOR XML AUTO", con);
System.Xml.XmlReader reader = cmd.ExecuteXmlReader();
while (reader.Read()) Console.WriteLine(reader.ReadOuterXml ());
reader.Close();
con.Close();
```

At the console the result could look like this:

```
<Employees EmployeeID="1" LastName="Davolio" FirstName="Nancy"/>
<Employees EmployeeID="3" LastName="Leverling" FirstName="Janet"/>
<Employees EmployeeID="5" LastName="Buchanan" FirstName="Steven"/>
...
```

Parameters

SQL statements and stored procedures use input and output parameters that can be set and retrieved via the property Parameters of IDbCommand (see Figure 5.5). The actual transfer of the parameters takes place when the command is executed. Then OLE DB types and MsSqlServer types (see enumerations System.Data.OleDb.OleDbType and System.Data.SqlDbType) are converted into .NET types (string, System.Int16, etc.), as illustrated in Table 5.2 at the end of this section. The IDataParameter property DbType contains the type of the corresponding data source.

The IDbCommand property Parameters is a collection of IDataParameter objects that represent the input and output parameters of the command objects. In the property CommandText placeholders identify the parameters as demonstrated in the next example. The format of such placeholders depends on the data provider implementation. MsSqlServer data provider implementations begin with a "@" (e.g. "@ID"). The placeholder symbol for OLE DB data provider implementations is a "?". The position of the placeholder in the CommandText corresponds to the index of the parameter in the Parameters collection. For example, the third occurrence of "?" refers to the third parameter in the property Parameters.

```
// CommandText for a data provider implementation for the MsSqlServer
cmd.CommandText = "DELETE FROM Employees WHERE EmployeeID = @ID";
// CommandText for a data provider implementation for OLE DB
cmd.CommandText = "DELETE FROM Employees WHERE EmployeeID = ?";
```

Stored procedures do not need explicit parameter names. Here the position of the actual parameters maps to the formal parameters. A call to cmd.Parameters.Add adds a IDataParameter object.

The following statement adds a System.Data.SqlClient.SqlParameter object with the name "@ID" and the MsSqlServer type bigint to the IDbCommand property Parameters:

```
cmd.Parameters.Add("@ID", new SqlParameter("@ID", SqlDbType.BigInt));
```

Under OLE DB, we add a parameter in the following way. This parameter could then be displayed as in the above DELETE statement. The parameter name "anID" is an arbitrary choice, defined only so that we can later access it via the statements cmd.Parameters[0] as well as cmd.Parameters["anID"].

```
cmd.Parameters.Add(new OleDbParameter("anID", OleDbType.BigInt));
```

@ID is an input parameter. The IDataParameter property Direction determines the direction (input or output) of the parameter. The default setting is ParameterDirection.Input which indicates an input parameter. Besides Input, the enumeration ParameterDirection contains Output (output parameter), ReturnValue (return value of a function or stored procedure), and InputOutput (input as well as output parameter).

With the IDataParameter property Value we can set the value of the input parameter @ID before the invocation, as shown in the following statement:

```
((IDataParameter) cmd.Parameters["@ID"]).Value = 1234;
```

The next example uses a table Contact that contains entries similar to a phone book, such as ID, FirstName, Name, NickName, EMail and Phone. The primary key is ID and its value is assigned automatically by the database. The example uses the MsSqlServer data provider implementation and adds a new row of data. We also show how to work with parameters. The method NewInsertCmd returns the INSERT command object and defines the formal SQL parameters. Finally, the method Execute inserts the new row of data. The string cmdStr in NewInsertCmd defines two SQL statements: the first for adding the new data row and the second for reading the assigned value of the primary key.

```
using System;
using System.Data;
using System.Data.SqlClient;

public class InsertContacts {

    static SqlConnection NewConnection() {
        return new SqlConnection("data source=(local)\\NetSDK; initial catalog=NETBOOK;
                                 user id=sa;");
    }

    SqlCommand NewInsertCmd() {
        string cmdStr =
            "INSERT INTO Contact (FirstName, Name, NickName, EMail, Phone)" +
            "VALUES (@FirstName, @Name, @Nick, @EMail, @Phone ); " +
            "SELECT @ID = @@IDENTITY";   // @@IDENTITY is MsSqlServer specific!
        SqlCommand cmd = new SqlCommand(cmdStr);
        cmd.Connection = NewConnection();
        cmd.CommandType = CommandType.Text;
        //----- set names and SQL types of the formal input parameters
        IDataParameterCollection pars = cmd.Parameters;
        pars.Add(new SqlParameter("@FirstName", SqlDbType.NVarChar) );
        pars.Add(new SqlParameter("@Name", SqlDbType.NVarChar) );
        pars.Add(new SqlParameter("@Nick", SqlDbType.NVarChar) );
        pars.Add(new SqlParameter("@EMail", SqlDbType.NVarChar) );
        pars.Add(new SqlParameter("@Phone", SqlDbType.NVarChar) );
        //----- set names and SQL types of the formal output parameters
        SqlParameter idPar = new SqlParameter("@ID", SqlDbType.BigInt);
        idPar.Direction = ParameterDirection.Output;
        pars.Add(idPar);
        return cmd;
    }

    void Execute( string firstName, string name, string nickName,
                  string email, string phone, out long id) {
        SqlCommand  cmd = NewInsertCmd();
        //----- set actual parameters
        cmd.Parameters["@FirstName"].Value = firstName;
        cmd.Parameters["@Name"].Value = name;
        cmd.Parameters["@Nick"].Value = nickName;
        cmd.Parameters["@EMail"].Value = email;
        cmd.Parameters["@Phone"].Value = phone;
        //----- insert new data row
        cmd.Connection.Open();
        cmd.ExecuteNonQuery(); // führt INSERT aus
        //----- query output parameters
        id = (long) cmd.Parameters["@ID"].Value;
        cmd.Connection.Close();
    }
```

```
public static void Main() {
    InsertContacts insert = new InsertContacts();
    long id;
    try {
        insert.Execute("Dietrich", "Birngruber", "Didi", "didi@dotnet.jku.at", "7133", out id);
        Console.WriteLine("Inserted new data row with the ID {0}", id);
    } catch (Exception e) {
        Console.WriteLine("Could not insert data row - {0}", e);
    }
}
}
```

For each new inserted data row the Contact table automatically assigns a new key that we can access with @@IDENTITY. @@IDENTITY is an MsSqlServer-specific property and is returned to the .NET application via the output parameter @ID. Inserting a new row of data and returning the automatically assigned key within a single SQL command is not a very elegant solution, because it depends on the database and works only for the MsSqlServer.

5.3.4   DataReader

The interfaces IDataReader and IDataRecord represent a connection-oriented cursor that can read data in a forward direction. The implementation of IDataReader depends on the specific data provider.

We use an IDataReader to access the result of SELECT statements. Therefore we must convert the data types of the data source into .NET data types too. The command object defines which columns and rows a query returns. Many commands can be executed via a single connection. As discussed in the previous section, a command can return several IDataReader objects with ExecuteReader. We must close all of them later with reader.Close().

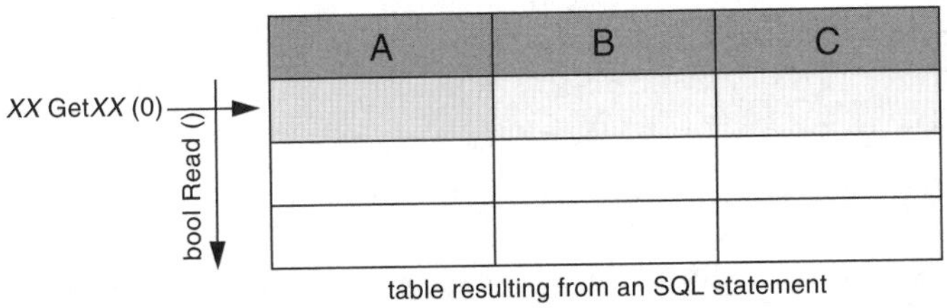

table resulting from an SQL statement

Figure 5.6 *Data access with IDataReader and IDataRecord*

After the creation of an IDataReader with ExecuteReader the cursor does not yet point to a row. This happens when we invoke the method Read. Read moves the cursor from one data row to the next. Read returns true as long as the cursor points to any data row (see Figure 5.6).

We describe some methods and properties of IDataReader and IDataRecord in the following interfaces. IDataReader itself does not offer any methods for reading the data of a row. These are already defined by the interface IDataRecord, which is the base type of IDataReader. We can access the data via the different Get*XX* methods of IDataRecord (*XX* stands for the corresponding .NET data type). The Get*XX* method needs a parameter with the index of the columns (e.g. byte b = reader.GetByte(idx);). The first column has the index 0. The indexer allows us to use the name of the column instead (e.g. byte b = (byte) reader["IsMale"];). With GetValues we can read the entire data record at once and with IsDBNull we can check whether a cell of a data row contains data or not.

```
public interface IDataRecord {
    //----- properties
    int FieldCount { get; }   // number of columns
    object this[int] { get; }   // access via the column index
    object this[string] { get; }   // access via the column name
    //----- some access methods
    bool GetBoolean(int idx);
    byte GetByte(int idx);
    IDataReader GetData(int idx);
    string GetDataTypeName(int i);
    string GetName(int idx);
    int GetOrdinal(string name);
    int GetValues(object[] values);
    bool IsDBNull(int idx);
    ...
}

public interface IDataReader : IDisposable, IDataRecord {
    //----- properties
    bool IsClosed { get; }
    ...
    //----- methods
    void Close();
    bool Read();
    ...
}
```

Besides the access methods and methods for moving the cursors, we can also obtain schema information about the resulting table. Schema information includes, among others, the number of columns (property FieldCount), the type of a certain column (method GetDataTypeName), the index (method GetOrdinal) or name of a column (method GetName). This schema information is especially important for tool developers or when processing data from arbitrary SELECT statements.

In the following example we use a stored procedure. Database procedures consist of a sequence of SQL statements that are stored in the database system. In our example we consider a database procedure for the MsSqlServer. Stored procedures can be invoked by command objects which also pass the parameters. The following stored procedure GetContacts returns all contacts with a certain last name or first letter. The queried name is determined by the input parameter @Name. The result of the SELECT statement in GetContacts is a table with the queried data records, or an empty table if no matching records are found.

```
CREATE PROCEDURE GetContacts
      @Name varchar(50) = null  -- Input parameter
AS
    SELECT    ID, FirstName, Name, NickName, EMail, Phone
    FROM      Contact
    WHERE     (Name LIKE (@Name+'%') )
```

The following method NewSelectCmd returns the command object which should later call the stored procedure.

```
IDbCommand NewSelectCmd() {
    SqlCommand cmd = new SqlCommand();
    cmd.Connection = NewConnection();
    cmd.CommandText = "GetContacts";   // name of the stored procedure
    cmd.CommandType = CommandType.StoredProcedure;
    // parameter of the stored procedure
    IDataParameterCollection pars = cmd.Parameters;
    pars.Add(new SqlParameter("@Name", SqlDbType.NVarChar) );
    return cmd;
}
```

In the following example we read the data records sequentially by transferring them from the database into the IDataReader. Therefore we access the fields (corresponding to the columns of the resulting tables) via the column index as well as the column name.

```
IDbCommand  cmd = NewSelectCmd();
cmd.Connection.Open();
((IDataParameter) cmd.Parameters["@Name"]).Value =  "B";
IDataReader r = cmd.ExecuteReader(CommandBehavior.CloseConnection);
while (r.Read()) {   // read ID, FirstName, Name, EMail, Phone
    StringBuilder buf = new StringBuilder();
    buf.Append(r.GetInt64(0)); buf.Append(","); // ID (read with access method)
    buf.Append(r.GetString(1)); buf.Append(",");// FirstName (read with access method)
    buf.Append(r[2]); buf.Append(",");           // Name (read with indexer)
    buf.Append(r[3]); buf.Append(",");           // Email (read with indexer)
    buf.Append(r["Phone"]);                      // Phone (read with indexer)
    Console.WriteLine(buf);
}
r.Close();   // closes the IDataReader and the connection
```

With the call to cmd.ExecuteReader we pass CommandBehavior.CloseConnection to specify that the connection to the database should be closed when the IDataReader r is closed with r.Close().

In the previous example we accessed the columns via their name or their index. However, if the schema of the resulting table is not known, the data can only be read by using schema information. The following example builds on the previous one and reads the data without knowing the schema by first reading the name of the column (r.GetName) and then the data records, which are then output on the console.

```
void PrintData(IDataReader r) {
    if (r.IsClosed) return;
    //----- print column names
    int cols = r.FieldCount;                                          // number of columns
    for (int i = 0; i < cols; i++) Console.Write(r.GetName(i) + " | ");    // name of column
    Console.WriteLine();
    //----- print data
    while (r.Read()) {   // read and print actual data records
        for (int i = 0; i < cols; i++) Console.Write (r.GetValue(i) +" | "); // value of column
        Console.WriteLine();
    }
}
```

On the console the result could look as shown below, where the column Phone is empty for the last data record. With r.IsDBNull(...) we can find out whether a field of a data record contains a null value.

```
ID | FirstName | Name | NickName | EMail | Phone |
1 | Dietrich | Birngruber | Didi | didi@dotnet.jku.at | 7133 |
4 | Wolfgang | Beer | Wutschgo | wutschgo@dotnet.jku.at |  |
```

Table 5.2 relates .NET types to their corresponding OLE DB and MsSqlServer types. The type conversions depend on the data provider implementation. The GetXX methods of IDataRecord implementations must return .NET types (e.g. string GetString(int idx)). As we have seen before, the types of the command parameters are determined with the enumerations OleDbType or SqlType (see Section 5.3.3).

Table 5.2 *Correspondence between .NET, OLE DB and MsSqlServer Types*

.NET data type	OLE DB data type	MsSqlServer data type
bool		bit
byte	DBTYPE_UI1	tinyint
byte[]	DBTYPE_BYTES	binary, image, timestamp, varbinary

Table 5.2 *Correspondence between .NET, OLE DB and MsSqlServer Types (cont.)*

.NET data type	OLE DB data type	MsSqlServer data type
DateTime	DBTYPE_DATE, DBTYPE_DBDATE, DBTYPE_DBTIME, DBTYPE_DBTIMESTAMP, DBTYPE_FILETIME	datetime, smalldatetime
DBNull	DBTYPE_NULL	null
Decimal	DBTYPE_CY, DBTYPE_DECIMAL, DBTYPE_NUMERIC	decimal, money, numeric, smallmoney
Double	DBTYPE_R8	float
ExternalExcep-tion	DBTYPE_ERROR	
Guid	DBTYPE_GUID	uniqueidentifier
Int16	DBTYPE_BOOL, DBTYPE_I2	smallint
Int32	DBTYPE_I4	int
Int64	DBTYPE_I8	bigint
not supported	DBTYPE_HCHAPTER, DBTYPE_UDT, DBTYPE_VARNUMERIC	
null	DBTYPE_EMPTY	
object	DBTYPE_IDISPATCH, DBTYPE_IUNKNOWN, DBTYPE_PROPVARIANT, DBTYPE_VARIANT	sql_variant
SByte	DBTYPE_I1	
Single	DBTYPE_R4	real
string	DBTYPE_BSTR, DBTYPE_STR, DBTYPE_WSTR	char, nchar, ntext, nvarchar, text, varchar
UInt16 (Int32)	DBTYPE_UI2	
UInt32 (Int64)	DBTYPE_UI4	
UInt64 (Int64)	DBTYPE_UI8	

5.4 Connectionless Access with DataSet

In Section 5.2 we explained the difference between connection-oriented and connectionless access. With connectionless access the data is read from the data source and stored in a DataSet. A DataSet can hold parts of a database in memory without knowing the original data source and thus it cannot maintain any connection with it. Modifications of the data in the DataSet or at the data source occur independently of each other. The application developer has to take care of synchronizing the data between DataSet and data source.

In order to fill a DataSet with data from a database (see "Fill" in Figure 5.7), we need a DataAdapter. If we have modified the data in the DataSet and want to incorporate these changes at the data source, we must again use a DataAdapter to synchronize the DataSet with the data source (see "Update" in Figure 5.7).

A DataSet contains multiple tables of type DataTable in the form of a DataTableCollection. A DataTable object has a schema and is made up of rows that hold the data itself (see DataRowCollection in Figure 5.7), similar to a database table. There can even be relations between DataTable objects. Such relations are managed by a DataRelationCollection. We can say that a DataSet is in a way a simplified database system in main memory. On a DataSet we can create arbitrary views of type DataView for filtering or searching the data.

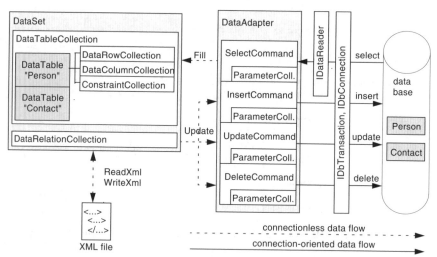

Figure 5.7 *Architecture of DataSet and DataAdapter*

Of course, a database system is more powerful than a DataSet, because it additionally offers users, roles, access rights, multi-user controls, indexes and so on. There are also no synchronization mechanisms within a DataSet. However, they are hardly necessary, because in general a DataSet is used only by one application, whereas a database system is, under normal conditions, used by multiple applications. If we still need to access a DataSet in parallel, we can use threads (see Section 4.3) and their synchronization mechanisms.

Another difference between DataSets and database systems is that DataSets are volatile. The data is not automatically made persistent on a hard disk. In case of a program crash the data will be lost and there is no recovery procedure as in a database system.

Besides types such as DataSet and DataTable, ADO.NET also offers the type DataAdapter. Adapters facilitate data transfer between a DataSet and the data sources. If we write back the data of a DataSet to the data source with an adapter, it will check for any data record, whether it has been modified, added or deleted in the DataSet. Depending on the type of the modification it executes a corresponding update (UpdateCommand), insert (InsertCommand) or delete (DeleteCommand) command. These commands are all of type IDbCommand (see Section 5.3.3).

DataSets cannot be synchonized with data sources directly, but only via DataAdapters. Therefore they are independent of the data source. In order to save a DataSet without an adapter, we must serialize it, for example, to an XML file. It is also possible to create DataSets from XML files and to write these, for example, into a database. Modern database systems can, of course, handle XML directly.

In the examples of the previous sections we have frequently used the table Contact. It contains the contacts of a certain person, but so far we have not described this data. Therefore we introduce a table Person with the columns ID, FirstName and Name. The primary key of the table Person is ID. The tables Person and Contact are related to each other such that a person can have multiple contacts and each contact is associated with exactly one person. Thus the table Contact has a column PersonID that works as a foreign key (see Figure 5.8). We will use this example more often throughout this section in order to explain how to work with DataSets.

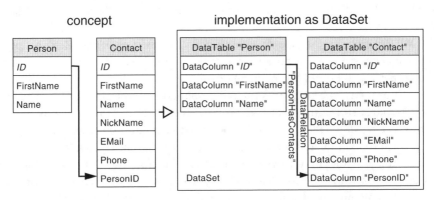

Figure 5.8 *The tables Person and Contact and their implementation as a DataSet*

When storing the data of the database tables Person and Contact in a DataSet, we naturally want to preserve the same organization as in the underlying database. As shown in Figure 5.7 a DataSet in not merely an arbitrary collection of data, but organizes the data as tables (property Tables). A table is implemented as a DataTable object that, like a database table, consists of columns (property Columns) and rows (property Rows). ADO.NET even guarantees *referential integrity* and manages it with the class DataRelationCollection as a collection of DataRelation objects. Referential integrity avoids insertion of inconsistent data into tables that are related to each other (e.g. 1:N or 1:1).

Let us look at an example: the attribute PersonID of the table Contact is a foreign key that maintains a 1:N relation between the tables Person and Contact: *one* person can have N contacts. Maintaining referential integrity now involves prohibiting the insertion of a data record into the Contact table if the table Person does not contain a corresponding data record. All values of Contact.PersonID must also exist as Person.ID. DataSets also offer this kind of behaviour.

The following subsections present the types DataSet and DataAdapter, as well as the integration of DataSet with XML in more detail. First we demonstrate how to work with DataSet and DataTable *without* a data source. Then we will look at how to synchronize the data between a DataSet and a database with a DataAdapter.

5.4.1 Creating and Using DataSets

The classes DataSet and DataTable are two of the most important classes in ADO.NET. A DataSet can be stored in an XML file or transformed into a byte stream and sent over a network in a distributed application. DataSet and DataTable are the only classes of ADO.NET that support sending data over a network. DataSet is also responsible for the integration of ADO.NET with other parts of the .NET Framework. Windows forms and web forms can, for example, use DataSets to display the contents of a database query on the screen (see Chapter 6).

We can broadly distinguish two groups of properties of DataSets: properties for managing data and properties for dealing with XML files. Figure 5.9 shows the properties and types for managing data.

The property Tables returns the tables that contain the actual data. The property Relations stores the DataRelation objects that model the relations between tables. ExtendedProperties allows the specification of additional, custom properties (e.g. when to load the data) that are important for the entire DataSet.

A table is made up of rows and columns. Therefore the class DataTable stores its data in DataRow objects. The property Columns contains schema information about the columns (see Figure 5.10) by maintaining a DataColumn object for each column. These DataColumn objects define the schema of a DataTable, that is, what data is allowed in each cell of a data row. A DataColumn object contains, among others, the name (ColumnName) and .NET type (DataType) of a column. We can also specify an aggregation function or a filter expression for a column (Expression). For example, a DataTable can contain two columns (DataColumns)

"Gross Price" and "Net Price". The contents of the column "Gross Price" are determined by the property Expression which is set to "Net Price" * 1.2.

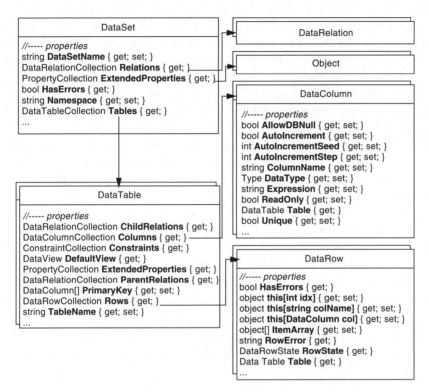

Figure 5.9 *Selected ADO.NET types and properties for data management*

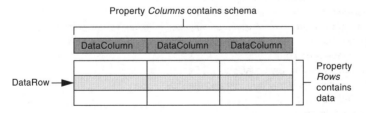

Figure 5.10 *Relation between DataColumn and DataRow in a DataTable*

In the following sections we will use the contact example to show how to work with DataSet, DataTable, DataColumn, DataRow and DataView independent of a data source. First, we will determine the schema of the tables Contact and Person in DataSet. Then we will manipulate the data in the DataSet: insert, delete, search and filter data records without, for example, using a database. We will discuss synchronizing the data of DataSets with data sources in Section 5.4.2.

Defining a Schema

In the following code fragment we will create a new DataSet "PersonContacts" and add an empty DataTable "Person" to it. The schema of the table Person of the example from the beginning of this section consists of the columns ID, FirstName and Name. Then we will determine the schema for the DataTable "Person". We create the columns as DataColumn objects. DataColumn "ID" will become the primary key of the DataTable "Person" (userTable.PrimaryKey). When inserting data records (that is, DataRow objects) into the DataTable "Person" later on, consecutive keys should be assigned to the new data records. We achieve this by setting the property AutoIncrement of DataColumn "ID" to true. In our example we will use only negative numbers starting at -1 (col.AutoIncrementSeed = -1) as keys. The consecutive values for the keys should decrease by 1 (col.AutoIncrementStep = -1). The key will only be assigned automatically if the value of ID in the inserted data record is null. If it is not null, the set value will be used.

Typically databases use positive primary keys. We use this trick here to be able to determine, in the DataSet, whether the data has been synchronized with a data source or not. By using negative keys in the DataSet we can immediately see if the positive primary keys assigned by the database have been correctly transferred from the data source to the DataSet. But more about synchronizing DataSets and data sources in Section 5.4.2.

```
DataSet ds = new DataSet("PersonContacts");
DataTable userTable = new DataTable("Person");
//----- create column ID, add it to the table and make it the primary key
DataColumn col = new DataColumn();
col.DataType = typeof(System.Int64);
col.ColumnName = "ID";
col.ReadOnly = true;   // allow only read access
col.Unique = true;   // allow only unique values
col.AutoIncrement = true;   // automatically assign key value
col.AutoIncrementSeed = -1;   // automatically assigned key values start at -1
col.AutoIncrementStep = -1;   // automatic key value will be reduced by 1
userTable.Columns.Add(col);
userTable.PrimaryKey = new DataColumn[] { col };
//----- create column FirstName and add it to the table
col = new DataColumn();
col.DataType = typeof(string);
col.ColumnName = "FirstName";
userTable.Columns.Add(col);
//----- create column Name and add it to the table
col = new DataColumn();
col.DataType = typeof(string);
col.ColumnName = "Name";
userTable.Columns.Add(col);
//----- add the table to the DataSet
ds.Tables.Add(userTable);
```

Setting the property Unique of the key column to true will lead to an exception if the inserted key values are not unique. From an implementation point of view this inserts an object of type UniqueConstraint into the Constraints collection of the DataTable "Person". This UniqueConstraint object checks, for each new data record, whether the key is unique. The property ReadOnly of the DataColumn "ID" specifies that the value of this column may not be modified.

In order to complete the contact example we still need to define the DataTable "Contact" analogously to the DataTable "Person" and add it to the Tables collection of the DataSet. We can later access the DataTable objects that we have added to ds.Tables via their names or their index, for example:

```
DataTable contactTable = ds.Tables["Contact"];
```

The relation between the tables Person and Contact requires an entry in the DataSet property Relations, as shown in the next example. Person and Contact are in a 1:N relation, which is expressed with the columns Person.ID and Contact.PersonID (see Figure 5.8). The DataRelation object with the name "PersonHasContacts" determines the referential integrity between the DataTable "Person" and the DataTable "Contact" by receiving these two columns in its constructor.

```
void DefineRelation(DataSet ds) {
    DataColumn parentCol = ds.Tables["Person"].Columns["ID"];
    DataColumn childCol = ds.Tables["Contact"].Columns["PersonID"];
    DataRelation rel = new DataRelation("PersonHasContacts", parentCol, childCol);
    ds.Relations.Add(rel);
}
```

Creating the DataRelation "PersonHasContacts" also adds an object of type ForeignKeyConstraint to the property Constraints of the DataTable "Contact". This ForeignKeyConstraint object then guards the referential integrity of the DataTable "Contact". We can assign various Constraint objects to the DataColumns and various DataRelation object to the tables. The actual checks of the data entries will be done by the Constraint objects.

If we look at the DataRelation "PeronHasContacts" as a tree, the person data record represents the parent node and the contact data records the child nodes. Therefore the DataTable "Person" contains an object of type DataRelation in its property ChildRelations (see Figure 5.9) and the DataTable "Contact" has a corresponding entry in its property ParentRelations. Based on this relation we can query each person data record for its contact data records and vice versa. We will present an example in the next subsection.

Adding, Searching and Deleting Data

After defining the DataTable objects, we can now insert data records in the form of DataRow objects into the tables. Because the DataTable "Person" has the columns

"ID", "FirstName" and "Name", each DataRow object of the DataTable "Person" also has three cells, of the types long, string and string.

There are two ways of inserting a data record into a DataTable: we can either create a new DataRow object with table.NewRow and add the appropriate cells via column index or column name there, or we can directly add an object array with the data to the Rows collection.

Thanks to the indexers, we can access the contents of a DataRow object via their index, the DataColumn object or the DataColumn name. The access via the index is faster, whereas the code becomes more readable by using the names.

As with a transaction, we can accept or reject any modification. Calling the method AcceptChanges tells a DataRow, a DataTable or an entire DataSet to accept all modifications. A DataSet will propagate the invocation of AcceptChanges to all its tables and data records. Calling RejectChanges rejects all modifications as in the case of a rollback. In database systems Commit or Rollback can fail, but AcceptChanges and RejectChanges are always executed—after all, the same application executes these methods on a DataSet in memory.

```
DataTable table = ds.Tables["Person"];
//----- insert first data record
DataRow row = table.NewRow();   // has 3 columns; column 0 (ID) is set automatically
row[1] = "Wolfgang";             // column 1: "FirstName"
row["Name"] = "Beer";            // column 2: "Name"
table.Rows.Add(row);
//----- insert second data record
table.Rows.Add(new object[] {null, "Dietrich", "Birngruber"});
System.Console.WriteLine ("new IDs {0} {1} ", row[0], table.Rows[1]["ID"]);
ds.AcceptChanges();   // equvalent to the "Commit" of a transaction
```

DataRow objects maintain a state that is made available via the property RowState and indicates whether the record has been inserted, modified or deleted in the course of the current "transaction". The enumeration DataRowState defines the possible states as Added, Deleted, Modified, Detached and Unchanged. Figure 5.11 gives an overview of the most important states and the transitions between them. We can even search for DataRow objects that are in a certain state. Therefore we need a DataView object (see next subsection).

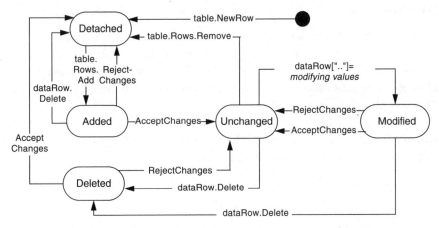

Figure 5.11 *Partial state diagram of a DataRow object*

After a DataTable has created a DataRow object with NewRow, the row will be in the state Detached. Now we can add the actual data to the DataRow object, which will then be in the state Added. Calling AcceptChanges for the DataTable will accept the modifications (in this case the new DataRow object with its data) and the row will be in the state Unchanged. A DataRow object always remembers the data from its last Unchanged states. Modifying the data will change the state from Unchanged to Modified. With RejectChanges these modifications can be undone by resetting the data record to the values stored from the last Unchanged state.

In the next example we look for a certain person in the Person table; then we query the person's contacts based on the relation "PersonHasContacts" with the method GetChildRows and output them to the console. The Find method of the DataRowCollection only accepts values for the primary key columns. Expressions like those in the WHERE clause of an SQL statement, where any column name may be used, are not allowed. For this we need a DataView object, which we will introduce in the next subsection.

```
//----- look for a person with a certain primary key
DataRow person = ds.Tables["Person"].Rows.Find(-11);    // look for person with ID=-11
if (person != null) {
    Console.WriteLine("Contacts of {0}:", person["Name"]);
    //----- print all contacts of the retrieved person
    foreach (DataRow contact in person.GetChildRows("PersonHasContacts")) {
        Console.WriteLine("{0}, {1}: {2}", contact[0], contact["Name"], contact["Phone"]);
    }
}
```

DataView

With DataView objects we can create various views of a DataTable (see Figure 5.12). DataViews are mainly employed when searching or filtering data records, similarly to the VIEW concept of SQL. While SQL VIEWs can be JOINed, this is not possible with DataViews. They are exclusively used for searching and filtering DataRow objects from a DataTable.

Many GUI elements in Windows forms and web forms can display the contents of DataView objects directly. The property DefaultView of a DataTable object provides quick access to a view of the table.

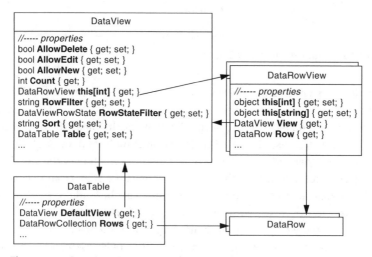

Figure 5.12 *Overview: DataView and DataRowView*

In the same way as DataTable objects contain a number of DataRow objects, a DataView object contains a number of DataRowView objects, each referring to a DataRow object. With the properties RowFilter and RowStateFilter of a DataView object we can filter the data from a table. For example, we can find all newly inserted data records of a table. RowFilter expects an expression containing a condition, similar to a WHERE clause of an SQL statement.

In the following example we look for all rows of the table Person where Name starts with "B", in order to delete their contacts. Therefore we first create a DataView object containing only the queried data records. Then we simply delete all contacts of the retrieved persons.

```
DataView view = new DataView(ds.Tables["Person"]);   // or Tables["Person"].DefaultView
//----- search for all persons whose name starts with 'B'
view.RowFilter = "Name LIKE 'B*'";   // always put strings in "
```

```
foreach (DataRowView person in view) {
    //----- delete all contacts of the retrieved persons
    foreach (DataRow contact in person.Row.GetChildRows("PersonHasContacts"))
        contact.Delete();
}
ds.AcceptChanges();   // commit all modifications
```

With DataView objects we can not only filter, but also sort data records by setting the columns to determine the order in the property Sort. For each attribute (column) we can also determine the sorting order with ASC (ascending) or DESC (descending). The next example sorts all contacts into ascending order according to Name and, within equal names, into descending order according to the phone number.

```
DataView view = ds.Tables["Contact"].DefaultView;
view.Sort = "Name, Phone DESC";
```

Working with Multiple DataSets

So far we have only manipulated a single DataSet. But it can also happen that the same data is modified in different DataSets. Then these must be merged to form one single DataSet.

Assume that the data from the contact example is stored on an application server (tier 2), are modified at the client (tier 1) and should then be sent back to the application server to be validated and stored there (see Figure 5.13).

In order to minimize the transferred amount of data, we want to send only the data modified in the DataSet. In this scenario we need not take any measures for schema evolution of the DataTables, because client and server use DataSets with the same structure (although not identical ones). For our purposes DataSet offers the methods GetChanges and Merge.

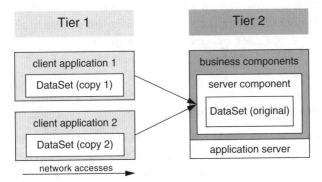

Figure 5.13 *Client/server scenario: different DataSets contain the "same" data*

In the example below, the method SendDataToServer gathers the modified data at the client and sends it to the server. There, the method MergeData stores the data modified at the client in a database and updates the original DataSet (which lies in main memory). DataSets and DataTables can be serialized, sent over a network and deserialized again at a server. In this example we will not cover the way in which the transmission works (for this see Section 4.4 and Chapter 7).

```
// method at the client
void SendDataToServer(DataSet ds) {
    // Assumption: ds.AcceptChanges has not been called yet!
    DataSet changedDS = ds.GetChanges();   // returns only the modified DataRows
    bool ok = serverProxy.MergeData(changedDS);
    if (ok) ds.AcceptChanges(); else ds.RejectChanges();
}

// method at the server
bool MergeData(DataSet changedDS) {
    if (!changedDS.HasChanges(DataRowState.Modified)) return true;
    StoreTable(changedDS, ...);    // stored changedDS (see later)
    origDS.Merge(changedDS);      // merge changes with original data
    bool ok = !origDS.HasErrors;  // Have there been errors during merging of the data?
    if (ok) origDS.AcceptChanges(); else origDS.RejectChanges();
    return ok;
}
```

ds.GetChanges() returns a DataSet that contains only the changes from ds. Thus the new DataSet is a subset of ds. Immediately after calling AcceptChanges or RejectChanges, GetChanges returns the empty set (see also the earlier discussion about DataRowState and Figure 5.11). At the server the method Merge is called for the original data (origDS) and the same modifications stored in changedDS are applied to origDS.

Let us assume that there is another DataTable "PersonMail" with the columns ID and EMail, whereas the DataTable "Person" considered so far has the columns ID, FirstName and Name. If we now want to add the column EMail to the DataTable "Person" and take over the e-mail data from the DataTable "PersonMail", we also have to modify the schema of Person as well as merging the data. We give an example of this in Section 5.5.2.

5.4.2 Database Access with DataAdapter

Up to now we have only created DataSets and manipulated data within them without ever synchronizing the data with a data source (e.g. a database). The class DataAdapter establishes a connection between a DataSet and a data source by offering methods such as Fill and Update (see Figure 5.14). Fill fills a DataSet with values from a database and Update writes the data from a DataSet back to a database.

As in the connection-oriented case, so with DataAdapter we must start with setting SQL commands (see Section 5.3.3) that specify which data to read or write. For this purpose DataAdapter provides the properties SelectCommand, DeleteCommand, UpdateCommand and InsertCommand. For a DataAdapter to know which DataTable corresponds to which table of the data source, we can specify appropriate associations in the form of ITableMapping objects in the property TableMappings of the DataAdapter.

A DataSet can contain data from tables of different databases. Table 1 can, for example, originate from an MsSqlServer, table 2 from an XML data stream and table 3 from an Oracle database. DataAdapter objects abstract from the type, schema and location of the data.

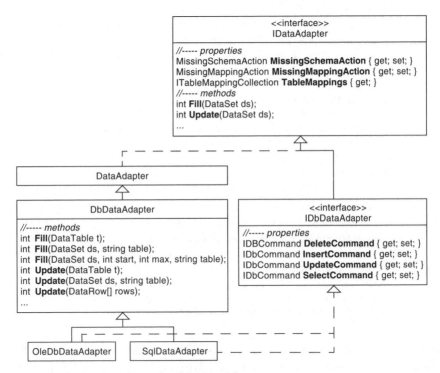

Figure 5.14 *Inheritance hierarchy of the DataAdapter types*

Each data provider has its own DataAdapter class which must implement the interface System.Data.IDataAdapter. Figure 5.14 shows the inheritance hierarchy and the most important methods and properties of DataAdapter for MsSqlServer and OLE DB. If data consumers want to stay independent of the data provider implementation, they should work with the types System.Data.DbDataAdapter and System.Data.IDbDataAdapter and not with concrete classes such as System.Data.SqlClient.SqlDataAdapter.

But unfortunately DbDataAdapter does not implement the interface IDbDataAdapter, although all subclasses of DbDataAdapter (e.g. SqlDataAdapter) must implement it. Thus a consumer cannot simply work with the abstract class DbDataAdapter, but must use either one of its subclasses (e.g. OleDbDataAdapter) or, in some cases, type cast from DbDataAdapter to IDbDataAdapter or vice versa. That is not a very clean solution from an object-oriented point of view.

Loading of Data and Schema Information

Now it is time to load data from a database into a DataSet. The result of a SELECT statement is, as we know, a table, and a DataSet contains DataTable objects. This means that we want to load the contents of a database table into a DataTable. Therefore we create a DataAdapter that can open a connection to a database, set its property SelectCommand and call its method Fill.

In the next example we fill the DataTable "Person" by means of a DataAdapter. This time we access the database server via OLE DB.

```
IDbCommand GetSelectPersonCmd() {
    OleDbCommand cmd = new OleDbCommand();
    cmd.Connection = new OleDbConnection("provider=SQLOLEDB; " +
            "server=127.0.0.1\\NetSDK; data source=netbook; user id=sa; password=;");
    cmd.CommandText = "SELECT * FROM Person";
    return cmd;
}

void LoadPersonData(DataSet ds) {
    // Assumption: ds contains the DataTable "Person"
    IDbDataAdapter adapter = new OleDbDataAdapter();
    adapter.SelectCommand = GetSelectPersonCmd();   // set the SELECT command
    ((DbDataAdapter)adapter).Fill(ds.Tables["Person"]);   // fill DataTable "Person"
    if (ds.HasErrors) ds.RejectChanges(); else ds.AcceptChanges();
    // adapter should be notified that it can free its resources
    if (adapter is IDisposable) ((IDisposable) adapter).Dispose();
}
```

In LoadPersonData we first create a DataAdapter. Its Fill method can only fill the Person table after we have set a valid SELECT command. If an error occurs while reading the data from the database, the property HasErrors of the DataSet will be set to true. With AcceptChanges the DataSet can accept the modifications and with RejectChanges it can reject them; the Fill method will not invoke these methods. After filling the DataTable we can access the loaded data as follows:

```
foreach (DataRow row in ds.Tables["Person"].Rows)
    Console.WriteLine("{0}, {1}, {2}", row["ID"], row["FirstName"], row["Name"]);
```

In the method LoadPersonData we have assumed that a DataSet with a DataTable "Person" already exists. The DataTable "Person" and the database table Person have a compatible schema. Attributes and DataColumns have the same name and the SQL types are assignment compatible with the .NET data types of each DataColumn. However, it would be even easier if the SELECT statement directly created a DateTable "Person" with the appropriate schema information and added this to the DataSet. If this were the case, we would not have to define the DataTables and DataColumns ourselves before filling them, as we have done in the previous subsection, and we could also read arbitrary database tables.

In the next example we will do exactly this: in the method GetSelectAllCmd we create one IDbCommand object with two SELECT statements, one for the table Person and one for the table Contact. We will use this command in the method LoadData for filling an empty DataSet that does not yet contain any DataTables.

In order for the DataAdapter to know how to add the two missing tables to the DataSet we set the DataAdapter property MissingSchemaAction to AddWithKey. This will not only add the missing tables, but also the constraints of its columns. Additionally the primary keys of the DataTables will be set. For each database table a DataTable object will be created and added.

If a table that does not yet exist is added to a DataSet via Fill, it will automatically be named "Table". For any further tables that are added, a number will be appended to the name (i.e. "Table", "Table1", "Table2", ...). Thus, one should not use the name "Table" for user-added DataTables such as "Person". We therefore define two mappings, in order to convert the generated names "Table" and "Table1" into the names "Person" and "Contact". We do this by adding corresponding entries to the DataAdapter property TableMappings.

```
IDbCommand GetSelectAllCmd() {
    OleDbCommand cmd = new OleDbCommand();
    cmd.Connection = new OleDbConnection ("provider=SQLOLEDB; " +
        "data source=(local)\\NetSDK; database=netbook; user id=sa; password=;" );
    cmd.CommandText = "SELECT * FROM Person; SELECT * FROM Contact";
    return cmd;
}

DataSet LoadData() {
    DataSet ds = new DataSet("PersonContacts");
    IDbDataAdapter adapter = new OleDbDataAdapter();
    adapter.SelectCommand = GetSelectAllCmd();
    //----- DataSet does not yet contain any tables, therefore add them with Fill!
    adapter.MissingSchemaAction = MissingSchemaAction.AddWithKey;
    //----- rename automatically created tables
    adapter.TableMappings.Add("Table", "Person");
    adapter.TableMappings.Add("Table1", "Contact");
    adapter.Fill(ds);   //----- load data from the database
    if (ds.HasErrors) ds.RejectChanges(); else ds.AcceptChanges();
    if (adapter is IDisposable) ((IDisposable) adapter).Dispose();
    return ds;
}
```

The only schema information that has not been added to the DataSet is the rela-tions between the database tables. The DataSet of the above example does not yet contain any information concerning the foreign-key relationship between the DataTable "Person" and the DataTable "Contact". If we also want to carry over the relations of the database tables from the database, we must query the system tables of the database. Every database stores the schema information in different ways. In most cases the schema information is held in so-called system tables. Normally only the database administrators or a user with special privileges may access these. The MsSqlServer offers the schema information in the views INFORMATION_SCHEMA.TABLES   and   INFORMATION_SCHEMA.COLUMNS, among others. In the case of OLE DB implementations we can access the database schema via the method OleDbConnection.GetOleDbSchemaTable.

Storing Data

As already pointed out, the connection to the database is closed after loading the data. However, data is typically not only loaded into a DataSet, but also modified there. In order to carry over those changes in the data source we must write back the data of the DataSet to the database via a DataAdapter. Possible modifications are adding, deleting and changing a data record. These correspond to the SQL statements INSERT, DELETE and UPDATE.

In an example of Section 5.4.1 we sent modified data from a client to the server and there we stored it in a database. However, the example did not show how this storing in the database works. Below we extend the example with that functionality.

```
bool MergeData(DataSet changedDS) {
    // Are there any changes?
    if (!changedDS.HasChanges(DataRowState.Modified)) return true;
    //----- store tables Person and Contact
    StoreTable(changedDS, "Person");
    if (!changedDS.HasErrors) StoreTable(changedDS, "Contact");
    if (changedDS.HasErrors) return false;
    //----- add changedDs to the original DataSet origDS
    origDS.Merge(changedDS);
    bool ok = !origDS.HasErrors;
    if (ok) origDS.AcceptChanges(); else origDS.RejectChanges();
    return ok;
}

// stores the data records of a table
void StoreTable(DataSet ds, string tableName) {
    OleDbConnection con = new OleDbConnection ("provider=SQLOLEDB; " +
        "data source=(local)\\NetSDK; database=netbook; user id=sa; password=;");
    //----- set SelectCommand, so that the OleDbCommandBuilder can automatically
```

```
//----- generate insert, update and delete commands
OleDbDataAdapter adapter = new OleDbDataAdapter("SELECT * FROM " +
                                                tableName, con);
OleDbCommandBuilder cmdBuilder = new OleDbCommandBuilder(adapter);
//----- store the data!
try {
    adapter.Update(ds, tableName);
} catch (DBConcurrencyException) {
    // database has been modified by another transaction, too!
    // ... react to the error! e.g. load DataSet anew!
}
adapter.Dispose();
}
```

In order for adapter.Update to be able to synchronize the modifications of the DataSet with the data source, the properties InsertCommand, UpdateCommand and DeleteCommand of the adapter must be set. However, in the above example we did not set them, but had an OleDbCommandBuilder generate them automatically. The generation happens when creating the OleDbCommandBuilder object. Without this object creation the DataAdapter method Update in this example would not work and would throw a System.InvalidOperationException.

We can employ a CommandBuilder where a DataTable exactly corresponds to a table of the database. The columns of the DataTable have the same name as the columns of the database table and their data types are compatible. From the provided SELECT command the CommandBuilder knows what the INSERT, UPDATE and DELETE commands have to look like. It will only automatically generate those commands that do not exist yet. If, for example, an INSERT command is already set, it will not generate a new one (see next example).

Because some time could have passed since the last update of the DataSet, other transactions might have modified the data. Thus, a modified DataRow contains two data records: the loaded original data record and the new, modified data record. If the original data record of a DataRow differs from the data record in the data source, a DBConcurrencyException will be thrown. This prevents already-modified data records being deleted or overwritten accidentally. When executing the method Update the isolation level IsolationLevel.Serializable (see Section 5.3.1) is used.

In the contact example the database assigned the keys for the Contact and Person data records. Because the automatically generated INSERT command does not produce any output parameters, the newly assigned key in the database can differ from the key in the DataSet. One way to get the assigned key from the insertion is to define a custom InsertCommand, in a similar way to the example from Section 5.3.3. Another way is to react to the result of event RowUpdated of the DataAdapter which is triggered for any modified tuple and read the generated value with a separate SQL command.

In the following example we use the custom-defined MsSqlServer procedure InsertPerson as the INSERT command. The update and delete command of the DataAdapter will be generated automatically.

```
CREATE PROCEDURE InsertPerson
    @FirstName nvarchar(50) = '',
    @Name nvarchar(50) = '',
    @ID bigint OUTPUT -- assigned key
AS
    INSERT INTO Person (FirstName, Name)
    VALUES      (@FirstName, @Name)
    SELECT @ID = @@IDENTITY -- return key of the new data record
```

We can use this procedure in C# like this:

```
OleDbConnection con = new OleDbConnection(conStr);
OleDbDataAdapter adapter = new OleDbDataAdapter("SELECT * FROM Person", con);
//----- set the stored procedure in the InsertCommand
adapter.InsertCommand = new OleDbCommand("InsertPerson");
adapter.InsertCommand.CommandType = CommandType.StoredProcedure;
adapter.InsertCommand.Connection = con;
//----- define parameters and assign them to the columns of the Person table
OleDbParameterCollection params = adapter.InsertCommand.Parameters;
params.Add ("@FirstName", OleDbType.VarWChar, 50, "FirstName");
params.Add ("@Name", OleDbType.VarWChar, 50, "Name");
params.Add ("@ID", OleDbType.BigInt, 8, "ID");
params["@ID"].Direction = ParameterDirection.Output;
//----- create update and delete commands
OleDbCommandBuilder cmdBuilder = new OleDbCommandBuilder(adapter);
//----- execute commands and store the data!
try {
  adapter.Update(ds, "Person");
} catch (DBConcurrencyException) { }
adapter.Dispose();
```

In this example we assign the separate DataColumns to the columns of the resulting table. The call

```
adapter.InsertCommand.Parameters.Add("@Name", OleDbType.VarWChar, 50, "Name");
```

for example, assigns the DataColumn "Name" to the parameter "@Name" of the database procedure. In the stored procedure the parameter "@Name" is defined as SQL type varchar of length 50. Therefore, we used the corresponding OleDbType VarWChar which is compatible to the SQL type of the stored procedure in the above example. By explicitly assigning each parameter to the columns' names the data columns may be named differently from the database columns. Furthermore the conversion between .NET types and OLE DB types is determined.

We can define a general mapping between DataTables and DataColumns to tables and columns of a data source with the DataAdapter property TableMappings.

TableMappings is a collection of ITableMapping objects that describe the actual mapping and are used by the method Fill and Update. If no matching ITableMapping object exists, a DataTable or DataColumn with the same name as the table or column of the data source is searched for.

5.5 Integration with XML

As already illustrated in Section 4.7 XML can be used for a platform-independent data exchange. Because of the interplay between DataSets and XML, DataSets can be converted into XML data and so, for example, sent via the Internet to a program on another computer. Also, web services take advantage of this platform independence of XML and the interplay with DataSets (see Chapter 7).

Since a DataSet is independent of a data source, it can be filled not only with data from, for example, a database, but also from data streams or XML documents. In a DataSet, XML data and XML schema information can even be combined with data and schema information from another data source (e.g. a database). We can access the data in a DataSet relationally via DataTables or hierarchically via XML navigators.

We can also store data in different formats, for example as database tables with DataAdapter or as XML files with XmlWriter. The schema information of the DataSet is stored in XSD format (*XML Schema*). If we assign an XML schema to a DataSet, we can access the data via user-friendly names. Microsoft also calls such DataSets strongly typed DataSets.

In this section we show how to store and read DataSets as XML documents. Additionally, we demonstrate how to apply XML schemas to DataSets. The example in this section is again based on the contact example of Section 5.4.

5.5.1 DataSets and XML Data

The class DataSet offers methods to read and write data and schema information in XML format. We can store a DataSet with the overloaded method WriteXml to a file, an output stream, a TextWriter or an XmlWriter, and then load it again with the method ReadXml.

```
public class DataSet : MarshalByValueComponent,
                       IListSource, ISupportInitialize, ISerializable {
    //----- methods to write and read XML data
    public void WriteXml(Stream dest);
    public void WriteXml(string fileName);
    public void WriteXml(TextWriter writer);
    public void WriteXml(XmlWriter writer);
    public void WriteXml(Stream dest, XmlWriteMode m);
    public void WriteXml(string fileName, XmlWriteMode m);
```

```
    public void WriteXml(TextWriter writer, XmlWriteMode m);
    public void WriteXml(XmlWriter writer, XmlWriteMode m);
    public XmlReadMode ReadXml(Stream dest);
    public XmlReadMode ReadXml(string fileName);
    public XmlReadMode ReadXml(TextReader reader);
    public XmlReadMode ReadXml(XmlReader reader);
    public XmlReadMode ReadXml(Stream dest, XmlReadMode m);
    public XmlReadMode ReadXml(string fileName, XmlReadMode m);
    public XmlReadMode ReadXml(TextReader reader, XmlReadMode m);
    public XmlReadMode ReadXml(XmlReader reader, XmlReadMode m);
    ...
}
```

It is relatively easy to read a DataSet from a database and store it as an XML file, as the following example shows. Here a DataSet ds, previously loaded from a database, is stored in the file data.xml.

```
    ds.WriteXml("data.xml");
```

The root element of the file data.xml is the name of the DataSet and contains a list of Person and Contact elements. The child XML elements of a Person or Contact element correspond to the column names such as ID, FirstName or Name. A part of data.xml might look like this:

```
<?xml version="1.0" standalone="yes"?>
<PersonContacts>    -- root element is the name of the DataSet
    <Person>   -- Person data record
        <ID>4</ID>
        <FirstName>Hanspeter</FirstName>
        <Name>Moessenboeck</Name>
    </Person>
    ...   -- further Person elements
    <Contact>   -- Contact data record
        <ID>1</ID>
        <FirstName>Wolfgang</FirstName>
        <Name>Beer</Name>
        <NickName>Wutschgo</NickName>
        <EMail>beer@dotnet.jku.at</EMail>
        <Phone>7132</Phone>
        <PersonID>4</PersonID>
    </Contact>
    ...   -- further Contact elements
</PersonContacts>
```

In the next example we create a new DataSet from the file data.xml. All created columns are of data type string, because the file data.xml does not contain any schema information. Even the DataColumn "ID" which actually should have the .NET type long is of type string. If data.xml also contained an XML schema, ReadXml would also load the schema information into the corresponding DataTable objects.

```
DataSet ds = new DataSet();
ds.ReadXml("data.xml", XmlReadMode.Auto);
```

The second parameter of ReadXml determines the XML format of the underlying data, and whether a schema should be read. The enumeration XmlReadMode has the values Auto, DiffGram, Fragment, IgnoreSchema, InferSchema and ReadSchema. The mode Auto specifies that a possibly available XML schema should be read in addition to the data. This is similar to what ReadSchema does. If the file does not contain a schema, Auto will proceed as InferSchema and attempt to infer a schema from the read data. With a similar parameter of the enumeration type XmlWriteMode, namely WriteSchema, we can specify for WriteXml that the schema information should be written as well as the data. Handling schema information becomes especially interesting when we try to add data from another XML source to an already filled DataSet. More about XML schemas and DataSets in Section 5.5.2.

We can access and manipulate the contents of a DataSet as a hierarchy like that of an XML document. For example, we can execute an XPath query (see Section 4.7.4) on an existing DataSet or manipulate the contents of a DataSet with XSL transformations (see Section 4.7.5). The classes DataSet and System.Xml. XmlDataDocument cooperate extremely well.

In the next example we create an XmlDataDocument from our DataSet. Afterwards we modify a record of the DataSet and then access the same record in the XML document. Although the modification in the DataSet has not yet been confirmed with AcceptChanges, it is already visible in the XML document! Finally we store the modified XML document to the file data2.xml.

```
XmlDataDocument xmlDoc = new XmlDataDocument(ds); // ds contains data + schema
//----- change the name of the person with ID=3 in the DataSet
DataTable table = ds.Tables["Person"];
table.Rows.Find(3)["Name"] = "Changed Name!";
//----- Is the modification already visible in the XML document?
XmlElement root = xmlDoc.DocumentElement;
XmlNode person = root.SelectSingleNode("descendant::Person[ID='3']");
Console.WriteLine("Access via XML: \n" + person.OuterXml);
xmlDoc.Save("data2.xml");   // store XML document
Console.WriteLine("Number of rows modified: {0}", table.GetChanges().Rows.Count);
```

The output to the console looks like this:

```
Access via XML:
<Person><ID>3</ID><FirstName>Dietrich</FirstName>
<Name>Changed Name!</Name></Person>
Number of rows modified: 1
```

Having multiple views of the same data poses the following question: if the data in the DataSet is changed, will the data in the XmlDataDocument also be changed? Does this also work the other way round? The answer is yes! Although DataSet and XmlDataDocument manage the data in different objects, they react to the appropriate events. If data in DataSet is modified, the modification will be immediately visible in XmlDataDocument and vice versa. If the XmlDataDocument has a schema that has not been taken from the DataSet, this synchronization only works if the schemas are compatible.

5.5.2   DataSets and XML Schemas

An XML schema describes the structure of an XML document, similarly to the way in which a relational schema specifies the make-up of the tables and their relation to each other. DataSet takes advantage of the similarity and offers methods to read, create and store XML schemas. Additionally, it is possible to integrate schemas from different data sources into a single DataSet. An existing XML schema can also be used as a template for generating a so-called typed DataSet.

An XML schema is itself described in XML [W3C]. These schema documents are typically stored in files with the extension .xsd. The schema namespace is http://www.w3.org/2001/XMLSchema.

In this section we will discuss how to load and store an XML schema, how to automatically create one, how to work with multiple schemas and how to create a typed DataSet.

Storing an XML Schema

We can store an XML schema with the overloaded method WriteXmlSchema to a file, to an output stream or to an XmlWriter.

```
public class DataSet : MarshalByValueComponent,
                        IListSource, ISupportInitialize, ISerializable {
    //----- methods to write XML schemas
    public void WriteXmlSchema(Stream dest)
    public void WriteXmlSchema(string fileName)
    public void WriteXmlSchema(TextWriter writer)
    public void WriteXmlSchema(XmlWriter writer)
    //----- methods to read XML data in order to create a schema from them
    public void InferXmlSchema(Stream dest, string[] namespaces)
    public void InferXmlSchema(string fileName, string[] namespaces)
    public void InferXmlSchema(TextWriter writer, string[] namespaces)
    public void InferXmlSchema(XmlWriter writer, string[] namespaces)
    //----- methods to read an existing XML schema
    public void ReadXmlSchema(Stream dest)
    public void ReadXmlSchema(string fileName)
    public void ReadXmlSchema(TextReader reader)
    public void ReadXmlSchema(XmlReader reader)

    ...
}
```

The following statement writes the schema of the DataSet ds (that is, information about the tables, columns, and relations) to the file contacts.xsd:

```
ds.WriteXmlSchema("contacts.xsd");
```

The contents of the resulting file look like this:

```xml
<?xml version="1.0" standalone="yes"?>
<xs:schema id="PersonContacts" xmlns=""
           xmlns:xs="http://www.w3.org/2001/XMLSchema"
           xmlns:msdata="urn:schemas-microsoft-com:xml-msdata">
  <xs:element name="PersonContacts" msdata:IsDataSet="true" msdata:Locale="de-AT">
    <xs:complexType>
      <xs:choice maxOccurs="unbounded">
        <xs:element name="Person">
          <xs:complexType>
            <xs:sequence>
              <xs:element name="ID" msdata:ReadOnly="true"
                          msdata:AutoIncrement="true"
                          msdata:AutoIncrementSeed="1" type="xs:long" />
              <xs:element name="FirstName" type="xs:string" minOccurs="0" />
              <xs:element name="Name" type="xs:string" minOccurs="0" />
            </xs:sequence>
          </xs:complexType>
        </xs:element>
        <xs:element name="Contact">
          <xs:complexType>
            <xs:sequence>
              <xs:element name="ID" msdata:ReadOnly="true"
                          msdata:AutoIncrement="true"
                          msdata:AutoIncrementSeed="1" type="xs:long" />
              <xs:element name="FirstName" type="xs:string" minOccurs="0" />
              <xs:element name="Name" type="xs:string" minOccurs="0" />
              <xs:element name="NickName" type="xs:string" minOccurs="0" />
              <xs:element name="EMail" type="xs:string" minOccurs="0" />
              <xs:element name="Phone" type="xs:string" minOccurs="0" />
              <xs:element name="PersonID" type="xs:long" minOccurs="0" />
            </xs:sequence>
          </xs:complexType>
        </xs:element>
      </xs:choice>
    </xs:complexType>
    <xs:unique name="Constraint1" msdata:PrimaryKey="true">
      <xs:selector xpath=".//Person" />
      <xs:field xpath="ID" />
    </xs:unique>
    <xs:unique name="Contact_Constraint1" msdata:ConstraintName="Constraint1"
                                          msdata:PrimaryKey="true">
      <xs:selector xpath=".//Contact" />
      <xs:field xpath="ID" />
    </xs:unique>
```

```
        <xs:keyref name="PersonHasContacts" refer="Constraint1">
          <xs:selector xpath=".//Contact" />
          <xs:field xpath="PersonID" />
        </xs:keyref>
      </xs:element>
    </xs:schema>
```

XSD already contains some predefined data types such as string or long. We will not go into the assignment compatibility between XSD types and .NET types here. This information can be found in the .NET online documentation or in Table 7.3 (on page 425).

Each DataTable object is stored as a separate, complex XML element (e.g. <xs:element name="Person">) with the columns (DataColumn objects) as XML child elements (e.g. <xs:element name="Name" type="xs:string" minOccurs="0"/>). If we do not want to store a DataColumn object as an XML child element, but rather as an XML attribute, we can specify this in the DataColumn property ColumnMapping. ColumnMapping is of the enumeration type System.Data.MappingType, which contains the constants Attribute, Element, Hidden and SimpleContent.

Loading an XML schema

To load the schema from contacts.xsd into a DataSet again, we can use the methods ReadXmlSchema or InferXmlSchema.

ReadXmlSchema reads schema information but no data, even if the XML file read contains both. For every complex XML data type (e.g. <xs:element name="Person">) it creates a DataTable object.

```
DataSet ds = new DataSet();
ds.ReadXmlSchema("contacts.xsd");
```

Like ReadXmlSchema, InferXmlSchema loads a schema from an XML data source in a DataSet. If the data source does not contain an explicit schema, it attempts to infer one based on the XML data.

Finally, there is the method ReadXml which reads data and schema information from an XML file. If the file does not contain a schema, it creates one from the data according to the following rules (see also .NET online documentation):

- ❑ *Tables* (DataTable) are created from elements with attributes, from elements with child elements or from repeated elements.
- ❑ *Columns* (DataColumn) are created from attributes or from single (not repeated) elements without attributes and without child elements.
- ❑ A relation (DataRelation) is created for a child element, if a table has been created for the child element as well as its parent element. The column names (foreign key as well as primary key) in both tables on which the relation is based must have the same names.

The file data.xml which we generated in the previous section does not contain any relation between Person and Contact. For this, the Contact elements would have to be child elements of the corresponding Person elements and the key of Person would have to be called PersonID, as in the following example:

```
<Person>   -- Person data record
   <PersonID>1</PersonID>   -- key
   <Contact>   -- Contact data record
      <ID>102</ID>   -- key
      ...   -- further elements (FirstName, Name, Phone, EMail)
      <PersonID>1</PersonID>   -- foreign key!!
   </Contact>
   ...   -- further Contact elements and the elements FirstName and Name
</Person>
```

❑ If an element that does not contain child elements and becomes a table contains text, a column with the name "*TableName*_Text" will be added, otherwise the text will be ignored.

In contrast to ReadXml, we can exclude XML elements and XML attributes of certain XML namespaces when creating a schema for a DataSet with InferXmlSchema. The method InferXmlSchema has two formal parameters: the first specifies the XML source, the second the namespaces to exclude. Here is an example of InferXmlSchema that excludes all elements and attributes that belong to the namespace http://dotnet.jku.at/ExcludeNamespace:

```
ds.InferXmlSchema( "other_data.xml",
                new string[] {"http://dotnet.jku.at/ExcludeNamespace"});
```

If a DataSet already contains a schema and data, the question arises as to how it can be combined with new data and a new schema. There are two ways to do this: we can either create a new DataSet and combine it with the existing one with the method Merge, or we can insert the new data into the existing DataSet with ReadXml and InferXmlSchema.

ReadXml and InferXmlSchema add those tables and columns to a DataSet that do not yet exist there. If conflicts arise between the existing DataTables in the DataSet and the ones to be inserted, for example if the tables have the same name but different namespaces, or if existing columns have a different type from that in the XML source, exceptions will be thrown. We now want to look at how to use ReadXml, InferXmlSchema and Merge.

The DataSet ds from the contact example contains a DataTable "Person" with the DataColumns "ID", "FirstName" and "Name". The following file personData.xml also contains an XML element—and thus a table—Person with the child elements or columns ID and EMail. Additionally, the file contains a schema for these data.

```
<?xml version="1.0"?>
<PersonContacts>
  <xs:schema id="PersonContacts" xmlns=""
                xmlns:xs="http://www.w3.org/2001/XMLSchema"
                xmlns:msdata="urn:schemas-microsoft-com:xml-msdata">
    <xs:element name="PersonContacts" msdata:IsDataSet="true">
      <xs:complexType>
        <xs:choice maxOccurs="unbounded">
          <xs:element name="Person">
            <xs:complexType>
              <xs:sequence>
                <xs:element name="ID" msdata:ReadOnly="true"
                                        msdata:AutoIncrement="true" type="xs:long" />
                <xs:element name="EMail" minOccurs="0">
                  <xs:simpleType>
                    <xs:restriction base="xs:string">
                      <xs:maxLength value="50" />
                    </xs:restriction>
                  </xs:simpleType>
                </xs:element>
              </xs:sequence>
            </xs:complexType>
          </xs:element>
        </xs:choice>
      </xs:complexType>
      <xs:unique name="Constraint1" msdata:PrimaryKey="true">
        <xs:selector xpath=".//Person" />
        <xs:field xpath="ID" />
      </xs:unique>
    </xs:element>
  </xs:schema>
  <Person>   -- 1st data record
    <ID>1</ID>
    <EMail>peter@dotnet.jku.at</EMail>
  </Person>
  <Person>   -- 2nd data record
    <ID>2</ID>
    <EMail>gogo@dotnet.jku.at</EMail>
  </Person>
</PersonContacts>
```

Figure 5.15 shows how applying the following three operations modifies the DataSet ds:

- ❏ ds.ReadXml("personData.xml", XmlReadMode.InferSchema);
- ❏ ds.InferXmlSchema("personData.xml", new string[0]);
- ❏ DataSet ds2 = new DataSet(); ds2.ReadXml("personData.xml"); ds.Merge(ds2);

Since personData.xml contains not only data but also an XML schema, InferXmlSchema can use this schema instead of generating a new one. With

ReadXml we can specify an XmlReadMode parameter. If the parameter has the value ReadSchema, the schema will be read from the XML file. If it is InferSchema, a new one will be generated.

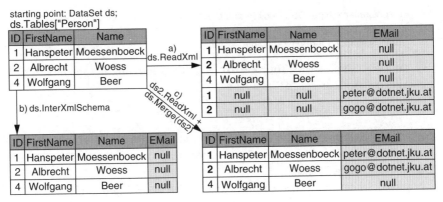

Figure 5.15 *Examples of schema and data migrations*

ReadXml appends data at the end of the table. If the column ID of the table Person is at the same time the key, this will lead to an exception in ReadXml, because the new data records have keys that already exist. ds.Merge(ds2) is only possible if Person has a key (ID) and only elements whose key (<ID>) also occurs in Person occur in the personData.xml.

Typed DataSets

So far we have always accessed the contents of a DataSet via various collections, for example:

```
//----- set name of Person data record with ID=3
ds.Tables["Person"].Rows.Find(3)["Name"]= "Joe";
```

It would be convenient for a developer to be able to access the contents of a table via typed properties. The code would gain readability and certain checks could be carried out as early as at compile time.

In order to achieve this, we could define custom classes that encapsulate the data or we could extend types such as DataSet and DataTable and offer such properties. Each way has its advantages, but all have a critical disadvantage: they take a lot of time and effort.

The .NET Framework contains a tool for exactly this purpose: xsd.exe. It processes an XSD schema and generates classes in C#, VB or JavaScript from it. The classes generated are made available in source code and can thus be edited manually later on. A command-line option of xsd.exe allows the developer to specify

whether DataSet or DataTable should be extended or whether completely independent classes should be generated.

In the following example we access a class PersonContacts which we generated
as a subclass of DataSet from the schema contained in contacts.xsd.

```
PersonContacts typedDS = new PersonContacts();
// ... Code to fill typedDS with data ...
typedDS.Person.FindByID(3).Name = "Joe";
```

We ran the command-line tool xsd.exe with the following parameters in order to
generate contacts.cs:

```
xsd contacts.xsd /dataset
```

contacts.cs contains the C# class PersonContacts, PersonDataTable, PersonRow,
PersonRowChangeEvent,   ContactDateTable,   ContactRow   and
ContactRowChangeEvent.

Visual Studio .NET also employs xsd.exe for accessing databases.

5.6   Exercises

1. **Database independence.** How does ADO.NET achieve independence from
   specific database implementations?

2. **OLEDB and MSSQL.** The .NET SDK offers data provider implementations
   for OLEDB and Microsoft SQL Server. Is it possible to access a Microsoft
   SQL Server database also via OLEDB? When would you use an OLEDB
   implementation and when a Microsoft SQL Server implementation?

3. **Data access modes.** Which ADO.NET interface is used for connection-
   oriented data access? Which class is used for connectionless data access?

4. **Data access modes.** Assume that several users want to access a database table
   at the same time. Would you suggest using a connection-oriented or a connectionless access protocol?

5. **Data update.** Are modifications to a DataSet or DataTable object automatically updated in the database? If yes, which mechanism is used? If not, how
   could the user accomplish this task?

6. **Connection-oriented data access.** This exercise uses a *contacts* database
   similar to the one that was used in Section 5.3. This time, however, we use
   Microsoft Access instead of MS SQL Server as the database provider. You can
   find this database under the name Contacts.mdb on the CD that comes with
   this book. It contains two tables with the following fields:

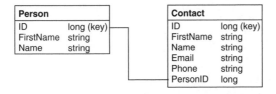

Write a program SqlBatch which reads a text file containing SQL commands and executes them. The text file starts with a connection string, which is followed by the SQL commands terminated by semicolons, for example:

```
Provider=Microsoft.Jet.OLEDB.4.0;Data Source=Contacts.mdb
SELECT * FROM Contact;
SELECT * FROM Person;
UPDATE Person SET Name = 'Modified' WHERE ID = 1;
SELECT * FROM Person;
```

The program should be called like this:

```
SqlBatch input.txt output.txt
```

The results, as well as any error messages, should be written to the specified output file. The results of SELECT commands should be printed in tabular form.

Process the SQL commands in connection-oriented mode using an IDataReader object. All commands in the input file should form a transaction. If one command fails, other commands already executed should be rolled back.

7. **Connectionless data access.** This exercise reuses the Contacts.mdb database from the previous exercise. Write a program DumpDB that reads certain tables of a database into a DataSet and displays their contents on the console. The tables to be listed should be specified by command-line arguments. For example, the command:

    ```
    DumpDB Contacts.mdb Person Contact
    ```

    should display the tables Person and Contact from the Contacts.mdb database.

8. **Storing a data set in an XML file.** Write a command-line tool ExportXML which reads all data from a database of your choice into a DataSet object and stores it in an XML file. The command should be called as

    ```
    ExportXML "connectionString" outputFileName
    ```

    The XML file should also contain the database schema.

9. **Efficiency.** Is the import of data from an XML file into a database efficient? If not, can you imagine an alternative solution?

6 ASP.NET

One of the major application areas of .NET is the Internet. ASP.NET is the part of the .NET technology which deals with Internet applications (as they occur, for example, in electronic commerce). At the heart of this stands the design of dynamic web pages with *server scripts* and *web forms*, two technologies which we will examine more closely in this chapter. Actually, *web services* are also considered to be part of ASP.NET, but we will discuss them on their own in Chapter 7.

ASP.NET is based on Microsoft's older ASP technology [Bus00]. Both names stand for *Active Server Pages*, a technique that allows the dynamic assembly of web pages from data available on a server. In this way it becomes possible to generate shopping catalogues, event schedules or stock market reports from up-to-date data at run time.

Although there are certain similarities with ASP, ASP.NET is radically different in its architecture and is also more powerful:

- ❑ **Object-orientation.** An ASP.NET page (also called aspx page) is compiled into a class which already inherits many useful features from a base class of the .NET Framework. The GUI (*graphical user interface*) elements such as buttons, text fields or lists that appear on web pages are also modelled as classes and are used by the page class.
- ❑ **Web controls.** There is a rich library of GUI elements (so-called *web controls*) that exceed by far the elements available in HTML, but can still be displayed by any web browser. Web controls can not only be used like HTML elements, but can also be accessed as objects from code fragments and can be configured in ways impossible in normal HTML.
- ❑ **Separation of layout and application logic.** While HTML and script code used to be heavily interwoven in older ASP pages, ASP.NET allows a clear distinction between the layout of a page, which is described inside an aspx file, and the application logic which exists as pure code (for example in C#, Visual Basic .NET or any other .NET language) in a separate file. Thus web designers and programmers can work on separate files.
- ❑ **Component-orientation.** Web controls are components that trigger events to which other components can react. Attributes of web controls can be set with properties in HTML-like tags.

❏ **Interactive design of web pages.** Visual Studio .NET supports the interactive creation of web pages with drag and drop, where properties and events of web controls can be edited without any programming effort. This mode of operation resembles the creation of user interfaces for local application with *Windows forms* (see Section 4.6).

❏ **Compilation instead of interpretation.** Whereas script code was *interpreted* in ASP (e.g. in VBScript or JavaScript), in ASP.NET it is written in a language such as C# or Visual Basic .NET, which is *compiled*. Therefore ASP.NET applications run substantially faster and have access to the entire .NET library.

❏ **Improved state management.** In the old ASP the state of GUI elements (for example the text of a text field) was not preserved automatically when a web page was updated. ASP programmers had tediously to restore the state on their own. In ASP.NET this happens automatically, so programmers no longer have to deal with this.

We will now work through ASP.NET step by step. Firstly, we will look at how to create simple web pages dynamically. Then we will turn our attention to the extensive domain of designing graphical user interfaces with web controls. Finally, we will deal with advanced topics such as validity checks, state management, and configuration.

6.1   Creating Dynamic Web Pages

Static HTML Pages

Most programmers will already have worked with HTML (*Hypertext Markup Language*) or will at least have seen HTML texts. HTML is a language for describing layouts of web pages. An example of a very simple HTML text is:

```
<html>
   <head>
      <title>Simple HTML Page</title>
   </head>
   <body>
      <h1>Welcome</h1>
      You are visitor number 1 to this page!
   </body>
</html>
```

It is made up of text pieces which are structured by pairs of tags (for example <html> ... </html>). The meaning of the tags is explained, for example, in [HTML], [HTML1]. If such a text is saved, for example, in a file First.html on a computer that has a web server running (e.g. Microsoft's *Internet Information Server* (IIS) [IIS]), it can be viewed with a web browser by navigating the browser to the address of the file, for example:

http://dotnet.jku.at/book/samples/6/First.html

The browser will then show the image of Figure 6.1.

Figure 6.1 *Representation of First.html in a web browser*

What happens here behind the scenes? The browser requests the HTML file from the server using the HTTP protocol [HTTP], a stateless client/server protocol that simply delivers the text of the requested file (see Figure 6.2). Subsequently the browser interprets this text and displays it with the appropriate formatting.

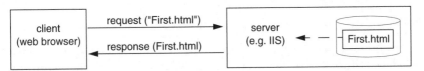

Figure 6.2 *Request of an HTML file*

First.html describes a *static web page*, which displays exactly the text that is in the file. Every visitor will thus find out that he is visitor number 1, which, of course, is not correct. It would be better if we could count the visits and display the result in the page. What we want therefore is a visitor counter, as can be found on many web pages.

Dynamic aspx Pages

In order to implement a visitor counter we need a *dynamic web page*, which does not hardcode the number of visits in its text, but inserts it into the text on demand. We can keep track of the current counter value, for example, in a file Counter.dat, which we read and update every time the page is requested. All we then need to do is to insert the current value of the counter into the page. For this ASP.NET offers ways to insert code fragments that calculate and inject certain values into the

HTML code of a page. These code fragments can be written in any .NET language and are enclosed by the character sequences <% and %>. Dynamic web pages are stored in files ending in aspx. We will name our page First.aspx. It looks as follows:

```
<%@ Page Language="C#" %>
<%@ Import Namespace="System.IO" %>
<html>
    <head> <title>Dynamic ASPX Page</title> </head>
    <body>
        <h1>Welcome</h1>
        You are visitor number <%
        FileStream s;
        s = new FileStream("D:\\Data\\Counter.dat", FileMode.OpenOrCreate);
        int n;
        try {
            BinaryReader r = new BinaryReader(s);
            n = r.ReadInt32();
        } catch { n = 0; }  // if file is empty
        n++;
        s.Seek(0, SeekOrigin.Begin);
        BinaryWriter w = new BinaryWriter(s);
        w.Write(n);
        s.Close();
        Response.Write(n);
        %> to this page!
    </body>
</html>
```

The parts necessary for calculating the current value of the counter are highlighted in bold face. The first two lines contain so-called *directives*, which indicate how to process the page. The Page directive, for example, says that the script code of the page is written in C#. The Import directive imports the namespace System.IO, which we need for file operations. It is equivalent to the using statement of C#. There are more directives, which we will introduce in the course of this chapter.

But now for the script code. It opens a file Counter.dat as a FileStream and attempts to read the counter value n with a BinaryReader. If the file is so far empty, an exception will be thrown and caught and n is set to 0. Subsequently the counter is increased and written back to the file with a BinaryWriter. Before that, we reset the writing position to the start of the file with Seek.

The last line of the script code is especially interesting. Response.Write(n) inserts the value of n into the HTML text at the position of the script code. Response is an object that represents the response of the server to the web browser. ASP.NET copies all HTML code from the file into this object automatically. The dynamically computed parts have to be inserted with Response.Write (see also Section 6.7.1).

Virtual Directories

Before we can test our new page, we have to create a *virtual directory* on our web server, into which we put the aspx file. A virtual directory contains all files that make up a web application (aspx pages, code, configuration files and so on). In order to create such a directory, we open the *Internet Information Services* (Control Panel | Administrative Tools | Internet Service Manager) as shown in Figure 6.3 (here under Windows 2000).

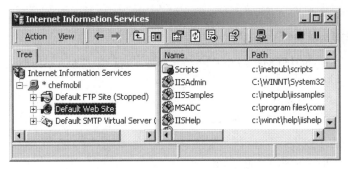

Figure 6.3 *Managing virtual directories under Windows 2000*

We right-click on Default Web Site and select New | Virtual Directory from the context menu that appears. This opens a wizard that leads us through the process of creating a virtual directory. Firstly, it wants us to provide an alias name for our directory. Here, for example, we enter the name samples and then click on Next. Then the wizard asks us to provide a path to a physical directory where our aspx files are stored (e.g. D:\book\samples). We enter this path and click Next. In the following dialog we can set access rights. For now, we will leave the default settings as they are and click Next (we can still change them later by right-clicking on the virtual directory and selecting Properties). After clicking on Finish, our new virtual directory appears as a subdirectory of Default Web Site. Assuming that the file First.aspx is in the directory samples (actually in its subdirectory 6, because we are in Chapter 6 of this book), we can navigate a web browser to it with the URI

    http://localhost/samples/6/First.aspx

If our computer has the domain name dotnet.jku.at we can also use the URI

    http://dotnet.jku.at/samples/6/First.aspx

This brings us to the page shown in Figure 6.4. On each visit to this page the counter is incremented by 1.

Figure 6.4 *Representation of First.aspx in a web browser*

What Happens Behind the Scenes?

If we take a look at the HTML source of Figure 6.4 via the *View* menu of the browser, it looks like this:

```html
<html>
   <head> <title>Dynamic ASPX Page</title> </head>
   <body>
      <h1>Welcome</h1>
      You are visitor number 3 to this page!
   </body>
</html>
```

There is no remaining trace of the script code or the directives. All we see is the HTML text which ASP.NET has generated from First.aspx and the counter file. Figure 6.5 illustrates what happens when an aspx page is requested.

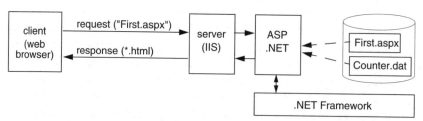

Figure 6.5 *Requesting a web page under ASP.NET*

The web server forwards the page request to ASP.NET which generates an HTML page from First.aspx and Counter.dat using the .NET Framework and returns this page to the client via the web server.

Server-side Script Code in aspx Files

Some readers might complain that the rather long embedded C# code obstructs their view of the surrounding HTML. Therefore we now show a slightly modified

version named Second.aspx, where the calculation of the counter value has been
extracted into a method which stands between <script> tags.

```
<%@ Page Language="C#" %>
<%@ Import namespace="System.IO" %>
<html>
  <head>
    <title>Visitor Counter</title>
    <script Language="C#" Runat="server">
      int CounterValue() {
        FileStream s;
        s = new FileStream("D:\\Data\\Counter.dat", FileMode.OpenOrCreate);
        int n;
        try {
          BinaryReader r = new BinaryReader(s);
          n = r.ReadInt32();
        } catch { n = 0; }
        n++;
        s.Seek(0, SeekOrigin.Begin);
        BinaryWriter w = new BinaryWriter(s);
        w.Write(n);
        s.Close();
        return n;
      }
    </script>
  </head>
  <body>
    <h1>Welcome</h1>
    You are visitor number <%= CounterValue() %> to this page!
  </body>
</html>
```

Between the tags <script> and </script> we can declare arbitrary methods and variables that we can then reference from the code fragments between <% and %>. We
also have to state the language of the script code and provide the attribute
Runat="server". This attribute is important and indicates that the script code
should not be executed on the client as with JavaScript, but on the server. It has to
run there in order to be able to read the counter value from the file Counter.dat.

Now the method CounterValue can be called at the appropriate point. The correct notation for writing the counter value into the HTML stream would be

```
<% Response.Write(CounterValue()); %>
```

but the abbreviated form

```
<%= CounterValue() %>
```

does exactly the same.

As we all know, a method always belongs to a class. But to which class does our method CounterValue belong? It belongs to the class Second_aspx, which ASP.NET creates from the file Second.aspx and which looks like this:

```
namespace ASP {
    ...
    using System.IO;

    public class Second_aspx : System.Web.UI.Page,
                               System.Web.SessionState.IRequiresSessionState {
        ...
        int CounterValue() {
            FileStream s;
            s = new FileStream("D:\\Data\\Counter.dat", FileMode.OpenOrCreate);
            ...
            return n;
        }
        ...
        private void __Render__control1( System.Web.UI.HtmlTextWriter __output,
                                         System.Web.UI.Control parameterContainer) {
            __output.Write("\r\n<html>\r\n\t<head>\r\n\t\t<title>");
            __output.Write("Visitor Counter</title>\r\n\r\n\r\n\t\t");
            __output.Write("\r\n\r\n\r\n\t</head>\r\n\t<body>\r\n\t\t<h1>");
            __output.Write("Welcome</h1>\r\n\t\t\tYou are visitor number ");
            __output.Write(CounterValue());
            __output.Write(" to this page!\r\n\t</body>\r\n</html>\r\n");
        }
    }
}
```

The parts in bold face are those that we have written, the rest has been generated. We see that the class Second_aspx extends System.Web.UI.Page. From there it inherits a lot of behaviour that is common to all aspx pages. The method __Render__control1 generates the HTML text for this page, including the counter value. The result in the web browser is again the same as in Figure 6.4.

Whenever a web browser requests the file Second.aspx, ASP.NET checks whether the class Second_aspx already exists in compiled form. If not, it will be generated as described above and compiled. Then ASP.NET creates a new object of this class which eventually calls its render method in order to generate the HTML text. This is then returned to the browser. Thus developers never explicitly compile their aspx files. This is done automatically in the background by ASP.NET.

Code-behind Files

To some readers even Second.aspx might still seem too bloated. It would be better to keep the C# code completely apart from the HTML code and write it into a separate file. In this way web designers and programmers would have separate documents which they could edit independently.

In ASP.NET this is possible in the following way: the class that ASP.NET generates from the aspx file is, as we have seen, derived from the class Page. But we can just as well derive it from a class that we have written ourselves (e.g. CounterPage) and that is derived from Page. This class CounterPage can be implemented in a separate file CounterPage.cs. Such files are called *code-behind files*. The generated page class inherits all fields and methods from CounterPage and can thus use them. The file CounterPage.cs looks like this:

```
using System.IO;

public class CounterPage : System.Web.UI.Page {
    public int CounterValue() {
        FileStream s = new FileStream("D:\\Data\\Counter.dat", FileMode.OpenOrCreate);
        int n;
        try {
            BinaryReader r = new BinaryReader(s);
            n = r.ReadInt32();
        } catch { n = 0; }
        n++;
        s.Seek(0, SeekOrigin.Begin);
        BinaryWriter w = new BinaryWriter(s);
        w.Write(n);
        s.Close();
        return n;
    }
}
```

In our third version of the counter page (Third.aspx) all we need to do is declare which class the page should be derived from and where to find the code of that class. These specifications are part of the Page *directive*. Thus Third.aspx shrinks to the following piece of code:

```
<%@ Page Language="C#" Inherits="CounterPage" Src="CounterPage.cs" %>
<html>
    <head>
        <title>Visitor Counter</title>
    </head>
    <body>
        <h1>Welcome</h1>
        You are visitor number <%= CounterValue() %> to this page!
    </body>
</html>
```

If we open Third.aspx in a web browser, we will again get the same picture as in Figure 6.4. From Third.aspx, ASP.NET generates a class Third_aspx which this time extends CounterPage (see Figure 6.6). The method CounterValue now belongs to the class CounterPage and is inherited by Third_aspx, so that it can be used there. The rest is as described above.

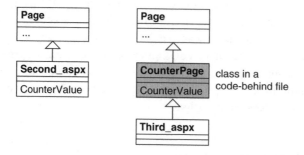

Figure 6.6 *Inheritance hierarchy of page classes without and with code-behind file*

6.2   Simple Web Forms

Most interactive web sites incorporate forms. They consist of text fields, list boxes, check boxes, and the like. The user fills out the form and then presses a button to send the data to a receiver that evaluates it.

In ASP.NET, forms (so-called *web forms*) play an important role. But in addition to web forms there are also the more basic HTML forms. Since web forms are constructed similarly, we will first look at HTML forms before we go into web forms.

HTML Forms

An HTML document can contain any number of forms, which are specified between <form> tags. Every HTML form is made up of elements such as

text fields	<input type="text" ...>	Text
buttons	<input type="button" ...>	click me
check boxes	<input type="checkbox" ...>	☐ check box
radio buttons	<input type="radio" ...>	○ radio button
drop-down-lists	<select ...> ... </select>	London ▾

A description of all these elements is beyond the scope of this book, but can be found for example in [HTML1]. For our purpose, an example of an HTML form should suffice.

```
...
<body>
    <form action="mailto:office@dotnet.jku.at" method="post">
        <input type="text" name="firstname"> First name<br>
        <input type="text" name="lastname"> Last name<br>
        <input type="radio" name="sex" value="male" checked> male
        <input type="radio" name="sex" value="female"> female<br><br>
        <input type="submit" value="Send">
    </form>
</body>
```

After storing this text into a file and then opening it with a web browser, we will see the picture shown in Figure 6.7.

Figure 6.7 *HTML form in a web browser*

If we now enter "Charlie" as first name and "Brown" as last name and click on "Send", the data is sent in an e-mail to office@dotnet.jku.at, as we have specified in the <form> element. The names and values of the form elements are encoded like this:

```
firstname=Charlie
lastname=Brown
sex=male
```

This encoding corresponds to the specification method="post": The data is written into the input stream of the receiver in the form of name–value pairs. If we had instead written

```
<form action="http://localhost/samples/Foo.asp" method="get">
```

the browser would have requested the page Foo.asp and the data would have been attached as name–value pairs to the address of the page, like this http://localhost/samples/Foo.asp?**firstname=Charlie&lastname=Brown&sex=male**

In both cases the receiver is responsible for reading and decoding the data, for which it usually has appropriate methods available. HTML forms allow three types of receivers:

❑ an e-mail recipient, e.g. action="mailto:office@dotnet.jku.at"
❑ a program, e.g. action="http://dotnet.jku.at/cgi-bin/myprog"
❑ a web site, e.g. action="http://dotnet.jku.at/foo/bar.asp"

Programs that evaluate form data can be written in any language, such as C, *Pascal,* or *Perl,* and are invoked by the web server via the CGI protocol (*Common Gateway Interface* [CGI]). After evaluating the form data, the program sends a new HTML page back to the browser, which displays it.

Form data can also be sent to a web site that is implemented with ASP (*Active Server Pages* [Bus00]), JSP (*Java Server Pages* [FK00]), or PHP (*Hypertext Processor* [PHP]). This web site then processes HTML and script code to generate a new HTML page, which is sent back to the browser.

Aside from the fact that writing CGI programs or ASP pages requires more effort than using ASP.NET, HTML forms offer only limited expressiveness. First of all, there is only a limited number of form elements available in HTML and these cannot be extended. Furthermore, HTML form elements do not fit into the object-oriented programming model of ASP.NET, where web pages as well as all controls contained in them are *objects* that can be referenced in C# programs like ordinary objects. In fact, HTML elements can be addressed like objects in scripting languages such as JavaScript, but not in compiled languages such as C#. For this reason ASP.NET offers its own set of form elements, which resemble those of HTML.

Sample Web Form

Web forms—like HTML forms—are described by <form> tags, which, however, must have the attribute Runat="server", meaning that they are evaluated on the server side. The controls in a web form (e.g. text fields, buttons, check boxes) are called *web controls* and have the general notation

<asp:*ClassName PropertyName*="*value*" ... Runat="server" > ... </asp:*ClassName*>

or also

<asp:*ClassName PropertyName*="*value*" ... Runat="server" />

Every control is implemented by a class from the namespace System.Web.UI.Web-Controls and is denoted by its class name in the form. The class Button, for example, is denoted as <asp:Button ...>. Every property of the control's class can be specified as an attribute of the <asp> element. A button, for example, has a property Text, which holds its caption and which can be set with <asp:Button Text="OK" ...>. All controls have a property ID that specifies their name. With this name the control can be accessed in the code like a variable.

As an example, suppose we wish to create a web form that allows us to add up amounts of money and display the current balance. We need a text field, where we can enter the amount, a button to confirm the input, and a static text to display the balance. These controls are already available through the classes TextBox, Button and Label. We just have to embed them in a <form> element and write this to an aspx file, which we call, for example, Adder.aspx.

```
<%@ Page Language="C#" Inherits="AdderPage" Src="Adder.aspx.cs" %>
<html>
    <head> <title>Balance</title> </head>
    <body>
        <form method="post" Runat="server">
            <b>Current balance:</b>
            <asp:Label ID="total" Text="0" Runat="server"/> Dollars<br><br>
            <asp:TextBox ID="amount" Runat="server"/>
            <asp:Button ID="ok" Text="Deposit" Runat="server" />
        </form>
    </body>
</html>
```

The three controls have the names total, amount and ok. The display of the current balance is initialized to "0" and the button shows the caption "Deposit". Be careful not to forget the attribute Runat="server", which must be specified with all controls, and the <form> element as well.

Some controls such as Label allow the following notation as an alternative to using the Text attribute:

```
<asp:Label ID="total" Runat="server"> 0 </asp:Label>
```

For every web form the programmer can implement a code-behind class, which contains all controls of the form as fields. In our example we call this class AdderPage and put it in a file Adder.aspx.cs which looks like this:

```
using System;
using System.Web.UI;
using System.Web.UI.WebControls;

public class AdderPage : Page {
    protected Label total;          // for <asp:Label ID="total" .../>
    protected TextBox amount;       // for <asp:TextBox ID="amount" .../>
    protected Button ok;            // for <asp:Button ID="ok" .../>

    ...
}
```

Please keep in mind that AdderPage must extend System.Web.UI.Page and is itself the superclass of the generated class Adder_aspx. In contrast to HTML pages, aspx pages have the restriction that they may only contain a single pair of <form> tags.

If we place Adder.aspx and Adder.aspx.cs in our virtual directory samples, we can navigate a browser to

http://localhost/samples/6/Adder.aspx

and get the picture shown in Figure 6.8. It will take a little longer to display the page for the very first time, because that is when the class Adder_aspx is generated and compiled. All subsequent requests of the page will be served considerably faster.

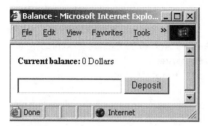

Figure 6.8 *Representation of Adder.aspx in a web browser*

Out of curiosity we look at the HTML code of the page via the *View* menu and are stunned. It contains nothing but HTML. All <asp> elements are gone and have been replaced with equivalent HTML tags:

```
<html>
   <head> <title>Balance</title> </head>
   <body>
      <form name="_ctl0" method="post" action="Adder.aspx" id="_ctl0">
         <input type="hidden" name="__VIEWSTATE"
            value="dDwxNTg0NTEzNzMyOzs+" />
         <b>Current balance:</b>
         <span id="total"> 0 </span>
         Dollars<br><br>
         <input name="amount" type="text" id="amount" />
         <input type="submit" name="ok" value="Deposit" id="ok" />
      </form>
   </body>
</html>
```

ASP.NET converts web controls to standard HTML elements. This guarantees that the documents delivered by the server can be displayed by any web browser. This works even in the case where C# and the .NET Framework have been used at the server side and are not available to the web browser at the client side.

In the above HTML code we see another noteworthy detail: There is an element <input type="hidden" ...> that contains a oddly encoded value. This is the page state where the values of the controls on the page are encoded. ASP.NET needs this information when the filled-out form is returned to the server. We will see more details about this in Section 6.7.2.

Up to now our page has merely been displayed, but has not accomplished anything useful. What we want to achieve is that a click on "Deposit" adds the amount entered in the text field to the current balance and displays the new value on the page.

Clicking on a button triggers an event which we can catch and handle. All we need to do is to assign an event handler (for example, a method called ButtonClick) to the Click event:

```
<asp:Button ID="ok" Text="Deposit" Runat="server" OnClick="ButtonClick" />
```

and implement it in Adder.aspx.cs:

```
using System; using System.Web.UI; using System.Web.UI.WebControls;

public class AderPage : Page {
    protected Label total;
    protected TextBox amount;
    protected Button ok;

    public void ButtonClick (object sender, EventArgs e) {
        int totalVal = Convert.ToInt32(total.Text);
        int amountVal = Convert.ToInt32(amount.Text);
        total.Text = (totalVal + amountVal).ToString();
    }
}
```

Now ASP.NET makes sure that a click on the button "Deposit" invokes the method ButtonClick. There we can access the values of the other controls (amount.Text and total.Text). We store their sum in total.Text and thus see the modified balance on our web site (see Figure 6.9).

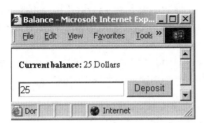

Figure 6.9 The web form of Figure 6.8 after adding 25 dollars

Note that the text field retains the value 25 even after clicking the button. ASP.NET retains the state of all controls, in contrast to the older ASP technology where the programmer had to take care of restoring the state of the controls before redisplaying the page.

So far, we have drawn a very simplified picture of how things work when the button "Deposit" is clicked. In the next section we want to look behind the scenes and find out how ASP.NET handles events.

6.3   Event Handling in ASP.NET

Web forms work according to an *event-driven model*. Every user interaction such as clicking a button, filling out a text field, marking a check box, or selecting an entry from a drop-down list triggers an event to which the program can react. Additionally, there are events that occur even without any intervention by the user, for example when loading a web page or immediately before a web control is rendered to HTML. In this section we will look at how events are triggered and handled.

Round Trip of a Web Page

Normally events are triggered by a user in a web browser. Then either the browser directly (that is the client) or the server can deal with them.

If the event should be handled at the client, the corresponding code must be written in a scripting language such as *JavaScript* or *VBScript*. This form of event handling, however, has nothing to do with ASP.NET and therefore we will not deal with it any further (see for example [Holz02] or [JS]).

If the event should be handled at the server, it must be sent to the server together with the contents of the page. There a handler method will be invoked that evaluates the page, possibly rewrites parts of it and returns it to the client which displays it anew in the web browser. This cycle is called a *round trip*.

Not all events cause a round trip but only so-called *postback events* do. They are essentially triggered by clicks on Button, ImageButton and LinkButton controls. If, on the other hand, a text field is modified, a check box marked or a list entry selected, the corresponding events will just be recorded and only treated at the next round trip. Such events are called *cached events*.

But in some situations even a cached event should immediately trigger a round trip. This can be achieved by specifying the attribute AutoPostBack="true" at the corresponding control, for example:

```
<asp:TextBox ID="amount" Runat="server" AutoPostBack="true" />
```

Modifying the contents of this text field and pressing the enter key or repositioning the cursor triggers a TextChanged event, which now instantly causes a round trip and thus allows the event to be handled at the server immediately.

On every round trip a new object of the page class is created and filled with new control objects. In order to be able to serve any number of clients the web server is *stateless*, that is, it does not remember what a page looked like previously. Rather, the state of the page and its controls is automatically encoded within the page itself and travels with the page on every round trip.

Event Handlers

Events lead to the invocation of methods that match the following delegate interface:

```
delegate void EventHandler(object sender, EventArgs args);
```

The first parameter refers to the object that triggered the event (for example the button that was clicked). The second parameter carries arguments of the event, in case it requires some, which most events do not. If there are no arguments, args has the value EventArgs.Empty and will be ignored.

Every control can trigger a number of events for which event handlers can be installed. The class Button, for example, has an event variable Click where event handlers for mouse clicks can be stored:

```
class Button : System.Web.UI.WebControl {
    public event EventHandler Click;
    ...
}
```

If we have declared a button named ok and a corresponding method ButtonClick in the code-behind file of a web page,

```
protected Button ok;

public void ButtonClick(object sender, EventArgs e) {
    ...
}
```

we can install the method by writing:

```
ok.Click += new EventHandler(ButtonClick);
```

The same happens when ASP.NET compiles the line

```
<asp:Button ID="ok"... OnClick="ButtonClick" />
```

ButtonClick is installed as an event handler for ok.

Types of Events

All web controls as well as the web page itself are derived from the class System.Web.UI.Control (see Figure 6.10).

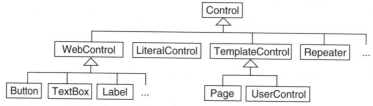

Figure 6.10 *Class* Control *and some of its subclasses*

Control declares a few common events, which all derived classes inherit and upon which they can react. These events are listed in Table 6.1.

Table 6.1 *Standard events of class* Control

Event	is triggered ...
Init	after a control object has been created. This event can be used for initializing the object.
Load	after the data sent from the browser has been assigned to the control object.
DataBinding	when the control object is bound to a certain data source (see Section 6.4.9).
PreRender	before the Render method of this control object is invoked, thus before HTML for this object is generated.
Unload	before the control object is released at the end of a round trip. Finalization tasks can be carried out here.

In addition to these standard events, certain controls can also trigger events of their own. Table 6.2 gives some examples.

Table 6.2 *Specific events of certain controls*

Control	Event	What does the event indicate?
Button	Click	The button has been clicked.
TextBox	TextChanged	The contents of the text field have changed.
CheckBox	CheckedChanged	The check box has been (un)checked.
ListControl	SelectedIndexChanged	A new list entry has been selected.
CustomValidator	ServerValidate	The validator is to execute its checks.

Click is a *postback event* that leads to a round trip of the page. All other events of Table 6.2 are *cached events* that will only be handled at the next round trip. The standard events of Table 6.1 occur automatically on every round trip and describe the *life cycle* of a page.

We can assign an event handler to every event *Evt* of a control *Ctrl*. We can do this either in the aspx page with

```
<asp:Ctrl ID="ctrlName" Runat="server" OnEvt="EvtHandler" />
```

or in the code-behind file with

```
ctrlName.Evt += new EventHandler(EvtHandler);
```

Life Cycle of an aspx Page

On every round trip a new page object is created. It is then processed in a series of steps and eventually generates an HTML stream that is sent back to the web browser. These steps define the *life cycle* of the page and the objects it contains.

1. **Creation.** The page object and all controls on the page are created and connected to form a hierarchy. The page from Figure 6.8, for example, leads to the tree shown in Figure 6.11.

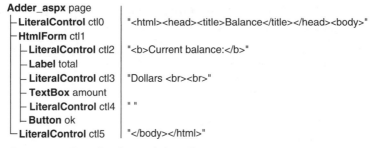

Figure 6.11 *Hierarchy of controls from Figure 6.8*

2. **Initialization.** An Init event is triggered for all controls and then for the page object itself. The objects can react by carrying out any initializations that are necessary.
3. **Loading.** Firstly, the state of all controls on the page before the last round trip is restored from the hidden field __VIEWSTATE which has been "smuggled into" the HTML code of the page. Then the data that the user has entered is assigned to the controls. Finally, a Load event is triggered for the page object and then for all controls.
4. **Event processing.** This phase is when the actual logic of the page is executed. First, all cached events for the controls on the page are handled (e.g.

TextChanged). Then, the postback event that caused the round trip is processed (e.g. Click).

5. **Rendering to HTML.** Now PreRender events are triggered topdown for all objects of the control tree (as shown in Figure 6.11). This gives the programmer a final opportunity to apply any changes before the objects are rendered to HTML. Next, the method SaveViewState is invoked on all objects in order to store their state in the hidden field __VIEWSTATE. Finally, the Render method is invoked on all the objects of the tree. This will generate the HTML code.

6. **Unloading.** In this ultimate phase the Dispose method is invoked on all objects and subsequently the Unload event is triggered, which allows possible finalization tasks to be carried out (for example closing files).

Besides System.Web.UI there are also other libraries of controls, for example the *Mobile Internet Toolkit* [MITK] which is used for mobile devices such as telephones. Such controls decide according to the browser type whether they should render to HTML or to WML (*Wireless Markup Language* [WML]) in phase 5.

We want to use the following example to convince ourselves that the events actually occur in the order given above. Therefore we write the event handlers for the page and the button in Adder.aspx so that they print out debug comments.

There is a simplified method for setting the event handlers of a page: if we specify the attribute AutoEventWireup="true" in the page directive of the aspx file, all methods with the name Page_*EventName* will automatically be bound to the event *EventName* of the page class. Adder.aspx thus looks like this:

```
<%@ Page  Language="C#" Inherits="AdderPage" Src="Adder.aspx.cs"
          AutoEventWireup="true" %>
<html>
   <head> <title>Balance</title> </head>
   <body>
      <form method="post" Runat="server">
         <b>Current balance:</b>
         <asp:Label ID="total" Runat="server"> 0 </asp:Label>
         Dollars<br><br>
         <asp:TextBox ID="amount" Runat="server" />
         <asp:Button ID="ok" Text="Deposit" Runat="server" OnInit="ButtonInit" />
      </form>
   </body>
</html>
```

The event handlers with the debug outputs are in the code-behind file Adder.aspx.cs:

```
using System;
using System.Web.UI;
using System.Web.UI.WebControls;
using System.IO;
```

```
public class AdderPage : Page {
    protected Label total;
    protected TextBox amount;
    protected Button ok;
    private StreamWriter w = File.CreateText("trace.txt");

    private void Put(string s) { w.WriteLine(s); }

    //----- automatically bound event handler of Page
    public void Page_Init(object sender, EventArgs e) {
        Put("Page.Init ");
        ok.Load += new EventHandler(ButtonLoad);
        ok.Click += new EventHandler(ButtonClick);
        ok.PreRender += new EventHandler(ButtonPreRender);
        ok.Unload += new EventHandler(ButtonUnload);
    }
    public void Page_Load(object sender, EventArgs e) { Put("Page.Load"); }
    public void Page_PreRender(object sender, EventArgs e) { Put("Page.PreRender"); }
    public void Page_Unload(object sender, EventArgs e) { Put("Page.Unload"); w.Close();}

    //----- in Page_Init manually bound event handlers of the Button ok
    public void ButtonClick(object sender, EventArgs e) {
        Put("Button.Click");
        int totalVal = Convert.ToInt32(total.Text);
        int amountVal = Convert.ToInt32(amount.Text);
        total.Text = (totalVal + amountVal).ToString();
    }
    public void ButtonInit(object sender, EventArgs e) { Put("Button.Init"); }
    public void ButtonLoad(object sender, EventArgs e) { Put("Button.Load"); }
    public void ButtonPreRender(object sender, EventArgs e) { Put("Button.PreRender"); }
    public void ButtonUnload(object sender, EventArgs e) { Put("Button.Unload"); }
}
```

AutoEventWireup causes Page_Init to be installed as event handler for the Init event. In this method we now install the event handlers for the button ok. The debug outputs are written to the file trace.txt and we get:

```
Button.Init
Page.Init
Page.Load
Button.Load
Button.Click
Page.PreRender
Button.PreRender
Button.Unload
Page.Unload
```

Please note that the Init event handler of the button ok cannot be set in Page_Init, because the Init event for the button occurs before the Init event of the page. Therefore we must assign it in Adder.aspx with OnInit="ButtonInit".

6.4 Web Server Controls

ASP.NET offers a wide range of web server controls of which we have so far only seen TextBox, Button and Label. Besides the predefined controls, programmers may develop their own controls, as long as ways can be found to map them to HTML (see Section 6.6). In this way it becomes possible to design highly customized web interfaces.

6.4.1 Control

The base class of all controls is System.Web.UI.Control, from which not only the web controls are derived but also the class Page, which is the base class for our web pages. Figure 6.11 shows a small excerpt of all classes derived from Control.

Control declares a number of properties, methods and events that all subclasses inherit. Here we see a part of its interface:

```
public class Control : IComponent,IDisposable,IParserAccessor,IDataBindingsAccessor {
    //----- properties
    public virtual string ID { get; set; }
    public virtual ControlCollection Controls { get; }
    public virtual Control Parent { get; }
    public virtual Page Page { get; set; }
    public virtual bool Visible { get; set; }
    protected virtual StateBag ViewState { get; }
    public virtual bool EnableViewState { get; set; }
    ...
    //----- methods
    public virtual bool HasControls();
    public virtual Control FindControl(string id);
    public void RenderControl(HtmlTextWriter w);
    public virtual void DataBind();
    protected virtual void LoadViewState(object savedState);
    protected virtual object SaveViewState();
    protected virtual void Render(HtmlTextWriter w);
    ...
    //----- events
    public event EventHandler Init;
    public event EventHandler Load;
    public event EventHandler DataBinding;
    public event EventHandler PreRender;
    public event EventHandler Unload;
    ...
}
```

Properties. The property ID holds the name that is used when this control is declared as a field of the page class in the code-behind file. Structured Control objects (for example ListBox or Page) contain inner controls that can be accessed via the property Controls. Conversely, Parent returns the parent control if one exists. The property Page returns the page to which the control belongs.

In order to hide a control on a web page one can set the property Visible to false. In this case the control is not rendered to HTML and is thus not displayed.

The server encodes the state of the page in a hidden HTML field and keeps it there from one round trip to the next. The data of the control is thereby automatically preserved and restored later. Additionally, the programmer can also put custom state information in the property ViewState of the Control object. If we want to remember how often a user has clicked on a button, we can do it like this:

```
public void ButtonClick(object button, EventArgs e) {
    int clicks = 0;
    if (this.ViewState["NumOfClicks"] != null) clicks = (int) this.ViewState["NumOfClicks"];
    this.ViewState["NumOfClicks"] = ++clicks;
}
```

Here the number of clicks is stored in the ViewState of the page itself. It will be preserved automatically and restored at the next round trip. ViewState has the accessibility protected, which is why we cannot use the ViewState of the button in this example. With custom controls, however, such information can be stored directly in the state of the controls. If we want to prevent the control from keeping its state until the next time, we set the property EnableViewState to false.

All public properties can be set not only in the code-behind file of a page, but also in the aspx file, for example:

```
<asp:Button ID="ok" EnableViewState="false" Runat="server" />
```

Methods. Developers will only rarely need the methods of a control. HasControls tells whether the control has inner elements. FindControl(id) searches for the inner control with the name id. Calling RenderControl activates the protected method Render, which translates the control to HTML.

The method DataBind is used to fill controls with data from a data source such as a database. We will discuss this in more detail in Section 6.4.9.

Among the protected methods we mention only LoadViewState and SaveViewState which are both invoked by ASP.NET. SaveViewState saves the state of a control in an object array and returns this. The array is encoded into the field __VIEWSTATE of the web page. On the next round trip the object array is extracted from __VIEWSTATE and given as a parameter to the method LoadViewState which restores the state of the control.

Events. We have already discussed the events Init, Load, DataBinding, PreRender and Unload in Section 6.3. They are declared in Control and inherited by all control element classes.

6.4.2   WebControl

For our purposes the most significant subclass of Control is WebControl. It is the base class for all graphic controls of a web page. Here is an excerpt of the classes derived from WebControl, where the class hierarchy is represented by indentation:

```
WebControl
  - Button
  - TextBox
  - Label
      - BaseValidator
          - RequiredFieldValidator
          - BaseCompareValidator
          - CustomValidator
          - RegularExpressionValidator
  - CheckBox
      - RadioButton
  - ListControl
      - ListBox
      - DropDownList
      - CheckBoxList
      - RadioButtonList
  - Image
      - ImageButton
  - HyperLink
  - LinkButton
  - Table
  - TableCell
      - TableHeaderCell
  - TableRow
      - DataGridItem
  - BaseDataList
      - DataList
      - DataGrid
  - DataListItem
  - AdRotator
  - Calendar
  - ValidationSummary
  - ...
```

We will discuss only the most important classes. But before that we want to see which properties WebControl offers. These are common to all web controls:

```
public class WebControl : Control, IAccessor {
    //----- properties
    public virtual Unit Width { get; set; }
    public virtual Unit Height { get; set; }
    public virtual FontInfo Font { get; set; }
    public virtual Color ForeColor { get; set; }
    public virtual Color BackColor { get; set; }
```

```
    public virtual Unit BorderWidth { get; set; }
    public virtual Color BorderColor { get; set; }
    public virtual BorderStyle BorderStyle { get; set; }
    public virtual bool Enabled { get; set; }
    public virtual short TabIndex { get; set; }
    public virtual string ToolTip { get; set; }

    ...
}
```

The properties Width and Height set the width and height of the control. They are of type Unit which, besides the value, also stores the unit of measurement:

```
public struct Unit {
    public Unit(double value, UnitType type);
    public double Value { get; }
    public UnitType Type { get; }

    ...
}
public enum UnitType { Cm, Em, Ex, Inch, Mm, Percentage, Pica, Pixel, Point }
```

In an aspx file these values can be encoded like this:

```
<asp:TextBox ID="text1" Width="100" Runat="server" />
<asp:TextBox ID="text2" Width="10cm" Runat="server" />
```

Values without a unit of measurement are considered to be in pixels. In a program these values can be set as follows:

```
text1.Width = 100;  // implicit conversion from int to Unit; default unit = pixel
text2.Width = new Unit(10, UnitType.Cm);
```

The property Font allows us to set the font for controls that contain text. FontInfo is defined as follows:

```
public sealed class FontInfo {
    public string Name { get; set; }
    public FontUnit Size { get; set; }
    public bool Bold { get; set; }
    public bool Italic { get; set; }
    public bool Underline { get; set; }

    ...
}
public struct FontUnit {
    public FontUnit(FontSize size);
    public FontUnit(int size);
    public FontSize Type { get; }
    public Unit Unit { get; }

    ...
}
public enum FontSize { AsUnit, XSmall, Small, Medium, Large, XLarge, ... }
```

All this information can be specified in the aspx file, for example:

```
<asp:Button  ID="button1"  Text="Button 1"  Runat="server"
              Font-Name="Arial" Font-Size="Large" Font-Bold="true" />
<asp:Button  ID="button2"  Text="Button 2"  Runat="server"
              Font-Name="Times" Font-Size="12px" Font-Italic="true" />
```

In a program, these values can be encoded as like this:

```
button1.Font.Name = "Arial";
button1.Font.Size = new FontUnit(FontSize.Large);
button1.Font.Bold = true;
button2.Font.Name = "Times";
button2.Font.Size = new FontUnit(12);
button2.Font.Italic = true;
```

The properties ForeColor and BackColor set the colour of the foreground (typically the colour of the text) and the background of a control. Usually, the colour is given as one of the predefined values Color.Red, Color.Green, Color.Blue and so on. But the type System.Drawing.Color allows also the definition of custom colours by means of an RGB value (proportions of red, green and blue). Here is an example:

```
<asp:Label ID="lab" Text="sample" ForeColor="Red" BackColor="Blue" Runat="server" />
```

In a program the colour is set in the following way:

```
lab.ForeColor = System.Drawing.Color.Red;
```

Most controls may have a border that can be defined with the properties BorderStyle, BorderWidth and BorderColor. BorderStyle can assume the following values whose visual representation is shown in Figure 6.12:

```
public enum BorderStyle {
    NotSet, None, Dotted, Dashed, Solid, Double, Groove, Ridge, Inset, Outset
}
```

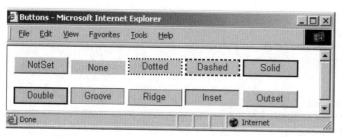

Figure 6.12 Types of borders for a control

In an aspx file these features can be encoded like this:

```
<asp:TextBox BorderStyle="Outset" BorderColor="Red" BorderWidth="4" Runat="server"/>
```

Setting the property Enabled of a control to false deactivates it. In this case the control will still be displayed, but does not react to user input. For example, a button will be dimmed and can no longer be clicked.

```
button.Enabled = false;
```

With the property TabIndex we can determine the order in which the controls of a page receive the focus when the tabulator key is pressed repeatedly. The value 0 indicates that the index has not been defined, a value greater than 0 determines the order. If we define three text fields like this

```
<asp:TextBox ID="box1" TabIndex="3" Runat="server" />
<asp:TextBox ID="box2" TabIndex="2" Runat="server" />
<asp:TextBox ID="box3" TabIndex="1" Runat="server" />
```

they get the focus in the order box3, box2 and box1.

Finally, the property ToolTip allows the definition of a documentation text that will be displayed in a popup window when the user makes the mouse cursor hover above the control.

```
<asp:Button Text="OK" Tooltip="submits the form" Runat="server" />
```

After this thorough treatment of the base classes of all controls, Control and WebControl, we will now look at the most important web controls such as Button, TextBox, CheckBox and so on.

6.4.3 Button

Nearly every web page contains one or more buttons for confirming a filled-out form or for executing commands. The class Button has the following interface:

```
public class Button : WebControl, IPostBackEventHandler {
    //----- properties
    public string Text { get; set; }
    public string CommandName { get; set; }
    public string CommandArgument { get; set; }
    public bool CausesValidation { get; set; }
    //----- events
    public event EventHandler Click;
    public event CommandEventHandler Command;
}
```

The property Text sets the caption of the button. We have already used it a couple of times in examples. The properties CommandName and CommandArgument will be discussed later in connection with the Command event. The property Causes-Validation can be used to deactivate the validation of all controls on a web page. We will talk about validation of controls in Section 6.5.

The principal event to which a button can react is the Click event. It is triggered when a user clicks the button. The Click event always leads to a round trip of the web page and can be caught by an appropriate event handler at the server. We have already seen in a few examples how to install such event handlers.

If a page contains more buttons, one might still want to define only one single event handler for all the buttons. For example, there could be three buttons that set the colour of a piece of text to red, green or blue, respectively. In order for the event handler to find out which button has actually been clicked, we can declare the buttons in such a way that they will trigger a Command event instead of a Click event. A Command event takes a command name and command parameters which the event handler can then evaluate. The following example demonstrates this:

```
<%@ Page Language="C#" %>
<html>
    <head>
        <script Language="C#" Runat="server">
            void ButtonClick(object sender, CommandEventArgs e) {
                text.ForeColor = System.Drawing.Color.FromName(e.CommandName);
            }
        </script>
    </head>
    <body>
        <form Runat="server">
            <asp:Label ID="text" Text="Sample text" Runat="server" /><br><br>
            <asp:Button Text="Red"    CommandName="Red"
                                      OnCommand="ButtonClick" Runat="server" />
            <asp:Button Text="Blue"   CommandName="Blue"
                                      OnCommand="ButtonClick" Runat="server" />
            <asp:Button Text="Green" CommandName="Green" 
                                      OnCommand="ButtonClick" Runat="server" />
        </form>
    </body>
</html>
```

Figure 6.13 shows how this page would appear in a browser. Clicking on the Blue button triggers a Command event that leads to the invocation of ButtonClick. e.CommandName holds the string "Blue" which is used to set the text colour.

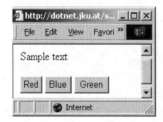

Figure 6.13 *Buttons for setting the text colour with a* Command *event*

In this example we did not use a command argument. However, such an argument could be assigned a value with CommandArgument="..." at the definition of the button and then accessed in ButtonClick with e.CommandArgument.

6.4.4   TextBox

Almost as important as buttons are text fields, where the user can enter values. Text fields are implemented in the class TextBox. There are single-line and multi-line text fields with different input modes. But let us first look at the interface of TextBox:

```
public class TextBox : WebControl, IPostBackHandler {
    //----- properties
    public virtual string Text { get; set; }
    public virtual TextBoxMode TextMode { get; set; }
    public virtual int MaxLength { get; set; }
    public virtual int Columns { get; set; }
    public virtual int Rows { get; set; }
    public virtual bool Wrap { get; set; }
    public virtual bool ReadOnly { get; set; }
    public virtual bool AutoPostBack { get; set; }
    //----- event
    public event EventHandler TextChanged;
}
```

The principal property is Text which allows getting and setting the contents of the text field. It can be initialized in one of the following two ways:

```
<asp:TextBox Text="Sample text" Runat="server" />
<asp:TextBox Runat="server">Sample text</asp:TextBox>
```

The text field can work as a single-line or multi-line plain-text field or as a single-line password field. This is determined by the property TextMode.

```
public enum TextBoxMode { SingleLine, MultiLine, Password }
```

In password fields each character entered is displayed as an asterisk.

For single-line text fields the maximum number of characters that can be entered is defined with MaxLength. This property does not have any effect on multi-line text fields. For these, we can instead set the number of characters per line and the number of lines with the properties Columns and Rows. Of course, we can also adjust the width and height of a text field with the inherited properties Width and Height, as well as the colour and font with ForeColor, BackColor and Font.

If the entered text is longer than the text field, moving the mouse will scroll the text. In multi-line text fields this can also be done with the displayed scroll bar.

The property Wrap indicates whether the text should be wrapped at the right edge of the field. For single-line text fields this does not have any effect.

The property ReadOnly can lock the text field so that it does not accept any input. This setting is mostly done from program code. But it can, of course, also be set in the aspx file.

If the contents of a text field are modified, a TextChanged event is triggered. Generally, this event does not send the page to the server and thus can only be handled at the next round trip (for example when a button is clicked). If we want to process the TextChanged event immediately, we must set the property Auto-PostBack to true. In this case the page will be sent to the server as soon as the input cursor is removed from the text field. For single-line text fields pressing the enter key also triggers the event. In multi-line text fields this only results in a line break.

The subsequent example shows a multi-line text field whose changes immediately lead to a round trip of the page. The event handler for TextChanged displays the properties of the text field on the page.

```
<%@ Page Language="C#" %>
<html>
   <head>
      <script Language="C#" Runat="server">
         void HandleText(object sender, EventArgs e) {
            label.Text =   "TextMode=" + box.TextMode +
                           ", Rows=" + box.Rows +
                           ", Columns=" + box.Columns +
                           ", Wrap=" + box.Wrap;
         }
      </script>
   </head>
   <body>
      <form Runat="server">
         <asp:Label ID="label" Runat="server" /><br>
         <asp:TextBox ID="box" TextMode="MultiLine" Rows="3" Columns="15"
                     OnTextChanged="HandleText" AutoPostBack="true"
                     Runat="server" />
      </form>
   </body>
</html>
```

Figure 6.14 shows what this page looks like.

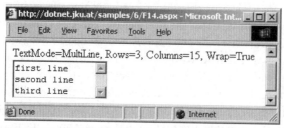

Figure 6.14 *Multi-line TextBox with its properties*

6.4.5 Label

The class Label implements static pieces of text on a web page, that is text which the user cannot edit. Accordingly, its interface is very simple:

```
public class Label : WebControl {
    public virtual String Text { get; set; }
}
```

There are two ways for setting the text of a Label object:

```
<asp:Label ID="lab1" Text="Monday" Runat="server" />
<asp:Label ID="lab2" Runat="server">Monday</asp:Label>
```

Of course, one can set the colour and font of a label, as with other controls, using ForeColor, BackColor and Font.

Label is the base class for all the validators that we will discuss in Section 6.5. A validator checks other controls for validity and, if necessary, generates an error message which is displayed as the text of the validator.

6.4.6 CheckBox

A check box is a user interface element that can assume two states: checked or unchecked (true or false).

```
public class CheckBox : WebControl, IPostBackHandler {
    //----- properties
    public virtual bool Checked { get; set; }
    public virtual string Text { get; set; }
    public virtual TextAlign TextAlign { get; set; }
    public virtual bool AutoPostBack { get; set; }
    //----- event
    public event EventHandler CheckedChanged;
}
```

The state of the check box can be defined with the property Checked: true means checked, false means unchecked.

Next to the check box there is usually a text describing its meaning. This can be set with the property Text. TextAlign determines whether to display the text on the left or on the right side of the check box. The default setting is the right side.

```
public enum TextAlign { Left, Right }
```

Modifying the state of a check box triggers a CheckedChanged event which is cached and will only be handled at the next round trip. In order to deal with it immediately, AutoPostBack must be set to true. Here is an example:

```
<%@ Page Language="C#" %>
<html>
  <head>
    <script Language="C#" Runat="server">
      void ButtonClicked(object sender, EventArgs e) {
        label.Text = "You bought: ";
        if (apples.Checked) label.Text += "Apples ";
        if (pears.Checked) label.Text += "Pears ";
        if (bananas.Checked) label.Text += "Bananas ";
      }
    </script>
  </head>
  <body>
    <form Runat="server">
      <asp:CheckBox ID="apples" Text="Apples" Runat="server" /><br>
      <asp:CheckBox ID="pears" Text="Pears" Runat="server" /><br>
      <asp:CheckBox ID="bananas" Text="Bananas" Runat="server" /><br>
      <asp:Button Text="Buy" OnClick="ButtonClicked" Runat="server" /> <br><br>
      <asp:Label ID="label" Runat="server" />
    </form>
  </body>
</html>
```

Figure 6.15 shows how this page would appear in a browser.

Figure 6.15 CheckBox *controls in a browser*

6.4.7   RadioButton

A radio button can be turned on and off with the mouse just like a check box. In contrast to a check box, however, it is never used on its own but always grouped together with other radio buttons. Switching on one radio button of such a group will automatically turn off all the others.

```
public class RadioButton : CheckBox {
    public virtual string GroupName { get; set; }
}
```

The property GroupName defines the name of the group to which the radio button belongs. All radio buttons with the same group name belong to the same group. Apart from this, RadioButton works just like CheckBox. The following example explains how to use radio buttons.

```
<%@ Page Language="C#" %>
<html>
<head>
   <script Language="C#" Runat="server">
      void RadioChanged(object sender, EventArgs e) {
         label.Text = "Method of payment: ";
         if (cash.Checked) label.Text += cash.Text;
         if (cheque.Checked) label.Text += cheque.Text;
         if (card.Checked) label.Text += card.Text;
      }
   </script>
</head>
<body>
   <form Runat="server">
      <p>Select method of payment:</p>
      <asp:RadioButton ID="cash" Text="cash" GroupName="payment"
                    OnCheckedChanged="RadioChanged"
                    AutoPostBack="true" Runat="server" /><br>
      <asp:RadioButton ID="cheque" Text="cheque" GroupName="payment"
                    OnCheckedChanged="RadioChanged"
                    AutoPostBack="true" Runat="server" /><br>
      <asp:RadioButton ID="card" Text="credit card" GroupName="payment"
                    OnCheckedChanged="RadioChanged"
                    AutoPostBack="true" Runat="server" /><br>
      <br>
      <asp:Label ID="label" Runat="server" />
   </form>
</body>
</html>
```

Figure 6.16 shows how this page would appear in a browser.

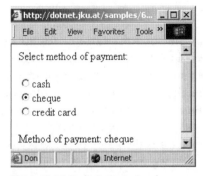

Figure 6.16 RadioButtons *in a browser*

6.4.8   ListControl

ListControl is the base class for various lists that can be displayed in a web form. Among them are simple lists (ListBox), drop-down lists (DropDownList) and lists of CheckBox and RadioButton controls.

A list is a set of name–value pairs. The browser only shows the names. Clicking on a name yields the corresponding value as a result.

Lists can be specified by enumerating the elements either in the aspx file, or in the code-behind file of the page. It is also possible to bind an existing collection of elements which, for example, has been filled with data from a database, to a list.

We will look at examples of lists in connection with ListBox. But first of all, here is the interface of ListControl:

```
public abstract class ListControl : WebControl {
    //----- properties
    public virtual ListItemCollection Items { get; }
    public virtual ListItem SelectedItem { get; }
    public virtual int SelectedIndex { get; set; }
    public virtual string DataTextFormatString { get; set; }
    public virtual object DataSource { get; set; }
    public virtual string DataTextField { get; set; }
    public virtual string DataValueField { get; set; }
    public virtual bool AutoPostBack { get; set; }
    ...
    //----- events
    public event EventHandler SelectedIndexChanged;
    ...
}
```

Properties. The property Items holds the set of elements that make up the list. Each element is of type ListItem, whose interface looks like this:

```
public sealed class ListItem : IStateManager, IParserAccessor, IAttributeAccessor {
    public string Text { get; set; }
    public string Value { get; set; }
    public bool Selected { get; set; }
    ...
}
```

The properties Text and Value describe the name and the value of the list item. Selected indicates whether the user has selected the list item with the mouse.

The property SelectedItem of ListControl points to the list item the user has selected. If none was selected, SelectedItem contains null. Some lists even allow more than one item to be selected. In this case SelectedItem refers to the first selected item of the list.

In analogy to SelectedItem, SelectedIndex returns the index of the selected list item, with the indices starting at zero. If no item was selected, SelectedIndex is -1.

The property DataTextFormatString allows us to specify the way the list item is to be displayed, using a format string, as described in Section 2.7.1 (for example "{0:f2}").

Event. Selecting a list element with the mouse triggers a SelectedIndexChanged event. This event will not be handled before the next round trip, unless AutoPostBack is set to true. In the event handler one can use SelectedItem or SelectedIndex in order to find out which element has been selected. If one needs to know whether more than one element has been selected, it is necessary to iterate over all Items and check the property Selected of each.

Binding to a data source. In order to fill a list with values from a database, one must create a view (DataView) of a data table (DataTable) and assign it to the property DataSource. A subsequent call to DataBind extracts the list items as name–value pairs from the columns of the data table denoted by the values of the properties DataTextField and DataValueField. We will give an example in Section 6.4.9.

DataSource can be not only initialized with a DataView object, but also with any object whose class implements the interface ICollection (e.g. Array, ArrayList or SortedList). For this we will also look at an example in Section 6.4.11.

6.4.9   ListBox

A ListBox is the most trivial subclass of ListControl. It simply displays the list items in multiple lines and allows the selection of one or more of them with the mouse. Each line is represented by an object of class ListItem.

```
public class ListBox : ListControl, IPostBackHandler {
    public virtual int Rows { get; set; }
    public virtual ListSelectionMode SelectionMode { get; set; }
}
```

Rows determines the number of lines to display in the browser. The width follows the widest list element. If the list has more entries than lines, scrolling will be enabled. SelectionMode indicates whether one or more lines can be selected.

```
public enum ListSelectionMode { Single, Multiple };
```

Statically Specified Lists

In the simplest case, all list items are specified statically in the aspx file with ListItem elements.

```
<%@ Page Language="C#" %>
<html>
  <head>
    <script Language="C#" Runat="server">
      void ButtonClick(object sender, EventArgs e) {
        lab.Text = "The selected country has the international car code ";
        if (list.SelectedItem != null) lab.Text += list.SelectedItem.Value;
      }
    </script>
  </head>
  <body>
    <form Runat="server">
      <asp:ListBox ID="list" Rows="3" Runat="server" >
        <asp:ListItem Text="United States" Value="USA" Runat="server" />
        <asp:ListItem Text="Great Britain" Value="GB" Runat="server" />
        <asp:ListItem Text="Germany" Value="D" Runat="server" />
        <asp:ListItem Text="France" Value="F" Runat="server" />
        <asp:ListItem Text="Italy" Value="I" Runat="server" />
      </asp:ListBox><br><br>
      <asp:Button OnClick="ButtonClick" Text="Show" Runat="server" /><br>
      <asp:Label ID="lab" Runat="server" />
    </form>
  </body>
</html>
```

Longer texts of a list item can also be written like this:

```
<asp:ListItem Value="D" Runat="server">Germany</asp:ListItem>
```

In the browser the page looks as shown in Figure 6.17.

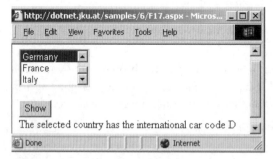

Figure 6.17 *Example of a* ListBox

Dynamically Generated Lists

In many situations we do not want to specify the list items statically, but would rather have the program generate them dynamically. The easiest way to do this is to put the desired items in a collection (for example SortedList) and then assign this collection to the property DataSource of the ListBox. We must not forget to call DataBind, in order to actually bind the data from the SortedList to the ListBox.

```
<%@ Import Namespace="System.Collections" %>
<%@ Page Language="C#" %>
<html>
   <head>
      <script Language="C#" Runat="server">
         void Fill(object sender, EventArgs e) {
            SortedList data = new SortedList();
            data["United States"] = "USA";
            data["Great Britain"] = "GB";
            data["Germany"] = "D";
            data["France"] = "F";
            data["Italy"] = "I";
            list.DataSource = data;
            list.DataTextField = "Key";    // take text from Key of SortedList elements
            list.DataValueField = "Value";// take value from Value of SortedList elements
            list.DataBind();
         }
      </script>
   </head>
   <body>
      <form Runat="server">
         <asp:ListBox ID="list" Rows="3" Runat="server" /><br><br>
         <asp:Button OnClick="Fill" Text="Fill" Runat="server" />
      </form>
   </body>
</html>
```

If the names and values of list items are the same, we can make it still easier for ourselves. In this case it is enough to assign an array of strings to DataSource:

```
list.DataSource = new string[] { "USA", "GB", "D", "F", "I"};
list.DataBind();
```

Generating the List from a Database

Now we want to look at how to fill a list with values from a database. For this example we use the *Northwind* database described in Chapter 5, which has a table Employees holding the employees of the company *Northwind*. The list should display the employee names. The value of each list item should be the respective employee number. This data corresponds to the columns LastName and EmployeeID from the database table.

If we want to display values from a database in a ListBox, we must do as described in Section 5.4: create a DataSet, fill it using a DataAdapter, create a DataView object from it, and finally assign this to the property DataSource of the

ListBox. Then we must specify the table columns that should correspond to the text and the value of the displayed list items using the properties DataTextField and DataValueField.

In the following example we separate the aspx file from the code-behind file for reasons of readability. The aspx file is then very simple and looks like this:

```
<%@ Page Language="C#" Inherits="BasePage" Src="List.aspx.cs" %>
<html>
   <body>
      <form OnInit="PageInit" Runat="server">
         <asp:ListBox ID="list" Runat="server" AutoPostBack="true"
                  DataTextField="LastName" DataValueField="EmployeeID"
                  OnSelectedIndexChanged="HandleSelect" /><br>
         <asp:Label ID="label" Runat="server" />
      </form>
   </body>
</html>
```

The corresponding code-behind file List.aspx.cs contains the class BasePage with two event handlers. One is for the Init event of the page; it fills the list with the values from the database. The other is for the SelectedIndexChanged event of the ListBox; it displays the selected list item.

```
using System;
using System.Data;
using System.Data.Common;
using System.Data.SqlClient;
using System.Web.UI;
using System.Web.UI.WebControls;

public class BasePage : Page {
   protected ListBox list;
   protected Label label;

   public void PageInit(object sender, EventArgs e) {
      DataSet ds = new DataSet();
      SqlConnection con = new SqlConnection("data source=127.0.0.1\\NETSDK; " +
         "initial catalog=Northwind; user id=sa; password=; Trusted_Connection=true");
      string cmdString = "SELECT * FROM Employees";
      SqlDataAdapter adapter = new SqlDataAdapter(cmdString, con);
      adapter.Fill(ds, "Employees");
      if (ds.HasErrors) ds.RejectChanges(); else ds.AcceptChanges();
      list.DataSource = ds.Tables["Employees"].DefaultView;
      list.DataBind();
   }

   public void HandleSelect(object sender, EventArgs e) {
      label.Text = "employee number = ";
      if (list.SelectedItem != null) label.Text += list.SelectedItem.Value;
   }
}
```

After we have created the DataSet ds and specified the connection con, we create an adapter with the appropriate SQL command and the desired connection. We then use this adapter to fill ds and create the table "Employees". The property DefaultView returns the default view of this table and we assign it to the property DataSource of the list. At the end we must not forget to call DataBind in order to transmit the values from the data source to the list. Figure 6.18 shows the result.

Figure 6.18 A ListBox *filled from a database*

6.4.10 DropDownList

The class DropDownList implements a drop-down list. It is displayed as a single line that shows the element selected most recently. Clicking on the arrow at the right-hand side of the line unfolds a list where one of the entries can be selected.

```
public class DropDownList : ListControl, IPostBackHandler {
    // same interface as ListControl
}
```

The following example shows that a DropDownList can be used in the same way as a ListBox. The only noteworthy thing is that by setting AutoPostBack="true" the selection of a list item will immediately lead to a round trip and will be handled by HandleSelect.

```
<%@ Page Language="C#" %>
<html>
    <head>
        <script Language="C#" Runat="server">
            void HandleSelect(object sender, EventArgs e) {
                lab.Text = "The selected country has the international car code ";
                if (list.SelectedItem != null) lab.Text += list.SelectedItem.Value;
            }
        </script>
    </head>
```

```
<body>
  <form Runat="server">
    <asp:DropDownList ID="list" OnSelectedIndexChanged="HandleSelect"
                      AutoPostBack="true" Runat="server" >
      <asp:ListItem Text="United States" Value="USA"/>
      <asp:ListItem Text="Great Britain" Value="GB"/>
      <asp:ListItem Text="Germany" Value="D"/>
      <asp:ListItem Text="France" Value="F"/>
      <asp:ListItem Text="Italy" Value="I"/>
    </asp:DropDownList>
    <br>
    <asp:Label ID="lab" Runat="server" />
  </form>
</body>
</html>
```

The result would be as shown in Figure 6.19.

Figure 6.19 *Example of a* DropDownList

Just as with ListBox, we can specify the list items of a DropDownList either statically, dynamically, or read them from a database, as shown in Section 6.4.9.

6.4.11 DataGrid

In addition to simple controls such as buttons or text fields ASP.NET also offers highly complex controls that hold structured information and can be manipulated in various ways. As an example for such a complex control we choose the class DataGrid.

A DataGrid is a table of rows and columns. In most cases it is filled from a database, but it can also be constructed manually. ASP.NET allows the programmer to display such tables in various formats and edit them, as well as add or delete rows. As a special feature it is possible to put buttons into the rows in order to implement commands for these rows.

Here we will present only a small subset of the functionality of DataGrid. Further details can be found in the online documentation of .NET [SDKDoc].

```
public class DataGrid : BaseDataList, INamingContainer {
   //----- properties
   public virtual object DataSource { get; set; }
   public virtual DataGridColumnCollection Columns { get; }
   public virtual bool AutoGenerateColumns { get; set; }
   public virtual DataGridItemsCollection Items { get; }
   public virtual DataGridItem SelectedItem { get; set; }
   public virtual int SelectedIndex { get; set; }
   public virtual GridLines GridLines { get; set; }
   public virtual int CellPadding { get; set; }
   public virtual int CellSpacing { get; set; }
   public virtual bool ShowHeader { get; set; }
   public virtual bool ShowFooter { get; set; }
   public virtual TableItemStyle AlternatingItemStyle { get; }
   public virtual TableItemStyle HeaderStyle { get; }
   public virtual TableItemStyle FooterStyle { get; }
   public virtual TableItemStyle ItemStyle { get; }
   public virtual TableItemStyle SelectedItemStyle { get; }
   ...
   //----- methods
   public override void DataBind();
   ...
   //----- events
   public event DataGridCommandEventHandler DeleteCommand;
   public event DataGridCommandEventHandler EditCommand;
   public event DataGridCommandEventHandler CancelCommand;
   public event DataGridCommandEventHandler UpdateCommand;
   public event DataGridCommandEventHandler ItemCommand;
   public event EventHandler SelectedIndexChanged;
   ...
}
```

DataGrid extends BaseDataList which in turn extends WebControl. Thus all characteristics of WebControl also apply to DataGrid.

Properties

As with ListControl we can use the property DataSource to specify the source from which the data can be retrieved. Subsequently, we must not forget to call DataBind in order to initiate the data transmission.

A DataGrid consists of multiple columns that can be accessed via the property Columns. If the property AutoGenerateColumns is true, the columns are generated directly from the data source (for example from the DataTable object). If it is false, programmers have to take care of this for themselves, either in the code-behind file of the page or in the aspx file (see example further down). Here are the most common column types:

❏ BoundColumn. A column that corresponds directly to a column of the data source. Properties allow the assigning of this column to a certain column of the data table and specifying its format. In general the default settings should suffice.

❏ ButtonColumn. A column that displays buttons which can execute commands for the corresponding rows of the DataGrid. Properties allow the specification of the type of the buttons, the names of the commands to execute, and the association with data from a database.

❏ EditCommandColumn. A column that displays an edit button per row that can be configured via properties. Clicking on an edit button triggers an EditCommand event and the edit button is replaced with a cancel and an update button. Clicking one of these triggers a CancelCommand or an UpdateCommand event, respectively.

❏ HyperLinkColumn. A column that displays hypertext links to another page. Properties allow the specification of the destinations of these links.

The property Items holds a collection of all rows of the DataGrid. For each row we can define its format and access its cells, for example:

```
foreach (DataGridItem row in myDataGrid.Items)
    foreach (TableCell cell in row.Cells)
        Console.WriteLine(cell.Text);
```

If we select a row of the DataGrid with the Select command (see example "Modifying a DataGrid" further below), it can then be accessed via the properties SelectedItem and SelectedIndex.

A DataGrid can be formatted in various ways. The property GridLines determines whether grid lines should be displayed. ShowHeader and ShowFooter switch headers and footers on and off. With CellPadding and CellSpacing we can adjust the space between the cell border and its contents and between two cells, as shown in Figure 6.20.

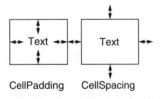

Figure 6.20 CellPadding *and* CellSpacing

Finally, we can set the font, colour, and other format information of the rows with the following properties:

HeaderStyle	determines the style of the header
FooterStyle	determines the style of the footer
ItemStyle	determines the style of the contents rows
SelectedItemStyle	detemines the style of the selected row
AlternatingItemStyle	determines the style of every other row

Events

Beside the general events such as Init, Load and PreRender that all web controls support, a DataGrid object can react to a number of additional events.

Most of these events are not triggered by DataGrid itself, but by one of the controls in its rows. Such events are, however, not handled by the triggering control or by the cell which contains it, but are forwarded to the DataGrid object, which then reacts. This forwarding is called *event bubbling*.

The conditions under which the different events are triggered are rather complicated. They depend on the type of column in which a button was clicked, as well as on the CommandName that has been installed in this button. Table 6.3 lists these conditions.

Table 6.3 *Conditions under which certain events are triggered*

column type		events
ButtonColumn	CommandName == "Select"	SelectedItemChanged
	CommandName == "Delete"	ItemCommand + DeleteCommand
	CommandName == other	ItemCommand
EditCommandColumn	EditText == "..."	EditCommand
	UpdateText == "..."	UpdateCommand
	CancelText == "..."	CancelCommand

Clicking a button in a ButtonColumn generally triggers an ItemCommand event, except in two cases: if the command name is "Select" a SelectedItemChanged event is triggered, while if the command name is "Delete" a DeleteCommand event is triggered in addition to an ItemCommand event.

In an EditCommandColumn either an edit button or an update button, as well as a cancel button, are visible. Depending on which one is clicked an EditCommand, UpdateCommand or CancelCommand event is triggered.

Example: Displaying a DataGrid

Now it is really time for an example. We start with a very simple case, where the data from the *Northwind* database (see Chapter 5) is displayed in a DataGrid. In this example the table is formatted very simply.

```
<%@ Page Language="C#" Inherits="BasePage" Src="DataGrid.aspx.cs" %>
<html>
  <body>
    <form OnInit="PageInit" Runat="server">
      <asp:DataGrid ID="grid" OnLoad="GridLoad" Runat="server" />
    </form>
  </body>
</html>
```

The code-behind file of this page is DataGrid.aspx.cs and contains the event handlers PageInit for the Init event of the page and GridLoad for the Load event of the DataGrid.

```
using System;
using System.Data;
using System.Data.Common;
using System.Data.SqlClient;
using System.Web.UI;
using System.Web.UI.WebControls;

public class BasePage : Page {
    protected DataGrid grid;
    DataView dataView;

    public void PageInit(object sender, EventArgs e) {
        DataSet ds = new DataSet();
        SqlConnection con = new SqlConnection("data source=127.0.0.1\\NETSDK; " +
            "initial catalog=Northwind; user id=sa; password=; Trusted_Connection=true");
        string sqlString = "SELECT EmployeeID, FirstName, LastName FROM Employees";
        SqlDataAdapter adapter = new SqlDataAdapter(sqlString, con);
        adapter.Fill(ds, "Employees");
        if (ds.HasErrors) ds.RejectChanges(); else ds.AcceptChanges();
        dataView = ds.Tables["Employees"].DefaultView;
    }

    public void GridLoad(object sender, EventArgs e) {
        grid.HeaderStyle.Font.Bold = true;
        grid.AlternatingItemStyle.BackColor = System.Drawing.Color.LightGray;
        grid.DataSource = dataView;
        grid.DataBind();
    }

}
```

PageInit fills a table "Employees" with data from the database, as described in Section 6.4.9. A view of this table is kept in the field dataView. GridLoad defines some formatting for the table (the header is printed in bold face and every other row in the table should have a grey background). Then the data source of the grid is set and DataBind is invoked. Figure 6.21 shows the result.

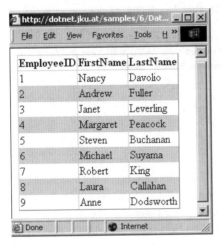

Figure 6.21 *A simple* DataGrid

Example: Modifying a DataGrid

Now we want to look at a more challenging example. We will again display data from the *Northwind* database in a DataGrid, but this time we provide a way to select or delete rows. Furthermore, the table and its columns should be formatted in a more appealing way than in the previous example.

This time we will not let ASP.NET generate the columns of the DataGrid automatically, but will explicitly specify them in the aspx file. This looks as follows:

```
<%@ Page Language="C#" Inherits="BasePage" src="DataGrid1.aspx.cs" %>
<html>
    <body>
        <form onLoad="PageLoad" Runat="server">
            <asp:DataGrid ID="grid" Runat="server"
                        AutoGenerateColumns="false"
                        CellPadding="3"
                        AlternatingItemStyle-BackColor="LightGray"
                        OnDeleteCommand="DeleteRow"
                        OnSelectedIndexChanged="SelectRow">
                <HeaderStyle BackColor="#aaaadd"/>
```

```
            <Columns>
                <asp:BoundColumn HeaderText="#" DataField="EmployeeID">
                    <ItemStyle HorizontalAlign="Right" />
                </asp:BoundColumn>
                <asp:BoundColumn HeaderText="First Name"
                                DataField="FirstName" />
                <asp:BoundColumn HeaderText="Last Name"
                                DataField="LastName" />
                <asp:ButtonColumn ButtonType="LinkButton" Text="delete"
                                CommandName="Delete" />
                <asp:ButtonColumn ButtonType="LinkButton" Text="select"
                                CommandName="Select" />
            </columns>
        </asp:DataGrid><br>
        <asp:Label ID="label" Runat="server" />
    </form>
  </body>
</html>
```

The DataGrid control contains the attribute AutoGenerateColumns="false", which means that the column information is not automatically generated from the database, but the columns are defined by <Columns> elements.

As we can see, there are five columns. The first three are of type BoundColumn, which means that they are each bound to a column of the data table whose name is specified by the attribute DataField. With the attribute HeaderText we can define a better readable header for the columns: instead of "FirstName" we use, for example, "First Name". For the first column we also specify that the data should be right-aligned. Instead of the nested <ItemStyle> element we could also use the attribute ItemStyle-HorizontalAlign="Right" in the <asp:BoundColumn> element.

The fourth column is of type ButtonColumn. It displays a link button with the caption "delete". Clicking it triggers a DeleteCommand event which the DataGrid handles with the method DeleteRow.

The fifth column is also of type ButtonColumn. It displays a link button with the caption "select". Clicking it triggers a SelectedItemChanged event which the DataGrid handles with the method SelectRow.

The DataGrid element has some more formatting attributes: CellPadding specifies the distance between the text and the border of a cell. AlternatingItemStyle-BackColor sets the background colour of every other row.

The code-behind file of this page is DataGrid1.aspx.cs and looks like this:

```
using System;
using System.Data;
using System.Data.Common;
using System.Data.SqlClient;
using System.Web.UI;
using System.Web.UI.WebControls;
```

```
public class BasePage : Page {
    protected DataGrid grid;
    protected Label label;
    DataView dataView;

    public void PageLoad(object sender, EventArgs e) {
        DataSet ds;
        if (!IsPostBack) {
            ds = new DataSet();
            SqlConnection con = new SqlConnection("data source=127.0.0.1\\NETSDK; " +
                "initial catalog=Northwind; user id=sa; password=; Trusted_Connection=true");
            string cmd = "SELECT EmployeeID, FirstName, LastName FROM Employees";
            SqlDataAdapter adapter = new SqlDataAdapter(cmd, con);
            adapter.Fill(ds, "Employees");
            if (ds.HasErrors) ds.RejectChanges(); else ds.AcceptChanges();
            Session["data"] = ds;
        } else ds = (DataSet) Session["data"];
        dataView = ds.Tables["Employees"].DefaultView;
        grid.DataSource = dataView;
        grid.DataBind();
    }

    public void DeleteRow(object sender, DataGridCommandEventArgs e) {
        dataView.RowFilter = "EmployeeID='" + e.Item.Cells[0].Text + "'";
        if (dataView.Count > 0) dataView.Delete(0); // delete data only in DataView objekt,
        dataView.RowFilter = "";                    // not in the database
        grid.DataSource = dataView;
        grid.DataBind();
    }

    public void SelectRow(object sender, EventArgs e) {
        grid.SelectedItemStyle.BackColor = System.Drawing.Color.Gray;
        label.Text = grid.SelectedItem.Cells[1].Text + " " + grid.SelectedItem.Cells[2].Text;
    }

}
```

On loading the page, the method PageLoad is called, which reads the data from
the database. The page will be reloaded on every round trip, but the data should
only be retrieved from the database when the page is loaded for the first time. This
can be achieved by checking the property IsPostBack of the Page object. It is false
when the page is loaded for the first time and true on any further round trip. In
order to preserve the DataSet until the next round trip we save it with

```
Session["data"] = ds;
```

in the state of the current session (see Section 6.7.3) under an arbitrary name (for
example "data"). On the next round trip the DataSet can be restored from the session state with

```
ds = (DataSet) Session["data"];
```

Clicking the button "delete" in one of the rows triggers a DeleteCommand event which leads to the invocation of DeleteRow. The affected row is passed along in the parameter e.Item. We restrict the view on the DataSet by setting the property RowFilter to "EmployeeID=...", where the employee number is taken from the affected row using e.Item.Cells[0].Text. Calling dataView.Delete(0) now will delete exactly that row which matches the RowFilter, that is, where the button has been clicked. Subsequently we reset the RowFilter, assign the new view to the DataGrid and invoke DataBind() to make the changes visible.

If the user clicks the "select" button in one of the rows, a SelectedIndexChanged event is triggered which leads to the invocation of SelectRow. There we set the background colour of the selected row to grey and write the text of columns 1 and 2 in a Label control. Figure 6.22 shows how the page looks in a browser.

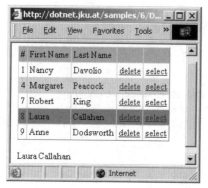

Figure 6.22 DataGrid with a selected row and several deleted rows (compared to Figure 6.21)

6.4.12 Calendar

Finally, we will look at a fancy, but often quite useful web control, namely a calendar, where a user can select a certain date. The Calendar control is complex. Therefore we do not present its entire interface but just an example. Details can be found in the online documentation of .NET.

The following aspx file contains a Calendar control with various format specifications as well as a Label control for displaying the selected date.

```
<%@ Page Language="C#" %>
<html>
  <script Runat="server">
    void ShowDate(object sender, EventArgs e) {
      DateTime date = cal.SelectedDate;
      lab.Text = date.ToShortDateString();
    }
  </script>
```

```
<body>
   <form Runat="server">
      <asp:Calendar ID="cal" OnSelectionChanged="ShowDate" Runat="server">
         <TitleStyle BackColor="Gray" />
         <DayStyle BackColor="LightGray" />
         <OtherMonthDayStyle ForeColor="Gray" />
         <SelectedDayStyle ForeColor="Red" Font-Bold="True" />
      </asp:Calendar><br>
      <asp:Label ID="lab" Runat="server" />
   </form>
</body>
</html>
```

A Calendar allows the definition of styles (font, colour, alignment) for different areas of the calendar:

TitleStyle	Style of the header line
DayStyle	Style of the days within the selected month
OtherMonthDayStyle	Style of the days outside the selected month
SelectedDayStyle	Style of the selected day
TodayDayStyle	Style of the current day
WeekEndDayStyle	Style of the days of the weekend

Furthermore, certain parts, such as the header line or the names of the days, can be hidden.

The user can now select a certain day with the mouse. This triggers a Selection-Changed event and an immediate round trip. The property SelectedDate now refers to the selected date. Figure 6.23 shows the calendar of this example.

Figure 6.23 A Calendar *control*

6.5 Validating User Input

Before processing a form it is wise to do some validity checks. For example, certain input fields should not be left empty, the age of a person should be a positive number, and an e-mail address should contain the character '@'. Because most such checks follow a similar pattern, ASP.NET offers some controls (so-called *validators*) that take the routine work of implementing those checks away from the programmer.

All validators extend the class BaseValidator which is itself a subclass of Label. Here is an overview of all validators:

```
BaseValidator
 – RequiredFieldValidator        checks whether an input field is empty
 – BaseCompareValidator
    – RangeValidator             checks whether a value is within the valid range
    – CompareValidator           compares two input values
 – RegularExpressionValidator    checks if a value matches a regular expression
 – CustomValidator               carries out a user-defined check
```

Every validator is assigned a control (for example a TextBox) which it has to check. The only exception is the CompareValidator, which is assigned two controls. If the check discovers an error, the text of the validator (which is a subclass of Label) is displayed where the validator appears in the web form. Additionally, a summary of all error messages on the page can be displayed in a ValidationSummary control. If an error occurs the property IsValid of the page is set to false. By querying this property other controls can react to the error. Here is a simple example of a RequiredFieldValidator for a text field:

```
<asp:TextBox ID="box" Runat="server" />
<asp:RequiredFieldValidator ControlToValidate="box"
                    ErrorMessage="You must enter a text." Runat="server" />
```

The validity checks are done at the next round trip of the page. In order to avoid erroneous input causing unnecessary round trips, there is a JavaScript implementation of the validators which is used if the browser understands JavaScript. JavaScript code is executed at the client before the round trip starts. If an error is detected, the round trip is held back and the error messages are displayed in the browser. If the browser does not understand JavaScript, the checks are carried out at the server.

6.5.1 BaseValidator

BaseValidator defines the behaviour that is common to all validators. Here is an extract of its interface:

```
public abstract class BaseValidator : Label, IValidator {
    //---- properties
    public string ControlToValidate { get; set; }
    public string ErrorMessage { get; set; }
    public bool IsValid { get; set; }
    public ValidatorDisplay Display { get; set; }
    public override bool Enabled { get; set; }
    public bool EnableClientScript { get; set; }
    //----- method
    public void Validate();
}
```

ControlToValidate contains the name of the control to be validated. Mostly, these controls are of kinds TextBox, ListBox and DropDownList.

If the validation fails, the property Text, which the validators inherit from Label, is displayed as an error message at the position of the validator. In ErrorMessage we can specify a more detailed description of the error that will be added to the report of the ValidationSummary control, if one exists. If the property Text is left undefined, ErrorMessage is also displayed at the position of the validator.

In case of an error, the property IsValid is set to false. The web page itself also has such a property whose value corresponds to the result of combining the IsValid properties of all the validators with a logical *and*.

With the property Display we can specify how the error message is inserted at the position of the validator. The value None means that the message is never inserted. Static indicates that the space for the error message is always kept free in the page. Finally, Dynamic does not reserve any space for the error message and thus other controls may move when the error message is actually inserted.

If the property Enable, inherited from WebControl, is set to false, the validation is suppressed. With EnableClientScript we can specify whether the validation should be carried out at the client or at the server. If we choose true here (which is the default), the client browser must support JavaScript.

By calling the method Validate we can explicitly initiate the validation, for example if we have modified a control from within the code-behind file and now want to validate it.

6.5.2 RequiredFieldValidator

In many situations all we want to do is make sure that the user has actually filled out a text field. For this purpose we can use a RequiredFieldValidator that displays an error message if the corresponding field is empty.

```
public class RequiredFieldValidator : BaseValidator {
    public string InitialValue { get; set; }
}
```

In InitialValue we can provide the initial value of the checked text field (for example "Please fill out"). If the text has not changed before the check, an error message is displayed. If we do not specify any InitialValue, the error message is displayed for an empty text field.

6.5.3 RangeValidator

This validator checks whether the value of a control lies within a certain range.

```
public class RangeValidator : BaseCompareValidator {
    public string MinimumValue { get; set; }
    public string MaximumValue { get; set; }
    public ValidationDataType Type { get; set; }
}
```

With MinimumValue and MaximumValue we define the valid interval. The property Type must specify whether the values under consideration are numbers, strings or of some other type. The default assumption is that we are dealing with strings.

```
public enum ValidationDataType { String, Integer, Double, Date, Currency }
```

6.5.4 CompareValidator

A CompareValidator allows comparison of two values with respect to a given operator.

```
public class CompareValidator : BaseCompareValidator {
    public string ControlToCompare { get; set; }
    public string ValueToCompare { get; set; }
    public ValidationCompareOperator Operator ( get; set; }
    public ValidationDataType Type { get; set; }
}
```

We can compare the control under consideration (ControlToValidate) with either another control (ControlToCompare) or with a constant value (ValueToCompare). However, it is illegal to define ControlToCompare and ValueToCompare at the same time. The property Operator specifies the comparison operator:

```
public enum ValidationCompareOperator { Equal, NotEqual,
    GreaterThan, GreaterThanEqual, LessThan, LessThanEqual, DataTypeCheck }
```

The order of comparison is ControlToValidate Operator ControlToCompare. Specifying DataTypeCheck as an operator will only check whether the validated controls have the required types.

The types of the values being compared are specified with the property Type, as with the RangeValidator.

6.5.5   CustomValidator

The most flexible kind of validator is the CustomValidator, which invokes a user-defined method where any sort of checks can be carried out.

```
public class CustomValidator : BaseValidator {
    public string ClientValidationFunction { get; set; }
    public event ServerValidateEventHandler ServerValidate;
}
```

The validation can be carried out either at the client or at the server. If it is to be done at the client, we have to specify the name of the method to be invoked in ClientValidationFunction. We must then implement this method in a scripting language that can be interpreted at the client (e.g. JavaScript or VBScript). In JavaScript, for example, the interface of such a method looks like this:

```
<script Language="JavaScript">
    function MyClientValidationFunction(source, arg) {
        ...
    }
</script>
```

The value of the control to validate is passed in arg.Value. The result of the validation (true or false) is returned in arg.IsValid. Of course, the web browser must support the scripting language used.

   If the validation should happen at the server, we do not set ClientValidationFunction, but define an event handler for the ServerValidate event. This can be written, for example, in C#, and it has access to all the control elements on the web page and the entire .NET library.

```
void MyServerValidationFunction(object sender, ServerValidateEventArgs arg) {
    ...
}
```

The passed parameter arg has the two properties Value and IsValid as in the client-side validation scenario.

6.5.6   Example

In the following example we use the four validators described above. Each validator checks a certain text field and displays an asterisk next to this field if its contents fails the validation. In addition to that, we specify detailed error messages which are collected in a ValidationSummary that we place at the end of the web page. For the sake of simplicity we have not formatted the page.

```
<%@ Page Language="C#" %>
<html>
   <script Runat="server">
      void HandleClick(object sender, EventArgs e) {
         if (IsValid) label.Text = "Everything OK"; else label.Text = "Error!";
      }
   </script>
   <script Language="JavaScript">
      function ValidateEmail(source, arg) {
         if (arg.Value.indexOf("@") < 0) arg.IsValid = false;
         else arg.IsValid = true;
      }
   </script>
<body>
   <form Runat="server">
      Name:
      <asp:TextBox ID="name" Runat="server" />
      <asp:RequiredFieldValidator ID="nameVal" ControlToValidate="name" Text="*"
         ErrorMessage="Please enter a name." Runat="server" /><br>
      Age:
      <asp:TextBox ID="age" Runat="server" />
      <asp:RangeValidator ID="ageVal" ControlToValidate="age" Text="*"
         MinimumValue="0" MaximumValue="120" Type="Integer"
         ErrorMessage="Age must be between 0 and 120." Runat="server" /><br>
      Years of membership:
      <asp:TextBox ID="memberSince" Runat="server" />
      <asp:CompareValidator ID="memberVal" Text="*"
         ControlToValidate="memberSince" Operator="LessThan"
         ControlToCompare="age" Type="Integer"
         ErrorMessage="Age is less than years of membership." Runat="server" /><br>
      Email:
      <asp:TextBox ID="email" Runat="server" />
      <asp:CustomValidator ID="emailVal" ControlToValidate="email" Text="*"
         ClientValidationFunction="ValidateEmail"
         ErrorMessage="Invalid E-mail address." Runat="server" /><br>
      <asp:Button ID="ok" Text="Send" OnClick="HandleClick" Runat="server" /><br>
      <asp:Label ID="label" Runat="server" /><br>
      <asp:ValidationSummary Runat="server" />
   </form>
</body>
</html>
```

If the browser displaying this page is Internet Explorer 4.0 or higher, ASP.NET will generate JavaScript code to do the validation at the client. In this case, if the form has not been filled out correctly, clicking on the button "Send" will not lead to a round trip, because the errors will already have been detected at the client. In Figure 6.24 we see that the event method HandleClick has not been executed, because otherwise the web page would display the text "Error!".

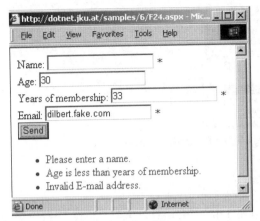

Figure 6.24 *Text fields with validators*

6.6   User-defined Controls

ASP.NET already offers a wide range of predefined web controls. However, on top of these users can still implement new controls and thus design web interfaces according to their own ideas. This is one of the advantages of ASP.NET in contrast to HTML. While HTML offers only a limited supply of controls, ASP.NET is extensible.

There are two ways to implement new controls. We can either compose them from existing controls or we can implement them as a completely new class that must extend System.Web.UI.Control or one of its subclasses. The first style is called *user controls* and the second *custom controls*. We will now describe them in more detail.

6.6.1   User Controls

A user control consists of a number of other controls and possibly HTML code. These are combined into a group and can then be used like a single control in an aspx file.

For example, we could combine a TextBox and a DropDownList to make a new control MoneyField, where amounts of money can be entered and then converted to another currency by selecting from the DropDownList (see Figure 6.25).

MoneyField can then be used as often as necessary (even several times per web page) as a stand-alone web control.

Figure 6.25 *User control consisting of a* TextBox *and a* DropDownList

ascx Files

The code of a user control is saved to a file with the extension ascx. For our example we will create a file MoneyField.ascx with the following contents:

```
<%@ Control Inherits="MoneyFieldBase" Src="MoneyField.ascx.cs" %>
<asp:TextBox ID="amount" Runat="server" />
<asp:DropDownList ID="currency" AutoPostBack="true"
                       OnSelectedIndexChanged="Select" Runat="server">
   <asp:ListItem Text="Euro" Value="1.0" Selected="true" />
   <asp:ListItem Text="US Dollar" Value="1.1489" />
   <asp:ListItem Text="Swiss Franc" Value="1.5725" />
   <asp:ListItem Text="British Pound" Value="0.6873" />
</asp:DropDownList>
```

As we can see, this file contains a TextBox and a DropDownList. The DropDownList stores the desired currencies and their exchange rates with respect to the euro (as of November 2003). Selecting a currency triggers a SelectedIndexChanged event which should be handled by the method Select.

Code-Behind File of a User Control

We could include the method Select as a server-side script code directly in MoneyField.ascx. However, in this example we have decided to store it in a code-behind file. Therefore we must specify this file in the Control directive of the ascx file, as we have done in the first line of our example. Our code-behind file is MoneyField.ascx.cs and contains a class MoneyFieldBase which is extended by our composite control element. MoneyFieldBase itself must be derived from System.Web.UI.UserControl in a similar way to what we have already seen with the code-behind files of aspx pages.

```
using System;
using System.Web.UI;
using System.Web.UI.WebControls;
using System.Globalization;
```

```
public class MoneyFieldBase : UserControl {
    protected TextBox amount;
    protected DropDownList currency;
    private CultureInfo culture = new CultureInfo("en-US");

    public string Text {
        get { return amount.Text; }
        set { amount.Text = value; }
    }

    public double OldFactor {
        get { return ViewState["factor"] == null ? 1 : (double) ViewState["factor"]; }
        set { ViewState["factor"] = value; }
    }

    public void Select(object sender, EventArgs arg) {
        try {
            double val = Convert.ToDouble(amount.Text, culture);
            double newFactor = Convert.ToDouble(currency.SelectedItem.Value, culture);
            double newVal = val / OldFactor * newFactor;
            amount.Text = newVal.ToString("f2", culture);
            OldFactor = newFactor;
        } catch (Exception) {
            amount.Text = "0";
        }
    }
}
```

In MoneyFieldBase we must declare the constituent controls as fields.

The method Select calculates the value to be displayed in the TextBox from its current value, the exchange rate of the target currency and the exchange rate of the source currency with respect to the euro. If the currently displayed amount is, for example, a US dollar value that should be converted to Swiss francs, the new value is computed as Value / 1.1489 * 1.5725.

Because the server does not maintain state information, the conversion factor of the currently displayed value (with respect to the euro) must be saved somewhere until the next round trip. For this we use the property ViewState of class UserControl which will automatically be stored in a hidden field of the HTML page sent to the browser. In order to simplify the access to ViewState our user control offers a property OldFactor, which accesses the stored value with ViewState["factor"].

The conversion of a string value (for example "1.1489") into a double value is done by the method Convert.ToDouble. We have given the decimal point as "." and not, for example, as "," which would be the German notation. In order to make sure that the conversion works we provide as a second parameter a CultureInfo object that recognizes the US notation for the decimal point. CultureInfo is declared in the namespace Globalization which is why we have to import this namespace.

As we can see, a user control may have its own properties and methods which can then be accessed from outside the class. The property Text of MoneyField allows us, for example, to set and query the value of the TextBox amount.

If an element of a user control triggers an event, this must be handled in the ascx file or the corresponding code-behind file. It is not possible to react to such an event in the page that contains the user control.

Using User Controls

We can now use our MoneyField control as often as we like in other web pages. The following aspx file, for example, contains two MoneyField controls that can be manipulated independently of each other:

```
<%@ Page Language="C#" %>
<%@ Register TagPrefix="my" TagName="MoneyField" Src="MoneyField.ascx" %>
<html>
<body>
  <form Runat="server">
    Amount 1: <my:MoneyField ID="field1" Text="100" Runat="server" /><br>
    Amount 2: <my:MoneyField ID="field2" Runat="server" />
  </form>
</body>
</html>
```

In order to make MoneyField known we need a Register directive. It specifies the name of the control (TagName) as well as its prefix (TagPrefix) which will then be used instead of the prefix asp which we use for the predefined elements. Additionally, the Src attribute specifies the ascx file in which this control is defined.

At the first occurrence of MoneyField we have also used the custom-defined property Text to set the initial value of the control's text field. Figure 6.26 shows how the browser displays the above aspx file.

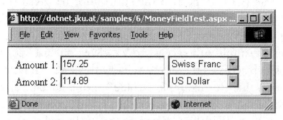

Figure 6.26 *Multiple user controls in a web page*

6.6.2   Custom Controls

Since controls such as TextBox, Button or DropDownList are nothing but ordinary classes, it is not surprising that we can implement our own classes and extend the library of controls with them. As long as the controls can somehow be rendered to HTML, we can do whatever comes to mind here.

A control that is implemented from scratch is called a *custom control*. It must extend the class Control or one of its subclasses (WebControl, Label, Button, etc.). If we derive it from Control, we have to implement its entire functionality ourselves, whereas deriving it from Label, for example, allows us to use the functionality of Label immediately. The only method that we must always override is Render. It produces the control's HTML code which is sent back to the browser.

Let us start with an example right away. Some editors allow folding of text pieces, that is, hiding them and displaying some background text instead. We now want to implement this functionality for a web browser as well. We will do this in a custom control implemented as class Fold. Figure 6.27 shows how the result should look in the browser.

A Fold control should consist of two small triangles which surround the text. Clicking on the first (left) triangle replaces the text with a background text (that is, the element is expanded; see the right side of Figure 6.27). Solid or hollow triangles indicate whether a Fold control is collapsed or expanded, respectively.

Figure 6.27 Fold *controls in a browser: collapsed (left), expanded (right)*

Implementing a Custom Control Class

First of all, we should think of what we need for implementing the Fold controls:

❏ A class Fold, which is best derived from ImageButton. An ImageButton shows an image (for example our opening triangle) and reacts when the user clicks on that image.

❏ Two properties, for storing the main and the background text, respectively. The class ImageButton already has a property AlternateText that we can use for the background text. For the main text we define a new property called Text. We also have to take care of preserving the contents of these properties from one round trip to the next. For AlternateText the class ImageButton already does this for us. For Text we have to do it ourselves by storing its value in ViewState of Fold.

❏ A method FoldClick that reacts to Click events. ImageButton already has an event named Click where we can install our event handler. In FoldClick we simply swap the contents of Text and AlternateText. Because this should also change the appearance of the triangles we define another property Icon which can assume the values "Solid" and "Hollow" and is also saved in ViewState.

❏ An implementation of the method Render where we generate the HTML.

❏ Four small images for the opening and closing triangles. We call them SolidLeft.gif, SolidRight.gif, HollowLeft.gif, and HollowRight.gif.

After these considerations we can go ahead and implement the class Fold and save its source code in a file Fold.cs.

```
using System; using System.Web.UI; using System.Web.UI.WebControls;

namespace Folds {

public class Fold : ImageButton {

    public string Text {   // property
        get { return ViewState["Text"] == null ? "" : (string) ViewState["Text"]; }
        set { ViewState["Text"] = value; }
    }

    public string Icon {   // property
        get { return ViewState["Icon"] == null ? "Solid" : (string) ViewState["Icon"]; }
        set { ViewState["Icon"] = value; }
    }

    public Fold() : base() {   // constructor
        Click += new ImageClickEventHandler(FoldClick);
    }

    void FoldClick(object sender, ImageClickEventArgs e) {   // event handler
        string s = Text;
        Text = AlternateText;
        AlternateText = s;
        if (Icon == "Solid") Icon = "Hollow"; else Icon = "Solid";
    }

    protected override void Render(HtmlTextWriter w) {   // generate HTML
        w.Write("<input type=image name=" + UniqueID);
        w.Write(" src='" + TemplateSourceDirectory + "/" + Icon + "Left.gif' border=0 />");
        w.Write(Text);
        w.Write("<img src='" + TemplateSourceDirectory + "/" + Icon + "Right.gif'>");
    }

}
}
```

Custom controls must be implemented in a specific namespace. We call ours Folds. The method Render generates the following HTML code:

```
<input type=image name=_ctl1 src='/samples/6/SolidLeft.gif' border=0 />
... background text...
<img src='/samples/6/SolidRight.gif'>
```

The <input> element describes an image button with the image SolidLeft.gif. The <img> element displays the triangle SolidRight.gif. The property UniqueID that we use in Render holds a unique name for the web control which is generated automatically by ASP.NET. In this example it is _ctl1. It is essential to use this also as the name for the generated HTML element, because ASP.NET connects an event with the corresponding web control according to its name. Render also uses the property TemplateSourceDirectory which holds the name of the virtual directory where the aspx file is stored. In our example this directory is "/samples/6".

The get and set accessors of the properties Text and Icon store their values in the ViewState of the Fold element. Between round trips ViewState is preserved in the HTML code that is sent to the client.

Before we can use our new custom control, we have to compile Fold.cs into a dll assembly and place this in a subdirectory bin under the virtual directory. All custom controls must lie in a dll assembly in the bin directory. But a dll assembly can hold more than one custom control. The compilation command would be:

```
csc /target:library /out:bin/Folds.dll Fold.cs
```

Using Custom Control s

Now we are ready to use our new Fold control in an aspx file. Using a Register directive we must specify the assembly and namespace where the control is to be found. Furthermore, we have to choose a prefix to use in front of the control instead of the standard asp.

```
<%@ Page Language="C#" %>
<%@ Register TagPrefix="my" Namespace="Folds" Assembly="Folds" %>
<html>
   <body>
      <form Runat="server">
         <my:Fold Text="Main text" AlternateText="Background text"
                  Runat="server" />
      </form>
   </body>
</html>
```

Since Fold extends ImageButton, we can set any other properties of ImageButton in the <Fold> element; we might, for example, assign a new event handler for mouse clicks:

```
<my:Fold OnClick="MyClickHandler" ... Runat="server" />
```

Clicking on the opening triangle of the Fold control now invokes not only the method FoldClick, but also the method MyClickHandler.

Controls With an Inner Structure

Some controls contain inner elements. ListBox, for example, consists of ListItem objects. Custom controls can also contain inner elements. How to implement this in general is described in the online documentation of .NET [SDKDoc]. We will demonstrate it here with the simple special case of a Fold element containing arbitrary text as an inner structure, something like this:

```
<my:Fold Text="Please read!" Runat="server">
    ASP.NET allows the development of custom controls that
    open up almost unlimited possibilities for new web functionality.
</my:Fold>
```

If a user specifies a Fold element in this way the inner text should be interpreted as the value of the attribute AlternateText. Therefore we have to do the following:

- ❏ Declare the class Fold with the attribute [ParseChildren(false)]. This attribute indicates that the web control is structured (ParseChildren) but does not contain any further controls except text (false).
- ❏ Override the method AddParsedSubObject which receives the inner text in the form of a parameter of type LiteralControl.

Now our class looks like this:

```
[ParseChildren(false)]
public class Fold : ImageButton {
    ...
    protected override void AddParsedSubObject(object obj) {
        if (obj is LiteralControl) AlternateText = ((LiteralControl) obj).Text;
    }
    ...
}
```

The inner text may contain arbitrary text, including HTML tags. The only tags not allowed are asp tags, because the text will be inserted into the returned HTML stream as it is and will thus be ignored by the ASP compiler.

Triggering Custom Events

Our Fold controls trigger Click events and react to these themselves. Click events already belong to the functionality of the base class ImageButton. But how can we get custom controls to trigger new events so that the application programmer can react to those?

In order to demonstrate this we will modify our Fold control a little: it should be possible to read the background text from a file whose name is specified with a leading '@' in the property AlternateText (for example "@background.txt"). When doing so, a file of the specified name might not be found. In this case we want to trigger a FileNotFound event to which the program might react, for example, by retrieving AlternateText from somewhere else.

First of all we have to understand the mechanism that leads to the triggering of events at the server. A page is sent from a client to the server, because a certain web control (for example a button) has initiated the round trip (postback). The server now checks whether the web control has a method RaisePostBackEvent and, if so, invokes it. This method then decides which events to trigger: an ImageButton, for example, calls its OnClick method and thus triggers a Click event. This goes something like this:

```
public class ImageButton : Image, IPostBackEventHandler, IPostBackDataHandler {
    public event ImageClickEventHandler Click;
    ...
    protected virtual void OnClick(ImageClickEventArgs e) {
        if (Click != null) Click(this, e);
        ...
    }
    ...
}
```

If we want Fold objects to trigger a FileNotFound event we must do the following:

❑ Declare an event named FileNotFound.
❑ Implement a method OnFileNotFound that triggers this event.
❑ Override the method OnClick and attempt to open the file specified in AlternateText. If this fails, OnFileNotFound has to be invoked.

The result is the following code:

```
[ParseChildren(false)]
public class Fold : ImageButton {
    public event EventHandler FileNotFound;

    protected virtual void OnFileNotFound(EventArgs e) {
        if (FileNotFound != null) FileNotFound(this, e);
    }
```

```
protected override void OnClick(ImageClickEventArgs e) {
    try {
        if (AlternateText.StartsWith("@")) {
            string fileName = Page.MapPath(TemplateSourceDirectory) + "/" +
                                AlternateText.Substring(1);
            FileStream s = File.OpenRead(fileName);
            StreamReader r = new StreamReader(s);
            AlternateText = r.ReadToEnd();
        }
    } catch (FileNotFoundException) {
        OnFileNotFound(EventArgs.Empty);
    } finally {
        base.OnClick(e);
    }
}
...
}
```

The property TemplateSourceDirectory which we use in OnClick indicates the virtual directory holding the aspx file (for example "/samples/6"). The method MapPath maps it to the corresponding physical directory where the aspx files actually reside and where we also expect to find the file with the background text.

In OnClick we must not forget to call the OnClick method of the base class ImageButton, because otherwise the Click event will not be triggered.

Now we can use the new Fold control in an aspx file and react to the event FileNotFound there.

```
<%@ Page Language="C#" %>
<%@ Register TagPrefix="my" Namespace="Folds" Assembly="Folds" %>
<html>
    <script Language="C#" Runat="server">
        void HandleNotFound(object sender, EventArgs e) {
            fold.AlternateText="File not found";
        }
    </script>
    <body>
        <form Runat="server">
            <my:Fold ID="fold" Text="Please read!" AlternateText="@background.txt"
                    OnFileNotFound="HandleNotFound" Runat="server"/>
        </form>
    </body>
</html>
```

6.7   State Management

Under ASP.NET web servers are stateless. That means they do not maintain any information about web pages, users or their data. The server handles every page request independently, without reference to any previous requests.

At least it is like this in principle. In practice, however, state management is very important. Users who visit the web pages of a book store do not want to have to authenticate themselves anew on every page. They also want to collect books in a shopping cart and proceed to the checkout with them when they have finished shopping. All this requires state information.

ASP.NET distinguishes between three categories of state. All of them can be maintained quite easily:

- ❏ **Page state.** This includes the values of all controls on a web page, for example the contents of text fields, the state of check boxes and so on. ASP.NET automatically stores the page state in a hidden field of the HTML page sent to the client. In this way the state information is maintained at the client instead of at the server, thus decreasing the server's workload. The programmer can also store custom data in the page state.
- ❏ **Session state.** All requests to a server that originate from the same client and arrive within a certain time interval make up a *session*. In its state a session can store, for example, a shopping cart, which is preserved while the client visits different pages of the server. The session state is managed at the server and identified by an automatically assigned session name.
- ❏ **Application state.** All web pages, code-behind files, and other resources that reside within one virtual directory make up an *application*. The application state is also managed at the server and is accessible for all sessions of that application.

Figure 6.28 shows how pages, sessions, applications and their states are interconnected.

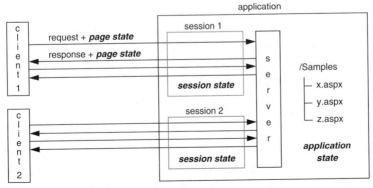

Figure 6.28 *Page state, session state and application state*

The next subsections will deal with each of the three state categories in more detail. But before that we will look at the Page class which represents a web page and provides access to all three kinds of state.

6.7.1 Class Page

We have already used the class System.Web.UI.Page a couple of times in the previous sections. It is the base class of all web pages and provides useful properties and methods for programming such pages. Here is an extract of its interface:

```
public class Page : TemplateControl, IHttpHandler {
    //----- properties
    public virtual ControlCollection Controls { get; }
    public ValidatorCollection Validators { get; }
    public bool IsValid { get; }
    public bool IsPostBack { get; }
    public virtual string TemplateSourceDirectory { get; }
    public HttpApplicationState Application { get; }
    public virtual HttpSessionState Session { get; }
    public HttpRequest Request { get; }
    public HttpResponse Response { get; }
    public HttpServerUtility Server { get; }
    public IPrincipal User { get; }
    //----- methods
    public string MapPath(string virtualPath);
    public virtual void Validate();
    //----- events: Init, Load, DataBinding, PreRender, Unload inherited from Control
    ...
}
```

Page extends TemplateControl which itself is derived from Control. That means that Page inherits all properties, methods and events from Control. So Page can, for example, react to the events Init, Load, DataBinding and so on. We have already done this a couple of times in the examples of the previous sections.

The property Controls contains a collection of all web controls of the page. A program can add new controls or search for a specific control.

Validators is a collection of all the validators of the page. We can iterate over the validators and enable or disable them individually. Every validator has a property IsValid. If one of them is false, then IsValid of the page will also be false. By calling the method Validate we can explicitly initiate a validation of the page, which means that all validators of the page will do their validity checks.

The property IsPostBack is true if the page has been sent from the client to the server during a round trip. This property is only false when the page has been requested for the first time. We have already used IsPostBack in Section 6.4.11, where we did the initialization only at the first visit of the page.

TemplateSourceDirectory provides the name of the current virtual directory that holds the aspx file of the current page (for example "/samples/6"). The method MapPath converts this name into the path to the corresponding physical directory.

The property Session provides the session state (see Section 6.7.3), the property Application provides the application state (see Section 6.7.4), and the property ViewState, which Page inherits from Control, provides the page state (see Section 6.7.2).

The two properties Request and Response are also interesting, which is why we will now take a closer look at them.

HttpRequest

If the client requests a web page from a server this request is packed into an HttpRequest object that holds all the information about the request. ASP.NET uses this object in order to create and initialize the page object with all its controls. However, the programmer can also access the HttpRequest object and gather interesting information from it. Here are its most important properties:

```
public sealed class HttpRequest {
    public string UserHostName { get; }
    public string UserHostAddress { get; }
    public string HttpMethod { get; }
    public HttpBrowserCapabilities Browser { get; }
    public NameValueCollection Form { get; }
    public NameValueCollection QueryString { get; }
    public HttpCookieCollection Cookies { get; }
    public NameValueCollection ServerVariables { get; }
    ...
}
```

UserHostName holds the DNS name of the client and UserHostAddress the corresponding IP number. HttpMethod specifies the method of the request (GET or POST). The property Browser contains information about the web browser used by the client, for example its name, version or ability to handle cookies or scripts.

The names and values of the controls on the current web page are encoded in the property Form of the HttpRequest object. We can access the name of the i-th control with Form.Keys[i] and its value with Form[i].

A URL can contain parameters in the form of a so-called *query string*:

http://www.fake.com/Mission.aspx**?id=007&agent=JamesBond**

These parameters are passed to the property QueryString. QueryString.Keys[1] then contains the name "agent"; QueryString[1] holds the value "JamesBond". It is also possible to access the elements of QueryString via their names: in our example QueryString["agent"] will return the value "JamesBond".

The property Cookies contains the names and values of possibly transmitted cookies. In ServerVariables we find information about the web server used.

HttpResponse

As a response to a page request, ASP.NET generates an HTML stream which is then returned to the client. The class HttpResponse contains properties and methods to build up that HTML stream.

```
public sealed class HttpResponse {
    //----- properties
    public string ContentType { get; set; }
    public TextWriter Output { get; }
    public int StatusCode { get; set; }
    public HttpCookieCollection Cookies { get; set; }
    ...
    //----- methods
    public void Write(string s);   // there are some overloaded versions of this
    public void Redirect(string newURL);
    ...
}
```

ContentType describes the MIME type of the HTML stream (the default is "text/html"). Output is a TextWriter that can be used to write into the HTML stream. It is passed as a parameter to the Render method of the controls, so that they can fill in their HTML representation. StatusCode provides information about the success of the request. The value 200, for example, means OK and the value 404 means that the requested page could not be found. In Cookies one can return cookies from the server to the client.

The method Write is a short form of Output.Write(...). It can be used to write into the HTML stream. In the following example we will write the IP number of the sender in the HTML stream of a web page:

```
<body>
    Client = <% Response.Write(Request.UserHostAddress); %>
</body>
```

Finally, the method Redirect offers a simple way to redirect a request to another web page. Any parameters can be passed as a query string in the URL of the page, for example:

```
Response.Redirect("http://localhost/Samples/Warning.aspx?id=3&name=Miller");
```

On the receiver side the parameters can then be read like this:

```
int id = Convert.ToInt32(Request.QueryString["id"]);   // sets id to 3
string name = Request.QueryString["name"];             // sets name to Miller
```

6.7.2 Page State

When the server sends a page to the browser, it packs the page state and the values of all controls into the HTML stream. When the page comes back, the server can construct the new page state from the old page state stored in the HTML stream and the newly entered values of the controls, which are stored in the property Form of HttpRequest.

The page state is encoded in a hidden HTML field named __VIEWSTATE which might, for example, look like this:

```
<input type="hidden" name="__VIEWSTATE" value="dDwxNzg3NTQzOTc5O3O3Q802">
```

ASP.NET automatically encodes the state in the attribute value without any need for the programmer to be involved.

But sometimes we want to put additional data into the page state in order to have it available at the next round trip (for example, values of custom-declared fields or properties of the page class). Such data can be added to the property ViewState manually.

The page and all its controls have a property ViewState which they inherit from Control and which is a collection where values can be stored under a custom name. In order to save, for example, a value named counter until the next round trip, we can write:

```
ViewState["counter"] = counter;
```

The value of counter is then stored under the name "counter" in the ViewState of the page and will be packed into the __VIEWSTATE field together with the other values. At the next round trip we can read it in again with

```
int counter = (int) ViewState["counter"];
```

It is considered good programming style to hide the access to ViewState in the get and set accessors of a property, for example:

```
int Counter {
    get { return (int) ViewState["counter"]; }
    set { ViewState["counter"] = value; }
}
```

Unfortunately, ViewState has the visibility protected so that the page cannot access the ViewState properties of its controls. Custom controls, however, can store their data in their own ViewState.

Maintaining the page state at the client decreases the load on the server and thus allows it to handle more concurrent page requests.

6.7.3 Session State

Multiple requests coming from the same client make up a *session* even if they target different pages of the same application. The requests of a session can store data such as a shopping cart in a *session state* object which is preserved during the entire session and is accessible from all requests of that session.

A session starts with the first access to a web page of a virtual directory and ends automatically after there have been no accesses for a certain period of time. This time-out is normally set to 20 minutes, but can be adjusted with the property Timeout of the class HttpSessionState (see below).

The session state can be accessed via the property Session of every web page. In order to store, for example, a shopping cart in the session state, we write:

```
Session["cart"] = shoppingCart;  // shoppingCart is of type DataTable, say
```

At the next round trip we can recover it with:

```
DataTable shoppingCart = (DataTable)Session["cart"];
```

where "cart" is a name we have chosen. Of course, the access to Session["cart"] should be hidden in a property as well.

The property Session returns an object of type HttpSessionState. Here is an extract from its interface:

```
public sealed class HttpSessionState : ICollection, IEnumerable {
    //----- properties and indexers
    public int Count { get; }
    public object this[string name] { get; set; }
    public object this[int index] { get; set; }
    public NameObjectCollectionBase.KeysCollection Keys { get; }
    public string SessionID { get; }
    public bool IsNewSession { get; }
    public int Timeout { get; set; }
    public SessionStateMode Mode { get; }
    ...
    //----- methods
    public void Abandon();
    public void Clear();
    public void Remove(string name);
    ...
}
```

Count returns the number of name–value pairs in the session state. The two indexers allow access to the values of the state via either their names or their indices. Keys[i] provides the name of the i-th state value.

Every session is assigned a unique session identifier which is provided in SessionID. IsNewSession indicates whether the currently processed request is the first of the session.

With Timeout we can set the time after which a session automatically ends and its session state can be deleted. The default value is 20 minutes after the last request. But we can also terminate a session explicitly at any time by calling the method Abandon.

The session state is usually kept in main memory. This has the advantage that it can be accessed quickly. However, the drawback is that it is lost in case of a server crash. If there are hundreds of parallel sessions that all maintain some state information, this can also become a bottleneck. Therefore we can use the property Mode to specify that the session state should be externalized in a database (however, we will not describe this in any more detail here).

Finally, calling the method Clear deletes the entire state of a session while Remove(n) deletes only the value stored under the name n.

6.7.4   Application State

All accesses to pages within a virtual directory form an *application*. An application can also have its own state which is accessible for all requests of the different sessions of the application.

The application state is stored in the property Application of every web page and is represented by a collection of name–value pairs just like the other kinds of state. For example, in order to store the name of a database in the application state, we write:

```
Application["database"] = databaseName;
```

We can then retrieve it with:

```
string databaseName = (string) Application["database"];
```

The property Application provides an object of type HttpApplicationState with the following interface:

```
public sealed class HttpApplicationState : NameObjectCollectionBase {
    //----- properties and indexers
    public override int Count { get; }
    public object this[string name] { get; set; }
    public object this[int index] { get; }
    public string[] AllKeys { get; }

    ...
    //----- methods
    public void Clear();
    public void Lock();
    public void Unlock();

    ...
}
```

Count returns the number of name–value pairs in the application state. With the help of the two indexers we can access a state value via its name or its index just as with the sessions. Strangely enough, and in contrast to a session state, we only get read-access when addressing the values via the index. AllKeys returns an array with all the names for the state values.

Clear deletes the entire application state. In contrast to a session state, it is not possible to remove a single value from the application state.

Since multiple sessions of an application can be active at the same time, they must be prevented from interfering with each other when writing to the application state. This can be achieved by locking the state during write accesses with Lock and UnLock, for example:

```
Application.Lock();
Application["database"] = databaseName;
Application.UnLock();
```

The first access to one of its web pages starts an application. Once started it cannot be stopped explicitly, but in principle runs until the web server is restarted.

6.8   ASP.NET Application Layer (Global.asax)

An ASP.NET application consists of one or more aspx files stored in a common virtual directory. Additionally, there can also be a source file named Global.asax, where session or application-level events can be handled and global objects of an application (for example, visit counters) can be created. An application can have at most one Global.asax file, which must reside in the root directory of the application. If Global.asax does not exist, ASP.NET assumes that no event handling on the session or application level exists.

At the first access to a web page of an application ASP.NET compiles the file Global.asax into a class that is derived from HttpApplication. In contrast to aspx files, users cannot view the file Global.asax in a web browser. Here is an example of the contents of Global.asax:

```
<%@ Language="C#" %>
<script Runat="server">
    void Application_Start(Object sender, EventArgs e) { ... }
    void Application_BeginRequest(Object sender, EventArgs e) { ... }
    void Session_Start(Object sender, EventArgs e) { ... }
    void Session_End(Object sender, EventArgs e) { ... }
    void Application_EndRequest(Object sender, EventArgs e) { ... }
    void Application_End(Object sender, EventArgs e) { ... }
</script>
```

If we separate the C# code from the HTML code, Global.asax holds only the following line:

```
<%@ Application Inherits="Global" Src="Global.asax.cs" %>
```

The C# code then resides in the code-behind file Global.asax.cs:

```
using System;
using System.ComponentModel;
using System.Web;
using System.Web.SessionState;

public class Global : HttpApplication {
    public Global() { ... }
    protected void Application_Start(Object sender, EventArgs e) { ... }
    protected void Application_BeginRequest(Object sender, EventArgs e) { ... }
    protected void Session_Start(Object sender, EventArgs e) { ... }
    protected void Session_End(Object sender, EventArgs e) { ... }
    protected void Application_EndRequest(Object sender, EventArgs e) { ... }
    protected void Application_End(Object sender, EventArgs e) { ... }

    ...
}
```

The events Application_Start and Session_Start are triggered at the start of an application or a session and are caught by event handlers with the same names in Global.asax.cs. Round trips of a page will trigger the events Application_BeginRequest and Application_EndRequest. Ending a session triggers the Session_End event.

As an example, we will show here how to count the visits to pages in an application with the event Application_BeginRequest. The number of different users can be derived from the number of started sessions. The contents of the file Global.asax stay unchanged; only the file Global.asax.cs is modified, like this:

```
using System; using System.ComponentModel;
using System.Web; using System.Web.SessionState;

public class Global : HttpApplication {

    protected void Application_Start(Object sender, EventArgs e) {
        Application["accesses"] = 0;
        Application["users"] = 0;
    }

    protected void Application_BeginRequest(Object sender, EventArgs e) {
        Application.Lock();
        Application["accesses"] = (int) Application["accesses"] + 1;
        Application.UnLock();
    }

    protected void Session_Start(Object sender, EventArgs e) {
        Application.Lock();
        Application["users"] = (int) Application["users"] + 1;
        Application.UnLock();
    }
}
```

```
        protected void Session_End(Object sender, EventArgs e) { }
        protected void Application_EndRequest(Object sender, EventArgs e) { }
        protected void Application_End(Object sender, EventArgs e) { }
    }
```

Since the file Global.asax is not an ASP.NET page, we still need a separate page to display the statistics (Statistics.aspx):

```
<%@ Page Language="C#"%>
<html>
    <body>
        <h1>Statistics:</h1>
        Accesses to the Page: <% Response.Write(Application["accesses"]); %><br>
        User Sessions:<% Response.Write(Application["users"]); %>
    </body>
</html>
```

Figure 6.29 shows how this file would be displayed in a browser.

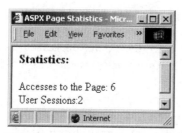

Figure 6.29 *Statistics collected by* Global.asax.cs

6.9 Configuration

ASP.NET applications can be configured with the XML file Web.config. The settings in this file apply to the virtual directory in which it is stored as well as to its subdirectories. But each subdirectory can have its own Web.config file. A Web.config in a subdirectory can extend the settings of the parent directory.

Web.config files are optional. If a directory does not have such a file, it inherits the settings of its parent directory. Under Windows 2000 the default settings for the entire web server are defined in the file:

```
c:\WINNT\Microsoft.NET\Framework\ [version] \CONFIG\Machine.config
```

All configuration files are continuously monitored for changes, which will then immediately take effect without restarting the Internet Information Server.

Web.config is used to configure security, authentification, databases, debugging, browsing, and web services. All settings are contained in the element <configuration> and consist of two parts: the *definition* of configuration sections and the *data* for those configuration sections.

6.9.1 Definition of Configuration Sections

In this part of Web.config or Machine.config we can define *configuration sections* (for example appSettings) whose contents will be specified later on. For each section we have to specify the name of a handler class that should process the configuration data of this section.

The definition part is located at the beginning of the configuration file. It may only appear once: either in Web.config or in Machine.config. If it is already defined in Machine.config, it may not be redefined in Web.config. Subordinate configuration files inherit these settings. The definition part starts with the <configSections> and contains <section> elements with the name of the configuration sections and their handlers:

```
<configuration>

  <configSections>
    <section name="appSettings"
             type=" System.Configuration.NameValueFileSectionHandler, System,
                 Version=1.0.3300.0, Culture=neutral,
                 PublicKeyToken=b77a5c561934e089"/>
  </configSections>

  <appSettings> ... </appSettings>
  ...
</configuration>
```

Normally, configuration sections are already defined in Machine.config, where sections that belong together are usually grouped with <sectionGroup> elements:

```
<configuration>
  <configSections>
    <sectionGroup name="system.web">
      <section name="browserCaps" ... />
      <section name="authorization" ... />

      ...
    </sectionGroup>
    ...
  </configSections>
  ...
</configuration>
```

6.9.2 Data of the Configuration Sections

In this part of Web.config or Machine.config we find the actual data of the sections defined under <configSections>. The section <appSettings> defined above, for example, allows us to pass name–value pairs to an application. It can look like this:

```
<configuration>
    <!-- Definition part -->
    <configSections>
        <!-- The definition of the section "appSettings" has already been done in the file
             Machine.config and must not be redefined here-->
    </configSections>
    <!-- Now follows the actual configuration -->
    <appSettings>
        <add key="DefaultHelpHomepage" value="www.help.com"/>
        <add key="AdminEmail" value="admin@nirwana.com"/>
    </appSettings>
</configuration>
```

The settings in this example define the help page and the e-mail address of the administrator for the application. In an ASP.NET application these settings can then be read like this:

```
<%@ Page Language="C#"%>
<%@ Import Namespace="System.Configuration" %>
<html>
    <script Language="C#" Runat="server">
        string GetHelpHomepage() {
            return ConfigurationSettings.AppSettings["DefaultHelpHomepage"];
        }
        string GetAdminEmail() {
            return ConfigurationSettings.AppSettings["AdminEmail"];
        }
    </script>
    <head>
        <title>ASPX Page with Configuration</title>
    </head>
    <body>
        <h1>Welcome</h1>
        For help refer to:
        <a href="<% Response.Write(GetHelpHomepage()); %>">
        <% Response.Write(GetHelpHomepage()); %></a><br>
        Web master:
        <a href="mailto:<% Response.Write(GetAdminEmail()); %>">
        <% Response.Write(GetAdminEmail()); %></a>        .
    </body>
</html>
```

Figure 6.30 shows how this file would be displayed in a browser.

Figure 6.30 *Passing configuration parameters to an application*

6.9.3 Overview of the Configuration Sections for ASP.NET

The configuration sections defined under <sectionGroup name="system.web"> are especially important for ASP.NET applications. We will provide an overview of these sections and explain some of them with examples. They are defined in Machine.config, and all Web.config files inherit them.

```
<configuration>
   <system.web>
      <authorization>
         <allow> <deny>
      <authentication>
         <forms> <credentials> <passport>
      <browserCaps>
         <result> <use> <filter> <case> <clientTarget> <add> <remove> <clear>
      <compilation>
         <compilers> <compiler> <assemblies> <add> <remove> <clear>
      <customErrors>
         <error>
      <globalization>
      <httpHandlers>
         <add> <remove> <clear>
      <httpModules>
         <add> <remove> <clear>
      <httpRuntime>
      <identity>
      <machineKey>
      <pages>
      <processModel>
      <securityPolicy>
         <trustLevel>
      <sessionState>
      <trace>
      <trust>
```

```
    <webServices>
        <protocols>
            <add> <remove>
        <serviceDescriptionFormatExtensionTypes>
            <add> <remove> <clear>
        <soapExtensionTypes>
            <add>
        <soapExtensionReflectorTypes>
            <add>
        <soapExtensionImporterTypes>
            <add>
        <WsdlHelpGenerator>
    </system.web>
<configuration>
```

authorization

The <authorization> section determines which users may access an ASP.NET application. The elements <allow users="..."> and <deny users="..."> specify which users always have access and which have to authenticate themselves (that is, login). The authentication always takes place before the authorization of a user, because the identity of the user has to be confirmed first. The attribute users can have the following values:

*	all users
?	anonymous users
[name]	explicit specification of users with their names

In order to force anonymous users to log in we insert the following in Web.config:

```
<authorization>
    <deny users="?"/>
</authorization>
```

authentication

In the section <authentication mode="..."> we can specify how to determine the identity of a user. The following kinds of authentication are available and can be specified in the attribute mode: None, Windows, Passport and Forms.

mode="None" is the default setting in Machine.config and means that no login is required.

mode="Windows" uses the Windows login which queries and checks the user data from the Windows server. However, the Windows login requires a high administrative effort and does not work outside a firewall.

mode="Passport" uses the Microsoft Passport service. If users request a web page that requires Passport authentication, they are automatically redirected to a page of the Passport server, where they are asked to enter their user data (of course, they must already have an account on the Passport server). After successful authentication the web page originally requested is displayed. The advantage of this kind of authentication is that a single account is enough to access all web pages that use this authentication scheme.

mode="Forms" allows the developer to implement a custom login form. Because the Forms login is a simple and flexible authentication technique that works independently of a firewall, it is the most frequently used kind of authentication. Figure 6.31 shows how it works.

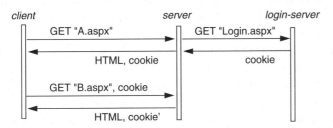

Figure 6.31 *Forms-based login*

Suppose a client requests the page A.aspx. Being not yet authenticated, the server redirects the request to the page Login.aspx, where the user is prompted for a user name and a password. If authentication succeeds the server generates a *cookie* (server-side piece of data) and sends it back to the client with the HTML code of the page A.aspx originally requested. There the cookie is automatically stored and then sent with all future page requests (for example, B.aspx) to the same server as a form of identification. From the information in the cookie the server can determine that the client has already been authenticated and it sends the requested page right away, together with a new cookie that replaces the previous one. Cookies do have an expiration date. If they are not replaced by a new one within a certain amount of time, they expire, and the client must reauthenticate itself at the login page on its next request.

We now want to demonstrate such a Forms login with an example. First of all we must create an appropriate configuration file Web.config:

```
<configuration>
 <system.web>

  <authorization>
   <deny users="?"/>
  </authorization>
```

```
<authentication mode="Forms">
  <forms name="MyCookie" loginUrl="Login.aspx" protection="All"
         timeout="20" path="/">
    <credentials passwordFormat="MD5">
      <user name="wolfgang" password="85C69322756E01FD4A7A22DE55E19743" />
      <user name="dietrich" password="85C69322756E01FD4A7A22DE55E19743" />
      <user name="peter" password="85C69322756E01FD4A7A22DE55E19743" />
      <user name="albrecht" password="85C69322756E01FD4A7A22DE55E19743" />
    </credentials>
  </forms>
</authentication>
</system.web>
</configuration>
```

The <authorization> section specifies that all anonymous users must be authenticated. If this restriction is missing in Web.config, the subsequent <authentication>
section is simply ignored.

The <forms> element contains the name of the cookie that will be sent to the
user if the authentication is successful. The value of the cookie is automatically
generated by the server. The attribute timeout determines after how many minutes
without requests the cookie will expire. Login.aspx is the page that asks the user for
his or her name and password and then tries to authenticate him or her according
to the user information provided under <credentials>. The passwords for each user
are encrypted in the selected format (here "MD5"). We have chosen the password
"dotnet" for all users and encrypted it in MD5 with the following utility program:

```
using System;
using System.Web.Security;

public class CryptPwd {
    public static void Main(string[] arg) {
        // arg[0] plain text representation of the password
        // arg[1] encryption format ("MD5")
        string pwd =
            FormsAuthentication.HashPasswordForStoringInConfigFile(arg[0],arg[1]);
        Console.WriteLine(pwd);
    }
}
```

We will now show a page Login.aspx where the user can enter his or her name and
password. These are then compared against the data provided under <credentials>
using the method FormsAuthentication.Authenticate(name, pwd). As an alternative,
the name and password could also be compared against a database, which is the
preferred technique if there are large numbers of users.

```
<%@ Page language='C#' %>
<%@ import namespace='System.Web.Security' %>
<html>
<script Runat='server'>
  void Login(Object sender, EventArgs eventArgs) {
    // compare name and pwd against the data provided in <credentials>.
    if (FormsAuthentication.Authenticate(name.Text, pwd.Text)) {
      // authentication ok: the user is redirected to the originally requested page
      FormsAuthentication.RedirectFromLoginPage(name.Text, permanent.Checked);
    } else {
      // authentication failed: the user remains on the login page and a message is printed.
      msg.Text = "Login failed!";
    }
  }
</script>
<head> <title>Login</title> </head>
</body>
  <form Runat="server">
    <table>
      <tr>
        <td>Username:</td>
        <td><asp:TextBox ID="name" Runat="server"/></td>
      </tr>
      <tr>
        <td>Password:</td>
        <td><asp:TextBox ID="pwd" TextMode="password" Runat="server"/></td>
      </tr>
    </table>
    <p>
      <asp:CheckBox ID="permanent" Runat="server"
                    Text="Store authorization permanently?"/>
    </p>
    <p> <asp:Label ID="msg" Runat="server"/> </p>
    <p> <asp:Button Text="Login" Runat="server" OnClick="Login"/> </p>
  </form>
</body>
</html>
```

If anonymous users now request an aspx page with Forms login, they will be redirected to the login page Login.aspx where they can authenticate themselves. If the authentication was successful they will be redirected to the page originally requested. Figure 6.32 shows the page Login.aspx.

compilation

In the <compilation> section we can enter settings that govern the compilation of an ASP.NET page. With the attribute <compilation debug="true">, for example, the browser will display detailed compilation error messages.

Figure 6.32 The login page Login.aspx

httpHandlers

In the <httpHandlers> section we can determine who is responsible for handling HTTP requests. Here is an excerpt from the <httpHandlers> section from the configuration file Machine.config:

```
<httpHandlers>
    <add verb="*" path="*.aspx" type="System.Web.UI.PageHandlerFactory"/>
    <add verb="*" path="*.config" type="System.Web.HttpForbiddenHandler"/>
    <!-- ... -->
</httpHandlers>
```

Requests for aspx pages are always forwarded to a PageHandlerFactory, but requests for configuration files (*.config) are forwarded to an HttpForbiddenHandler. Because the publication of configuration files is undesirable, the HttpForbidden-Handler prohibits all accesses to files with the extension .config.

6.10 Programming Web Pages with Visual Studio .NET

So far we have created all web pages in this chapter without using Visual Studio .NET, because this tool hides from the user many things that are important for understanding ASP.NET.

On the other hand, the development of graphical web pages is one of the strengths of Visual Studio .NET. This is why we want to take a quick look at this tool at the end of this chapter. In contrast to the .NET Framework SDK, Visual Studio .NET is not free of charge. However, Microsoft offers a free alternative in the form of *ASP.NET Web Matrix*, which is on the CD that comes with this book. Web Matrix provides approximately the same functionality as Visual Studio .NET when it comes to developing ASP.NET pages.

As an example, we will now create a web application in Visual Studio .NET that allows users to enter two numbers in text fields and then add them by clicking a button.

Creating a new ASP.NET project in Visual Studio .NET works like this: we select File | New | Project and get the window shown in Figure 6.33, where we can choose the type of the project to create.

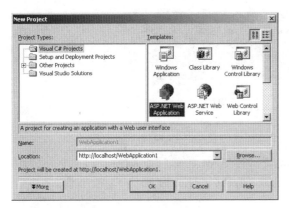

Figure 6.33 *Creating a new ASP.NET project*

We select *ASP.NET Web Application*. Under Location we provide the name of a virtual directory for our application (here http://localhost/WebApplication1) and click OK. Now a new ASP.NET project is created. Visual Studio .NET will also create the virtual directory on the IIS, if it does not yet exist.

In addition, all configuration files (Web.config, Global.asax and so on) are generated and filled with default values. A list of the generated files is displayed in the Visual Studio *Solution Explorer* (see Figure 6.34). Each file can be opened with a double click.

Figure 6.34 *List of generated files in the solution explorer*

Our web form has been given the default name WebForm1.aspx, which we can, of course, change. WebForm1.aspx is displayed in a design view with a dotted grid and a tool box to the left where we can select GUI elements and drag them into the design area. We can move and resize all elements and thus build the desired user interface. In the example shown in Figure 6.35 we have placed two text fields and a button in this way.

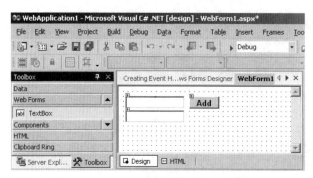

Figure 6.35 *Design view and toolbox with GUI elements*

We can edit the properties of the GUI elements in a property window in the lower-right corner of the screen (see Figure 6.36). For example, we set the name of the button to addButton and its caption to Add.

Figure 6.36 *Property window (left: property view; right: event view)*

While we do this, Visual Studio .NET generates the C# code for the page and its GUI elements in the background. By clicking on the "HTML" tab to the right of the "Design" tab in Figure 6.35, we switch from the design view to the code view, which now looks like this:

```
<%@ Page language="c#" Codebehind="WebForm1.aspx.cs" AutoEventWireup="false"
        Inherits="WebApplication1.WebForm1" %>
<!DOCTYPE HTML PUBLIC "-//W3C//DTD HTML 4.0 Transitional//EN" >
```

```
<html>
  <head>
    <title>WebForm1</title>
    ...
  </head>
  <body MS_POSITIONING="GridLayout">
    <form id="Form1" method="post" runat="server">
      <asp:TextBox id="Opd1" style="Z-INDEX: 101; LEFT: 12px; POSITION: absolute;
          TOP: 15px" runat="server" Width="100px" Height="20px"></asp:TextBox>
      <asp:Button id="addButton" style="Z-INDEX: 102; LEFT: 120px;
          POSITION: absolute; TOP: 16px" runat="server" Width="50px" Text="Add"
          Font-Bold="True" Height="20px"></asp:Button>
      <asp:TextBox id="Opd2" style="Z-INDEX: 103; LEFT: 12px; POSITION: absolute;
          TOP: 38px" runat="server" Width="100px" Height="20px"></asp:TextBox>
    </form>
  </body>
</html>
```

This code is in the file WebForm1.aspx. Additionally, a file WebForm1.aspx.cs is created which at first does not do anything special and looks like this:

```
using System;
using System.Collections;
using System.ComponentModel;
using System.Data;
using System.Drawing;
using System.Web;
using System.Web.SessionState;
using System.Web.UI;
using System.Web.UI.WebControls;
using System.Web.UI.HtmlControls;

namespace WebApplication1 {
    public class WebForm1 : System.Web.UI.Page {
        protected System.Web.UI.WebControls.TextBox opd1;
        protected System.Web.UI.WebControls.TextBox opd2;
        protected System.Web.UI.WebControls.Button addButton;

        private void Page_Load(object sender, System.EventArgs e) {
            // Put user code to initialize the page here
        }

        override protected void OnInit(EventArgs e) {
            InitializeComponent();
            base.OnInit(e);
        }

        private void InitializeComponent() {
            this.Load += new System.EventHandler(this.Page_Load);
        }
    }
}
```

Next we have to catch the Click event with an appropriate event handler. Therefore we click on the lightning icon in the tool bar of the property window (see Figure 6.36) in order to switch to the event view. We then select the event Click and on
the right enter the name for the event handler (for example, OnClick). Now Visual
Studio .NET automatically inserts an empty method OnClick into the file
WebForm1.aspx.cs and displays it for us to edit. We fill it with the following code:

```
private void OnClick(object sender, System.EventArgs e) {
    opd1.Text = (Convert.ToInt32(opd1.Text) + Convert.ToInt32(opd2.Text)).ToString();
}
```

Furthermore, Visual Studio .NET inserts the line

```
this.addButton.Click += new System.EventHandler(this.OnClick);
```

in the method InitializeComponent. This registers the method as an event handler.
After compiling the project with Build I BuildSolution and directing a browser to
http://localhost/WebApplication1/WebForm1.aspx it will display our adder (see Figure
6.37).

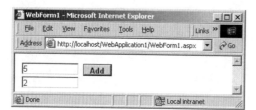

Figure 6.37 *Adder in a browser*

6.11 Exercises

1. **Registration form.** Implement a web form that can be used to register a user
   for a .NET course. In addition to text fields for the user's name and e-mail
   address the form should also contain a check box for specifying whether the
   user would like to participate in a workshop (in addition to the course), as
   well as radio buttons for specifying the user's profession (for example, programmer, manager, web designer, etc.). The data entered should be appended
   to a log file. Implement the web form with a code-behind file.

2. **Number format conversions.** Implement a web page with a text field in which
   the user can enter a positive integer number either in decimal format (e.g.
   127), in hexadecimal format (e.g. 0x3f), in octal format (e.g. 0o177), or in binary format (e.g. 0b11111111). The web page should have buttons that can be
   used to convert the number entered into any of the other formats and display

it in the text field again. If the input is syntactically wrong an error message should be displayed on the page.

3. **Image album.** Implement a web page on which the user can view images. The image to be displayed should be selectable from a dropdown list containing the image names. An image on the page is represented by the web control class System.Web.UI.Image. Its property ImageUrl specifies the URL of the desired image.

4. **Displaying HTTP request parameters.** The property Page.Request which is of type HttpRequest contains information about the current page request. Implement a web page with a DataGrid control, which displays various elements of the request (for example, UserHostName, UserHostAddress, HttpMethod, browser version, etc.). Hint: Store the data in a DataTable object and assign its DataView property to the DataSource property of the DataGrid. Don't forget to call the DataBind method for the grid in order to make the data visible on the page. Examples can be looked up in the online documentation of the .NET SDK.

5. **User controls.** Implement a user control which consists of two text fields, one holding a basic price and one the corresponding final price (i.e. the basic price plus taxes). If the user changes the basic price the final price should change accordingly, and vice versa. The tax rate should be specifiable as an attribute of the user control (e.g. Rate="1.2" for a tax rate of 20%). Also implement a web page which contains your new user control.

6. **Validity checks.** Use a RangeValidator to check whether a text field contains a positive integer. If the check fails an error message should be displayed on the page.

7. **Validity checks.** Use a CustomValidator to check whether a text field contains a valid date. A date can be entered in the format mm/dd/yy (e.g. 01/20/04) or dd-mmm-yyyy (e.g. 20-Jan-2004). If the check fails an error message should be displayed on the page. The check should be performed on the server and not on the client.

8. **Page counter.** Implement a web page counter, which counts the visits to a page. Its value should be stored in the application state of ASP.NET.

9. **ASP.NET Web Matrix.** Use ASP.NET Web Matrix which is on the CD that accompanies this book to create a page Adder.aspx, as described in Section 6.10. After starting the tool, select *ASP.NET Web Page*, type in a directory path for the location of the project and the file name Adder.aspx. Select C# as the source language and click OK. Drag two text boxes and a button into the designer window and name them appropriately (e.g. Opd1 and Opd2) using the properties window. Double-click on the button. This opens a code

window for entering the event handler for the button click. Type in something like:

```
int res = Convert.ToInt32(Opd1.Text) + Convert.ToInt32(Opd2.Text);
Opd1.Text = res.ToString();
Opd2.Text = "";
```

Save the project and press F5 to compile and run the ASP.NET page.

7 Web Services

Web services combine several technologies for accessing services from different providers in distributed systems. This chapter introduces web services and deals with tools and libraries offered by .NET that support the creation and use of web services.

7.1 Overview

Although web services are a core element of .NET, they are not .NET-specific, but can, for example, also be used in a Java environment. Web services are simply heterogeneous, distributed services that can be used by any application. Web services rely on the existing infrastructure of the Internet (e.g. HTTP, SMTP, web server) for the transport of the data, and use XML to describe the transmitted data.

Web services are a network of software services that can be created and used independently of operating system, programming language and binary transmission protocol. The *web* part in the name *web* service does not necessarily indicate the involvement of internet technologies, such as HTTP or HTML.

CORBA (*Common Object Request Broker Architecture* [OMG01]) offers similar independence. The fundamental difference lies in the fact that web services do not define a new binary protocol (such as IIOP or TCP/IP) for the communication, but use an XML-based protocol named SOAP (*Simple Object Access Protocol* [SOAP]). Furthermore, SOAP does not insist on its own distributed object model, but supports arbitrary data structures that can be described using XML.

SOAP calls are essentially nothing more than text files that travel between a client and a server. Thus the existing network infrastructure can be used. For example, a SOAP call can be sent via the internet protocol HTTP (*Hypertext Transfer Protocol*) or via SMTP (*Simple Mail Transfer Protocol*) in the form of a simple e-mail message, and can then be processed by programs that have been written in any (not necessarily object-oriented) programming language. The only requirement for such programming languages is that they must be able to handle XML documents. A web service can, for example, be implemented with object-oriented languages, such as C# or Java, or using script languages, such as Perl or Python (see Figure 7.1).

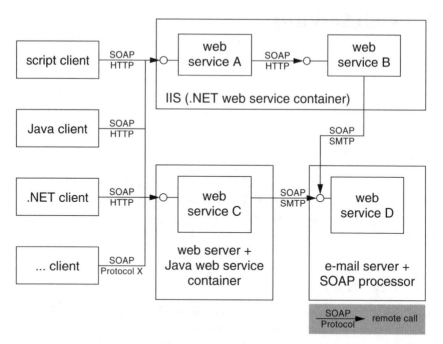

Figure 7.1 *Application scenario for web services*

So the communication is done with SOAP; but how do we know what operations a web service offers, and how they should be invoked? What we need here is a description of a web service that does what the IDLs (*Interface Description Language*) do for DCOM (*Distributed Component Object Model* [EdEd98]) or CORBA, that is, specify the available operations and types. This description is also offered in an XML format called WSDL (*Web Service Description Language* [WSDL]).

Concrete web service implementations are typically stateless and live within a web service container (e.g. MS IIS). The container's responsibility is to forward the SOAP calls sent to the server to the actual implementation. If necessary, the container also activates the web service implementation (e.g. by creating an object) or deactivates it (e.g. by freeing memory).

How a web service can be called is defined by SOAP. What a web service offers is established by a WSDL description. And where to reach the web service is determined by its URI.

A vast number of web pages make people use so-called search engines in order to query for information on the Net. The same concept could be applied to finding web services. But while today's search engines make a rich interface available for human users, they offer hardly any, or only a proprietary, programming interface that could be used by software applications.

That is why companies such as Microsoft, IBM and Ariba are trying to establish with UDDI (*Universal Description, Discovery and Integration* [UDDI]) a standard service for searching web services according to certain criteria. In this way it should be made possible for applications to extend their functionality at run time by simply looking for an appropriate web service and then using it for the new task. A UDDI database might store, among others, the URIs of web services, but also information such as a company's address or the URI of the company's web page.

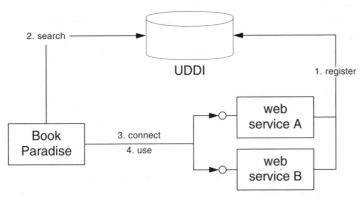

Figure 7.2 *UDDI and web services scenario*

Let's look at an example: a web shop for books called "Book Paradise" wants to integrate the products of arbitrary publishers inside a uniform web interface. Visitors to Book Paradise's home page can look for books, compare prices and even order books. Publishers A and B each offer a web service for retrieving their product catalogue. These two web services (we'll call them web service A and web service B) offer the same web service "interface", that is, their WSDL descriptions are the same. If a user now looks for a book at Book Paradise and then wants to order it, Book Paradise does the following (see also Figure 7.2):

1. Precondition: All publishers have registered their web services at some UDDI database.
2. Book Paradise contacts a UDDI database and searches for web services that implement the service *Product Catalog* for books. UDDI returns the URIs for web services A and B.
3. Book Paradise establishes a connection to web service A and web service B.
4. Book Paradise uses the two web services and displays the result to the user on a nice-looking web site.
5. The user eventually decides to buy one of publisher A's books. Book Paradise now looks for a service *Order* belonging to publisher A, so that it can process the order for the user electronically.

6. Book Paradise could not find any web service named *Order* in the UDDI database, but instead it discovered an address and telephone number for faxing the order to publisher A. Now Book Paradise asks for a web service named *Fax* in order to be able to transmit fax messages. Then Book Paradise show a generated order fax and the postal address of publisher A to the user. The user accepts the order and Book Paradise sends the fax to the web service *Fax* of the company FaxWorld, which finally faxes it to publisher A.

This example should demonstrate the strength of web services: the integration of heterogeneous systems. In order to preserve this interoperability into the future, SOAP and WSDL have been submitted to the W3C for standardization.

Besides solving the integration problem technologically with web services, economic and contractual agreements are required in order to settle questions concerning royalty payments, fail safety and so on. Therefore the principal area of application for UDDI and web services will more likely lie in the integration of heterogeneous systems within one company (Enterprise Application Integration (EAI)) rather than in the integration of global services from an arbitrary provider.

Microsoft pays special attention to web services and is developing services for private and enterprise use. *MyServices*, also known as *Microsoft .NET Services*, is a collection of web services that allow users to access their personal data (address book, calendar, mail box, documents, profiles, etc.) independently of location and device. The *Microsoft .NET Alerts* service, for example, supplies customers, friends, etc. with information that will be sent only at a certain point in time (e.g. on 12 August) or when a condition is fulfilled (e.g. fewer than 10 units are left in stock). For this to work, it does not matter on what device (PC, cellular phone, ...), with what software (e-mail client, SMS program, ...) the recipients process these messages—they only need to be able to handle XML texts. Additionally, Microsoft will extend the web service infrastructure, based on SOAP, with aspects such as security and transactions [WSE].

What has not been discussed yet is the efficiency of the transmission. Intuitively, we can claim that SOAP calls are slower than calls that go over a binary protocol, because they have to be packed into XML and then unpacked again. This takes a long time, especially when sending large amounts of data, and also increases the amount of data to transmit even more.

So if we implement both the client and the server of a distributed application and the server will not be used by any other external clients, we will still use binary protocols (e.g. a custom-defined protocol over a TCP/IP socket). Distributed applications whose clients and server are developed under .NET can use either sockets (see Section 4.4) or .NET Remoting (see [Ram02]). Server applications that will communicate with different clients will offer a web service as a façade [GHJV95].

7.2   A Simple Web Service under .NET

In this section we will create a simple web service under .NET and it will be used by two different clients. The example introduced here will reappear in some of the subsequent sections.

We will begin with a look at the support for web service in the .NET library. Table 7.1 describes the namespace System.Web.Services and its sub-namespaces which contain attributes, interfaces and classes for creating and using web services.

Table 7.1 *Namespaces for web services*

Namespace	Description
System.Web.Services	contains the class WebService and additional attributes for creating web services.
System.Web.Services.Configuration	contains attributes for configuring the XML description of a web service and extending SOAP.
System.Web.Services.Description	offers classes for creating and processing the WSDL description of a web service.
System.Web.Services.Discovery	contains classes that implement XML Web Service Discovery (DISCO) and can be used to find web services.
System.Web.Services.Protocols	contains classes that realize the protocols for communication (e.g. SOAP-HTTP).

The ASP.NET infrastructure (see Chapter 6) also supports web services. Web services can just as well be implemented with other technologies, such as .NET Remoting (see [Ram02]), but we will use the ASP.NET infrastructure. Therefore we have to create a virtual directory on the IIS for our web service.

We now want to develop a web service that returns the current time at the server to the client. Essentially this requires the following steps:

❏ Prepare the web service container: MS IIS must be available. As in the case of ASP.NET, either a virtual directory must be created for the web service or it must be copied into a virtual directory of an existing ASP.NET application.
❏ Develop the web service: We create a file with the extension .asmx. This contains the implementation of the web service, which has to extend the class System.Web.Services.WebService.
❏ Test the web service: Simply use a web browser to invoke the methods of the web service.

How to start IIS and how to create a virtual directory have already been explained in Chapter 6. For our example we create the virtual directory "time" on the IIS of our local machine.

We implement our web service in the file TimeService.asmx, which we place in the physical directory (e.g. C:\Inetput\wwwroot\time) to which our virtual directory points. As with ASP.NET, we can also apply the *code behind* technique here. TimeService.asmx will then contain nothing but a reference to the actual implementation of the web service in the code-behind file.

In TimeService.asmx we now implement the class TimeService which contains a method GetTime. Every .asmx file begins with the directive @WebService which contains the chosen programming language, the name of the web service and, if the code-behind technique is used, also the name of the assembly file.

```
<%@ WebService Language="C#" Class="TimeService" %>
using System.Web.Services;
public class TimeService : WebService {
   [WebMethod(Description="Returns the current time")]
   public string GetTime() { return System.DateTime.Now.ToLongTimeString(); }
}
```

Every method of the web service that is to be called remotely by a client is simply marked with the attribute [WebMethod]. As can be seen, TimeService must be derived from the class System.Web.Services.WebService which looks as follows:

```
public class WebService : System.ComponentModel.MarshalByValueComponent {
   //----- properties
   public HttpApplicationState Application {get;}  // ASP.NET application state
   public HttpContext Context {get;}   // ASP.NET HTTP context of the current request
   public HttpSessionState Session {get;}   // ASP.NET session state
   public IPrincipal User {get;}   // ASP.NET user object for authorization
   ...
}
```

Now it is time to test our web service. In .NET, web services will be automatically compiled at the first invocation of one of their methods. For every call, IIS creates an object of the web service class (here TimeService), forwards the call (here GetTime) to the created object and sends the result (here the current time) back to the client.

Our web service can be reached at the URI http://localhost/time/TimeService.asmx. If we enter this URI in a browser, it will display a description of the web service with all its methods, as shown in Figure 7.3. If we click on "Service Description", we will get the WSDL of the web service, which we can also directly request with http://localhost/time/TimeService.asmx?WSDL.

TimeService

The following operations are supported. For a formal definition, please review the <u>Service Description</u>.

- <u>GetTime</u>
  Returns the current time

This web service is using http://tempuri.org/ as its default namespace.

Recommendation: Change the default namespace before the XML Web service is made public.

Figure 7.3 *Excerpt from the generated description of TimeService.asmx*

Clicking on "GetTime" takes us to a detailed description of this web service method (see Figure 7.4). It contains information about how the method can be invoked via different protocols (HTTP-GET, HTTP-POST or SOAP). If it supports HTTP-GET, we will also find a way to actually test it (see button "Invoke").

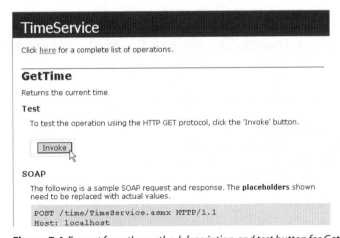

TimeService

Click <u>here</u> for a complete list of operations.

GetTime

Returns the current time

Test

To test the operation using the HTTP GET protocol, click the 'Invoke' button.

[Invoke]

SOAP

The following is a sample SOAP request and response. The **placeholders** shown need to be replaced with actual values.

```
POST /time/TimeService.asmx HTTP/1.1
Host: localhost
```

Figure 7.4 *Excerpt from the method description and test button for GetTime*

The result of the method invocation is again wrapped in XML. The latest generation of internet browsers, such as MS Internet Explorer (version 5.0 or higher), can display XML directly. For our example this may look as shown in Figure 7.5.

```
<?xml version="1.0" encoding="utf-8" ?>
<string xmlns="http://tempuri.org/">16:32:53</string>
```

Figure 7.5 *Result of the HTTP-GET method call of GetTime as displayed in MS IE*

Now our web service is ready to receive calls from any client application.

7.2.1 A Simple .NET Client

Because of the object-oriented nature of .NET, it would be helpful, when implementing a client, if we could treat the web service like a local object, that is, if we
could simply create a local TimeService object and invoke its GetTime method. For
this purpose distributed applications use so-called *proxies*.

A proxy works as a placeholder for a remote web service. It represents the
functionality of the web service as described in the WSDL in the form of a .NET
class, transforms the .NET data types to XML data and initiates the invocation of
the web service method over the network. A more detailed discussion of this process can be found in Section 7.3.

In order to use our TimeService we need such a proxy. The tool wsdl.exe gener-
ates a proxy class in the languages C#, Visual Basic or JavaScript from a given
WSDL file. After we have generated the proxy class, we need to compile it to
MSIL. wsdl.exe is a console application and comes with the .NET SDK. It is in the
directory [C:\Program Files\Microsoft Visual Studio .NET]\FrameworkSDK\Bin\, where
[C:\Program Files\Microsoft Visual Studio .NET] is the directory in which Visual Studio
.NET or the .NET SDK resides, respectively.

Once the proxy class has been generated and compiled, the client can use it by
creating an object of the class TimeClient.TimeService and calling its method GetTime
as follows:

```
using System;
using TimeClient;   // namespace of the generated proxies
public class NetClient {
    public static void Main(string[] args) {
        TimeService service = new TimeService();
        Console.WriteLine("Current time at server is: ");
        string time = service.GetTime();
        Console.WriteLine(time);
    }
}
```

wsdl.exe requires the URI of a WSDL or DISCO description (see Section 7.5) in
order to generated the proxies. To generate the file TimeServiceProxy.cs for our
example we ran wsdl.exe with the following parameters:

```
wsdl /namespace:TimeClient /out:TimeServiceProxy.cs
     http://localhost/time/TimeService.asmx?WSDL
```

TimeServiceProxy.cs contains the class TimeClient.TimeService in C# source code
and can thus be edited manually at any time. The TimeService proxy has the
method GetTime. Additionally, it also offers methods for the asynchronous call of
GetTime.

Table 7.2 lists the different parameters of wsdl.exe.

Table 7.2 *Command-line parameters of wsdl.exe*

Parameter	Description
/language:	sets the language in which the proxies are generated. Valid values: CS (C#), VB (Visual Basic) and JS (JavaScript). Default setting: CS
/namespace:	sets the namespace for the generated code.
/out:	sets the name of the file for the generated code.
/protocol:	sets the protocol for the communication. Valid values are SOAP (default setting), HTTP-GET, HTTP-POST.
/username:	sets the user name, if the web service container needs one for authentification.
/password:	sets the password, if the web service container needs one for authentication.
/domain:	sets the domain, if the web service container needs one for authentication.

7.2.2   A Simple Java Client

When creating a client in Java we essentially go through the same steps as under .NET: we generate a proxy from the WSDL and then use it.

For Java there are several web service containers and tools like wsdl.exe. But instead of using a tool, we will manually create a simple Java client that sends a SOAP call via HTTP-POST to our TimeService and outputs the SOAP response to the console. The transmitted SOAP call corresponds to the SOAP call from the HTML description of GetTime that we showed in Figure 7.4.

```
import java.io.*;  import java.net.*;   // NOTE: this is Java code!
/** Simple web service client in Java.
      The web service is invoked via SOAP-HTTP and
      the SOAP result is printed to the console. */
public class JavaClient {
    public static void main(String[] args) {
        try {
            URL url = new URL("http://localhost/time/TimeService.asmx");
            //----- open HTTP connection to the service
            HttpURLConnection connection = (HttpURLConnection) url.openConnection();
            connection.setRequestMethod("POST");
            connection.setDoOutput(true);
            connection.setDoInput(true);
            //----- build SOAP request
            connection.setRequestProperty("Content-type", "text/xml; charset=utf-8");
            connection.setRequestProperty("SOAPAction", "http://tempuri.org/GetTime");
            //----- build SOAP request string for GetTime - see detailed description of GetTime
            //----- at: http://localhost/time/TimeService.asmx?op=GetTime
```

```
String msg =
    "<?xml version=\"1.0\" encoding=\"utf-8\"?>\n" +
    "<soap:Envelope" +
    " xmlns:soap=\"http://schemas.xmlsoap.org/soap/envelope/\">\n" +
    "  <soap:Body>\n" +
    "    <GetTime xmlns=\"http://tempuri.org/\" /> \n" +
    "  </soap:Body>\n" +
    "</soap:Envelope>";
//----- send SOAP request (triggered by out.write(...);)
byte[] bytes = msg.getBytes();
connection.setRequestProperty("Content-length", String.valueOf(bytes.length));
OutputStream out = connection.getOutputStream();
out.write(bytes);
out.close();
//----- read and print SOAP response
BufferedReader in =
    new BufferedReader(new InputStreamReader(connection.getInputStream()));
System.out.println("SOAP response:");
String inputLine = in.readLine();
while (inputLine != null) {
    System.out.println(inputLine);
    inputLine = in.readLine();
}
in.close();
} catch (Exception e) {
    System.out.println("ERROR:" + e.getMessage());
}
    }
  }
}
```

The command javac JavaClient.java compiles the file JavaClient.java given above.
We start the resulting executable file with java JavaClient and get the following
output:

```
SOAP response:
<?xml version="1.0" encoding="utf-8"?>
<soap:Envelope xmlns:soap="http://schemas.xmlsoap.org/soap/envelope/"
    xmlns:xsi="http://www.w3.org/2001/XMLSchema-instance"
    xmlns:xsd="http://www.w3.org/2001/XMLSchema">
    <soap:Body>
        <GetTimeResponse xmlns="http://tempuri.org/">
            <GetTimeResult>16:56:32</GetTimeResult>
        </GetTimeResponse>
    </soap:Body>
</soap:Envelope>
```

This communication would usually be done by a proxy similar to the one from the
previous .NET example, and the result 16:56:32 would be returned in the form of a
string. But more about SOAP in the next section.

7.3 SOAP

SOAP is an XML-based protocol for packing data for transmission over a transport protocol (such as HTTP). It offers a uniform model for simple and platform-independent data exchange as well as remote procedure calls. SOAP is currently defined in version 1.2 in a W3C recommendation [SOAP]. Until version 1.2, "SOAP" was an acronym for *Simple Object Access Protocol*. But as we will see, SOAP does not have much to do with objects in the object-oriented sense. Therefore (and because of legal issues concerning trade marks), beginning with version 1.2, SOAP became a name in its own right and is no longer an acronym. This section summarizes the SOAP specification 1.1, because version 1.1 of the .NET Framework does not yet support SOAP 1.2.

When sending a letter, we compose the contents (for example a poem) and put them in an envelope that shows the address of the recipient, the sender, and maybe other information (for example "confidential"). Then we hand the envelope with its contents over to some delivery service that carries it from one station to the next until it reaches its destination.

This is essentially what SOAP is all about: an asynchronous "one way" protocol that defines envelope and contents in XML and allows transportation from a sender via arbitrary intermediate stations to the designated receiver using a protocol of choice. Here "one way" means that the message is sent only in one direction from the sender to receiver without waiting for a response. Combining such "one way" messages allows emulation of the different modes of message exchange (*one-way, request/response, multicast*, etc.) of the various transport protocols.

HTTP, for example, uses the *request/response* mode. Putting this into effect with SOAP requires combining two "one way" calls. The first call represents the HTTP request, the second the HTTP response. In Section 7.3.2 we will go into a little more detail about SOAP and HTTP.

SOAP defines neither an object model nor a model for distributed callbacks. It also does not specify how distributed garbage collection should be implemented. All it describes is how to send "one way" messages that hold data.

The analogy to the letter example above is also reflected in the XML structure of SOAP calls, as outlined in the following excerpt:

```
<soap:Envelope xmlns:soap=...>
   <soap:Header>   <!-- optional & extensible -->
      <m:myInfo xmlns:m="anURI" soap:mustUnderstand="0" soap:actor="next" /> ...
   </soap:Header>
   <soap:Body>   <!-- data or fault element (see below) -->
      <soap:Fault>
         <faultcode> soap:Server or soap:Client </faultcode>
         <faultstring> description of the error </faultstring>
      </soap:Fault>
   </soap:Body>
</soap:Envelope>
```

Every call has to contain the root element <Envelope> as well as the <Body> element. In between these two there can be an optional <Header>, which, analogously to the letter example, holds additional information for the recipient (for example user name, password, information about the current transaction, routing directives for intermediate stations). All child elements of <Header> are also called *header elements*. The <Envelope> element itself may contain additional XML attributes that are application specific, and thus not specified by SOAP.

A header element may have an attribute mustUnderstand to indicate whether the receiver must understand it (value 1) or not (value 0). If a recipient is obliged to understand a header element, but does not know what to do with it, it has to return an error message to the sender and abort the processing of the current SOAP message.

A SOAP message can pass several intermediate stations such as fire walls, SOAP preprocessors, etc. before reaching the designated receiver. For each of these intermediate stops dedicated header elements may carry helpful information for correctly interpreting the contents of the <Body> element. The header element XML attribute actor describes how to forward the message from one station to the next.

What XML elements the <Header> and <Body> elements actually contain depends on the concrete application. That is why one has to specify to which XML namespaces the child elements of <Header> and <Body> belong. An XML namespace can be any URI name under which more XML elements are gathered (for example, http://dotnet.jku.at). By assigning XML namespaces, XML elements and attributes with the same name can still be distinguished. The XML namespace for SOAP-specific elements is http://schemas.xmlsoap.org/soap/envelope/. At this URI you also find the XML schema of SOAP.

The actual data—the letter itself—is encoded in child elements of <Body>. In case of an error, however, the <Body> element will not contain any data, but only a <Fault> element that details the error. In principle, two participants can be responsible for the error. Either it is the client's fault (soap:Client), because it sent invalid data or a wrongly formulated SOAP message, or it is the receiver's (soap:Server), because it cannot process the message. Which one actually caused the error is stated in the element <faultcode> (e.g. <faultcode>soap:Client</faultcode>).

In .NET, exceptions and <Fault> elements interoperate smoothly. If a SOAP method call causes an exception of type System.Web.Services.Protocols. SoapException at the .NET server, it is automatically converted into a <Fault> element of the response message and sent back to the caller. At the caller site the original exception is restored from the <Fault> element and can then be caught inside a try-block.

The encoding format determines how to serialize data (for example, an array) (see Section 7.3.1). What XML elements the data are packed into depends on the message format selected as well as on the application and the receiver. For this reason all elements must specify their XML namespace. Just as a letter has to be written in a language the recipient understands, so have the child elements of the <Body> element also to be comprehensible to the receiver (see <GetTime> element in the Java client example and Figure 7.4 in Section 7.2).

7.3.1 SOAP Message Formats for Web Services

In the .NET client example in Section 7.2 we implemented a proxy that serves as a local representative for the actual web service. It encodes the method call with its parameters by packing the .NET data types of the parameters and the method call itself (for example, GetTime()) in SOAP (*marshalling*). Subsequently, the SOAP message so generated is transformed into a byte stream and sent to the receiver via HTTP-POST. The server then has to unpack the data stream in order to invoke the actual web service method (*unmarshalling*).

In the course of this procedure the parameters passed are copied from the client to the server and exist in the two separate processes at least for the duration of the method call. Note also that only data are transmitted and not objects. The server is therefore not allowed to invoke methods of the passed parameter objects, as it is possible in the case of local object-oriented applications. We cannot even assume that the server will create object representations for the unpacked parameters! Web services do not define a uniform distributed object model as CORBA, Java-RMI or DCOM does.

The proxy is now waiting for the response from the web service and it converts this into the return value for the method GetTime. If we use, for example, a Java client, it will utilize its own Java proxy (see Figure 7.6) which handles the same tasks as the .NET proxy for the Java client.

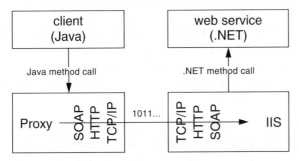

Figure 7.6 *Web service method call with a proxy*

Message Formats

In order for sender and receiver to know how the header elements and the data are encoded in the SOAP message, they have to agree upon a common message format. Message formats indicate how data is serialized and encoded, marshalled and unmarshalled. The WSDL (see Section 7.5) of a web service basically defines two message formats for SOAP calls: *document* and *rpc*. They determine the format of the child elements of the <Body> element. For the header elements a message format can, but does not have to be used.

- ❑ *document*. Data and method call are sent as an XML document. SOAP does not define any rules about how the contents should be represented. Arbitrary XML elements may be sent—as long as the receiver can handle them. This format is favoured when sending large amounts of data.
- ❑ *rpc*. The structure of the <Body> child elements is set according to SOAP rules. The <Body> element contains essentially the name of the method as well as its parameters as XML child elements (see example below).

Encoding Types

How the actual parameters and the data itself are serialized as XML text depends on the chosen encoding type. In principle, arbitrary rules can be applied to serializing the data. In addition to the two message formats (*document*, *rpc*), SOAP offers the two encoding types *literal* and *encoded*.

- ❑ *literal*. The data are encoded based on some XML schema (XSD). SOAP does not define any rules for this. Client and server do not exchange objects or arrays, but XML data.
- ❑ *encoded*. The data are encoded according to SOAP rules, which are based on the rules for XML schemas, that is, all simple data types (e.g. xsd:string) can be used, as they appear in other XML documents as well, but certain restrictions apply. Additionally, structs and arrays are supported. The SOAP encoding rules are optional for web service containers and are described in Chapter 5 of the SOAP specification 1.1 [SOAP]. If an encoding type is used, this is expressed by the XML attribute encodingStyle in the <Body> element that contains the XML namespace of the selected encoding (see example below). The namespace for the SOAP encoding is http://schemas.xmlsoap.org/soap/encoding/. The XML schema for the SOAP encoding is also available for that URI.

Most SOAP messages are encoded either *rpc/encoded* or *document/literal*. Of course, we can define a custom type of serialization for document and rpc formatted calls. The default setting for web services in .NET is *document/literal*.

We now extend our TimeService with the method GetTime2(shortForm). The Boolean parameter shortForm determines whether the time is to be returned in a short or a long format. SOAP calls must have distinct names; that means we cannot overload the method GetTime. The service will use the message format *rpc/ encoded*. The *rpc/encoded* SOAP message for the call of GetTime2(true) via HTTP looks like this:

```
... HTTP header for POST request ...
<?xml version="1.0" encoding="utf-8"?>
<soap:Envelope xmlns:soap="http://schemas.xmlsoap.org/soap/envelope/"
    xmlns:soapenc="http://schemas.xmlsoap.org/soap/encoding/"
    xmlns:tns="http://tempuri.org/" xmlns:types="http://tempuri.org/encodedTypes"
    xmlns:xsi="http://www.w3.org/2001/XMLSchema-instance"
    xmlns:xsd="http://www.w3.org/2001/XMLSchema">
    <soap:Body soap:encodingStyle="http://schemas.xmlsoap.org/soap/encoding/">
        <tns:GetTime2>
            <shortForm xsi:type="xsd:boolean">true</shortForm>
        </tns:GetTime2>
    </soap:Body>
</soap:Envelope>
```

Naturally, the result is also returned in the *rpc/encoded* format:

```
Content-Type:text/xml; charset=utf-8
<?xml version="1.0" encoding="utf-8"?>
<soap:Envelope xmlns:soap="http://schemas.xmlsoap.org/soap/envelope/"
    xmlns:soapenc="http://schemas.xmlsoap.org/soap/encoding/"
    xmlns:tns="http://tempuri.org/" xmlns:types="http://tempuri.org/"
    xmlns:xsi="http://www.w3.org/2001/XMLSchema-instance"
    xmlns:xsd="http://www.w3.org/2001/XMLSchema">
    <soap:Body soap:encodingStyle="http://schemas.xmlsoap.org/soap/encoding/">
        <types:GetTime2Response>
            <GetTime2Result xsi:type="xsd:string">10:07</GetTime2Result>
        </types:GetTime2Response>
    </soap:Body>
</soap:Envelope>
```

In .NET the attribute [SoapRpcService] extends the web service to understand the message format *rpc/encoded* (see also Section 7.4).

```
<%@ WebService Language="C#" Class="TimeService" %>
using System; using System.Web.Services; using System.Web.Services.Protocols;
[SoapRpcService]    // web service uses the message format rpc/encoded
public class TimeService : WebService {
    [WebMethod (Description="Returns the current server time")]
    public string GetTime() {
        return System.DateTime.Now.ToLongTimeString();
    }
```

```
[WebMethod (Description="Returns the current server time in a long or short format")]
public string GetTime2(bool shortForm) {
    if (shortForm) return DateTime.Now.ToShortTimeString();
    return this.GetTime();
}
}
```

7.3.2   HTTP Binding

SOAP calls can be carried out over diverse transport protocols. However, the SOAP specification 1.1 contains exactly one *binding* to a certain protocol, and that is HTTP (*Hypertext Transfer Protocol*). This default binding describes how to conduct SOAP-encoded remote procedure calls (RPCs) via HTTP.

In our TimeService example the web service method can be invoked via HTTP-GET, HTTP-POST and SOAP, where SOAP uses HTTP as well. The difference between these three alternatives lies in the encoding of the call.

HTTP-GET sends the call to the service not SOAP encoded, but as a URI that any browser understands. The method name and the input parameters are embedded in the URI (e.g. http://localhost/time/TimeService.asmx/GetTime2? shortForm=false). This form of invocation is very simple, yet somewhat limited. It must be possible to represent the actual parameters in a URI-encoded format, because they have to adhere to the encoding rules for HTTP-GET requests.

HTTP-POST also does not send a SOAP-encoded call to the service, but a URI, similarly to HTTP-GET. However, the parameters are not visible in the URI, but are transmitted in a data stream, exactly like the data of an HTTP form (see Chapter 6).

SOAP encodes the call in XML and uses HTTP to transmit it. If, for example, a *SOAP header* is required, SOAP must be used. Here we again show the complete *document/literal* encoded SOAP-HTTP-POST request with the *HTTP headers* for GetTime from our TimeService example:

```
POST /time/TimeService.asmx HTTP/1.1
Content-type: text/xml; charset=utf-8
SOAPAction: http://tempuri.org/GetTime
Content-length: 198
User-Agent: Java1.4.0
Host: localhost
Accept: text/html, image/gif, image/jpeg, *; q=.2, */*; q=.2
Connection: keep-alive
<?xml version="1.0" encoding="utf-8"?>
<soap:Envelope  xmlns:soap="http://schemas.xmlsoap.org/soap/envelope/">
   <soap:Body>
      <GetTime xmlns="http://tempuri.org/" />
   </soap:Body>
</soap:Envelope>
```

In the following we summarize the rules for the binding of SOAP to HTTP:

❑ SOAP uses HTTP-POST and not HTTP-GET for transmission.

❑ A SOAP-HTTP-POST request is identified by the HTTP header (not SOAP header!) SOAPAction, which contains a URI and can therefore also be empty. The URI of the SOAP call specifies the receiver (e.g. http://localhost/time/TimeService.asmx), whereas the URI in the SOAPAction header contains a reference to the method to be executed (e.g. http://tempuri.org/GetTime). (Note: in SOAP 1.2 the HTTP header SOAPAction is no longer mandatory.)

❑ The content type for SOAP is text/xml. (Note: SOAP 1.2 defines the content type for SOAP as application/soap.)

❑ A successfully executed SOAP call typically returns with code 200. On errors, only HTTP response code 500 is admissible, which indicates that an error has occurred and that the response to the caller will thus contain a <Fault> element in its body. The .NET proxies convert a fault element into a System.Web.Services.Protocols.SoapException. (Note: SOAP 1.2 allows more HTTP response codes in case of an error.)

HTTP is a connectionless protocol. After the server has received an HTTP request (POST or GET) and returned the response, it "forgets" whose request it has just processed. The server cannot distinguish between calls from different clients. Moreover, SOAP assumes a stateless SOAP receiver.

HTTP cookies are one way to associate several HTTP requests with one client. A cookie is like an identification assigned by the server to a client. It contains data that the client sends with every HTTP request. Cookies make sessions (see Section 6.7) available to HTTP.

However, this pure HTTP solution cannot be applied if, for example, a SOAP-HTTP message is sent to a web service A that triggers another SOAP call on its part. Web service A now sends a SOAP call to web service B which does not use HTTP, but, for instance, SMTP, as the transport protocol. In this case the association between a client and its call (i.e. the HTTP cookie) gets lost. A pure SOAP solution would be to identify calls from the same client in a SOAP header. So the client information is carried in a header element instead of an HTTP cookie. The drawback of this approach is that all participating clients and servers need to understand those header elements.

7.4 SOAP and .NET

For developers of web services and clients SOAP offers different options for setting the message format (*document/literal*, *rpc/encoded* or custom) and header elements. But these options come at a price: once set, you have to live with your decisions. .NET offers various classes and attributes to realize these decisions, which we will briefly introduce now.

7.4.1 Determining the SOAP Message Format

The .NET attributes described here determine the SOAP message format. They are applied to the web service or the client proxy. Attributes ending in "Service" always affect an entire class, whereas attributes ending in "Method" operate only on methods. The attributes stem from the namespace System.Web.Services.Protocols.

❏ The .NET attributes for *document/literal* encoding are SoapDocumentMethod and SoapDocumentService with the property Use=Literal. This is the default setting for .NET web services. The SoapDocumentMethod attribute also sets the URI for the SOAPAction header (Action) and the names and namespaces of the XML elements for the method call (Request...) and the return values (Response...). This is an example:

```
[SoapDocumentMethod(Use=SoapBindingUse.Literal,
    Action="http://dotnet.jku.at/Sample/AddAddressDocLit",   // SOAPAction
    RequestNamespace="http://dotnet.jku.at/Sample/Request",
    RequestElementName="AddAddressDocLitRequest",   // SOAP element name
    ResponseNamespace="http://dotnet.jku.at/Sample/Response",
    ResponseElementName="AddAddressDocLitResponse")]   // SOAP element name
[WebMethod(Description="Adds an address DataSet for the specified user")]
public void AddAddressDocLit(long userID, Address address) { ... }
```

❏ The .NET attributes for *document/encoded* encoding are SoapDocumentMethod and SoapDocumentService with the property Use=Encoded. Here is another example:

```
[SoapDocumentService(Use=SoapBindingUse.Encoded)]
public class TimeService : WebService { ... }
```

❏ The .NET attributes for *rpc/encoded* encoding are SoapRpcMethod and SoapRpcService. For example:

```
[SoapRpcMethod(Action="http://dotnet.jku.at/Sample/AddAddressRpc",
    RequestNamespace="http://dotnet.jku.at/Sample/Request",
    RequestElementName="AddAddressRpcRequest",   // SOAP element name
    ResponseNamespace="http://dotnet.jku.at/Sample/Response",
    ResponseElementName="AddAddressRpcResponse")]   // SOAP element name
[WebMethod(Description="Adds an address DataSet for the specified user")]
public void AddAddressRpc(long userID, Address address) { ... }
```

.NET does not offer attributes to set *rpc/literal* encoding. You will find more detailed descriptions of the individual attribute classes in the online documentation.

7.4.2 SOAP Encoding of .NET Data Types

If the messages are sent SOAP-encoded (e.g. *rpc/encoded*), the types of the parameters contained (e.g. int, Array) have to be serialized and deserialized according to the SOAP encoding rules (see Chapter 5 of the SOAP specification 1.1 [SOAP]). However, when using *document/literal* encoding the serialized objects have to conform to an XML schema.

Setting the appropriate .NET attributes determines the encoding type (e.g with [SoapRpcMethod]) and allows it to be further adapted (e.g. with [SoapAttribute], see below). ASP.NET encodes and decodes the dispatched data automatically. But the automatic SOAP encoding cannot achieve everything and so cannot always be applied to all .NET objects. For example, objects of type System.Data.DataSet (see Section 5.4) can be encoded in the *document/literal* message format, but not in *rpc/encoded*.

In this section we introduce the .NET attribute for setting the SOAP encoding. Some of these .NET attribute classes such as [SoapAttribute] and [SoapElement] can be found in the namespace System.Xml.Serialization (see below).

If *rpc/encoded* is the chosen message format, .NET will encode the public fields and properties of objects and structs by default as their child elements. Consequently, such objects can be used as parameters as well. So we can, for example, extend our TimeService with the method GetTimeDesc() which returns a TimeDesc object of the following kind:

```
public struct TimeDesc {
    public string TimeLong, TimeShort, TimeZone;
}
```

The response to the *rpc/encoded* SOAP call of GetTimeDesc looks like this:

```
...
<soap:Envelope xmlns:soap="http://schemas.xmlsoap.org/soap/envelope/"
               xmlns:soapenc="http://schemas.xmlsoap.org/soap/encoding/"
               xmlns:tns="http://dotnet.jku.at/time/"
               xmlns:types="http://dotnet.jku.at/time/"
               xmlns:xsi="http://www.w3.org/2001/XMLSchema-instance"
               xmlns:xsd="http://www.w3.org/2001/XMLSchema">
  <soap:Body soap:encodingStyle="http://schemas.xmlsoap.org/soap/encoding/">
    <types:GetTimeDescResponse>
      <GetTimeDescResult href="#id1" />
    </types:GetTimeDescResponse>
    <types:TimeDesc id="id1" xsi:type="types:TimeDesc">
      <TimeLong xsi:type="xsd:string">10:00:25</TimeLong>
      <TimeShort xsi:type="xsd:string">10:00</TimeShort>
      <TimeZone xsi:type="xsd:string">1</TimeZone>
    </types:TimeDesc>
  </soap:Body>
</soap:Envelope>
```

The .NET type TimeDesc has been mapped to the XML element <types:TimeDesc> with the child elements <TimeLong>, <TimeShort> and <TimeZone>. As can be seen in the following code fragment, we have defined the namespace for the types TimeService and TimeDesc with [WebService(Namespace="http://dotnet.jku.at/time/")]. If we had not done that, .NET would have put the types into the standard namespace http://tempuri.org/. This should, however, only be done for testing purposes.

```
<%@ WebService Language="C#" Class="TimeService" %>
using System; using System.Web.Services; using System.Web.Services.Protocols;
using System.Xml.Serialization;
[SoapRpcService]
[WebService(Namespace="http://dotnet.jku.at/time/", Description="Returns the time")]
public class TimeService : WebService {
    // ... other methods
    [WebMethod(Description="Returns the time description of the server")]
    public TimeDesc GetTimeDesc() { ... }
}
public struct TimeDesc { ... }
```

The namespace System.Xml.Serialization contains the following attribute classes, which are used to set the SOAP encodings. These adaptations will only take effect when using the transport protocol SOAP-HTTP.

❑ SoapAttributeAttribute can be applied to public fields, properties, parameters and return values. It indicates that a member shall not be encoded as a child element, but as an XML attribute of its type. For large amounts of data this is more efficient than wrapping everything in child elements. You can use the property DataType to set the XML type (see Table 7.3) of the attribute and the property AttributeName to change its name. The declaration

```
public struct TimeDesc {
    [SoapAttribute] public string TimeLong;
    [SoapAttribute] public string TimeShort;
    [SoapAttribute (DataType="nonNegativeInteger", AttributeName = "ZoneID")]
    public string TimeZone;
}
```

is encoded in SOAP as

```
<types:TimeDesc id="id1" xsi:type="types:TimeDesc"
  types:TimeLong="10:00:25" types:TimeShort="10:00" types:ZoneID="1" />
```

❑ SoapElementAttribute can be applied to public fields, properties, parameters and return values. It expresses that a member shall be encoded as an XML element instead of an XML attribute. This is the default setting. In the next example we adapt the TimeDesc property TimeZone:

```
public struct TimeDesc {
    public string TimeLong;
    public string TimeShort;
    [SoapElement (DataType="nonNegativeInteger", ElementName = "ZoneID")]
    public string TimeZone;
}
```

to the following SOAP encoding of TimeDesc:

```
<types:TimeDesc id="id1" xsi:type="types:TimeDesc">
    <TimeLong xsi:type="xsd:string">18:19:00</TimeLong>
    <TimeShort xsi:type="xsd:string">18:19</TimeShort>
    <ZoneID xsi:type="xsd:nonNegativeInteger">1</ZoneID>
</types:TimeDesc>
```

❑ SoapEnumAttribute can be applied to public constants of an enumeration
type in order to change their name.
❑ SoapIgnoreAttribute can be applied to public fields and properties. It indicates that the marked fields should not be serialized.
❑ SoapIncludeAttribute can be applied to web service classes and public web-
service methods. It indicates that a certain type shall be embedded in the
description of the web service. For example, including subclass B of a class
A that is used in the web service allows parameters of static type A but
dynamic type B to be serialized as B objects. A related attribute is the
[XmlIncludeAttribute] which is used for encoding calls via HTTP (GET/POST).
The subsequent example shows a method Find(ssn), which returns the
Person with the given social security number ssn. The dynamic type of this
Person object can be one of the subclasses Employee or Customer.

```
<%@ WebService Language="C#" Class="PersonService" %>
using System;
using System.Web.Services;
using System.Web.Services.Protocols;
using System.Xml.Serialization;

public class PersonService : WebService {
    [WebMethod] [SoapRpcMethod]
    // include subtypes of Person for calls via SOAP-HTTP
    [SoapInclude(typeof(Customer)), SoapInclude(typeof(Employee))]
    // include subtypes of Person for calls via HTTP-GET/-POST
    [XmlInclude(typeof(Customer)), XmlInclude(typeof(Employee))]
    public Person Find(string ssn) {
        Person p = null;
        if (ssn == "1") p = new Customer(ssn, "Max Customer", "EMP-33");
        else p = new Employee(ssn, "Tom Employee");
        return p;
    }
}
```

```
public abstract class Person {
    public string SSN; public string Name;
    public Person() { }
    public Person(string ssn, string name) { this.SSN = ssn; this.Name = name; }
}
public class Customer : Person {
    public string EmpSSN;
    public Customer() { EmpSSN = "??"; }
    public Customer(string ssn, string n, string e): base(ssn, n) { EmpSSN = e; }
}
public class Employee : Person {
    public Employee() { }
    public Employee(string ssn, string name) : base(ssn, name) { }
}
```

❑ SoapTypeAttribute can be applied to public types. It indicates that the
marked type shall be serialized as a public, named XML type and included
in the XML schema. The following code renames the type Employee to
EmployeeType.

```
[SoapType("EmployeeType")]
public class Employee : Person { ... }
```

If a parameter or return value needs to be serialized, the web service has to know
its dynamic type. Otherwise the type must be explicitly included in the description
with the attribute [SoapInclude(type)] or [XmlInclude(type)]. In our example we extend the PersonService with a method GetAll that returns an array of Person, which
contains elements of the subclasses Customer and Employee.

```
[SoapRpcMethod] [WebMethod]
// include subtypes of Person for calls via ...
[SoapInclude(typeof(Customer)), SoapInclude(typeof(Employee)))]   // ... SOAP-HTTP
[XmlInclude(typeof(Customer)), XmlInclude(typeof(Employee)))]   // ... HTTP-GET/-POST
public Person Find(string ssn) { ... }
```

```
[SoapRpcMethod] [WebMethod]
public Person[] GetAll() {
    Person[] data = new Person[2];
    data[0] = new Customer("1", "Max Customer", "EMP-33");
    data[1] = new Employee("EMP-33", "Tom Employee");
    return data;
}
```

The *rpc/encoded* response of GetAll is an array of type Person[] and the dynamic
types Customer and Employee are also included in the response message. Note that
no SoapInclude or XmlInclude attributes have been applied to GetAll, because this
has been done by the method Find and thus the XML schemas for the types
Customer and Employee are already contained in the WSDL. The response for
GetAll for this example looks like this:

```
...
<soap:Envelope xmlns:soap="http://schemas.xmlsoap.org/soap/envelope/" ... >
    <soap:Body soap:encodingStyle="http://schemas.xmlsoap.org/soap/encoding/">
        <tns:GetAllResponse>
            <GetAllResult href="#id1" />
        </tns:GetAllResponse>
        <soapenc:Array id="id1" soapenc:arrayType="types:Person[2]">
            <Item href="#id2" />
            <Item href="#id3" />
        </soapenc:Array>
        <types:Customer id="id2" xsi:type="types:Customer">
            <SSN xsi:type="xsd:string">1</SSN>
            <Name xsi:type="xsd:string">Max Customer</Name>
            <EmpSSN xsi:type="xsd:string">EMP-33</EmpSSN>
        </types:Customer>
        <types:Employee id="id3" xsi:type="types:Employee">
            <SSN xsi:type="xsd:string">EMP-33</SSN>
            <Name xsi:type="xsd:string">Tom Employee</Name>
        </types:Employee>
    </soap:Body>
</soap:Envelope>
```

Table 7.3 shows the default conversion relation between simple XML schema types [XSD] and their corresponding .NET types. If this default conversion is unsatisfactory, we can choose a specific XML type with [SoapElement(DataType = "*XML type*")] and [SoapAttribute(DataType = "*XML type*")].

Table 7.3 Correlation between simple .NET types and XML schema types

.NET type	XML schema type (case sensitive)
System.Boolean	boolean
System.SByte	byte
System.Int16	short
System.Int32	int
System.Int64	long
System.Byte	unsignedByte
System.UInt16	unsignedShort
System.UInt32	unsignedInt
System.UInt64	unsignedLong
System.Single	float
System.Double	double
System.Decimal	decimal
System.Byte[]	base64Binary, (hexBinary)
System.DateTime	dateTime, (date, time)
System.Xml.XmlQualifiedName	QName

Table 7.3 *Correlation between simple .NET types and XML schema types(cont.)*

.NET type	XML schema type (case sensitive)
System.String	string, (anyURI, ENTITY, ENTITIES, gDay, gMonth, gMonthDay, gYear, gYearMonth, ID, IDREF, IDREFS, Name, NCName, negativeInteger, NMToken, NMTokens, normalizedString, nonNegativeInteger, nonPositiveInteger, NOTATION, positiveInteger, recurringDate, duration, token)

The XML schema types between parentheses (e.g. hexBinary) can be explicitly demanded, but will not be selected by .NET by default, because the more general XML type (e.g. base64Binary) will be used.

7.4.3 Developing and Using SOAP Header Entries

Every SOAP message (no matter whether sent from client to server or the other way round) can contain a <Header> element with several header entries. Some of these must be comprehensible to the recipient of the message, others not. In .NET header entries are modelled by the class System.Web.Service.Protocols.SoapHeader.

```
public class SoapHeader {
    //----- properties
    public string Actor { get; set; }           // URI for the recipient of the header entry
    public bool DidUnderstand { get; set; }      // true, if web service method knows how to
                                                 // process the header entry
    public bool MustUnderstand { get; set; }     // value of the XML attribute mustUnderstand
    public string EncodedMustUnderstand { get; set; }  // actual value ("0" or "1") of the
                                                 // XML attribute mustUnderstand
    ...
}
```

The properties Actor and EncodedMustUnderstand correspond to the XML attributes actor and mustUnderstand of a header entry. If, for example, a web service method must understand a header entry (MustUnderstand is true), but does not know how to handle it, it sets DidUnderstand to false. This causes a <Fault> element to be inserted into the response. If and how a web service method uses a header entry is determined by the attribute [SoapHeader].

We will now extend TimeService such that clients may only call the method GetTime if they send a header entry <AuthHeader> that contains an appropriate cookie. This entry is modelled as class AuthHeader and contains a public field cookie of type string.

```
public class AuthHeader : SoapHeader { public string cookie; }
```

TimeService gets another method Login(user, pwd) which authenticates a user and returns a cookie which can then be used in <AuthHeader>. The SOAP call of GetTime contains our new header entry <AuthHeader> and—as it did before—the actual invocation of GetTime in <Body>.

```xml
<?xml version="1.0" encoding="utf-8"?>
<soap:Envelope xmlns:soap="http://schemas.xmlsoap.org/soap/envelope/" ... >
    <soap:Header>
        <AuthHeader xmlns="http://dotnet.jku.at/time/">
            <cookie>aewt12348cvNNgrt55</cookie>
        </AuthHeader>
    </soap:Header>
    <soap:Body>
        <GetTime xmlns="http://dotnet.jku.at/time/" />
    </soap:Body>
</soap:Envelope>
```

In order for the <AuthHeader> entry to take effect, we have to do the following two things: we must configure the method GetTime such that it always requires a <AuthHeader> entry. Furthermore, GetTime needs be able to access the <cookie> element. Therefore we declare a public field curUser of type AuthHeader in the web service. The attribute [SoapHeader("curUser")] of the method GetTime indicates that the <AuthHeader> entry sent by the client will be stored in curUser. If the SOAP message does not contain an <AuthHeader> entry, curUser is set to null. In .NET 1.0 the ASP.NET run-time environment throws an exception if a required header is missing.

```csharp
<%@ WebService Language="C#" Class="HeaderTimeService" %>
using System; using System.Web.Services; using System.Web.Services.Protocols;
// implementation of the header entry as a class
public class AuthHeader : SoapHeader { public string cookie; }
[WebService(Namespace="http://dotnet.jku.at/time/", Description="SOAP header demo")]
public class HeaderTimeService : WebService {
    public AuthHeader curUser;   // header entry <AuthHeader>

    [WebMethod(Description="Returns the current time")]
    [SoapHeader("curUser")]    // entry of type AuthHeader is stored in curUser
    public string GetTime() {
        if (curUser != null && ValidateCookie(curUser.cookie))   // user validated?
            return System.DateTime.Now.ToLongTimeString();
        else throw new SoapHeaderException( "Access denied!",   // client error!
                            SoapException.ClientFaultCode);
    }

    [WebMethod (Description="Authenticates the user")]
    public string Login(string user, string pwd) { ... create cookie ... }
    bool ValidateCookie(string cookie) { ... validate cookie ... }
}
```

If an error occurs while processing the header entry, a SoapHeaderException is thrown. This causes a <Fault> element to be inserted into the <Body> of the SOAP response. The parameter ClientFaultCode indicates that the client is responsible for the error, because it is not entitled to execute this method. If it was the server's fault, SoapException.ServerFaultCode would be used.

Because we now require a SOAP header entry, we can no longer invoke the method GetTime via HTTP-GET or HTTP-POST, but only via SOAP-HTTP. In order to test it, we develop a command-line client that uses the types HeaderTimeService and AuthHeader. We let wsdl.exe (see Section 7.2) generate the proxy HeaderTimeService and the header entry AuthHeader. During this, the proxy receives a field of type AuthHeader, to refer to the header entry. We can set the value of a header entry of type T in a proxy p with p.TValue = ..., as shown in the following example, where we create an object entry of type AuthHeader and before the call assign it to the proxy with proxy.AuthHeaderValue = entry;.

```
HeaderTimeService proxy = new HeaderTimeService();
AuthHeader entry = new AuthHeader();
entry.cookie = proxy.Login(user, pwd);   // cookie for header entry
proxy.AuthHeaderValue = entry;
Console.WriteLine(proxy.GetTime());   // Note: GetTime might throw an Exception
```

In this example the client has to set the header entry explicitly, because it is sent from the client to the server. However, it would be more convenient for the developer of the client if the server returned the complete AuthHeader at the login, instead of only the cookie. Then the client would no longer have to assign the header entry to the proxy explicitly. To achieve this we have to adjust the methods Login and GetTime at the web service. The return value of the Login method is now no longer a cookie, but only a Boolean value that indicates whether the authentication has been successful or not. This simplifies the client code:

```
HeaderTimeService proxy = new HeaderTimeService();
if (proxy.Login(user, pwd)) Console.WriteLine(proxy.GetTime());
```

We adapt the methods Login and GetTime so that they both use the same header entry, which is set in the field curUser of type AuthHeader. Additionally, the direction of transmission of the header entry has to be indicated: with Login it is sent from the server to the client and with GetTime from the client to the server.

```
[WebService(Namespace="http://dotnet.jku.at/time/", Description="SOAP header demo")]
public class HeaderTimeService : WebService {
    public AuthHeader curUser;   // header entry

    [WebMethod (Description="Authentificates the user")]
    [SoapHeader("curUser", Direction=SoapHeaderDirection.Out)]
    public bool Login(string user, string pwd) {
        curUser = new AuthHeader();   // create entry to be returned
        if (Authenticate(user, pwd)) {
            curUser.cookie = CreateCookie(user);   // user is known, so set cookie!
            return true;
        } else return false;
    }
```

```
[WebMethod(Description="Returns the current time")]
[SoapHeader("curUser", Direction=SoapHeaderDirection.In)]
public string GetTime() {
    if (ValidateCookie(curUser.cookie))   // user validated?
        return System.DateTime.Now.ToLongTimeString();
    else throw new SoapHeaderException("Access denied!",   // client error!
                                    SoapException.ClientFaultCode);
}

    bool ValidateCookie(string cookie) { ... validate cookie ... }
    bool Authenticate(string usr, string pwd) { ... is the user known? ... }
    string CreateCookie(string user) { ... create cookie ... }
}
```

The direction of transmission of the SOAP header is indicated by the property Direction. Valid values include SoapHeaderDirection.In (from client to server), SoapHeaderDirection.Out (from server to client) and SoapHeaderDirection.InOut (both ways). SoapHeaderDirection.In is the default setting and therefore need not be explicitly specified.

7.4.4 Life Cycle of a Web Service

Since a web service is usually represented by an object, questions arise: when is this object created, used and destroyed again? Does the server create a new object for every method call and destroy it again right after the method has been executed? Is the state of the object (i.e. its fields) still available after the method call? In short: what does the life cycle of a web-service object in .NET look like?

.NET assumes stateless web-service objects that are created for one method call and destroyed after the method has terminated. If data must be kept for more than one invocation of a web service method it has to be stored in the state of the current session or application, by accessing the properties Session or Application (see Section 6.7).

Every object of type WebService automatically has access to the Application object. If a web service method needs to access a Session object, the property EnableSession of the attribute [WebMethod] must be set to true.

The following example illustrates the usage of the properties Application and Session. The class StateDemo offers two methods. IncApplication accesses the Application property and increases a counter. IncSession accesses the Session property and increases another counter there.

```
<%@ WebService Language="C#" Class="StateDemo" %>
using System.Web.Services;

[WebService(Namespace="http://dotnet.jku.at/StateDemo/")]
public class StateDemo : WebService {
```

```
[WebMethod()]
public int IncApplication() {
    int hit = (Application["Hit"] == null) ? 0 : (int) Application["Hit"];
    hit++;
    Application["Hit"] = hit;
    return hit;
}

[WebMethod(EnableSession=true)]
public int IncSession() {
    int hit = (Session["Hit"] == null) ? 0 : (int) Session["Hit"];
    hit++;
    Session["Hit"] = hit;
    return hit;
}
}
```

In order to test this service, we open two browsers and navigate to the StateDemo service. Invoking IncApplication increases a shared counter, whereas an invocation of IncSession operates on separate counters for each browser (i.e. a separate counter for each session).

7.5   Web Services Description Language

WSDL (*Web Services Description Language*) is an XML-based notation for describing the functionality of web services. Hardly any developer should ever have to write a WSDL description of their web service by hand, because most web service containers (e.g. IIS) will do this for them. However, during the integration of several different web services it might come in handy to understand their WSDL structure. In order to facilitate the use of web services that run on different platforms, Ariba, IBM and Microsoft have submitted WSDL to the W3C for standardization [WSDL]. The XML namespace of WSDL is http://schemas.xmlsoap.org/wsdl/. You can also get the XML schema of WSDL there. This section presents an overview of the structure of WSDL 1.1.

A web service offers methods that have parameters of various types and can be invoked via various protocols (e.g. SOAP-HTTP, SOAP-SMTP, HTTP-GET). This, exactly, is what WSDL describes:

❑ What services offer what methods?
❑ Which ports, protocols and messages can be used to invoke these methods?
❑ What name and what parameters does a message have?
❑ What data types does a message use?

The structure of a WSDL description more or less reflects the items from the above list. A WSDL description is built up hierarchically and contains five sections designated by the XML elements <types>, <messages>, <portType>, <binding> and

<service>. Each section depends on the previous sections. For example, the element <message> refers to the data types defined in the XML schema and in <types>.

```
<definitions>
    <types>                    ... XML description of the data types used
        <xsd:schema>
    </types>
    <message>                  ... description of a message (name and parameters)
        <part>                     "<message>" can appear more than once.
    </message>
    <portType>                 ... describes for each protocol what messages form a
        <operation>                complete operation (input and output message).
            <input>                Thus it also describes all operations that can be reached
            <output>               on this "port".
        </operation>
    </portType>
    <binding>                  ... binds a protocol to a port and describes how the data are
        Protocolinfo               encoded and serialized (e.g. SOAP, rpc/encoded).
        <operation>
    </binding>
    <service>                  ... connects the name of a service with a URI and a binding
        <port>
    </service>
</definitions>
```

The sections <binding> and <service> describe which URI (element <port>) and protocols a web service can be reached through and how data is serialized and encoded. The first three sections describe the operations and data types used, independent of a protocol or service. Thus a WSDL description is also split into an abstract part (<types>, <message>, <portType>) and a concrete part (<binding>, <service>).

The <types> element follows immediately after the root element <definitions> and contains those data types (e.g. TimeDesc) that will later be used in the messages (<message>). A WSDL description always has exactly one <types> element, but may contain many <message> elements.

The section <portType> describes operations. An operation (<operation>) consists of up to two messages. As a reminder: SOAP always sends only "one way" messages from the sender to the receiver. If a response is to be returned to the sender, an incoming message (<input>) is connected to an outgoing message (<output>) to form an operation. Of course, only messages from the <message> section can be used here. Finally, multiple operations form a port type. A WSDL description can contain many <portType> elements.

The section <binding> describes what transport protocol to use (e.g. SOAP and/or HTTP-GET) and how to encode the data of the various operations (e.g. *rpc* or *document*). The encoding is specified for each message of an operation (input and output). The <binding> section connects a protocol via its operations to a <portType>. For example, a <binding> that describes HTTP-GET can bind to fewer operations or even different operations than another one describing SOAP. There is one <binding> element for each transport protocol supported.

The <service> element describes at what URI and via which protocol a service can be reached.

Let us take our TimeService example in its simplest form: it offers only the method GetTime and uses SOAP and the message format *rpc/encoded*.

```
<%@ WebService Language="C#" Class="TimeService" %>
using System.Web.Services; using System.Web.Services.Protocols;

[SoapRpcService]
[WebService( Namespace="http://dotnet.jku.at/time/",
                Description="Simple web service for querying the time")]
public class TimeService : WebService {
    [WebMethod(Description="Returns the current server time")]
    public string GetTime() { return System.DateTime.Now.ToLongTimeString(); }
}
```

The TimeService has been configured (see Section 7.7) to accept only SOAP calls. The WSDL description of our web service is:

```
<?xml version="1.0" encoding="utf-16"?>
<definitions xmlns:soap="http://schemas.xmlsoap.org/wsdl/soap/"
                xmlns:tns="http://dotnet.jku.at/time/"
                xmlns:s="http://www.w3.org/2001/XMLSchema"
                xmlns:http="http://schemas.xmlsoap.org/wsdl/http/"
                xmlns:mime="http://schemas.xmlsoap.org/wsdl/mime/"
                xmlns:soapenc="http://schemas.xmlsoap.org/soap/encoding/"
                targetNamespace="http://dotnet.jku.at/time/"
                xmlns="http://schemas.xmlsoap.org/wsdl/">

    <types />

    <message name="GetTimeSoapIn" />
    <message name="GetTimeSoapOut">
        <part name="GetTimeResult" type="s:string" />
    </message>

    <portType name="TimeServiceSoap">
        <operation name="GetTime">
            <documentation>Returns the current server time</documentation>
            <input message="tns:GetTimeSoapIn" />
            <output message="tns:GetTimeSoapOut" />
        </operation>
    </portType>
```

```
<binding name="TimeServiceSoap" type="tns:TimeServiceSoap">
  <soap:binding transport="http://schemas.xmlsoap.org/soap/http" style="rpc" />
  <operation name="GetTime">
    <soap:operation soapAction="http://dotnet.jku.at/time/GetTime" style="rpc" />
    <input>
      <soap:body use="encoded" namespace="http://dotnet.jku.at/time/"
           encodingStyle="http://schemas.xmlsoap.org/soap/encoding/" />
    </input>
    <output>
      <soap:body use="encoded" namespace="http://dotnet.jku.at/time/"
           encodingStyle="http://schemas.xmlsoap.org/soap/encoding/" />
    </output>
  </operation>
</binding>

<service name="TimeService">
  <documentation>Simple web service for querying the time</documentation>
  <port name="TimeServiceSoap" binding="tns:TimeServiceSoap">
    <soap:address location="http://localhost/time/TimeService.asmx" />
  </port>
</service>
</definitions>
```

The interested reader will find more detailed descriptions of XML in general, WSDL, and how WSDL can be combined with SOAP at the web pages of [W3C], as well as in books such as [WaLa01].

7.6 Discovery of Web Services

In Section 7.1 we introduced a scenario for a shopping portal of a book store that searches for web services at run time and then uses the services so discovered. The search component we briefly presented that offers this kind of flexibility was UDDI (*Universal Description, Discovery and Integration*).

The namespace System.Web.Services.Discovery offers techniques to discover web services. It contains classes that use DISCO instead of UDDI to find web services. DISCO is a mechanism developed by Microsoft that, like UDDI, enables the dynamic integration of web services. The principal differences between DISCO and UDDI are:

❑ DISCO is mainly supported by Microsoft, while UDDI is a multi-corporation initiative (which includes Microsoft).
❑ DISCO resembles a bookmark list. That means it is simply an XML document with references (URIs) to WSDL documents. This information is typically stored in a file.

❑ DISCO and UDDI both enable the dynamic discovery of web services. However, UDDI allows more complex queries than DISCO; for example, for location, company, "interface type", and so on.

❑ UDDI databases offer special web services for searching and registering web services.

❑ UDDI databases store not only the URI and the kind or type of web services, but also information about the line of business, company, location, etc. of a web service provider.

❑ DISCO files can be published via a custom-developed web service, sent directly to clients, or retrieved from a UDDI database. Clients connect to a web service based on a DISCO document. For example, they read the URI from the DISCO document and thus determine where to find the web service. There is no centralized place for finding DISCO entries as there is for UDDI.

The .NET SDK comes with the command-line tool disco.exe which creates XML documents for web services, such as DISCO and WSDL descriptions, that can help in finding the web service. .NET web services can also generate a DISCO description directly, by appending ?DISCO as a parameter, similarly to the WSDL generation. If we would like to retrieve, for example, a DISCO description for our TimeService, we need only navigate a web browser to http://localhost/time/TimeService.asmx?DISCO and we get:

```
<?xml version="1.0" encoding="utf-8"?>
<discovery xmlns:xsd="http://www.w3.org/2001/XMLSchema"
          xmlns:xsi="http://www.w3.org/2001/XMLSchema-instance"
          xmlns="http://schemas.xmlsoap.org/disco/">
   <contractRef ref="http://localhost/time/TimeService.asmx?wsdl"
      docRef="http://localhost/time/TimeService.asmx"
      xmlns="http://schemas.xmlsoap.org/disco/scl/" />
   <soap address="http://localhost/time/TimeService.asmx"
      xmlns:q1="http://dotnet.jku.at/time/"
      binding="q1:TimeServiceSoap" xmlns="http://schemas.xmlsoap.org/disco/soap/" />
</discovery>
```

A DISCO description consists of the root element <discovery> and the child elements <contractRef> and <soap>. <contractRef> points to the WSDL description and the documentation for the web service. <soap> indicates the URI and the binding information for sending SOAP messages.

The classes of the namespace System.Web.Services.Discovery encapsulate DISCO documents and allow them to be loaded via the Internet. We want, for example, to develop a client application that switches at run time between different TimeService implementations. The DISCO documents will tell our client where to find those services. For the communication we will use a proxy that has been generated with wsdl.exe http://localhost/time/TimeService.asmx?WSDL.

Before we start, we create two additional web services as variants of our current TimeService and store them in the files TimeService1.asmx and TimeService2.asmx.

```
// TimeService1.asmx:
<%@ WebService Language="C#" Class="TimeService1" %>
using System.Web.Services;
[WebService(Namespace="http://dotnet.jku.at/time/", Name="TimeService")]
public class TimeService1 : WebService {
    [WebMethod(Description="Returns the current server time")]
    public string GetTime() { return System.DateTime.Now.ToLongTimeString(); }
}

// TimeService2.asmx:
<%@ WebService Language="C#" Class="TimeService2" %>
using System.Web.Services;
[WebService(Namespace="http://dotnet.jku.at/time/", Name="TimeService")]
public class TimeService2 : WebService {
    [WebMethod]
    public string GetTime() { return "I don't know the time!"; }
}
```

Both web services have the same name (Name="TimeService") and live inside the same namespace (Namespace="http://dotnet.jku.at/time/"). Therefore their interfaces are considered equal and we can use the same proxy for both services in our client application DiscoSample.exe.

Our client application receives DISCO-URIs from the command line and uses them to load DISCO documents with an object of type System.Web.Services.Discovery.DiscoveryClientProtocol. The retrieved documents are returned in the property Documents, a dictionary whose keys are the URIs and whose values the loaded DISCO documents of type DiscoveryDocument.

Afterwards, the <contractRef> element is extracted from each DiscoveryDocument and converted into ContractReference objects whose property DocRef corresponds to the docRef attribute of a <contractRef> element. The URI of our current TimeService proxy is set to the URI of the new web service. We use the URI from the docRef attribute, because for .NET web services the URI for the documentation is identical to the URI of the web service itself. With proxy.Discover() we tell the proxy to use the new web service from now on. If the new web service cannot be used for some reason, proxy.Discover() will throw an exception of type System.Exception.

```
using System;
using System.Web.Services.Discovery;
using System.Collections;
```

```
public class DiscoSample {

    public static void Main(string[] args) {
        // load the DISCO files
        DiscoveryClientProtocol discoClient = new DiscoveryClientProtocol();
        foreach (string uri in args) {
            discoClient.Discover(uri);   // load DISCO document
        }
        Print(discoClient.Documents.Count + " documents found");
        if (discoClient.Documents.Count > 0) {
            // check all URIs contained in all the documents
            discoClient.ResolveAll();
            TimeService proxy = new TimeService();
            // discoClients.Documents: key = URI, value = document
            foreach (object obj in discoClient.Documents.Values) {
                DiscoveryDocument dDoc = obj as DiscoveryDocument;
                if (dDoc != null) {
                    // look for <contractRef> element
                    ContractReference contr = null;   // encapsulate <contractRef> element
                    IEnumerator it = dDoc.References.GetEnumerator();
                    while (contr == null && it.MoveNext())
                        contr = it.Current as ContractReference;
                    if (contr != null) {   // found <contractRef>!
                        proxy.Url = contr.DocRef;   // reference to new web service
                        Print("Connecting proxy to " + proxy.Url);
                        proxy.Discover();   // connect proxy with new web service
                        Print("Result of GetTime: " + proxy.GetTime());
                    }
                }
            }
        }
    }

    static void Print(string msg) { System.Console.WriteLine(msg); }
}
```

We run DiscoSample.exe with the URIs for the DISCO documents for the two web services. In our example, these DISCO documents reside in the directory c:\Temp\Disco:

```
> DiscoSample file://C:/Temp/Disco/TimeService1.disco
             file://C:/Temp/Disco/TimeService2.disco
```

This produces the following output at the console:

```
2 documents found
Connecting proxy to http://localhost/time/TimeService1.asmx
Result of GetTime: 11:39:13
Connecting proxy to http://localhost/time/TimeService2.asmx
Result of GetTime: I don't know the time!
```

For dealing with UDDI, Microsoft offers specific .NET classes and COM components as well as a special UDDI database for testing. These UDDI SDKs have to be downloaded separately from Microsoft (URI see Section 7.8) and are not considered any further here. Since some UDDI servers return DISCO documents as results of queries, these can be used as described in this section.

7.7 Configuration of Web Services under .NET

In Section 6.9 we introduced the configuration of ASP.NET applications. Web services build upon the ASP.NET infrastructure and thus also use the file Web.config for their configuration. The following shows the structure of the configuration section <webServices>:

```
<configuration>
   <system.web>
      <webServices>
         <protocols>
            <add/> <remove/>
         </protocols>
         <serviceDescriptionFormatExtensionTypes>
            <add/> <remove/> <clear/>
         </serviceDescriptionFormatExtensionTypes>
         <soapExtensionTypes>
            <add/>
         </soapExtensionTypes>
         <soapExtensionReflectorTypes>
            <add/>
         </soapExtensionReflectorTypes>
         <soapExtensionImporterTypes>
            <add/>
         </soapExtensionImporterTypes>
         <wsdlHelpGenerator href="..."/>
      </webServices>
   </system.web>
</configuration>
```

Here we present two of these configuration subsections in more detail.

<protocols>

With <protocols> you can add and remove transport protocols such as SOAP, HTT-POST and HTTP-GET. Additionally, ASP.NET defines a protocol for documentation. As a reminder: if we navigate a web browser to the URI of a web service (e.g. http://localhost/time/TimeService.asmx), we will see its documentation (see Section 7.2).

Possible child elements of <protocols> are <add name="*ProtocolName*"/> and <remove name="*ProtocolName*"/>. Valid protocol names are "Http-Soap" for SOAP, "HttpPost" for HTTP-POST, "HttpGet" for HTTP-GET and "Documentation" for the HTML documentation. The default setting for <protocols> in Machine.config is:

```
<protocols>
    <add name="HttpSoap"/>
    <add name="HttpPost"/>
    <add name="HttpGet"/>
    <add name="Documentation"/>
</protocols>
```

If, for example, we want to allow only SOAP and the documentation as transport protocols for our TimeService, we create a file Web.config with the following contents in the directory of the file TimeService.asmx:

```
<configuration>
    <system.web>
        <webServices>
            <protocols>
                <add name="HttpSoap"/>
                <add name="Documentation"/>
                <remove name="HttpGet"/>
                <remove name="HttpPost"/>
            </protocols>
        </webServices>
    </system.web>
</configuration>
```

The two <add> elements are not really necessary, because HttpSoap and Documentation have already been added system-wide in Machine.config. They are only provided to be on the safe side, in case one of the protocols is removed by a higher-level configuration file.

<wsdlHelpGenerator>

<wsdlHelpGenerator href="*URI of help pages*"> can provide a URI where HTML help pages for a web service are generated. In Machine.config this is already set to

```
<wsdlHelpGenerator href="DefaultWsdlHelpGenerator.aspx"/>
```

If this entry is not overridden in an application's Web.config file, the appearance of all web service description pages will be determined by the page DefaultWsdlHelpGenerator.aspx, which lies in the directory \WINNT\Microsoft.NET\ Framework\[Version]\CONFIG\. ([Version] refers to the version of the .NET SDK, e.g. v1.0.3705.)

7.8 Tools and Resources

Besides wsdl.exe (see Section 7.2.1), there are several other useful tools that ease the creation and use of web services. In this section we will present one more such tool and provide references to some web resources about web services.

7.8.1 .NET Web Service Studio

.NET Web Service Studio (which you can find on the enclosed CD-ROM) aims to support web-service developers who want to test their web services without implementing a separate test client. The tool takes only a WSDL description and generates a proxy and a possible test client from it—both in C#.

So far we have used wsdl.exe to generate a proxy. .NET Web Service Studio offers a GUI for wsdl.exe (see Figure 7.7). It allows invocation of individual web service methods and displays the corresponding SOAP messages (request, response).

The tool is a .NET application and can be downloaded from [GotD].

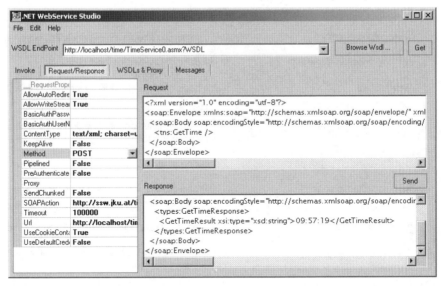

Figure 7.7 .NET Web Service Studio

7.8.2 Helpful Web Addresses

Internet resources about web services can principally be split into two categories: They either offer a collection of web services (see Table 7.4) or provide information for developers of web services or clients (see Table 7.5).

Table 7.4 *Web Service Directories*

URI	Description
www.uddi.org	home page of the UDDI initiative
www.xmethods.com	directory of various web services according to various interfaces like UDDI and DISCO
uddi.microsoft.com, www-3.ibm.com/services/uddi	public UDDI databases of Microsoft and IBM. The Microsoft UDDI page also contains references to their UDDI SDKs that provide .NET classes and COM components for accessing UDDI.
test.uddi.microsoft.com	Microsoft UDDI database for testing purposes

Table 7.5 *Resources for Developers*

URI	Description
www.gotdotnet.com	.NET resources about web services, among others
www.microsoft.com/netservices	home page of Microsoft's .NET Services
www.w3.org	home page of the W3C. Source for various specifications (SOAP, WSDL, etc.)
www.webservices.org	collection of articles and information about web services, server producers, discussion forums, etc.
groups.yahoo.com/group/soapbuilders	discussion group about SOAP and web services
www.pocketsoap.com	SOAP client COM component for Windows and PocketPC as well as a collection of useful tools
www.vbws.com/book	book about web services for VB.NET programmers
www.soapware.org	collection of sources for specifications, tutorials, etc. for various platforms
msdn.microsoft.com/library/ default.asp?URL=/library/en-us/ dnsoap/html/soap1and2.asp	Microsoft's SOAP toolkit for VB6 and C++ (for Visual Studio .NET)
www.csharphelp.com	articles, tutorials, etc. about various C# topics
xml.apache.org/axis/	web service server based on Apache and Java
www.themindelectric.com	GLUE: a web service server in Java

7.9   Exercises

1.   **Stock quotes.** Write a web service that has a method

     double GetQuote(string symbol) { }

   which returns the value of a stock symbol that is given as a string (for example, "MSFT" for Microsoft or "AMZN" for Amazon.com). For reasons of simplicity, the web service should keep the stock values in a hash table instead of reading them from a database.

   Generate a proxy class for your web service using the command-line tool wsdl.exe. Use this proxy to call the web service from a test program.

2.   **Testing a web service.** If the web service from the previous exercise was stored in a file called StockTicker.asmx you can use Internet Explorer to test it. Simply direct the browser at

     http://localhost/*yourVirtualDirectory*/StockTicker.asmx

   You will get a page that allows you to call your web-service method. Look at the generated WSDL description by entering the following address into your browser:

     http://localhost/*yourVirtualDirectory*/StockTicker.asmx?WSDL

3.   **Web services on the Web.** The site www.xmethods.com contains one of the largest collections of free web services that one can find on the Internet. Go to this site and browse through the web services that are offered there.

4.   **Fail-safe web service usage.** In this advanced exercise, you should implement an ASP.NET web page that always displays the current exchange rate between US dollars and euros. In a web browser this could look as follows:

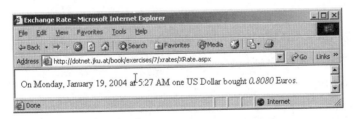

   The actual exchange rate should be retrieved from a web service. For example, xmethods.com offers such a web service whose WSDL can be obtained from

     http://www.xmethods.net/sd/2001/CurrencyExchangeService.wsdl

   You can generate the source code for a proxy class for the web service with the *Web Service Description Language Utility* (wsdl.exe). Then you need to put the compiled assembly library in the bin\ subdirectory of your application directory.

Since the exchange rate page accesses the web service via the Internet each time the page is displayed, this might fail in one way or another. In order to be able to display some sensible data even in case of a network failure, you should implement the following fail-safe strategy:

❑ Every time your application successfully receives data from the web service, it should store the exchange rate together with a current time stamp in some local file (XML, serialization, ...).
❑ Now when the application fails to access the web service it can still display the last valid data by reading it from the local file.

5. **Using the Google web service.** The search engine Google can be used as a web service. Go to http://www.google.com/apis/ and download the WSDL, sample code and the documentation. Before you can use this web service you have to apply for a key, which you must then use on every web service call to Google. Create a web service proxy from the downloaded file GoogleSearch.wsdl:

```
wsdl /out:GoogleProxy.cs GoogleSearch.wsdl
```

Write a test program that looks something like this:

```
public class Search {
    public static void Main(string[] arg) {
        GoogleSearchService service = new GoogleSearchService();
        GoogleSearchResult result = service.doGoogleSearch(
            "--yourKey--", arg[0], 0, 10, false, "", false, "", "", ""
        );
        foreach (ResultElement elem in result.resultElements)
            Console.WriteLine(elem.URL);
    }
}
```

Compile both your test program and the proxy:

```
csc Search.cs GoogleProxy.cs
```

and call it like this:

```
Search dotnet
```

The downloaded documentation explains how to use all the parameters of doGoogleSearch() as well as the other web methods that come with this service.

6. **Webservice Studio.** Invoke and test the Google web service that was described in the previous exercise using the tool *Webservice Studio* which comes with the CD included in this book. Start the tool by double-clicking the file WebServiceStudio\bin\WebServiceStudio.exe. Browse for GoogleSearch.wsdl which was downloaded as described in the previous exercise and click the Get

button. A proxy will be generated and all web service methods will be displayed. Select the method doGoogleSearch and fill its parameters as described in the previous example. Then click the Invoke button. The web-service method will be called and the results will be shown.

8 Working with the .NET Framework SDK

In this chapter we wish to look at some of the tools and aids that play a role in the most important activities of the development phase—coding, compiling and debugging. We will concentrate on the tools that are contained in the .NET Framework SDK and that are not part of Visual Studio .NET, because a detailed discussion of this development environment could fill an entire book.

8.1 Overview of the .NET Tools

The .NET SDK is delivered with a range of programs that support the developer's work. Table 8.1 shows an overview of these tools with a brief description. More detailed descriptions for all the tools (with a few exceptions) can be found in the .NET online documentation [SDKDoc] by searching for their name (as displayed in Table 8.1) in the index. The file names in boldface are of programs that are directly executable. Unless otherwise indicated, the program files are situated in one of these two directories:

- [c:\Program Files\Microsoft.NET]\FrameworkSDK\Bin\
- [c:\WINNT]\Microsoft.NET\Framework\[v1.1.4322]\

where [c:\Program Files\Microsoft.NET] stands for the installation directory of the .NET Framework SDK, [c:\WINNT] for the Windows installation directory and [v1.1.4322] for the version number.

Table 8.1 .NET Tools (overview)

Tool name	Program file
short description	
.NET Framework Configuration Tool	mscorcfg.msc
Microsoft Management Console (MMC) plug-in that allows you to manage and configure assemblies in the Global Assembly Cache, adjust code access security policy and adjust remoting services.	
.NET Services Installation Tool	**regsvcs**.exe
Performs the following actions for installing Windows services: – Loads and registers an assembly. – Generates, registers and installs a type library into a specified COM+ 1.0 application. – Configures services that you have added programmatically to your class.	

Table 8.1 *.NET Tools (overview) (cont.)*

Tool name short description	Program file
Assembly Cache Viewer	shfusion.dll
Windows shell extension that allows you to view and manipulate the contents of the global assembly cache using Windows Explorer (see Section 8.5.3).	
Assembly Binding Log Viewer	**fuslogvw**.exe
Displays details for failed assembly binds, which typically show up as a TypeLoadException. This information helps you diagnose why the .NET Framework cannot locate an assembly at run time.	
Assembly Linker	**al**.exe
Generates a file with an assembly manifest (see Section 3.6) from one or more files that are either modules or resource files.	
Assembly Registration Tool	**regasm**.exe
Reads the metadata within an assembly and adds the necessary entries to the registry. Once a class is registered, any COM client can use it as though the class were a COM class.	
Certificate Creation Tool	**makecert**.exe
Generates X.509 certificates for testing purposes only.	
Certificate Manager Tool	**certmgr**.exe
Manages certificates, certificate trust lists (CTLs) and certificate revocation lists (CRLs).	
Certificate Verification Tool	**chktrust**.exe
Checks the validity of a file signed with an Authenticode certificate.	
Code Access Security Policy Tool	**caspol**.exe
Enables users and administrators to modify security policy for the machine policy level, the user policy level and the enterprise policy level (see Section 3.8.1).	
Common Language Runtime Minidump Tool	**mscordmp**.exe
Creates a file containing information that is useful for analyzing system problems in the run-time.	
File Signing Tool	**signcode**.exe
Signs a portable executable (PE) file (.dll or .exe file) with an Authenticode digital signature. You can sign either an assembly or an individual file contained in a multi-file assembly. Running signcode.exe without specifying any options launches a wizard that helps with signing.	
Global Assembly Cache Utility	**gacutil**.exe
Allows viewing and manipulation of the contents of the global assembly cache and the download cache.	
Installer Tool	**installutil**.exe
Allows you to install and uninstall server resources by executing the installer components in a specified assembly. This tool works in conjunction with classes in the System.Configuration. Install Namespace.	
Isolated Storage Tool	**storeadm**.exe
Lists or removes all existing stores for the current user (see Section 4.2.3).	

Table 8.1 .NET Tools (overview) (cont.)

Tool name short description	Program file
JScript Compiler	**jsc**.exe
Microsoft JScript .NET (v7.0) compiler. Produces executable (.exe) files and dynamic-link libraries (.dll).	
License Compiler	**lc**.exe
Reads text files that contain licensing information and produces a .licenses file that can be embedded in a common language runtime executable as a resource.	
Management Strongly Typed Class Generator	**mgmtclassgen**.exe
Enables you to quickly generate an early-bound managed class (in C#, Visual Basic or JScript) for a specified Windows Management Instrumentation (WMI) class.	
Microsoft CLR Debugger	**dbgclr**.exe
Is intended as an interim tool for debugging applications written and compiled for the Microsoft .NET runtime (see Section 8.4.2). The Microsoft CLR Debugger, and the accompanying documentation, is based on work being done for the Microsoft Visual Studio .NET debugger.	
Microsoft Program Maintenance Utility	**nmake**.exe
32-bit tool that builds projects based on commands contained in a description file.	
MSIL Assembler	**ilasm**.exe
Generates a portable executable (PE) file from MSIL assembly language.	
MSIL Disassembler	**ildasm**.exe
Is a companion tool to the MSIL Assembler (ilasm.exe). It takes a portable executable (PE) file that contains Microsoft intermediate language (MSIL) code and creates a text file suitable as input to ilasm.exe or to display the CIL and metadata in a GUI (see Section 8.5.1).	
Native Image Generator	**ngen**.exe
Creates a native image from a managed assembly and installs it into the *native image cache* on the local computer (see Section 3.7.4).	
Permissions View Tool	**permview**.exe
Is used to view the minimal, optional and refused permission sets requested by an assembly. Optionally, you can use permview.exe to view all declarative security used by an assembly (see Section 3.8.1).	
PEVerify Tool	**peverify**.exe
Helps developers who generate Microsoft intermediate language (MSIL) (such as compiler writers, script engine developers and so on) to determine whether their MSIL code and associated metadata meet type safety requirements.	
Resource File Generator	**resgen**.exe
For conversion between .txt, .resx (XML-based resource format) and common language runtime binary .resources files that can be embedded in a runtime binary executable or compiled into satellite assemblies.	
Runtime Debugger	**cordbg**.exe
Helps tools vendors and application developers find and fix bugs in programs that target the .NET Framework common language runtime (see Section 8.4.1).	

Table 8.1 *.NET Tools (overview) (cont.)*

Tool name	Program file
short description	

Security Tool	**secutil**.exe

Extracts strong name (see Section 3.6.2) information or the public key for an X.509 certificate from an assembly and converts this information into a format that can be incorporated into code.

Set Registry Tool	**setreg**.exe

Allows you to change the registry settings for public key cryptography. These keys, called the Software Publishing State Keys, control the behaviour of the certificate verification process.

Soapsuds Tool	**soapsuds**.exe

Helps you compile client applications that communicate with XML web services using a technique called remoting. It creates XML schemas describing services exposed in a common language runtime assembly, or creates runtime assemblies to access services described by XML schemas.

Software Publisher Certificate Test Tool	**cert2spc**.exe

Creates a Software Publisher's Certificate (SPC) from one or more X.509 certificates for test purposes only.

Strong Name Tool	**sn**.exe

Helps sign assemblies with strong names (see Section 8.5.2). It provides options for key management, signature generation and signature verification.

Type Library Exporter	**tlbexp**.exe

Generates a type library that describes the types defined in a common language runtime assembly.

Type Library Importer	**tlbimp**.exe

Converts the type definitions found within a COM type library into equivalent definitions in a common language runtime assembly.

Visual Basic Compiler	**vbc**.exe

Microsoft Visual Basic .NET (v7) compiler.

Visual C# Compiler	**csc**.exe

Microsoft's compiler for the new .NET programming language C# (see Section 8.2).

Visual C++ Compiler	**cl**.exe

32-bit tool that controls the Microsoft C and C++ compilers and linker. The compilers produce Common Object File Format (COFF) object (.obj) files. The linker produces executable (.exe) files or dynamic-link libraries (DLLs).

Web Services Discovery Tool	**disco**.exe

Discovers the URLs of XML web services located on a Web server (see Section 7.6) and saves documents related to each XML web service on a local disk.

Web Services Description Language Tool	**wsdl**.exe

Generates code for XML web services and XML web service clients from WSDL contract files, XSD schemas and .discomap discovery documents (see Section 7.2.1).

Table 8.1 *.NET Tools (overview) (cont.)*

Tool name	Program file
short description	
Windows Forms ActiveX Control Importer	**aximp**.exe
Converts type definitions in a COM type library for an ActiveX control into a Windows Forms control.	
Windows Forms Class Viewer	**wincv**.exe
Allows quick look-up of information about a class or series of classes, based on a search pattern. The class viewer displays information by using reflection on the type using the common language runtime reflection API.	
Windows Forms Resource Editor	**winres**.exe
Visual layout tool that helps localization experts localize Windows Forms forms.	
XML Schema Definition Tool	**xsd**.exe
Generates XML schema or common language runtime classes from XDR, XML and XSD files, or from classes in a run-time assembly (see Section 5.5.2).	

In the following sections of this chapter we will write parts of the command options in italics to indicate that these parts can be omitted. For example, */target:* means that this option can either be written in full as /target: or abbreviated to /t:.

8.2   The C# Compiler (csc.exe)

We have already given a first introduction to the compilation of C# programs with the C# compiler in Chapter 2. Here we will go further into some of the compiler options.

/target:

The option */target:* determines which sort of output the C# compiler produces:

❑ *Directly executable program* (.exe): These can only be created from source code that contains a Main method; otherwise the compiler reports an error.

csc */target:*exe MyApp.cs
creates the console application MyApp.exe. The option */target:*exe is the default setting; csc MyApp.cs alone gives the same result.

csc */target:*winexe MyWinApp.cs
creates the GUI application MyWinApp.exe.
If a Windows GUI application is compiled with the option */target:*exe then starting the program with a double click on the .exe file opens a command-line window, before the GUI appears. When this extra window is closed, the application is closed and ended.

❑ *Dynamic link library* (.dll): These are created with /*target*:library. The only difference from the first category is that the library has no entry point and can therefore only be used from a running program.

    csc /*target*:library MyLib.cs
    creates the library assembly MyLib.dll.

❑ *.NET module* (.netmodule): Whereas the previous variants represent complete assemblies, a .NET module lacks a manifest.

    csc /*target*:module MyModule.cs
    create the module MyModule.netmodule.

/reference:

Assemblies can reference other assemblies by using them. When compiling an assembly we must specify all the assemblies that it references. This is done with the /*reference*: option. The assemblies that are referenced must be given by their full file name (including extension) and separated by a comma or a semicolon. We can also give an individual /*reference*: option for each assembly that is referenced.

    csc /*reference*:MyLib.dll MyApp.cs
    creates an assembly file MyApp.exe and embeds the metadata from the manifest of MyLib.dll. The assembly mscorlib.dll, which contains the most important types of the namespace System, is always bound in, so the following commands are equivalent to the one above:
    csc /reference:MyLib.dll,**mscorlib.dll** MyApp.cs
    csc /reference:MyLib.dll /*reference*:**mscorlib.dll** MyApp.cs
    We can remove this referencing of mscorlib.dll by using the option /nostdlib.

For .NET modules it is not enough to reference them from another assembly; they must be added to an assembly using the option /addmodule:.

    csc /**addmodule:MyModule.netmodule** MyApp.cs
    creates the console application MyApp.exe and binds in the module MyModule.

/out:

The name of the created file can be specified by the /out: option.

    csc /*target*:module /**out:MyMod.mod** MyModule.cs
    creates a module in the form of the file MyMod.mod instead of using the default file name MyModule.netmodule.

It is possible to compile several source code files into one assembly or module file. To achieve this they must merely be listed one after another.

```
csc MyApp.cs MyLib.cs MyModule.cs
csc MyLib.cs MyApp.cs MyModule.cs
```

Both variants create an assembly file MyApp.exe that contains the compiled version of MyLib.cs and MyModule.cs.

```
csc /target:library MyModule.cs MyLib.cs
```

creates an assembly file MyModule.dll.

The default name of the generated file is based on the name of the first file in the list. However, if an executable file (.exe) is created, then the name of the assembly corresponds to the name of the file that contains the Main method. If there are several files in the list that define types with a Main method, we must specify which Main method should serve as entry point. This is done by giving the type, using the /main: option. But the name of the created file then again corresponds to the name of the first file in the list.

```
csc /main:WinApp MyLib.cs MyApp.cs MyWinApp.cs
```

creates a file MyLib.exe with the Main method of the type WinApp (which is defined in the file MyWinApp.cs) as entry point. Despite this, the assembly file is named after the first file name in the list.

Response Files (*.rsp)

To avoid typing the compiler options for every compilation, the C# compiler offers the possibility of putting all the options in a so-called response file (*.rsp). On calling the compiler we simply give the name of the corresponding file after an @ symbol and then all the options from this file are used for this compilation. In the following example the response file MySwitches.rsp specifies that a Windows-GUI application should be created in the file MyApp.exe and that the library assembly MyLib.dll and the module MyModule.netmodule should be bound in.

```
Response file MySwitches.rsp:
    /target:winexe
    /out:MyApp.exe
    /reference:MyLib.dll
    /addmodule:MyModule.netmodule
```

The following call compiles the C# file MyWinApp.cs using the options from MySwitches.rsp.

```
csc @MySwitches.rsp MyWinApp.cs
```

There are also two special response files, which the compiler automatically reads for the compilation. Both are called csc.rsp. One determines the global options that are used for every compilation. It lies in the same directory as csc.exe ([c:\WINNT]\Microsoft.NET\Framework\[v1.1.4322]\). In addition, we can install a local csc.rsp file that must lie in the directory from which the compiler is called. The global options are overridden by local ones and they in turn by those given on the command line. If we change the name of the above file MySwitches.rsp to csc.rsp then csc MyWinApp.cs has the same effect as above. The option /noconfig prohibits the options from the csc.rsp files being used.

8.3   Configuration

Under .NET the behaviour of applications can be influenced by the settings of configuration files. Configuration files are XML files that can be handled with any text editor. On each execution of an application its run-time behaviour is adapted according to the settings in configuration files without having to compile the application afresh. Among others, it allows the following to be set:

- ❑ security policy
- ❑ version of the CLR which should execute the application
- ❑ automatic memory management (*garbage collection*)
- ❑ redirection of assembly references to different versions
- ❑ location of assemblies (*codebase*)
- ❑ remoting behaviour
- ❑ ...

In addition, there are different levels for configuration settings. These are distinguished by their scope. The most important ones are:

- ❑ *Machine configuration* (Machine.config): Settings from this file hold for the entire system, and so for all applications that are run on this machine. The machine configuration file is located in the directory [c:\WINNT]\Microsoft.NET\Framework\[v1.1.4322]\CONFIG\.
- ❑ *Application configuration*: The name of the application configuration file is based on the name of the application file to be configured with the extension .config. MyApp.exe is thus configured by the file MyApp.exe.config, which must be in the same directory as MyApp.exe. The settings from the application configuration file only hold for this application. In ASP.NET applications, this file is always called Web.config (see Section 6.9).
- ❑ *Security configuration*: For the configuration of security policy there are separate files that determine security on three different levels (see also Section 3.8):

- *enterprise-wide security policy*: the file enterprisesec.config in directory [c:\WINNT]\Microsoft.NET\Framework|[v1.1.4322]\CONFIG\.
- *machine-wide security policy*: the file security.config in directory [c:\WINNT]\Microsoft.NET\Framework\[v1.1.4322]\CONFIG\.
- *user-specific security policy*: the file security.config in the directory c:\Documents and Settings\[User]\Application Data\Microsoft\CLR Security Config\[v1.1.4322]\.

Despite the different levels of settings all configuration files have the same uniform format: their root element is always

```
<configuration> ... </configuration>
```

Within this are all the elements that describe actual settings. One must, however, keep in mind that not all elements may be used in all configuration files. For example, the <probing> element can only appear in an application configuration file. We do not wish here to give an exhaustive list of all possible XML elements (please find these in the online documentation), but only a brief example, to show how an application can be configured:

```
<configuration>
  <runtime>
    <gcConcurrent enable="true"/>
    <assemblyBinding xmlns="urn:schemas-microsoft-com:asm.vl>
      <probing privatePath="bin;subdir/bin"/>
      <dependentAssembly>
        <assemblyIdentity  name="MyLib"
                           publicKeyToken="320a40fec32d32d2"
                           culture="en-US"/>
        <bindingRedirect oldVersion="1.0.0.0-2.0.0.0" newVersion="3.0.111.2"/>
        <codeBase version="3.0.111.2" href="http://dotnet.jku.at/MyLib.dll">
      </dependentAssembly>
    </assemblyBinding>
  </runtime>
</configuration>
```

Settings in the <runtime> element affect the run-time behaviour of a program, for example the automatic memory management (<gcConcurrent>) or the binding of assembly references to actual assemblies (<assemblyBinding>). In the <probing> element privatePath specifies the subdirectories of the applications directory in which the CLR should look for assemblies at run time. Further, with the element <dependentAssmbly> we can give the location (<codeBase>) or the version to be used (<bindingRedirect>) of individual assemblies of an application (<assemblyIdentity>).

8.4   Debugging

Searching for errors in a program is mostly a complicated and unpleasant activity. Therefore any support is welcome. Alongside the debugging facilities of Visual Studio .NET, which we are not going into for reasons of space, .NET offers three further debugging aids. They are delivered with the .NET SDK and are described in the next three sub-sections.

In order to be able to debug a program in a meaningful way, we must first create additional information during compilation. This is used to relate the machine code produced by the JIT compiler to the CIL code and then to the source code. The mapping of machine code to CIL code is called *JIT tracking*. It must be activated so that we can jump into a running process with the debugger. Information about the mapping of CIL code to source code is written into a separate file (*.pdb, *program database*) by the compiler. The creation of debugging information can be directed by the following compiler options:

- ❏ no debug information: /debug- or no /debug entry (= default)
- ❏ only PDB file: /debug:pdbonly
- ❏ PDB file and JIT tracking: /debug, /debug+, /debug:full

8.4.1   Command-line Debugger (cordbg.exe)

Because the .NET Framework also offers a GUI debugger even without Visual Studio .NET, we might ask why we need a command-line debugger. The command-line debugger has three advantages compared to its graphical counterpart.

Firstly, it is more frugal with system resources, secondly, it allows the user to call certain debug information automatically via a script, and last, but not least, the source code for this debugger is delivered with the SDK (in directory [c:Program Files\Micordosft.NET]\FrameworkSDK\Tool Developers Guide\Samples\ debugger\). This can be useful if we wish to tailor it to special requirements or simply to see how issues are solved internally in order to understand the functioning of the debugger or the debugging interface of the CLR better.

For the commands and options of the command-line debuggers please consult the online documentation. We can also start the command-line debugger with cordbg and learn more about the debug command by using help.

8.4.2   GUI Debugger (dbgclr.exe)

If we wish to use the Windows debugger to search for errors in a .NET Windows application, we must do the following:

1. Start the debugger: the program file DbgCLR.exe is located in the directory [c:\Program Files\Microsoft.NET]FrameworkSDK\GuiDebug\. For regular use, we recommend installing a link in the Windows start menu.

2. In the dialog Debug | Program To Debug ... select the program to be examined (.exe file), and set the program arguments and the work directory.

3. Either start the program with F10 (*Step Over*) (the program will halt after the first step of the Main method) or open the source code in the debugger, set breakpoints (for example, through clicking the region left of the code line) and start the execution with F5 (it will stop on reaching the first breakpoint).

If you have already worked with a GUI debugger, you should find this straightforward. Otherwise we recommend the tutorial delivered with the online documentation (navigate to .NET Framework SDK | Tutorials | Debugging with the .NET Framework SDK in the table of contents). There you will find a step-by-step introduction to the use of the most important functions of the GUI debugger by means of a simple GUI application (*Integer Calculator*) and an ASP.NET application (*Resources and Localization*).

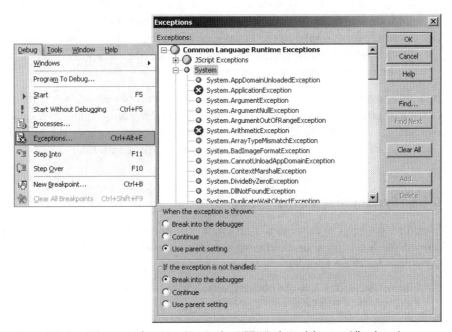

Figure 8.1 *Special support for exceptions in the .NET Windows debugger (dbgclr.exe)*

Exceptions in the Debugger

We will now describe a special feature of the .NET debugger. Microsoft has not stopped at supporting exception handling with the CLR, but has continued this comprehensively as far as the Windows debugger. As Figure 8.1 shows, Debug I Exceptions ... offers a dialog window in which all exceptions known to the debuggers are listed as a tree structure ordered by namespace.

Underneath this display there are two groups of radio buttons. With these we can determine, for selected exceptions, what should happen if

1. the exception is thrown;
2. the exception is not handled in any catch statement and the program execution would terminate with an *"unhandled exception"*.

The following actions can be chosen:

❑ *Break into the debugger*: The program execution will be halted at the corresponding position, so that work with the debugger can commence from there.

❑ *Continue*: The program execution will carry on as usual (if no debugger is involved).

❑ *Use parent settings*: The settings of the parent are applied. The problem with this is that the tree structure in the dialog does not represent the inheritance hierarchy of the exception classes, but only the grouping by namespaces. Applying the behaviour of the base class would make much more sense for exceptions, not least because the exception filters (catch statements) function in this manner.

It is also possible to introduce new exceptions: to do this we must select the root of the exception tree (*Common Language Runtime Exceptions*) and then click on the Add ... button. In the dialog window that this opens, we give the full name (including namespace) of the new exception and confirm with OK.

8.4.3 System.Diagnostics.Debug

Everyone who has ever written a computer program and tried to run it will be familiar with one form or another of the following style of "debugging" (we use C# syntax for this example):

```
System.Console.WriteLine("In method CalcResult()");
System.Console.WriteLine("x = {0}", x);
...
```

We introduce trace output at the critical point in the program either to reconstruct the program's path or to determine the values of variables. After all the errors have been dealt with, the trace output is typically removed from the source code since, naturally, it should not occur in the final program. If we find a new error at a later time then we have to reintroduce the trace output.

The class System.Diagnostics.Debug makes this functionality available conveniently and with some extra features:

```
public sealed class Debug {
    //----- properties
    public static TraceListenerCollection Listeners { get; }
    public static int IndentLevel { get; set; }
    public static int IndentSize { get; set; }
    //----- methods
    public static void Assert(bool cond, string msg);
    public static void Indent();
    public static void Unindent();
    public static void Write(string msg)
    public static void WriteIf(bool cond, string msg);
    ...
}
```

The most important advantages of the Debug methods with respect to the "old-fashioned" trace output are the following:

- ❏ Reports can be sent to any number of destinations (*listeners*).
- ❏ The formatting of output (indentation) is directly supported.
- ❏ The user is informed about unfulfilled assertions.
- ❏ The compilation of the method calls for the trace output can be removed without changing the source code (*conditional compilation*).

Listeners

The static Write methods of the class Debug do not write directly to a medium but pass on the report to all registered System.Diagnostics.TraceListeners. By default, a System.Diagnostics.DefaultTraceListener is registered. It passes received information to the Log method of the class System.Diagnoistics.Debugger (and to a default debug output). So this information is not shown on the console during program execution, but instead, along with other output, in the output window of the .NET GUI debugger, if it has started the application (see Figure 8.2).

There is also an EventLogTraceListener in the .NET class library (for writing into Windows event logs) and a TextWriterTraceListener that passes its received reports to a System.IO.TextWriter or a System.IO.Stream. For example, if we wish both to receive debugging information on the console and to store it in a file, we must introduce the following two lines of code:

```
Debug.Listeners.Add(new TextWriterTraceListener(Console.Out));
Debug.Listeners.Add(new TextWriterTraceListener(File.Create("MyLog.txt")));
```

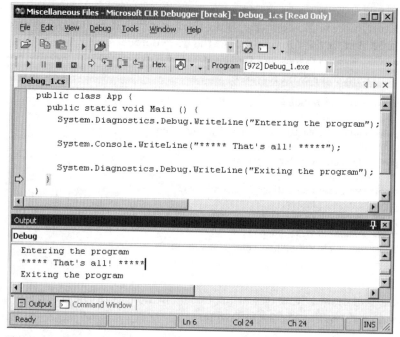

Figure 8.2 *Output of the DefaultTraceListener in the Windows debugger*

Formatting of the Output

We can use the methods Indent and Unindent to format the output clearly. For example, before each method call we can increase the IndentLevel by IndentSize (Indent()) and return to the former settings on return from the call (Unindent()). The following example calculates the Fibonacci numbers recursively and uses the Debug methods to display the recursive calls on the console.

```
using System;
using System.Diagnostics;

public class App {

    public static void Main(string[] args) {
        Debug.Listeners.Add(new TextWriterTraceListener(Console.Out));
        Debug.WriteLine("Entering program: " + DateTime.Now);
        int result = Fib(Convert.ToInt32(args[0]));
        Console.WriteLine("Fib({0}) = {1}", args[0], result);
        Debug.WriteLine("Exiting program: " + DateTime.Now);
    }
```

```
public static int Fib(int n) {
    int fib = n;
    Debug.Write("Fib(" + n + ") ");
    if (n > 1) {
        Debug.WriteLine("");
        Debug.Indent();
        fib = Fib(n-1) + Fib(n-2);
        Debug.Unindent();
    }
    Debug.WriteLine("= " + fib);
    return fib;
}
```

For example, the calculation of the third Fibonacci number produces the following output on the console (the parts shown in boldface are debug output):

```
> Fib 3
Entering program: 12/29/2003 12:49:32 AM
Fib(3)
   Fib(2)
      Fib(1) = 1
      Fib(0) = 0
   = 1
   Fib(1) = 1
= 2
Fib(3) = 2
Exiting program: 12/29/2003 12:49:32 AM
```

Conditional Output and Assertions

The methods WriteIf and Assert work according to a similar principle: They first test a condition and then print the output or do nothing, depending on the result of this test. The difference between these two types of methods is the following: the WriteIf methods—like the Write methods—notify all registered listeners if the condition is fulfilled.

The Assert methods, on the other hand, open a dialog window if the condition is *not* fulfilled. There the user must decide whether to continue or interrupt the program's execution or whether the program should be investigated with a debugger. Figure 8.3 shows the "Assertion Failed" dialog that is created by the program line

```
Debug.Assert(x != 0, "Division by Zero!");
```

in the case where x has the value 0.

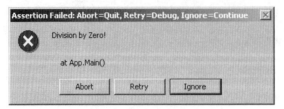

Figure 8.3 *"Assertion Failed" dialog*

Implicit Conditional Compilation

The special feature of all these calls to methods of the class Debug is that they are only translated by the compiler under a certain condition (*conditional compilation*). That means that the C# compiler actually generates code for these method calls only when the pre-processor symbol DEBUG is defined. In C# a pre-processor symbol can be defined in two ways:

❑ in the source code itself: #define DEBUG
❑ with a compiler option: /*define*: DEBUG

The nice thing about this is that we do not have to strew the source code with #ifdef and similar pre-processor statements. As a demonstration we compare the results (as CIL code) of two compilations of the Main method of the test program Debug_1.cs, shown in Figure 8.2:

```
csc Debug_1.cs                          csc /define:DEBUG Debug_1.cs

==>                                     ==>

                                        ldstr "Entering the program"
                                        call System.Diagnostics.Debug::WriteLine(string)
ldstr "***** That's all! *****"         ldstr "***** That's all! *****"
call System.Console::WriteLine(string)  call System.Console::WriteLine(string)
                                        ldstr "Exiting the program"
                                        call System.Diagnostics.Debug::WriteLine(string)
ret                                     ret
```


The Twin Class System.Diagnostics.Trace

There is yet a further class (System.Diagnostics.Trace) that offers the same functionality as Debug. The two are thus identical twins that are distinguished only by their names. The reason for having two functionally equivalent classes is that they are activated by different pre-processor symbols. Whereas the DEBUG symbol controls the compilation of the Debug methods, the Trace methods use the symbol TRACE. Thus we can distinguish outputs that are really only intended for debugging from others that should be used in every program execution. If you wish to make use of these we recommend using #define TRACE in the source code so as to be sure that all trace methods are always compiled. The debug methods should only be activated through the compiler option /define: DEBUG.

8.5   Further Tools

We have selected a few more tools from Table 8.1 to describe further. These are ones that appear to us to be particularly important.

8.5.1   IL Disassembler (ildasm.exe)

We warmly recommend the IL disassembler to anyone who likes to know what code the compiler has generated from their program. This tool lets you see clearly all the information in the metadata as well as the entire CIL code of each .NET type. This is available in a GUI platform or also as a text file or directly on the console.

To give an impression of this we have implemented an example type SomeType in C#. This is not actually a meaningful example, but it shows some of the possible components of a type.

```
class SomeType {
    const float MyConstant = 1.0f;
    static long MyStaticField = 2;
    static void MyStaticMethod (int firstParam) { MyStaticField += 3; }
    int MyField;
    float MyMethod () { return MyConstant; }
    int MyProperty { get { return 2; } set { System.Console.WriteLine(value); } }
    event System.EventHandler MyEvent;
}
```

The following two statements compile this program, held in the file ildasmDemo.cs, into the .NET module ILdasmDemo.mod and show its contents with the IL disassembler (see Figure 8.4):

```
csc /target:module /out:ILdasmDemo.mod ildasmDemo.cs
ildasm ILdasmDemo.mod
```

Each element of a type is represented by a particular symbol that reflects the kind of element. So methods are shown with squares, fields with diamonds, properties with different triangles; static components are additionally marked with an "S". After the symbol comes the name of the component, followed by its signature, which is separated from the name by a colon.

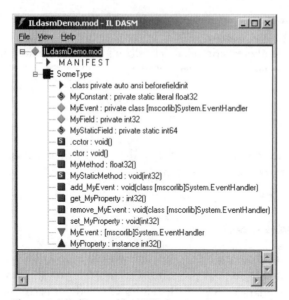

Figure 8.4 *IL disassembler (GUI) showing the contents of a module*

The IL disassembler view also shows that the compilers create many additional components that do not appear explicitly in the source code. For example, the compiler has generated a default constructor .ctor and a class constructor .cctor. In addition, we find further methods such as get_MyProperty or add_MyEvent that are necessary to implement properties and events.

Double-clicking on a component opens a further window that shows the CIL code of the component, as Figure 8.5 does for the method MyMethod and Figure 8.6 for the property MyProperty.

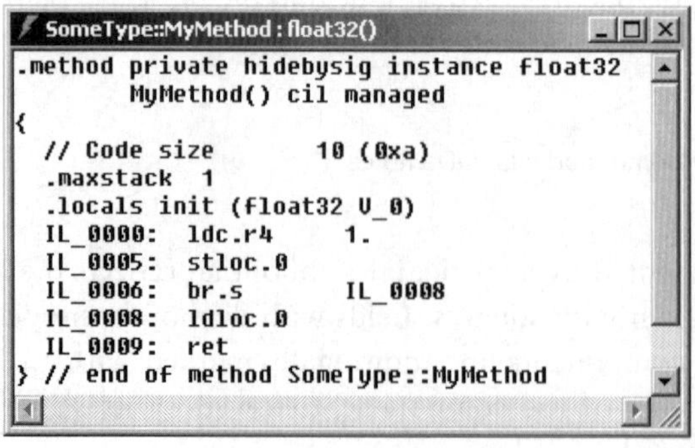

```
/ SomeType::MyMethod : float32()                    _ □ ×
.method private hidebysig instance float32
        MyMethod() cil managed
{
  // Code size          10 (0xa)
  .maxstack  1
  .locals init (float32 V_0)
  IL_0000:   ldc.r4       1.
  IL_0005:   stloc.0
  IL_0006:   br.s         IL_0008
  IL_0008:   ldloc.0
  IL_0009:   ret
} // end of method SomeType::MyMethod
```

Figure 8.5 *IL disassembler showing CIL code and metadata for a method*

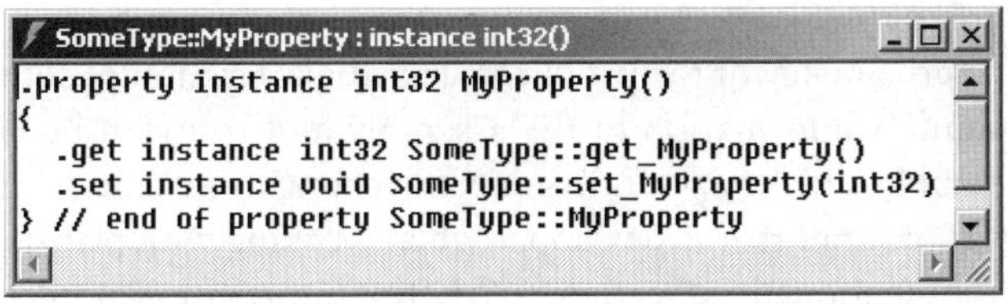

Figure 8.6 *IL disassembler showing CIL code and metadata for a property*

This additional information that is so conveniently arranged by the IL disassembler can often give the developer valuable evidence when trying to find an error in a program. It can also help one to understand the functioning of the CLR better and thus to write more efficient programs.

A good comprehensive overview of the metadata of a .NET module is obtained through the extended menu options by starting the IL disassembler with option /advance and then selecting View | MetaInfo | Show! from the menu (or by pressing control-M).

Customizing CIL Code Directly

The majority of programming languages support only a subset of the CTS (see Section 3.2). This means that the developer cannot exploit all the functions and characteristics of the CLR when using just one programming language. The IL disassembler can help here: for example, we can compile a C# program into an equivalent IL assembler program by using the /out=*filename* option for the disassembler, so that it will not start the graphical interface but instead will write the output to a text file. Because CIL is the language of the CLR itself, it actually supports all the subtleties of the CLR. It is possible to improve a program by making changes direct to the CIL code and then translating this to a .NET PE file by using the MSIL assembler (ilasm.exe).

8.5.2 Strong Name Tool (sn.exe)

Assemblies that are only used in the application directories—as private assemblies (see Section 3.6.2)—do not need strong names and as a rule you should try to use private assemblies because they are considerably easier to manage.

In many cases you will nonetheless wish to install an assembly in the Global Assembly Cache, distinguish different versions of an assembly or ensure that an assembly has not been altered by a third party. For these reasons you must underwrite an assembly with a digital signature through which it obtains a *strong name* (see Section 3.6.2) and can be used as a shared assembly. It is thus not sufficient merely to provide the four constituents (assembly name, version number, culture attribute and producer's public key). An assembly name only becomes "strong" when it is signed by the private key of the producer. This digital signature contains a hash value of the manifest information of the assembly and so it can be determined whether the assembly's files have undergone any change since the signing.

The *Strong Name Tool* supports the developer when working with private and public keys. As already mentioned in Section 3.6.2, the information needed for composing a strong name can be specified either by user-defined attributes in the source code or via options of the assembly linker (al.exe). Here we are only going into the attributes, because with these we can create a signed assembly with the compiler alone and without needing to use any further tool.

To be able to sign an assembly we first need a pair of private and public keys. Calling sn.exe with the -k option generates such a key pair and stores it in a file:

```
sn -k mykeys.snk
```

This command creates a 596-byte-long file mykeys.snk, which contains a 436-byte-long private key and a 128-byte-long public key (the remaining 32 bytes are used by header information). We now cross-reference this file with the option /keyfile for al.exe or with the attribute System.Reflection.AssemblyKeyFileAttribute in the source code so that the assembly linker or the compiler creates a signed assembly with a strong name:

```
In source code file MyLib.cs:
    [assembly: AssemblyKeyFile("mykeys.snk")]
csc /target:library MyLib.cs
```

However, this procedure is often not optimal because every developer must have access to the private key of an enterprise, which as a rule is something to be avoided. The private key should be accessed only once—namely immediately before distribution—by particularly trustworthy persons in order to sign the end product. This is described in the following section.

Delay Signing

To delay the signing we must first separate the public key from the private. This is achieved by using the /p option:

```
sn -p mykeys.snk mypubkey.snk
```

The file mypubkey.snk then contains only the public key and can be distributed to all developers without concern (they need the public key in order to create valid assembly references). The file mykeys.snk, which contains both the public and the private keys, is used later for signing. The developers use the public key as follows:

In source code file *MyLib.cs*:
```
[assembly: AssemblyKeyFile("mypubkey.snk")]
[assembly: AssemblyDelaySign(true)]
csc /target:library MyLib.cs
```

The attribute AssemblyDelaySign activates delay signing. The C# compiler finds only the public key in the file mypubkey.snk passed with AssemblyKeyFile and inserts it in the created assembly. Instead of the signature, the corresponding place in the assembly file is left empty. This can be filled by a digital signature at any later time. To do this we call sn.exe with the -R option:

```
sn -R MyLib.dll mykeys.snk
```

Now the assembly MyLib is fully signed and can be distributed. Figure 8.7 once again emphasizes the difference between direct signing during compilation and delay signing.

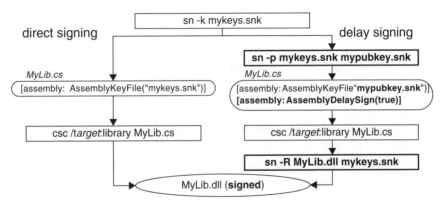

Figure 8.7 *Overview: difference between direct and delay signing of assemblies*

A more important difference between fully and partially signed assemblies is that partially signed assemblies can indeed be compiled and referenced from other assemblies but cannot be executed or installed in secure environments. A secure environment checks their signature before loading or installing assemblies. So, for example, a partially signed assembly cannot be installed in the Global Assembly Cache and applications that use such assemblies may not load them. If we wish to use one nonetheless, for test purposes, we must switch off the checking of the assembly's signature:

```
sn -Vr MyLib.dll
```

We can also give * here as the assembly file name in order to switch off the verification of the signatures for all assemblies. *,035a6638e5079673 suppresses the verification only for assemblies with a public key that corresponds to the given public key token. Optionally, a list of user names for which this setting should hold can follow the assembly name. The option -Vu reactivates the verification for the given assembly, -Vx for all assemblies, and -Vl lists all assemblies for which the checking has been de-activated. A short example of this: after the statement sequence

```
sn -Vr * Administrator
sn -Vr *,035a6638e5079673 Developer,Tester
sn -Vr MyLib.dll Tester
```

sn -Vl produces the following output:

```
Assembly/Strong Name              Users
==============================================
*,*                               Administrator
*,035a6638e5079673                Developer Tester
MyLib,035a6638e5079673            All users
```

This means that signature checking of MyLib.dll has been de-activated for all users. Assemblies with the public key token 035a6638e5079673 are not checked when used by Developer or Tester and the testing is generally omitted for administrators.

8.5.3   Assembly Cache Viewer (shfusion.dll)

As we have briefly mentioned in Section 3.6.2, assemblies can be registered with a strong name in a global data structure and are then available for all applications on the system. This data structure is called the *Global Assembly Cache* (GAC) and is held in the directory [c:\WINNT]\assembly. A special extension (plug-in) for Windows Explorer, the *Assembly Cache Viewer* (shfusion.dll), displays the assemblies in the GAC as if they were ordinary files with some special attributes (see Figure 8.8).

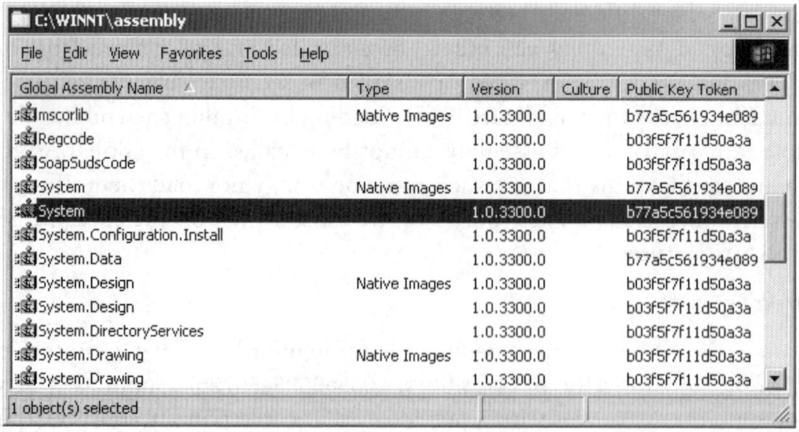

Figure 8.8 *Assembly Cache Viewer displays Global Assembly Cache in the Windows Explorer*

In Figure 8.8 it appears as if all the assemblies lie in the same directory. Because the version, culture and public key are not reflected in the file name of an assembly (which, by the way, must be identical to the assembly name), the GAC must maintain its own internal directory structure which allows assembly files with the same name to be distinguished. Anyone who wishes to know exactly what the directory structure looks like can simply navigate through the GAC directory from the command line. So the assembly System highlighted in Figure 8.8 is, for example, actually in the following place:

c:\WINNT\assembly\GAC\System\1.0.3300.0__b77a5c561934e089\System.dll

Thus each assembly name has its own directory. The names of the directories underneath are determined by the version number, culture code and public key token together. It is in these directories that the actual assembly files are stored.

The Assembly Cache Viewer supports drag-and-drop installation of assemblies in the GAC. Removal of assemblies from the GAC functions just like the familiar files in Windows Explorer.

Native image cache. Under .NET it is also possible to translate assemblies completely to machine code at the time of installation so as to avoid the delays caused by JIT compilation (with the *Native Image Generator*, ngen.exe). Such precompiled assemblies are similarly collected in a subdirectory of [c:\WINNT]\assembly and shown by the Assembly Cache Viewer with their type given as *Native Images*. The most important assemblies of the .NET Framework class library (for example, System (see Figure 8.8 above the highlighting)) also exist in pre-compiled versions.

Downloaded assembly cache. The Assembly Cache Viewer shows a subdirectory Download in the GAC directory. Here assemblies that have been downloaded from a server at run time are stored.

8.5.4 Global Assembly Cache Utility (gacutil.exe)

The *Global Assembly Cache Utility* is a tool that supports developers in managing the GAC. They can inspect the contents of the GAC (option -l), install assemblies in the GAC (-i) and de-install (-u) them. The downloaded assembly cache can also be managed: -ldl for showing the contents, -cdl for deleting all downloaded assemblies. This tool is very attractive for developers because they can automate the management of the GAC through scripts and so need not always do everything manually, as with the Assembly Cache Viewer (see Section 8.5.3). The following command line

gacutil -i GlobalLib.dll

installs the assembly file GlobalLib.dll in the GAC and

```
gacutil -u GlobalLib
```

removes the assembly GlobalLib from the GAC. The problem with this style of installing is that you never know whether there are still applications that are using the assembly and so will no longer function after the de-installation. For this reason you should use only the options -i and -u for testing during development. For installation for the end user Microsoft generally recommends the use of the *Microsoft Windows Installer* from version 2.0 (as delivered with Visual Studio .NET for example), because it keeps track of which global assemblies are used by which applications and removes an assembly from the GAC if it is no longer referenced by any other assembly.

But similar reference counters can be carried out with an option from gacutil. An r is appended to the corresponding operation, so -ir, -ur, -lr. After this come the four parameters: *Assembly, Scheme, Id, Description. Assembly* describes the name of the assembly, or—during installation—the name or path of the assembly file. *Scheme* defines the type of the reference, which can have the following values and on which the specification of the *Id* parameter depends:

❑ UNINSTALL_KEY: This type should be used by applications that register themselves during installation in the "Add/Remove Programs" dialog, which is achieved by an entry under HKEY_LOCAL_MACHINE\SOFTWARE\ Microsoft\Windows\CurrentVersion. The *Id* parameter must correspond exactly to the name of this registry entry. A program that has registered itself as ...\CurrentVersion**MyApp** in the registry installs the assembly MyLib.dll in the GAC in the following manner:

```
gacutil -ir MyLib.dll UNINSTALL_KEY MyApp "description"
```

❑ FILEPATH: This type should be used by applications that do not register themselves in the registry as described above. Here the parameter *Id* gives the complete path to the application file.

```
gacutil -ir MyLib.dll FILEPATH c:\Program Files\MyApp\MyApp.exe "description"
```

❑ OPAQUE: In the case that neither of the variants above seems suitable, here the *Id* parameter can contain any information. It must present this input in double quotes.

```
gacutil -ir MyLib.dll OPAQUE "arbitrary ID information" "description"
```

The concluding *Description* parameter can contain any description of the reference. It will be shown in the listing of references by gacutil -lr. To de-install a reference the same values of *Scheme, Id* and *Description* as were given on installation must be used. *Assembly* can only give the assembly name.

We will now look at a more detailed example.

```
gacutil -ir GlobalLib.dll FILEPATH c:\apps\MyApp.exe App
gacutil -ir GlobalLib.dll FILEPATH c:\libs\MyLib.dll Lib
```

These two installation statements place the assembly file GlobalLib.dll in the GAC only once, but note two references to it.

```
gacutil -ur GlobalLib FILEPATH c:\apps\MyApp.exe App
```

removes one of the two previously installed references to GlobalLib. However, the assembly remains in the cache. The following report is produced:

```
Assembly:  GlobalLib, Version=1.2.0.0, Culture=neutral,
            PublicKeyToken=035a6638e5079673, Custom=null
Removed reference:
    SCHEME: <FILEPATH>  ID: <c:\apps\MyApp.exe> DESCRIPTION : <App>
Pending references:
    SCHEME: <FILEPATH>  ID: <c:\libs\MyLib.dll>  DESCRIPTION : <Lib>

Number of items uninstalled = 0
Number of failures = 0
```

Now all assemblies that are still referenced can no longer be accidentally deleted. The command

```
gacutil -u GlobalLib
```

produces the following error report:

```
Assembly:  GlobalLib, Version=1.2.0.0, Culture=neutral,
            PublicKeyToken=035a6638e5079673, Custom=null
Unable to uninstall: assembly is required by one or more applications
Pending references:
    SCHEME: <FILEPATH>  ID: <c:\libs\MyLib.dll>  DESCRIPTION : <Lib>

Number of items uninstalled = 0
Number of failures = 0
```

Here, it is interesting to note that the reference was actually tested. That means that if the file c:\libs\MyLib.dll had not existed, then the assembly GlobalLib would have been deleted (however, this is not tested on installation!). Naturally, the user also has the power to enforce the deletion of an assembly (adding f for force).

```
gacutil -uf GlobalLib
```

removes the assembly from the GAC in all circumstances, without concern for how many applications might still reference it.

8.6   Exercises

1. **Strong name tool (sn.exe).** Make a file MyLib.cs that contains the follow code:

    ```
    public class MyLib {
        public static int getTen () { return 10; }
    }
    ```

    If you want to install this file into the *Global Assembly Cache* (GAC) it needs a strong name and a signature. Use the *Strong Name Tool* (sn.exe) to generate a public/private key pair and then adapt the source code such that the compiler will produce the signed assembly MyLib.dll.

2. **Global assembly cache utility (gacutil.exe).** Now use the *Global Assembly Cache Utility* (gacutil.exe) to install the assembly MyLib.dll produced in the previous exercise. Then list the contents of the GAC to check that your assembly has actually been installed. Finally, delete it from the GAC.

    Also try to install the original *unsigned* version of MyLib.dll to verify that this does not work.

3. **Delay signing.** Here you can again use the public/private key pair file and the original source code of MyLib.cs from Exercise 1. Extract the public key from the key file and adapt the source code so that the compiler does not sign the assembly immediately but rather prepares it for delay signing using only the public key.

    Now try installing the unsigned assembly in the GAC. This should fail. Therefore, delay sign the assembly with the original key file. Now installation in the GAC should work. Try it, but do not forget to remove your test assembly from the GAC when you have finished the exercise.

4. **Debug output.** The following program creates a little GUI with a text box to enter integer amounts, a button, and a label to display the result of adding the amount in the text box to the current total after the button has been clicked.

    ```
    using System; using System.Windows.Forms;

    class Adder : Form {
        TextBox amount = new TextBox();
        Button b = new Button();
        Label total = new Label();

        Adder () {
            amount.Left = 10; amount.Top = 10;
            Controls.Add(amount);

            b.Text = "ADD";
            b.Left = 10; b.Top = 40;
            b.Click += new EventHandler(Add);
            Controls.Add(b);
    ```

```
                total.Text = "0";
                total.Left = 10; total.Top = 70;
                Controls.Add(total);
            }

            private void Add (object sender, EventArgs eargs) {
                total.Text = ( Convert.ToInt32(amount.Text) +
                            Convert.ToInt32(total.Text)).ToString();
            }

            public static void Main () { Application.Run(new Adder()); }
        }
```

Extend this program so that it logs all entered amounts in a file "amount.log".
You should always reuse the same file, once it has been created. Each logging
session shows the current date and time in a header line and then lists the
amounts, each in a separate line and indented from the header line. The contents of a sample log file could look like this:

```
1/19/2004 8:42:50 AM
    78
    5
    0
    -43
1/19/2004 8:43:54 AM
    6
    9
    9
1/19/2004 8:44:24 AM
    -45
    0
    12
```

5. **Assert dialogs.** Use the source code from the previous example and extend it
   in such a way that it will display an assertion-fail dialog if a negative amount
   is entered in the text box, and a different dialog, if the input does not represent an integer number.

9 A Preview of .NET 2.0

Microsoft .NET is an evolving system that is continuously improved and extended. In late 2003 Microsoft announced .NET 2.0 (codename *Whidbey*) as a major new version of .NET; a beta release of it will be available in spring 2004. Version 2.0 will offer a wealth of new features in almost every part of .NET. There are language extensions to C# and the other .NET languages, new library classes, and improved functionality for ADO.NET, ASP.NET and web services.

At the time when this book was written, .NET 2.0 was only available as an alpha release. Since there are probably many details that will change before the final release, we decided not to integrate the new features into the regular chapters of our book but instead to provide you with a separate preview chapter that shows you what to expect from .NET in the future.

9.1 New Features in C#

The major new features in C# 2.0 are *generics*, *anonymous methods*, *iterators* and *partial types*. We will have a look at them now.

9.1.1 Generics

In many cases a class should be able to work with arbitrary types of data. The common solution to this is to let the class work with elements of type object, with which all data types are compatible. The problem, however, is that the compiler cannot guarantee that those elements are of a particular type. Furthermore, when an element is retrieved from the class you have to apply a type cast in order to convert it from object to its real data type. Generics are a better solution to this problem.

A generic type is a class, struct, interface or delegate that is parameterized with one or more other types. The type parameters are *placeholders* for concrete types such as int or string that are provided later.

Let us look at an example. If we want to implement a generic Buffer class, we could do it like this:

```
class Buffer<Element> {
   private Element[] data = ...;
   public void Put(Element x) {...}
   public Element Get() {...}
}
```

Element is a placeholder that is written in angle brackets after the class name. It can be used like an ordinary type in the declaration of the data array or the parameters of Put and Get.

When Buffer is used in a declaration (i.e. when it is *instantiated*) its placeholder must be substituted by a real type, for example:

```
Buffer<int> intBuf = new Buffer<int>();
intBuf.Put(3);
int x = intBuf.Get();
```

This example declares a buffer whose elements are statically defined to be of type int. This means that the compiler can check that all values that are passed to Put are of type int. Likewise, the method Get returns an int value (not an object value that has to be cast to an int value first). This not only makes the program more readable but also more efficient, since type casts become unnecessary. Of course, we could also use Buffer to declare a buffer of strings:

```
Buffer<string> stringBuf = new Buffer<string>();
stringBuf.Put("John");
string s = stringBuf.Get();
```

Again, the compiler makes sure that only strings are passed to Put and it knows that the value returned by Get is a string.

Not only classes but also structs, interfaces and delegates can be declared to be generic by parameterizing them with a placeholder type:

```
struct Stack<ElemType> {...}
interface ITokenReader<TokenType> {...}
delegate bool Matches<T>(T value);
```

Constraints

Our class Buffer just stores the elements in the data array but does not perform any operations on them. If the elements are to be compared, however, or if some methods are to be called on them, the compiler must know which operations can be applied to Element variables. This can be specified with a *constraint* that declares the placeholder to be of some minimum type.

Assume that we want to have a class OrderedBuffer which stores a collection of elements sorted by priorities. The priorities can be of any type but they must be comparable. Thus we have to declare OrderedBuffer with a constraint on the placeholder Priority:

```
class OrderedBuffer<Element, Priority> where Priority: IComparable {
    const int size = 100;
    Element[] data = new Element[size];
    Priority[] prio = new Priority[size];
    int lastElem = -1;

    public void Put(Element x, Priority p) { // insert x and p sorted by priority
        int i = lastElem;
        while (i >= 0 && p.CompareTo(prio[i]) > 0) {
            data[i+1] = data[i]; prio[i+1] = prio[i];
            i--;
        }
        data[i+1] = x; prio[i+1] = p;
        lastElem++;
    }

    public void Get(out Element x, out Priority p) {
        x = data[lastElem]; p = prio[lastElem]; lastElem--;
    }
}
```

The where clause in the header of the class specifies that the placeholder Priority must implement the interface IComparable. Therefore the compiler knows that the method CompareTo can be applied to the parameter p in the method Put. If OrderedBuffer is instantiated in a declaration like this:

```
OrderedBuffer<string, int> buf = new OrderedBuffer<string, int>();
```

the compiler checks that the type that is substituted for Priority implements the interface IComparable (which is the case for int). We can use the variable buf now to enter data and priorities:

```
buf.Put("network", 10);
buf.Put("printer", 5);
string device; int priority;
buf.Get(out device, out priority);   // device == "network", priority == 10
```

We can also specify multiple constraints for the placeholders:

```
class OrderedBuffer<Element, Priority>
    where Element: MyBaseClass
    where Priority: IComparable, ISerializable {
    ...
}
```

In this example the type substituted for Element must be derived from a class MyBaseClass and the type substituted for Priority must implement the interfaces IComparable and ISerializable.

In addition to classes and interfaces a constraint can also specify a *constructor clause* which is written as new(), for example:

```
class Buffer<Element> where Element: ISerializable, new() {...}
```

This means that the placeholder must be substituted by a class with a parameter-less constructor so that Buffer can create and initialize Element objects.

Generic Types and Inheritance

Like normal classes, a generic class can inherit from another class and implement several interfaces. Both the base class and the interfaces can be generic. Our class Buffer<Element>, for example, could be derived from a class List<Element>, which provides the methods Add and Remove for implementing the buffer:

```
class Buffer<Element>: List<Element> {
    ...
    public void Put(Element x) { this.Add(x); } // Add is inherited from List
}
```

The type that is substituted for Element in Buffer is also substituted for Element in List.

A generic type can inherit from a normal type, from an instantiated generic type, or from a generic type with the same placeholder, so:

```
class A<X>: B {...}          // extending a normal type
class A<X>: B<int> {...}     // extending an instantiation of a generic type
class A<X>: B<X> {...}       // extending a generic type with the same placeholder
```

A normal class, however, can never inherit from a generic type. The following declaration is therefore illegal:

```
class A: B<X> {...}
```

In the same way that classes can be derived from generic types, interfaces can be derived from generic interfaces.

Assignment Compatibility Between Generic Types

Generic subtypes are compatible with their base types. Assume that we have the following declarations:

```
class B<X>: A {...}
class C<X>: B<X> {...}
```

We can perform the assignments:

```
A a = new B<int>();             // OK, B<int> is a subtype of A
a = new C<string>();            // OK, C<string> is an indirect subtype of A
B<float> b = new C<float>();    // OK, C<float> is a subtype of B<float>
```

However, the assignment

```
B<int> b = new C<short>();
```

is illegal, because C<short> is not a subtype of B<int>. The compiler will report an error.

Overriding Methods in Generic Classes

If a method of an instantiated generic base type is overridden in a subtype, any placeholder that appears as a parameter type in the base method is substituted by the corresponding concrete type:

```
class MyBuffer: Buffer<int> {
    public override void Put(int x) {...}        // Element is substituted by int
}
```

However, if a method from a non-instantiated generic base type is overridden, the placeholder is not substituted:

```
class MyBuffer<Element>: Buffer<Element> {
    public override void Put(Element x) {...} // Element is not substituted
}
```

Run-time Checks

Like any other type, an instantiated generic type (for example, Buffer<int>) can be used in type tests and type casts:

```
Buffer<int> buf = new Buffer<int>();
object obj = buf;            // the dynamic type of obj is Buffer<int>
...
if (obj is Buffer<int>)        // run-time type test; returns true here
    buf = (Buffer<int>) obj;    // type cast
```

Generic types can even be used in reflection, for example:

```
Type t = typeof(Buffer<int>);
Console.WriteLine(t.FullName);// prints Buffer[[System.Int32,...]]
```

Generic Methods

Although methods are not types, they too can be generic, that is, they can be parameterized with other types. In this way it is possible to implement a method that is applicable to data of arbitrary types. Here is an example of a Sort routine that can be used to sort any array whose elements implement the interface IComparable.

```
static void Sort<T>(T[] a) where T: IComparable {
    for (int i = 0; i < a.Length-1; i++) {
        for (int j = i+1; j < a.Length; j++) {
            if (a[j].CompareTo(a[i]) < 0) { T x = a[i]; a[i] = a[j]; a[j] = x; }
        }
    }
}
```

This method can now be used as follows:

```
int[] a = {5, 4, 7, 3, 1};
Sort<int>(a);
```

The C# compiler is even clever enough to derive the type that should be substituted for the placeholder from the type of the parameter a, so we can just write:

```
Sort(a);
```

Notice that we could also have implemented Sort as a non-generic method Sort(object[] a). The difference is that the compiler can check that the parameter of the generic method is an int array while for the non-generic case the compiler cannot even check that the elements of the parameter array support the interface IComparable.

Null Values

For any placeholder T there is a value T.default that denotes the null value of the corresponding concrete type:

```
class A<T> {
    T a = 0;            // illegal; the compiler reports an error
    T b = null;         // illegal; the compiler reports an error
    T c = T.default;    // OK; assigns 0, null, false, or '\0' depending on the concrete type
}
```

If x is declared with a placeholder type T the check

```
if (x == null) ...
```

does a null check if T was substituted by a reference type, otherwise it yields false.

How Generic Types are Implemented

If we declare a generic class Buffer<Element> the compiler generates CIL code that serves as a template for later instantiations. When the class is instantiated the JIT compiler creates code for different concrete classes depending on whether the placeholder was substituted by a value type or by a reference type.

For every value type V that is substituted for the placeholder Element the JIT compiler creates a concrete class Buffer<V>, whereas all reference types R that are substituted for Element share a common implementation of the class Buffer<R>:

```
Buffer<int> a = new Buffer<int>();          // creates a class Buffer<int>
Buffer<int> b = new Buffer<int>();          // reuses Buffer<int>
Buffer<float> c = new Buffer<float>();       // creates a class Buffer<float>
Buffer<string> d = new Buffer<string>();     // creates a class Buffer<refType>
Buffer<Person> e = new Buffer<Person>();     // reuses Buffer<refType>
```

9.1.2 Anonymous Methods

Anonymous methods simplify the use of delegates. Let us explain this with an example. Assume that we have a dialog window with a text box and a button. Whenever the button is clicked the numeric value of the text box should be added to a local sum. Thus we install a delegate for the Click event of the button:

```
public class Sample {
    Button button = new Button("Add");
    TextBox amount = new TextBox();
    int sum = 0;

    void AddAmount(object sender, EventArgs e) {
        sum += Convert.ToInt32(amount.Text);
    }
    public void Run() {
        ...
        button.Click += new EventHandler(AddAmount);
    }
}
```

This works fine, but it is slightly inconvenient, since we have to declare a method AddAmount just to execute a single statement in response to a button click. We have to invent a name for this method. Even worse, the method cannot be local to Run and so the variables that are accessed in AddAmount cannot be local either.

Anonymous methods allow us to specify the body of AddAmount right at the place where it is assigned to the Click event:

```
public class Sample {
    public void Run() {
        Button button = new Button("Add");
        TextBox amount = new TextBox;
        int sum = 0;
        button.Click = delegate (object sender, EventArgs e) {
            sum += Convert.ToInt32(amount.Text);
        };
    }
}
```

An anonymous method consists of the keyword delegate, an optional formal parameter list and a method body. No name has to be invented for such a method and
its body can access the local variables of the enclosing method Run. If the formal
parameters are not used in the body of the anonymous method (as in our example)
they can be omitted, so we can just write:

```
button.Click = delegate { sum += Convert.ToInt32(amount.Text); };
```

While speaking about delegates it is worth mentioning that the creation of delegate objects is simplified in C# 2.0. Instead of having to write

```
button.Click += new EventHandler(AddAmount);
```

we can just write

```
button.Click += AddAmount;
```

The compiler will derive the type of the delegate object that is to be created from
the type of the Click event.

9.1.3   Iterators

The foreach loop is a convenient way to iterate over collections. In order to be
able to do this, however, the collection has to implement the interface IEnumerable
from the namespace System.Collections. This requires the methods MoveNext and
Reset to be implemented, as well as the property Current (see Section 4.1.1). C#
2.0 offers a simpler solution for that. If a class has a method

```
public IEnumerator GetEnumerator() {...}
```

that contains one or more *yield statements* then it is possible to apply a foreach
statement to objects of this class. Let us look at an example. Assume that we have
a class Store that maintains a set of fruits. If we want to iterate over these fruits we
have to implement a method GetEnumerator as follows:

```
class Store {
    Fruit apple = new Fruit("apple", ...);
    Fruit orange = new Fruit("orange", ...);
    Fruit banana = new Fruit("banana", ...);

    public IEnumerator GetEnumerator() {
        yield return apple;
        yield return orange;
        yield return banana;
    }
}
```

The yield statements return a sequence of fruits and the foreach loop can be used
to iterate over them:

```
Store store = new Store();
foreach (Fruit fruit in store) Console.WriteLine(fruit.name); // apple, orange, banana
```

Note that the class Store no longer has to implement IEnumerable but just provides a GetEnumerator method, which is automatically transformed into a method that returns an object of a compiler-generated class _Enumerator:

```
class _Enumerator: IEnumerator {
    public object Current { get {...} }
    public bool MoveNext() {...}
    public void Dispose() {...}
}
```

The above foreach loop is then translated to:

```
IEnumerator _e = store.GetEnumerator();
try {
    while (_e.MoveNext()) Console.WriteLine(((Fruit)_e.Current).name);
} finally {
    if (_e != null) _e.Dispose();
}
```

Every call to MoveNext runs to the next yield statement, which stores the yielded value in a private field from where it can be retrieved by Current.

Instead of IEnumerator, the method GetEnumerator should preferably use the return type IEnumerator<Fruit> (declared in System.Collections.Generic). In this way the property Current will return a value of type Fruit instead of type object and the type cast in the translated form of the foreach loop can be omitted.

The yield statement comes in two forms. The statement

```
yield return expression;
```

yields a value for the next iteration of the foreach loop. The type of *expression* must be T if the return type of GetEnumerator is IEnumerator<T>, otherwise a value of type object is returned. The statement

```
yield break;
```

terminates the foreach loop and does not yield a value.

Specific Iterators

In addition to the standard iterator GetEnumerator, a class can also implement any number of more specific iterators, which are methods or properties with the type IEnumerable (or IEnumerable<T>) that contain a yield statement. The following class demonstrates this by providing three ways for iterating over a private data array:

```
class MyList {
    int[] data = ...;

    public IEnumerator<int> GetEnumerator() {        // standard iterator
        for (int i = 0; i < data.Length; i++) yield return data[i];
    }

    public IEnumerable<int> Range(int from, int to) {    // specific iterator method
        for (int i = from; i <= to; i++) yield return data[i];
    }

    public IEnumerable<int> Downwards {                // specific iterator property
        get {
            for (int i = data.Length-1; i >= 0; i--) yield return data[i];
        }
    }
}
```

Note that specific iterators return IEnumerable<T> while a standard iterator returns IEnumerator<T>. These iterators can now be used as follows:

```
MyList list = new MyList();
foreach (int x in list) Console.WriteLine(x);
foreach (int x in list.Range(2, 7)) Console.WriteLine(x);
foreach (int x in list.Downwards) Console.WriteLine(x);
```

For those who are interested in the implementation of all this: the method Range is transformed into a method that returns a compiler-generated object of type IEnumerable<int>, which has a GetEnumerator method that returns a compiler-generated object of type IEnumerator<int>, which is then used in the foreach loop as explained above. Quite tricky, isn't it? But as a programmer you don't have to care about it.

9.1.4 Partial Types

Classes, structs and interfaces are usually implemented in a single file, which is good, because it promotes readability and maintainability. In some cases, however, it makes sense to split up a type's implementation into several files. In C# 2.0 this can be done by declaring a type with the modifier partial.

The following example shows a type C whose source code is split into two parts implemented in the files Part1.cs and Part2.cs.

```
// this code is in file Part1.cs
public partial class C {
    int x;
    public void M1() {...}
}
```

```
// this code is in file Part2.cs
public partial class C {
    string y;
    public void M2() {...}
}
```

Although the separation of a type into several files should be the exception it can have advantages occasionally:

❑ The members of a type can be grouped according to their functionality.
❑ Several developers can work on a type concurrently because each of them is using his or her own file.
❑ Parts of a type can be generated by a program while others can be written by hand. In this way it is easier to separate machine-generated parts from hand-written ones. If the generated parts are re-created they don't have to be merged with the hand-written parts.

9.2   New Features in the Base Class Library

The Base Class Library (BCL) provides a rich set of types for rapid application development. Under .NET 2.0 some weaknesses of this library were removed and new functionality was added. Existing features were improved (for example, better graphics performance, simplified file access and a more powerful class Console) and new features were added (for example, a web browser control for Windows forms, as well as new namespaces for generic collections and for data protection). In this section we will go through a few of the most important new features.

9.2.1   Generic Collections

The new namespace System.Collections.Generic provides support for generic collections, which offer a better performance for strongly typed elements than traditional collections do. The most important classes of this namespace are List<T>, Stack<T>, Queue<T>, Dictionary<T, U> and SortedDictionary<T, U>. They offer the same methods as the traditional collection classes with the exception that all elements in the collections are strongly typed. The following example shows the creation and use of a List (which is the generic counterpart of ArrayList):

```
// create a list of strings
List<string> list = new List<string>();
// add three strings
list.Add("Mike");
list.Add("Andrew");
list.Add("Susan");
```

```
// retrieve an element from the list
string s = list[0]; // no type cast necessary!
Console.WriteLine(s);
// sort the list
list.Sort();
foreach(string s in list) Console.WriteLine(s);
```

Here are the most important methods of class List:

```
class List<T> : IList<T>, ICollection<T>, IEnumerable<T>, IList, ICollection, IEnumerable {
    public virtual T this[int pos] {get; set;}        // indexer
    public virtual void Clear();                       // clears the list
    public virtual int Add(T item);                    // adds an element
    public void AddRange(ICollection<T> c);            // adds the collection c
    public virtual void Insert(int pos, T item);       // inserts an element at position pos
    public void InsertRange(int pos, ICollection<T> c); // inserts the collection c at pos
    public virtual void Remove(T item);                // removes an element
    public virtual void RemoveAt(int pos);             // removes an element at pos
    public virtual bool Contains(T item);              // checks if item is in the list
    public virtual int IndexOf(T item);                // returns the first position of item
    public int LastIndexOf(T item);                    // returns the last position of item
    public List.Enumerator<T> GetEnumerator();         // returns a generic enumerator
    public int BinarySearch(T item);                   // searches for the element item
    public void Sort();              // sorts the list using the elements' CompareTo method
    public void CopyTo(T[] array); // copies the elements into a existing array of type T
    public T[] ToArray();          // converts the list to a new array of type T[]
    ...
}
```

Reflection Support for Generic Types

The classes of the namespace System.Reflection now also support the introspection of generic types and their members as well as dynamic loading of such types, instance creation and method invocation. In addition to that, the class System.Type adds properties and methods for reading information about generic types:

```
public abstract class Type : MemberInfo, IReflect {
    // checks if this type is a generic (non-instantiated) type
    public virtual bool IsGenericTypeDefinition {get;}:
    // checks if this generic type has type parameters (concrete types or placeholders)
    public virtual bool HasGenericParameters {get;}:
    // returns the type parameters of a generic type (both instantiated and non-instantiated)
    public virtual Type[] GetGenericParameters()
    // checks if this type is a placeholder of a generic type
    public virtual bool IsGenericParameter {get;}
    // returns the position of this placeholder type in a list of generic parameter types
    public virtual int GenericParameterPosition {get;}
    ...
}
```

9.2.2 New Features of Class Console

The current version of System.Console has methods for reading from and writing to the console. The new version offers additional features such as text positioning, foreground and background colours and the ability to move text within the screen buffer. It is even possible to set the size of the console window and the screen buffer programmatically. The property KeyAvailable allows waiting for user input without a blocking read operation. The following example shows how the new features improve text output:

```
// save the properties of the console window
int wWidth  = Console.WindowWidth;
int wHeight = Console.WindowHeight;
int sbWidth = Console.BufferWidth;
int sbHeight = Console.BufferHeight;

// set the new size of the console window and screen buffer
Console.SetWindowSize(24, 9);
Console.SetBufferSize(24, 9);

Console.Clear();
Console.WriteLine("Press key to continue...");
Console.ForegroundColor = ConsoleColor.Yellow;
for(int i = 3; i < 6; i++) {
    Console.SetCursorPosition(11, i);
    Console.Write("@ @ @");
}
while (!Console.KeyAvailable) {}

// restore the original settings
Console.ResetColor(); // restores the original system colours
Console.SetBufferSize(sbWidth, sbHeight);
Console.SetWindowSize(wWidth, wHeight);
```

Figure 9.1 shows the output of this program.

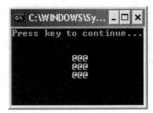

Figure 9.1 *New console features (the block of @@@ is written in yellow)*

9.2.3 New Network Protocols

The namespaces System.Net and System.Net.Sockets which are used for network communication were extended by new protocols that come in addition to the already existing file protocol (FileWebRequest, FileWebResponse) and HTTP protocol (HttpWebRequest, HttpWebResponse).

Managed FTP Support

System.Net now offers a managed FTP (file transfer protocol) implementation. The classes FtpWebRequest and FtpWebResponse extend the abstract classes WebRequest and WebResponse to allow FTP connections. The following example shows how to establish an FTP connection and get the size of a file myfile.exe by using the FTP command GetFileSize:

```
Uri serverUri = new Uri("ftp://dotnet.jku.at/myfile.exe");
FtpWebRequest request = WebRequest.Create(serverUri) as FtpWebRequest;
request.Method = FtpMethods.GetFileSize;
FtpWebResponse response = request.GetResponse() as FtpWebResponse;
Console.WriteLine("file size: " + response.ContentLength);
```

The struct type FtpMethods defines the various FTP commands as strings:

```
public struct FtpMethods {
    public const string AppendFile;
    public const string DeleteFile;
    public const string DownloadFile;
    public const string GetFileSize;
    public const string ListDirectory;
    public const string UploadFile;
}
```

A Simple Managed Web Server

The new class HttpWebListener represents a simple managed web server, which is able to listen to HTTP requests. At the time when this book was written, this web server was only supported for the *Windows Server 2003* operating system family. The following code creates a managed web server instance:

```
HttpWebListener listener = new HttpWebListener();
// adds a URI, which this server is intended to handle
listener.AddPrefix(@"http://localhost:8080/");
// starts the server in order to listen for incoming HTTP requests
listener.Start();
```

After the server has been started and URI prefixes added, the server waits for incoming HTTP requests. A request can be handled as follows:

```
// wait for a HTTP request
ListenerWebRequest request = listener.GetRequest();
// when a request is received we use a response object to send back an HTML page
ListenerWebResponse response = request.GetResponse();
// create a byte array that contains an HTML page
byte[] buf = Encoding.UTF8.GetBytes("<HTML><BODY>Simple managed web server" +
    "</BODY></HTML>");
// write the buffer to the response stream
response.ContentLength = buf.Length;
Stream rs = response.GetResponseStream();
rs.Write(buf, 0, buf.Length);
// close the stream, the response and request connection
rs.Close();
response.Close();
request.Close();
```

Network Information

The new namespace System.Net.NetworkInformation allows the collecton of network statistics. Its classes can be used to get information about UDP, TCP/IP and ICMP listeners on the local host as well as statistics about local network interfaces (e.g. Ethernet cards or wireless cards). The class NetworkInformation is the main class of this namespace. It offers the following properties, methods and events:

```
public class NetworkInformation {
    // properties
    public string DomainName {get;}
    public string HostName {get;}

    ...
    // methods
    public ActiveUdpListener[] GetActiveUdpListeners();
    public IcmpV4Statistics GetIcmpV4Statistics();
    public IcmpV6Statistics GetIcmpV6Statistics();
    public bool GetIsConnected();
    public NetworkInterface[] GetNetworkInterfaces();
    public TcpConnection[] GetTcpConnections();
    public TcpStatistics GetTcpStatistics(AddressFamily family);
    public UdpStatistics GetUdpStatistics(AddressFamily family);

    ...
    // events
    NetworkInformation.AddressChangedEventHandler AddressChanged;
}
```

The following example shows how to use the class NetworkInformation to gather information about the TCP protocol stack:

```
// create a NetworkInformation instance
NetworkInformation ni = new NetworkInformation();
// retrieve the TCP information according to the IPv4 (Internet protocol version 4) family
```

```
TcpStatistics tcpStats = ni.GetTcpStatistics(AddressFamily.InterNetwork);
// print the no. of accepted connections as well as the no. of segments sent and received
Console.WriteLine("Connections accepted: {0}", tcpStats.ConnectionsAccepted);
Console.WriteLine("Segments sent: {0}", tcpStats.SegmentsSent);
Console.WriteLine("Segments received: {0}", tcpStats.SegmentsReceived);
```

The ouput of this program could look as follows:

```
Connections accepted: 2
Segments sent: 110
Segments received: 109
```

9.2.4   Data Protection API (DPAPI)

The current BCL version contains a namespace System.Security.Cryptography that helps developers to protect their applications by cryptography. In the new BCL this namespace is enhanced to allow the use of the *data protection API*, which is provided by Windows 2000 and its successors. The classes ProtectedData and ProtectedMemory allow users to protect data by calling the methods Protect and Unprotect, which encrypt or decrypt data arrays using just a single line of code. Both ProtectedData and ProtectedMemory are managed wrappers for the native DPAPI functionality. The DPAPI uses the machine or user credentials to protect or unprotect the given data. The interface of the class ProtectedData is shown here:

```
public sealed class ProtectedData {
    public static byte[] Protect(byte[] data, byte[] optEntropy, DataProtectionScope s);
    public static byte[] Unprotect(byte[] data, byte[] optEntropy, DataProtectionScope s);
}
```

The methods take an array data, which represents the data to be protected. The array optEntropy may contain arbitrary bytes that are used as an additional key when encrypting and decrypting data. Both methods return a byte array, which contains the encrypted or decrypted data. The enumeration s of type DataProtectionScope specifies in which context the data is allowed to be decrypted:

```
public enum DataProtectionScope {
    CurrentUser,   // the encrypted data is associated with the current user context
    LocalMachine  // the encrypted data is associated with the local machine
}
```

In contrast to ProtectedData, the class ProtectedMemory encrypts and decrypts the data directly in data without returning a new byte array:

```
public sealed class ProtectedMemory {
    public static void Protect(byte[] data, MemoryProtectionScope scope);
    public static void Unprotect(byte[] data, MemoryProtectionScope scope);
}
```

The enumeration MemoryProtectionScope is defined as follows:

```
public enum MemoryProtectionScope {
    CrossProcess,   // all code in any process can unprotect the data
    SameLogon,      // all code within the same user context can unprotect the data
    SameProcess     // all code within the same process can unprotect the data
}
```

The following example shows how to protect a data array with DPAPI calls:

```
using System;
using System.Text;
using System.Security.Cryptography;

public class DPAPI_Example {
    public static void Main() {
        byte[] secret = Encoding.ASCII.GetBytes("secret data!");
        byte[] entropy = { 0, 1, 3, 8 };
        try {
            Console.WriteLine("Data to encrypt: {0}\n",
                    Encoding.ASCII.GetString(secret));
            // get the encrypted data
            byte[] cypher = ProtectedData.Protect(secret, entropy,
                    DataProtectionScope.CurrentUser );
            Console.WriteLine("Encrypted data: \n{0}\n",
                    Encoding.ASCII.GetString(cypher));
            // now unprotect the data again
            byte[] plain = ProtectedData.Unprotect(cypher, entropy,
                    DataProtectionScope.CurrentUser );
            Console.WriteLine("Decrypted data: {0}\n", Encoding.ASCII.GetString(plain));
        } catch (CryptographicException) {
            Console.WriteLine("Data was not encrypted!");
        }
    }
}
```

The result is shown in Figure 9.2.

Figure 9.2 *Console output of the DPAPI example*

9.2.5   Graphics and Windows Forms Improvements

.NET 2.0 offers a multitude of enhancements for the development of graphical user interfaces under Windows. While the BCL 1.1 provides a basic set of Windows forms controls, the BCL 2.0 enriches this set by new controls and by adding new functionality to some existing controls. We give just a few examples here.

WinBar

The new WinBar control replaces the existing ToolBar control and adds the possibility to customize the visual representation of a toolbar. Whereas a ToolBar can only contain basic controls such as buttons, the WinBars also allow combo boxes, text fields, drop-down lists and many other controls. The old ToolBar still exists in the new BCL for backward compatibility. The following example shows a ComboBox as a member of a WinBar:

```
using System.Windows.Forms;

public class WinBarExample : Form {

  public WinBarExample() {
    WinBar wb = new WinBar();
    wb.Controls.Add(new ComboBox());
    this.Controls.Add(wb);
  }

  public static void Main(string[] args) {
    Application.Run(new WinBarExample());
  }
}
```

The result is shown in Figure 9.3.

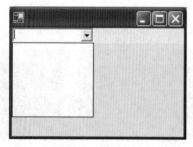

Figure 9.3 *WinBar with a ComboBox*

Layout Enhancements

A set of new classes simplifies the layout of controls in a Windows form. The class SplitContainer, for example, is able to represent two controls that are separated by a horizontal or vertical splitter bar, which can be moved by the user to change the split view. The classes FlowLayoutPanel and TableLayoutPanel offer new layout styles that decrease the amount of code for placing controls in a window.

Additional Features

An interesting new feature of TextBoxes and ComboBoxes is the AutoCompleteMode, which allows these controls to complete the user's input automatically by choosing from a given collection of text sources or from previously entered input texts.

The new Flash method of the Windows Form class enables the form to give the user a visual notification by flashing the title bar of the form until the method StopFlash is called.

9.3   New Features in ADO.NET

ADO.NET 2.0 offers several new features. Some of them extend the current ADO.NET and XML API, others are added for a tighter integration with the next Microsoft SQL server version (codename *Yukon*). The most important new features are:

- ❏ bulk copy of data;
- ❏ *Multiple Active Result Sets* (*MARS*), which allows an application to have more than one DataReader open on a connection;
- ❏ asynchronous execution of database operations;
- ❏ batch processing for reducing the round trips when updating a DataTable;
- ❏ paging the result of a database cursor, which allows a better integration with user interface controls, for example in ASP.NET;
- ❏ support for the next generation of MS SQL server: in-process cursors and user-defined data types (because Yukon hosts the .NET CLR), classes for an OO-relational mapping (*ObjectSpaces*), notifications about changes made to data stored in MS SQL server when the data was modified outside the application.

The namespace System.Xml has new features, too. Some of them are related to ADO.NET. For example, System.Xml contains classes for using *XQuery*, *XSLT* and *XPath* from W3C. It adopts the concepts of views and offers XML views. With XML views a non-XML data source can be mapped to an XML document. This can be used, for example, to generate XML documents from relational databases, or to query relational data using *XQuery*.

The above list is a non-exhaustive summary. We will now briefly sketch a subset of these features and provide several examples. Some of the new features of ADO.NET require MDAC 9.0 (*Microsoft Data Access Components*).

9.3.1 Bulk Copy Operations

Bulk copy allows an application to efficiently insert a large amount of data into an MS SQL server database. Currently only MS SQL server is supported as the output target but an application can use multiple input data sources as long as they can be accessed via a DataReader. The main class for performing bulk copy operations is System.Data.SqlClient.SqlBulkCopyOperation. The methods of this class read data from a DataReader or DataTable and write data to an MS SQL server database.

The following example shows a simple copy operation in which we copy the data of the whole Customers table located in the *Northwind* database to the Copy_Customers table. We created the Copy_Customers table in advance with the same schema as the source table. Both tables are located in the same database.

```
// STEP 1: define source
SqlConnection sourceCon = new SqlConnection(conString);
sourceCon.Open();
SqlCommand sourceCmd = new SqlCommand("SELECT * FROM Customers",sourceCon);
IDataReader sourceReader = sourceCmd.ExecuteReader();

// STEP 2: define target
SqlConnection targetCon = new SqlConnection(conString);
targetCon.Open();

// STEP 3: copy source to target
SqlBulkCopyOperation bulkCmd = new SqlBulkCopyOperation(targetCon);
bulkCmd.DestinationTableName = "Copy_Customers";
bulkCmd.WriteDataReaderToServer(sourceReader);

// STEP 4: release resources
bulkCmd.Close(); targetCon.Close();
sourceReader.Close(); sourceCon.Close();
```

The methods WriteDataReaderToServer and WriteDataTableToServer(DataTable) copy all rows from the specified data source to the MS SQL server. Typically, the schemas of the source and the target are not identical. The SqlBulkCopyOperation class uses properties such as DestinationTableName and associated classes such as SqlBulkCopyColumnAssociator for defining the mapping of the source schema to the target schema. Because the execution time of a bulk copy operation can be quite long, the class SqlBulkCopyOperation offers an event notification service. The SqlRowsCopied event is fired when a certain number of rows have been processed.

9.3.2 Multiple Active Result Sets and Asynchronous Operations

Multiple Active Results Sets (MARS) allow an application to have more than one DataReader opened for single database connection and to access all those readers concurrently. The Yukon version of MS SQL server supports MARS directly. For older versions of MS SQL server (e.g. for MS SQL Server 2000) ADO.NET simulates this functionality. The MARS technology, as well as the asynchronous execution of database commands, requires the MDAC 9 library.

The following example uses two readers that share a connection to retrieve customers and orders from the *Northwind* database concurrently.

```
SqlConnection con = new SqlConnection(conStr);
con.Open();

//--- create two commands and associate them with the same connection
SqlCommand custCmd = new SqlCommand("SELECT CustomerId, CompanyName " +
    "FROM Customers ORDER BY CustomerId", con);
SqlCommand ordCmd = new SqlCommand("SELECT CustomerId, OrderId, OrderDate " +
    "FROM Orders ORDER BY CustomerId, OrderDate", con);

//--- execute the commands
SqlDataReader custRdr = custCmd.ExecuteReader();
SqlDataReader ordRdr = ordCmd.ExecuteReader();

//--- read data from both DataReaders
string custID = null;
while(custRdr.Read()) { // use the first reader
    custID = custRdr.GetString(0);
    while(ordRdr.Read() && ordRdr.GetString(0) == custID ) { // use the second reader
        ...
    }
}
con.Close();
```

Database commands are normally executed synchronously. This means that the caller blocks until the command is finished. In order to avoid this, a command can also be executed asynchronously: the caller starts the command and continues with other tasks while the command is being executed on the server. When the command finishes the caller collects the results. Under .NET 1.1 an asynchronous database command had to be simulated by executing a synchronous command as a separate thread. Besides, it was not possible to start multiple commands over a single database connection. Both restrictions were removed in .NET 2.0. There is now an explicit API for asynchronous database commands, and several such commands can share a single connection.

The ADO.NET API for executing commands asynchronously resembles other asynchronous APIs in the .NET Framework, such as the file or network I/O API. It supports executing commands and opening connections.

In the following example we execute a long-running stored procedure and want to be notified when it is finished. Therefore we execute it asynchronously using an AsyncCallback delegate.

```
using System;
using System.Data;
using System.Data.SqlClient;

public class Async {

    SqlCommand cmd; // command to be executed asynchronously

    public void CallCmdAsync() {
        SqlConnection con = new SqlConnection("Data Source=(local)\\NetSDK;" +
            "database=northwind;integrated security=true; use MDAC9=true; async=true");
        cmd = new SqlCommand("MyLongRunningStoredProc", con);
        cmd.CommandType = CommandType.StoredProcedure;
        con.Open();
        // execute the command asynchronously
        cmd.BeginExecuteNonQuery(new AsyncCallback(AsyncCmdEnded), null);
        // continue with other work or simply return
        ...
    }

    // this callback method is executed when the SQL command is finished
    public void AsyncCmdEnded(IAsyncResult result) {
        cmd.EndExecuteNonQuery(result);
        // optionally do some work based on results
        ...
    }
}
```

In the connection string we used two additional parameters: The parameter use MDAC9=true tells ADO.NET to use the MDAC 9 library (in the final release of .NET 2.0 this parameter should no longer be necessary). With the parameter async=true we explicitly enable the asynchronous mode.

9.3.3   Batch processing

Batch processing improves performance by reducing the number of round trips to the MS SQL server, especially when updating a DataSet. Before ADO.NET 2.0, a separate update command had to be sent and executed on the server for every DataRow that had to be modified.

In ADO.NET 2.0 the DataAdapter class is extended with batch processing functionality. Of course, the underlying data source has to support batch processing, too. If the property DataAdapter.UpdateBatchSize is set to a value other than 1 batch processing is enabled. Setting the value to 0 will execute a single (and probably very slow) batch command. If the underlying data source does not support batch processing this property is silently ignored.

In the following example the property UpdateBatchSize is set to 50 before the DataTable "Categories" is updated.

```
void UpdateCategories(DataSet ds, SqlConnection con) {
    // create an adapter with select and update commands
    SqlDataAdapter da = new SqlDataAdapter("SELECT * FROM Categories", con);
    // the command builder creates the missing UPDATE, INSERT and DELETE commands
    SqlCommandBuilder cb = new SqlCommandBuilder(da);
    // set the batch size != 1
    da.UpdateBatchSize = 50;
    // execute the update in batch mode
    da.Update(ds.Tables["Categories"] );
}
```

Depending on the application certain values of UpdateBatchSize are more efficient than others. Therefore you should test for the optimum setting.

9.3.4   Paging

This feature allows programmers to retrieve a subset of rows when paging through the results of a query. This is especially useful if the feature is combined with user interface controls such as an ASP.NET DataGrid. The method

SqlDataReader ExecutePageReader(CommandBehavior b, int startRow, int pageSize)

of the class SqlDataReader offers a way to retrieve a set (or *page*) of data rows. The parameter startRow defines the starting position of the read operation (the first row has number 1). The parameter pageSize defines the number of returned rows.

9.3.5   ObjectSpaces

ObjectSpaces bridges the gap between object-oriented programs and relational databases. It maps .NET classes to database relations that are stored either in Yukon or in MS SQL Server 2000. At the time of writing, the ObjectSpaces technology was in an early stage. Thus, we confine ourselves to an overview.

ObjectSpaces provides several classes for loading, querying, mapping, updating and storing objects to MS SQL server databases. It comes with a new query language called *OPath* which is based on *XPath*. The main classes are shown below. They belong to the namespace System.Data.ObjectSpaces.

❑ The class ObjectSpace is the main class of this namespace and is used to communicate with data sources.

❏ The class ObjectSources maintains a list of connections that are used by an ObjectSpace object.

❏ The class ObjectQuery is used for querying objects using the *OPath* query language.

❏ The class ObjectReader allows one to read the stream of objects that is returned by a query.

❏ The class ObjectSet contains copies of persistent objects similarly to the way that a DataSet contains tables and rows.

❏ The classes ObjectList and ObjectHolder are collections which support delayed loading of persistent objects.

Any .NET class can be mapped by ObjectSpaces without having to implement a certain interface or having to be annotated with a special .NET attribute. In the following example all Customer objects with an Id greater than 'T' are retrieved from an object space that is mapped to the *Northwind* database.

```
using System; using System.Data.ObjectSpaces; using System.Data.SqlClient;

// mapped class
public class Customer {
    public string Id; // primary key
    public string Name;
    public string Company;
    public string Phone;
}

public class ObjectSpaceSample {

    public static void Main() {
        // load the mapping and data source information and create the ObjectSpace.
        SqlConnection con = new SqlConnection("Data Source=(local)\\NetSDK;" +
            " Integrated Security=SSPI; Database=northwind");
        ObjectSpace os = new ObjectSpace("map.xml", con);

        // query for objects
        ObjectQuery oQuery = new ObjectQuery(typeof(Customer),"Id >= 'T'", "");
        ObjectReader reader = os.GetObjectReader(oQuery);

        // print result
        foreach (Customer c in reader) {
            Console.WriteLine(c.GetType() + ":");
            Console.WriteLine("Id: " + c.Id);
            Console.WriteLine("Name: " + c.Name);
            Console.WriteLine("Phone: " + c.Phone);
        }

        reader.Close();
        con.Close();

    }
}
```

The mapping between our Customer class and the Customer table in the database is described by the XML file map.xml which is stored in the application directory. Its format, however, is beyond the scope of this overview section.

9.4   New Features in ASP.NET

ASP.NET 2.0 comes with a large number of new features such as

- ❑ Master pages for a consistent layout of web sites
- ❑ Site maps for easy navigation within a web site
- ❑ Themes and skins for selecting the look and feel of web controls
- ❑ Personalization for storing user data in a database
- ❑ Controls and classes for user authentication and membership management
- ❑ Controls for simpler visualization of external data

A full coverage of all these topics would need a book of its own. Since this is a preview chapter and ASP.NET 2.0 will still evolve until the final release, we will just illustrate the basic ideas with some examples.

9.4.1   Master Pages

A master page is a template that defines the common layout of a set of web pages. It looks like a normal ASP.NET page but has a Master directive instead of a Page directive and the file extension .master instead of .aspx. A master page contains one or more ContentPlaceHolder controls, which define areas that are to be filled in by web pages that are based on this master. Figure 9.4 sketches a master page with a header area, a sidebar with links and a placeholder area.

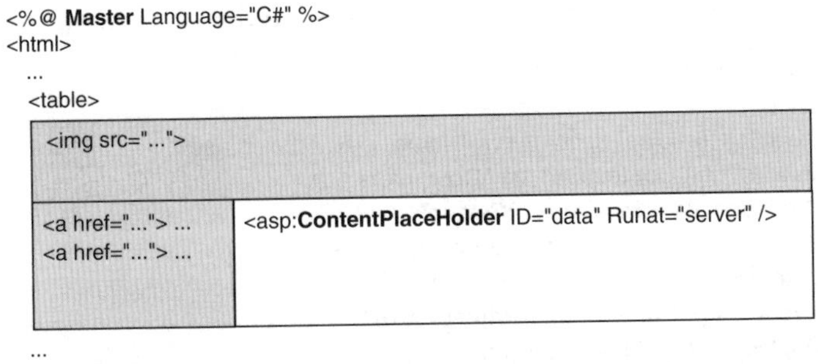

```
<%@ Master Language="C#" %>
<html>
   ...
   <table>
```

<img src="...">	
<a href="..."> ... <a href="..."> ...	<asp:ContentPlaceHolder ID="data" Runat="server" />

```
   ...
```

Figure 9.4 *A master page* MyApp.master *with a ContentPlaceHolder*

Assume, for example, that this master page is stored in a file MyApp.master. We can now base other web pages on it. For each ContentPlaceHolder control in the master page the dependent pages must contain a Content control specifying the contents of the placeholder (see Figure 9.5).

```
<%@ Page Language="C#" Master="MyApp.master" %>

<asp:Content ContentPlaceHolderID="data" Runat="server">

    ...

</asp:Content>
```

Figure 9.5 *A web page* MyPage.aspx *with a Content control based on* MyApp.master

The Content control may contain arbitrary HTML code or ASP.NET controls. If the page is stored in a file MyPage.aspx we can direct a web browser to it

http://*domainName/virtualDirectory/*MyPage.aspx

and obtain a combination of the master page and the contents. Master pages thus allow us to define a consistent layout for all web pages of an application.

Master pages can also be nested. We could have a company-wide master page and then a sub-master for employee pages and client pages. An employee master page, for example, could look as follows:

```
<%@ Master Language="C#" Master="MyApp.master" %>
<asp:Content ContentPlaceHolderID="data" Runat="server">

    ...

    <asp:ContentPlaceHolder ID="subdata" Runat="server" />
</asp:Content>
```

9.4.2 Navigation with Site Maps

Web applications usually have dozens of pages. Navigating through them can be a nightmare and one can easily get lost. As a solution to this problem ASP.NET 2.0 allows the definition of page hierarchies as XML site map files, for example:

```
<?xml version="1.0" encoding="utf-8" ?>
<siteMap>
    <siteMapNode title="Articles" description="Home" url="Articles.aspx" >
        <siteMapNode title="Computers" url="Computers.aspx">
            <siteMapNode title="PCs" url="PCs.aspx" />
            <siteMapNode title="Notebooks" url="Notebooks.aspx" />
        </siteMapNode>
        <siteMapNode title="Printers" url="Printers.aspx">
            <siteMapNode title="Laser" url="Laser.aspx" />
            <siteMapNode title="InkJet" url="InkJet.aspx" />
```

```
      </siteMapNode>
    </siteMapNode>
  </siteMap>
```

Every <siteMapNode> specifies the name and the URL of a web page. We can now display this site map by using a TreeView control which takes its data from a SiteMapDataSource. By default, a SiteMapDataSource is bound to the XML file app.sitemap in the application directory but we can also specify any other site map file as an attribute.

```
<asp:SiteMapDataSource ID="ds" Runat="server" />
<asp:TreeView DataSource="ds" Runat="server" />
```

The result is shown in Figure 9.6. The individual nodes can be expanded and collapsed, and every node is a link to the specified web page.

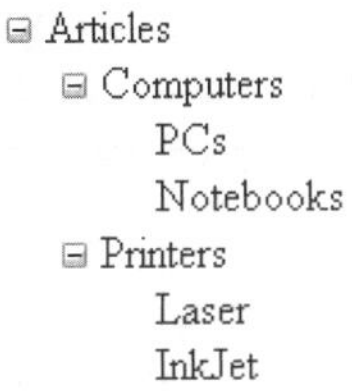

```
⊟ Articles
    ⊟ Computers
          PCs
          Notebooks
    ⊟ Printers
          Laser
          InkJet
```

Figure 9.6 *A site map visualized as a TreeView*

It is recommended that the TreeView control is used on the master page on which all other pages of the application are based. This makes site navigation available on all web pages.

Another useful navigation aid is the SiteMapPath control which shows the path through a site map from its root to the current page. It is declared as

```
<asp:SiteMapPath Runat="server" />
```

and looks like Figure 9.7.

Articles > Computers > PCs

Figure 9.7 *A SiteMapPath control*

Again, it is recommended that this control should be placed on the master page so that it is available on all web pages of the application.

9.4.3 Themes and Skins

Some users prefer to have their own look and feel for buttons, text boxes or drop-down lists. Of course, the style of all web controls (for example, their colour or size) can be configured with attributes in ASP.NET but it is tedious to do this again and again for all web pages of an application. Furthermore, static styles would not allow every user to have his or her own look and feel for web controls. This problem is solved with themes and skins in ASP.NET 2.0.

A *skin* is a sample web control that is configured with all the desired attributes, for example:

```
<asp:Label ForeColor="#585880" Font-Size="0.9em" Font-Name="Verdana" />
```

Several such skins can be stored in a file with the extension .skin. Usually, this file contains skins for different controls, but it can also have several skins for the same kind of controls, which are then distinguished by a SkinID attribute:

```
<asp:Label SkinID="red" ForeColor="#FF0000" Font-Name="Arial" Font-Bold="true" />
```

Any property that is not explicitly defined by an attribute retains its default value.

A *theme* is a collection of skin files and other resources such as icons or cascading style sheets. It is stored in a directory whose name is the theme name. An application can have several themes which are stored in the subdirectory Themes of the application directory (see Figure 9.8).

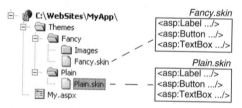

Figure 9.8 Themes *directory with two themes: Fancy and Plain*

A theme can be applied to one or several web pages. In this way the controls on those pages get the look and feel that is specified in the respective skin file. Controls that are not defined in the skin file retain their default style. There are three ways in which a theme can be associated with a web page:

❑ It can be set globally for all pages of the application by making an entry in the application's Web.config file:

```
<configuration>
    <system.web>
        <pages theme="Fancy" />
        ...
    </system.web>
</configuration>
```

❑ It can be set statically for a web page in the Page directive:

```
<%@ Page Language="C#" Theme="Fancy" %>
```

❑ It can be set dynamically for a web page in response to its PreInit event.

```
public void Page_PreInit(object sender, EventArgs e) {
    Theme="Fancy";
}
```

The PreInit event is new in ASP.NET 2.0. It is raised before the Init event, which would be too late for setting the theme, because all controls on the page have already been created at this point.

If a web page has the theme Fancy, which declares two skins for a label, say one with the SkinID="red" and one without a SkinID, we can choose between the skins in the following way:

```
<asp:Label Runat="server">Label without a SkinID</asp:Label>
<asp:Label SkinID="red" Runat="server">Label with the SkinID="red"</asp:Label>
```

Instead of using SkinIDs in the skin file we could also have several skin files for a theme (for example, Fancy.skin and Fancy2.skin both in the subdirectory Fancy), each of them setting different attributes for labels, buttons and so on. We could then make the selection between those skin files as follows:

```
<asp:Label Runat="server">Label from Fancy.skin</asp:Label>
<asp:Label SkinID="Fancy2" Runat="server">Label from Fancy2.skin</asp:Label>
```

9.4.4   Personalization

ASP.NET 2.0 allows a web application to store data about every user in a database. Which data is to be stored is defined in the application's Web.config file:

```
<system.web>
    <personalization>
        <profile>
            <property name="User" type="System.String" />
            <property name="LastVisit" type="System.DateTime" />
        </profile>
    </personalization>
</system.web>
```

The <profile> element defines the user data as a set of name–value pairs by specifying the name and the type of the values. The Page class has a new property Profile which can be accessed in the code of a web page like this:

```
label.Text = "Welcome " + Profile.User;
Profile.LastVisit = DateTime.Now;
```

By default, the user data is automatically stored in a Microsoft Access database file with the name AspNetDB.mdb in the /data directory of the application. However, we can also select SQL Server as the database provider or even implement a cus-tom provider class that stores the data in some custom-specific way.

Of course, the user has to provide the data to be stored (for example, on a reg-istration page) if it cannot be derived automatically from the request. The users are identified either by cookies or by URL rewriting.

The reader may argue that user data could also be stored in the session state that is already available in ASP.NET 1.1; however, there are some important dif-ferences. Personalization data is *statically typed*, so the program does not have to apply type casts as for session state items. Furthermore, personalization data is stored *permanently* in a database, whereas session state data is disposed of when the session ends. Finally, personalization data is only loaded *on request*, whereas session state data is reloaded on every page request.

Personalization can, for example, also be used to store a specific theme for every user. Whenever the user visits a page of this application, the personal theme is set and the page appears in the user's personalized look and feel.

9.4.5   Authentication and Membership Management

Many web pages require a user to register at the first visit and log in at all subse-quent visits. Registration and login pages can, of course, be implemented with ASP.NET 1.1 already; however, it is a tedious task and occurs again and again. Therefore, ASP.NET 2.0 provides a set of prefabricated web controls and utility classes that simplify this job.

Login Controls

The LoginStatus control displays a link with the text Login if the user has not signed in already and a link with the text Logout otherwise. It is declared as follows:

```
<asp:LoginStatus Runat="server" />
```

The Login link leads to a login page that is specified in Web.config:

```
<system.web>
  <authentication mode="Forms">
    <forms loginUrl="login.aspx" />
  </authentication>
</system.web>
```

The LoginStatus control is often used together with a LoginView and a LoginName control. A LoginView declares two texts, one of which is displayed if the user has not logged in yet, and the other is displayed if the user has already signed in. The LoginName displays the name of the logged-in user. Here is an example:

```
<asp:LoginView Runat="server">
    <AnonymousTemplate>
        You are not logged in. Click the Login link.
    </AnonymousTemplate>
    <LoggedInTemplate>
        You are logged in. Welcome,
        <asp:LoginName Runat="server" />
    </LoggedInTemplate>
</asp:LoginView>
```

In Web.config we specified login.aspx as the login page. This page should display a dialog where the user can enter his or her name and password. ASP.NET should verify that the user credentials are correct and should redirect the user to the page originally requested. All these tasks are automatically performed by the Login control, which—in its simplest form—can be written like this:

```
<asp:Login Runat="server" />
```

The resulting dialog is shown in Figure 9.9.

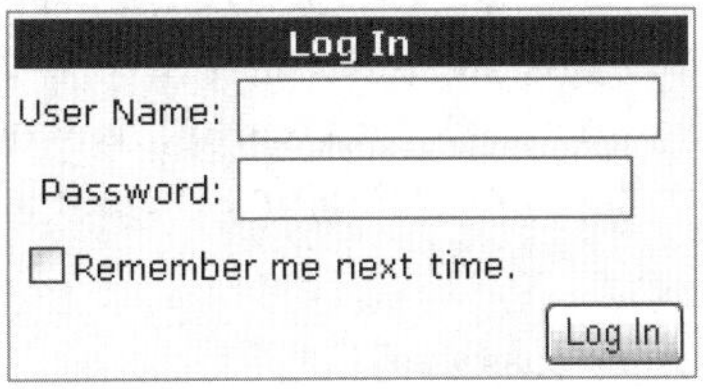

Figure 9.9 *A login dialog resulting from a Login control*

The programmer can customize this dialog in many ways, for example by specifying an error text that appears when the login fails, or by providing links to a help page or to a password recovery page. The dialog also raises some events (e.g. BeforeLogin, AfterLogin, LoginError, etc.) that can be handled by the programmer.

For users who have forgotten their password ASP.NET 2.0 provides the PasswordRecovery control, which is yet another nice feature that eliminates routine coding. It displays a dialog where the user can request that his or her password should be sent to him or her by e-mail. Here is how this control is specified:

```
<asp:PasswordRecovery Runat="server">
    <MailDefinition from="mailto:admin@dotnet.jku.at" cc="your password" />
</asp:PasswordRecovery>
```

Figure 9.10 shows how this control is displayed.

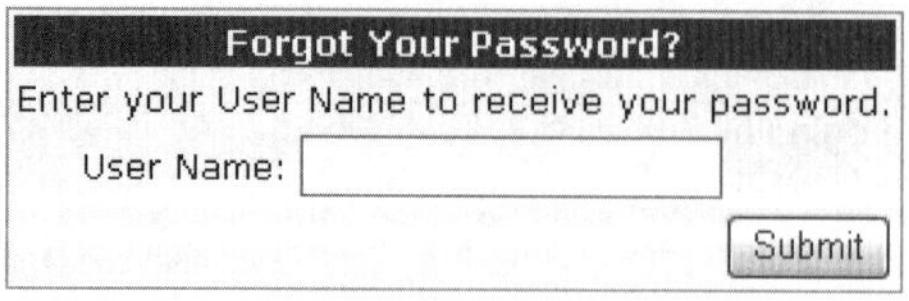

Figure 9.10 *A PasswordRecovery control*

But how does the system know the e-mail address of the user, and even more general: how does it know the names and passwords of all the users when processing the login dialog? This information can be maintained with the membership classes of ASP.NET 2.0.

Membership Classes

The class Membership which is declared in the namespace System.Web.Security maintains data about registered users. This data is automatically stored in a database. By default, this is a Microsoft Access file with the name AspNetDB.mdb that is stored in the application's /data directory. But the user can also select SQL Server as the database provider or even implement his or her own membership provider class.

The Membership class contains a set of static methods for creating new users, looking them up in the database, updating their data and validating them. Here is an extract of its interface:

```
static MembershipUser CreateUser(string name, string password) {...}
static MembershipUser GetUser(string name) {...}
static void UpdateUser(MembershipUser user) {...}
static bool DeleteUser(string name) {...}
static bool ValidateUser(string name, string password) {...}
```

The ValidateUser method is used in the login dialog to validate the data that is entered by the user. The methods CreateUser and GetUser return a MembershipUser object which stores user data such as the user's name, password, e-mail address, the last login date or a password recovery question. Of course, there must be a registration page where a new user can enter all this data.

Member Pages

Many web sites provide member pages that are protected from unauthorized access. ASP.NET 2.0 makes it easy to specify that only registered users can access such pages. The administrator simply has to collect all member pages in a subdirectory of the application (for example, /members) and provide a Web.config file in this directory that has an <authorization> element like this:

```
<configuration>
  <system.web>
    <authorization>
      <deny users="?" />
    </authorization>
  </system.web>
</configuration>
```

This <authorization> element specifies that unregistered users are denied access. If a user that has not logged in tries to access a page in the /members directory he or she is automatically redirected to the login page specified in the application's Web.config file. As long as the login fails, the user stays there. If the login was successful the user is redirected to the member page that he or she originally requested. All this happens automatically without the programmer having to write a single line of code.

In addition to individual users, access rights can also be based on *roles*. The namespace System.Web.Security contains a class Roles with a set of static methods for role management:

```
static void CreateRole(string roleName) {...}
static void AddUserToRole(string userName, string roleName) {...}
...
```

If we had created a role with the name "Admin" and had added the users "Peter" and "Albrecht" to this role, we could define a set of administration pages to which only users with the role "Admin" have access. For this, we have to collect the administration pages in a separate directory of the application (for example, /admin) and provide a Web.config file for this directory. This file must contain an <authorization> element as well as a <roleManager> element that enables roles:

```
<system.web>
  <roleManager enabled="true" />
  <authorization>
    <allow roles="Admin" />
    <deny users="*" />
  </authorization>
<system.web>
```

This configuration specifies that all users are denied access to the pages in the directory /admin except those users that have the role "Admin".

9.4.6   New Controls for Database Access

A lot of web pages display data that is extracted from a database. ASP.NET 1.1 already offers a DataGrid control that allows programmers to bind a DataView object to it and show its contents in tabular form. However, programmers still have to write code to connect to the database, retrieve the DataView object and bind it to the DataGrid. ASP.NET 2.0 provides an easier way to do this, by allowing the specification of the database and the SELECT command declaratively in a web control. The data is then retrieved automatically without having to write any code.

Let us explain this with an example, which uses an AccessDataSource control that connects to a Microsoft Access database. We simply have to specify the database file name and the SELECT command, for example:

```
<asp:AccessDataSource ID="data" Runat="server"
    DataFile="db.mdb"
    SelectCommand="SELECT id, name, subject FROM Students" />
```

This control retrieves a DataSet from the table Students of the database db.mdb. In addition to AccessDataSource there is also an SqlDataSource for retrieving data from an SQL server database or an XmlDataSource for retrieving data from an XML file.

Now that we have the DataSet we can display it with the new GridView control of ASP.NET 2.0, which is as simple as this:

```
<asp:GridView DataSourceID="data" AllowSorting="true" Runat="server" />
```

The GridView is connected to a data source using the DataSourceID attribute. AllowSorting specifies that we would like to be able to sort the GridView by clicking on one of the column headers. Figure 9.11 shows how the GridView is displayed.

id	name	subject
9955004	Miller	Computer Science
9934128	Johnson	Economics
9955332	Howard	Computer Science
9882076	Keen	Physics
9834524	Feldman	Economics

Figure 9.11 *A GridView control showing the data from an AccessDataSource*

Note that we did not have to write a single line of code for that. Everything was specified declaratively, and the defaults of the control properties are set such that we hardly have to specify anything for the most common cases. Of course, there are many options for formatting the GridView or for requesting additional features.

The DataSource controls can be bound not only to a GridView but also to any of the existing web controls that hold a set of values such as a ListBox or a DropDownList, for example:

```
<asp:AccessDataSource ID="data" Runat="server"
    DataFile="db.mdb"
    SelectCommand="SELECT DISTINCT subject FROM Students" />
<asp:DropDownList DataSourceID="data" DataTextField="subject" Runat="server" />
```

Sometimes the SELECT command needs parameters, for example to extract only those students that have "Computer Science" as their subject. Such parameters can be specified in the <SelectParameters> section of the AccessDataSource control. The parameter values can be taken from another web control such as a text box:

```
<asp:TextBox ID="tb" AutoPostBack="true" Runat="server" />
<asp:AccessDataSource ID="data" Runat="server"
    DataFile="db.mdb"
    SelectCommand="SELECT id,name,subject FROM Students WHERE subject=@par">
    <SelectParameters>
        <asp:ControlParameter name="par" ControlID="tb" PropertyName="Text" />
    </SelectParameters>
</asp:AccessDataSource>
<asp:GridView DataSourceID="data" Runat="server" />
```

This results in the picture shown in Figure 9.12.

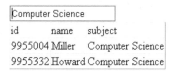

Computer Science		
id	name	subject
9955004	Miller	Computer Science
9955332	Howard	Computer Science

Figure 9.12 *A filtered GridView of students with the subject Computer Science*

The GridView control is much more powerful than we have shown so far. We can, for example, use it to delete rows of the table or to update their values. For that we have to specify also a DeleteCommand and an UpdateCommand in the Access-DataSource control:

```
<asp:AccessDataSource ID="data" Runat="server"
    DataFile="db.mdb"
    ShareMode="ReadWrite"
    SelectCommand="SELECT id, name, subject FROM Students"
    DeleteCommand="DELETE FROM Students WHERE id=@id" />
    UpdateCommand="UPDATE Students SET name=@name, subject=@subject
        WHERE id=@id" />
<asp:GridView ID="grid" DataSource="data" Runat="server"
    DataKeyNames="id"
    AutoGenerateDeleteButton="true"
    AutoGenerateEditButton="true" />
```

The DataKeyNames attribute specifies the primary key of the data set. The Auto-GenerateDeleteButton and AutoGenerateEditButton attributes request that a Delete button and an Edit button are displayed in every row. If nothing else is specified the column names of the GridView are taken from the column names of the database, and these names can also be used as parameter names for the UPDATE and DELETE command. The result of all this is shown in Figure 9.13.

		id	name	subject
Edit	Delete	9955004	Miller	Computer Science
Edit	Delete	9934128	Johnson	Economics
Edit	Delete	9955332	Howard	Computer Science
Edit	Delete	9882076	Keen	Physics
Edit	Delete	9834524	Feldman	Economics

Figure 9.13 *A GridView with Edit and Delete buttons*

If we click on the Edit button of a row the fields of this row that are not primary keys are displayed for editing (see Figure 9.14).

		id	name	subject
Edit	Delete	9955004	Miller	Computer Science
Update	Cancel	9934128	Johnson	Economics
Edit	Delete	9955332	Howard	Computer Science
Edit	Delete	9882076	Keen	Physics
Edit	Delete	9834524	Feldman	Economics

Figure 9.14 *Editing fields of a GridView*

In addition to the GridView there is also another new web control in ASP.NET 2.0 called a DetailsView. It is used for displaying the records of a database row by row, for example if a database record has so many fields that they cannot be displayed in a single line on the screen. Like a GridView, a DetailsView can be bound to any DataSource control. Here is an example:

```
<asp:AccessDataSource ID="data" Runat="server"
    DataFile="db.mdb"
    SelectCommand="SELECT id, name, subject FROM Students" />
<asp:DetailsView DataSourceID="data" Runat="server"
    DataKeyNames="id"
    AllowPaging="true"
    PagerSettings-Mode="NextPrevFirstLast" />
```

The AllowPaging attribute specifies that buttons should be displayed to navigate through the rows of the data source. More specifically, the PagerSettings-Mode attribute says that we want to have a *next* button (>), a *previous* button (<), a *first* button (<<) and a *last* button (>>). The result is shown in Figure 9.15.

id	9955332
name	Howard
subject	Computer Science
<< < > >>	

Figure 9.15 *A DetailsView control*

9.5   New Features for Web Services

The next release of the .NET Framework will include major changes to the way you implement and work with web services. A whole new group of namespaces will be introduced under the name *Indigo*. Indigo will not only cover web services, but also include what is now known as .NET Remoting and .NET Enterprise Services, that is, all facets of (network) communication will become the responsibility of only one part of the .NET class library.

Therefore, a better title for this section would be "New Features for Communication", because Web Services, .NET Remoting and .NET Enterprise Services will grow together almost inseparably. The great advantage of this integration under a common umbrella is that programming in any of these—up to now, distinct—realms becomes uniform, meaning that whether you want to use a web service method or instantiate and use a remote object will only require minor changes in your code and configuration files. Even adding things such as security, reliability and durability to your network communication will not require a great deal of work on your code, but will often be as simple as using another attribute for your class or method.

Through this, Indigo allows for great flexibility in programming loosely coupled applications that need to communicate with other applications: as the distinction between web services, enterprise services and remoting vanishes, so does the need for an early decision on which to use in your application. You can now simply add "features" (such as encryption) to your communication channels as you go along.

9.5.1   What is Indigo?

According to [Rec04] (where most of the information found here was taken from), Indigo is an implementation of a messaging system that enables secure, reliable, transacted messaging over multiple transports and across heterogeneous systems. It is a set of .NET technologies for building and managing *service-oriented* systems and exposes a unified programming model to the developer.

Indigo adds the following features to the current web services, .NET remoting and MS Enterprise Services infrastructure:

- ❑ *Transactions*.
- ❑ *Reliable* communication:
  - – message buffering;
  - – disconnected messaging;
  - – message sequencing.

❏ *Secure* communication:
  – confidentiality (encryption of messages) and integrity (digital signing);
  – authentication and authorization (access control for services).
❏ *Protocol independence*: Indigo has built-in support for TCP, HTTP and IPC (Interprocess Communication).
❏ *Host independence*: Indigo service applications can be hosted in any type of application, which means they do not have to be hosted in ASP.NET as today's web services do, but can, for example, be run by a stand-alone command-line application.
❏ *Message-based activation* of the server: The application at the server side does not have to be running when a request arrives. Indigo service applications that are hosted in ASP.NET can be activated automatically when a message arrives for them.

This enhancement of functionality is only possible because Indigo applications now support two forms of communication:

❏ **Stateless communication.** This is how today's web services work and should be used for non-critical communication only. Here, almost no guarantees can be made for the delivery of the messages.
❏ **Stateful communication.** A session state is maintained and thus valuable characteristics such as reliability, durability, security and transactions that are essential for enterprise applications become possible.

9.5.2   Indigo Architecture

The classes of the Indigo namespaces (for example, System.MessageBus) build a layered architecture of which developers usually touch only the top layer. This so-called *service layer* reveals to them a managed API which is used on both the service and the client side. The developers use common programming abstractions such as methods, events and delegates which the lower layers of the Indigo architecture convert into messages which are ultimately transmitted to the communication partner. Figure 9.16 shows the participants of each level in the Indigo architecture at the sender side of a communication connection.

Indigo understands *messages* as in-memory SOAP envelopes, but while one usually pictures such SOAP envelopes as long strings of nested, angle-bracketed XML text, this does not have to be case for Indigo messages. The SOAP specification actually defines them at the XML Infoset level which describes a hierarchical structure for information, but says nothing about angle brackets. Thus XML Infoset messages can be more compact than their familiar XML-formatted representation. Separate formatters determine the actual serialization of the Indigo messages.

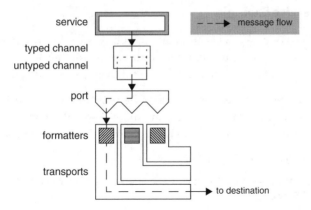

Figure 9.16 *Sender side of an Indigo communication connection*

Indigo messages travel between the *services* of the service layer. They pass their messages on to so-called *typed channels* that represent type-safe wrappers around *untyped channels* whose job is the actual transmission of the messages. These untyped channels implement particular message exchange strategies. For example, a datagram channel does not provide any guarantees for message delivery, whereas a dialog channel enables reliable communication.

The untyped channels feed the messages into *ports* which define named locations in the network space and so form the communication endpoints of the Indigo messaging framework. Each port resides within a single application domain. A port contains a pipeline of one or more untyped channels and has one or more affiliated transports.

Transports are adapters for the underlying wire protocol (TCP, HTTP, ...) and handle connections, addressing, and flow control. The serialization of the messages is left to *formatters*. So at the sender a transport accepts a message from a port, requests a formatter to serialize it and then sends it to its destination port. At the receiver the transport passes the received message to a formatter for deserialization and feeds it to the port's message pipeline. Only the transports deal with message formats; all higher levels work only with message objects.

What has been omitted in Figure 9.16 are the *managers* that control each of the displayed participants and other parts. For example, Indigo offers the classes ServiceManager, RemotingManager, SecurityManager, PolicyManager, Transaction Manager and many more. They can be configured via application configuration files, attributes in the source code or properties of their corresponding objects. The managers hide all the complexity of the underlying components from the developer: so an Indigo application may, for example, simply request from a service the ability to send a message and wait for the response. The underlying managers now make sure that the message is actually sent and, in the case of a time-out, re-send it, until the required response arrives.

9.5.3   Indigo Web Service Example

Now, let us look at some code. We want to create a web service that offers one simple method which returns the current time at the server in the form of a System.DateTime object. Therefore, we need to do the following at the *server side*:

1. Implement the web service class TimeService. We must apply the attribute DatagramPortType to the class and the attribute ServiceMethod to the method to be published. The file TimeService.cs holds the following code:

   ```
   using System; using System.MessageBus.Services;

   [DatagramPortType(Name="TimeService", Namespace="http://dotnet.jku.at/WS")]
   public class TimeService {

       [ServiceMethod]
       public DateTime GetTime() {
           DateTime now = DateTime.Now;
           Console.WriteLine ("Time request at {0}", now);   // to monitor server
           return now;
       }
   }
   ```

2. Compile the service into TimeService.dll with

   ```
   csc /target:library /reference:System.MessageBus.dll TimeService.cs
   ```

3. Create WSDL and XSD files for the clients to download. From these descriptions clients can then generate interfaces to access the web service. wsdlgen.exe (part of the Windows Longhorn SDK) generates the files dotnet_jku_at.WS.wsdl and dotnet_jku_at.WS.xsd:

   ```
   wsdlgen TimeService.dll
   ```

4. Implement an application that hosts the web service and will receive the incoming messages and forward them to the web service. This can be a simple console application such as the following from the file Server.cs:

   ```
   using System; using System.MessageBus;

   class Server {
       static void Main () {
           ServiceEnvironment se = null;
           try {
               se = ServiceEnvironment.Load();
               se.Open();
               Console.WriteLine("Press enter to stop the service ...");
               Console.ReadLine();
           } finally { if (se != null) se.Close(); }
       }
   }
   ```

The host just opens a ServiceEnvironment and thereby lets Indigo take care of all the processing of the messages. All we still need to do is to

5. Configure the host application in a file Server.exe.config:

```
<configuration>
  <system.messagebus>
    <serviceEnvironments>
      <serviceEnvironment name="main">
        <port>
          <identityRole>
            soap.tcp://localhost:12345/TimeService/
          </identityRole>
        </port>
        <remove name="securityManager"/> <!-- Security disabled!!! -->
        <policyManager>
          <areUntrustedPolicyAttachmentsAccepted> true
          </areUntrustedPolicyAttachmentsAccepted>
          <isPolicyReturned> true </isPolicyReturned>
        </policyManager>
        <serviceManager>
          <activatableServices>
            <add type="TimeService, TimeService" />
          </activatableServices>
        </serviceManager>
      </serviceEnvironment>
    </serviceEnvironments>
  </system.messagebus>
</configuration>
```

In the section <system.messagebus> any number of service environments can be set up. We only need one and give it the name main, because this will be loaded by the parameterless ServiceEnvironment.Load method by default. Then we define a port mapped to the URL given in the <identityRole> element. Finally, the <activatableServices> element contains all the types (fully qualified and with the full name of the assembly) that Indigo can load and activate when a message for this service arrives.

For this example we deactivated any security measures that Indigo provides per default. This is not recommended for real-life services.

6. After compiling our host application into a console application with

```
csc /reference:System.MessageBus.dll Server.cs
```

7. we can start the host application and let it wait for incoming requests.

Now we turn to the *client side*, where the following steps are required:

1. Obtain the WSDL and—if available—XSD descriptions of the web service and generate a proxy class from them. This is again done with wsdlgen.exe.

```
wsdlgen dotnet_jku_at.WS.wsdl dotnet_jku_at.WS.xsd
```

produces the file dotnet_jku_at.WS.cs which defines an interface ITimeService
that exposes all the service methods, and an interface ITimeServiceChannel
that is the strongly typed channel to communicate with the web service.

2. Compile the interfaces into dotnet_jku_at.WS.dll.

```
csc /target:library /reference:System.MessageBus.dll dotnet_jku_at.WS.cs
```

3. Implement a client application (Client.cs) that uses the interfaces to access
   the web service.

```
using System; using System.MessageBus; using System.MessageBus.Services;
using dotnet_jku_at.WS;   // namespace of the generated interfaces

public class Client {
    public static void Main () {
        ServiceEnvironment se = null;
        try {
            se = ServiceEnvironment.Load();
            ServiceManager sm = se[typeof(ServiceManager)] as ServiceManager;
            if (sm == null) throw new Exception("ServiceManager is not available.");
            se.Open();
            Uri uri = new Uri("soap.tcp://localhost:12345/TimeService/");
            // get a channel to the web service from the default service manager
            ITimeServiceChannel channel = (ITimeServiceChannel)
                    sm.CreateChannel(typeof(ITimeServiceChannel), uri);
            Console.WriteLine(channel.GetTime());   // invoke web service method
        } catch (Exception e) { Console.WriteLine(e);
        } finally { if (se != null) se.Close(); }
    }
}
```

4. Compile the client application to a Windows console application:

```
csc /reference:System.MessageBus.dll,dotnet_jku_at.WS.dll Client.cs
```

5. Configure the client application with a file Client.exe.config. The only differences from the above Server.exe.config is that it defines another port
   identity (soap.tcp://localhost:54321/TimeClient/) and does not have the element <serviceManager> with the <activatableServices> element.

6. Run the client to retrieve the current time from the server. A sample session
   could look like this:

```
//----- Client                          //----- Server
                                         > Host.exe
                                         Press enter to stop the service ...

> Client.exe
1/29/2004 3:35:51 PM                     Time request at 1/29/2004 3:35:51 PM
>
```

9.5.4 Security

Indigo service application can be effectively secured in two ways:

1. Securing access to published methods
2. Securing content of sent messages

In order to secure access to the published methods of a service, Indigo first needs to determine the identity of the user that requests access to the service. For this, Indigo has some built-in authentication services available, such as Microsoft Windows authentication, X.509 certificate authentication, or basic user name and password authentication.

For securing the contents of the transmitted messages, so that third parties cannot read or modify them, Indigo supports encryption using both symmetric and asymmetric algorithms. Similarly, Indigo is capable of using digital signatures to protect the integrity of the sent messages and to verify the authenticity of the sender.

Indigo provides many default security schemes that can easily be controlled through attributes in the source code or configuration files. Indigo client applications can automatically adapt to the security requirement of the server. So, often only the server side needs to specify security requirements and the clients simply use default security schemes, and thus let Indigo take care of meeting the requirements.

Typically, each port has its own SecurityManager attached that defines the security requirements for incoming and outgoing messages.

9.5.5 Reliability and Durability

Indigo can provide delivery assurances about messages and so make communication reliable. We can demand that messages arrive at least once, at most once, or exactly once, or that they arrive in the order in which they were sent. Indigo will take all the necessary steps without the developer having to bother about the communication problems involved. Indigo also provides automatic failure detection and recovery.

Indigo applications can also be configured so that they save the state of their communications in a non-volatile memory. Thus, they protect themselves against the consequences of service failures and support long-running applications. Especially in connection with message-based activation, it becomes possible for applications to shut themselves down after a certain period of inactivity and be reactivated when another message arrives for them. Since all messages can be made persistent on arrival and departure, a service application can pick up processing messages exactly where its predecessor instance left off, for example after a program crash. This makes Indigo service applications highly durable.

In order to take advantage of these benefits the developer does not have to do much more than declare the service class to be a so-called Indigo *dialog*. This is as simple as attaching the attribute DialogPortType (instead of the stateless DatagramPortType) to the service class declaration.

9.5.6   Transactions

For enterprise applications it is often essential to make sure that critical sequences of operations are either executed entirely or not at all. Therefore we want to combine such operations to form transactions.

With Indigo this becomes possible even for widely distributed applications that use web services. The namespace System.Transactions provides the necessary types for handling transactions. There is a Transaction class and a TransactionManager which can both be used to create new transactions that can then be committed or rolled back. Furthermore, it is possible to register interest in numerous events a transaction can fire, such as TransactionCompleted or TransactionOutcome.

References

[ASU86]	Alfred Aho, Ravi Sethi, Jeffrey Ullman: *Compilers – Principles, Techniques and Tools*. Addison-Wesley, 1986
[Bus00]	David Buser et al.: *Beginning Active Server Pages 3.0*. Wrox, 2000
[C#Std]	Standard ECMA-334: C# Language Specification http://www.ecma-international.org/publications/standards/ Ecma-334.htm
[CGI]	Common Gateway Interface Specification http://www.w3.org/CGI/
[CLI]	Standard ECMA-335: Common Language Infrastructure (CLI) http://www.ecma-international.org/publications/standards/ Ecma-335.htm
[EdEd98]	Guy Eddon, Henri Eddon: *Inside Distributed COM*. Microsoft Press, 1998
[ElNa00]	Ramez Elmasri, Shamkant Navathe: *Fundamentals of Database Systems*. 3rd ed., Addison-Wesley, 2000
[FK00]	Duane K. Fields, Mark A. Kolb: *Web Development with Java Server Pages*. Manning Publication Company, 2000
[Fow03]	Martin Fowler: *UML Distilled*. 3rd ed., Addison-Wesley, 2003
[GHJV95]	Erich Gamma, Richard Helm, Ralph Johnson, John Vlissides: *Design Patterns – Elements of Reusable Object-Oriented Software*. Addison-Wesley, 1995
[GotD]	GotDotNet: .NET Framework community http://www.gotdotnet.com
[Gou02]	John Gough: *Compiling for the .NET Common Language Runtime* (CLR). Prentice Hall PTR, 2002
[Holz02]	Steve Holzner: *Inside JavaScript*. New Riders, 2002
[HTML]	Hypertext Markup Language Specification http://www.w3.org/MarkUp/

[HTML1]	Hypertext Markup Language Reference http://www.netzwelt.com/selfhtml.html
[HTTP]	Hypertext Transfer Protocol (HTTP) http://www.w3.org/Protocols/rfc2616/rfc2616.html
[IIS]	Internet Information Server Home http://www.microsoft.com/iis/
[JS]	Javascript specification and resources http://www.swtech.com/script/javascript/lang/
[JKU]	Web site for this book with various .NET topics http://dotnet.jku.at
[LBK01]	Philip Lewis, Arthur Bernstein, Michael Kifer: *Database and Transaction Processing*. Addison-Wesley, 2001
[MeSi92]	Jim Melton, Alan Simon: *Understanding the New SQL: A Complete Guide*. Morgan Kaufmann Publishers, 1992
[MeSz01]	Erik Meijer, Clemens Szyperski: What's in a Name? .NET as a Component Framework, Aug 2001 http://research.microsoft.com/users/cszypers/pub/Components.pdf
[MITK]	Mobile Internet Toolkit http://www.asp.net/mobile/
[Mono]	Information and resources around the Mono project http://www.go-mono.com
[MSBiz]	Microsoft BizTalk Server http://www.microsoft.com/biztalk/
[MSData]	Microsoft web site about accessing data sources http://www.microsoft.com/data/
[MSDL]	Microsoft Developer Network (MSDN) downloads http://msdn.microsoft.com/downloads/
[MSSQL]	Microsoft SQL Server http://www.microsoft.com/sql/
[OMG01]	Object Management Group: The Common Object Request Broker: Architecture and Specification, editorial revision: CORBA 2.6, December 2001 http://www.omg.org/technology/documents/formal/corba_iiop.html
[ONE]	Sun Open Network Environment http://www.sun.com/sunone/

[Pass]	Microsoft .NET Passport http://www.passport.com
[PHP]	PHP: Hypertext Processor http://www.php.net
[Ram02]	Ingo Rammer: *Advanced .NET Remoting*. Apress, 2002
[RFC]	Internet Engineering Task Force (IETF), Request For Comments (RFC) http://www.ietf.org/rfc.html
[Rec04]	Brent Rector: *Introducing Longhorn for Developers*. Microsoft Press, 2004
[Rich00a]	Jeffrey Richter: Garbage Collection: Automatic Memory Management in the Microsoft .NET Framework. *MSDN Magazine*, November 2000
[Rich00b]	Jeffrey Richter: Garbage Collection - Part 2: Automatic Memory Management in the Microsoft .NET Framework. *MSDN Magazine*, December 2000
[Rich02]	Jeffrey Richter: *Applied Microsoft .NET Framework Programming*. Microsoft Press, 2002
[RJB99]	James Rumbaugh, Ivar Jacobson, Grady Booch: *The Unified Modeling Language Reference Manual*. Addison-Wesley, 1999
[SDKDoc]	Documentation of the .NET Framework, which is part of the .NET SDK on the CD in this book. You can also find it at http://www.microsoft.com/net
[SMTP]	Simple Message Transfer Protocol (SMTP), RFC2821
[SOAP]	SOAP Version 1.2 http://www.w3c.org/TR/SOAP/
[SSCLI]	Microsoft Shared Source Implementation of the Common Language Infrastructure (Rotor) http://msdn.microsoft.com/net/sscli
[Szy97]	Clemens Szyperski: *Component Software: Beyond Object-Oriented Programming*. Addison-Wesley, 1997
[UDDI]	Universal Description, Discovery and Integration (UDDI) http://www.uddi.org
[UNC]	Universal Naming Convention (UNC), Microsoft Developer Network (MSDN) http://msdn.microsoft.com/library/en-us/off2000/html/defunc.asp

[UniC]   Unicode character set
                  http://www.unicode.org

[URI]   Unified Resource Identifier, www.w3c.org/Addressing

[W3C]   World Wide Web Consortium (W3C)
                  http://www.w3.org

[WaLa01]   Lonnie Wall, Andrew Lader: *Building Web Services and .NET
                  Applications.* Osborne, 2001

[Wir96]   Niklaus Wirth: *Compiler Construction.* Addison-Wesley, 1996

[WML]   Wireless Markup Language Home
                  http://www.wapforum.org/

[WSDL]   Web Service Description Language Specification
                  http://www.w3.org/TR/wsdl.html

[WSE]   Microsoft Web Service Enhancement
                  http://msdn.microsoft.com/webservices/building/wse

[XML]   Extensible Markup Language Specification
                  http://www.w3.org/XML/

[XPath]   XPath
                  http://www.w3c.org/TR/xpath

[XSD]   XML Schema
                  http://www.w3.org/XML/Schema

Additional literature for each chapter

General

- ❑ DevHood: .NET training modules
  http://www.devhood.com/training_modules/
- ❑ GotDotNet: examples, tutorials, links
  http://www.gotdotnet.com
- ❑ Microsoft .NET home
  http://www.microsoft.com/net
- ❑ Microsoft Developer Network on .NET
  http://msdn.microsoft.com/net

Chapter 1: What is .NET?

- ❑ David S. Platt: *Introducing Microsoft .NET.* 3rd edn, Microsoft Press, 2003
- ❑ Thuan Thai, Hoang Lam: *.NET Framework Essentials.* O'Reilly, 2002

Chapter 2: The Language C#

- ❑ Ben Albahari, Peter Drayton, Brad Merrill: *C# Essentials.* 2nd edn, O'Reilly, 2002
- ❑ Tom Archer: *Inside C#.* Microsoft Press, 2002
- ❑ Eric Gunnerson: *A Programmer's Introduction to C#.* Apress, 2001
- ❑ Charles Petzold: *Programming Windows with C#.* Microsoft Press, 2001
- ❑ Simon Robinson et al.: *Professional C#.* 2nd edn, Wrox-Press, 2002
- ❑ Andrew Troelsen: *C# and the .NET-Platform.* 2nd edn, Apress, 2003

Chapter 3: The .NET Architecture

- ❑ Keith Brown: Security in .NET: Enforce Code Access Security with the Common Language Runtime. *MSDN Magazine,* February 2002
- ❑ Andrew Gordon, Don Syme: *Typing a Multi-Language Intermediate Code. POPL'01.* ACM Press, 2001
- ❑ John Gough: Stacking Them Up: A Comparison of Virtual Machines. *ACSAC'01,* February 2001
- ❑ John Gough: *Compiling for the .NET Common Language Runtime (CLR).* Prentice Hall PTR, 2002

❑ Erik Meijer, John Gough: Technical Overview of the Common Language Runtime. 2001 (revised edition)
http://research.microsoft.com/~emeijer/Papers/CLR.pdf

❑ Microsoft Shared Source Implementation of the Common Language Infrastructure (Rotor)
http://msdn.microsoft.com/net/sscli

❑ Jeffrey Richter: *Applied Microsoft .NET Framework Programming*. Microsoft Press, 2002

❑ Jeffrey Richter: Microsoft .NET Framework Delivers the Platform for an Integrated, Service-Oriented Web. *MSDN Magazine*, September 2000

❑ Jeffrey Richter: Part 2: Microsoft .NET Framework Delivers the Platform for an Integrated, Service-Oriented Web. *MSDN Magazine*, October 2000

❑ Jeffrey Richter: .NET Framework: Building, Packaging, Deploying, and Administering Applications and Types. *MSDN Magazine*, February 2001

❑ Jeffrey Richter: .NET Framework: Building, Packaging, Deploying, and Administering Applications and Types - Part 2. *MSDN Magazine*, March 2001

❑ Damien Watkins, Sebastian Lange: An Overview of Security in the .NET Framework. *Microsoft Developer Network (MSDN)*, January 2002
http://msdn.microsoft.com/library/en-us/dnnetsec/html/netframesecover.asp

❑ Jason Whittington: Rotor: Shared Source CLI Provides Source Code for a FreeBSD Implementation of .NET. *MSDN Magazine*, July 2002

Chapter 4: The .NET Class Library

❑ Jason Bell: *Professional Windows Forms*. Wrox-Press, Oktober 2001

❑ Don Box, John Lam, Aaron Skonnard: *Essential XML, Beyond MarkUp*. Addison-Wesley, July 2000

❑ Ingo Rammer: Advanced .NET Remoting. *Apress*, April 2002

❑ Jeffrey Richter: *Applied Microsoft .NET Framework Programming*. Microsoft Press, 2002

❑ Mike Snell, Lars Powers: *Visual Basic Programmer's Guide to the .NET Framework Class Library*. Sams, 2002

❑ Thuan Thai: *.NET Framework Essentials*. O'Reilly UK, 2002

❑ Richard Weeks: *.NET Windows Forms Custom Controls*. Sams, 2002

Chapter 5: ADO.NET

❑ Bob Beauchemin: *Essential ADO.NET*. Addison-Wesley, 2002.

❑ Jim Buyens: *Web Database Development—Step by Step—.NET Edition*. Microsoft Press, 2002

❏ Richard Hundhausen, Steven Borg: *Programming ADO.NET*. Wiley & Sons, 2002
❏ Rebecca M. Riordan: *Microsoft ADO.NET—Step by Step*. Microsoft Press, 2002
❏ David Sceppa: *Microsoft ADO.NET. Core Reference*. Microsoft Press, 2002

Chapter 6: ASP.NET

❏ Marco Bellinaso, Kevin Hoffman: *ASP.NET Website Programming: Problem – Design – Solution*. Wrox, 2002
❏ Dino Esposito: *Building Web Solutions with ASP.NET and ADO.NET*. Microsoft Press, 2002
❏ Jesse Liberty, Dan Hurwitz: *Programming ASP.NET*. O'Reilly, 2002
❏ Jeffrey Richter: *Applied Microsoft .NET Framework Programming*. Microsoft Press, 2002
❏ Dan Wahlin: *XML for ASP.NET Developers*. Sams, 2001
❏ General web site on ASP.NET
http://www.asp.net
❏ Sample implementation of a Web shop with ASP.NET
http://www.asp.net/IBS_Store/

Chapter 7: Web-Services

❏ Frank P. Coyle: *XML, Web Services, and the Data Revolution*. Addison-Wesley, 2002
❏ Bill Evjen: *XML Web Services for ASP.NET*. Wiley, 2002
❏ Eric Newcomer: *Understanding Web Services: XML, WSDL, SOAP, and UDDI*. Addison-Wesley, 2002
❏ Scott Seeley: *SOAP: Cross Platform Web Services Development Using XML*. Prentice Hall, 2001
❏ Scott Short: *Building XML Web Services for the Microsoft .NET Platform*. Microsoft Press, 2002

Index

Microsoft product available with this book:
ASP.NET Web Matrix Project, which includes:

- Web Matrix Project
- .NET Framework Software Development Kit
- .NET Framework Service Pack 1
- Microsoft SQL Server Desktop Engine, MSDE
- Mobile Internet Toolkit, MMIT
- IBuySpy Solution Kits

Product name and associated trademark:
Microsoft® ASP.NET Web Matrix Project

Environment:
Microsoft Windows®

System requirements:
The ASP.NET Web Matrix Project runs on the following platforms:
- Microsoft Windows 2000 Professional and Server (SP 2 recommended)
- Microsoft Windows XP Professional or Home Edition
- Microsoft Internet Explorer 5.5 or later
  NOTE: IE 5.5+ is a requirement on the developer machine only. Applications running on
  ASP.NET may target any browser.

In addition, ASP.NET Web Matrix requires:
- .NET Framework version 1.0

Optional components:
To build data driven applications, a local copy of Microsoft SQL Server Desktop Engine,
MSDE (a SQL Server-compatible database engine) is required.

To create Mobile Web Applications and extend ASP.NET applications to mobile phones, PDAs
and other mobile devices Microsoft Mobile Internet Toolkit, MMIT, must be installed.

Documentation:
Online help only, no printed documentation. http://www.asp.net